STUDY GUIDE

for Stiglitz and Boadway's

Economics and the Canadian Economy

STUDY GUIDE

for Stiglitz and Boadway's

Economics and the Canadian Economy

ALAN HARRISON
McMaster University

LAWRENCE W. MARTIN
Michigan State University

W. W. NORTON & COMPANY · NEW YORK · LONDON

ISBN 0-393-96521-X

W. W. Norton & Company, Inc., 500 Fifth Avenue, New York, N.Y. 10110
W. W. Norton & Company Ltd., 10 Coptic Street, London WC1A 1PU

CONTENTS

PREFACE

This Study Guide is designed to help you understand the material in Joseph Stiglitz and Robin Boadway's *Economics and the Canadian Economy*. Each chapter in this volume corresponds to the equivalently numbered chapter in the main text.

There are three parts to each Study Guide chapter. The first part contains a *Chapter Review* and sections on *Essential Concepts* and *Behind the Essential Concepts.*

The second part provides a self-test, with three sorts of questions, plus answers to every question. There are true-or-false questions, multiple-choice questions, and completion questions. Attempting the self-test after reading each chapter of *Economics and the Canadian Economy* and the first part of the associated chapter in the Study Guide should help you to determine how well you understand the material.

The final part of each chapter is entitled *Doing Economics: Tools and Practice Problems,* which is designed to teach you the basic skills of economics. The exercises are sets of related problems, and working through them is intended to help you to apply what you have learned. For each type of problem, there is a *Tool Kit* that gives step-by-step instructions, followed by a worked problem and several practice problems. Again, answers are provided in all cases.

We hope you find the Study Guide helpful to your understanding of the material in Stiglitz and Broadway's *Economics and the Canadian Economy,* and we hope too that you enjoy studying economics. Good luck with your course.

Part One

Introduction

Chapter 1

THE AUTOMOBILE AND ECONOMICS

Chapter Review

The story of the automobile is a rich one, introducing as it does the principal ideas of economics. The dominant idea is that economics is about the choices made by the three major groups of participants: individuals or households, firms, and government. These choices control the allocation of resources, another central concern of economics. The automobile story also highlights the three markets on which this book focuses: product, labour, and capital. The chapter closes with a discussion of how economists use models and theories to describe the economy and why they sometimes disagree. This chapter sets the stage for the introduction of the basic economic model in Chapter 2.

ESSENTIAL CONCEPTS

1 The brief history of the automobile given here illustrates the broad and varied subject matter of economics and many of the important themes of this book. We see the importance of investors and entrepreneurs and the risks they face, and the central roles of research, technological advance, and patents. The problem of in-

centives appears both in the conflicting interests of Henry Ford and his investors and in the effect of high wages on his workers. The upheavals caused by oil price increases in the 1970s and the influx of competition from foreign producers show us how the Canadian economy now functions in the world economy. Finally, a large and growing government presence has mandated environmental and safety regulations, and provided protection against foreign competition. Indeed, in the United States, it has even supplied money to bail out a major producer.

2 Economics studies how **choices** are made by individuals, firms, governments, and other organizations and how those choices determine the allocation of resources. **Scarcity,** the fact that there are not enough resources to satisfy all wants, requires that choices must be made by individuals and by the economy as a whole. The fundamental questions that an economy must answer are the following:

   a What is produced, and in what quantities?
   b How are these goods produced?
   c For whom are these goods produced?
   d Who makes economic decisions, and by what process?

3 The Canadian economy is a mixed one that relies primarily on private decisions to answer the basic economic questions. **Markets,** which exist wherever and whenever exchanges occur, influence the choices of individuals and firms, but government also plays a prominent role. The government sets the legal structure within which market forces operate. It also regulates private activity, collects taxes, produces some goods and services, and provides support for the elderly, poor, and others.

4 Trade takes place between individuals and firms in three major markets: the **product market,** the **labour market,** and the **capital market.** Figure 1.1 sketches the interactions. Notice that in general, individuals buy goods and services from firms; they also supply labour and funds for investment to firms.

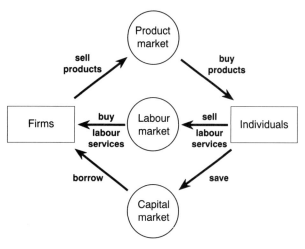

Figure 1.1

5 There are two broad branches in economics. **Microeconomics** studies the product, labour, and capital markets, focusing on the behaviour of individuals, households, firms, and other organizations that make up the economy. **Macroeconomics** looks at the performance of the economy as a whole and at such aggregate measures as unemployment, inflation, growth, and the balance of trade.

6 Economics uses models and theories, which are sets of assumptions and conclusions, to understand and predict the behaviour of the economy. Economists want to discover and interpret relationships among economic variables and especially to distinguish where there is causation and where there is only correlation.

7 Economists are frequently asked to give advice regarding public policy, and sometimes they disagree. When this happens, there are two major reasons: they disagree about what is the appropriate theoretical model of the economy and about the effects a policy will have.

BEHIND THE ESSENTIAL CONCEPTS

1 In this book you will learn many economic theories and models. Models and theories are simplified representations of the vast and complex economic world. The way that a model is made simple and workable is through assumptions. We assume that only certain factors are relevant to the problem at hand. Then we derive conclusions from the assumptions and test the model by comparing its predictions with what we know of the world.

You need to do two different things with the models that you will come across in your study of economics. First, you must understand how the model works—specifically, what is assumed and how the conclusions follow. The second task is to evaluate how well the model explains what it is supposed to explain. As you read the many arguments and pieces of evidence, keep in mind how they fit with the model's basic assumptions and conclusions.

2 Economic **variables** are measurable, and they change. The price of potatoes is an economic variable; so is the rate of unemployment. We look for two types of relationships among these variables. First, we are interested in whether certain economic variables move together. For example, workers who have received more years of education are paid higher incomes. Levels of schooling and wages are **correlated.** But we are also interested in whether a change in one variable **causes** a change in another variable. Specifically, does more education cause higher wages (perhaps by raising workers' productivity)? Before economists make conclusions, they require a sound model that shows how a change in an economic variable was caused and also some evidence that the model's assumptions are appropriate and that its predictions proved accurate.

3 **Positive economics** focuses on questions about how the economy works. What does it do, and why does it do it? **Normative economics,** on the other hand, typically asks what should be done. Keep in mind, however, that normative economics cannot prescribe which value to hold; it describes the appropriate policy given the value.

4 Microeconomics and macroeconomics are two ways of looking at the economy. Microeconomics looks from the bottom up; it starts with the behaviour of individuals and firms and builds to an understanding of markets and the economy as a whole. Macroeconomics, on the other hand, is a top-down look, beginning with a description of the performance of aggregate economic variables and then constructing explanations. Micro- and macroeconomics must fit together. The models that explain how individuals, firms, and markets work must be consistent with the models that we use to describe the economy as a whole. An important theme of this book is that the microeconomics in Parts One, Two, and Three provides a firm foundation for the macroeconomics to follow in Parts Four, Five, and Six.

SELF-TEST

exclusive right w/ regard to an invention

True or False

F 1   Henry Ford patented the internal combustion engine.

F 2   Henry Ford paid his workers especially high wages because he wanted them to earn enough to buy his cars.

T 3   Patents give exclusive rights to market an innovation for a limited period of time.

F 4   The import restrictions negotiated by the U.S. and Canadian governments on exports of Japanese automobiles to North America allowed North American automakers to regain their lost market share.

T 5   The Canada-U.S. Auto Pact allows for specialization by each country's production plants in different vehicle product lines and free trade between the countries in the automobiles and trucks produced.

T 6   Economics studies how individuals, firms, governments, and other organizations make choices and how those choices determine the allocation of the economy's resources.

T 7   The four basic questions concerning how economies function are ① what is produced and in what quantities, ② how are the goods produced, ③ for whom are they produced, and ④ who makes the decisions?

F 8   Most resource allocation decisions are made by governments in the Canadian economy.

T 9   In centrally planned economies, most decisions are made by the government.

F 10   The three major markets are the product, labour, and insurance markets.   *capital*

F 11   *macro* Microeconomics focuses on the behaviour of the economy as a whole.

F 12   *micro* Macroeconomics studies the behaviour of firms, households, and individuals.

T 13   If two economic variables are correlated, there may not be a systematic relationship between them; if there is a systematic relationship between them, they are correlated.

F 14   When two variables are correlated, it is because *causation* changes in one cause changes in the other.

F 15   *positive* Normative economics deals with questions concerning how the economy actually works.

Multiple Choice

1   Henry Ford paid his workers more than the going rate chiefly because

   a   he feared that the government would set minimum wages if he paid low wages.

   b   he could thereby obtain a high-quality, hard-working labour force.

   c   he did not care about profits, only the well-being of his workers.

   d   his highly paid workers would buy more of his cars.

   e   his highly paid workers would pay more taxes.

2   Which of the following is not true of patents?

   a   Patents give inventors exclusive rights to produce and market their inventions for a limited time.

   b   Patents allow inventors to charge high prices without fear of competition.

   c   Patents provide incentives to encourage new inventions.

   d   Patents are awarded for innovations, not ideas.

   e   None of the above.

3   In the 1980s, the U.S. and Canadian governments negotiated limitations on exports of Japanese automobiles to North America. As a result,

   a   prices of Japanese automobiles rose but prices of North American automobiles were unchanged.

   b   prices of Japanese automobiles were unchanged but prices of North American automobiles rose.

   c   prices of both Japanese and North American automobiles were unchanged.

   d   prices of both Japanese and North American automobiles rose.

   e   North American automobile producers were taken over by Japanese automobile producers.

4   The Canada-U.S. Auto Pact

   a   requires that every automobile purchased in Canada must be produced in Canada.

   b   imposes restrictions on all trade in automobiles and automotive parts between Canada and the United States.

   c   allows duty-free import of U.S.-produced vehicles and parts into Canada as long as the manufacturer produces other vehicles and parts in Canada, with minimum requirements on the ratio of production to total sales.

   d   affects only trade in automobiles between Canada and the United States, not trade in automotive parts.

   e   affects only trade in automotive parts between Canada and the United States, not trade in automobiles.

5   Because resources are scarce,

   a   questions must be answered.

   b   choices must be made.

   c   all except the rich must make choices.

   d   governments must allocate resources.

   e   some individuals must be poor.

6   In market economies, the four basic questions are answered

   a   by elected representatives.

   b   in such a way as to ensure that everyone has enough to live well.

   c   by private individuals and firms, interacting in markets.

   d   according to the traditional way of doing things.

   e   by popular vote.

7   In market economies, goods are consumed by those who

    a   are most deserving.
    b   work the hardest.
    c   are politically well connected.
    d   are willing and able to pay the most.
    e   produce them.

8   Which of the following is one of the three major markets?

    a   a supermarket
    b   the labour market
    c   the foreign exchange market
    d   the European Common Market
    e   the Hamilton farmers' market

9   The detailed study of firms, households, individuals, and the markets where they transact is called

    a   macroeconomics.
    b   microeconomics.
    c   normative economics.
    d   positive economics.
    e   aggregate economics.

10   The study of the behaviour of the economy as a whole, especially such factors as unemployment and inflation, is called

    a   macroeconomics.
    b   microeconomics.
    c   normative economics.
    d   positive economics.
    e   market economics.

11   An economic theory or model is a

    a   mathematical equation.
    b   prediction about the future of the economy.
    c   recommended reform in government policy that pays attention to the laws of economics.
    d   set of assumptions and conclusions derived from those assumptions.
    e   small-scale economic community set up to test the effectiveness of a proposed government program.

12   If those with more education are also generally better paid,

    a   forcing people to stay in school longer will result in their receiving higher wages when they leave school.
    b   this is an example of causation.
    c   raising people's wages will encourage them to go back to school.
    d   this is an example of correlation.
    e   we can conclude that there is a systematic relationship between the levels of education and wages.

13   Which of the following is an example of correlation?

    a   The high budget deficits of the 1980s caused the trade deficits.
    b   Taxes are too high.

14   Which of the following is an example of normative economics?

    a   The high budget deficits of the 1980s caused the trade deficits.
    b   During recessions, output falls and unemployment increases.
    c   Lower interest rates would encourage investment.
    d   Interest rates should be reduced to encourage investment.
    e   Expansionary monetary policy will reduce interest rates.

15   Which of the following is an example of positive economics?

    a   Taxes are too high.
    b   Canadian savings rates are too low.
    c   Lower interest rates would encourage investment.
    d   Interest rates should be reduced to encourage investment.
    e   There is too much economic inequality in Canada.

16   In Canada, the question of what is produced and in what quantities is answered

    a   primarily by private decisions influenced by prices.
    b   by producing what was produced the previous year.
    c   primarily by government planning.
    d   randomly.
    e   according to majority vote.

17   In centrally planned economies, most decisions concerning what is produced, how, and for whom are made by

    a   consumers.
    b   firms.
    c   government.
    d   workers.
    e   private investors.

18   Choices must be made because

    a   resources are scarce.
    b   human beings are choice-making animals.
    c   government regulations require choices to be made.
    d   economic variables are correlated.
    e   without choices, there would be no economics as we know it.

19   Anything that can be measured and that changes is

    a   a correlation.
    b   a causation.
    c   a variable.
    d   a value.
    e   an experiment.

c   During recessions, output falls and unemployment increases.
d   In mixed economies, there is a role for markets and a role for government.
e   Economics studies choices and how choices determine the allocation of resources.

20 In the labour market,

   a households purchase products from firms.
   b firms purchase the labour services of individuals.
   c firms raise money to finance new investment.
   d households purchase labour services from firms.
   e borrowing and lending are coordinated.

Completion

1 Exchanges take place in _markets_ .

2 In a _mixed_ economy, some decisions are made chiefly by government and others by markets.

3 All the institutions involved in borrowing and lending money make up the _capital_ market.

4 The behaviour of the economy as a whole, and especially of certain aggregate measures such as unemployment and inflation, is called _macroeconomics_ .

5 The branch of economics that focuses on firms, households, and individuals and studies product, labour, and capital markets is called _microeconomics_ .

6 The statement that crime rates are higher in low-income areas is an example of _correlation_ .

7 The statement that poverty leads to crime is an example of _causation_ .

8 Economists use _theories or models_ , which are sets of assumptions, conclusions, and data, to study the economy and evaluate the consequences of various policies.

9 _normative_ economics rests on value judgments; _positive_ economics describes how the economy behaves.

10 The four basic questions that economists ask about the economy are (1) what is produced and in what quantities, (2) _How the goods are produced_ , (3) for whom are they produced, and (4) who makes the decisions?

Answers to Self-Test

True or False

1	f	6	t	11	f
2	f	7	t	12	f
3	t	8	f	13	t
4	f	9	t	14	f
5	t	10	f	15	f

Multiple Choice

1	b	6	c	11	d	16	a
2	e	7	d	12	b	17	c
3	d	8	b	13	c	18	a
4	c	9	b	14	d	19	c
5	b	10	a	15	c	20	b

Completion

1 markets
2 mixed
3 capital
4 macroeconomics
5 microeconomics
6 correlation
7 causation
8 theories or models
9 Normative, positive
10 how are these goods produced

Chapter 2

THINKING LIKE AN ECONOMIST

Chapter Review

The concept of scarcity discussed in Chapter 1 implies that choices must be made. This chapter begins to explain how economists think about choice, and how choices are influenced and coordinated by markets. A basic economic assumption is that of rational choice, which simply says that people select the alternative they prefer most from among all those that are available. The alternatives available to any particular firm or individual, of course, depend upon the choices made by other firms and individuals. All these rational choices must somehow fit together, and markets serve the function of coordinating them. How they do so is the subject of Chapters 3 through 5.

ESSENTIAL CONCEPTS

1   The **basic economic model** includes three elements: individuals, firms, and markets. Economic decisions such as what and how much of each type of good to produce, how to produce them, what kind of career to pursue, and how to spend one's earnings are made by **rational, self-interested individuals** and **rational, profit-maximizing firms. Markets** serve the economic role of coordinating these decisions.

2   The basic economic model assumes that markets are **perfectly competitive.** In competitive markets, there are many consumers and firms, and each is small relative to the size of the overall market. One key feature of perfect competition is that any firm charging more than the going price will lose all its customers. Without any ability to influence the market price, the firm is a **price taker.** (Later in this book, we will encounter monopolists and others known as **price makers,** who have the power to charge higher prices without losing all their customers.)

3   Even though the price is treated by firms and individuals as **exogenous** (that is, outside their control), it is determined by, or **endogenous** to, the market as a whole. The **equilibrium price** is the outcome of the interaction of all buyers and all sellers.

4   Private **property rights** play an important role in the basic model. They include the right to use resources in certain ways and the right to sell them in markets. These two aspects of property rights provide in-

centives to use resources efficiently and to transfer resources to their most valuable use. Inefficiencies can arise when property rights are ill-defined or restricted.

5 When compensation is tied to performance, people have strong incentives to work hard and be productive, but those who are more fortunate and successful also will earn higher incomes. On the other hand, distributing the output more equally undermines incentives. This **incentive-equality trade-off** is one of the basic questions facing societies: how should the tax and welfare system be constructed to balance the competing ends of providing strong incentives and promoting equality?

6 **Scarcity** implies that not everyone who desires a good or resource can have it. There is an allocation problem. In market economies, goods are allocated to the highest bidder. Another solution to the allocation problem is to **ration.** Rationing schemes include queues, first-come first-served, lotteries, coupons, and rationing by government regulation. Unless supplemented by markets, rationing schemes will likely lead to inefficiencies.

7 The basic economic model assumes that decisions are made rationally: this simply means that individuals and firms balance the benefits and costs of their decisions. Economists see rational decision making as a two-step process. First, find what alternatives are possible. This step is the construction of the **opportunity set.** Next, select the best alternative from those within the opportunity set.

8 The chapter presents three types of opportunity sets. The **budget constraint** shows what combinations of goods can be consumed with a limited amount of money. The **time constraint** indicates to what uses limited time can be put. Finally, the **production possibilities curve** depicts the combinations of goods that a firm or an entire economy can produce given its limited resources and the quality of the available technology.

9 The best alternatives in an opportunity set will lie along the outer edge. This is because people prefer more goods to fewer. Operating on the outer edge also implies that there will be a **trade-off**: more of one option means less of another. For example, on the budget constraint, consuming more of one good means that less money is available to spend on another good. On the time constraint, if an individual devotes more time to one activity, there is less time available for other endeavours. A society that chooses to produce more of one good must settle for less production of other goods.

10 The **opportunity cost** of a good or activity is the option forgone. The opportunity cost of consuming more of one good is consuming less of some alternative good. The opportunity cost of an activity is the other endeavour that would have been, but now cannot be, undertaken. The opportunity cost of producing one good is the necessarily lower production of another.

11 The opportunity cost, not the price, is the proper measure of the economic cost of any choice. For example, in addition to the ultimate purchase price, the opportunity cost of buying an automobile includes the time and expense devoted to investigating alternatives, searching for the best deal, and negotiating the terms.

12 Opportunity costs are measured in total and at the margin. When a firm is deciding where to locate its plant, it compares the **total costs** at each location. When a firm is considering how large a plant to build, it looks at the costs of increasing or decreasing the size. These are the **marginal costs,** the costs of a little bit more or a little bit less.

BEHIND THE ESSENTIAL CONCEPTS

1 The basic competitive model introduced in this chapter is critical to your understanding of economics. It will be expanded and applied in all the chapters that follow, but you should master the concepts given in this chapter: rational individuals choose the best combinations of goods along their budget constraints, firms maximize profits, and trading takes place in competitive markets, where each individual and firm is a price taker.

2 The opportunity set itself shows all the alternatives that are available. Because more is generally preferred to less, however, economists focus on the outer boundary of the opportunity set. For example, Figure 2.1 shows an opportunity set for an agricultural firm that must divide its resources between growing corn and growing wheat. The entire shaded area shows all the combinations that are possible. The economist's attention is drawn to the outer edge, the production possi-

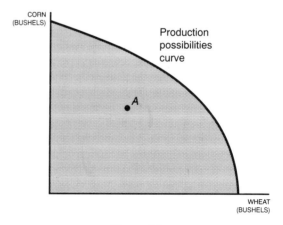

Figure 2.1

bilities curve, because to choose a combination inside (such as point *A*) would be inefficient.

3 The terms "opportunity set," "budget constraint," "trade-off," and "opportunity cost" are related, but they are distinct, and you should take care to understand each one. Figure 2.2 shows the opportunity set for a student who consumes hamburgers and pizzas. The **opportunity set** shows all the combinations of hamburgers and pizzas that are affordable. Points *A* and *B* are affordable; they lie within the opportunity set, but have the critical characteristic of lying along its outer edge, which is the budget constraint. The trade-off is that more hamburgers mean fewer pizzas. If Joe chooses *B* rather than *A,* he eats another pizza and exactly two fewer hamburgers. The trade-off between any two points measures the opportunity cost. In this case, the opportunity cost of this extra pizza is the two forgone burgers. When the outer edge of the opportunity set is a straight line, the trade-offs will be the same all along the line; when it is a curve, the trade-offs will change.

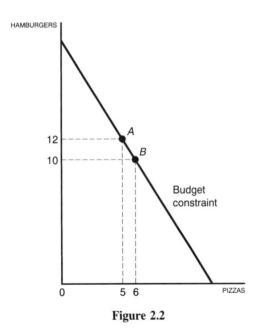

Figure 2.2

4 Opportunity costs are forgone alternatives—not money, not time, and not resources. For example, if you spend one hour in class tomorrow, the opportunity cost of attending that class is not the hour itself. That hour will pass whether you go to the class or not. The opportunity cost is what you would have done with that hour. It is the activity you give up. Strictly speaking, the opportunity cost of buying a book for $20 is not the money, but what would have been purchased with the $20 if it had not been spent on the book.

5 **Sunk costs,** outlays that cannot be recovered, are not opportunity costs. Because these expenditures are not affected by the choice of any alternative, they do not represent the opportunity cost of any alternative. For

example, suppose that you sign a one-year lease on an apartment and are forbidden to sublet it. When you consider whether to stay in town for the summer or travel abroad, the rent owed your landlord is irrelevant. You cannot do anything about it. Regardless of which alternative you choose, you must pay the rent. The rent is a sunk cost, not an opportunity cost.

6 Be clear about the difference between total costs and marginal costs. Marginal costs are the costs of a little more or a little less of some activity. Before considering going into business, you evaluate the total opportunity costs of the enterprise—all the costs of setting up the plant, designing and producing the product, and locating the market. When you are considering whether to produce another unit of output, however, it is the marginal opportunity cost that is important. The marginal cost of producing a little bit more is just the added cost incurred when producing more with the plant already set up, the product designed, and the market found. These latter costs are not marginal.

7 **Diminishing returns** can be confusing at first. What the term means is that as more inputs are used in a production process, output increases at a diminishing rate. For example, suppose more workers are hired to pick apples. Each additional worker results in more apples being picked in total, but the marginal contribution of the newest worker, how many extra apples are picked when that worker is hired, is not as great as that of the previously hired new workers. We can also say that the opportunity cost of increasing output—the marginal cost—is higher as output increases.

8 Another way to approach diminishing returns is to think about why the output of the marginal input is declining. The extra inputs are just as good at producing; however, as more are used, the production process becomes crowded. For example, when more workers are hired to pick apples, there are fewer apple trees per worker, and it is more difficult to pick apples.

SELF-TEST

True or False

1 The basic model of economics seeks to explain why people want what they want.

2 A rational decision maker may choose to decide among alternatives without seeking good information, if she expects the costs of becoming informed are higher than the benefits.

3 A rational decision maker always forecasts the future correctly.

4 A firm selling in a perfectly competitive market is a price taker because any increase in price would cause it to lose all its customers.

outside their control

T 5 Both the right to use a resource in certain ways and the right to transfer that resource are important aspects of private property rights.

F 6 Common ownership of property is the reason for diminishing returns.

7 A legal entitlement—that is, the right to use a resource in certain ways—often prevents the resource from going to its highest valued use.

8 Lotteries are an inefficient means of allocating resources because they do not allocate goods to the highest bidder.

9 Rationing by queues wastes the time spent waiting in line.

10 The opportunity set includes only the best available alternative.

11 The production possibilities curve shows the boundary of the opportunity set.

12 The principle of diminishing returns says that as more units of any input are added to a production process, total output eventually falls.

13 If an economy is not using its resources in the most productive way, economists say that there is inefficiency.

T 14 Sunk expenditures do not represent opportunity costs.

15 If one pizza sells for $8 but two pizzas can be purchased for $12, the marginal cost of the second pizza is $6.

Multiple Choice   15/20

1 Individuals and firms in the economy must make choices because of

　a　diminishing returns.
　b　rationality.
　c　scarcity.
　d　economic efficiency.
　e　sunk costs.

behave / think rationally

2 The concept of rationality refers to

　a　the fact of scarcity.
　b　the principle of diminishing returns.
　c　the assumption that individuals have sensible goals.
　d　the assumption that individuals and firms weigh the costs and benefits of their choices.
　e　the assumption that individuals and firms are certain of the consequences of their choices.

3 A firm that cannot influence the price it sells its product for is called a

　a　price maker.
　b　price taker.
　c　rational decision maker.
　d　monopolist.
　e　none of the above.

4 In a competitive market, equilibrium price is

　a　exogenous to each of the individuals and firms, which means that it is fixed without reference to market conditions. *determined by*
　b　endogenous to each of the individuals and firms, which means that any single individual's or firm's actions will influence price.
　c　exogenous to each of the individuals and firms, but endogenous to the market as a whole, that is, all individuals and firms.
　d　endogenous to each of the individuals and firms, but exogenous to the market as a whole, that is, all individuals and firms.
　e　set by the largest firm.

outside their control / determined by

5 In a pure market economy, incentives to work hard and produce efficiently are provided by

　a　the profit motive alone.
　b　government regulations.
　c　private property rights alone.
　d　both the profit motive and private property rights.
　e　the profit motive, private property rights, and government regulations.

6 When property is owned in common, users

　a　do not maximize profits.
　b　violate the principle of rationality.
　c　ignore the principle of diminishing returns.
　d　have little incentive to maintain and preserve the value of the property.
　e　give it away.

7 If owners are not allowed to sell their resources, then

　a　the resources will not go to the highest value users.
　b　the owners will not act rationally.
　c　their choices will not be limited to their opportunity sets.
　d　the market will be perfectly competitive.
　e　the owners give them away.

8 Allocating goods by lotteries, queues, and coupons are examples of

　a　rationing.
　b　selling to the highest bidder.
　c　efficient ways of allocating resources.
　d　the profit motive.
　e　competitive markets.

9 Rationing by queues

　a　leads to an efficient allocation of resources.
　b　allocates goods to those willing to pay the most money.
　c　wastes the time spent waiting in line.
　d　is an efficient way of allocating scarce goods.
　e　is the only way to sell movie tickets.

10 When goods are rationed by coupons and the coupons are not tradable,

　a　the goods go to the individuals who value them most.

b a black market may be established.

c individuals will not act rationally.

d the coupons have no value.

e resources are efficiently allocated.

11 Which of the following is *not* related to opportunity cost?

 a the production possibilities curve

 b diminishing returns

 c budget constraints

 d scarcity

 e sunk costs

12 Fred has $10 to spend on baseball cards and hamburgers. The price of baseball cards is $0.50 per pack. Hamburgers sell at a price of $1.00 each. Which of the following possibilities is not in Fred's opportunity set?

 a 10 hamburgers and 0 packs of baseball cards

 b 5 hamburgers and 10 packs of baseball cards

 c 3 hamburgers and 16 packs of baseball cards

 d 1 hamburger and 18 packs of baseball cards

 e none of the above

13 The production possibilities curve is not a straight line because of

 a scarcity.

 b diminishing returns.

 c rationality.

 d sunk costs.

 e none of the above.

14 Henry spends an hour shopping and buys one sweater for $30. The opportunity cost of the sweater is

 a one hour.

 b $30.

 c one hour plus $30.

 d the next-best alternative uses of the hour and the $30.

 e a jacket.

15 Renting an apartment, Bill signs a lease promising to pay $400 each month for one year. He always keeps his word, and therefore he will pay the $400 each month whether he lives in the apartment or not. The $400 each month represents

 a an opportunity cost.

 b a sunk cost.

 c a trade-off.

 d a budget constraint.

 e diminishing returns.

16 One box of Nature's Crunch Cereal sells for $2.55. Each box comes with a coupon worth $.50 off the purchase price of another box of Nature's Crunch Cereal. The marginal cost of the second box of this product is

 a $2.55.

 b $3.05.

 c $2.05.

 d $1.55.

 e none of the above.

17 If the price of a 12-ounce glass of beer is $2.50 and the price of a 20-ounce glass of beer is $4, the difference in price is

 a the opportunity cost of a 12-ounce glass of beer, because that's what you would buy if you didn't buy a 20-ounce glass.

 b the opportunity cost of a 20-ounce glass of beer, because that's what you would buy if you didn't buy a 12-ounce glass.

 c the sunk cost of 8 ounces of beer.

 d the marginal cost of an extra 8 ounces of beer.

 e the marginal cost of 12 ounces of beer.

18 Fred is considering renting an apartment. A one-bedroom apartment rents for $400, and a two-bedroom apartment for $500. The $100 difference is

 a the opportunity cost of the two-bedroom apartment.

 b the marginal cost of the second bedroom.

 c a sunk cost.

 d the marginal cost of an apartment.

 e none of the above.

19 If a firm changes from paying commissions on total sales to paying each member of its sales force a fixed salary, it will likely

 a experience lower total sales.

 b experience higher sales.

 c see no difference because compensation is a sunk cost.

 d see no difference because incentives do not matter.

 e none of the above.

20 The Canadian government has invested billions of taxpayers' dollars in the Hibernia oil field off the coast of Newfoundland. Which of the following statements about the money already spent is true?

 a It represents the opportunity cost of Hibernia because it would cost this much to develop another oil field.

 b It represents the marginal cost of the first barrel of oil that will eventually flow from Hibernia.

 c It is irrelevant to a decision on whether to continue development of Hibernia because it represents a sunk cost.

 d It does not represent a sunk cost until and unless development of Hibernia is permanently halted.

 e It represents the marginal cost of all the oil that will ever flow from Hibernia.

Completion

1 Economists assume that people make choices _____ taking into consideration the costs and benefits of their alternatives.

2 A market with large numbers of buyers and sellers, each of whom cannot influence the price, is an example of _____.

3 The right of an owner of a resource to use it in certain ways and to sell it is called a _____.

4 Allocating goods and services by some means other than selling to the highest bidder is called *rationing*

5 The collection of all available opportunities is called the *opportunity set*

6 *Constraints* limit choices.

7 The amount of goods that a business firm is able to produce is called its *production possibilities*

8 The idea that as more inputs are used in a production process each successive input eventually adds less to output is an example of the principle of *diminishing returns*

9 The fact that more time spent studying means less time available for other activities illustrates a *trade-off*

10 An expenditure that cannot be recovered is a *sunk* cost.

Answers to Self-Test

True or False

1 f	4 t	7 t	10 f	13 t
2 t	5 t	8 t	11 t	14 t
3 f	6 f	9 t	12 f	15 f

Multiple Choice

1 c	6 d	11 e	16 c
2 d	7 a	12 c	17 d
3 b	8 a	13 b	18 b
4 c	9 c	14 d	19 a
5 d	10 b	15 b	20 c

Completion

1 rationally
2 perfect competition
3 property right
4 rationing
5 opportunity set
6 constraints
7 production possibilities
8 diminishing returns
9 trade-off
10 sunk

Doing Economics: Tools and Practice Problems

For the problem sets in this section, we reach into the economist's tool box for five important techniques, each of which will reappear throughout the remainder of the book. Three relate to the opportunity set: budget and time constraints, for which the outer edge of the opportunity set is a straight line; multiple constraints involving, for example, limits on both time and money; and production possibilities curves, which can be straight lines but more often exhibit

diminishing returns and are curved. The remaining two techniques relate to costs: the distinction between sunk and opportunity costs, and the use of marginal analysis to balance costs and benefits.

Tool Kit 2.1: Plotting the Straight-Line Opportunity Set

The budget constraint shows what combinations of goods can be purchased with a limited amount of money. It can be drawn given the size of the budget and the prices of the goods.

The time constraint shows what combinations of time-consuming activities can be undertaken with a limited amount of time. To plot the time constraint, you must know the total time available and the time requirements of each activity.

Step one: Draw a set of coordinate axes. Label the horizontal axis as the quantity of one good or activity and the vertical axis as the quantity of the other good or activity.

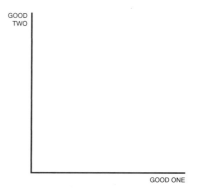

Step two: Calculate the maximum quantity of the good or activity measured on the horizontal axis. Plot this quantity along the horizontal axis.

Step three: Calculate the maximum quantity of the good or activity measured on the vertical axis. Plot this quantity along the vertical axis.

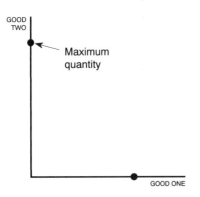

Step four: Draw a line segment connecting the two points. This line segment is the relevant part of the opportunity set.

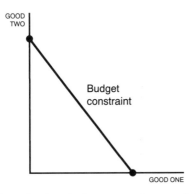

Step five: The slope is the opportunity cost of the good or activity measured on the horizontal axis. In the case of the budget constraint, it is called the relative price, the ratio of the price of the good measured on the horizontal axis divided by the price of the good measured on the vertical axis.

1 (Worked problem: budget constraint) Diana has an entertainment budget of $200 each month. She enjoys lunches with friends and going to the movies. The price of a typical lunch is $10. Movie tickets are $5 each. Construct her opportunity set.

Step-by-step solution

Step one: Draw coordinate axes and label the horizontal one "Lunches" and the vertical one "Movies." (There is no rule as to which good goes where. It would be fine if lunches were measured on the vertical axis and movies on the horizontal.)

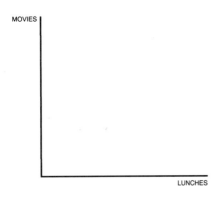

Step two: Calculate the maximum quantity of lunches. This number is $200/$10 = 20 lunches. Plot this quantity along the horizontal axis.

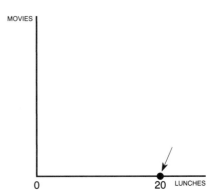

Step three: Calculate the maximum quantity of movies. This number is $200/$5 = 40 movie tickets. Plot this quantity along the vertical axis.

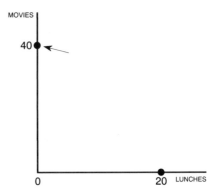

Step four: Draw a line segment connecting these two points. This line segment is the budget constraint.

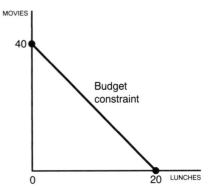

Step five: The slope of the budget constraint is 40/20 = 2. The price ratio is $10/$5 = 2. (Strictly speaking, these slopes are negative, but we follow the practice of dropping the negative sign as long as there is no confusion.)

2 (Practice problem: budget constraint) Velma Thomas must pay for both prescription medicine and nursing care for her elderly father. Each bottle of pills costs her $40, and the price of nursing care is $100 per day. She has been able to scrape together $1,000

each month for these expenses. Construct her opportunity set, going through all five steps.

3 (Practice problem: budget constraint) Construct the following opportunity sets.

    a Clothing budget per year = $900; price of suits = $300; price of shoes = $90.

    b Food budget = $200 per week; price of restaurant meals = $20; price of in-home meals = $5.

    c University expense budget = $1,200 per term; price of books = $50; price of courses = $200.

    d Annual provincial transportation department budget = $100,000; cost of fixing potholes = $200; cost of replacing road signs = $500.

4 (Worked problem: time constraint) Ahmed likes to visit his invalid father across town. Each visit, including transportation and time with Dad, takes 3 hours. Another of Ahmed's favourite activities is his tango lessons. These are given downstairs in his apartment building and take only an hour each. With work and night school, Ahmed has only 15 hours each week to divide between visiting his father and tango lessons. Construct his opportunity set.

Step-by-step solution

Step one: The time constraint works very much like the budget constraint. Plot coordinate axes and label the horizontal one "Visits" and the vertical one "Lessons."

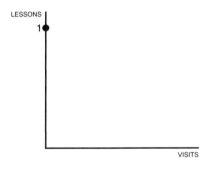

Step two: Calculate the maximum number of visits to his father. This number is 15/3 = 5 visits. Plot this quantity along the horizontal axis.

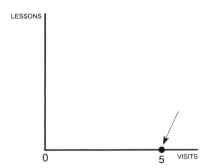

Step three: Calculate the maximum number of tango lessons. This number is 15/1 = 15 lessons. Plot this quantity along the vertical axis.

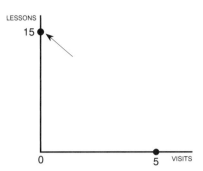

Step four: Draw a line segment connecting these two points. This line segment is the time constraint.

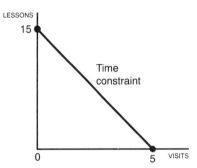

Step five: The slope of the time constraint is 15/5 = 3. The time-requirement ratio is 3/1 = 3.

5 (Practice problem: time constraint) Michael Terranova has 2 hours to make his house as clean as possible. The place needs vacuuming and dusting. He can dust one piece of furniture in 10 minutes. Each room takes 20 minutes to vacuum. Plot his time constraint.

6 (Practice problem: time constraint) Construct the following opportunity sets.

    a Total time available = 6 hours; time required to iron each shirt = 15 minutes; time required to iron each dress = 30 minutes.

    b Total time available = 20 days; time required to study each chapter = 1/2 day; time required to write book reports = 2 days.

    c Total time available = 40 hours; time required to counsel each disturbed teenager = 2 hours; time required to attend each meeting = 1 hour.

    d Total time available = 8 hours; time required to visit each client = 4 hours; time required to telephone each client = 10 minutes.

When the opportunity set involves production, its boundary is called the production possibilities curve. What can be produced is limited by the resources that can be used and the technology, which tells how much of the goods can be produced given the resources.

7 (Worked problem: production possibilities curve) First, assume that there is one resource, which can be used in the production of either of two goods, and that there are no diminishing returns. In this case, the production possibilities curve is a straight line, and we treat it just as we did the budget and time constraints.

There are 25 farm workers employed at a vegetable farm. Each worker can pick 4 bushels of cucumbers an hour. Alternatively, each worker can pick 1 bushel of peppers an hour. Each worker can work 8 hours a day. Plot the daily production possibilities curve.

Step-by-step solution

Step one: Plot coordinate axes and label the horizontal one "Cucumbers" (measured in bushels) and the vertical one "Peppers."

Step two: Calculate the maximum number of cucumbers that can be picked each day. This number is 25 (workers) × 8 (hours) × 4 (bushels an hour) = 800 bushels of cucumbers. Plot this number along the horizontal axis.

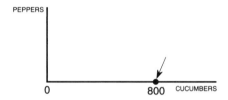

Step three: Calculate the maximum number of peppers that can be picked each day. This number is 25 (workers) × 8 (hours) × 1 (bushel an hour) = 200 bushels of peppers. Plot this number along the vertical axis.

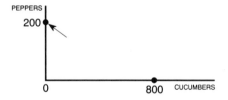

Step four: Draw a line segment connecting these two points. This line segment is the production possibilities curve.

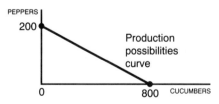

Step five: The slope is 200/800 = 1/4, which means that the opportunity cost of 1 bushel of cucumbers is 1/4 bushel of peppers.

8 (Practice problem: production possibilities curve) Coach Hun has four assistant coaches. They make re-cruiting visits and also run clinics for local youth. Each can make 32 recruiting visits a week. Alternatively, each can run 8 clinics in a week. Plot the production possibilities curve.

9 (Practice problem: production possibilities curve) Construct the following opportunity sets.

   a Total amount of land available = 10 hectares of land; output of corn per hectare = 2,000 bushels; output of wheat per hectare = 1,000 bushels.

   b Total amount of labour available = 40 hours; output of donuts per hour = 150; output of sweet rolls per hour = 50.

   c Total amount of floor space available = 1,000 square metres; sales of women's sportswear per square metre = $500; sales of housewares per square metre = $200.

   d Total amount of fuel available = 5,000 litres; kilometres per litre for tank travel = 3; kilometres per litre for armoured personnel carriers = 9.

Tool Kit 2.2: Plotting Multiple Constraints

Individuals often face more than one constraint. For example, many activities cost money and take up time. This means that the opportunity set includes only those alternatives that do not exceed both the budget and time constraints. To plot the opportunity set when more than one constraint applies, follow this three-step procedure.

Step one: Plot the first constraint. (For example, this might be the budget constraint.)

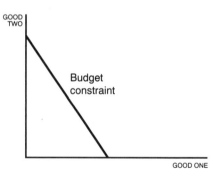

Step two: Plot the second constraint. (For example, this might be the time constraint.)

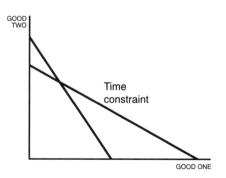

Step three: Darken the section of each constraint that lies under the other constraint. This is the outer edge of the opportunity set.

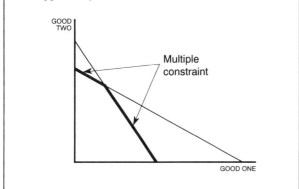

10 (Worked problem: multiple constraints) Out of work for six months, Donna feels that it is time to start looking for a job. Her father (gently) suggests that she apply in person to several of the retail stores on the west side of town. Each store application would require $5 in out-of-pocket expenses for transportation and dry cleaning. (She realizes that only those who wear clean clothes stand any chance of receiving an offer.) Each trip would require 5 hours.

   Donna's mother (not so gently) says that she should mail letters of application to a wide variety of potential employers. Each letter of application would require only $1 in mailing and copying costs and 1/2 hour of time.

   Donna can devote 30 hours and $50 dollars each week to her job search campaign. Plot her opportunity set.

Step-by-step solution

Step one: Follow the procedure for plotting her budget constraint. Label the horizontal axis "Personal applications" and the vertical one "Mail applications." Your answer should look like this.

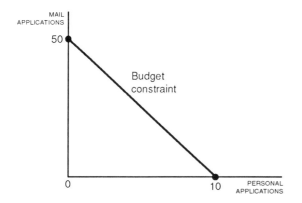

Step two: Follow the procedure for plotting her time constraint. Your answer should look like this.

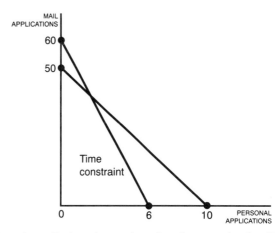

Step three: Darken the section of each constraint that lies under the other constraint. Notice that between points *A* and *B* on the diagram, it is the budget constraint that is binding, but between *B* and *C*, the time constraint is the limiting one.

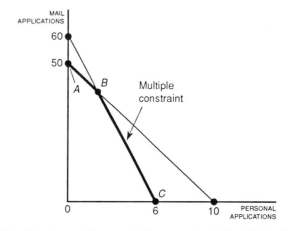

11 (Practice problem: multiple constraints) Harold's leaf-raking business is taking off. He has so many jobs to do that he is thinking of renting a leaf blower. This would cost him $20 per day. With a leaf blower, he could clean 10 lawns each day. He can only do 4 each day with his trusty rake, which costs nothing. Harold works 7 days each week, but has only $100 to spend. Plot his opportunity set for the week. (Hint: The axes should be labelled as lawns cleaned with a leaf blower and lawns raked by hand.)

12 (Practice problem: multiple constraints) The maintenance department at Alberti Van and Storage has 8 mechanic-hours to tune truck engines and replace the mufflers. It takes 1 hour to tune an engine and 1/2 hour to replace the muffler. In addition, the parts budget is only $100, the parts required to tune an engine cost $10, and each muffler costs $20. Construct the department's opportunity set.

13 (Practice problem: multiple constraints) Lamont tests swimming pools and cleans locker rooms for local country clubs. He has 20 hours available, and it takes him 1 hour to test each pool and 1/2 hour to clean each locker room. He has a budget of $50 to spend. It costs him $10 to test each pool and $1 to clean each locker room. Construct his opportunity set.

Tool Kit 2.3: Plotting the Production Possibilities Curve with Diminishing Returns

Diminishing returns mean that as more of some resource is used in production, the extra (or marginal) output declines. Follow this five-step procedure to plot the production possibilities curve with diminishing returns.

Step one: Draw and label a set of coordinate axes.

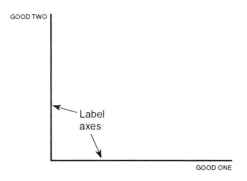

Step two: Calculate the total amount of the good measured on the horizontal axis that can be produced if all the resource is used. Plot this quantity along the horizontal axis.

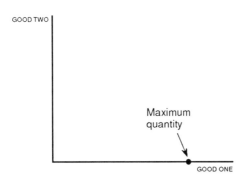

Step three: Calculate the total amount of the good measured on the vertical axis that can be produced if all the resource is used. Plot this quantity along the vertical axis.

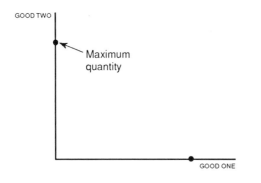

Step four: Calculate and plot several other feasible combinations.

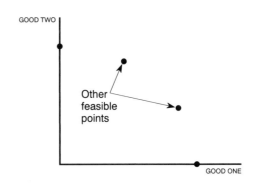

Step five: Draw a smooth curve connecting these points. This curve is the production possibilities curve.

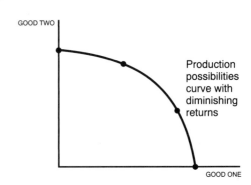

Step six: Verify that the slope is increasing along the curve. Since the slope is the marginal opportunity cost of the horizontal axis good, this reflects diminishing returns.

14 (Worked problem: production possibilities curve) Iatrogenesis, a medical laboratory, employs 4 lab technicians. Each is equally adept at analyzing throat cultures and distilling vaccines. The table below shows output per day for various numbers of lab technicians.

Technicians doing cultures	Throat cultures	Technicians doing vaccines	Vaccines
1	50	1	20
2	90	2	35
3	120	3	45
4	140	4	50

Plot the production possibilities curve for Iatrogenesis.

Step-by-step solution

Step one: Draw coordinate axes. Label the horizontal one "Throat cultures" and the vertical one "Vaccines."

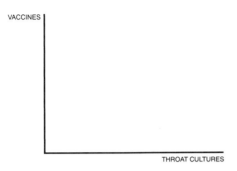

Step two: Calculate the maximum number of throat cultures. If all 4 technicians do throat cultures, the number is 140. Plot this number.

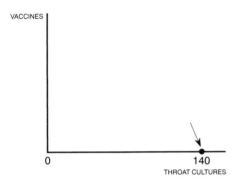

Step three: Calculate the maximum number of vaccines. If all 4 technicians do vaccines, the number is 50. Plot this number.

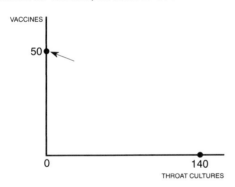

Step four: Calculate several other feasible points. For example, if 1 technician does throat cultures, then 3 can do vaccines. Reading off the table, we see that the combination produced is 50 throat cultures and 45 vaccines. Similarly, if 2 do throat cultures and 2 do vaccines, the outputs are 90 throat cultures and 35 vaccines. Another feasible combination is 120 cultures and 20 vaccines. Plot these points.

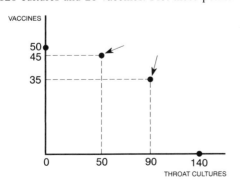

Step five: Draw the production possibilities curve through the points that have been plotted.

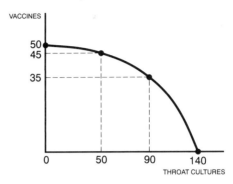

Step six: Observe that, as expected, the slope gets steeper as the number of throat cultures is increased. This indicates diminishing returns.

15 (Practice problem: production possibilities curve) Mulroney Memorial University has a crime problem. Members of the criminal element have stolen many bicycles and a great deal of stereo equipment. To address this crime wave, the campus police has hired 5 new officers. The following table gives the expected number of thefts for various assignments for these new officers.

New police officers assigned to bicycle duty	Reduction in bicycle thefts	New police officers assigned to dorm patrol	Reduction in thefts of stereo equipment
1	25	1	10
2	45	2	18
3	60	3	25
4	70	4	31
5	75	5	36

Plot the production possibilities curve.

16 (Practice problem: production possibilities curve) Movaway Company has employed 4 maintenance inspectors for their fleet of trucks and forklifts. The following table shows how assigning inspectors leads to fewer breakdowns.

Inspectors assigned to check trucks	Reduced number of truck breakdowns	Inspectors assigned to check forklifts	Reduced number of forklift breakdowns
1	5	1	3
2	9	2	5
3	12	3	6
4	14	4	6

Plot Movaway's production possibilities curve, and verify that it shows diminishing returns.

17 (Practice problem: production possibilities curve) The Don Getty vegetable farm (located on erstwhile corn-growing land in Alberta) has 800 tonnes of fertilizer. The following table shows how output of endive and

bib lettuce is expected to respond to different amounts of fertilizer.

Fertilizer used on endive crop (tonnes)	Output of endive (bushels)	Fertilizer used on lettuce crop (tonnes)	Output of bib lettuce (bushels)
0	1,400	0	2,000
200	2,400	200	3,400
400	3,200	400	4,200
600	3,600	600	4,700
800	4,000	800	5,000

Plot the farm's production possibilities curve, and verify that it exhibits diminishing returns.

Tool Kit 2.4: Distinguishing Opportunity Costs and Sunk Costs

Rational individuals make choices by carefully weighing the benefits and costs of their alternatives. Doing this requires a clear understanding of exactly what an opportunity cost is. Expenditures that cannot be recovered are not true opportunity costs. They are sunk costs and should not affect decisions.

Opportunity costs are forgone alternatives. To find the opportunity cost of an action, it is necessary to see what is changed by undertaking that action rather than its alternative. Follow this four-step procedure.

Step one: To find the opportunity cost of an action, first specify the next-best alternative. This is what would be done if the action in question were not chosen.

Step two: Calculate the total cost for the action and its alternative.

Step three: Calculate the opportunity cost. Subtract the cost for the alternative from the cost for the action. This difference is the opportunity cost of the action.

Step four: Calculate the sunk costs. Any costs that are the same for both the chosen action and its alternative are sunk costs.

---

18 (Worked problem: opportunity cost and sunk costs) Bruce Peninsula Airlines is studying the question of when to cancel flights for its Toronto to Tobermory route. Flying nearly empty planes seems like bad business. The company wants to know the opportunity cost of going ahead with a scheduled round-trip flight. There are two scheduled flights each day. Here are some relevant cost data.

Salaries of crew	$1,000 per day
Fuel	$ 400 per round trip
Mortgage on plane	$ 100 per day
Landing fees	$ 50 in Tobermory
	$ 100 in Toronto
Other in-flight costs	$ 100 per round trip

Calculate the opportunity cost of each round trip.

Step-by-step solution

Step one: The next-best alternative to going ahead with the scheduled round-trip flight is not flying.

Step two: Calculate the total cost for going ahead with the flight and cancelling it. If the flight is made, the expenditures are all those listed above. If the flight is cancelled, the company saves on fuel, landing fees, and other in-flight costs. The salaries of the crew and the mortage must be paid whether the flight happens or not.

Expenditures if flight is not cancelled =

$1,000 + $400 + $100 + $150 + $100 = $1,750.

Expenditures if flight is cancelled = $1,000 + $100 = $1,100.

Step three: Calculate the opportunity cost of the flight: $1,750 − $1,100 = $650.

Step four: Calculate the sunk costs. The remaining $1,100 for salaries and mortgage are sunk costs. Whether or not the flight is cancelled, these cannot be recovered.

19 (Practice problem: opportunity cost and sunk costs) Often during the summer term, courses are scheduled but cancelled at Mulroney Memorial University's downtown education building. In order to see whether this is a good policy, the administration needs to know the opportunity cost of going ahead with a scheduled course offering. Here are some cost data.

Compensation for instructor	$4,000
Air conditioning and lighting	$1,000
Custodial services	$2,000
Property taxes	$2,500

Each course requires one room. Any rooms not used for summer courses can be rented to local groups for $1,200 for the summer term.

a Find the opportunity cost of offering a course.
b How much are sunk costs?

20 (Practice problem: opportunity cost and sunk costs) The Bank of Canada is downsizing under Governor Raven. It is considering offering early retirement to 8 bureaucrats. Each is 2 years from regular retirement age. (For simplicity, you may ignore discounting the second year's dollars in this problem.)

Salaries	$50,000 each (per year)
Fringe benefits	$20,000 each (per year)
Office space for all 8	$10,000 annually (lease signed for 1 more year)
Pension benefit	$20,000 each if retired (per year)

a If the 8 bureaucrats do receive early retirement, what is the opportunity cost?
b How much are sunk costs?

Tool Kit 2.5: Using Marginal Benefit and Marginal Cost

The rational individual always considers the benefit and cost of any activity. Once you decide to do something, however, there is the question of how much of it to do. Answering this question involves looking at the benefit and cost of a little more or a little less, the marginal benefit and marginal cost. To determine how much of any activity to do, follow this four-step procedure.

Step one: Identify the objective of the activity and the benefit and cost of various levels of the activity.

Step two: Calculate the marginal benefit. This is the extra gain from a little bit more of the activity.

Step three: Calculate the marginal cost. This is the extra cost from a little bit more of the activity.

Step four: Choose the level of the activity for which the marginal benefit equals the marginal cost.

21 (Worked problem: marginal cost and marginal benefit) A new inoculation against Honduran flu has just been discovered. Presently, 55 people die from the disease each year. The new inoculation will save lives, but unfortunately, it is not completely safe. Some of the recipients of the shots will die from adverse reactions. The projected effects of the inoculation are given in Table 2.1.

Table 2.1

Percent of population inoculated	Deaths due to the disease	Deaths due to the inoculations
0	55	0
10	45	0
20	36	1
30	28	2
40	21	3
50	15	5
60	10	8
70	6	12
80	3	17
90	1	23
100	0	30

How much of the population should be inoculated?

Step-by-step solution

Step one: Identify the objective, benefit, and cost. The objective is to minimize total deaths from the disease and the inoculations, and the problem is to choose the percentage of the population to inoculate. The benefit is reduced deaths caused by the disease, and the cost is the deaths caused by the shots.

Step two: Calculate the marginal benefit. The first 10 percent of the population inoculated reduces deaths caused by disease from 55 to 45. The marginal benefit of the first 10 percent is 10. From the second 10 percent (increasing the percentage from 10 to 12), the marginal benefit is $45 - 36 = 9$. The schedule of the marginal benefit is given in Table 2.2.

Table 2.2

Percent of population	Marginal benefit
10	10
20	9
30	8
40	7
50	6
60	5
70	4
80	3
90	2
100	1

Step three: Calculate the marginal cost. Inoculating the first 10 percent causes no deaths. The second 10 percent (increasing the percent of the population getting the shots from 10 to 20 percent) causes 1 death. The schedule for the marginal cost is shown in Table 2.3.

Table 2.3

Percent of population	Marginal cost
0	0
10	1
20	1
30	1
40	1
50	2
60	3
70	4
80	5
90	6
100	7

Step four: Choose the level of inoculation percentage for which marginal benefit equals marginal cost. The percentage of the population to inoculate is 70. To see why this is correct, notice that inoculating 10 percent of the population saves 10 lives (marginal benefit = 10) and causes no deaths (marginal cost = 0). The net savings in lives is 10. Increasing the percentage to 20 percent saves 9 lives at a cost of 1 death. The net savings is 9 lives. Continuing as long as deaths do not rise gives 70 percent. Notice that increasing the percentage to 80 percent saves fewer people (marginal benefit = 2) than it kills (marginal cost = 4). This is a bad idea. We should stop at 70 percent.

22 (Practice problem: marginal cost and marginal benefit) The transportation department has 10 workers fixing potholes. It is considering allocating some of these workers to reprogram traffic lights. Each activity saves travel time for commuters, and this is the objective of the transportation department. Table 2.4 gives time savings of each activity as the number of

workers assigned to it varies. Remember that if a worker is assigned to reprogram lights, he cannot fix potholes.

Table 2.4

Workers assigned to reprogramming	Total time saved	Workers assigned to fix potholes	Total time saved
1	100	1	125
2	190	2	225
3	270	3	305
4	340	4	365
5	400	5	415
6	450	6	455
7	490	7	485
8	520	8	510
9	540	9	530
10	550	10	540

How should the workers be assigned? (Hint: Let the number of workers assigned to reprogramming be the activity. What is the cost of assigning these workers?)

23 (Practice problem: marginal cost and marginal benefit) Bugout pesticide kills insects that eat lettuce leaves. Currently 11 leaves per head are eaten by the insects. In the right concentrations, Bugout can be effective. On the other hand, there are side effects. When the concentration is too great, leaves fall off the lettuce head. Table 2.5 shows the relationship between concentrations of Bugout, leaves eaten, and leaves fallen. What concentration should the manufacturer recommend?

Table 2.5

Concentration (parts per million)	Leaves eaten per head	Leaves fallen per head
1	7	0
2	4	1
3	2	3
4	1	6
5	0	10
6	0	15

Answers to Problems

2
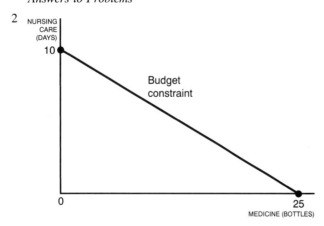

3
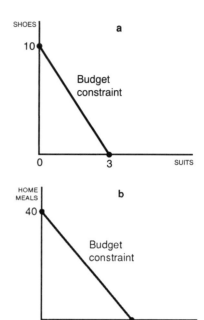

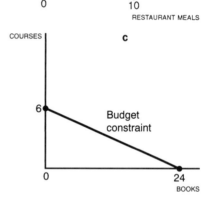

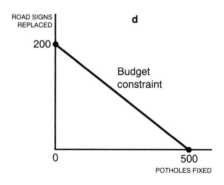

5
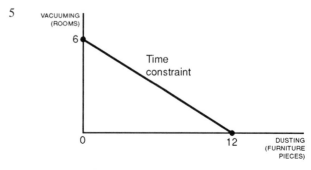

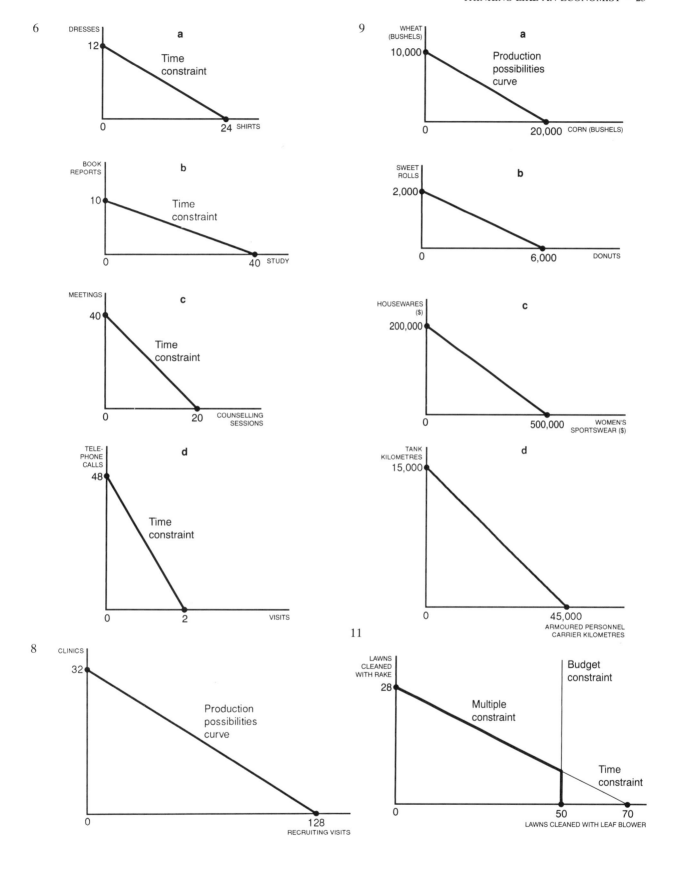

12
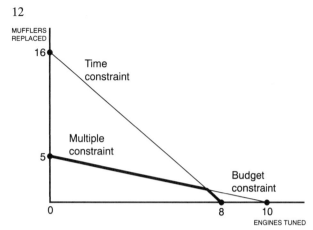

13
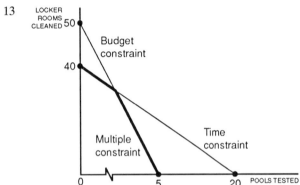

15

Reduction in bicycle thefts	Reduction in thefts of stereo equipment
0	36
25	31
45	25
60	18
70	10
75	0

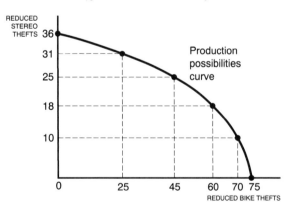

16

Reduced number of truck breakdowns	Reduced number of forklift breakdowns
0	6
5	6
9	5
12	3
14	0

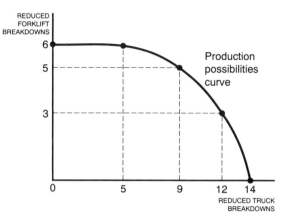

17

Endive (bushels)	Lettuce (bushels)
1,400	5,000
2,400	4,700
3,200	4,200
3,600	3,400
4,000	2,000

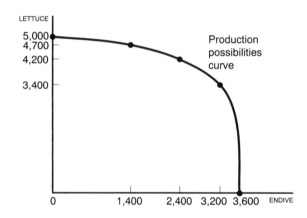

19

	Costs of holding class	Costs of cancelling class
Compensation for instructor	$4,000	0
Air conditioning and lighting	$1,000	$1,000
Custodial services	$2,000	$2,000
Property taxes	$2,500	$2,500
Rent	0	– $1,200
Total	**$9,500**	**$4,300**

a   Opportunity cost = $9,500 – $4,300 = $5,200.
b   Sunk costs = $4,300.

20

	Costs of early retirements	Costs of retaining bureaucrats
Salaries	0	$50,000 × 8 × 2
Fringe benefits	0	$20,000 × 8 × 2
Office space for all 8	$ 10,000	$20,000
Pension benefit	$ 20,000 × 8 × 2	0
	$330,000	$1,140,000

a   Opportunity cost = $1,140,000 − $330,000 = $810,000.

b   Sunk costs = $330,000.

22   The marginal benefit of assigning a worker to reprogram the lights is the time saved; the marginal cost is the time lost because the worker was not assigned to fix potholes.

Worker assigned to reprogramming	Marginal benefit	Marginal cost
1	100	10
2	90	20
3	80	25
4	70	30
5	60	40
6	50	50
7	40	60
8	30	80
9	20	100
10	10	125

Assign 6 to reprogramming and 4 to fixing potholes.

23   The benefit of recommending higher concentrations of pesticides is the fewer leaves eaten; the cost is the leaves that fall off.

Concentration of pesticide	Marginal benefit	Marginal cost
1	4	0
2	3	1
3	2	2
4	1	3
5	1	4
6	0	5

The manufacturer should recommend a concentration of 3 ppm.

EXCHANGE AND PRODUCTION

Chapter Review

Chapter 3 takes up the key feature of markets: exchange. The fundamental aspect of market-based economies is voluntary trade. By definition, voluntary trade is mutually beneficial; it creates a surplus for both buyer and seller. If this were not true, the trade would not take place! An important insight of trade theory is the principle of comparative advantage, which shows how individuals and countries can specialize in production and thereby increase the gains they receive from trade. Economists emphasize these gains from trade and see little sense in protectionist arguments that trade between countries should be limited. The next two chapters will show how markets help realize some of the potential gains from trade.

ESSENTIAL CONCEPTS

1 Voluntary trade between rational individuals is **mutually beneficial;** it is good for both buyer and seller. Naturally, the buyer would like a lower price, and the seller prefers a higher price. Both might also benefit from better information. Nevertheless, the fact that the exchange takes place implies that given the information each has at the time of the transaction, both judge that they are better off trading than not trading.

2 Trade between individuals within a country and trade between individuals in different countries take place in markets. The three broad classes of markets are the product, labour, and capital markets. These three markets are all integrated internationally; this has led to a high degree of economic interdependence among nations.

3 Trade is many-sided, or multilateral. A typical person sells labour to an employer and uses the wages earned both to purchase goods and services from many other firms and to save for future consumption. Similarly, a country may import more from some trading partners and export very little to those countries. With other trading partners, the country may export more than it imports. A country may also buy more goods and services than it sells abroad, and make up the difference by borrowing in capital markets or sending its workers to foreign labour markets.

4 The principle of **comparative advantage** says that in-

dividuals and countries will specialize in those goods that they are relatively more efficient in producing. To be relatively efficient means to have a lower opportunity cost. Countries will have comparative advantages in different goods. Each can import certain goods from abroad for a lower opportunity cost than it would incur producing them at home. Similarly, each can export to foreign countries those goods for which it has a comparative advantage.

5 Comparative advantage leads to **specialization** in trade, but specialization itself increases productivity and further lowers opportunity costs. First, individuals and countries grow more efficient at their specialties through practice. Second, producing for others allows a larger scale of operations, more **division of labour** into separate tasks, and more specialization. Finally, specialization creates conditions in which invention and innovation flourish.

6 Different countries and individuals have comparative advantages in different activities. Reasons for a comparative advantage can include natural endowments such as climate (for a country) or manual dexterity (for a tailor), human or physical capital, knowledge, and experience. These factors may be gifts of nature, or they may be the result of investment, experience, -education, training, or other past actions.

7 **Protectionism** is the idea that the economy needs safeguarding against the perceived harmful effects of trade. Proponents of protectionism use many arguments; chief among them are the loss of domestic jobs, the vulnerability to foreign influences, the unfair trade practices of foreign governments, trade imbalances, and the potential damage to weak economies. To economists, none of these arguments is convincing.

8[1] Some of the benefits of economic interdependence come from exchange; some are the result of working together in organizations. Each type of activity has its costs as well. The costs of exchanging are called **transactions costs.** These include the costs of bringing buyers and sellers together, holding inventories of unsold goods, advertising, and determining prices. The costs of organizations include problems of providing incentives, communicating and coordinating information, selecting people for different tasks, and simply making the decisions that organizations must make.

BEHIND THE ESSENTIAL CONCEPTS

1 An exchange creates and divides a surplus. The surplus is the difference between the value to the seller of what is traded and its value to the buyer. If there is no surplus, the exchange does not take place; the seller simply refuses to trade if he thinks the good is worth more than the buyer is willing to pay. The division of

the surplus is another matter. Both the buyer and seller will receive some of the surplus. This is what economists mean when they say that trade is mutually beneficial: each party receives some of the surplus. The buyer pays somewhat less than the maximum she is willing to pay, and the seller receives somewhat more than the minimum he is willing to accept. Of course, whatever the division of the surplus, each would prefer to receive more.

2 When individuals trade, both buyer and seller gain. Each is better off with the trade than he or she would be if the trade did not take place. Likewise, countries also gain from trade. Trade allows specialization on the basis of comparative advantage, and countries benefit from more goods and services. But although each country as a whole gains from trade, not every individual in each country is better off. Some businesses lose out to foreign competition, and some workers lose jobs. Other businesses gain new markets, and new jobs are created. Thus, international trade creates both gains and losses, but overall, the gains outweigh the losses.

3 The problem with protectionism is that it looks only at the losers from international trade. Tariffs, quotas, and other protectionist policies can, at least temporarily, protect the losers, but only by limiting the trade. Limiting the trade means limiting the gains as well as the losses. Because the gains from trade exceed the losses, protectionism can only make matters worse for the economy as a whole.

4 To gain a better understanding of comparative advantage, it helps to distinguish it from **absolute advantage.** A country has an absolute advantage in the production of a good or service if it requires fewer inputs to produce the good than another country. Comparative advantage, on the other hand, pertains to opportunity cost. As we have seen, the opportunity cost is not the inputs used in production; rather, it is the alternative use of those inputs. Thus, a country (or individual) has the comparative advantage in the production of a good or service if it has the lower opportunity cost.

For instance, assume that only labour is required to produce tomatoes or bookcases. Workers in country A can produce a carload of tomatoes in 40 hours, while workers in country B require 80 hours. Country A has an absolute advantage in producing tomatoes. To determine comparative advantage, however, we must look at how productive those workers are elsewhere in the economy. If the 40 hours of labour in country A produce 2 bookcases, but 80 hours in country B produce only 1, then country B has a comparative advantage in tomatoes. Why? Because a carload of tomatoes has an opportunity cost of 1 fewer bookcase in country B.

5[2] Economists see the balancing of benefits and costs in many areas. For example, what determines which tasks will be done within an organization and which will be

[1]This topic is covered in the appendix to Chapter 3.

[2]This topic is covered in the appendix to Chapter 3.

purchased in markets? For a firm, this is the make-or-buy decision: should the firm make it or buy it from someone else? If it chooses to buy, there are transactions costs. On the other hand, if it chooses to make, there are the costs of organization.

SELF-TEST

True or False

F 1 Unless the gain from trade is divided equally between buyer and seller, an exchange cannot be mutually beneficial. F

F 2 Because of problems of information, problems of estimating risks, and difficulties in forming expectations about the future, many exchanges are not mutually beneficial. F

T 3 With multilateral trade, imports from a particular country may not equal exports to that country. T

F 4 The country that can produce a good with the least amount of labour is said to have a comparative advantage in the production of that good. F

F 5 Trade on the basis of comparative advantage leads to complete specialization.

T 6 The extent of the division of labour is limited by the size of the market. T

T 7 Comparative advantage is determined by the endowment of natural resources, human and physical capital, knowledge, and the experience that comes from specialization. T

T 8 Opposition to trade between nations is called protectionism.

F 9 A country that exports more than it imports will run a trade deficit. F

T 10 Although trade benefits the country as a whole, many individuals may lose from trade in a particular product.

T 11 A country that runs a trade deficit must borrow from abroad.

T 12 Transactions costs in the market may be so large that the economic interaction takes place within organizations.

T 13 Incentive problems arise whenever the decision maker does not receive the full benefits and costs of the decision. T

T 14 Organizations face a selection problem, in that someone must decide who should do which tasks. T

T 15 In centralized systems, more control is exercised by top management. T

[3]Questions 12–15 are covered in the appendix to Chapter 3.

Multiple Choice

1 Voluntary trade between two rational individuals

a benefits the buyer only.
b benefits the seller only.
c benefits the buyer or the seller but not both.
d benefits both the buyer and the seller.
e none of the above.

2 The gain from trade, that is, the difference between the value of a good to the buyer and its value to the seller,

a accrues entirely to the seller.
b accrues entirely to the buyer.
c is always divided equally.
d accrues to the government.
e none of the above.

3 When economists argue that both parties benefit from voluntary trade, they are assuming

a that both parties are well-informed.
b that both parties place the same value on the traded good.
c that both parties desire the same price.
d that the surplus is divided evenly between buyer and seller.
e none of the above.

4 Goods produced in Canada and sold in foreign countries are called

a imports.
b exports.
c either imports or exports.
d capital flows.
e none of the above.

5 If Japan buys oil from Saudi Arabia, Saudi Arabia buys grain from Canada, and Canada buys cars and televisions from Japan, this is an example of

a multilateral trade.
b bilateral trade.
c absolute advantage.
d selection.
e incentive problems.

6 If Canada has a comparative advantage in the production of a good, then

a fewer resources are required to produce the good in Canada.
b Canada also has an absolute advantage in the production of the good.
c the relative cost of producing the good is lower in Canada.
e none of the above.

7 The principle of comparative advantage

a applies only to international trade.
b always leads to complete specialization.
c forms the basis for the division of labour.
d is relevant only in the absence of protection.
e none of the above.

8 Which of the following is not a reason why specialization increases productivity?

    a Workers and countries grow more efficient by repeating the same tasks.

    b Specialization saves time needed to switch from one task to another.

    c Specialization allows larger-scale production with greater efficiency.

    d Specialization allows the assignment of tasks to those who have a comparative advantage.

    e none of the above.

9 Which of the following is not an important source of comparative advantage?

    a natural endowments

    b human and physical capital

    c superior knowledge

    d experience

    e protectionism

10 If two countries have identical relative opportunity costs,

    a there will never be any basis for trade.

    b they might specialize in the production of certain goods and acquire a comparative advantage in those goods over time.

    c each will gain from protectionist policies.

    d the country with an absolute advantage will reap all of the gains from trade.

    e none of the above.

11 When two countries trade,

    a all individuals and firms in both countries benefit.

    b all individuals and firms in at least one country benefit.

    c no individuals or firms in either country benefit.

    d particular groups in each country may be hurt by trade in some goods.

    e none of the above.

12 Increased immigration of unskilled workers into Canada is likely to

    a raise wages of unskilled workers already in Canada, lower consumer goods prices, and make Canadian firms more competitive in international markets.

    b lower wages of unskilled workers already in Canada, raise consumer goods prices, and make Canadian firms less competitive in international markets.

    c raise wages of unskilled workers already in Canada, raise consumer goods prices, and make Canadian firms less competitive in international markets.

    d lower wages of unskilled workers already in Canada, lower consumer goods prices, and make Canadian firms more competitive in international markets.

    e none of the above.

13 If a country runs a trade deficit for several years,

    a it imports more goods and services than it exports and must borrow from abroad.

    b it exports more goods and services than it imports and must borrow from abroad.

    c it imports more goods and services than it exports and must lend money abroad.

    d it exports more goods and services than it imports and must lend money abroad.

    e another country must have a trade surplus of an identical amount.

14 The passage about the production of pencils (p. 67 in the text) illustrates

    a the law of diminishing returns.

    b the principle of scarcity.

    c the benefits from specialization.

    d the fact that incentive problems are caused by imperfect and costly information.

    e none of the above.

15[4] Which of the following are transaction costs?

    a wages paid to skilled workers at the factory

    b interest payments

    c marketing costs

    d costs of complying with government regulations

    e none of the above

16 Incentive problems arise whenever costs and benefits do not accrue to the person making the decision. In which of the following cases is there no incentive problem?

    a a family considers participating in voluntary recycling

    b a man rents an apartment that provides free electricity

    c an office allows its employees uncontrolled use of its telephones

    d a household pays a fixed rate (that is, independent of usage) for water

    e none of the above

17 Which of the following is not one of the basic problems of economic organizations?

    a providing incentives to subordinates

    b communicating and coordinating dispersed information

    c selecting which person should do each task

    d taking decisions with imperfect information

    e none of the above

18 Which of the following is not an advantage of decentralized decision making?

    a an ability to respond quickly to changes in the environment

    b better incentives for subordinates

    c better motivation

    d the ability to coordinate decisions

    e none of the above

[4]Questions 15–20 are covered in the appendix to Chapter 3.

19 In a mixed economy,

    a all economic decisions are taken centrally.

    b problems concerning the communication and co-ordination of information are unimportant.

    c there is considerable decentralization of decision making, and the powers of government are limited.

    d the state controls the means of production.

    e there is no role for government.

20 In large organizations,

    a production is more efficient because of the principle of diminishing returns.

    b centralized decision making solves all incentive and information problems.

    c basic problems such as selection, coordination, and incentives arise from the fact that information is imperfect and costly.

    d decentralized decision making solves all incentive and information problems.

    e comparative advantage does not apply.

Completion

1 The difference between what a person is willing to pay for an item and what she has to pay is a gain from trade, or _surplus_.

2 If a country is relatively more efficient at producing a good than its trading partners, then that country is said to have an _comparative advantage_ in the production of that good.

3 Because of trade possibilities, individuals and countries can produce more of what each has a comparative advantage in. This specialization or division of labour is limited by the _size_ of the market.

4 _Natural endowments_ such as location, natural resources, and climate are bases of comparative advantage.

5 Acquired endowments, such as physical and human _capital_, represent other sources of comparative advantage.

6 The doctrine that the economy of a country is injured by trade is called _protectionism_

7[5] The costs of buying and selling in markets are called _transaction costs_

8 _Incentive_ problems arise when individuals do not receive the full benefits and costs of their decisions.

9 The delegation of responsibility to subordinates is an example of _decentralized_ decision making.

10 The fundamental problems of organizations—incentives, communication and coordination, selection, and decision making—arise because _information_ is imperfect and costly.

[5]Questions 7–10 are covered in the appendix to Chapter 3.

Answers to Self-Test

True or False

1 f	4 f	7 t	10 t	13 t
2 f	5 f	8 t	11 t	14 t
3 t	6 t	9 f	12 t	15 t

Multiple Choice

1 d	6 c	11 d	16 e
2 e	7 c	12 d	17 e
3 e	8 e	13 a	18 d
4 b	9 e	14 c	19 c
5 a	10 b	15 c	20 c

Completion

1 surplus
2 comparative advantage
3 size
4 Natural endowments
5 capital
6 protectionism
7 transactions costs
8 Incentive
9 decentralized
10 information

Doing Economics: Tools and Practice Problems

This chapter introduces comparative advantage, a very important concept. The principle of comparative advantage illustrates how individuals, firms, and countries can benefit by specializing in performing tasks or producing goods and trading with each other. This problem set will help you to identify comparative advantage and to see why comparative advantage determines the division of labour and the pattern of trade. You will also study the gains from trade when they proceed according to comparative advantage. Finally, you will use the idea of comparative advantage to construct the production possibilities curve for the case in which resources differ.

1 (Worked problem: comparative advantage) Workers in Canada and Brazil can produce shoes and computers. The annual productivity of a worker in each country is given in the table below.

Country	Computers	Shoes
Canada	5,000	10,000
Brazil	200	5,000

    a Which country has a comparative advantage in computers? in shoes?

    b Predict the pattern of trade.

    c Indicate the range of possible relative prices that would bring about this pattern of trade.

Step-by-step solution

Step one (a): Plot the production possibilities curves. In this problem, the production possibilities curve for one worker in

Tool Kit 3.1: Identifying Comparative Advantage

When a country or individual has a comparative advantage in performing some task or producing some good, that country or individual is relatively more efficient, which means that the country or individual has the lower opportunity cost. The following procedure shows how to identify comparative advantage and predict the pattern of trade. It is written for the case of two-country trade.

Step one: Plot the production possibilities curve for each country. Be sure to be consistent and measure units of the same good along the horizontal axis in each case.

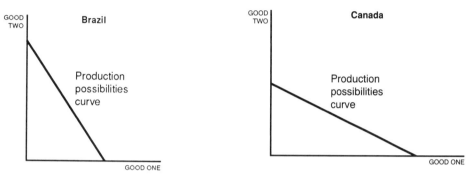

Step two: The slope of the production possibilities curve is the opportunity cost of the good on the horizontal axis, and it indicates the trade-off. The flatter slope implies a comparative advantage for producing the good on the horizontal axis.

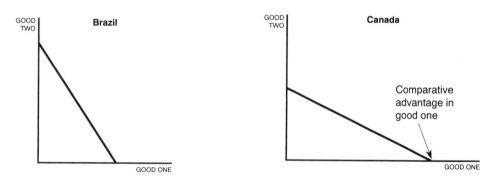

Step three: The steeper slope indicates a comparative advantage for producing the good on the vertical axis.

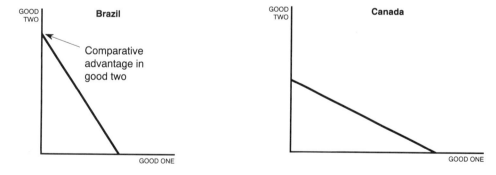

Step four: In a system of free trade, each country will produce more of the good in which it has a comparative advantage, and the relative price will lie somewhere between the opportunity costs of the two countries.

each country will suffice. Measure computers on the horizontal axis.

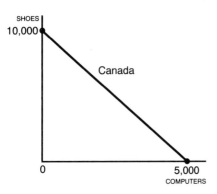

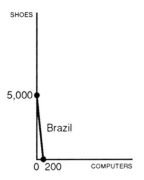

Step two: The production possibilities curve for Canada has the flatter slope; therefore, the Canadian worker has a comparative advantage in the production of computers.

Step three: The production possibilities curve for Brazil is steeper, and the Brazilian worker has a comparative advantage in shoes.

Step four (b and c): Brazil will trade shoes for Canadian computers. The relative price must lie between 2 shoes per computer (the Canadian opportunity cost) and 25 shoes per computer (the Brazilian opportunity cost).

2 (Practice problem: comparative advantage) Workers in Nigeria and neighbouring Niger produce textiles and sorghum. The productivities of each are given in the table below.

Country	Textiles (bales)	Sorghum (bushels)
Nigeria	100	500
Niger	50	400

 a Which country has a comparative advantage in textiles? in sorghum?
 b Predict the pattern of trade.
 c Indicate the range of possible relative prices that would bring about this pattern of trade.

3 (Practice problem: comparative advantage) For each of the following, determine which country has a comparative advantage in each good, predict the pattern of trade, and indicate the range of possible relative prices consistent with this pattern of trade.

a Country	Fish	Wheat (bushels)
Greece	60	80
Poland	35	70

b Country	Heart bypass operations	Auto parts (containers)
United States	5,000	10,000
Canada	3,000	9,000

c Country	Scrap steel (tonnes)	Finished steel (tonnes)
Thailand	20	20
Laos	10	2

d Country	Wine (barrels)	Wool (bales)
Portugal	2	2
Great Britain	4	8

4 (Worked problem: gains from trade) This problem builds upon problem #1. Show that a worker in Brazil and a worker in Canada can benefit by trading on the basis of comparative advantage.

Step-by-step solution

Step one: Identify the country with a comparative advantage in each good and the trade-offs for each country. The Canadian worker has a comparative advantage in computers, and the trade-off is 2 shoes per computer. The Brazilian worker has a comparative advantage in shoes, and the trade-off is 25 shoes per computer.

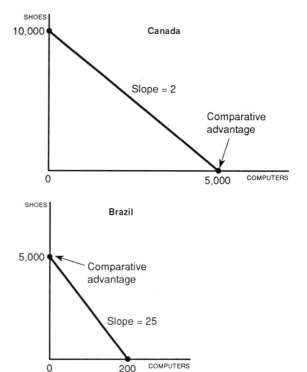

Step two: Choose a relative price between the trade-offs. Let's choose 20 shoes per computer.

Tool Kit 3.2: Showing the Gains from Trade

When the pattern of trade is based upon comparative advantage, both countries can gain. Specifically, they each can consume a bundle of goods that lies beyond their own production possibilities curve.

Step one: Draw the production possibilities curve for each country, identify the country with a comparative advantage in each good, and identify the trade-offs for each country.

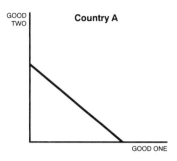
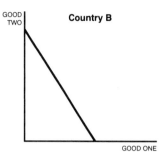

Step two: Choose a relative price between the trade-offs.

Step three: For the country with the comparative advantage in the horizontal-axis good, label the horizontal intercept *A* and draw a line segment from *A* with a slope equal to (−) the relative price. This line segment shows the bundles of goods that the country can consume by trading at the given relative price.

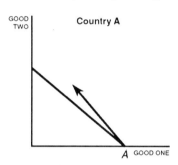
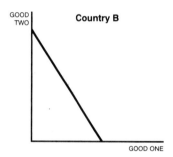

Step four: For the country with the comparative advantage in the vertical-axis good, label the vertical intercept *A* and draw a line segment from *A* with a slope equal to (−) the relative price. This line segment shows the bundles of goods that this country can consume by trading at the given relative price.

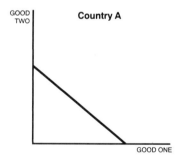
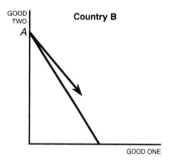

Step five: Pick a pair of consistent points, where A's exports equal B's imports, one on each line segment, and show how each country can benefit from trade.

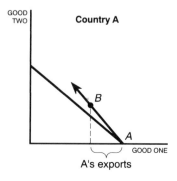
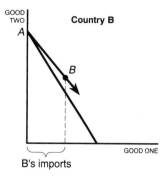

Step three: For the country with the comparative advantage in computers, which is Canada, label the horizontal intercept *A* and draw a line segment from *A* with a slope equal to –20. This line segment shows the bundles of goods that Canada can consume by trading at the given relative price.

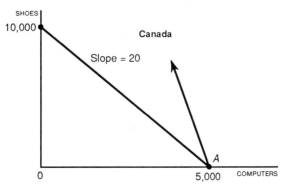

Step four: For the country with the comparative advantage in shoes, which is Brazil, label the vertical intercept *A* and draw a line segment from *A* with a slope equal to –20. This line

segment shows the bundles of goods that Brazil can consume by trading at the given relative price.

Step five: Pick a pair of consistent points, one on each line segment, and show how each country can benefit from trade. Let the Canadian worker produce 4,800 computers for domestic consumption. This leaves 200 for trade. At a relative price of 20 shoes, the 200 computers trade for 4,000 shoes. Plot the point (4,000, 4,800) and label it *B*. The Brazilian

---

Tool Kit 3.3: Plotting the Production Possibilities Curve When Resources Are Different

Free trade assigns to each country the task of producing those goods in which it has a comparative advantage. The same is true for trade between individuals. To see why this is efficient, we now consider the joint production possibilities curve in the case where there are two or more different types of resources that can be used in the production of two goods. The problems will illustrate that it is necessary to assign resources to produce the good in which the resources themselves have a comparative advantage.

Step one: Draw a set of coordinate axes. Label the horizontal axis as the quantity of one good and the vertical axis as the quantity of the other good.

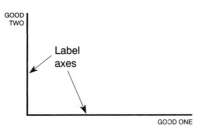

Step two: Calculate the maximum quantities of each good that can be produced. Plot the quantity along the vertical axis and label the point *B*. Plot the quantity along the horizontal axis and label this point *A*.

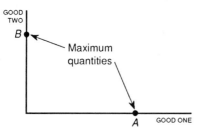

Step three: Identify the resource with the comparative advantage for each good.

Step four: Choose the resource with the comparative advantage in the horizontal-axis good and assign it to produce this good, while keeping the other resource producing the vertical-axis good. Calculate the total quantities produced, and plot this point. Label it *C*.

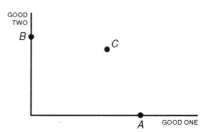

Step five: Connect the points *BCA* with line segments. This is the production possibilities curve.

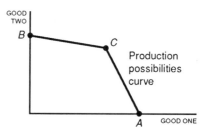

Step six: Verify that the slope is increasing. Because the slope measures the opportunity cost of the horizontal-axis good, this means that the opportunity cost is increasing; this implies the principle of diminishing returns.

worker must then produce 4,000 shoes for trade. This leaves 1,000 shoes for domestic consumption. The 4,000 shoes trade for 200 computers. Plot the point (200, 1,000) and label it *B*. At this point, Canada exports 200 computers and imports 4,000 shoes, while Brazil imports 200 computers and exports 4,000 shoes. Trade is balanced, and each country consumes beyond its production possibilities curve.

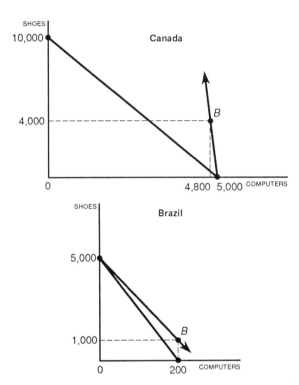

5 (Practice problem: gains from trade) This problem builds upon problem #2. Show that workers in Nigeria and Niger can benefit by trading according to comparative advantage.

6 (Worked problem: production possibilities curve) Harrigan and her daughter have formed a two-person firm to handle business incorporations and real estate transactions. The hours required for each type of task are given below. Each works 48 hours every week.

Lawyer	Hours required to perform each incorporation	Hours required to complete each transaction
Harrigan	4	8
Daughter	8	24

Plot their weekly production possibilities curve.

Step-by-step solution

Step one: Draw and label a set of coordinate axes. Put real estate transactions on the horizontal axis and incorporations on the vertical.

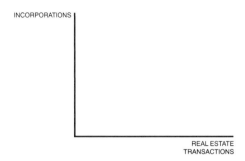

Step two: Calculate the maximum number of incorporations they can do in a week. For Harrigan, this number is 48/4 = 12; for her daughter, it is 48/8 = 6. The pair can complete 18 incorporations. Plot this point along the vertical axis, and label it *A*. Concerning real estate transactions, Harrigan can do 48/8 = 6; her daughter, 48/24 = 2. The pair can do 8. Plot this point along the horizontal axis, and label it *B*.

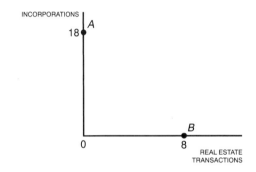

Step three: Identify the resource with the comparative advantage for each good. Since it takes Harrigan 8 hours to complete each real estate transaction but only 4 to do an incorporation, each real estate transaction requires enough time to do 2 incorporations. The opportunity cost of a real estate transaction for Harrigan is, then, 2 incorporations. By the same argument, the opportunity cost for her daughter is 24/8 = 3 incorporations; thus, Harrigan has the comparative advantage in real estate transactions, while her daughter has the comparative advantage in incorporations.

Step four: We assign to Harrigan the task of real estate transactions, leaving her daughter to do the incorporations. With this assignment, they can do 6 incorporations and 6 real estate transactions (see step two). Plot this point, and label it *C*.

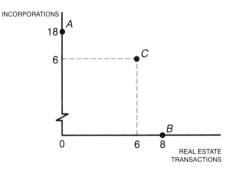

Step five: Draw line segments connecting the points. This is the production possibilities curve.

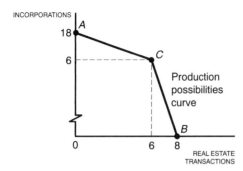

Step six: Note that between *A* and *C* the slope is 2, but between *C* and *B* the slope increases to 3. The shape of the production possibilities curve thus indicates diminishing returns.

7 (Practice problem: production possibilities curve) A farmer has 3 hectares of land. Owing to various characteristics of the land, his ability to produce his two cash crops (corn and soybeans) differs on each hectare. The technology of production is given in the table below.

Maximum outputs of each crop per hectare (bushels)

	Hectare #1	Hectare #2	Hectare #3
Corn	200	200	100
Soybeans	400	200	50

These figures represent the maximum output of each crop, assuming that only one crop is grown on the hectare. That is, hectare #1 can produce either 200 bushels of corn or 400 bushels of soybeans. Of course, the farmer can also divide the hectare into one part corn and one part soybeans. For example, he can grow 100 bushels of corn and 200 bushels of soybeans on hectare #1. Plot the production possibilities curve.

8 (Practice problem: production possibilities curve) Plot the following production possibilities curves.

a Maximum harvest of each type of fish per trawler (tonnes)

	Trawler #1	Trawler #2	Trawler #3
Salmon	2	3	4
Tuna	2	6	6

b Maximum amounts of pollutants removed (parts per million [ppm])

	Smokestack scrubbers	Coal treatment
Sulphur	100	50
Particulates	500	100

Answers to Problems

2 *a* Nigeria has a comparative advantage in textiles. Niger has a comparative advantage in sorghum.
 b Nigeria will trade its textiles for sorghum from Niger.

c The relative price will lie between 8 and 5 bushels of sorghum per bale of textiles.

3 *a* Greece has a comparative advantage in fish. Poland has a comparative advantage in wheat. Greece will trade its fish for Polish wheat. The relative price will lie between 4/3 and 2 bushels of wheat per fish.
 b The United States has a comparative advantage in heart bypass operations, and Canada in auto parts. The United States will trade heart bypass operations for Canadian auto parts. The relative price will lie between 2 and 3 containers of auto parts per operation.
 c Thailand has a comparative advantage in finished steel, Laos in scrap steel. Thailand will trade its finished steel for Laotian scrap steel. The relative price will lie between 1 and 5 tonnes of scrap steel per tonne of finished steel.
 d Portugal has a comparative advantage in wine, Great Britain in wool. British wool will be traded for Portuguese wine. The relative price will lie between 1 and 2 bales per barrel of wine.

5 Choose, for example, 6 bushels of sorghum per bale of textiles as the relative price. Nigeria can produce 100 bales of textiles and trade 20 to Niger for 120 bushels of sorghum. The point (80, 120) lies outside its production possibilities curve. Niger can produce 400 bushels of sorghum and trade 120 bushels to Nigeria for 20 bales of textiles. The point (20, 280) lies outside its production possibilities curve.

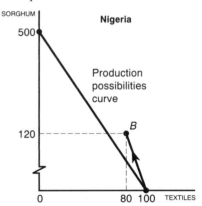

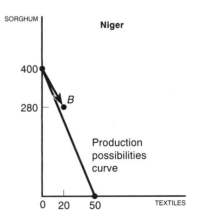

7

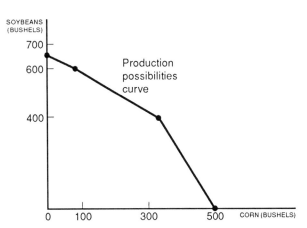

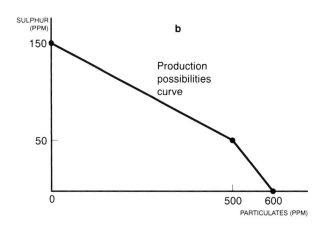

8

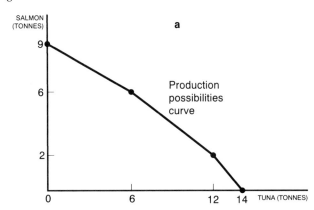

DEMAND, SUPPLY, AND PRICES

Chapter Review

Trade, the markets in which it occurs, and the gains it provides for both buyers and sellers are all important concepts from Chapter 3. Chapter 4 discusses the basic model of markets, which is the supply and demand model. The focus is on prices and quantities—how they are determined and how they change when other factors change. Chapter 5 then applies the supply and demand model to major areas of concern to economists: what happens to the quantity demanded or supplied when prices change, and what happens when prices do not adjust, as when the government sets price floors or ceilings.

ESSENTIAL CONCEPTS

1 Consumers **demand** goods and services. They are willing and able to pay, and given a price, they will buy a certain quantity. Several factors influence demand, but the most important is **price.** As the price falls, people buy more of the good or service; as the price rises, they purchase less. The entire relationship between the price and the quantity that a person buys is called the individual **demand curve.**

2 Adding all the individual demand curves gives the **market demand curve.** For every price, ask how much each individual will buy. Add these quantities. The result is the market demand curve, which shows the total amount of the good that will be purchased by all individuals at each price.

3 Firms **supply** goods and services. They are willing and able to produce and sell the good, and at a given price, they will sell a certain quantity. Several factors influence the supply, but the most important is price. As the price rises, producers will supply more; as the price falls, producers will supply less. The entire relationship between the price and the quantity that the producer will sell is called the individual **supply curve.**

4 Adding all the individual supply curves gives the **market supply curve.** For every price, ask how much each producer will sell. Add these quantities. The result is the market supply curve, which shows how much of the good will be sold by all producers at each price.

5 The price at which consumers want to buy exactly the

quantity that firms want to sell is the **equilibrium price.** This quantity, which is the same for demand and supply, is the **equilibrium quantity.** It is an equilibrium because there are no forces that would cause it to change.

6   If the price were higher than the equilibrium price, firms would want to sell more than consumers would buy. Unable to sell all their goods, many firms would compete, by lowering prices, to attract the relatively few consumers. Because this higher price would change, it is not an equilibrium. Similarly, if the price were lower than the equilibrium price, consumers would want to buy more than firms would sell. Seeing the glut of consumers, firms would raise their prices. In sum, if the price is above equilibrium, it falls; if it is below equilibrium, it rises. When price equals the equilibrium price, it does not change.

7   Many factors affect the demand and supply. For demand, these factors include changes in income, prices of substitutes and complements, the composition of the population, and people's tastes. This is only a partial list. When one of these factors—or anything else that affects the willingness to pay for the good—changes, the entire demand curve **shifts,** and a new equilibrium must be found.

Supply is affected by changes in technology and input price—more generally, anything that causes costs to change. Again, changes in these factors **shift** the supply curve and lead to a new equilibrium.

BEHIND THE ESSENTIAL CONCEPTS

1   The demand curve is the entire range, or schedule, that indicates how many goods will be purchased at each price. At a given price, this number is called the quantity demanded. In diagrams of demand curves, the quantity demanded is measured along the horizontal axis. To find the quantity demanded, simply read it off the demand curve at the current price. Economists, students, and sometimes professors are sloppy and say "change in demand" without being clear whether they mean a shift in the demand curve or a change in the quantity demanded. The latter is brought about by a change in price, and it involves only a movement along the same demand curve. To guard against confusion in stressful situations (like tests!), say "demand curve" when you refer to the entire schedule of prices and quantities and "quantity demanded" when you want to indicate the number of goods purchased.

2   It is very important to understand why the market demand curve is drawn as it is. When the price rises, the market quantity demanded falls for two reasons. First, each individual buys less. The principle of substitution says that other available goods and services can serve as alternatives, and at higher prices, people switch to

consume these substitutes. Second, some individuals find the price to be too high altogether, and they leave the market completely. When the price falls, the opposite happens. People substitute away from other goods and buy more of the one with the lower price. Furthermore, the lower price attracts new consumers to the market.

3   The market supply curve slopes upwards. This means that as the price rises, more is offered for sale. Again, there are two reasons. First, firms are willing to sell more at higher prices. Second, higher prices attract new products to the market.

4   Other factors that shift the demand curve include consumer income, tastes, prices of substitutes and complements, and the composition of the population. The supply curve shifts with changes in technology or input prices. While these factors are the most common causes of shifts, they are not a complete list. Anything that affects the willingness and ability to pay for goods shifts the demand curve, and anything that affects costs shifts the supply curve. For example, if it rains in April, the supply of crops may increase, and the demand for umbrellas may also increase.

5   Successful supply and demand analysis proceeds in four steps:

   a   Start with an equilibrium.
   b   Figure out which curve shifts.
   c   Shift the curve and find the new equilibrium.
   d   Compare the price and quantity at the original and new equilibria.

Be careful to avoid a common pitfall. Suppose you are asked to show the effect of a change in tastes that shifts demand to the right. The failing student's analysis goes like this: "Demand shifts to the right; this increases quantity and price, but the increase in price leads producers to want to supply more, so the supply also shifts to the right." What is wrong with this answer? Stop before the "but." True, the demand shift does raise price and quantity, but that is the end of the story. The increase in price does lead producers to want to supply more. As they supply more, there is a movement along the supply curve, but not a shift. Changes in the price of a good *never shift* the demand curve for that good or the supply curve for that good; rather, changes in the price of a good cause a *movement* along the demand curve or supply curve. There is more discussion on this point and lots of practice problems in the "Doing Economics" section of this chapter.

SELF-TEST

True or False

1   Prices provide incentives to help the economy use resources efficiently.

2   As the price falls, the quantity demanded decreases.

3   The market demand curve is the sum of the quantities and prices of each individual demand.

4   The individual demand curve is an example of an equilibrium relationship.

5   One reason why the supply curve slopes upwards is that at higher prices, more producers enter the market.

6   In equilibrium, there is neither excess demand nor excess supply.

7   If the price is above the equilibrium price, consumers can buy as much as they are willing to buy.

8   If the price is below the equilibrium price, sellers cannot sell as much as they are willing to sell.

9   The law of supply and demand says that the equilibrium price will be that price at which the quantity demanded equals the quantity supplied.

10 The individual supply curve is an example of an identity.

11 The price of diamonds is higher than the price of water because diamonds have a higher value in use.

12 A change in a consumer's income will shift her demand curve.

13 A change in the price of a good will shift its market demand curve to the right.

14 An increase in the price of a substitute will shift the demand curve for the good in question to the right.

15 A decrease in the price of a complement will shift the demand curve for the good in question to the left.

Multiple Choice

1   The level of a market price reflects

    a   how necessary the commodity is.
    b   how much of a luxury the commodity is.
    c   how heavy market demand is for the commodity.
    d   the interaction of the forces of supply and demand.
    e   none of the above.

2   The individual demand curve for a good or service

    a   gives the quantity of the good or service the individual would purchase at each price.
    b   gives the equilibrium price in the market.
    c   shows which other goods or services will be substituted according to the principle of substitution.
    d   gives the amount of money the individual would spend on the good at each price.
    e   none of the above.

3   The idea that there are other goods or services that can serve as reasonably good alternatives to a particular good or service is called the

    a   law of demand.
    b   principle of substitution.
    c   market demand curve.
    d   principle of scarcity.
    e   none of the above.

4   If you knew the individual demand curve of each consumer, you could find the market demand curve by

    a   taking the average quantity demanded at each price.
    b   adding all the prices.
    c   adding, at each price, the quantities purchased by each individual.
    d   taking the average of all prices.
    e   none of the above.

5   As the price rises, the quantity demanded decreases along an individual demand curve because

    a   the individual substitutes other goods and services, and hence buys fewer units.
    b   some individuals exit the market, and hence buy fewer units.
    c   some individuals enter the market, but they buy fewer units.
    d   the quantity supplied decreases.
    e   the individual substitutes other goods and services, and hence buys fewer units, *and* some individuals exit the market.

6   As the price rises, the quantity demanded decreases along the market demand curve because

    a   individuals substitute other goods and services, and hence buy fewer units, but no individual exits the market.
    b   some individuals exit the market, but no individual substitutes other goods and services and hence buys fewer units.
    c   some individuals enter the market, but they buy fewer units.
    d   the quantity supplied decreases.
    e   individuals substitute other goods and services, and hence buy fewer units, and some individuals exit the market.

7   As the price rises, the quantity supplied increases along an individual supply curve because

    a   higher prices give the firm an incentive to supply more units.
    b   some firms exit the market, but those that remain supply more units.
    c   some firms enter the market, and hence supply more units.
    d   the quantity demanded increases.
    e   higher prices give the firm an incentive to supply more units *and* some firms enter the market.

8   As the price rises, the quantity supplied increases along the market supply curve because

    a   higher prices give firms an incentive to supply more units.

b some firms exit the market, but those that remain supply more units.

c some firms enter the market, and hence supply more units.

d the quantity demanded increases.

e higher prices give firms an incentive to supply more units *and* some firms enter the market.

9 If the market price is below equilibrium, then

a there is excess demand.

b there is excess supply.

c consumers will want to raise the price.

d firms will want to lower the price.

e none of the above.

10 If the market price is at equilibrium, then

a the quantity that consumers are willing to buy equals the quantity that producers are willing to sell.

b there is excess demand.

c there is excess supply.

d the market price will rise.

e the market price will fall.

11 If the market price is above equilibrium, then

a supply equals demand.

b there is excess demand.

c firms will not be able to sell all that they would like.

d consumers will not be able to buy all that they would like.

e none of the above.

12 The law of supply and demand is an example of

a an identity.

b an equilibrium relationship.

c a behavioural relationship.

d a criminal offence.

e none of the above.

13 The statement that market supply is equal to the sum of individual firms' supplies is an example of

a an identity.

b an equilibrium relationship.

c a behavioural relationship.

d a disequilibrium relationship.

e none of the above.

14 A diamond sells for a higher price than a litre of water because

a luxuries always have higher prices than necessities.

b only a few people demand diamonds, but everyone needs water.

c the total use value of diamonds exceeds the total value of water.

d the total cost of diamond production exceeds the total cost of water production.

e none of the above.

15 Stationary exercise bicycles and stair-stepper ma-

chines are substitutes, according to the aerobically correct. An increase in the price of exercise bicycles will

a shift the demand for stair-stepper machines to the left.

b increase the price of stair-stepper machines.

c lower the quantity of stair-stepper machine sales.

d shift the supply curve of stair-stepper machines to the left.

e none of the above.

16 As people have grown more concerned about saturated fat in their diets, the demand for beef has shifted to the left. The quantity of beef sold has also fallen. This change is a

a movement along the demand curve for beef.

b shift to the right in the supply curve for beef.

c movement along the supply curve for beef.

d shift to the left in the supply curve for beef.

e none of the above.

17 Which of the following is not a source of shifts in market demand?

a an increase in consumer income

b a change in tastes

c an increase in the population

d a technological advance

e none of the above

18 If the price of an input falls,

a supply shifts to the left.

b demand shifts to the right.

c demand shifts to the left.

d supply shifts to the right.

e none of the above.

19 If ski-lift tickets and skiing lessons are complements, then an increase in the price of lift tickets

a shifts demand for skiing lessons to the left.

b shifts demand for skiing lessons to the right.

c shifts supply of skiing lessons to the left.

d shifts supply of skiing lessons to the right.

e none of the above.

20 A recent regulation requires tuna fishing companies to use nets that allow dolphins to escape. These nets also allow some tuna to escape. This regulation causes

a the supply of tuna to shift to the left.

b the demand for tuna to shift to the right.

c the demand for tuna to shift to the left.

d the supply of tuna to shift to the right.

e none of the above.

Completion

1 _____ is defined as what is given in exchange for a good or service.

2 If the price of a good or service falls, the quantity demanded _____.

3   The quantity of the good or service purchased at each price is given by the _____.

4   The quantity of the good or service offered for sale at each price is given by the _____.

5   In an economic equilibrium, there are no forces for _____.

6   The law of supply and demand says that at the equilibrium price, the _____ equals the _____.

7   The statement that market supply equals market demand is an example of an _____.

8   The statement that market supply is the total of all individual supplies is an example of an _____.

9   An increase in the price of a good leads to a _____ its demand curve.

10 A change in technology leads to a _____ the supply curve.

Answers to Self-Test

True or False

1	t	4	f	7	t	10	f	13	f
2	f	5	t	8	f	11	f	14	t
3	f	6	t	9	t	12	t	15	f

Multiple Choice

1	d	6	e	11	c	16	c
2	a	7	a	12	b	17	d
3	b	8	e	13	a	18	d
4	c	9	a	14	e	19	a
5	a	10	a	15	b	20	a

Completion

1   Price
2   increases
3   demand curve
4   supply curve
5   change
6   quantity demanded, quantity supplied
7   equilibrium relationship
8   identity
9   movement along
10 shift in

Doing Economics: Tools and Practice Problems

Three techniques receive attention in this section. The first technique shows how to add individual demand and individual supply curves to get market demand and market supply curves. The next technique involves finding the equilibrium price and quantity, where the market clears. Finally, some general instructions about supply and demand analysis are given and developed in several problems. Each of these techniques is fundamental and will appear repeatedly throughout this book.

Tool Kit 4.1: Calculating Market Demand and Supply

The market demand is the sum of the individual demands. The market supply is the sum of the individual supplies. This tool kit shows how to add the individual demands and supplies.

Step one: Make two columns. Label the left-hand column "Price" and the right-hand column "Quantity."

Price   Quantity

Step two: Choose the highest price at which goods are demanded. Enter this in the first row of the price column.

Price   Quantity
p_1

Step three: Find how many goods each individual will purchase. Add these quantities. Enter the total in the first row of the quantity column.

Price	Quantity
p_1	$Q_1 = Q_a + Q_b + Q_c + \cdots$

Step four: Choose the second highest price, and continue the process.

---

1   (Worked problem: market demand) The individual demands of Jason and Sheila for economics tutoring are given in Table 4.1. Calculate the market demand. (Jason and Sheila are the only two individuals in this market.)

Table 4.1

Jason		Sheila	
Price	*Quantity*	*Price*	*Quantity*
$10	6	$10	4
$ 8	8	$ 8	5
$ 6	10	$ 6	6
$ 4	12	$ 4	7

Step-by-step solution

Step one: Make and label two columns.

Price   Quantity

Step two: Choose the highest price. This is $10. Enter this in the first row under price.

Price   Quantity
$10

Step three: Find the market quantity. Jason would buy 6; Sheila would buy 4. The total is 6 + 4 = 10. Enter 10 in the corresponding quantity column.

Price   Quantity
$10   10

Step four: Repeat the process. The next lower price is $8. Jason would buy 8; Sheila would buy 5. The total is 8 + 5 = 13. Enter $8 and 13 in the appropriate columns.

Price	Quantity
$10	10
$ 8	13

Continue. The entire market demand is given below.

Price	Quantity
$10	10
$ 8	13
$ 6	16
$ 4	19

2 (Practice problem: market demand) Gorman's tomatoes are purchased by pizza sauce makers, by submarine sandwich shops, and by vegetable canners. The demands for each are given in Table 4.2. Find the market demand.

Table 4.2

	Pizza sauce		Submarine shops		Vegetable canners
Price	Quantity (bushels)	Price	Quantity (bushels)	Price	Quantity (bushels)
$5	25	$5	5	$5	55
$4	35	$4	6	$4	75
$3	40	$3	7	$3	100
$2	50	$2	7	$2	150
$1	80	$1	7	$1	250

Tool Kit 4.2: Finding the Equilibrium Price and Quantity

The equilibrium price in the demand and supply model is the price at which the buyers want to buy exactly the quantity that sellers want to sell. In other words, the quantity demanded equals the quantity supplied. The equilibrium quantity in the market is just this quantity. Here is how to find the equilibrium in a market.

Step one: Choose a price. Find the quantity demanded at that price and the quantity supplied.

Step two: If the quantity demanded equals the quantity supplied, the price is the equilibrium. Stop.

Step three: If the quantity demanded exceeds the quantity supplied, there is a shortage. Choose a higher price and repeat step one. If the quantity demanded is less than the quantity supplied, there is a surplus. Choose a lower price and repeat step one.

Step four: Continue until the equilibrium price is found.

---

3 (Practice problem: market supply) The technique for finding the market supply curve is the same as for the market demand. Simply sum the quantities supplied at each price. There are three law firms that will draw up partnership contracts in the town of Pullman. Their individual supply curves are given in Table 4.3. Find the market supply curve.

Table 4.3

Jones		Jones and Jones		Jones, Jones, and Jones	
Price	Quantity	Price	Quantity	Price	Quantity
$200	0	$200	6	$200	4
$220	0	$220	8	$220	8
$240	0	$240	12	$240	10
$260	8	$260	24	$260	11

4 (Worked problem: equilibrium price and quantity) The supply curve and demand curve for cinder blocks are given in Table 4.4. The quantity column indicates the number of blocks sold in one year.

Table 4.4

Demand		Supply	
Price	Quantity	Price	Quantity
$2.00	50,000	$2.00	200,000
$1.50	70,000	$1.50	160,000
$1.00	100,000	$1.00	100,000
$0.75	150,000	$0.75	50,000
$0.50	250,000	$0.50	0

a Find the equilibrium price and quantity.
b If the price is $1.50, is the market in equilibrium? Will there be a surplus or a shortage? If so, what is the size of the surplus or shortage? What will happen to the price? Why?
c If the price is $0.75, is the market in equilibrium? Will there be a surplus or a shortage? If so, what is the size of the surplus or shortage? What will happen to the price? Why?

Step-by-step solution

Step one (a): Choose a price. At a price of, say, $2.00, the quantity demanded is 50,000 and the quantity supplied is 200,000.

Step two: The quantities are not equal.

Step three: There is a surplus. The equilibrium price will be lower.

Step four: Continue. Try other prices until the quantity supplied equals the quantity demanded. The equilibrium price is $1.00, where the quantity equals 100,000. We can now see the answers to parts b and c.

Step five (b): If the price is $1.50, the quantity demanded is 70,000, and it is less than the quantity supplied, which is 160,000. There is a surplus of 90,000 (160,000 – 70,000). The price will fall because producers will be unable to sell all that they want.

Step six (c): If the price is $0.75, the quantity demanded is 150,000, and it is greater than the quantity supplied, which is 50,000. There is a shortage of 100,000 (150,000 – 50,000). The price will rise because producers will see that buyers are unable to buy all that they want.

5   (Practice problem: equilibrium price and quantity) The demand curve and supply curve in the market for billboard space adjacent to a highway are given in Table 4.5. The price is the monthly rental price. The quantity column shows numbers of billboards.

Table 4.5

Demand		Supply	
Price	Quantity	Price	Quantity
$100	5	$100	25
$ 80	8	$ 80	21
$ 60	11	$ 60	16
$ 40	14	$ 40	14
$ 20	22	$ 20	3

a   Find the equilibrium price and quantity.
b   If the price is $20, is the market in equilibrium? Will there be a surplus or a shortage? If so, what is the size of the surplus or shortage? What will happen to the price? Why?
c   If the price is $80, is the market in equilibrium? Will there be a surplus or a shortage? If so, what is the size of the surplus or shortage? What will happen to the price? Why?

6   (Practice problem: equilibrium price and quantity) Find the equilibrium price and quantity in each of the following markets.

a   The supply and demand curves for new soles (shoe repair) are given in Table 4.6.

Table 4.6

Demand		Supply	
Price	Quantity	Price	Quantity
$35	17	$35	53
$30	21	$30	37
$25	25	$25	25
$20	30	$20	15
$15	35	$15	0

b   The supply and demand curves for seat cushions are given in Table 4.7.

Table 4.7

Demand		Supply	
$8	4	$8	32
$7	8	$7	28
$6	12	$6	22
$5	16	$5	19
$4	17	$4	17

Tool Kit 4.3: Using Supply and Demand

Supply and demand analysis provides excellent answers to questions of the following form: "What is the effect of a change in _____ on the market for _____?" You are well on your way to success as a student of economics if you stick closely to this procedure in answering such questions.

Step one: Begin with an equilibrium in the relevant market. Label the horizontal axis as the quantity of the good or service and the vertical axis as the price. Draw a demand and a supply curve and label them *D* and *S*, respectively.

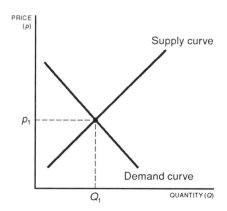

Step two: Figure out whether the change shifts the supply curve, the demand curve, or neither.

Step three: Shift the appropriate curve.

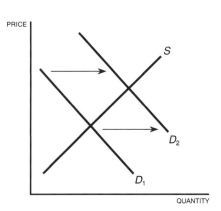

Step four: Find the new equilibrium, and compare it with the original one.

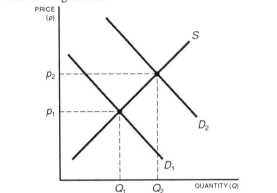

7 (Worked problem: using supply and demand) In response to concern about the fumes emitted by dry cleaning establishments, regulations have been issued requiring expensive filtering systems. How will this regulation affect the dry cleaning market?

Step-by-step solution

Step one: Start with an equilibrium.

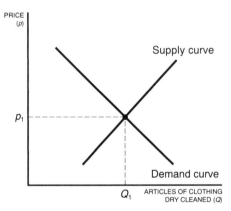

Step two: Figure out which curve shifts. The mandated filtering systems increase the dry cleaning firm's costs, and so shift the supply curve to the left.

Step three: Shift the curve.

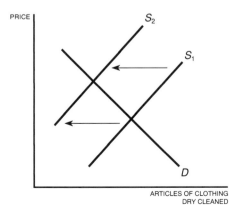

Step four: Find the new equilibrium and compare. The effect of the regulation is to raise the price and lower the quantity of clothes dry cleaned.

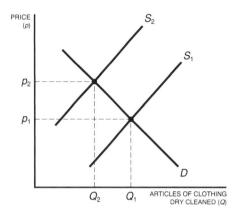

8 (Practice problem: using supply and demand) As the oil market comes to the realization that Kuwait's production will not return to prewar levels, the price of oil has increased by $4 per barrel. Explain the effect of this oil price increase on the market for natural gas.

9 (Practice problem: using supply and demand) For each of the following, show the effects on price and quantity. Draw the diagrams and follow the procedure.

a an increase in income
b an increase in the price of a substitute
c a decrease in the price of a substitute
d an increase in the price of a complement
e a decrease in the price of a complement
f an increase in the price of an input
g a decrease in the price of an input
h an improvement in technology

Answers to Problems

2	Price	Quantity (bushels)
	$5	85
	$4	116
	$3	147
	$2	207
	$1	337

3	Price	Quantity
	$200	10
	$220	16
	$240	22
	$260	43

5 a Equilibrium price = $40; quantity = 14.
   b If the price is $20, there is a shortage of 22 − 3 = 19. The price will be driven up.
   c If the price is $80, there is a surplus of 21 − 8 = 13. The price will be driven down.

6 a Price = $25; quantity = 25.
   b Price = $4; quantity = 17.

8 Oil and natural gas are substitutes, and therefore the demand curve shifts to the right, the price increases, and the quantity increases.

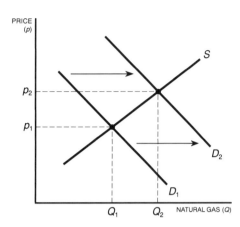

9 a Demand shifts to the right; this drives the price up and increases the quantity.

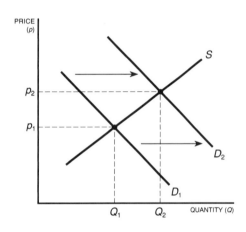

b Demand shifts to the right; this drives the price up and increases the quantity.

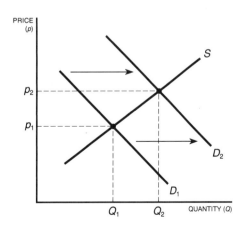

c Demand shifts to the left; this drives the price down and decreases the quantity.

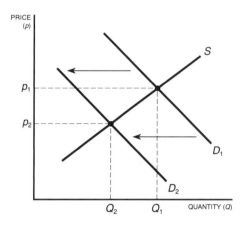

d Demand shifts to the left; this drives the price down and decreases the quantity.

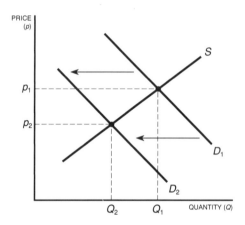

e Demand shifts to the right, this drives the price up and increases the quantity.

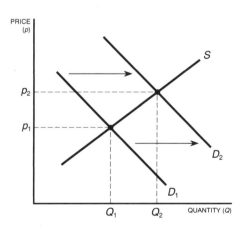

f Supply shifts to the left; this increases the price but decreases the quantity.

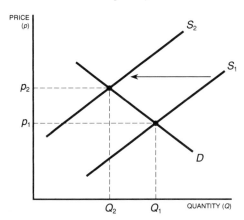

h Supply shifts to the right; this decreases the price but increases the quantity.

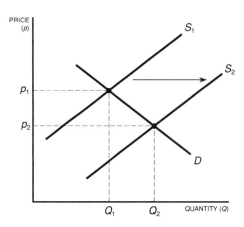

g Supply shifts to the right; this decreases the price but increases the quantity.

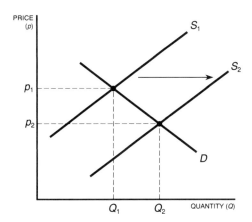

Chapter 5

USING DEMAND AND SUPPLY

Chapter Review

The model of demand and supply introduced in Chapter 4 is one of the most useful in all the social sciences. The ideas of demand and supply form the basis of all economic study, and will be used throughout this text. This chapter develops the model in more detail and introduces the concept of elasticity. Elasticity is best thought of as "sensitivity." The price elasticity of demand, for instance, measures how sensitive the quantity demanded is to a change in price. The chapter then applies the model to the study of the effects of taxes and price controls. Chapter 6 extends the supply and demand framework to markets in which future goods and risk are exchanged.

ESSENTIAL CONCEPTS

1   When price falls, quantity demanded increases. If the demand curve is steep, the increase in quantity is smaller than it would be if the curve were flat. Although it might seem natural to measure how the quantity responds to price changes by the slope of the demand curve, economists employ the concept of **elasticity.** They do so because elasticity will produce the same measure no matter what units are used. The **price elasticity of demand** is the percentage change in the quantity demanded brought about by a 1 percent change in price.

2   The **price elasticity of supply** is the percentage change in the quantity supplied brought about by a 1 percent change in price. It is the basic measure of how sensitive the quantity supplied is to changes in price.

3   The price elasticity of demand is greater when there are good, close substitutes available. Usually it is greater when the price is higher, because at higher prices, only those who consider the good essential remain in the market. Both the price elasticity of demand and the price elasticity of supply are greater in the long run because individuals and firms have more time to find substitutes and make adjustments.

4   The economic effects of a tax are seen by focusing on the market affected by the tax. For example, a tax on the sale of gasoline shifts the supply curve up (vertically) by the amount of the tax, raises consumer prices, and reduces the quantity of gasoline sold. Ex-

cept in a case where supply or demand is perfectly inelastic or perfectly elastic, the increase in consumer price is less than the amount of the tax. This means that producers are able to pass on only part of the tax to their customers and must bear some of the burden themselves.

5   **Price ceilings,** when set below the market-clearing price, lead to shortages, which means the quantity demanded exceeds the quantity supplied. **Price floors,** when set above the market-clearing price, result in surpluses; in this case, the quantity demanded is less than the quantity supplied. In each case, the quantity actually exchanged is less than it is at the market-clearing price.

BEHIND THE ESSENTIAL CONCEPTS

1   The concept of elasticity appears many times throughout the text, and is worth mastering. Suppose that price falls by 1 percent. We know that quantity will increase as consumers substitute towards the lower price, but by how much? The price elasticity provides the answer. It is the percent change in quantity brought about by a 1 percent change in price.

2   The relationship between elasticity and total revenue is very important. Total revenue is just price multiplied by quantity. If the price of a bicycle is $200 and there are 20 sold, then total revenue is $200 × 2 = $4,000. When price falls, total revenue is pushed down because each unit sells for less money; however, total revenue is pushed up because more units are sold. Whether on balance total revenue rises or falls depends on the elasticity. Table 5.1 helps to keep the relationship between elasticity and total revenue straight.

Table 5.1

If price rises,
   total revenue *falls* if the price elasticity of demand is greater than 1 (elastic).
   total revenue *rises* if the price elasticity of demand is less than 1 (inelastic).
   total revenue *does not change* if the price elasticity of demand equals 1 (unitary elasticity).

If price falls,
   total revenue *rises* if the price elasticity of demand is greater than 1 (elastic).
   total revenue *falls* if the price elasticity of demand is less than 1 (inelastic).
   total revenue *does not change* if the price elasticity of demand equals 1 (unitary elasticity).

3   What makes the demand for some goods (like motor boats) elastic, while the demand for others (like milk) is inelastic? The most important factor is the availability of substitutes. The **principle of substitution** says that consumers will look for substitutes when the price rises. If there are good, close substitutes available, then finding substitutes will be easy and consumers will switch. If good, close substitutes are not available, the consumers are more likely to swallow the price increase and continue purchasing the good.

4   Suppose that the government levies a tax on the supply of hotel rooms. Who pays the tax? While it is natural to think that the hotel pays the tax because it actually writes the cheque to the government, when you look at the issue through the lens of supply and demand, you see the value of economics. The tax increases the hotel's costs, and therefore it shifts the supply curve up and raises the price. Because they must pay higher prices for hotel rooms, consumers pay some of the tax.

5   Price ceilings only make a difference if they are set below the market-clearing price (where the supply and demand curves intersect). A price ceiling set above the market-clearing price has no effect. Similarly, a price floor set below the market-clearing price does not do anything.

6   Price floors and ceilings also affect the quantity traded in the market. If there is a price ceiling, then the quantity demanded exceeds the quantity supplied. The supply is the short side of the market, and although consumers would like to buy more of the good, the quantity traded is what producers are willing to sell. This is shown in Figure 5.1A. With price floors, the opposite is true. The demand is the short side of the market, and the quantity traded equals the amount that consumers are willing to buy, as shown in panel B. In each case, we say that the short side of the market determines the actual quantity traded, and the actual quantity traded is less than the market-clearing quantity.

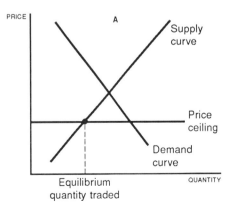

Figure 5.1

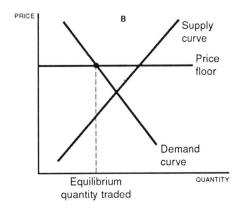

Figure 5.1

SELF-TEST

True or False

1 The price elasticity of demand is greater for goods and services that have better close substitutes.

2 The price elasticity of demand is always constant along the demand curve.

3 Total revenue increases as price falls when the demand is elastic.

4 A horizontal demand curve is perfectly elastic.

5 A vertical supply curve is perfectly inelastic.

6 If the supply curve is unitary elastic, then total revenue is constant as price changes.

7 If the supply curve is upward sloping, a rightwards shift in the demand curve increases the equilibrium price and the equilibrium quantity.

8 If the demand curve is downward sloping, a rightwards shift in the supply curve increases the equilibrium price and the equilibrium quantity.

9 When the demand curve is very elastic, relatively more of a tax on the production of some good or service will be borne by producers.

10 A tax on the sale of beer shifts the supply curve vertically by the amount of the tax.

11 When prices are sticky, shortages and surpluses can result in the short run.

12 A price ceiling set above the equilibrium price will have no effect on the market.

13 A price ceiling set below the equilibrium price will have no effect on the market.

14 A price floor set above the equilibrium price in the milk market will lead to a surplus of milk.

15 When demand and supply are more elastic, minimum wages set above the equilibrium wage lead to relatively more unemployment.

Multiple Choice

1 The quantity demanded is more sensitive to price changes when

  a supply is relatively inelastic.
  b close substitutes are available.
  c consumers are rational.
  d consumers are relatively more informed about quality for some goods.
  e none of the above.

2 Suppose that price falls by 10 percent and the quantity demanded rises by 20 percent. The price elasticity of demand is

  a 2.
  b 1.
  c 0.
  d 1/2.
  e 20.

3 Suppose that the price elasticity of demand is 1/3. If price rises by 30 percent

  a quantity demanded rises by 10 percent.
  b quantity demanded falls by 10 percent.
  c quantity demanded rises by 90 percent.
  d quantity demanded falls by 90 percent.
  e quantity demanded does not change.

4 Suppose that the price elasticity of demand is 1.5. If price falls, total revenue will

  a remain the same.
  b fall.
  c rise.
  d double.
  e fall or rise depending on the price elasticity of supply.

5 Suppose that the price elasticity of demand is 0.7. The demand for this good is

  a perfectly inelastic.
  b inelastic.
  c unitary elastic.
  d elastic.
  e perfectly elastic.

6 Which of the following is a true statement concerning the price elasticity of demand?

  a The price elasticity is constant for any demand curve.
  b Demand is more price elastic in the short run than in the long run.
  c If total revenue rises as price increases, the demand is relatively inelastic.
  d If total revenue falls as price increases, the demand is relatively inelastic.
  e None of the above.

7 If the supply curve is vertical, then the price elasticity of supply is

  a 0.
  b inelastic.

c 1.
d elastic.
e infinite.

8 Suppose that supply is perfectly elastic. If the demand curve shifts to the right, then

a price and quantity will increase.
b quantity will increase, but price will remain constant.
c price will increase, but quantity will remain constant.
d neither price nor quantity will increase.
e price will increase, but quantity will decrease.

9 Suppose that demand is perfectly inelastic, and the supply curve shifts to the left. Then

a price and quantity will increase.
b quantity will increase, but price will remain constant.
c price will increase, but quantity will remain constant.
d neither price nor quantity will increase.
e price will increase, but quantity will decrease.

10 The price elasticity of demand for tires is 1.3, and the supply curve is upward sloping. If a $1-per-tire tax is placed on the production of tires, then the equilibrium price will

a not change because the tax is on production and not on consumption.
b increase by $1.
c increase by less than $1.
d fall by less than $1.
e fall by $1.

11 For a given upward-sloping supply curve, consumers bear more of a tax when the demand is

a relatively inelastic.
b unitary elastic.
c relatively elastic.
d such that consumers always bear the entire burden.
e none of the above.

12 Which of the following is not true of a tax?

a Consumers always finish up paying the tax.
b The relative burden of the tax on consumers and firms depends on the price elasticities of demand and supply.
c Consumers pay all the tax if supply is perfectly elastic.
d Firms absorb all the tax if demand is perfectly elastic.
e Consumers bear a larger relative burden of the tax in the long run if the price elasticity of supply is greater in the long run than in the short run but the price elasticity of demand is the same in the long run as it is in the short run.

13 Suppose that the supply of a good is perfectly inelastic. A tax of $1 on that good will raise the price by

a less than $1.
b $1.
c more than $1.
d $.50.
e none of the above.

14 A price ceiling set below the equilibrium price will

a create a shortage.
b increase the price.
c create a surplus.
d cause a shift to the left in the demand curve.
e have no effect.

15 A price ceiling set above the equilibrium price will

a create a shortage.
b increase the price.
c create a surplus.
d cause a shift to the left in the demand curve.
e have no effect.

16 A price ceiling set below the equilibrium price will

a increase the quantity demanded.
b increase the quantity supplied.
c decrease the quantity supplied.
d cause a shift to the left in the demand curve.
e have no effect.

17 Which of the following is not true of rent controls?

a They create a shortage of rental housing.
b They create larger shortages of rental housing in the long run than in the short run.
c They lower rents for those who already have apartments.
d They make it more difficult for those who do not already have apartments to find apartments, and more difficult for those with apartments to move to different apartments.
e Governments quickly see their harmful effects and remove them.

18 A price ceiling on insurance rates will

a shift demand to the left.
b shift demand to the right.
c shift supply to the left.
d shift supply to the right
e none of the above.

19 Which of the following is not a cause of surpluses or shortages?

a price ceilings
b price floors
c taxes
d sticky prices
e none of the above

20 Recently, the demand for housing has fallen in parts of Canada. Housing prices are sticky, and therefore

   a temporary shortages of housing have appeared.
   b temporary surpluses of housing have appeared.
   c the housing market has cleared.
   d supply has also shifted to the left.
   e none of the above.

Completion

1   The percentage change in the quantity demanded as a result of a 1 percent price change is called the

   _____.

2   Price changes have no effect on revenue if the price elasticity of demand is _____.

3   If the price elasticity of demand lies between 0 and 1, then we say that demand is relatively _____.

4   A horizontal demand curve indicates that demand is

   _____.

5   If the supply curve is vertical, then the price elasticity of supply equals _____.

6   A $.50-per-litre tax on the production of gasoline can normally be expected to raise price by _____.

7   If demand is relatively inelastic, most of the tax is borne by _____.

8   A price ceiling set below the equilibrium price will create a _____.

9   A price floor set above the equilibrium price will create a _____.

10   The minimum wage is an example of a _____.

Answers to Self-Test

True or False

1	t	4	t	7	t	10	t	13	f
2	f	5	t	8	f	11	t	14	t
3	t	6	f	9	t	12	t	15	t

Multiple Choice

1	b	6	c	11	c	16	d
2	a	7	a	12	a	17	d
3	d	8	e	13	b	18	e
4	c	9	b	14	a	19	c
5	b	10	c	15	e	20	b

Completion

1   price elasticity of demand
2   1
3   inelastic
4   perfectly elastic
5   zero
6   less than $.50
7   consumers
8   shortage
9   surplus
10   price floor

Doing Economics: Tools and Practice Problems

Three techniques receive attention in this section. You'll first learn how to calculate elasticity, then how to measure the effects of taxes, and finally how to analyze the effects of price controls.

Tool Kit 5.1: Calculating Elasticity

Elasticity measures how sensitive the quantity is to changes in price. This section shows how to calculate elasticity. We will confirm the relationship between the price elasticity of demand and total revenue and observe the fact that elasticity is not constant along the demand curve.

Step one: To find the elasticity between two points on the demand curve, let p_1 and Q_2 be the price and quantity at the second point.

Step two: Substitute the prices and quantities into the formula

   elasticity = $(Q_1 - Q_2)(p_1 + p_2)/(Q_1 + Q_2)(p_1 - p_2)$.

---

1   (Worked problem: calculating elasticity) The demand curve for bulletin boards is given below.

Price	Quantity
$35	800
$30	1,000
$25	1,200
$20	1,300

   a Calculate total revenue for each price.
   b Calculate the price elasticity of demand between $35 and $30, between $30 and $25, and between $25 and $20. Does elasticity change along this demand?
   c Verify the relationship between elasticity and total revenue.

Step-by-step solution

Step one (a): Total revenue at $35 is 800 × $35 = $28,000. Total revenue at $30 is 1,000 × $30 = $30,000. Continue, and enter the numbers in the table.

Price	Quantity	Total revenue
$35	800	$28,000
$30	1,000	$30,000
$25	1,200	$30,000
$20	1,300	$26,000

Step two (b): Let $35 = p_1, 800 = Q_1, $30 = p_2, and 1,000 = Q_2. Substituting into the formula gives

elasticity = $(35 + 30)(1,000 - 800)/(800 + 1,000)(35 - 30)$
     = 1.44, which is elastic.

Step three: Between $30 and $25,

elasticity = (30 + 25)(1,200 − 1,000)/(1,000 + 1,200)(30 − 25)
= 1, which is unitary elastic.

Step four: Between $25 and $20,

elasticity = (25 + 20)(1,300 − 1,200)/(1,200 + 1,300)(25 − 20)
= 0.36, which is inelastic.

Clearly, the elasticity is not constant. The demand curve is less elastic at lower prices.

Step five (c): Between $35 and $30, where the demand is elastic, total revenue rises from $28,000 to $30,000 as price falls. Between $30 and $25, where the demand is unitary elastic, total revenue is constant at $30,000 as the price falls. Between $25 and $20, where the demand is inelastic, total revenue falls from $30,000 to $26,000 as the price falls. Check Table 5.1 to verify that these numbers are consistent with the general relationship between price elasticity of demand and total revenue.

2 (Practice problem: calculating elasticity) The demand curve for bookends is given below.

Price	Quantity
$10	70
$ 8	90
$ 6	120
$ 4	130

 a Calculate total revenue for each price.
 b Calculate the price elasticity of demand between each of the adjacent prices. Does elasticity change along this demand?
 c Verify the relationship between elasticity and total revenue.

3 (Practice problem: calculating elasticity) For each of the following, calculate the total revenue for each price and the price elasticity for each price change, and verify the relationship between elasticity and total revenue.

 a | Price | Quantity |
| --- | --- |
| $12 | 6 |
| $10 | 8 |
| $ 8 | 10 |
| $ 6 | 12 |

 b | Price | Quantity |
| --- | --- |
| $100 | 80 |
| $ 80 | 85 |
| $ 60 | 90 |
| $ 40 | 95 |

 c | Price | Quantity |
| --- | --- |
| $9 | 10 |
| $8 | 8 |
| $7 | 6 |
| $6 | 4 |

Tool Kit 5.2: Using Supply and Demand for Tax Incidence

The economic effects of taxes can be analyzed using the method of supply and demand introduced in Chapter 4. The key idea is that the burden of a tax—its incidence—does not necessarily fall on the person or firm that must deliver the money to the government. Taxes affect exchanges, and their impact must be analyzed by looking at the markets where the affected exchanges occur. The basic conclusions of this analysis are that except when demand or supply is perfectly elastic or perfectly inelastic, consumers and producers share the burden of the tax, that taxes reduce the level of economic activity, and, perhaps surprisingly, that the effects of the tax are the same whether the supplier or the demander pays.

Step one: Start with an equilibrium in the relevant market.

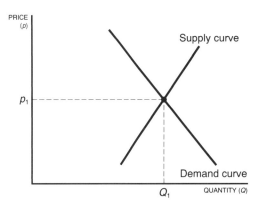

Step two: Identify whether the demander or supplier must pay the tax.

Step three: If the supplier must pay the tax, shift the supply curve up (vertically) by exactly the amount of the tax. If the demander must pay the tax, shift the demand curve down by exactly the amount of the tax.

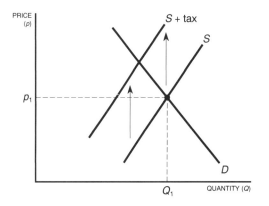

Step four: Find the new equilibrium.

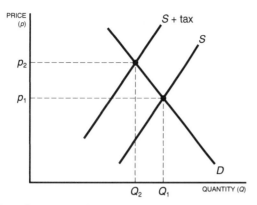

Step five: Determine the economic incidence of the tax. If the supplier must pay the tax, then use the following formulas to calculate economic incidence.

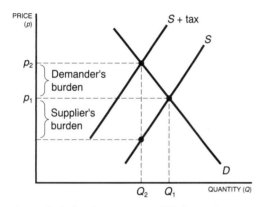

demander's burden = new equilibrium price
                        – original equilibrium price.

supplier's burden = original equilibrium price
                      – new equilibrium price + tax.

If the demander must pay the tax, use the following formulas to calculate tax incidence.

demander's burden = new equilibrium price + tax
                        – original equilibrium price.

supplier's burden = original equilibrium price
                      – new equilibrium price.

4 (Worked problem: tax incidence) The demand curve and supply curve for two-bedroom apartments in Halifax are given in Table 5.2.

Table 5.2

Demand		Supply	
Price	Quantity	Price	Quantity
$800	100	$800	500
$750	200	$750	500
$700	300	$700	450
$650	400	$650	400
$600	500	$600	300

a Find the equilibrium price and quantity.
b Suppose that landlords are required to pay $100 per apartment in a renter's tax to the city government. Use supply and demand analysis to determine the incidence of the tax.
c Now suppose that rather than being paid by the sellers of an apartment, the tax must be paid by the demanders. Use supply and demand analysis to determine the incidence of the tax.
d Does it matter who pays the tax?

Step-by-step solution

Step one (a): Find the no-tax equilibrium. When the price is $650, the market clears with 400 apartments rented. This is the answer to part a.

Step two (b): Identify whether the demander or supplier must pay the tax. For part b, the supplier pays the tax.

Step three: Because the tax is paid by sellers, the supply curve shifts up by $100, the amount of the tax. The new supply curve is found by adding $100 to the price column, as in Table 5.3.

Table 5.3

Supply	
Price	Quantity
$900	500
$850	500
$800	450
$750	400
$700	300

Step four: Find the new equilibrium. The market clears at a price of $700 and a quantity of 300.

Step five: Determine the economic incidence of the tax.

demander's burden = new equilibrium price
                      – original equilibrium price.
            = $700 – $650 = $50.
supplier's burden = original equilibrium price
                    – new equilibrium price + tax.
            = $650 – $700 + $100 = $50.

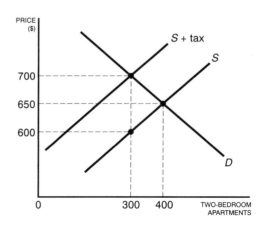

Step six (c): To answer part c, we repeat the procedure for the case where the demander must pay the tax.

Step seven (one): The original no-tax equilibrium is the same with the price equal to $650 and 400 apartments rented.

Step eight (two): In this case, the demanders pay the tax.

Step nine (three): We shift the demand curve down by $100. The new demand curve is given in Table 5.4.

Table 5.4

Demand	
Price	Quantity
$700	100
$650	200
$600	300
$550	400
$500	500

Step ten (four): The market clears at a price of $600 and a quantity of 300.

Step eleven (five): We determine the incidence as follows.

demander's burden = new equilibrium price
+ tax − original equilibrium price.
= $600 + $100 − $650 = $50.
supplier's burden = original equilibrium price
− new equilibrium price
= $650 − $600 = $50.

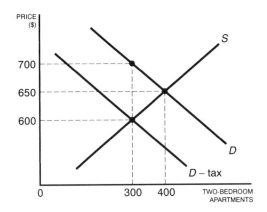

Step twelve (d): It does not matter who pays the tax! In either situation, the total amount that demanders pay is $700, the net amount that sellers receive is $600, and the equilibrium quantity is 300. The diagrams illustrate the solution.

5   (Practice problem: tax incidence) The demand curve and supply curve for unskilled labour are given in Table 5.5.

Table 5.5

Demand		Supply	
Wage	Quantity	Wage	Quantity
$6.50	1,000	$6.50	1,900
$6.00	1,200	$6.00	1,800
$5.50	1,400	$5.50	1,700
$5.00	1,600	$5.00	1,600
$4.50	1,800	$4.50	1,500
$4.00	2,000	$4.00	1,400

a   Find the equilibrium wage and quantity hired.
b   Consider the effect of the unemployment insurance tax. Suppose that it equals $1.50 per hour and is paid by the employers (they are the demanders in this market). Use supply and demand analysis to determine the incidence of this tax.
c   Now suppose that rather than being paid by the employers, the tax must be paid by the workers. Use supply and demand analysis to determine the incidence of this tax.
d   Does it matter who pays the tax?

Tool Kit 5.3: Using Supply and Demand for Price Controls

When the government interferes with the law of supply and demand and sets price controls, the effects can be analyzed with the basic method of supply and demand. To see the effects, start with an equilibrium.

The price control (if it is effective) will change the price without changing either the demand curve or the supply curve. The new equilibrium occurs at the price set by the government, but the quantity demanded is read off the demand curve, and the quantity supplied is read off the supply curve. The actual quantity transacted is always the short side of the market (the smaller of the quantity demanded and the quantity supplied).

The basic results of this analysis are that price ceilings, when set below the market-clearing price, lower the price, cause shortages, and reduce the quantity transacted. Price floors, when set above the market-clearing price, raise the price, cause surpluses, and reduce the quantity transacted.

Step one: Start with a market-clearing equilibrium.

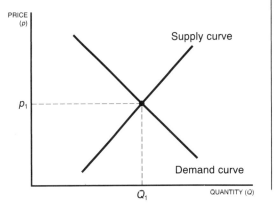

Step two: Identify the controlled price, and decide whether it is a floor or a ceiling.

Step three: Find the new equilibrium price. If it is a price floor set below the market-clearing price or a price ceiling set above the market-clearing price, then the equilibrium is the market-clearing one found in step one. If it is a price floor set above the market-clearing price or a price ceiling set below market clearing, then the controlled price is the equilibrium price.

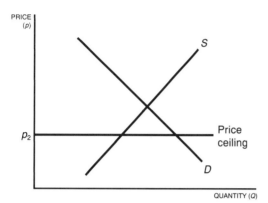

Step four: Determine the shortage or surplus. For a price floor set above the market-clearing price, there is a surplus:

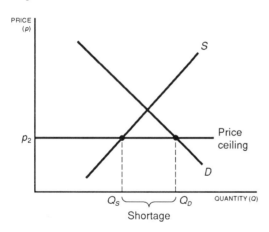

shortage = quantity supplied – quantity demanded.

For a price ceiling set below the market-clearing price, there is a shortage:

surplus = quantity demanded – quantity supplied.

6   (Worked problem: price controls) Dental bills in Toothache City rose again last year. The City Council is considering a bill to place a ceiling on fees that dentists can charge for teeth cleaning. The supply curve and demand curve for teeth cleanings are given in Table 5.6.

Table 5.6

Demand		Supply	
Price	*Quantity*	*Price*	*Quantity*
$65	100	$65	190
$60	120	$60	180
$55	140	$55	170
$50	160	$50	160
$45	180	$45	150
$40	200	$40	140

a   Find the equilibrium price and quantity for teeth cleanings in Toothache City.

b   The City Council passes a price ceiling ordinance, setting the maximum price at $40 per cleaning. Use supply and demand analysis to determine the effects of the price control.

Step-by-step solution

Step one (a): Find the equilibrium price and quantity. The market clears at a price of $50 and quantity equal to 160.

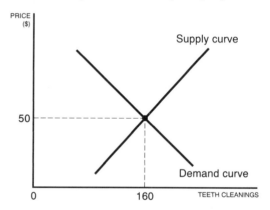

Step two (b): Identify the controlled price and whether it is a floor or a ceiling. The price control is a price ceiling set at $40.

Step three: Determine the new equilibrium price. The ceiling is below the market-clearing price; therefore, the new price is equal to the ceiling price of $40.

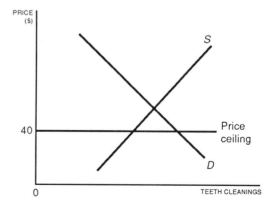

Step four: Determine the shortage or surplus. When the price is $40, the quantity demanded is 200 and the quantity supplied is 140. Although consumers would like more, there are only 140 cleanings actually performed. This results in a shortage of 200 − 140 = 60 teeth cleanings. The diagram illustrates the solution.

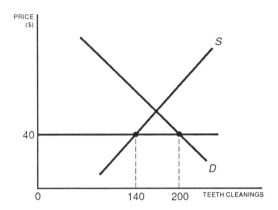

7 (Practice problem: price controls) The legislature in the state of Canute is considering price ceilings on automobile insurance premiums. The supply curve and demand curve for automobile insurance policies ($250 deductible on liability, no collision) are given in Table 5.7.

Table 5.7

Demand		Supply	
Price	Quantity	Price	Quantity
$800	1,000	$800	1,800
$750	1,100	$750	1,500
$700	1,200	$700	1,200
$650	1,400	$650	900
$600	1,600	$600	600

a Find the equilibrium price and quantity.
b Suppose that a price ceiling of $650 is imposed. Use supply and demand analysis to determine the effects of the price control.

8 (Practice problem: price controls) Fearful of a restless urban population, Corporal Thug, the new supreme ruler of Costa Guano, attempts to mollify the masses with a wage increase. Thug mandates that employers must pay at least $8 per day. The supply and demand curves for urban labour are given in Table 5.8.

Table 5.8

Demand		Supply	
Wage	Quantity	Wage	Quantity
$8.50	400	$8.50	4,000
$8.00	600	$8.00	3,200
$7.50	700	$7.50	2,600
$7.00	800	$7.00	2,200
$6.50	900	$6.50	1,800
$6.00	1,000	$6.00	1,000

a Find the quantity demanded, the quantity supplied, and the size of the surplus or shortage, if any.
b Democracy comes to Costa Guano! Corporal Thug is overthrown and the minimum wage repealed. Use supply and demand analysis to determine the effects of the price control.

Answers to Problems

2 a
Price	Quantity	Revenue
$10	70	$700
$ 8	90	$720
$ 6	120	$720
$ 4	130	$520

b Between $10 and $8,
elasticity = (10 + 8)(90 − 70)/(10 − 8)(90 + 70)
= 1.125.
Between $8 and $6,
elasticity = (8 + 6)(120 − 90)/(8 − 6)(120 + 90)
= 1.
Between $6 and $4,
elasticity = (6 + 4)(130 − 120)/(6 − 4)(130 + 120)
= 0.2.
c When elasticity is 1.125, the demand curve is elastic, and total revenue rises from $700 to $720 as price falls. When elasticity is 1, the demand curve is unitary elastic, and total revenue remains constant at $720 as price falls. Finally, when elasticity is 0.2, the demand curve is inelastic, and total revenue falls from $720 to $520 as price falls.

3 In the following tables, the number in the elasticity column corresponding to each price refers to the elasticity over the interval between that price and the next highest price.

a
Price	Quantity	Total revenue	Elasticity
$12	6	$72	
$10	8	$80	1.57
$ 8	10	$80	1.00
$ 6	12	$72	0.64

b
Price	Quantity	Total revenue	Elasticity
$100	80	$8,000	
$ 80	85	$6,800	0.26
$ 60	90	$5,400	0.20
$ 40	95	$3,800	0.14

c
Price	Quantity	Total revenue	Elasticity
$9	10	$ 90	
$8	14	$112	2.430
$7	18	$126	1.875
$6	22	$132	1.300

5 a Wage = $5.00; quantity = 1,600.
b The new supply is given in Table 5.9.

Table 5.9

Supply	
Wage	Quantity
$8.00	1,900
$7.50	1,800
$7.00	1,700
$6.50	1,600
$6.00	1,500
$5.50	1,400

The new equilibrium wage = $5.50; quantity = 1,400. Demander's burden = $5.50 − $5.00 = $0.50; supplier's burden = $5.00 + $1.50 − $5.50 = $1.00.

  c The new demand curve is given in Table 5.10. The new equilibrium wage = $4.00; quantity = 1,400. Demander's burden = $4.00 + $1.50 − $5.00 = $0.50; supplier's burden = $5.00 − $4.00 = $1.00.

Table 5.10

Demand	
Wage	Quantity
$5.00	1,000
$4.50	1,200
$4.00	1,400
$3.50	1,600
$3.00	1,800
$2.50	2,000

  d No. The demander's burden, supplier's burden, and equilibrium quantity are the same in each case.

7 a Price = $700; quantity = 1,200.
    b Price = $650; quantity demanded = 1,400; quantity supplied = 900; shortage = 1,400 − 900 = 500.

8 a Wage = $8.00; quantity demanded = 600; quantity supplied = 3,200; surplus = 3,200 − 600 = 2,600.
    b Price = $600; quantity = 1,000.

Chapter 6

TIME AND RISK

Chapter Review

When trades involve the future, as they do when individuals borrow money or buy a house, people must be concerned with the time value of money and with the risk that the trade will not proceed as stipulated. Time and risk therefore affect today's demand and supply curves. This chapter explores markets for risk and insurance along with the broad class of capital markets (stock markets, foreign exchange markets, and so on) where firms raise funds to finance investment and where people transfer risks. Chapter 7 closes the introductory part of the book, with a look at the public sector and the large role government plays in the economy.

ESSENTIAL CONCEPTS

1   The value of a dollar today is greater than the value of a dollar to be received in the future. In other words, money has a time value. Any decision that involves present and future dollars must account for the time value of money. Economists calculate the present discounted value; they convert future dollars to their present equivalent. The formula is as follows:

present value = future dollars/$(1 + $ interest rate$)^n$,

where n represents the number of years in the future.

2   The market for loanable funds brings together all those who want to borrow and those who want to save. The price in this market is the **interest rate.** Figure 6.1 shows the demand curve for loanable funds sloping downwards; this indicates that at lower interest rates, more borrowers would like to borrow more funds. The supply curve slopes upwards because at higher interest rates, individuals will save more. The interest rate adjusts to clear the market, and the equilibrium quantity of savings equals the equilibrium quantity of borrowing.

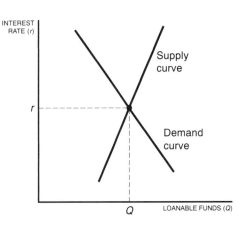

Figure 6.1

3 **Assets,** such as land, housing, stocks, and bonds, last a long time and can be bought today and sold in the future. The prices of assets are determined by supply and demand; however, supply and demand are affected by both today's conditions and what people expect future prices to be. Buyers and sellers of assets must form their **expectations** and make forecasts with care; nevertheless, they are likely to make mistakes, disagree, and revise their expectations. Changing expectations explain large changes in asset prices and make asset markets volatile and risky.

4 Most people are **risk averse** and would prefer to reduce the uncertainty about future economic conditions. The **market for risk** is a whole set of institutions and arrangements by which risk is transferred. One such institution is the **insurance market,** where individuals purchase policies that protect against the risk of loss associated with specific events, such as disability or accidents. Sometimes, however, insurance markets do not offer such protection. One reason is adverse selection, which means that the riskiest customers are the most likely to buy insurance. Another problem, moral hazard, arises because people who have bought insurance have less incentive to take other precautions that would protect themselves against loss.

5 Firms can raise capital in two ways. First, they can borrow, either from a bank or by issuing bonds; in both cases they promise to pay a certain sum in the future and interest periodically. Loans and bonds are risky because the borrower may default. Lenders charge higher interest rates, or **risk premiums,** to compensate for greater default risks. Second, they can raise **equity capital,** chiefly by selling shares of stock. Because stockholders own a share of the firm, they bear the risk that the firm will not be profitable. Stockholders do have limited liability, which means that they can lose no more than their investment.

6 One of the most fundamental **trade-offs** in the economy involves **risk and incentives.** In markets for both risk and capital, when risks are reduced, so are incentives. Figure 6.2 shows the trade-off. At point A, there is low risk and limited incentives. Both risk and incentives increase by moving from A to B.

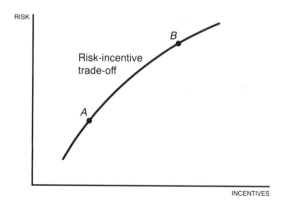

Figure 6.2

7 Entrepreneurs introduce new products, develop new ways of producing goods, and create new businesses. These activities are very risky, but they are not insurable. An important function for entrepreneurs is bearing the risks of these necessary endeavours.

BEHIND THE ESSENTIAL CONCEPTS

1 The distinction between real and nominal interest rates is very important, especially in macroeconomics. When you deposit money in your bank account, the bank pays you the nominal interest rate. Say it is 5 percent. Your money grows at 5 percent each year, but your purchasing power may not, because each year prices may also be changing. Suppose that the inflation rate (the rate of increase in the general price level) is 4 percent. This means that each year goods become 4 percent more expensive, and you can buy only 5 percent – 4 percent = 1 percent more goods. The 1 percent is the real interest rate, and also the rate of increase in your purchasing power.

2 Many economic activities, from purchasing an asset to making an investment, are oriented towards the future. Households and firms must form expectations about the future. Economists distinguish three ways of forming expectations. If you think that tomorrow will be like today, then your expectations are **myopic.** You have **adaptive expectations** if you think that current trends will continue. Finally, you have **rational expectations** (and are well on your way to becoming an economist) if you use all available information, including what you learn in economics.

3 **Adverse selection** and **moral hazard** are important problems, and you should be clear about the difference. Adverse selection occurs when the mix of customers is affected by the insurance contract. For example, an insurance company may find that its policyholders have more accidents than the population at large. The company reasons that high-risk people buy more insurance. **Moral hazard,** on the other hand, involves the behaviour of the insured. People who have insurance may not take the same precautions as those without insurance. They may fail to buckle up or may even drive recklessly.

4 Adverse selection, moral hazard, and the risk-incentive trade-off are not limited to the insurance industry. They are pervasive in the economy. If you are a banker and charger higher interest rates, then you may find that only risky borrowers apply for loans. We say that the pool of applicants for your loans is adversely selected. It may be wise for you to move along the risk-incentive trade-off. You can do this by requiring collateral. This increases the borrower's risk—the collateral will be forfeited if the borrower defaults— but it gives better incentives to repay the loan.

Here is another example. Suppose that you own a business and you pay your sales force a fixed salary. You may find that they do not work as hard as you would like, and sales decline. Because it is the behaviour of your sales force that changes, it is called moral hazard. Again, you can move along the risk-incentive trade-off by replacing the fixed salary with commission pay based on how much each employee sells. This policy exposes your sales force to more risk, but gives them incentives to work hard.

SELF-TEST

True or False

1 A 10 percent mortgage is more costly for the borrower when compounded monthly rather than annually.

2 The nominal interest rate is the real interest rate minus the inflation rate.

3 The present discounted value of a future dollar is what one would pay today for that future dollar.

4 The interest rate is the price in the market for loanable funds.

5 Current prices of assets are based upon expectations about their future prices.

6 Someone who always expects that what is true today will be true tomorrow has myopic expectations.

7 Individuals demand insurance because they are risk averse.

8 The adverse selection problem arises because insurance companies are not sure about the riskiness of their customers.

9 The moral hazard problem arises because insured individuals have less incentive to protect against loss.

10 A deductible is an example of how an insurance company adjusts an individual's position on the risk-incentive trade-off.

11 Governments can generally borrow money at lower interest rates than individuals because there is less risk of a government's defaulting on the loan.

12 Bonds are riskier than stocks because stocks have limited liability.

13 When risks are higher, so are incentives to protect against losses.

14 The individuals who are responsible for creating new businesses, new products, and new production processes are called entrepreneurs.

15 Most of the risks faced by entrepreneurs, such as the risk that the business will not succeed, cannot be insured against.

Multiple Choice

1 If you deposit $1,100 in the bank today and the interest rate on your deposit is 10 percent, how much money will be in your account at the end of one year?

a $1,200
b $1,210
c $121
d $1,000
e none of the above.

2 If you are to receive $1,100 from a client one year from today, what is the present discounted value of that future receipt?

a $1,100
b $1,000
c $1,200
d $979
e none of the above

3 If the interest rate increases, the present discounted value of the future returns from investment projects

a increases.
b remains unchanged.
c decreases.
d may rise or fall depending on how the change in the interest rate alters the future returns from the investment projects.
e none of the above.

4 If you borrow $4,000 for a used car purchase at 11 percent interest, the 11 percent is the

a real rate of interest.
b rate of inflation.
c nominal rate of interest.
d real rate of interest – nominal rate of interest.
e nominal rate of interest – rate of inflation.

5 Suppose that the interest rate offered for certificates of deposit is 8 percent. The inflation rate is expected to be 5 percent. What is the real rate of interest?

a 8 percent
b 5 percent
c 13 percent
d 3 percent
e none of the above

6 When market prices for assets change dramatically, it is usually because of

a changes in the supply of assets.
b government price floors.
c changes in expectations about future prices.
d changes in tastes.
e changes in income.

7 People who use all available information to form expectations about the future are said to have

a   myopic expectations.
b   adaptive expectations.
c   rational expectations.
d   insider expectations.
e   random walk expectations.

8   Most people are risk averse. This means they

a   try to avoid or minimize serious risks.
b   have myopic expectations.
c   never take risks.
d   focus on the nominal rate of interest.
e   enjoy taking risks.

9   Which of the following is not true of the insurance market?

a   Buyers of insurance are risk averse.
b   Insurance companies spread risks among their many customers.
c   Insurance companies can usually forecast accurately the annual amount of claims.
d   Insurance companies will insure against all types of risk, including business failure.
e   Insurance companies will sometimes require that those buying the insurance bear part of the risk.

10   For insurance companies, the selection problem refers to

a   selecting the best employees to hire.
b   selecting the right premium to charge.
c   selecting the best risks to insure.
d   selecting the best corporate logo.
e   none of the above.

11   Which of the following is not true? Adverse selection

a   is a consequence of the fact that the insurance company has limited information about the riskiness of individual customers.
b   implies that those more likely to buy insurance tend to be the higher risk.
c   causes those customers with lower risk to avoid insurance at high rates.
d   makes the fraction of customers who will have an accident larger when premiums are higher.
e   causes those customers who insure to become less concerned to avoid the loss against which they are insured.

12   If the average loss per policy is always less than the premium, then

a   an insurance market for this risk is not viable.
b   insurance firms must increase the premium.
c   insurance buyers are not risk averse.
d   insurance companies are not sharing risks.
e   none of the above.

13   Moral hazard means that

a   insurance buyers are risk averse.
b   insurance companies can predict losses accurately.
c   higher-risk individuals demand more insurance at higher prices.
d   insured individuals have less incentive to avoid accidents.

e   the premium must include an allowance for false claims.

14   If an individual who sometimes drives recklessly has a higher demand for automobile insurance as a result, this is an example of

a   adverse selection.
b   moral hazard.
c   risk aversion.
d   adaptive expectations.
e   none of the above.

15   After buying more malpractice insurance, a doctor spends less time with each patient. This is an example of

a   adverse selection.
b   moral hazard.
c   risk aversion.
d   adaptive expectations.
e   none of the above.

16   Which of these is *not* a means of raising capital?

a   issuing stocks
b   selling bonds
c   taking out loans
d   purchasing insurance
e   none of the above

17   Limited liability means

a   limits are placed on how much debt corporations can issue in the form of bonds.
b   limits are placed on how much corporations can borrow in the form of loans.
c   limits are placed on how much money corporations can raise in the form of equity.
d   limits are placed on the ratio of debt to equity.
e   individuals who buy equity in a corporation are not responsible for any debts the corporation incurs beyond the amount they have invested in equity.

18   Stocks are riskier than bonds because

a   the nominal interest rate is greater than the real interest rate.
b   investors are risk averse.
c   bondholders bear only the risk of default, while the amount that stockholders receive depends upon how profitable the firm is.
d   the liability of stockholders is limited to the amount invested.
e   interest is tax deductible, but dividends are not.

19   Which factor did not contribute to the savings and loan crisis in the United States?

a   Higher interest rates in the 1970s reduced the present discounted value of mortgages.
b   Federal deposit insurance protected depositors against loss and encouraged them to deposit money in risky savings and loans.
c   S & L's, whose depositors were insured, issued risky loans.

d Regulations encouraged moral hazard in managing risks.

e None of the above.

20 The risk-incentive trade-off shows that

a insurance buyers have adaptive expectations.

b bonds are riskier than stocks.

c fully insured individuals have less incentive to protect against risk.

d as risk is decreased, the moral hazard problem becomes less severe.

e none of the above.

Completion

1 The return received for giving up current consumption in exchange for increased future consumption is called _____.

2 The _____ of a dollar to be received in the future shows how much that future dollar is worth today.

3 The formula used to calculate the present value of $1 next year is _____.

4 When the interest rate rises, the present discounted value of future income _____.

5 The interest rate is the price in the market for _____.

6 A savings account that pays 10 percent compounded daily will return _____ to the saver than another savings account that pays 10 percent compounded monthly.

7 The interest rate that indicates how much consumption tomorrow must be forgone for extra consumption today is the _____ interest rate.

8 The real interest rate is the nominal interest rate minus the _____.

9 Current prices of assets, such as land, depend upon _____ about their future prices.

10 The fact that insured individuals have less incentive to take precaution against accident is called _____.

Answers to Self-Test

True or False

1	t	6	t	11	t
2	f	7	t	12	f
3	t	8	t	13	t
4	t	9	t	14	t
5	t	10	t	15	t

Multiple Choice

1	b	6	c	11	e	16	d
2	b	7	c	12	a	17	e
3	c	8	a	13	d	18	c
4	c	9	d	14	a	19	e
5	d	10	c	15	b	20	c

Completion

1 interest rate
2 present value
3 1/(1 + interest rate)
4 falls
5 loanable funds
6 more
7 real
8 inflation rate
9 expectations
10 moral hazard

Doing Economics: Tools and Practice Problems

Tool Kit 6.1: Calculating the Present Discounted Value

Payments to be received in the future are not worth as much as payments received today. This statement reflects the fact that there is a time value of money. To compare the worth of present and future payments, it is necessary to compute the present discounted value, which is the current dollar equivalent of an amount to be rendered in the future.

Step one: Make a table with four columns, and label them as shown.

Year	Amount	Discount factor	Present discounted value

Step two: For every payment or receipt, enter the year and the amount. Let Y_1 be the amount in the first year, Y_2 the amount the second year, and so on.

Year	Amount	Discount factor	Present discounted value
1	Y_1		
2	Y_2		

Step three: Calculate the discount factor for each year. The formula is $1/(1 + r)^n$, where r is the interest rate and n is the number of years until the payment or receipt. Enter these discount factors in the table.

Year	Amount	Discount factor	Present discounted value
1	Y_1	$1/(1 + r)$	
2	Y_2	$1/(1 + r)^2$	

Step four: Multiply the number in the amount column by the corresponding discount factor. Enter the product in the present discounted value column.

Year	Amount	Discount factor	Present discounted value
1	Y_1	$1/(1 + r)$	$Y_1 \times 1/(1 + r)$
2	Y_2	$1/(1 + r)^2$	$Y_2 \times 1/(1 + r)^2$

Step five: Add the numbers in the right-hand column. The sum is the present discounted value.

Year	Amount	Discount factor	Present discounted value
1	Y_1	$1/(1 + r)$	$Y_1 \times 1/(1 + r)$
2	Y_2	$1/(1 + r)^2$	$Y_2 \times 1/(1 + r)^2$

Present discounted value =
$Y_1 \times 1/(1 + r) + Y_2 \times 1/(1 + r)^2$

1 (Worked problem: present discounted value) Ethel has two years before retirement from a career of teaching unruly high school delinquents. Her salary is $40,000, paid at the end of each year. The school board has offered her $70,000 now to retire early. The relevant interest rate is 7 percent. In monetary terms alone, is working worth more than retiring?

Step-by-step solution

First, calculate the present discounted value of continuing to work.

Step one: Make a table with four columns, and label them as shown.

Year	Amount	Discount factor	Present discounted value

Step two: For every payment or receipt, enter the year and the amount. Ethel receives $40,000 each year for two years.

Year	Amount	Discount factor	Present discounted value
1	$40,000		
2	$40,000		

Step three: Calculate the discount factor for each year. For the first year, the discount factor is $1/(1 + .07) = 0.93$, and for the second year it is $1/(1 + .07)^2 = 0.86$. Enter these discount factors in the table.

Year	Amount	Discount factor	Present discounted value
1	$40,000	0.93	
2	$40,000	0.86	

Step four: Multiply the number in the amount column by the corresponding discount factor. Enter the product in the present discounted value column.

Year	Amount	Discount factor	Present discounted value
1	$40,000	0.93	$37,380
2	$40,000	0.86	$34,400

Step five: Add the numbers in the right-hand column. The sum is the present discounted value.

Year	Amount	Discount factor	Present discounted value
1	$40,000	0.93	$37,380
2	$40,000	0.86	$34,400

Present discounted value = $71,780.

Next, compare the lump-sum payment with the present discounted value of continuing to work. Ethel can postpone retirement and increase the present discounted value of her earnings by only $1,780. The reason that the gain is so little is that earnings come in the future and must be discounted, while the retirement bonus is paid now.

2 (Practice problem: present discounted value) The Transportation Department is considering the bids of two paving companies for repaving South Street. The Do-It-Rite firm will do the job for $200,000, and they will guarantee that their new process will make the road free of potholes for 3 years. The Let-It-Go company only charges $100,000, but estimated pothole repair costs are $40,000 each year. The interest rate is 8 percent.

   a Calculate the present discounted value of the entire cost with the Let-It-Go firm.
   b Which is the less expensive bid?

3 (Practice problem: present discounted value) Calculate the present discounted value of each of the following.

   a Interest rate equals 10 percent.

Year	Amount	Discount factor	Present discounted value
1	$10,000		
2	$15,000		

   b Interest rate equals 5 percent.

Year	Amount	Discount factor	Present discounted value
1	$ 0		
2	$20,000		

   c Interest rate equals 15 percent.

Year	Amount	Discount factor	Present discounted value
1	$5,000		
2	$5,000		
3	$5,000		

   d Interest rate equals 5 percent.

Year	Amount	Discount factor	Present discounted value
1	$ 5,000		
2	$ 0		
3	$25,000		

Answers to Problems

2 *a*

Firm	Cost
Do-It-Rite	$200,000
Let-It-Go	$100,000 + \dfrac{\$40,000}{1.08} + \dfrac{\$40,000}{(1.08)^2} + \dfrac{\$40,000}{(1.08)^3} = \$203,083$

   b The Do-It-Rite bid.

3 *a* $21,488.
   b $18,141.
   c $12,447.
   d $26,358.

Chapter 7

THE PUBLIC SECTOR

Chapter Review

The text's focus so far has been on private markets. This is overly simple, as the history of the automobile given in Chapter 1 illustrates. While the North American automobile industry consists of private firms, governments have played a large role throughout the industry's history, from issuing patents and regulating safety and environmental standards to occasionally protecting domestic manufacturers from foreign competition and providing unemployment benefits to laid-off workers. This blend of the public and private sectors is called a mixed economy.

This chapter considers the economic role of the public sector and how it operates differently from the private sector. Important roles for the public sector include improving the market's allocation of resources, stabilizing the overall performance of the economy, and redistributing income. The chapter also discusses government policies and emphasizes that government action may not always succeed in correcting market failures.

ESSENTIAL CONCEPTS

1 The Canadian government has a **federal structure,** with national, provincial, and municipal levels, and sometimes a regional level between the provincial and municipal levels. Government actions at all levels pervade the economy—providing goods, regulating the private activity of individuals and firms, collecting taxes, and overseeing the money supply, to name a few. Government differs from private institutions in that its decisions are made by elected representatives or their appointed officers, and government has the power to force compliance with some of its orders.

2 Government's economic role arises when it has the opportunity to improve on **market failures,** to stabilize the overall level of economic activity, or to redistribute income to those unable to provide for themselves. Private markets will generally do a poor job of providing public goods or allocating resources when there are **externalities.**

3 The **public sector** has a variety of instruments with which to accomplish its goals. It can take direct action, either produce the good or service itself or purchase it from private firms. It can **mandate** private sector action, **regulate** private activity, or **ban** certain behaviours altogether. Finally, with a somewhat lighter hand, the government can provide incentives to increase or decrease certain types of actions through the use of its tax and subsidy powers.

4   In Canada, government spending at all levels amounts to nearly 45 percent of gross domestic product (GDP), higher than the average for developed countries. Canadian government spending has grown dramatically in recent decades. Much of the growth of government spending is accounted for by transfers to the elderly, transfers to the provinces in the areas of health and welfare, and interest on the growing national debt.

BEHIND THE ESSENTIAL CONCEPTS

1   **Externalities** exist whenever individuals or firms do not face the full costs and benefits of their decisions, and left alone, externalities create incentive problems. Negative externalities are costs borne by others, such as pollution, congestion, and noise. Positive externalities are benefits received by others, such as contributions for medical and other research, innovation, public parks, and endangered species preservation. Because decision makers can ignore the costs that spill over onto others, private firms overproduce negative externalities. Similarly, because they are not compensated, producers of positive externalities do not create enough. Governments can improve the allocation of resources by inducing individuals to produce fewer negative and more positive externalities.

2   **Public goods** have two important characteristics. Once they are provided, the marginal cost of another consumer's enjoying the good is zero. For example, a second, third, or fourth person can view a public statue without affecting the first person's enjoyment. The second characteristic is that it is costly to exclude individuals from enjoying the public good. Placing the statue in a private viewing area and charging admission misses the point of a monument. This feature makes it difficult for private individuals to collect enough funds to provide public goods. The fact that people can choose to enjoy public goods without paying for them is called the free-rider problem, and it is one reason economists often recommend that the public sector take a role in providing public goods.

3   When the private market fails to allocate resources efficiently, there is a potential role for government action. For example, when a public good such as a traffic light is needed, the government is the natural choice to provide it. When negative externalities are present, such as pollution, the government may be able to discourage them. The income distribution produced by private markets may be unacceptable, and the government may be able to redistribute it. Governments are large organizations, however, and policies do not always work as intended.

4   The existence of market failures prompts the call for more government intervention. **Government failures**

justify calls for less intervention. Often what is needed is different, better government action, which harnesses market incentives to bring about a better allocation of resources.

SELF-TEST

True or False

1   In a federal governmental structure, government activities take place at several levels: national, provincial, and municipal.

2   Government action is distinguished from private sector action in that government always has better information.

3   Externalities are present whenever an individual or a firm can take an action without bearing all the costs and benefits.

4   The marginal cost of an additional consumer is zero for a public good.

5   The marginal cost of production is zero for a public good.

6   It is impossible to exclude those who do not pay from consuming private goods.

7   Markets for new inventions fail if those who benefit from new inventions do not pay the inventor.

8   The free-rider problem implies that private markets may not provide public goods efficiently.

9   If the private market provides too little of some good or service, then government can increase the quantity provided by subsidizing the good or service.

10 In the last decade, there has been an increase in the amount of nationalization in Canada.

11 The federal government takes most of the responsibility for education in Canada.

12 One category that has increased as a share of the federal budget since 1950 is interest on the national debt.

13 As countries spend a larger fraction of GDP through government, per capita income always increases.

14 Even though markets may fail to allocate resources efficiently, government action may make matters worse.

15 The government plays a substantial role in the economy of almost every industrialized country.

Multiple Choice

1   Which of the following is not one of the four basic questions an economy must answer?

 a   What is produced, and in what quantities?
 b   How are goods and services produced?

c For whom are the goods and services produced?

d Who makes the decisions?

e Who elects the government?

2 Private institutions, such as business firms and not-for-profit organizations, are distinguished from government in that

a private decision makers are rational.

b government decision makers have adaptive expectations.

c governments are not rational.

d government has certain powers of coercion.

e none of the above.

3 The economic system in Canada is best described as a

a mixed economy with a federal system of government.

b system with central control over all economic functions.

c purely market economy.

d nationalized economy with a federal system of government.

e mixed economy with a single central government.

4 In his book *The Wealth of Nations,* Adam Smith argued that the public interest is best promoted by

a government control of the economy.

b the benevolence of well-meaning citizens.

c individuals pursuing their own self-interest.

d adherence to time-honoured traditions.

e none of the above.

5 The Great Depression of 1929–1939 led the federal government to take a more active role in

a reallocating resources.

b redistributing income.

c stabilizing the level of economic activity.

d nationalizing private business firms.

e none of the above.

6 Which of the following is not a legitimate role of government?

a solving the problem of scarcity

b redistributing income

c stabilizing the level of economic activity

d correcting market failures

e seeking reelection

7 Which of the following is not an example of an externality?

a environmental pollution

b research and development

c restoring buildings in decaying areas

d contributions to philanthropic organizations

e eating a tomato

8 When farmers irrigate their crops with water provided by the government at subsidized prices, there is

a an externality.

b a public good.

c a market.

d a patent.

e none of the above.

9 Which of the following is not true of pure public goods?

a The marginal cost of an additional individual using the good is zero.

b It is impossible to exclude people from receiving the good.

c They are efficiently provided through the interaction of supply and demand.

d They are inefficiently provided through the interaction of supply and demand.

e none of the above.

10 Private markets have difficulty supplying public goods because

a of the free-rider problem.

b of the federal system of government.

c the level of private activity fluctuates.

d the income distribution is inequitable.

e all markets are efficient.

11 One advantage that government has in the provision of public goods is that it

a is not subject to scarcity.

b does not face uncertainty about the demand for public goods.

c can coerce citizens to pay for them.

d need not always be rational.

e none of the above.

12 The free-rider problem refers to

a the idea that public transportation always runs large deficits.

b the idea that when people can enjoy a public good without paying for it, they often do not contribute.

c the idea that markets fail to allocate resources efficiently when there are externalities.

d the idea that the marginal cost of an additional consumer enjoying a pure public good is zero.

e none of the above.

13 Which of the following is not an example of direct government action to correct market failure?

a A country nationalizes its banking system.

b Tax breaks are offered for exploring for new deposits of oil.

c A large city builds shelters for the homeless.

d The army purchases tanks from a private firm.

e None of the above.

14 Which of the following is not an example of mandating private sector action?

a Tuna fishers are required to use nets with larger openings so that captured dolphins may escape.

b Electric utilities are required to install scrubbing devices in smokestacks.

c Trucking firms are required to install antipollution devices in their vehicles.

d Nationalization.

e None of the above.

15 Consumer sovereignty means that

a individuals are the best judges of what is in their own interest.

b there is no role for government in product-safety regulations.

c consumers always have good information.

d consumers are rational decision makers.

e none of the above.

16 Delegating to the private sector activities previously done by government is called

a deregulation.

b nationalization.

c privatization.

d subsidization.

e none of the above.

17 Since 1950, which category has increased most in proportionate terms in the federal budget?

a defence

b grants to other governments

c debt charges

d transfers to persons and business

e capital investment

18 Which of the following is true of Canada?

a Government expenditures represent nearly 45 percent of GDP.

b Canada spends relatively less on government than most other developed countries.

c Government spending as a fraction of GDP has remained constant since 1950.

d Defence spending is about 20 percent of GDP.

e Governments have only spent what they raise in taxes.

19 Which of the following is an example of market failure?

a Housing is expensive.

b The poor often cannot afford adequate health care.

c The ostentatious displays of wealth by the rich and famous are offensive.

d Periodic episodes of high unemployment trouble market economies.

e None of the above.

20 The right to seize private property (with proper compensation) for public use is called

a diminishing returns.

b taxation.

c deregulation.

d nationalization.

e eminent domain.

Completion

1 The failure of private markets to produce economic efficiency is called _____.

2 When an individual or firm can take an action without bearing the full costs and benefits, there is said to be an _____.

3 Goods for which it costs nothing extra to have an additional individual enjoy are called _____.

4 Because it is difficult to exclude those who do not pay from benefiting from public goods, the private markets do a poor job of providing public goods. This is the _____ problem.

5 If the government seeks to encourage some activity, such as recycling, it can _____ the activity.

6 Delegating functions previously run by the government to the private sector is called _____.

7 When resources are idle, the economy is operating _____ its production possibilities curve.

8 Three legitimate economic roles of government are to redistribute income, stabilize the economy, and _____.

9 During the late 1970s and early 1980s, many regulations were reduced or eliminated in transportation, telecommunications, and banking. This process is an example of _____.

10 Three instruments of government for economic purposes are taking direct action, mandating private action, and providing _____ to the private sector through taxes and subsidies.

Answers to Self-Test

True or False

1	t	4	t	7	t	10	f	13	f
2	f	5	f	8	t	11	f	14	t
3	t	6	f	9	t	12	t	15	t

Multiple Choice

1	e	6	a	11	c	16	c
2	d	7	e	12	b	17	c
3	a	8	a	13	b	18	a
4	c	9	c	14	d	19	d
5	c	10	a	15	a	20	e

Completion

1 market failure

2 externality

3 public goods

4 free-rider

5 subsidize

6 privatization

7 inside

8 reallocate resources

9 deregulation

10 incentives

Doing Economics: Tools and Practice Problems

When an activity causes positive externalities, or external benefits, the government can often improve matters through subsidies. This section explores two questions. First, how do subsidies encourage more of the subsidized activity? Our analysis will be very much like the treatment of the economic effects of taxation in Chapter 5. The other issue is why decisions are likely to be inefficient when there are externalities. This is an application of the technique of balancing marginal benefits and marginal costs introduced in Chapter 2.

Tool Kit 7.1: Using Supply and Demand to Determine the Effects of Subsidies

Many goods and services receive subsidies from various levels of government. Sometimes, as in the case of home ownership, the demanders benefit directly. In other cases, as with federal water projects, the subsidies are paid to the suppliers. Subsidies obtain their effects by shifting supply or demand curves, and bringing about new equilibrium quantities.

Step one: Start with a no-subsidy equilibrium in the appropriate market.

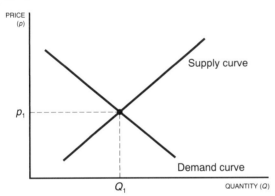

Step two: Identify the magnitude of the subsidy and whether it is paid directly to the demanders or suppliers.

Step three: If the subsidy is paid to demanders, shift the demand curve up (vertically) by exactly the amount of the subsidy. If the subsidy is paid to suppliers, shift the supply curve down by exactly the amount of the subsidy.

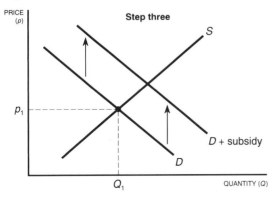

Step four: Find the new equilibrium and compare it with the original equilibrium.

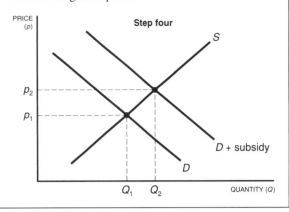

1 (Worked problem: effects of subsidies) Home ownership is treated very favourably by the Canadian tax system, since capital gains earned by selling at more than the purchase price are not taxed. To see how the subsidy affects the housing market, consider the market for three-bedroom bungalows in Little Spoon. The market demand and supply curves without the subsidy are given in Table 7.1.

Table 7.1

Demand		Supply	
Price	Quantity	Price	Quantity
$125,000	10	$125,000	50
$100,000	14	$100,000	42
$ 90,000	25	$ 90,000	31
$ 80,000	28	$ 80,000	28
$ 70,000	31	$ 70,000	20

a Find the equilibrium price and quantity.
b The tax advantages accruing to the home owner amount to $20,000 over the life of the occupancy. Calculate the demand curve with the subsidy included.
c Find the equilibrium price and quantity with the subsidy in place. How does the subsidy change the number of bungalows sold in Little Spoon?

Step-by-step solution

Step one (a): Start with a no-subsidy equilibrium in the appropriate market. The price is $80,000; the market clears with 28 houses sold. This is the answer to part a.

Step two (b): Identify the magnitude of the subsidy and whether it is paid directly to the demanders or suppliers. The subsidy is $20,000, paid to demanders.

Step three: Because it is paid to demanders, the subsidy causes the demand curve to shift vertically by $20,000. To calculate this, add $20,000 to each entry in the price column of the demand curve. The new demand curve is given in Table 7.2, which is the answer to part b.

Table 7.2

Demand	
Price	Quantity
$145,000	10
$120,000	14
$110,000	25
$100,000	28
$ 90,000	31

Step four (c): Find the new equilibrium and compare it with the original equilibrium. The new equilibrium price is $90,000, and the market clears at 31 houses sold. The subsidy has increased the number of home owners in Little Spoon from 28 to 31. The price is $10,000 higher, so the $20,000 subsidy makes home owners only $10,000 better off. Producers share in the benefits with a $10,000 higher price. The solution is illustrated in the diagram.

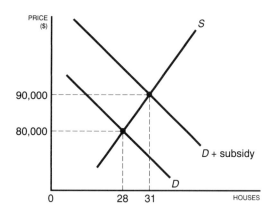

2 (Practice problem: effects of subsidies) Eyes brightening at the thought of thousands of stressed, child-raising voters, a politician has proposed child care grants of $10,000 per family. The demand and supply curves for child care services (measured in days) are given in Table 7.3.

Table 7.3

Demand		Supply	
Price (thousands)	Quantity (days)	Price (thousands)	Quantity (days)
$50	50,000	$50	100,000
$45	60,000	$45	80,000
$40	70,000	$40	70,000
$35	80,000	$35	60,000
$30	100,000	$30	50,000

a Find the equilibrium price and quantity without the subsidy.
b Calculate the demand with the subsidy.
c Find the equilibrium price and quantity with the

subsidy. Compare the equilibria, and explain the effects of the subsidy.

3 (Practice problem: effects of subsidies) To promote conversion to renewable sources of energy, the government has offered various tax deductions and credits for the purchase and installation of solar water heaters. The value to a typical taxpayer of the tax provisions is $3,000. The supply and demand curves for solar water heaters are given in Table 7.4.

Table 7.4

Demand		Supply	
Price	Quantity	Price	Quantity
$8,000	1,000	$8,000	10,000
$7,000	3,000	$7,000	9,000
$6,000	5,000	$6,000	8,000
$5,000	7,000	$5,000	7,000
$4,000	9,000	$4,000	6,000
$3,000	11,000	$3,000	5,000

a Find the equilibrium price and quantity without the subsidy.
b Calculate the demand with the subsidy.
c Find the equilibrium price and quantity with the subsidy. Compare the equilibria, and explain the effects of the subsidy.

Tool Kit 7.2: Showing How Positive Externalities Lead to Inefficiencies

Individuals make decisions by balancing their private benefits and costs at the margin, but efficiency requires that all benefits and costs, not only the private ones, be included in the decision. Thus, when there are externalities, there are costs or benefits ignored by the individual making the decision, and this fact leads to inefficient decisions. This tool kit focuses on positive externalities and the inefficiencies that result.

Step one: Find the private marginal benefits and costs of the relevant activity.

Step two: Find the equilibrium level of the activity, which is the level at which private marginal benefits equal marginal cost.

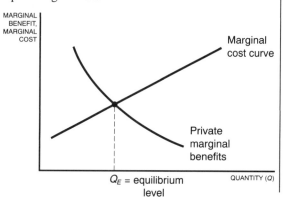

Step three: Calculate the social marginal benefits by adding the external benefit to the private marginal benefit at each level of the activity.

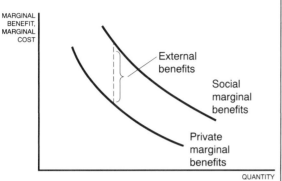

Step four: Find the efficient level of the activity, which is the level at which social marginal benefits equal marginal cost.

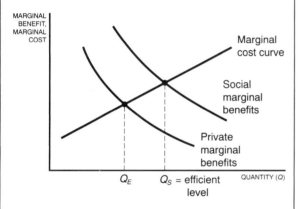

Step five: Compare the equilibrium and efficient levels of the activity.

4 (Worked problem: positive externalities) An important example of an activity that generates positive externalities is worker training. When firms train their employees, the employees not only become more productive in the job, they can also earn higher wages elsewhere. This increase in earning power is a positive externality. The QXV Corporation is considering sending some of its white-collar employees to computer school. The cost is $1,000 per week, and the private marginal benefits to QXV are given in Table 7.5. Also, the value of the external benefit is $500 per week.

Table 7.5

Weeks at school	Private marginal benefits
1	$1,500
2	$1,250
3	$1,000
4	$ 750
5	$ 500
6	$ 250

a How many weeks of computer schooling will the company provide?
b Find the social marginal benefits of computer schooling.
c What is the efficient number of weeks of schooling?

Step-by-step solution

Step one (a): Find the private marginal benefits and costs of the relevant activity. The private marginal benefits are in Table 7.5; the private marginal cost is $1,000 per week.

Step two: Find the equilibrium level of the activity. Private marginal benefits equal $1,000 at 3 weeks.

Step three (b): Calculate the social marginal benefits by adding the external benefit to the private marginal benefit at each level of the activity. The answer is in Table 7.6.

Table 7.6

Weeks at school	Private marginal benefits	Social marginal benefits
1	$1,500	$2,000
2	$1,250	$1,750
3	$1,000	$1,500
4	$ 750	$1,250
5	$ 500	$1,000
6	$ 250	$ 750

Step four (c): Find the efficient level of the activity. Social marginal benefits equal marginal cost at 5 weeks.

Step five: Compare the equilibrium and efficient levels of the activity. The equilibrium number of weeks is 3, which is less than the efficient number, which is 5. The number of weeks provided is too low because the firm ignores the externality.

5 (Practice problem: positive externalities) ZZZX Pharmaceuticals is considering how many scientists to put to work researching a new drug for Angolan flu. Each scientist, complete with equipment and assistance, costs $200,000. The research will bring profits to ZZZX, but it will also bring about advances in viral research that other companies may build on in their own research. The private benefits are given in Table 7.7. The external marginal benefits are $150,000.

Table 7.7

Scientists	Private benefits
1	$400,000
2	$600,000
3	$700,000
4	$750,000
5	$750,000

a How many scientists will the company use? (Hint: First find the private marginal benefits.)

b Find the social marginal benefits of research scientists.

c What is the efficient number of scientists?

6 (Practice problem: positive externalities) Hillside Country farmers have been advised to erect earthen dikes for erosion control. Each dike costs $2,000. The private marginal benefits are given in the second column of Table 7.8, but they do not include the external benefit that one farmer's erosion control efforts provide to neighbours. The external benefits appear in the third column of the table.

Table 7.8

Dikes	Private marginal benefits	External marginal benefits
1	$3,000	$8,000
2	$2,000	$7,000
3	$1,500	$6,000
4	$1,000	$5,000
5	$ 500	$4,000
6	$ 0	$3,000
7	$ 0	$2,000

a How many dikes will each farmer erect?

b Find the social marginal benefits of a farmer's dikes.

c What is the efficient number of dikes?

Answers to Problems

2 *a* Price = $40; quantity = 70,000.

b The new demand curve is given in Table 7.9.

Table 7.9

Demand	
Price	Quantity
$60	50,000
$55	60,000
$50	70,000
$45	80,000
$40	100,000

c The new equilibrium price is $45,000, and the quantity is 80,000. The subsidy increases the quantity from 70,000 to 80,000. Consumers are better off by $5,000 ($10,000 subsidy – $5,000 increase in price), and firms are better off by $5,000, which is the increase in price.

3 *a* Price = $5,000; quantity = 7,000.

b The new demand curve is given in Table 7.10.

Table 7.10

Demand	
Price	Quantity
$11,000	1,000
$10,000	3,000
$ 9,000	5,000
$ 8,000	7,000
$ 7,000	9,000
$ 6,000	11,000

c The new equilibrium price is $7,000, and the quantity is 9,000. The subsidy increases the quantity from 7,000 to 9,000. Consumers are better off by $1,000 ($3,000 subsidy – $2,000 increase in price), and firms are better off by $2,000, which is the increase in price.

5 *a* 2 scientists.

b The social marginal benefits are given in Table 7.11.

Table 7.11

Scientists	Private benefits	Private marginal benefits	Social marginal benefits
1	$400,000	$400,000	$550,000
2	$600,000	$200,000	$350,000
3	$700,000	$100,000	$250,000
4	$750,000	$ 50,000	$200,000
5	$750,000	$ 0	$150,000

c The efficient number is 4 scientists. The company chooses only 2 because it ignores the externality.

6 *a* 2 dikes.

b The social marginal benefits are given in Table 7.12.

Table 7.12

Dikes	Private marginal benefits	External marginal benefits	Social marginal benefits
1	$3,000	$8,000	$11,000
2	$2,000	$7,000	$ 9,000
3	$1,500	$6,000	$ 7,500
4	$1,000	$5,000	$ 6,000
5	$ 500	$4,000	$ 4,500
6	$ 0	$3,000	$ 3,000
7	$ 0	$2,000	$ 2,000

c The efficient number of dikes is 7. Farmers only erect 2 because they ignore the external benefits.

Part Two

Perfect Markets

Chapter 8

THE CONSUMPTION DECISION

Chapter Review

The detailed study of microeconomics, the branch of economics that focuses on the behaviour of individuals and firms and builds to an understanding of markets, begins in this chapter and continues throughout Parts Two and Three of the text. The basic competitive model of the private economy developed here is one you'll use throughout this course. Chapters 8 to 14 build on this model; they explore first the decisions individuals make—how much to consume, save, invest, and work—and then the decisions firms take—what and how much to produce and by what method. The entire model is put together in Chapter 14.

ESSENTIAL CONCEPTS

1   The consumer's decisions about how much of each good to purchase—that is, the demand for each—are made in a two-step procedure. First, the consumer finds how much can be consumed given the amount of money available. This step is the construction of the **opportunity set,** the outer edge of which is the **budget**

constraint. Second, the consumer chooses the best alternative along the budget constraint. Figure 8.1 depicts a budget constraint.

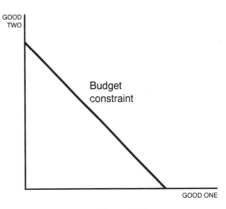

Figure 8.1

2   The budget constraint shows how much of each good can be purchased with the money available. The **slope** of the budget constraint is the **relative price** of the good measured on the horizontal axis. This relative

price indicates the **trade-off**: how much of one good must be forgone to consume one more unit of the other.

3   The benefit or utility that a consumer derives from a good is measured by how much the consumer is willing to pay. Consumers focus on the margin (the next unit) and continue to purchase more of the good until the *marginal benefit equals the price.*

4   When income increases, the budget constraint shifts out, but its slope does not change. Consumers buy more normal goods. Goods that people buy less of as income increases are called inferior goods, but these are the exceptions. The **income elasticity of demand** measures how much the quantity demanded changes as income changes. It is positive for **normal goods** and negative for **inferior goods.**

5   When price changes, the budget constraint rotates: it becomes steeper if the price of the good on the horizontal axis rises and flatter if it falls. The **price elasticity of demand** measures how much the quantity demanded changes as price changes. If this number is greater than 1, the demand is elastic. If it is less than 1, the demand is inelastic. If there are many good substitutes available, the price elasticity tends to be high. Conversely, demand is price inelastic when substitution is difficult.

6   Price changes cause substitution and income effects. Suppose the price of a good rises. Because the good is relatively more expensive, the principle of substitution says that consumers will shift some of their consumption to other goods. This change is the **substitution effect.** At the same time, because the price is higher, the consumer's purchasing power is lower. This causes the consumer to buy less if the good is normal but more if the good is inferior. This change is the **income effect.**

7   **Utility** is the term economists use for the benefits that individuals receive for consuming goods. As people consume more of a particular good, they get smaller increments of utility. In other words, there is diminishing marginal utility. When the consumer has chosen the best bundle of goods, the consumer's utility is maximized and the marginal utility of each good equals its price.

8   **Consumer surplus** equals the difference between what the consumer is willing to pay for goods and the price (what the consumer has to pay). Figure 8.2 shows a demand curve for apples, which also represents what the consumer is willing to pay for apples. When the price is $.25, the consumer purchases 8 apples per week. The consumer surplus, shown as the area between the demand curve and the price, measures the consumer's gain from trade.

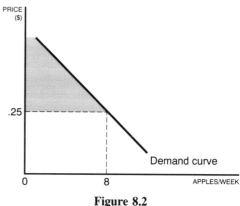

Figure 8.2

BEHIND THE ESSENTIAL CONCEPTS

1   The budget constraint shows what quantities of goods are affordable. If you know the prices of goods and an individual's income, you can draw that individual's budget constraint. As you might expect, people who have the same income and must pay the same prices have the same budget constraint. As price changes, each individual's budget constraint changes in the same way. The budget constraint indicates opportunities; it says nothing about the value that the consumer places on the goods. Individual tastes only come into the picture when the actual choices are made.

2   The slope of the budget line depends only on prices, not on income. Therefore, changes in income cannot change the slope of the budget line. Changes in income bring about a parallel shift in the budget constraint. Price changes, on the other hand, do change the slope. The budget constraint rotates when price changes.

3   Economists measure the responsiveness of quantity to income or price changes by using elasticities. In this chapter, there are two elasticities: the income elasticity of demand and the price elasticity of demand. Elasticities are relative percentage changes. The income elasticity equals the percentage that the quantity demanded changes when income changes by 1 percent. The price elasticity tells the percentage change in quantity demanded as the result of a 1 percent change in price.

4   The basic economic model says that individuals balance the benefits and costs of their decisions. It emphasizes choice at the margin, for the next unit of a good or service. Individuals continue buying until the marginal benefit equals the marginal cost. For the consumer, the marginal benefit (called the marginal utility) is just how much the consumer is willing to pay for another unit. The marginal cost is the price. When marginal utility equals price, the consumer has realized all the possible gains from the purchase of the good.

5   There are two important diagrams in this chapter: the budget constraint and the demand curve. Although

each is downward sloping, they should not be confused. The budget constraint drawn in Figure 8.1 shows the combination of goods that a person can afford. Quantities of goods are measured on each axis. The demand curve drawn in Figure 8.2 shows how much of *one* good will be purchased at each price. The quantity of the good is measured on the horizontal axis, and the price is measured on the vertical.

SELF-TEST

True or False

1 The budget constraint indicates that the amount spent on goods cannot exceed income.

2 The slope of the budget constraint shows the trade-off between two goods.

3 Income determines the slope of the budget constraint.

4 The amount that an individual is willing to pay for coffee is called the marginal utility of coffee.

5 The amount that an individual is willing to pay for an extra cup of coffee is called the marginal utility of coffee.

6 A rational individual will increase consumption of a good until the marginal utility equals the price.

7 When income increases, the budget constraint rotates and becomes flatter.

8 When income increases, the consumer demands more of inferior goods.

9 If an individual demands more of a good when income falls, the good is a complement.

10 If the income elasticity is less than zero, then the good is an inferior good.

11 The long-run income elasticity of demand is greater than the short-run income elasticity of demand.

12 If when the price of one good rises the demand for another also rises, the goods are substitutes.

13 If when the price of one good falls the demand for another also falls, the goods are complements.

14 When the price of a good falls, the substitution effect encourages more consumption of that good.

15 When the price of a normal good falls, the income effect encourages more consumption of that good.

Multiple Choice

1 Assuming that there is no saving or borrowing and income is fixed, a consumer's budget constraint

   a defines that consumer's preferences.
   b indicates that total expenditures cannot be greater than total income.

   c shows that marginal utility is decreasing.
   d is vertical.
   e none of the above.

2 Suppose that the price of a movie ticket is $5 and the price of a pizza is $10. The trade-off between the two goods is

   a one pizza for one movie ticket.
   b two movie tickets for one pizza.
   c two pizzas for one movie ticket.
   d $2 per movie ticket.
   e none of the above.

3 The marginal utility of a good indicates

   a that the usefulness of the good is limited.
   b the willingness to pay for an extra unit.
   c that the good is scarce.
   d that the slope of the budget constraint is the relative price.
   e none of the above.

4 Diminishing marginal utility means that

   a the usefulness of the good is limited.
   b the willingness to pay for an extra unit decreases as more of that good is consumed.
   c the good is less scarce.
   d the slope of the budget constraint is flatter as more of that good is consumed.
   e none of the above.

5 If Fred is willing to pay $100 for one espresso maker and $120 for two, then the marginal utility of the second espresso maker is

   a $20.
   b $120.
   c $100.
   d $60.
   e $50.

6 When the income of a consumer increases, that consumer's budget constraint

   a shifts outwards parallel to the original budget constraint.
   b rotates and becomes steeper.
   c rotates and becomes flatter.
   d shifts inwards parallel to the original budget constraint.
   e none of the above.

7 The percentage change in quantity demanded resulting from a 1 percent increase in income is

   a 1.
   b greater than 0.
   c the income elasticity of demand.
   d the price elasticity of demand.
   e none of the above.

8 If the share of income that an individual spends on a good decreases as the individual's income increases, then the income elasticity of demand is

   a greater than 1.

b   between 0 and 1.

c   0.

d   less than 0.

e   less than 1.

9   In the long run,

   a   the price elasticity of demand is greater than in the short run.

   b   the income elasticity of demand is greater than the price elasticity of demand.

   c   the price elasticity of demand is less than in the short run.

   d   the income elasticity of demand is less than in the short run.

   e   none of the above.

10   When the price of a good (measured along the horizontal axis) falls, the budget constraint

   a   rotates and becomes flatter.

   b   rotates and becomes steeper.

   c   shifts out parallel to the original budget constraint.

   d   shifts in parallel to the original budget constraint.

   e   none of the above.

11   If demand for a good falls as income rises, then

   a   the good is a normal good.

   b   the good is an inferior good.

   c   the income elasticity is undefined.

   d   the income elasticity is between 0 and 1.

   e   none of the above.

12   When the price of a good falls, the substitution effect

   a   encourages the individual to consume more of the good.

   b   encourages the individual to consume less of the good.

   c   leads to more consumption if the good is an inferior good, but less if the good is a normal good.

   d   leads to less consumption if the good is an inferior good, but more if the good is a normal good.

   e   none of the above.

13   When the price of a good falls, the income effect

   a   encourages the individual to consume more of the good.

   b   encourages the individual to consume less of the good.

   c   leads to more consumption if the good is an inferior good, but less if the good is a normal good.

   d   leads to less consumption if the good is an inferior good, but more if the good is a normal good.

   e   none of the above.

14   If the price of one good falls and the demand for another good rises, the goods are

   a   inferior.

   b   complements.

   c   substitutes.

d   normal goods.

e   none of the above.

15   If the price of one good rises and the demand for another good rises, the goods are

   a   inferior.

   b   complements.

   c   substitutes.

   d   normal goods.

   e   none of the above.

16   In general, the price elasticity of demand is greater when

   a   the good is an inferior good.

   b   there are good, close substitutes available.

   c   there are good, close complements available.

   d   the income elasticity of demand is less.

   e   none of the above.

17   For normal goods, when income rises,

   a   the budget constraint shifts out, parallel.

   b   the demand curve shifts to the left.

   c   quantity demanded falls.

   d   less money is spent on the good.

   e   none of the above.

18   For normal goods, as price rises,

   a   the substitution effect encourages more consumption.

   b   the income effect encourages less consumption.

   c   the quantity demanded rises.

   d   the demand for substitute goods falls.

   e   none of the above.

19   For inferior goods, as price rises,

   a   the substitution effect encourages less consumption.

   b   the income effect encourages less consumption.

   c   the substitution effect encourages more consumption.

   d   the quantity demanded rises.

   e   none of the above.

20   The slope of the budget constraint depends on

   a   the relative price of the goods.

   b   the income of the consumer.

   c   the availability of substitute goods.

   d   whether the good is normal or inferior.

   e   none of the above.

Completion

1   The opportunity set for the consumer is defined by the _____, which says that expenditures cannot exceed income.

2   The slope of the budget line equals the _____ of the two goods.

3   The benefits of consumption are called _____.

4   The willingness to pay for an extra unit of some good is its _____.

5   When income increases, the budget constraint shifts outwards in a _____ way.

6   The _____ of demand measures how consumption of a good changes in response to a change in income.

7   When the price of a good changes, the budget constraint _____.

8   The _____ of demand measures how consumption of a good changes in response to a change in price.

9   When the price of a good falls, the _____ effect always encourages more consumption of the good.

10 If an increase in the price of one good leads to a decrease in the consumption of another good, then the goods are _____.

Answers to Self-Test

True or False

1	t	4	f	7	f	10	t	13	f
2	t	5	t	8	f	11	t	14	t
3	f	6	t	9	f	12	t	15	t

Multiple Choice

1	c	6	a	11	b	16	b
2	b	7	c	12	a	17	a
3	b	8	e	13	d	18	b
4	b	9	a	14	b	19	a
5	a	10	a	15	c	20	a

Completion

1   budget constraint
2   relative price
3   utility
4   marginal utility
5   parallel
6   income elasticity
7   rotates
8   price elasticity
9   substitution
10 complements

Doing Economics: Tools and Practice Problems

The most important model in this chapter is the opportunity set for the consumer: the budget constraint. This section will first review how to construct the budget constraint and then explain how the budget constraint changes when price and income change. A somewhat more advanced topic follows, as we explore how to illustrate the substitution and income effects of price changes. Finally, there are some applications: in-kind transfers and tax-subsidy schemes.

Tool Kit 8.1: Plotting the Budget Constraint

The budget constraint shows what combinations of goods can be purchased with a limited amount of money. Constructing the budget constraint is one of the essential techniques needed in Part Two.

When either income or price changes, the budget constraint moves. The basic technique here is to first draw the budget constraint using the original income and prices, and then draw a new budget constraint using the new income and prices. Compare the two budget constraints and verify that the shift is parallel when income changes, but the budget constraint rotates when price changes.

Step one: Draw a set of coordinate axes. Label the horizontal axis as the quantity of one good consumed and the vertical axis as the quantity of a second good consumed.

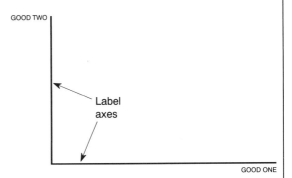

Step two: Calculate the quantity of the good measured on the horizontal axis that can be purchased if all the consumer's money is spent on it. Plot this quantity along the horizontal axis.

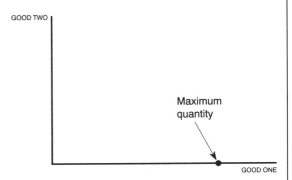

Step three: Calculate the quantity of the good measured on the vertical axis that can be purchased if all the consumer's money is spent on it. Plot this quantity along the vertical axis.

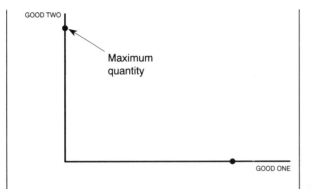

Step four: Draw a line segment connecting the two points. This line segment is the budget constraint.

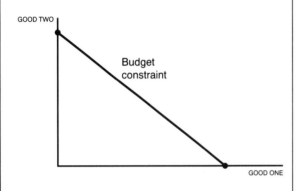

Step five: Verify that the slope of the budget constraint is (minus) the price of the good measured on the horizontal axis divided by the price of the good measured on the vertical axis.

1 (Worked problem: budget constraint) Dick has a budget of $500 to paint and paper the rooms in his new condominium. The price of enough paint for 1 room is $25; the price of wallpaper is $50 per room. Draw Dick's budget constraint.

Step-by-step solution

Step one: Draw a set of coordinate axes, and label the horizontal one "Rooms painted" and the vertical one "Rooms papered." (There is no rule as to which good goes on which axis. It is fine either way.)

Step two: Calculate how many rooms can be painted with the entire $500. This number is $500/$25 = 20 rooms. Plot this quantity along the horizontal axis.

Step three: Calculate how many rooms can be papered with the entire $500. This number is $500/$50 = 10 rooms. Plot this quantity along the vertical axis.

Step four: Draw a line segment connecting these two points. This line segment is the budget constraint.

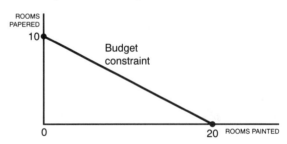

Step five: Verify the slope. The slope of the budget constraint is 10/20 = 1/2. The price ratio is $25/$50 = 1/2.

2 (Practice problem: budget constraint) Dean Lewis would like to have some of the practice pianos tuned in the charming but decaying music building. The dean could use some of the $1,000 in the supplies and services budget, but that money must pay for repairing broken lockers. The piano tuner charges $50 per piano, and the carpenter charges $40 per locker. Plot the dean's budget constraint and verify that the slope is the relative price.

3 (Practice problem: budget constraint). Draw the following budget constraints.

a Budget for hiring groundskeepers = $100,000; price of a full-time employee = $20,000; price of a part-time employee = $8,000.

b Budget for food = $250; price of microwave snacks = $2.00. (Plot expenditures on all other food on the vertical axis.)

c Budget for landscaping = $2,000; price of lilac bushes = $50; price of cherry trees = $80.

d Budget for library acquisitions = $50,000; price of books = $40; price of journal subscriptions = $100.

4 (Worked problem: budget constraint with income and price changes) Bill Kutt, a somewhat lazy student, has decided to take a course on the nineteenth-century American novel. Many books are assigned, and all are available in the abridged "Fred's Notes" versions at $8 each. The unabridged versions are $3 each. Bill has $72 to spend.

a Plot his budget constraint.
b Show how it changes when Bill finds that he has another $24 (for a total of $96).

Step-by-step solution

Step one (a): Plot Bill's budget constraint using the procedure outlined above. He can afford $72/$8 = 9 abridged and $72/$3 = 24 unabridged notes. Note that the slope is 9/24 = $3/$8, which is the ratio of the prices.

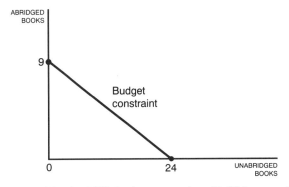

Step two (b): Plot Bill's budget constraint with $96 to spend. He can now afford $96/$8 = 12 abridged and $96/$3 = 32 unabridged notes.

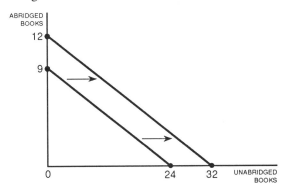

Step three: Verify that the shift in the budget constraint is parallel. The slope is 12/32 = $3/$8, which is the ratio of the prices. Because the prices have not changed, the slope has not changed. The income increase causes a parallel shift.

5 (Practice problem: budget constraint with income and price changes) Helen is nervous about graduate school. She is considering hiring a tutor for her economics course at $10 per hour. Another possibility is to attend sessions on how to improve the score of her GMAT test. These cost $30 each. She has $90.

a Plot her budget constraint.
b Oops! Unexpectedly stuck with the tab at Ernie's Ice House, Helen now has only $60 to spend. Plot her new budget constraint.

6 (Worked problem: budget constraint with income and price changes) Dissatisfied with his social life, Horatio has budgeted $400 for self-improvement. He is considering elocution lessons at $25 per hour and ballroom dancing classes at $10 each.

a Plot Horatio's budget constraint.
b Good news! A new elocution studio offers lessons at the introductory price of $20. Plot the new budget constraint.

Step-by-step solution

Step one (a): Plot the budget constraint at the $25 price. Horatio can afford $400/$25 = 16 elocution lessons or $400/$10 = 40 classes. Note that the slope is 40/16 = $25/$10, which is the ratio of the prices.

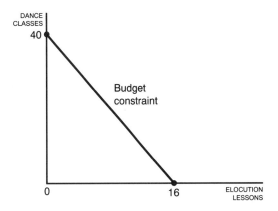

Step two (b): Plot the budget constraint at the $20 price. Horatio can now afford $400/$20 = 20 elocution lessons, which is 4 more, but he still can only buy 40 dance lessons.

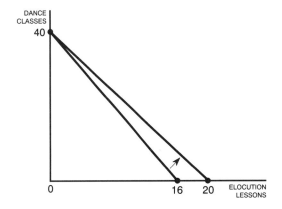

Step three: Verify that the budget constraint rotates. The slope is now 40/20 = $20/$10, which is the ratio of the new prices and is flatter. The price decrease rotated the budget constraint. The point at 0 elocution lessons and 40 dance classes does not change, because when no elocution lessons are purchased, the price change makes no difference.

7 (Practice problem: budget constraint with income and price changes) With some of her extra cash ($100 each month), Sho-Yen buys meals and blankets and donates them to the nearby shelter for the homeless. The meals cost $2 each, and the blankets $5 each.

a Plot Sho-Yen's budget constraint.
b The supplier of meals cuts the price to $1. Plot the new budget constraint.

8 (Practice problem: budget constraint with income and price changes) For each of these problems, draw the budget constraints before and after the change. Plot "Expenditures on other goods" on the vertical axis.

a Income = $400; price of potatoes = $1 per sack; price of potatoes rises to $2 per sack.
b Income = $5,000; price of therapy sessions = $100 per hour; income rises to $6,000.
c Income = $450; price of housecleaning = $45; income falls to $225.
d Income = $100; price of pizzas = $5; price increases to $10.

Tool Kit 8.2: Distinguishing between Substitution and Income Effects

When the price of a good changes, there are two effects: substitution and income. These can be illustrated using the budget constraint.

Step one: Draw the budget line with the original price.

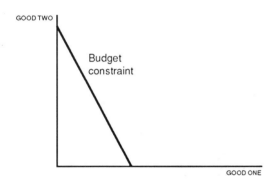

Step two: Find the chosen quantities along the budget line. Label this point A.

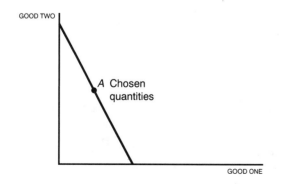

Step three: Draw the budget line with the new price.

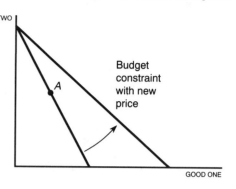

Step four: Draw a dashed line through point A and parallel to the *new* budget line.

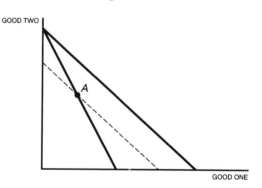

Step five: Darken the portion of the dashed line that lies above the original budget line. The points along this darkened segment represent the quantities not previously attainable. The change to the new quantity the consumer chooses is the substitution effect of the price change. Note that the substitution effect is necessarily in the opposite direction to the price change.

Arbitrarily select a point for the new consumption resulting from the substitution effect. Label this point B. The income effect is the change from B to the quantity the consumer chooses on the new budget line drawn in step three. If good one is normal, the income effect will result in higher consumption relative to B, for example, point C. If good one is inferior, the income effect will result in lower consumption relative to B, for example, point D.

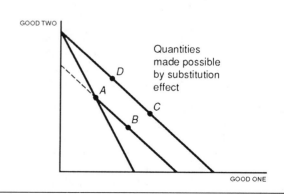

9 (Worked problem: substitution and income effects) Always diligent in keeping up with out-of-town friends and acquaintances, Lurleen budgets $30 per month for postage and phone calls. A long-distance call costs her $2 on average, and the price of a stamped envelope is $.30. She makes 6 calls and mails 60 letters each month.

   a Plot her budget constraint, and label the point that she has chosen.
   b Headline news! The price of a stamped envelope falls to $.20. Illustrate the substitution and income effects of the price change.

Step-by-step solution

Step one (a): Draw the original budget constraint. The maximum quantity of calls is $30/$2 = 15, and the maximum quantity of letters is $30/$.30 = 100.

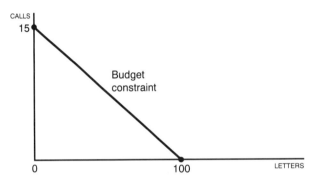

Step two: Plot and label the chosen point (6 calls, 60 letters). Note that this is on the budget constraint because (6 × $2) + (60 × $.30) = $30. Label this point *A*.

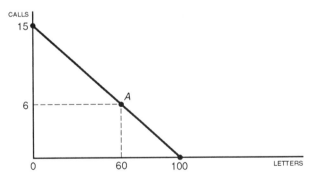

Step three (b): Draw the new budget constraint. The maximum quantities are 15 calls and 30/$.20 = 150 letters.

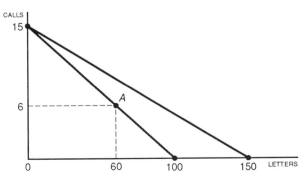

Step four: Draw a dashed line segment through *A* parallel to the new budget constraint.

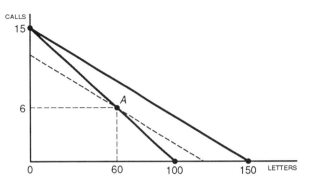

Step five: Darken the portion of the dashed line segment that lies above the original budget constraint. Notice that the substitution effect would lead Lurleen to choose a point like *B* along this segment, where the quantity of letters is greater. We say that the substitution effect of a price decrease is always to increase the quantity demanded. The income effect moves this darkened segment out to the new budget constraint. Lurleen would write more letters if letters were a normal good, but she would write fewer if letters were inferior. The income effect can go either way in principle, although most goods are normal.

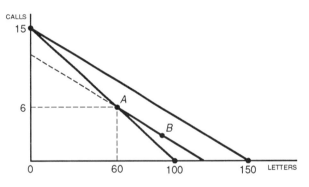

10 (Practice problem: substitution and income effects) Yves loves to wear whites for tennis. He sends his outfits to the cleaners at a price of $3.60 each. Playing tennis also requires new balls, which cost $2. Yves' tennis budget is $36 per week, which allows him his current consumption levels of 8 cans of balls and 5 clean outfits.

   a Plot his budget constraint, and show his current consumption choice.
   b The price of tennis balls has risen to $4.50. Illustrate the substitution and income effects of this price increase.

11 (Practice problem: substitution and income effects) For each of the following, illustrate the substitution and income effects of the price change. Plot "Expenditures on other goods" on the vertical axis, and pick any point on the original budget line as the quantities consumed before the price change.

a   Income = $100; price of bricks = $.10 each; price changes to $.20.

b   Income = $1,000; price of haircuts = $20; price changes to $25.

c   Income = $500; price of pies = $5; price changes to $4.

d   Income = $10; price of baseball cards = $.50; price changes to $.25

12 (Worked problem: applications) Many government programs deliver benefits in kind to people. For example, the U.S. government issues food stamps, which can only be used to buy food. Economists often argue that cash transfers are better. The typical food stamp recipient has $200 per week in income in addition to $80 per week in food stamps.

a   Draw the budget constraint.

b   One proposal is to substitute $80 in cash for the stamps. Draw the budget constraint that results from this proposal.

c   Which would the recipient prefer? Why?

Step-by-step solution

Step one (a): Draw the budget constraint with the food stamps. Label the axes "Food" and "Other goods." The slope is 1 because $1 less spent on other goods means $1 spent on food. Note that no more than $200 may be spent on other goods.

Step two (b): Draw the budget constraint with the cash grants replacing the food stamps.

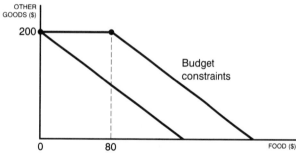

Step three (c): Compare. The difference is that the cash grant allows the recipient to choose the points between *A* and *B*. Many recipients would not choose these low levels of food consumption anyway; so there would be no difference. Some might, however, and these people would prefer the cash.

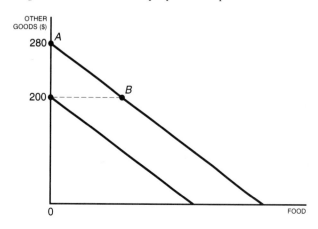

13 (Practice problem: applications) The city of Arbor recently planted 2 trees (worth $20 each) in every yard. The typical Arbor resident has $4,000 in disposable income this summer.

a   Plot the budget constraint with the in-kind transfer of 2 trees.

b   Plot the budget constraint with the $40 refunded through the tax system.

c   Which opportunity set is preferred? How could the tree planting be justified?

15 (Worked problem: applications) When less consumption of some good or service is needed, economists often recommend putting a tax on the good or service. One objection is that the taxes lead to higher prices, which make people worse off. If the tax revenue is refunded, however, people can be approximately as well off, yet still face higher prices for the good or service. In essence, it is possible to put the substitution effect to work and reduce consumption of the good or service without reducing the well-being of consumers very much. The city of Pleasantville is running out of room at the dump. The typical resident purchases 6 bags weekly at $.10 each.

a   Plot the budget constraint for the typical resident, and show the current consumption choice.

b   In an effort to encourage recycling and discourage disposal, the city institutes a user fee of $1.90 per trash bag. (Trash bags now cost $2.) Keeping to their "no new taxes" pledge, the city council members vote to combine the user fee with a tax refund. Each citizen receives a tax refund of $1.90 × 6 = $11.40. Plot the new budget constraint.

c   Discuss the user fee–tax refund plan.

Step-by-step solution

Step one (a): Plot the budget constraint with neither a user fee nor a tax refund. Label the resident's chosen point *A*.

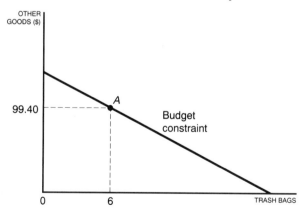

Step two (b): Plot the budget constraint with the user fee and tax refund.

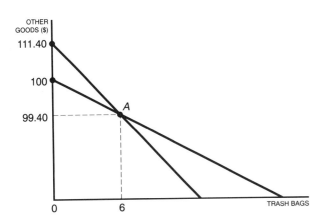

Step three (c): We see that the net effect of the entire user fee–tax refund scheme is only the substitution of the increase in the price of bags to $2. The resident is no worse off (because he can still consume as he did before the user fee), but he will be motivated to use fewer bags. (One minor flaw in the program is that as people substitute away from trash bags, they will pay less in user fees than is needed to finance the tax relief.)

16 (Practice problem: applications) Since the Gulf War, gasoline consumption has been on the mind of Adam Smith, M.P. He proposes a $1-per-litre tax on gasoline, which currently sells for $1. Assume that this tax will increase the price of gas to $2. The member also proposes refunding the gas-tax revenues through an income tax cut large enough to allow consumers to buy the same amount of gas as before the tax.

   a Plot the budget constraint with no added gas tax.
   b Plot the budget constraint with the gas tax and the refund.
   c Columnist Ann Frotheringham writes, "This plan will have no effect. The government takes money away with one hand and gives it back with the other." Is she right? Why or why not?

Answers to Problems

2

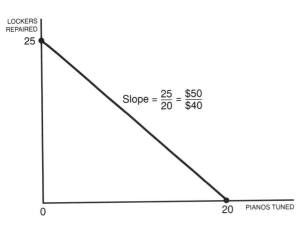

3

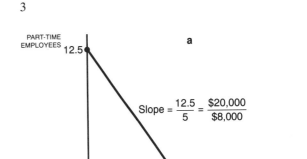

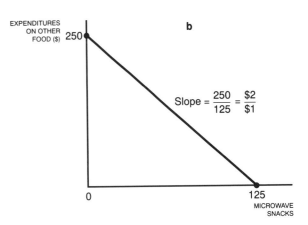

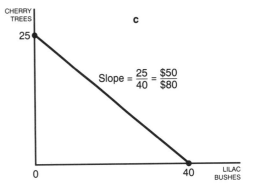

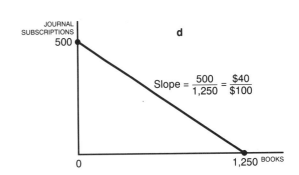

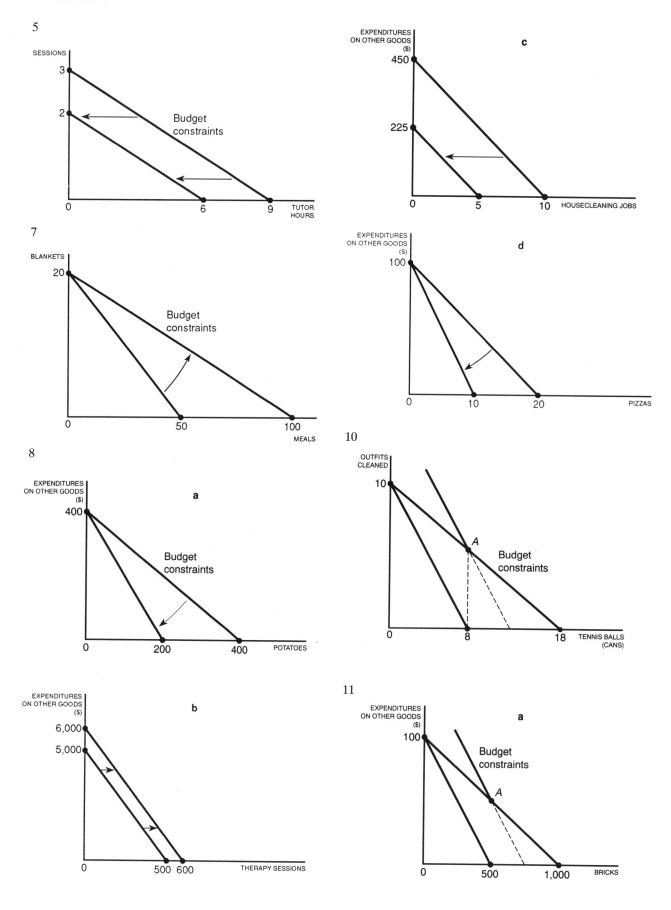

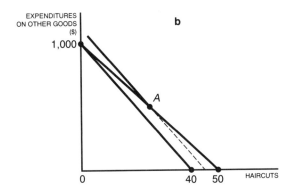

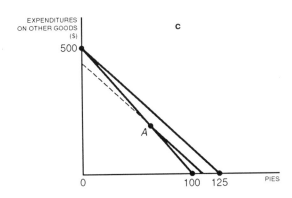

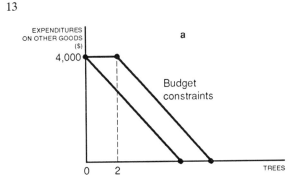

13

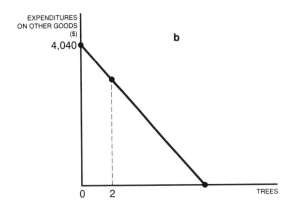

c The budget constraint with the tax refund, which is shown in part b, is preferred because it allows more choices. If desired, the resident can spend as much as $4,040 on other goods, and with the in-kind transfer of trees, the resident can spend a maximum of $4,000 on other goods.

16

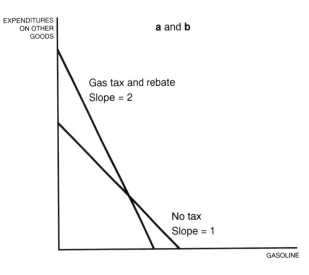

c She is wrong. The gas tax and rebate program results in a budget constraint with more alternatives that involve less gasoline consumption. It motivates individuals to substitute other goods for gasoline.

THE SAVINGS DECISION

Chapter Review

Chapter 8 explored the individual's decision to spend income; Chapter 9 examines the decision to save for the future or to borrow from future income to consume today. Borrowing and saving take place in the capital market, where the price is the interest rate. This chapter adapts the analysis of Chapter 8 to examine how the amount of savings (or borrowings) is affected by the interest rate.

In order to apply the budget constraint to the savings decision, think of the savings decision as the choice between two goods. Instead of building a budget constraint between two goods today, individuals choose between consuming goods today and consuming them tomorrow. Chapter 10 continues the discussion by looking at what the household does with the money it saves and how asset prices are determined in the capital market.

ESSENTIAL CONCEPTS

1   The **savings decision** is basically a decision about *when* to consume; households choose whether to spend all their income now or save it for future consumption. The **two-period budget constraint** employs the techniques we learned in Chapter 8 to show what combinations of consumption in the present and consumption in the future are affordable, given present and future incomes and the interest rate. As in Chapter 8, the slope of the budget constraint indicates the *trade-off*, and it equals the relative price. Since current consumption is measured on the horizontal axis, the slope is the **relative price of current consumption,** which is **1 plus the interest rate.**

2   When the interest rate changes, the budget constraint rotates; it becomes steeper if the interest rate increases and flatter if it decreases. In exactly the same manner as in Chapter 8's analysis of the consumption decision, the change in the budget constraint causes income and substitution effects. Higher interest rates make savers better off, and because current consumption is a normal good, the *income effect* makes them want to consume more today, and thus reduces savings. On the other hand, higher interest rates lower the relative price of future consumption. The resulting *substitution effect* increases savings. In the decision to save, the substitution and income effects work in opposite directions.

3 There are several motives for saving. People save during their working lives to provide for retirement. This is called **life-cycle savings.** People set aside **precautionary savings** to guard against the chance of accident or illness. The **bequest motive** leads people to save for their heirs. The **permanent income motive** causes people to save more in high-income years to provide money for consumption in low-income years. Finally, people save to meet a particular goal, such as buying a house or starting a business. We call this motive **target savings.**

4 The fall in the savings rate in Canada may be due in part to easier access to funds for borrowers.

5 Government policies affect savings; some encourage saving, others do not. For example, unfunded public pension benefits tend to reduce life-cycle savings because people do not feel as compelled to save for retirement. Taxes on interest lower the after-tax rate of interest and thus provide less incentive to save. In much the same way, taxes on **capital gains** reduce the net return to savings when an asset is sold. A plan designed to stimulate savings is the Registered Retirement Savings Plan (RRSP), which allows households to make limited annual deposits in special tax-exempt accounts; these accounts are subject to penalties for early withdrawal. The pros and cons of these policies can be analyzed by looking at how they change the two-period budget constraint.

BEHIND THE ESSENTIAL CONCEPTS

1 The basic diagram in this chapter is the two-period budget constraint shown in Figure 9.1. It is important to see how similar this diagram is to the consumer's budget constraint of Chapter 8. There, the trade-off was between consuming different goods. Here, the trade-off involves consuming at different time periods.

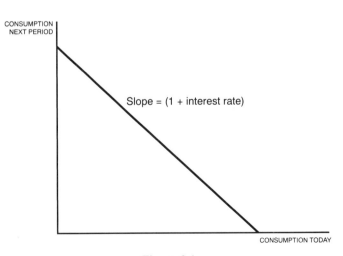

Figure 9.1

In each case, the slope is the relative price. When the relative price changes, there are substitution and income effects. Price changes rotate the budget constraint, but income changes bring about a parallel shift. This basic approach will also be used later for the labour supply decision and for other issues throughout the course.

2 Think about the slope of the two-period budget constraint. To consume more in the future, an individual can save today. One dollar saved today results in (1 plus the interest rate) dollars of consumption in the future. That is, the individual can buy $(1 + r)$ dollars of future consumption at an opportunity cost of only 1 dollar today. Conversely, to buy 1 more dollar of current consumption, the individual must give up $(1 + r)$ dollars of future consumption. The relative price of current consumption is, then, 1 plus the interest rate.

3 One plus the interest rate is also the slope of the budget constraint; therefore, only changes in the interest rate can change the slope. If the interest rate rises, the budget constraint becomes steeper. If the interest rate falls, the budget constraint becomes flatter. Income changes, either now or in the future, only shift the budget constraint in a parallel way.

4 Table 9.1 may help you keep the substitution and income effects straight.

Table 9.1

If the interest rate rises,
 the *substitution* effect leads to more savings because current consumption is relatively more expensive.
 the *income* effect leads to reduced savings because the saver is better off and desires to consume more today.
If the interest rate falls,
 the *substitution* effect leads to reduced savings because current consumption is relatively less expensive.
 the *income* effect leads to more savings because the saver is worse off and desires to consume less today.

5 The government policies addressed in this chapter are analyzed by considering how the budget constraint is affected. This is a pattern in economics. For the most part, economists concentrate on opportunities rather than on tastes. The decline in savings by individuals is attributed to factors that change the two-period budget constraint, not factors that lead people to change their tastes. The most effective government policies are those that affect the budget constraint, not those that attempt to change the minds of savers and borrowers.

SELF-TEST

True or False

1 The slope of the budget constraint equals the rate of interest.

2 As income increases, the income effect leads individuals to save less.

3 As the interest rate increases, the substitution effect leads people to save less.

4 As the interest rate increases, the budget constraint shifts out in a parallel way.

5 An increase in unfunded public pension benefits will increase national savings.

6 One reason for the low savings rate in Canada is that a greater percentage of the population are in the stage of life when they save less.

7 People whose income fluctuates from year to year save more during high-income years and less during low-income years in order to smooth consumption.

8 RRSPs allow individuals to put aside a certain amount each year for retirement and accumulate interest on the balance without paying taxes.

9 When the interest rate changes, the income and substitution effects work in the same direction.

10 A cut in interest taxes matters because people are concerned with the after-tax rate of interest.

11 In a perfect capital market, the rate of interest charged to borrowers equals the rate of interest charged to savers.

12 One reason for the fall in the savings rate in Canada is that borrowing has become easier.

13 When the interest rate rises, the relative price of future consumption also rises.

14 When an individual sells an asset for more than the individual paid, the difference is called a capital gain.

15 Public pensions in Canada are financed on a pay-as-you-go basis.

Multiple Choice

1 Using the budget constraint to analyze the savings decision underscores the fact that the individual is really deciding

a when to consume.
b what the slope of the budget constraint should be.
c without knowing what the future will bring.
d what the interest rate should be.
e none of the above.

2 The slope of the budget constraint

a equals the interest rate.

b shows the trade-off between consuming now and waiting to consume.
c is independent of the interest rate.
d indicates an individual's willingness to give up current consumption in return for future consumption.
e none of the above.

3 If the interest rate falls, the budget constraint

a shifts to the left in a parallel way.
b shifts to the right in a parallel way.
c rotates and becomes steeper.
d rotates and becomes flatter.
e none of the above.

4 If the interest rate falls, the substitution effect

a encourages people to consume more in the future, because the relative price of future consumption is lower.
b leads people to want to consume more both now and in the future, because they are better off.
c leads people to want to consume less both now and in the future, because they are worse off.
d encourages people to consume less in the future, because the relative price of current consumption is lower.
e none of the above.

5 If the interest rate rises, the income effect

a encourages people to consume more in the future, because the relative price of future consumption is lower.
b leads people to want to consume more both now and in the future, because they are better off.
c leads people to want to consume less both now and in the future, because they are worse off.
d encourages people to consume less in the future, because the relative price of current consumption is lower.
e none of the above.

6 If the interest rate rises, the substitution effect increases life-cycle savings because

a the relative price of future consumption is higher.
b people are better off and want to consume more today.
c the budget constraint rotates and becomes flatter.
d people are worse off and want to consume more today.
e none of the above.

7 Savings put aside to provide for consumption during retirement are called

a precautionary savings.
b bequest savings.
c life-cycle savings.
d speculative savings.
e none of the above.

8 Individuals whose income fluctuates from year to year will

a set consumption independently of income.

b save more in high-income years in order to smooth consumption.

c save less for bequests to their heirs.

d save less in high-income years in order to enjoy the benefits of their good years.

e none of the above.

9 Transfers to the elderly in Canada come

a solely from a fund created by investing the pension contributions paid during their working years.

b solely out of general tax revenues.

c solely from pension contributions paid by those currently working.

d solely from revenue raised through taxing corporations.

e none of the above.

10 Pension payments from the Canada (or Quebec) Pension Plan to the elderly come

a solely from a fund created by investing the pension contributions paid during their working years.

b solely from pension contributions paid by those currently working.

c partly from a fund created by investing the pension contributions paid during their working years and partly from general tax revenues.

d partly from pension contributions paid by those currently working and partly from general tax revenues.

e partly from a fund created by investing the pension contributions paid during their working years and partly from the pension contributions paid by those currently working.

11 In a perfect capital market,

a the interest rate is zero.

b the interest rate equals the inflation rate.

c the interest rate for borrowers equals the interest rate for savers.

d the interest rate for borrowers is greater than the interest rate for savers.

e the interest rate for savers is greater than the interest rate for borrowers.

12 The fact that the interest rate for borrowers exceeds the interest rate for savers

a makes the budget constraint a straight line.

b puts a kink in the budget constraint at the point where the individual neither saves nor consumes.

c makes the budget constraint shift in a parallel way.

d rotates the entire budget constraint and makes it flatter.

e rotates the entire budget constraint and makes it steeper.

13 One explanation of the fall in the savings rate in Canada in recent years is that

a interest rates for borrowers have risen relative to those paid to savers.

b the increased popularity of credit cards means that borrowers are now paying higher interest rates than they used to.

c people feel it is less important than it once was to leave bequests for their children.

d access to capital markets has become easier and so has facilitated borrowing.

e inflation is lower.

14 A cut in taxes on interest earnings will

a have no effect on the budget constraint between current and future consumption.

b shift the budget constraint out in a parallel way.

c rotate the budget constraint and make it flatter.

d rotate the budget constraint and make it steeper.

e put a kink in the budget constraint.

15 Taxes on interest

a reduce savings through the income effect.

b have no effect on savings because individuals care about the before-tax interest rate.

c reduce savings through the substitution effect.

d increase savings through the substitution effect.

e none of the above.

16 Which of the following cannot be characterized, at least in part, as an attempt to encourage saving?

a the Goods and Services Tax (the GST)

b Registered Retirement Savings Plans (RRSPs)

c Registered Pension Plans (RPPs)

d increases in the size of the lifetime exemption from the capital gains tax

e none of the above

17 The Registered Retirement Savings Plans (RRSPs)

a exempt all retirement savings from taxation.

b allow individuals to put aside a certain amount of money into a special account and exempt only the interest from taxation.

c allow individuals to put aside a certain amount of money into a special account and exempt both the amount invested and the interest from taxation.

d allow individuals to put aside a certain amount of money into a special account and exempt only the amount invested from taxation.

e exempt from taxation all payments from the plans that are received by the holder after retirement.

18 For those who invest in Registered Retirement Savings Plans (RRSPs) there is

a only a substitution effect.

b only an income effect.

c both an income effect and a substitution effect.

d either an income effect alone or a substitution effect and an income effect, depending on how much saving the individual would have done in the absence of the plan.

e neither an income effect nor a substitution effect.

19 Cutting the capital gains tax rate would

   a reduce savings through the substitution effect.

   b reduce savings through the income effect.

   c increase savings through the income effect.

   d increase savings through both the substitution and income effects.

   e have no effect.

20 In Canada, capital gains are

   a not taxed.

   b taxed but at a lower rate than other income.

   c taxed at the same rate as other income.

   d taxed only on that part of the gain not caused by inflation.

   e taxed but at a higher rate than other income.

Completion

1 The relative price of consumption today and consumption tomorrow is 1 plus the _____.

2 If the interest rate increases, the budget constraint for the savings decision becomes _____.

3 The income effect of higher interest rates _____ savings.

4 Savings for the purpose of consuming during retirement are called _____ savings.

5 A(n) _____ pension plan is one in which benefits received by older retirees are financed through taxes paid by younger workers.

6 An increase in unfunded pension benefits will _____ national savings.

7 In a perfect capital market, the interest rate paid to the saver _____ the interest rate paid by the borrower.

8 The _____ motive leads individuals to set aside savings to leave to heirs.

9 The _____ motive leads individuals to set aside savings against the chance of an unforeseen accident or illness.

10 The increase in the value of an asset between the times at which it is purchased and sold is called a _____.

Answers to Self-Test

True or False

1	f	4	f	7	t	10	t	13	f
2	t	5	f	8	t	11	t	14	t
3	f	6	t	9	f	12	t	15	f

Multiple Choice

1	a	4	d	7	c	10	e
2	b	5	b	8	b	11	c
3	d	6	e	9	e	12	b

13	d	15	c	17	c	19	b
14	d	16	e	18	d	20	b

Completion

1 interest rate
2 steeper
3 reduces
4 life-cycle
5 unfunded
6 reduce
7 equals
8 bequest
9 precautionary
10 capital gain

Doing Economics: Tools and Practice Problems

As in Chapter 8, the most important model of this chapter is the opportunity set: the two-period budget constraint. Given the wealth or income of the household and the interest rate, we can construct the two-period budget constraint. We see how the budget constraint is altered when income (either present or future) and interest rates change. We show the substitution and income effects by using the rotation and shift technique introduced in the last chapter. Finally, we learn some applications: different borrowing and lending interest rates, individual retirement, university and housing accounts, and how unfunded public pension benefits affect savings.

> **Tool Kit 9.1**: Plotting the Two-Period Budget Constraint
> The two-period budget constraint shows what combinations of consumption in each period are possible, given the income and interest rate.
>
> *Step one*: Draw a set of coordinate axes. Label the horizontal axis "Consumption in period one" and the vertical axis "Consumption in period two."
>
>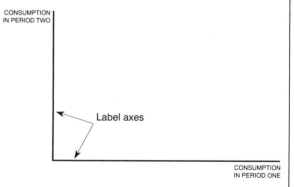
>
> *Step two*: Calculate the maximum possible consumption in period one. (This quantity is the present discounted value of income.) Plot this quantity along the horizontal axis.

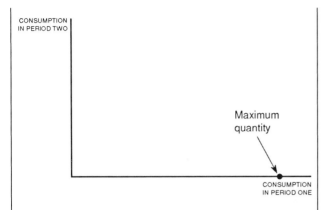

Step three: Calculate the maximum possible consumption in period two. (This quantity is the future value of income.) Plot this quantity along the vertical axis.

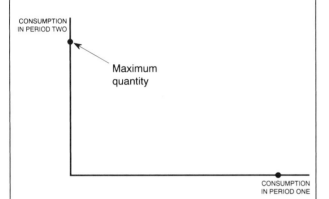

Step four: Draw a line segment connecting the two points. This line segment is the two-period budget constraint.

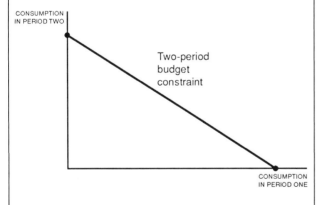

Step five: Verify that the slope of the budget constraint is (minus) $1 + r$, where r is the interest rate.

---

1 (Worked problem: two-period budget constraint) Nancy won the lottery! It is only $5,000, but that looks pretty good to someone making $18,000 per year. Her interest rate is 6 percent, and the capital market is perfect. Plot her two-period budget constraint.

Step-by-step solution

Step one: Draw coordinate axes, labeling the horizontal axis "Consumption now" and the vertical axis "Consumption next year."

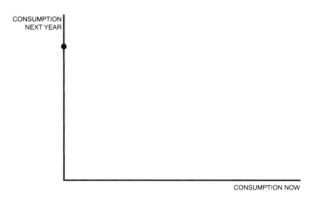

Step two: The maximum consumption today is the present discounted value of all income. Make the following table, and compute and plot the amount along the horizontal axis.

Year	Income	Discount factor	Present discounted value
Now	$23,000	1	$23,000
Next year	$18,000	1/(1.06)	$16,980

Present discounted value = $39,980.

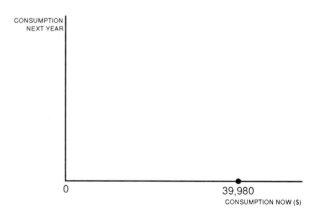

Step three: The maximum consumption next year is

$$\$23,000 \ (1 + .06) + \$18,000 = \$42,380.$$

Plot this point.

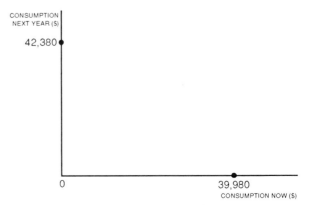

Step four: Draw a line segment connecting the two points.

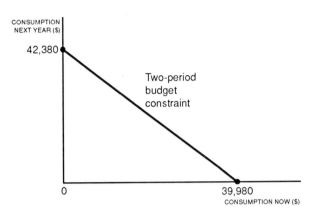

Step five: Verify that the slope equals 1 plus the interest rate. It is 42,380/39,980 = 1.06 = 1 + *r*.

2 (Practice problem: two-period budget constraint) Current income is $40,000. Retirement income is $15,000. The interest rate for the period between now and retirement is 150 percent. Plot the two-period budget constraint.

3 (Practice problem: two-period budget constraint) Plot the two-period budget constraints for the following.

	Interest rate	Present income	Future income
a	100%	$100,000	$ 25,000
b	50%	$ 40,000	$ 10,000
c	250%	$ 20,000	$ 0
d	80%	$ 0	$150,000

4 (Worked problem: two-period budget constraint) When the interest rate, current income, or future income changes, the two-period budget constraint moves. The basic technique here is to draw the two-period budget constraint using the original incomes and interest rate, and then draw a new two-period budget constraint using the new incomes and interest rate. Compare the two budget constraints and verify that the shift is parallel when either current or future income changes, but the budget constraint rotates when the interest rate changes. Michael is earning $25,000 as an executive assistant and expects to earn the same in the future. His interest rate is 5 percent.

a Plot his two-period budget constraint.
b He receives word that his aunt is sick and has one year to live. She plans to leave him $50,000. Plot his two-period budget constraint.

Step-by-step solution

Step one (a): Follow the procedure to plot the two-period budget constraint. The slope is 1 + *r* = 1.05, and it passes through the point $25,000 now and $25,000 next year.

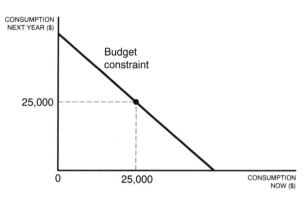

Step two (b): Plot the new budget constraint. Because the interest rate is the same, the slope does not change. The new budget constraint passes through the point $25,000 now and $75,000 next year.

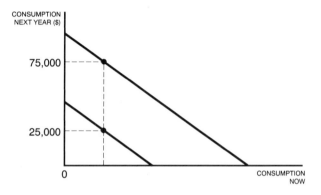

5 (Practice problem: two-period budget constraint) Boris currently takes home $45,000 as a skilled lathe operator. His union contract guarantees him the same salary next year. The credit union at the plant pays 8 percent interest.

a Plot his two period budget constraint.
b Boris' employer is experiencing low profits this year. She proposes that Boris accept $35,000 this year and $55,000 next year. Plot his two-period budget constraint. Does his employer's offer shift Boris' budget constraint? How?

6 (Practice problem: two-period budget constraint) Monica plans to retire in 20 years. She now takes home $40,000 and expects $20,000 in retirement income. The interest rate for the 20 years is 180 percent.

a Plot her budget constraint.
b A new broker promises her a 20-year return of 250 percent. She believes him. Plot her new budget constraint.

7 (Practice problem: two-period budget constraint) The Coddingtons now take home $375,000 per year, but they have no retirement income planned. Their portfolio will earn them 100 percent over the 12 years left until retirement.

a Plot their budget constraint.

Tool Kit 9.2: Distinguishing between Substitution and Income Effects of Changes in Interest Rates

When the interest rate changes, there are two effects: substitution and income. These effects can be illustrated by using the two-period budget constraint. This technique shows why the savings supply curve may bend backwards when the income effect works strongly enough to offset the substitution effect.

Step one: Draw the two-period budget line with the original interest rate.

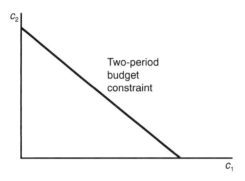

Step two: Find the chosen current and future consumption level along this budget line. Label this point *A*.

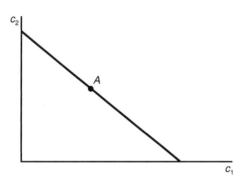

Step three: Draw the two-period budget line with the new interest rate.

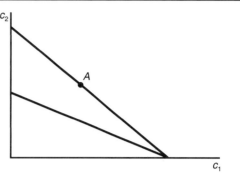

Step four: Draw a dashed line segment through point *A* and parallel to the *new* budget line.

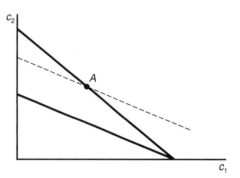

Step five: Darken the portion of the dashed line that lies above the original budget line. The points along this darkened segment represent the quantities made possible by the substitution effect of the interest rate change. The income effect is the response to moving from this new budget line to the lower, parallel budget line drawn in step three.

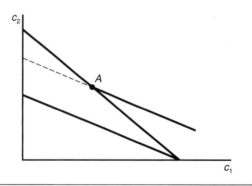

b Tax increases reduce their after-tax return to 60 percent. Plot their new budget constraint.

8 (Practice problem: two-period budget constraint) Plot the budget constraints before and after the change.

	Current income	Future income	Interest rate	Change
a	$100,000	$ 0	40%	interest rate = 60%
b	$100,000	$ 0	40%	future income = $100,000
c	$ 0	$50,000	10%	current income = $25,000
d	$ 60,000	$80,000	50%	interest rate = 20%

9 (Worked problem: substitution and income effects) Show the substitution and income effects of the change in the rate of return for Monica's portfolio in problem 6. She is currently saving $5,000 per year.

Step-by-step solution

Step one: Draw the two-period budget constraint with the interest rate equal to 180 percent. It must pass through the point ($40,000, $20,000).

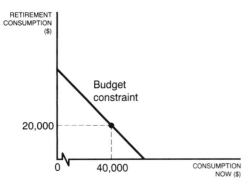

Step two: Label Monica's current consumption ($40,000 – $5,000 = $35,000) point *A*.

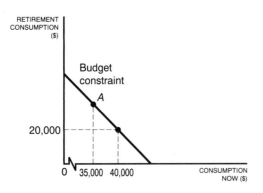

Step three: Draw the two-period budget constraint with the interest rate equal to 250 percent. It also must pass through the point ($40,000, $20,000).

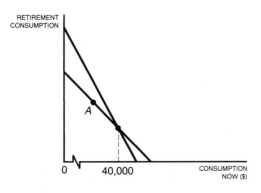

Step four: Draw a dotted line with a slope of 1 + 2.50 = 3.50 through *A*.

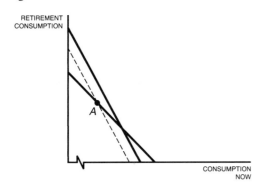

Step five: Darken the portion of the dashed line that lies above the original budget constraint drawn in step one. These are the alternatives made possible by the substitution effect of the interest rate change. All these involve more savings; thus, the substitution effect of an increase in the interest rate is an increase in savings. The income effect shifts this darkened line segment out parallel to the budget constraint drawn in step two and reduces savings.

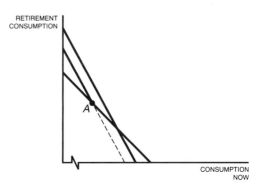

10   (Practice problem: substitution and income effects) Show the substitution and income effects for the change in the Coddingtons' after-tax interest rate in problem 7. Currently they have no savings.

11   (Practice problem: substitution and income effects) Show the substitution and income effects for parts a through d in problem 8. In each case, savings equal $10,000 before the interest rate changes.

12   (Worked problem: applications) If the capital market were perfect, then the interest rates for borrowing and lending would be the same. The rates for borrowing, however, are higher. Haywood and Myrna take home $40,000 each year. They can earn 4 percent on any savings, but they must borrow at 14 percent. Plot their two-period budget constraint.

Step-by-step solution

This is an application of the opportunity set with multiple constraints introduced in Chapter 2.

Step one: Plot the budget constraint with the 4 percent interest rate. The slope is 1.04, and it passes through the point $40,000 now and $40,000 next year.

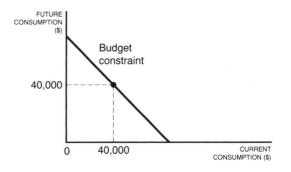

Step two: Plot the budget constraint with the 14 percent interest rate. The slope is 1.14, and it passes through the point $40,000 now and $40,000 next year.

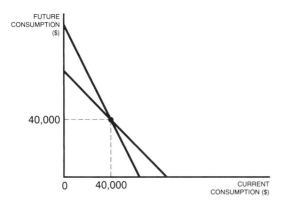

Step three: Darken the portion of each budget constraint that lies under the other constraint.

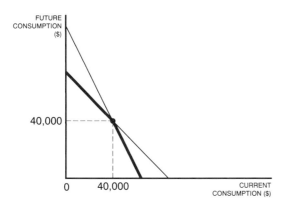

13 (Practice problem: applications) Bob takes home $20,000 this year, but he anticipates taking home $30,000 next year. He can earn 8 percent on savings, but he has a poor credit rating and must pay 19 percent to borrow. Plot his two-period budget constraint.

14 (Worked problem: applications) The Davidsons take home $100,000 per year after taxes and save $3,500. Their son, David, will enter university in three years' time if he can improve his grades sufficiently. The Davidsons are offered the opportunity to participate in a new government plan that will make it easier to pay for David's education: a special university savings account in which up to $3,000 can be deposited without attracting taxes so long as any money withdrawn is used to pay for university tuition.

   a Draw the Davidsons' two-period budget constraint if the real rate of return over the three-year period is 25 percent before taxes.
   b The Davidsons face a 40 percent marginal tax rate. Draw their budget constraint if their interest were taxed at this rate.
   c Draw the Davidsons' budget constraint after the introduction of the university savings plan.
   d Use the concepts of income and substitution effects to explain how their savings will be affected by the plan.

Step-by-step solution

Step one (a): Plot the two-period budget constraint. The slope is 1 + 0.25 = 1.25, and the budget constraint must pass through the point where current and future income are each $100,000.

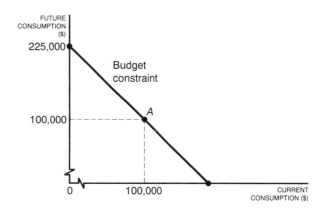

Step two (b): Plot the two-period budget constraint with the tax on interest. Taxes take 40 percent of the interest, so their after-tax interest rate for the three years is 15 percent. The slope is now 1.15. Interest taxes make the budget constraint flatter.

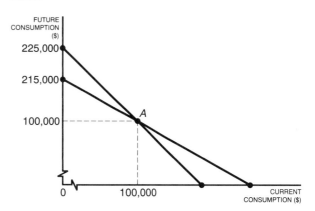

Step three (c): The university savings plan allows the Davidsons to save along the tax-free budget constraint, where the slope is 1.25 until their savings reach $3,000. At that point (*B*), there is a kink, and the slope of the budget constraint returns to the flatter after-tax slope of 1.15.

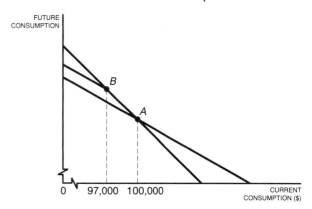

Step four (d): Since the Davidsons save more than $3,000, the program will have only an income effect. The program will not change their after-tax marginal rate of return, because only the first $3,000 of savings is tax exempt.

15 (Practice problem: applications) The Johnsons do not know where they will find the money to send their four bright children to university in 5 years. They make $26,000 per year and have been unable to save a nickel. Their marginal tax rate is 20 percent, and they could earn 40 percent interest on savings over the 5-year period.

    a Plot the Johnsons' two-period budget constraint ignoring the tax on interest.

    b Plot their two-period budget constraint including the tax on interest.

    c Plot their two-period budget constraint under the university savings plan spelled out in problem 14.

    d Use the concepts of substitution and income effects to explain how their savings will be affected by the university savings plan.

16 (Worked problem: applications) Unfunded pension benefits reduce the incentives for individuals to save for retirement. Melissa is already fantasizing about retirement, even though it is 40 years away. She estimates that a dollar deposited today will return $3.50 in interest when she retires. She currently takes home $25,000 after paying $3,250 annually in taxes and expects to draw $14,625 in pension benefits. Although she is thinking about retirement, Melissa has no savings.

    a Calculate the present discounted value of Melissa's pension benefits.

    b Draw her two-period budget constraint, and label her levels of consumption now and in the future.

    c Suppose that the future pension benefits and current taxes are eliminated. Draw her two-period budget constraint.

    d How much does Melissa save?

Step-by-step solution

Step one (a): The present discounted value of her benefit payment is $14,625/(1 + r) = $3,250, which is exactly her taxes.

Step two (b): Draw Melissa's two-period budget constraint. Label the axes "Current consumption" and "Consumption 40 years in the future." The slope is 1 + r, and the interest rate for the 40-year period is 350 percent. Also, the budget constraint must pass through her current choice: $25,000 now and $14,625 in 40 years.

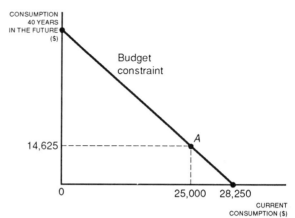

Step three (c): Eliminating pension benefits reduces her future income to $0, but because she no longer pays taxes, her current income rises to $28,250. Because the present discounted value of her two-period income does not change, the budget constraint does not change. (In general, this would shift out the budget constraint for low-income people and shift it in for high-income people.)

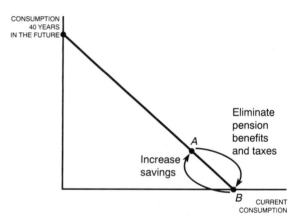

Step four (d): Because Melissa has the same budget constraint, she chooses the same point. This means that she must save $3,250 (which returns $14,625 in 40 years), which is exactly the amount she now pays in taxes. Eliminating pensions and taxes would (for Melissa) lead to the same consumption, but greater savings.

17 (Practice problem: applications) Melissa's uncle is only 10 years from retirement. He can expect to receive $1 in interest for every $1 saved for retirement. He takes home $50,000 annually, saves $10,000, and expects benefits of $20,000 when he retires.

    a Plot his two-period budget constraint.

    b Suppose there is a 50 percent increase in benefits. Taxes also rise, so that the budget constraint of Melissa's uncle does not change. How will his savings change? How will his consumption now and during retirement change?

Answers to Problems

2

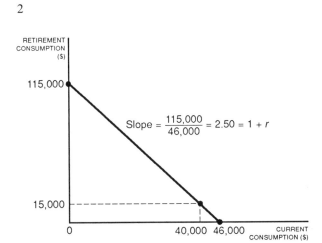

3

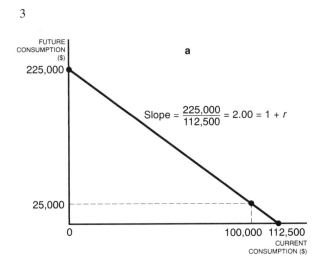

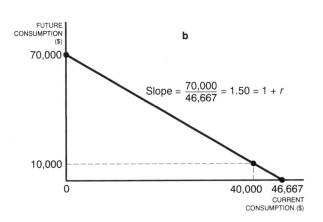

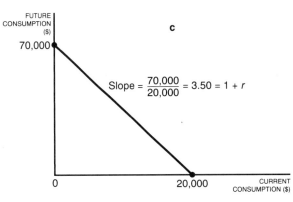

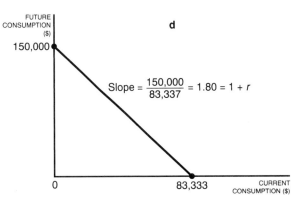

5

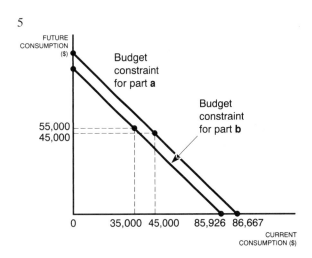

6

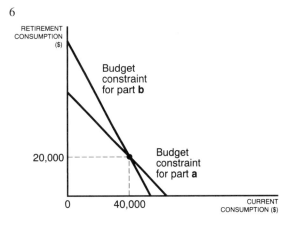

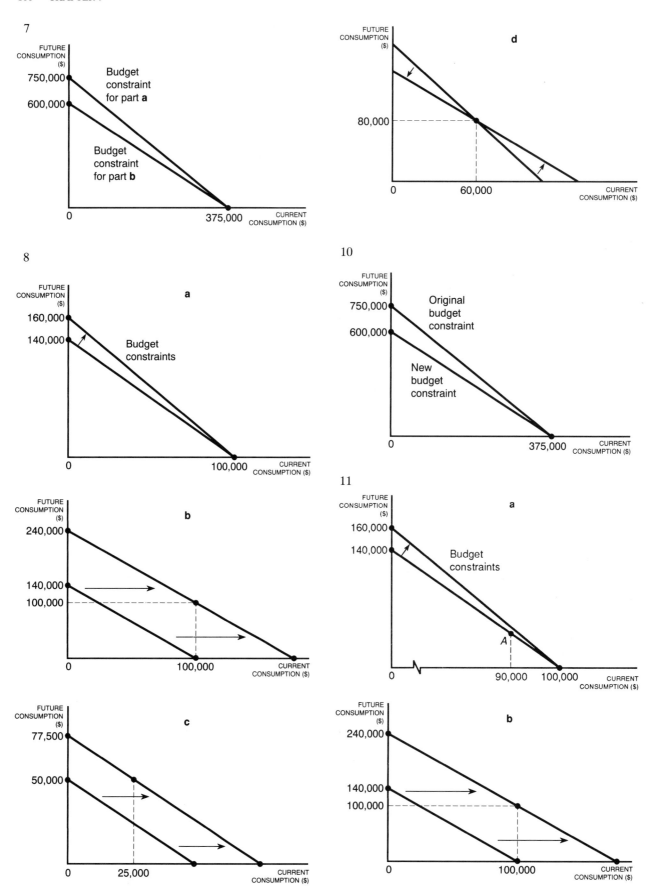

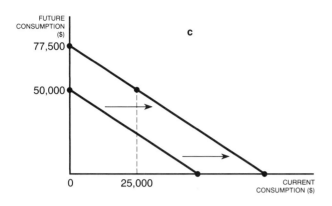

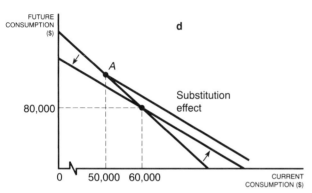

13

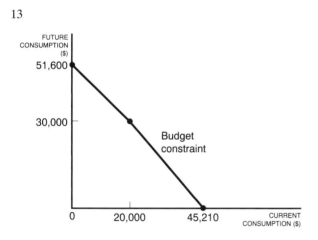

15

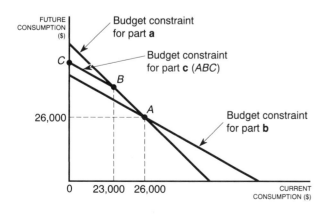

d If the Johnsons save less than $3,000, the program has both substitution and income effects. If they save more than $3,000, there is only an income effect.

17

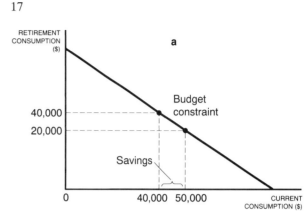

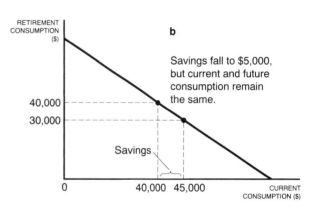

A STUDENT'S GUIDE TO INVESTING

Chapter Review

Chapter 10 takes a break from the budget constraint to explore what the household does with its savings. This is the investment decision. Financial markets offer a wide array of investment opportunities, from savings accounts to Treasury bills to corporate stock, all with different characteristics. Why investors value certain characteristics of assets and how returns to assets reflect these characteristics form the central focus of this chapter. Chapter 10 completes the discussion of the household's role in capital markets. Chapter 11 resumes the discussion of budget constraints and applies them to the household's decision of how much labour to supply.

ESSENTIAL CONCEPTS

1   **Financial investments** are purchases of financial assets in the expectation of receiving a return. Bank accounts, money market accounts, bonds, stocks, mutual funds, and housing are all examples of some of the more common financial investments. More exotic financial investments include preferred stock, convertible bonds, and options. Investors receive returns in the form of interest, dividends, and capital gains.

2   There are four important properties of financial investments: expected return, risk, tax treatment, and liquidity.

   a   Since returns are uncertain, the investor must balance the high returns with the low. The **expected return** is calculated by multiplying the possible returns by the probability each will occur.
   b   Assets with a greater chance of very low and very high returns are **risky.** Most individuals are **risk averse**; they prefer safer assets. An important risk characteristic of an investment is how its returns vary with the market as a whole. Assets that pay high returns when the economy is weak are in greater demand because they allow the investor to reduce the riskiness of the overall portfolio.
   c   The returns from some assets, such as housing and municipal bonds, are taxed less than the returns from other assets. The **tax advantages** make these assets more appealing to investors.
   d   The ease with which an investment can be converted to cash is called **liquidity.** Bank accounts are very liquid; housing is illiquid. Most investors prefer liquidity.

3 The **efficient market theory** says that market prices reflect the characteristics of assets, incorporate all currently available information, and change unpredictably. An important implication of this theory is that without inside information, investors cannot continue to earn more than average returns.

4 The chapter closes with some investment advice. Although unlikely to appear on a test, this advice is immensely valuable.

   a Carefully evaluate the characteristics of each asset you own as it relates to your personal situation.

   b Diversify. Give your portfolio a broad base.

   c Consider all your risks, not just those in your financial investment portfolio.

   d Think again before you imagine that you can beat the market.

BEHIND THE ESSENTIAL CONCEPTS

1 What do investors want from their financial assets? In addition to high expected returns, individuals value the characteristics of investments with low risk, favourable tax treatment, and liquidity. The demand for investments with these characteristics is higher; therefore, their price is higher. The fact that market prices are higher for assets with desirable characteristics—in other words, that asset prices reflect these characteristics—is one of the central ideas of efficient market theory.

2 Assets that pay higher returns in bad times are especially valuable. When the economy is in recession, the typical individual loses money on investments. People do not like to see their wealth fluctuate and are willing to pay something to smooth out these ups and downs. Assets that pay higher returns when the economy is weak help to stabilize the overall portfolio. Again, efficient market theory predicts that the prices of these assets will be higher.

3 Efficient market theory says that prices also reflect all available information. For example, when Iraq invaded Kuwait in August 1990, the prices of oil and oil stocks shot up immediately. The new information that oil would be in short supply in the future made firms that owned large oil reserves worth more, and their stock prices immediately reflected this additional worth.

4 Many people are mystified by the notion that in an efficient market, asset prices change randomly. Once you understand the logic, however, you can see why this must be true. Since market prices reflect available information, you can only beat the market if you have information others do not. Anyone who had known in April 1990 that Iraq would invade Kuwait could have bought oil stocks before their prices rose. Once the invasion happened, however, it was too late. Prices had

already risen. Since the invasion was a surprise, the sudden changes in the prices of oil stocks were also surprises. This is what is meant by random movements in prices: the changes are unpredictable, though they are not without rational cause.

SELF-TEST

True or False

1 The ease with which an asset can be converted to cash is called its liquidity.

2 To find the expected return, simply take the average of the possible returns.

3 Housing is a tax-favoured investment because interest is tax deductible and capital gains taxes may be postponed.

4 If the interest rate rises, bond prices fall.

5 Bondholders bear no risk from inflation.

6 If a company goes bankrupt, bondholders are paid before stockholders.

7 The portion of a company income not paid to stockholders in dividends is called retained earnings.

8 Risky assets pay higher rates of return on average.

9 Illiquid assets pay lower rates of return on average.

10 The right to purchase a share of stock at a specified price for some time in the future is called an option.

11 If stock prices vary randomly, then the market cannot be efficient.

12 Owing to the quality of their research staffs, most mutual funds continue to earn more than the market rate of return year after year.

13 Because most people prefer safe, tax-favoured, liquid assets, those assets yield higher returns.

14 A fund that gathers money from many investors and purchases a range of assets is called a mutual fund.

15 If stock prices reflect all available information, then changes in price must result from unanticipated events and must be random.

Multiple Choice

1 Which of the following is not a financial investment?

   a stocks

   b bonds

   c money market accounts

   d certificates of deposit

   e none of the above

2 Which of the following are real investments?

a preferred stock
b mutual funds
c purchases of new factories
d bank accounts
e none of the above

3 Liquidity refers to

a the correlation of the return on an asset and the market return.
b the term to maturity of a bond.
c the ease with which an asset can be converted into cash.
d the likelihood that an investor will be repaid if a corporation goes bankrupt.
e none of the above.

4 Which of the following is not a risk borne by bond-holders?

a The market interest rate may rise and cause the price of the bond to fall.
b Inflation may lower the real value of the fixed return.
c A corporation may go bankrupt and default on the bond.
d At the end of the term, even if it does not default, a company may not pay a bondholder what that bondholder expected to receive.
e None of the above.

5 Junk bonds are

a highly risky bonds usually issued by firms with high debt levels.
b bonds that must be held by the original purchaser and cannot be sold.
c bonds that have procyclical returns.
d bonds that are not convertible into stock.
e bonds issued by firms in the used vehicle industry.

6 The amount of a firm's earnings not paid out to stockholders as dividends is called

a economic profits.
b the average return.
c retained earnings.
d liquidity.
e accounting profits.

7 If an investor sells a share of stock for more than he paid for it, he earns a

a liquidity premium.
b capital gain.
c retained earnings.
d risk premium.
e procyclical return.

8 Who is repaid after owners of common stock when the firm goes bankrupt?

a bondholders
b owners of preferred stocks
c creditors

d Revenue Canada
e none of the above

9 Suppose that an antique automobile purchased for $25,000 is to be sold next year. The investor thinks that the sales price may be $20,000 or $40,000, and the probability of each price is one-half. What is the average return?

a $5,000
b $30,000
c $35,000
d −$5,000
e none of the above

10 If there were no differences between assets other than the ways in which they produced returns, then

a the average returns to all assets would be the same.
b the returns to stock ownership would exceed the returns to bond holding.
c assets that paid returns through capital gains would pay more than assets that paid returns through interest or dividends.
d no investor would hold bonds.
e none of the above.

11 Stocks are risky financial investments. Which of the following is not consistent with this statement?

a The price of the stock may go up or down.
b The amount of the dividend payment may go up or down.
c The firm may go bankrupt.
d Investors in stocks will look for higher expected returns than from Treasury bills.
e None of the above.

12 Most investors are risk averse. This means that they will

a never purchase risky assets.
b look only at the risk of an investment, not the expected return.
c always prefer bonds to stocks.
d always prefer bank accounts to bonds because bank accounts are guaranteed by the Canadian Deposit Insurance Agency, an agency of the federal government.
e only purchase assets that can be costlessly converted into cash.

13 A risk-neutral individual

a always invests in a wide variety of financial instruments.
b only cares about the expected return, not the risk.
c only cares about the risk, not the expected return.
d cares about both the expected return and the risk.
e none of the above.

14 Assets that yield high returns when the economy is in a recession

a are procyclical.

b   are less desirable than similar assets that yield low returns when the economy is in a recession.

c   allow owners to reduce the riskiness of their overall wealth.

d   are never purchased by risk-averse investors.

e   none of the above.

15 An asset with a return that is exempt from taxes

a   will be priced lower than a comparable asset with a taxable return.

b   will have the same price as a comparable asset with a taxable return.

c   will be priced highter than a comparable asset with a taxable return.

d   is more highly valued by those paying low rates of tax.

e   is less highly valued by those paying high rates of tax.

16 Housing in Canada is a tax-favoured investment in that

a   mortgage interest is tax deductible.

b   housing is liquid.

c   it is possible to avoid capital gains taxes on housing.

d   housing is financed by municipal bonds.

e   none of the above.

17 Which of the following assets is most liquid?

a   stocks

b   bonds

c   bank accounts

d   housing

e   mutual funds

18 Which of the following is not an attribute of an asset?

a   its liquidity

b   its expected returns

c   its risk

d   its tax treatment

e   the efficiency of the market in which it is traded

19 Efficient market theory says that

a   all assets are perfectly liquid.

b   all assets are treated the same by the tax system.

c   asset characteristics are perfectly reflected in their prices.

d   average returns are equal for all assets.

e   none of the above.

20 The advice to diversity your portfolio means

a   own a wide variety of assets with different risks.

b   stay away from risky assets.

c   choose only assets with procyclical returns.

d   follow a random walk strategy.

e   none of the above.

Completion

1   Purchases of new factories and machinery are examples of _____.

2   Purchases of stocks and bonds and deposits in money market accounts are examples of _____ investment.

3   _____ refers to the ease with which an investment can be turned into cash.

4   An unexpected decline in the rate of interest causes the prices of bonds to _____.

5   Because most individuals are _____, risky assets must offer a higher average return than safe assets.

6   In general, stocks that go up in value when the economy is weak are worth _____ than stocks that go up in value during good economic times.

7   An asset with a return that is exempt from tax will have a _____ price than a comparable asset with a taxable return.

8   The demand for an asset depends upon its average return, _____, tax treatment, and liquidity.

9   To find the average return on an asset, multiply the possible returns by the corresponding _____.

10 The theory that market prices perfectly reflect the characteristics of assets is called the _____ theory.

Answers to Self-Test

True or False

1	t	6	t	11	f
2	f	7	t	12	t
3	t	8	t	13	f
4	t	9	f	14	t
5	f	10	t	15	t

Multiple Choice

1	e	6	c	11	e	16	c
2	c	7	b	12	e	17	c
3	c	8	e	13	b	18	e
4	d	9	a	14	c	19	c
5	a	10	a	15	c	20	a

Completion

1   capital goods
2   financial
3   Liquidity
4   rise
5   risk averse
6   more
7   higher
8   risk
9   probabilities
10 efficient market

Doing Economics: Tools and Practice Problems

The concept of expected returns appears for the first time in this chapter. We study how to calculate the expected return on an investment and what it means. We go on to consider the opportunity set for the investor and learn how the investor perceives trade-offs of risk and expected return, and also liquidity and returns. The last issue we take up is the relationship between bond prices and interest rates. A few problems use the concept of present value (introduced in Chapter 6) to show why an increase in interest rates leads to a decrease in bond prices.

Tool Kit 10.1: Calculating Expected Returns

Because the returns on financial investments come in the future, at the time the decision is made an investor is uncertain about what the returns will actually be. Good investors think carefully about all the possibilities and calculate the expected returns.

Step one: Make a three-column table showing all the possible returns in the left-hand column and the corresponding probabilities in the middle column.

Returns	Probability	Product
r_1	P_1	
r_2	P_2	

Step two: Multiply each possible return by its probability, and enter the product in the right-hand column.

Returns	Probability	Product
r_1	P_1	$r_1 \times P_1$
r_2	P_2	$r_2 \times P_2$

Step three: Add the numbers in the right-hand column. The sum is the expected return.

Returns	Probability	Product
r_1	P_1	$r_1 \times P_1$
r_2	P_2	$r_2 \times P_2$

Average returns = $(r_1 \times P_1) + (r_2 \times P_2)$.

---

1 (Worked problem: expected returns) Envious of his brother's life-style, Dr. Mendez is considering investing in one of his brother's real estate ventures. His brother promises a return of 100 percent in one year, but Dr. Mendez thinks the probability that this will happen is only 1/4. More likely (probability = 1/2) is a return of 8 percent. Finally, there is another 1/4 probability that the project will go under and the doctor will lose all his money (return = −100 percent). Calculate the expected return.

Step-by-step solution

Step one: Make a table, and enter the possible returns and the corresponding probabilities.

Returns	Probability	Product
100%	1/4	
8%	1/2	
−100%	1/4	

Step two: Multiply each return by its probability, and enter the result.

Returns	Probability	Product
100%	1/4	25%
8%	1/2	4%
−100%	1/4	−25%

Step three: Add the numbers in the right-hand column.

Returns	Probability	Product
100%	1/4	25%
8%	1/2	4%
−100%	1/4	−25%

Expected returns = 4%.

Thus, in spite of the considerable risk, the investment pays an average of only 4 percent. The good doctor should stick to medicine and put his money in a safe investment.

2 (Practice problem: expected returns) Climax, flush with a consultant's prediction of its future as a high-technology center, is issuing bonds for a new city government building. The bonds pay 20 percent. Most financial analysts think the probability of default is 1/10. In case of default, the bondholders lose their investments (returns = −100 percent). Calculate the expected return on the Climax bond.

3 (Practice problem: expected returns) Calculate the expected return on each of the following.

a	Returns	Probability	Product
	50%	1/4	
	12%	5/8	
	−100%	1/8	

b	Returns	Probability	Product
	10%	1/4	
	20%	3/4	

c	Returns	Probability	Product
	200%	1/3	
	40%	1/3	
	−100%	1/3	

d	Returns	Probability	Product
	50%	1/3	
	12%	2/3	

4 (Worked problem: expected returns) There are four desirable characteristics of financial investments: expected returns, risk, tax treatment, and liquidity. Seeking the best combination of these characteristics, an

investor faces trade-offs. The table below gives the returns on six bond issues if there is no default, and also the probabilities of default for each. If there is a default, the investor loses all invested money (return = –100 percent). Also, note that if the probability of default is .1, then the probability of not experiencing a default must be .9.

a   Compute the expected return for each bond.
b   Measure risk as the probability of default. Construct the opportunity set, and interpret its outer edge as the risk-return trade-off.
c   Are there any bonds a rational investor would never buy? Why or why not?

Company	Returns (if no default)	Probability of default
Do Music Co.	5%	0
Re Music Co.	19%	0.1
Mi Music Co.	30%	0.2
Fa Music Co.	12%	0.05
Sol Music Co.	8%	0.02
Fred's Music Co.	15%	0.07

Step-by-step solution

Step one (a): Calculate the expected returns for each bond. Follow the procedure for calculating expected returns.

Do Music Co.	$(5\% \times 1) - (100\% \times 0) = 5\%$
Re Music Co.	$(19\% \times .9) - (100\% \times .1) = 7.1\%$
Mi Music Co.	$(30\% \times .8) - (100\% \times .2) = 4\%$
Fa Music Co.	$(12\% \times .95) - (100 \times .05) = 6.4\%$
Sol Music Co.	$(8\% \times .98) - (100\% \times .02) = 5.84\%$
Fred's Music Co.	$(15\% \times .93) - (100\% \times .07) = 6.95\%$

Step two (b): Plot the expected returns on the vertical axis and risk (measured as the probability of default) on the horizontal. This is the risk-return trade-off.

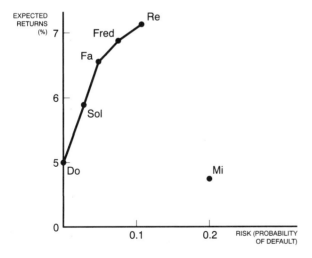

Step three (c): Since Mi Music Co.'s bonds do not lie on the outer edge, no one will buy them. All of the other issues offer higher average returns and lower risk, as shown in the figure.

5   (Practice problem: expected returns) The four hospitals in Greenville are racing to install the latest medical technologies. Each is trying to raise money in the bond market, and their returns and default risks are given below. If there is a default, the return is –100 percent.

a   Calculate the expected returns for each.
b   Plot the risk-return trade-off.

Hospital	Returns (if no default)	Probability of default
Northside	6%	0
Southside	18%	0.09
Eastside	22%	0.1
Westside	12%	0.05

6   (Practice problem: expected returns) The Kannapans have set aside some money in case of emergency. They are considering where to invest it, but they are concerned about how quickly they will have access to the money when it is needed. The four possible assets, their returns, and the times needed to withdraw the principal (or sell the asset) are given below. Construct the liquidity-return trade-off.

Asset	Returns	Waiting period
Bank account	5%	none
Bond	7%	2 days
Diamonds	4%	1 week
Rental housing	9%	1 month

7   (Worked problem: expected returns) When interest rates rise, bond prices fall. This fact of financial markets follows from the concept of present discounted value, introduced in Chapter 6. The market price for a bond is the present discounted value of the promised repayments. Bonds issued by Hitek, Inc., promise to pay $100 at the end of the year for 2 years. In addition, the face value equal to $1,000 is repaid at the end of 3 years. The market interest rate is 8 percent.

a   Calculate the present discounted value of the bond.
b   The interest rate rises to 10 percent. Recalculate the bond value.

Step-by-step solution

Step one (a): Make a table, and enter the years and the payments.

Year	Amount	Discount factor	Present discounted value
1	$ 100		
2	$ 100		
3	$1,000		

Step two: Calculate and enter the discount factors for each year. For the first year, the discount factor is $1/(1 + .08) = 0.92$. For the second year, it is $1/(1 + .08)^2 = 0.85$, and for the third, it is $1/(1 + .08)^3 = 0.78$.

Step three: Multiply the amounts by the corresponding discount factor. Enter the product in the right-hand column.

Step four: Add the numbers in the right-hand column.

Year	Amount	Discount factor	Present discounted value
1	$ 100	0.92	$ 92
2	$ 100	0.85	$ 85
3	$1,000	0.78	$780

Present discounted value = $957.

Step five (b): Repeat the procedure for a 10 percent interest rate. The table looks like this.

Year	Amount	Discount factor	Present discounted value
1	$ 100	0.90	$ 90
2	$ 100	0.81	$ 81
3	$1,000	0.73	$730

Present discounted value = $901.

The rise in the interest rate from 8 percent to 10 percent causes the bond price to fall by $56 ($957 – $901). It should be clear why ripples in interest rates cause waves in the bond market.

8 (Practice problem: expected returns) Deuce Hardwear, a franchiser of motorcycle clothing, has issued a bond that promises to pay $800 at the end of each of the next two years and $12,000 at the end of the third year. The interest rate is 7 percent.

   a Calculate the present discounted value of the bond.
   b The interest rate falls to 6 percent. How much does the price of the bond change?

9 (Practice problem: expected returns) For each of the following, calculate the change in the price of the bond.

   a The interest rate falls from 10 percent to 8 percent.

Year	Amount	Discount factor	Present discounted value
1	$ 88		
2	$ 88		
3	$1,000		

   Present discounted value = $
   b The interest rate rises from 10 percent to 13 percent.

Year	Amount	Discount factor	Present discounted value
1	$ 800		
2	$ 700		
3	$13,000		

   Present discounted value = $

Answers to Problems

2 Expected return = $(9 \times 20) - (.1 \times 100) = 8\%$.

3 a 7.5%
   b 17.5%
   c 46.7%
   d 24.7%

5 a The expected returns for each bond are given in the table.

Hospital	Returns (if no default)	Probability of default	Expected returns
Northside	6%	0	6%
Southside	18%	0.09	7.38%
Eastside	22%	0.1	9.8%
Westside	12%	0.05	6.4%

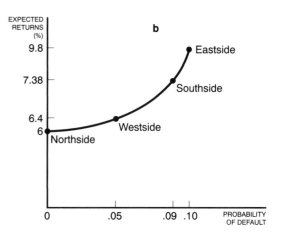

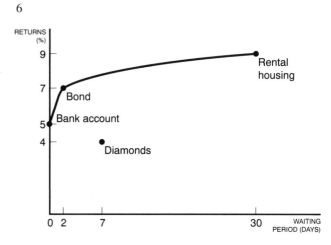

8 a Present discounted value = $800/(1.07) + $800/(1.07)^2 + $12,000/(1.07)^3 = $11,243
   b Present discounted value = $11,542

9 a Price of the bond rises from $904 to $950.
   b Price of the bond falls from $11,073 to $10,263.

Chapter 11

THE LABOUR SUPPLY DECISION

Chapter Review

This chapter concludes the discussion of household decision making. Along with Chapters 8 and 9, it is the third chapter to apply the budget constraint. Here, the focus is on the labour supply decision; the choice is between leisure and the income needed for consumption. As with the consumption and savings decisions in Chapters 8 and 9, the individual chooses the best alternative in an opportunity set: how much labour time to offer, what type of job to seek, and how much training to undertake.

ESSENTIAL CONCEPTS

1   The decision to supply labour is primarily a time-allocation problem. Individuals have only so much time available, and they must divide their time between working and other activities. Any time not devoted to working and earning money, whether it is spent in recreation, sleep, chores, or errands, is called leisure. The income earned while working is available for consumption; therefore, the *trade-off* is between **leisure** and **consumption,** between consuming time and consuming goods.

2   The chapter focuses on the budget constraint between leisure and consumption, shown here in Figure 11.1. The slope is the wage rate, and changes in the wage rate rotate the budget constraint and cause income and

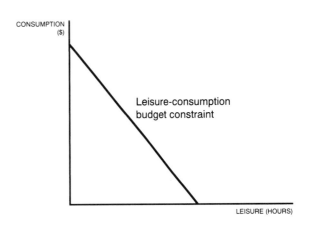

Figure 11.1

substitution effects. When an individual's wage increases, leisure becomes more expensive; thus, the *substitution effect* encourages less leisure and more work. On the other hand, the *income effect* leads the individual to want to consume more leisure, which results in less work. Because the income and substitution effects work in opposite directions, the supply curve for labour may slope upwards or even bend backwards.

3   There are more dimensions to labour supply than hours worked. Individuals choose whether or not to participate in the work force. They must also decide what sort of job to pursue, how much education and training to acquire, and when to retire. Finally, in the long run, the labour supply for the economy depends upon how many children families decide to have, a decision that, perhaps surprisingly, is quite subject to the influence of economic forces. Each of these decisions can be understood as the choice of the best alternative within an appropriately specified budget constraint.

4   Government policy also affects labour supply. Taxation reduces the consumption that a given amount of labour will yield. Both the substitution and income effects of the welfare system encourage recipients to work less or not at all. Each of these policies is analyzed in terms of how it alters the leisure-consumption budget constraint.

5   According to **human capital** theory, individuals invest in education and training to acquire human capital, or skills that increase their productivity and wages. Another view is that education signals to employers which potential workers are innately more productive. The belief in this signal leads to credentials competition, the process by which people gather degrees not for any learning that takes place, but rather to show that they will be productive if hired.

BEHIND THE ESSENTIAL CONCEPTS

1   The basic diagram of the chapter is the budget constraint for leisure and consumption. It is important to understand that this diagram is very much like the consumer's budget constraint in Chapter 8 and the two-period budget constraint in Chapter 9. Each shows which combinations are affordable. The slopes are the relative prices; in this case, the relative price of leisure is the wage rate. If the individual wants to consume another hour of leisure, the opportunity cost is the money that could be earned in that hour. Changes in nonwage income, such as investment returns, bring about a parallel shift in the budget constraint, but changes in the wage rate rotate it. Again, this is very similar to the other budget constraints.

2   Changes in the wage rate rotate the budget constraint and cause substitution and income effects. The income effect leads to more leisure (less work) when the wage

rate increases. The substitution effect, on the other hand, causes less leisure (more work) when the wage rate increases. As with the savings decision, the substitution and income effects of wage changes work in opposite directions. For consumption, however, they work in the same direction. Thus, while the demand curves for goods and services is downward sloping, the supply curves for savings and labour may be upward sloping or bend backwards.

3   Table 11.1 may help you keep straight the substitution and income effects.

Table 11.1

If the wage rate rises,
   the *substitution* effect leads to more work because leisure is more expensive.
   the *income* effect leads to less work because the worker is better off and demands more leisure.

If the wage rate falls,
   the *substitution* effect leads to less work because leisure is less expensive.
   the *income* effect leads to more work because the worker is worse off and demands less leisure.

---

4   Be sure not to confuse the budget constraint with the labour supply curve. The budget constraint shows the combinations of leisure and consumption the individual can afford given the wage rate and any nonwage income. The labour supply curve shows the quantity of labour supplied at each wage rate. As usual, it is important to pay attention to what is measured along each axis.

5   **Compensating differentials** are the higher wages that must be paid by risky jobs or jobs with unpleasant working conditions. You can compare these with differences in rates of return for assets, such as risk and liquidity premiums. Individuals seek desirable characteristics in both their assets and their jobs. Competition for good characteristics in assets drives the rates of return down for safe or liquid assets. Similarly, competition for jobs with desirable characteristics drives these jobs' wages down. In equilibrium, the relatively higher wages will compensate for the undesirable characteristics.

SELF-TEST

True or False

1   The percentage change in labour supply resulting from a 1 percent change in the wage is the elasticity of the supply of labour.

2 The income effect of a decrease in wages is to increase the quantity of labour supplied.

3 The substitution effect of a decrease in wages is to increase the quantity of labour supplied.

4 Investment in education is an example of human capital.

5 An increase in nonwage income rotates the budget constraint.

6 An increase in unfunded pension benefits will lead people, on average, to retire later.

7 Welfare programs reduce labour supply through both the income and substitution effects.

8 A cut in marginal income taxes should cause labour supply to increase by 50 percent.

9 The female elasticity of labour supply is no different from the male elasticity of labour supply.

10 As the wealth of a country increases, its birthrate also increases.

11 Having children is a profoundly personal decision, unaffected by economic incentives.

12 The labour force participation of women has increased since World War II.

13 Under a voucher system, parents would receive a voucher that could be used at any accredited school, public or private.

14 Jobs that are generally less attractive must pay compensating differentials, in the form of higher wages.

15 According to human capital theory, education increases the productivity of students and enables them to earn more in the labour market.

Multiple Choice

1 If a person can earn $10 per hour, then the slope of the leisure-consumption budget constraint is

  a   1/10.
  b   10.
  c   .01.
  d   .10.
  e   none of the above.

2 If nonwage income increases, then the budget constraint

  a   rotates and becomes steeper.
  b   rotates and becomes flatter.
  c   shifts out parallel.
  d   shifts in parallel.
  e   none of the above.

3 If the wage increases, then the budget constraint

  a   rotates and becomes steeper.
  b   rotates and becomes flatter.
  c   shifts out parallel.
  d   shifts in parallel.
  e   none of the above.

4 An increase in nonwage income will usually lead to

  a   a decrease in the quantity of labour supplied through the substitution effect.
  b   a decrease in the quantity of labour supplied through the income effect.
  c   an increase in the quantity of labour supplied through the substitution effect.
  d   an increase in the quantity of labour supplied through the income effect.
  e   none of the above.

5 The substitution effect of a wage increase leads to

  a   a decrease in the quantity of labour supplied.
  b   an increase in the quantity of labour supplied.
  c   an increase in leisure.
  d   a parallel shift in the budget constraint.
  e   none of the above.

6 The labour supply curve for an individual

  a   is always upward sloping.
  b   is always downward sloping.
  c   may slope upwards or downwards depending upon the strength of the substitution and income effects.
  d   is vertical because the substitution and income effects exactly offset each other.
  e   none of the above.

7 A decrease in the marginal income tax rate will

  a   cause a big increase in the quantity of labour supplied because the income effect is weaker than the substitution effect.
  b   cause a big decrease in the quantity of labour supplied because the substitution effect is weaker than the income effect.
  c   lead to little change in the quantity of labour supplied.
  d   have no effect on the quantity of labour supplied because taxes do not affect the budget constraint.
  e   none of the above.

8 Currently in Canada, the elasticity of female labour supply is

  a   higher than the elasticity of male labour supply.
  b   lower than the elasticity of male labour supply.
  c   equal to the elasticity of male labour supply.
  d   perfectly inelastic.
  e   irrelevant, because few women work.

9 Increased labour-force participation of women in Canada can be characterized as

  a   solely a movement along their labour supply curve.
  b   solely a shift of their labour supply curve.
  c   partly a movement along, partly a shift of, their labour supply curve.
  d   solely a response to higher relative wages for women.
  e   solely a response to greater job opportunities for women.

10 Increased lifetime wealth leads to

a earlier retirement through the income effect.
b later retirement through the substitution effect.
c earlier retirement through the substitution effect.
d later retirement through the income effect.
e none of the above.

11 Welfare programs

a reduce the labour supply of recipients through the income effect.
b increase the labour supply of recipients through the substitution effect.
c increase the labour supply of recipients through the income effect.
d increase the labour supply of recipients through both the income and substitution effects.
e reduce the labour supply of recipients through both the income and substitution effects.

12 Which of the following is not an example of investment in human capital?

a formal schooling
b on-the-job learning
c technical training
d plant and equipment
e none of the above

13 Which of the following statements is consistent with the theory that education provides a signal to employers about the innate productivity of a job applicant?

a In university, students learn skills that make them more productive in the workplace.
b Students learn a kind of perseverance that is highly valued in the business world.
c Innately brighter individuals find university easier, more pleasant, and more satisfying.
d Innately brighter individuals are no more likely than anyone else to do well at university.
e None of the above.

14 Which of the following is an example of a compensating differential?

a Long-distance truck drivers make $5,000 per year more than truck drivers who drive local routes.
b Union workers make 30 percent more than non-union workers.
c The average factory worker in Canada makes over three times what the average Mexican factory worker receives.
d Women doing identical jobs to men often receive lower wages.
e None of the above.

15 Many positions in government carry little risk of job loss. On the other hand, some similar jobs in the private sector offer much less job security. Which of the following is most likely?

a The government jobs will pay more because government workers have more human capital.

b Private sector jobs will pay more as a compensating differential for the lower job security.
c Each type of job will pay the same.
d No one will choose to work in the private sector.
e None of the above.

16 The opportunity costs of attending university do not include

a tuition expenses.
b costs of materials and books.
c room and board.
d forgone earnings while attending class and studying.
e travelling to and from university.

17 Typically, as the wealth of a country increases, the birthrate

a declines.
b does not change.
c increases.
d doubles.
e may rise or fall because there is no typical relationship between wealth and the birthrate.

18 Most capital in Canada is

a human capital.
b credentials.
c capital goods.
d compensating differentials.
e none of the above.

19 If an employer hires only liberal arts graduates, the employer is practising

a compensating differentials.
b signalling.
c screening.
d investment in human capital.
e none of the above.

20 If a university student switches his major to history in order to show that he is intelligent, he is practising

a compensating differentials.
b signalling.
c screening.
d investment in human capital.
e none of the above.

Completion

1 The decision concerning how much labour to supply is a choice between _____ and _____.

2 The slope of the budget line is equal to (minus) the _____.

3 When the nonwage income of an individual decreases, the individual's labour supply _____.

4 The _____ effect of a wage decrease leads individuals to decrease their labour supply.

5 If an individual's labour supply is backward bending, then the _____ effect is stronger.

6 The labour supply of women is usually _____ elastic than the labour supply of men.

7 The view that education raises wages because it increases productivity is called _____.

8 Another view is that higher levels of education _____ to employers that an individual is innately more productive.

9 Higher wages needed to attract workers to unpleasant jobs are called _____.

10 The economic model predicts that as wages received by women increase, the birthrate will _____.

Answers to Self-Test

True or False

1	t	4	t	7	t	10	f	13	t
2	t	5	f	8	f	11	f	14	t
3	t	6	f	9	f	12	t	15	t

Multiple Choice

1	b	6	c	11	a	16	c
2	c	7	c	12	d	17	a
3	a	8	a	13	c	18	a
4	b	9	c	14	a	19	c
5	b	10	a	15	b	20	b

Completion

1 income, consumption
2 wage
3 increases
4 substitution
5 income
6 more
7 human capital
8 signal
9 compensating differentials
10 fall

Doing Economics: Tools and Practice Problems

The most important model in this chapter is the opportunity set for the labour supply decision: the leisure-consumption budget constraint. In this section, we first review how to construct the budget constraint. We then see how the budget constraint changes when the wage rate or nonwage income changes. As in previous chapters, the substitution and income effects of wage changes can be illustrated using the budget constraint. Finally, there are some applications. The effects of many government programs and also of many private sector incentive schemes, such as overtime pay and attendance bonuses, become much clearer when you understand how they alter the leisure-consumption budget constraint. Several problems explore how to use the budget constraint to analyze these issues. You'll notice that some are quite similar in form to some problems in Chapters 8 and 9. This fact underscores how valuable it is to see the similarities between

the consumer's budget constraint of Chapter 8, the saver's two-period budget constraint of Chapter 9, and the leisure-consumption budget constraint of this chapter.

Tool Kit 11.1: Plotting the Leaisure-Consumption Budget Constraint

The budget constraint shows what combinations of leisure and consumption can be afforded given the wage rate and the amount of nonwage income. To plot the budget constraint, follow this five-step procedure.

Step one: Draw a set of coordinate axes. Label the horizontal axis as the quantity of leisure consumed and the vertical axis as the consumption level.

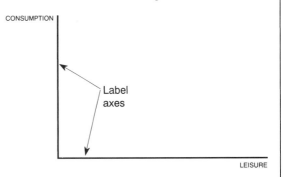

Step two: If an individual chooses to do no work, leisure equals the total time available, and consumption is equal to the nonwage income. Plot this point.

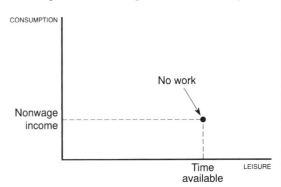

Step three: Calculate the maximum earnings if the individual consumes no leisure. Add this amount to the nonwage income, and plot this quantity along the vertical axis.

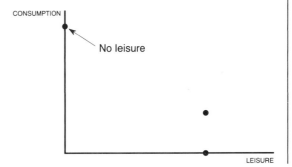

Step four: Draw a line segment connecting the two points. This line segment is the leisure-consumption budget constraint.

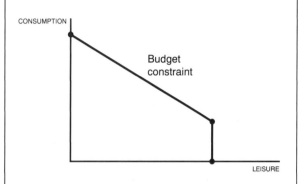

Step five: Verify that the slope of the budget constraint is (minus) the wage rate.

1 (Worked problem: leisure-consumption budget constraint) In his spare time, Mike, a student at Magic Johnson University, referees intramural basketball games. Each game pays $7, and if he could stand the abuse, Mike could referee as many as 60 each month. On average, each game takes 1 hour. This is not Mike's only source of income; each month his parents send him $200 for expenses.

   a Construct Mike's budget constraint.
   b Suppose that Mike chooses to referee 20 games. Label his chosen alternative, and indicate his total income, income from refereeing, hours worked, and leisure.

Step-by-step solution

Step one (a): Draw the two axes, and label the vertical one "Consumption" and the horizontal one "Leisure."

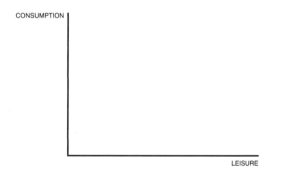

Step two: Plot the no-work consumption point. If Mike referees no games, he consumes all 60 hours as leisure. This leaves him $200 (from his parents) for consumption. Plot this point.

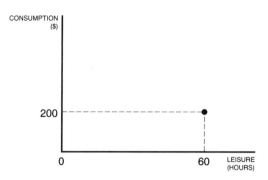

Step three: Calculate total income if Mike works all the time available. If he referees the maximum number of games, 60, he earns $420 from refereeing and retains the $200 from his parents. This leaves him with $620 for consumption but no time for leisure. Plot this point.

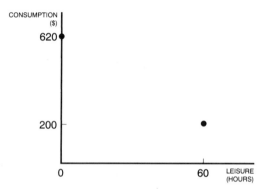

Step four: Draw a line segment between the two plotted points. This is the budget constraint.

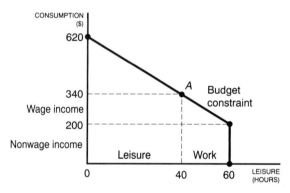

Step five: The slope of the budget constraint is (620 − 200)/60 = 7, which is the wage.

Step six (b): If Mike referees 20 games, then he is left with 40 hours of leisure, and earns $140 in wage income for a total of $340. Plot the point, and label appropriately.

2 (Practice problem: leisure-consumption budget constraint) University professors can earn extra cash by reviewing papers for journals. Editors pay around $50 per paper for an academic opinion about whether it should be accepted for publication. Reviewing a paper takes 1 hour. Professor Cavendish has 15 hours available each month for outside work such as re-

viewing. She draws $3,000 monthly from Eastern University and that is her only other source of income.

a Plot Professor Cavendish's budget constraint.
b Suppose that the professor reviews 6 papers in March. Plot and label her chosen alternative.

3 (Practice problem: leisure-consumption budget constraint) For each of the following, draw a budget constraint. Also, choose a point along the budget constraint, and show the corresponding amount of leisure, work, nonwage income, and wage income.

	Wage	Total time	Nonwage income
a	$25/hour	80 hours	$ 1,000
b	$200/day	30 days	$ 0
c	$1,000/week	50 weeks	$15,000
d	$5/hour	100 hours	$ 0

4 (Worked problem: leisure-consumption budget constraint) When either nonwage income or the wage rate changes, the budget constraint moves. The basic technique here is to draw the budget constraint using the original nonwage income and wage rate, following the procedure shown above. Then draw a new budget constraint using the new nonwage income and wage rate. Compare the two budget constraints, and verify that the shift is parallel when nonwage income changes, but the budget constraint rotates when the wage rate changes. Art supplements his pension by repairing automatic teller machines. Each service call takes an hour, and he receives $50 per call. His pension and other nonwage income is $200 per week. Art has 30 hours available and can work as much as he likes.

a Plot Art's budget constraint.
b His pension fund has done well with its investments and increases Art's nonwage income to $300. Plot his new budget constraint.
c How will Art change his work effort?

Step-by-step solution

Step one (a): Plot his budget constraint in the usual way. If he consumes all 30 hours as leisure, Art can consume $200. If he works all 30 hours, he can consume $200 + ($50 × 30) = $1,700. Note that the slope is (1,700 − 200)/30 = 50, which is the wage.

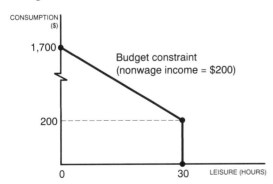

Step two (b): Plot his budget constraint with nonwage income equal to $300. His no-work consumption is now $300 + (30 × $50) = $1,800, if he works all the available time. Note that the nonwage income increase brings about a parallel shift.

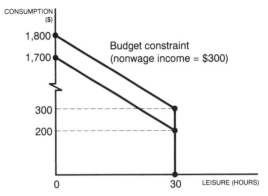

Step three (c): The change in the budget constraint is an income effect. The income effect reduces work effort when income rises. Art will work less.

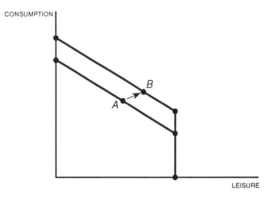

5 (Practice problem: leisure-consumption budget constraint) Liza's job as a broker requires making unsolicited, or "cold," calls to potential clients in an attempt to persuade them to put their portfolios in her hands. On average, cold calls earn Liza $10 each. She can make 4 per hour, and she can work as many as 80 hours per week. Her base salary (nonwage income) is $100 per week.

a Plot her budget constraint.
b Suppose that the firm offers her an increase in the base salary to $150 per week. Plot her new budget constraint.
c Will Liza make more or fewer cold calls? Why?

6 (Practice problem: leisure-consumption budget constraint) Sara is offered a position as tour guide for a local museum. She can conduct 2 tours per hour and earn $10 each. She has no nonwage income, but she must pay 25 percent of her salary in taxes. The museum will allow her to work as many as 20 hours each week.

a Plot her budget constraint.
b Taxes are reduced to 20 percent. Plot her budget constraint.

7 (Practice problem: leisure-consumption budget constraint) Theodore tutors some of his fellow students in

Tool Kit 11.2: Distinguishing between
Substitution and Income Effects
of Wage Changes

When the wage rate changes, there are two effects: substitution and income. These can be illustrated using the leisure-consumption budget constraint. This technique clarifies the fact that, as in the case of savings, the substitution and income effects work in opposite directions.

Step one: Draw the budget line with the original wage.

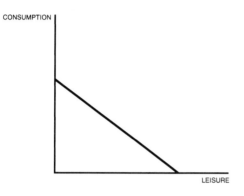

Step two: Find the chosen point along this budget line. Label this point *A*.

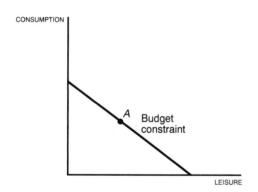

Step three: Draw the budget line with the new wage.

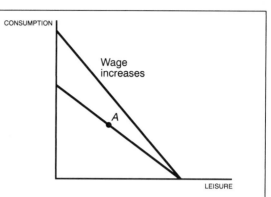

Step four: Draw a dashed line segment through point *A* and parallel to the *new* budget line.

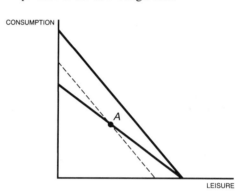

Step five: Darken the portion of the dashed line segment that lies above the original budget line. The points along this darkened segment represent the new alternatives made possible by the substitution effect of the wage change. The income effect shifts out this line in a parallel fashion to the new budget line drawn in step three.

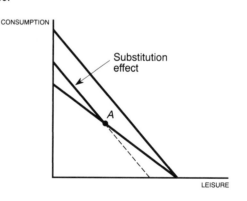

economics for $10 per hour. He also receives $2,000 in expense money per semester from his scholarship. He can work as many as 100 hours per semester.

a   Plot his budget constraint.
b   Students realize that there is a plethora of semi-intelligent grad students who will take less pay. Theodore now only receives $8 per hour. Plot his new budget constraint.

8   (Practice problem: leisure-consumption budget constraint) For each of the following, plot the budget constraint before and after the change.

a   Nonwage income = $100; wage = $20/hour; total time available = 40 hours; nonwage income changes to $0.
b   Nonwage income = $0; wage = $500/week; total

time available = 52 weeks; wage changes to $300/week.

c   Nonwage income = $10,000; wage = $40/hour; total time available = 50 hours; available time increases to 60 hours.

d   Nonwage income = $500; wage = $200/week; total time available = 52 weeks; wage changes to $400/week.

9   (Worked problem: wage changes/applications) John currently works 45 hours per week tuning pianos at a wage of $20 per hour. This is his only income. He is offered a raise to $30 per hour. He has 80 hours available for work each week.

a   Draw the budget constraint at $20 per hour. Label his chosen alternative along this budget line.

b   Draw the budget constraint at $30 per hour.

c   Show the substitution effect of the wage increase. Why must the substitution effect lead John to work no less at the new, higher wage?

Step-by-step solution

Step one (a): Draw the budget constraint at the original wage. We label the horizontal axis "Leisure" and the vertical one "Consumption." If John does not work, he has 80 hours of leisure and no consumption. If he works all 80 hours (leisure = 0), he consumes $1,600. Draw John's budget constraint connecting the two points.

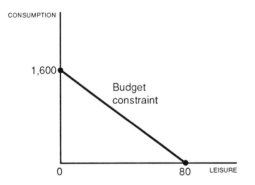

Step two: Find the chosen point along this budget constraint line. John chooses 80 – 45 = 35 hours of leisure, which give him 45 × $20 = $900. Label this point *A*, and note that it does lie along the budget constraint.

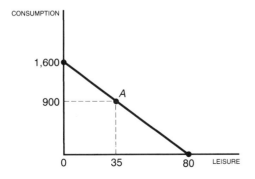

Step three (b): Draw the budget constraint when the wage is $30. The no-work alternative still offers consumption equal to $0, but now if John works the 80 hours available, he consumes $30 × 80 = $2,400. Plot and connect the two end points.

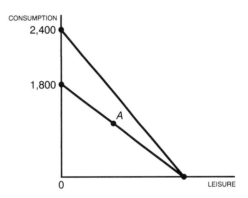

Step four (c): Draw a dashed line parallel to the $30 budget constraint through point *A*.

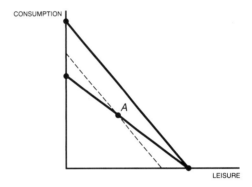

Step five: Darken the portion that lies above the budget constraint drawn in step one. These are the alternatives made possible by the substitution effect of the wage increase. All these points involve more work than at point *A*, the alternative chosen when the wage is $20.

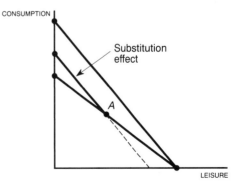

10 (Practice problem: applications) Arna loves her job as a design consultant. She can earn $60 per hour and has been able to work as much as she likes up to 50 hours per week. She has no nonwage income. She is currently working 15 hours per week.

a Plot her budget constraint. Find her chosen alternative, and label the point *A*.

b A new provincial income tax of 10 percent is passed. Arna now takes home only $54 per hour. Plot her new budget constraint.

c Show the substitution effect of the wage decrease.

11 (Practice problem: applications) For each of the following, draw the budget constraint with the wage in the first column and a new budget line with the wage in the second column. Pick an alternative along the first budget constraint, and show the substitution effect. There is no nonwage income.

	Old wage	New wage	Total time
a	$ 25/hour	$ 50/hour	80 hours
b	$ 200/day	$ 100/day	30 days
c	$1,000/week	$1,500/week	50 weeks
d	$ 5/hour	$ 4/hour	100 hours

12 (Worked problem: applications) In Smithsville, the welfare system pays $100 per week. Anyone in Smithsville can earn the minimum wage of $4 per hour at the local pickle plant, but welfare recipients cannot receive more than $100 per week. This means that any earnings are subtracted from welfare benefits. There are 80 hours available for work.

a Draw the budget constraint for a Smithsville welfare recipient.

b A new proposal would substitute a job subsidy for the welfare system. Under the job subsidy proposal, the town pays nothing to those who do not work and $.50 for every dollar earned, up to a total payment of $100. Draw the new budget constraint.

Step-by-step solution

Step one (a): Draw a set of axes labelled "Leisure" and "Consumption." If the recipient does no work, he consumes $100. Plot this point, and label it *A*.

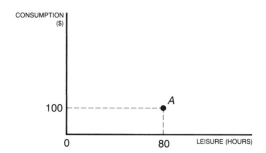

Step two: If the recipient earns $100, he loses all his benefits and still consumes $100. At $4 per hour, $100 is earned in $100/$4 = 25 hours, which leaves 80 − 25 = 55 hours of leisure. Plot the point (100, 55). Label this point *B*.

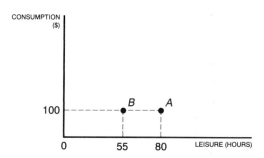

Step three: If the recipient works all 80 hours, he consumes $4 × 80 = $320. Plot this point, and label it *C*.

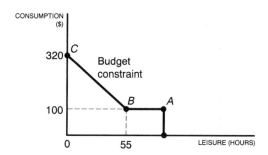

Step four: Draw line segments connecting points *A* and *B* and points *B* and *C*. This is the budget constraint under the welfare system.

Step five (b): Under the job subsidy program, if the person works no hours, he consumes nothing. Plot the point (0, 80). Label it *D*.

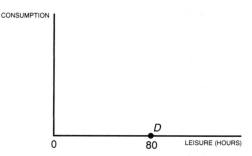

Step six: If the person earns $200, he receives the maximum subsidy, which is $100. The total consumption is then $300. To earn $200 (and consume $300) takes $200/$4 = 50 hours of work; this leaves 80 − 50 = 30 hours of leisure. Plot the point (300, 30), and label it *E*.

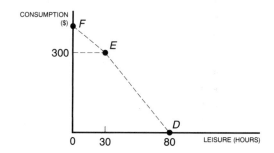

Step seven: If the person works all 80 hours, he consumes $100 + (80 × $4) = $420. Plot the point (420, 80), and label it *F*.

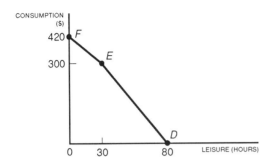

Step eight: Draw line segments connecting *DEF*. This is the budget constraint for job subsidies.

13 (Practice problem: applications) The management at Acme Manufacturing is disturbed that although the typical factory worker is required to work 250 days each year, most only work 230. It proposes a $100 bonus for any employee who works more than 240 days each year. The wage of the typical factory worker is $120 per day.

   a Draw the budget constraint without the attendance bonus.
   b Draw the budget constraint with the attendance bonus. How is attendance likely to change for the typical factory worker?
   c Suppose that the company simply gives each worker $100. How is the opportunity set different from the one with the attendance bonus?
   d Under which scheme will the typical worker work more? Why?

14 (Practice problem: applications) The Quantity Bakery Company has paid its workers $6 per hour to make donuts, cakes, and pies. There are always sweets to make, and the workers can work as many hours as they choose, up to 80 hours per week. Recently, the company union won a new contract that, although it keeps the wage at the same level, now allows for overtime pay of "time and a half" for any hours worked in excess of 40 per week.

   a Draw the budget constraint under the old contract with no provision for overtime pay.
   b Draw the budget constraint with the overtime pay.
   c What is likely to happen to the number of hours that Quantity Bakery workers work under the new contract? Explain.

15 (Practice problem: applications) Assume that earnings below $20,000 are taxed at 15 percent. Any earnings above $20,000 incur a 28 percent tax rate. Lucinda Gamez, a private investigator, earns $800 per week, and she has 50 weeks per year available for work.

   a Draw her budget constraint if she pays no taxes.
   b Draw her budget constraint under the schedule de-

scribed above. How do progressive income taxes shape the budget constraint?

16 (Practice problem: applications) Harry Gold makes $5,000 by working 20 days each month as a plumber. His wage is $250 per day, and he can work as many as 30 days each month (except February, of course). The income tax rate for Harry is 20 percent. Also, he pays $1,000 monthly in property taxes on a very nice condo down by the river. His nonwage income is $4,000 per month. (Hint: Review the solutions to problems 15 and 16 of Chapter 8.)

   a What is Harry's net wage after taxes?
   b Draw his budget constraint.
   c The new government proposes eliminating the income tax and increasing property taxes. Harry figures that his property tax bill will rise to $2,000. Draw his budget constraint under the government's proposed tax changes.
   d Will Harry work more or less under the new tax plan? Why?
   e Is Harry better off under the new tax plan? Why or why not?

17 (Practice problem: applications) After 10 miserable years, Al and Norma Bennet are getting a divorce. They have agreed that Norma will retain custody of their two children. Al makes $50 per hour from his job as a marriage counsellor, and this is his only income. Although he could work as many as 40 hours, Al is only working 20 hours currently. The court has ruled that Al must pay $250 per week in child support regardless of his earnings. (Hint: Review the solutions to problems 15 and 16 of Chapter 8.)

   a Draw Al's (postdivorce) leisure-consumption budget constraint.
   b Many U.S. states (for example, Wisconsin and Michigan) have established fixed guidelines for child support payments. Suppose the guideline requires that noncustodial parents pay 25 percent of their income per child. Draw Al's budget line for this child care payment.
   c Under which plan will Al work more? Why?

Answers to Problems

2

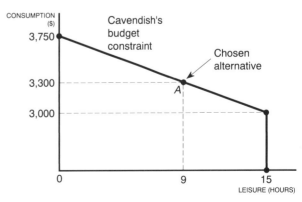

3

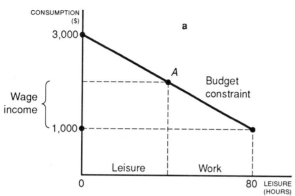

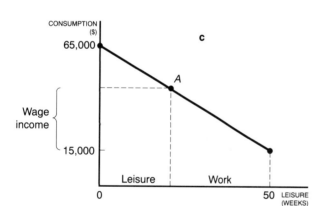

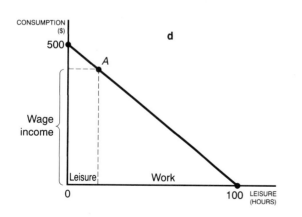

5

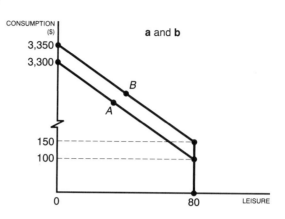

c Liza will make fewer cold calls; she will consume
   more leisure when her income increases, as
   shown by the movement from point A to point B.

6

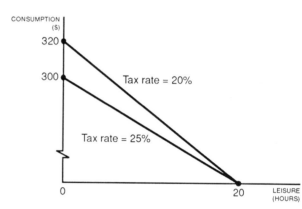

7

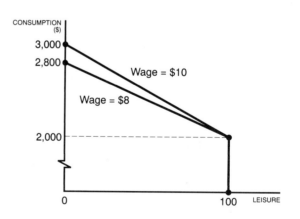

8

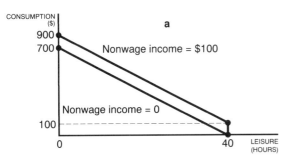

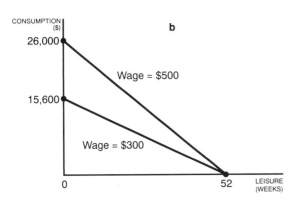

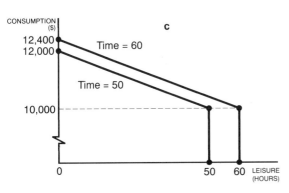

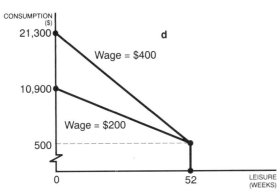

10

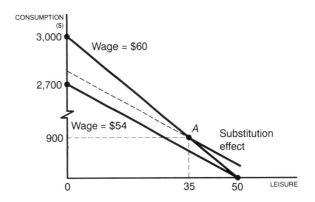

11

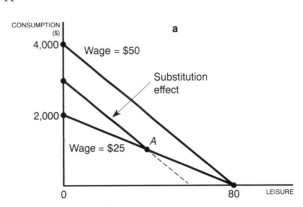

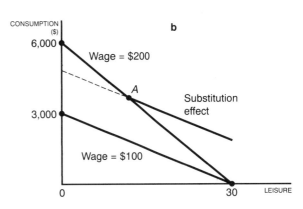

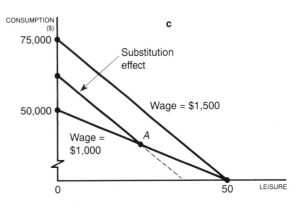

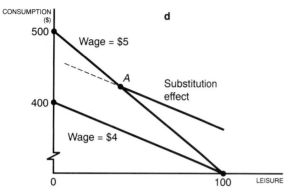

13

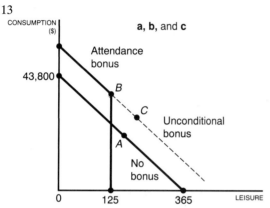

d An unconditional bonus of $100 simply shifts the budget constraint up in a parallel way, and so causes an income effect. The typical worker consumes more leisure at point C. The attendance bonus does not offer the points along the dashed budget constraint. Point B or another point involving even more work will be chosen. Clearly, there is a greater incentive to work with the attendance bonus.

14

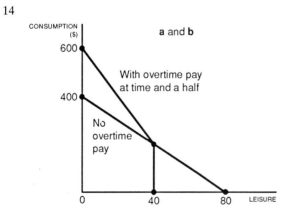

c All the new alternatives made possible by the overtime provision involve working more than 40 hours. Work time probably will increase.

15

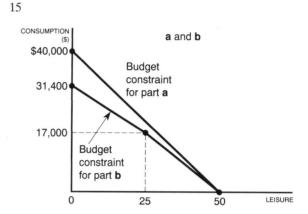

16 a $200/day.

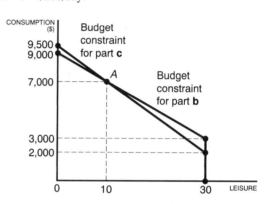

d He will work more because the tax change offers him new alternatives with more work. In effect it leaves him with the substitution effect of a wage increase; the income effect is cancelled by the property tax increase.

e He is better off because he can continue to choose point A, but he also has some new alternatives.

17

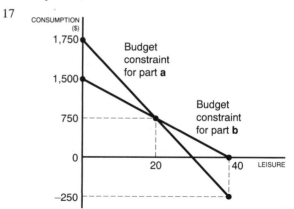

c Al will likely work more under the lump-sum child care requirement. The other system leaves him with the substitution effect of a wage decrease.

Chapter 12

THE FIRM'S COSTS

Chapter Review

With the labour supply decision in Chapter 11, one side of the competitive model, the household's, is complete. Business enterprises—firms—occupy the other side. This chapter begins the discussion of the role of firms in a market-based economy. We learn about the production function, which summarizes the relationship between the inputs that the firm demands (especially in the labour market) and the outputs that it supplies in the product market. Payments to purchase inputs make up most of the firm's costs, and this chapter treats these costs in depth. How the costs are balanced against revenues is the subject of Chapter 13.

ESSENTIAL CONCEPTS

1   In the basic competitive model, the firm's objective is to maximize its market value. Because the value of the firm depends on its profit-making potential, another way to put this is to say the firm's objective is to maximize its (long-term) profits. **Profits** equal revenues minus costs, and revenues are simply price times quantity.

2   The **production function** shows the relationship between inputs and outputs. The increase in output resulting from a small increase in the use of an input is called the **marginal product.** The **principle of diminishing returns** states that as more of one input is used, holding other inputs fixed, the marginal product declines. While diminishing returns represent the usual case, some production functions exhibit **increasing returns,** where the marginal product increases as more of an input is used. If doubling the input doubles the output, then there are **constant returns.** Inputs that do not change as output changes are called **fixed** or **overhead inputs**; inputs that do change with output are called **variable inputs.**

3   There are costs associated with each type of input: either **fixed costs,** which do not change when output changes, or **variable costs,** which do. The important concept to grasp is how the various measures of costs change as output changes. The **average cost** curve is typically U-shaped; the **marginal cost** curve lies below it when average cost falls, equals average cost at the minimum, and lies above it when average cost increases.

4   The **principle of substitution** says that as the price of an input increases, firms substitute other inputs. The

firm always chooses the least-cost production technique. In the long run, all inputs are variable; the firm has more choices. The **long-run average cost curve** is the lower boundary of all possible short-run average cost curves.

5   In the long run, there are **constant returns to scale** if output increases in the same proportion. If output increases by less, there are **decreasing returns to scale. Increasing returns to scale** imply that output increases by a greater proportion than do inputs. **Economies of scope** refer to the cost savings from producing several goods together rather than separately.

BEHIND THE ESSENTIAL CONCEPTS

1   Of the many diagrams in this chapter, there are four that you should particularly take care to master. Each is explained below. Notice how the economic idea (such as diminishing returns or increasing returns to scale) determines the shape of the curves.

   a   The first diagram to master is the production function (Figure 12.1, which is similar to Figure 12.4 in the text). The production function indicates how output (measured on the vertical axis) changes as the quantity of the variable input (measured on the horizontal axis) changes. There are two important facts to know. The first is that the shape indicates whether the production function has diminishing, constant, or increasing returns. Over the range of outputs for which the function in Figure 12.1 is drawn, there are diminishing returns. Also, the slope of the line from the origin to the curve is equal to the average product. The slope of the line drawn in Figure 12.1 therefore measures average product at L_0. Average product is actually at its highest at L_0; that is, the slope of this line is steeper than any other you can draw through the origin to any other point on the production function. If this is not obvious to you, you should try drawing

additional lines through the origin to other points on the function to demonstrate it to yourself.

   b   The total cost curves are shown in Figure 12.2 (which summarizes Table 12.5 A, B, and C of the text). Output is measured along the horizontal axis, and cost along the vertical one. Again, there are two important features to observe. First, total cost is the sum of fixed and variable costs. By definition, fixed costs do not change (otherwise they would not be fixed!). It follows that the variable cost curve and the total cost curve will be parallel to one another, since the difference between them is the total of the fixed costs. The second feature is that the total cost curve inherits its shape from the production function. This will be explored in the analysis part of this chapter.

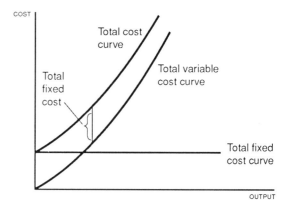

Figure 12.2

   c   Third, there is the average cost–marginal cost diagram, shown in Figure 12.3 (which duplicates Figure 12.6 in the text). The important concept here is the relationship between the marginal and average cost curves. The average cost curve is typically U-shaped. When marginal cost is below average cost, average cost is downward sloping. Marginal cost equals average cost at the minimum of average

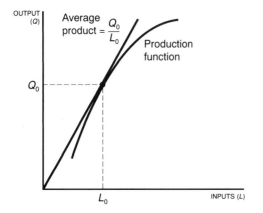

Figure 12.1

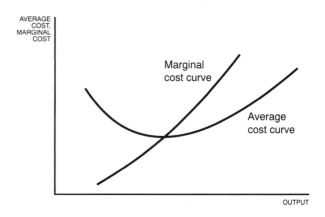

Figure 12.3

cost, and marginal cost is above average cost when average cost is upward sloping. Average cost falls as fixed costs are spread over more units. Average cost rises because diminishing returns drive the marginal cost curve above the average cost curve.

   d   Finally, there is the long-run average cost curve. For every production process, there are fixed inputs and an associated average cost curve. The long-run average cost curve is the lower boundary, as shown in Figure 12.4 (which duplicates Figure 12.14 in the text). The curve is drawn flat, which represents constant returns of scale.

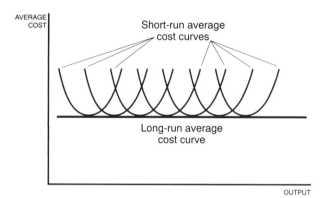

Figure 12.4

2   In reviewing these four diagrams, keep in mind three pointers.

   a   Remember to note what is measured along each axis. It's easy to make the mistake of memorizing the shapes of the curves while forgetting how to label the axes.

   b   Note the relationships among the curves, especially the marginal cost and average cost relationship.

   c   The shapes of the curves illustrate the economic properties. It's important to be able to recognize economic properties like diminishing returns and economies of scale in the diagrams of production functions and cost curves.

3   Diminishing returns refer to production processes in which some, but not all, inputs are variable. Diminishing returns imply that the marginal product decreases as more inputs are used. Economists add the words "to scale" when describing a production process in which all inputs are variable. Thus, decreasing returns to scale mean that as all inputs are increased in a certain proportion, output increases by less.

SELF-TEST

True or False

1   According to the basic competitive model, firms maximize the value of the firm.

2   The largest business sector of the Canadian economy is durable and nondurable manufacturing.

3   The marginal product is the last unit of output.

4   The principle of diminishing returns says that as more of one input is added, while other inputs remain unchanged, the marginal product of the added input diminishes.

5   With constant returns, if all inputs are increased by one-third, then output increases by one-third.

6   Costs associated with inputs that change as output changes are called variable costs.

7   Total costs are the sum of average and marginal costs.

8   If labour is the only variable input, then marginal cost equals the wage divided by the marginal product.

9   The average variable cost curve lies below the average total cost curve.

10   The marginal cost curve intersects the average cost curve at the minimum of the marginal cost curve.

11   If the price of an input rises, the firm will substitute other inputs to some extent, but its cost curves will still shift up.

12   Short-run average cost curves are typically U-shaped.

13   If there are economies of scale, the long-run average cost curve slopes downwards.

14   The level of output at which the average cost curve reaches its minimum depends on the relative sizes of fixed and variable costs.

15   Relatively larger fixed costs imply that the minimum average cost occurs at a relatively lower output level.

Multiple Choice

1   In the basic competitive model, a firm that charges more than the going price

   a   will lose some of its customers slowly over time.
   b   will lose all its customers.
   c   may keep its customers if its goods are of higher quality than those of its competitors.
   d   will lose no customers if its price equals its marginal cost.
   e   none of the above.

2   The dominant business sector in the Canadian economy is

   a   wholesale and retail trade.
   b   nondurable manufacturing.
   c   construction.
   d   agriculture.
   e   finance, real estate, and insurance.

3   According to the basic competitive model,

a managers of large corporations may sometimes behave in ways that do not maximize the firm's market value.

b firms maximize their short-run profits but ignore the long-run effects of current decisions.

c firms maximize their profits, considering both the long and short run.

d firms maximize their sales.

e none of the above.

4 The marginal product of an input is

a the cost of producing one more unit of output.

b the extra output that results from hiring one more unit of the input.

c the cost required to hire one more unit of the input.

d output divided by the number of inputs used in the production process.

e none of the above.

5 According to the principle of diminishing returns,

a as more of one input is added, the marginal product of the added input diminishes.

b as more of one input is added, holding other inputs unchanged, the marginal product of the added input diminishes.

c as more of the output is produced, the cost of production diminishes.

d as more of the output is produced, the marginal cost of production diminishes.

e none of the above.

6 If the production function exhibits increasing returns,

a the marginal product of input increases with the amount produced.

b the marginal cost increases with output.

c productivity is higher.

d the production function is downward sloping.

e none of the above.

7 If, when the total quantity of all inputs is doubled, output exactly doubles, the production function exhibits

a constant returns.

b diminishing returns.

c increasing returns.

d economies of scale.

e none of the above.

8 Fixed or overhead inputs are

a inputs that cannot be moved.

b inputs that can be purchased in only one fixed configuration.

c inputs that can be purchased at a fixed price.

d inputs that do not depend on the level of output.

e none of the above.

9 Fixed or overhead costs

a are the costs associated with only fixed inputs.

b are the costs that do not change with output, regardless of whether the associated inputs are fixed or variable.

c are the costs associated with only variable inputs.

d are the costs of building ceilings.

e none of the above.

10 The relationship between the marginal product of labour and the marginal cost of output is the following.

a Marginal cost is the inverse of marginal product.

b Marginal cost equals the wage divided by the marginal product.

c Marginal cost is downward sloping when marginal product is downward sloping.

d Marginal cost is constant, but marginal product is subject to diminishing returns.

e None of the above.

11 The principle of diminishing returns implies that

a marginal product diminishes as more of the input is hired.

b marginal cost falls with the level of output.

c productivity is higher in large firms.

d output is lower in large firms.

e none of the above.

12 Total cost equals

a the sum of fixed and variable costs.

b the product of fixed and variable costs.

c the ratio of fixed and variable costs.

d the sum of average costs and average variable costs.

e none of the above.

13 When the marginal cost curve is above the average cost curve,

a the average cost curve is at its minimum.

b the marginal cost curve is at its maximum.

c the marginal cost curve is downward sloping.

d the average cost curve is downward sloping.

e the average cost curve is upward sloping.

14 According to the principle of substitution,

a marginal cost equals average cost at the minimum of average costs.

b an increase in the price of an input will lead the firm to substitute other inputs.

c a decrease in the price of an input will lead the firm to substitute other inputs.

d if the firm does not know its marginal cost curve, it can substitute its average cost curve.

e none of the above.

15 The difference between the long run and the short run is

a that there are constant returns in the short run but not in the long run.

b that all inputs can be varied in the long run.

c three months.

d that average cost is decreasing in the short run but increasing in the long run.

e approximately 32 kilometres.

16 In the short run, the typical average cost curve is

  a upward sloping.
  b downward sloping.
  c U-shaped.
  d horizontal.
  e none of the above.

17 The long-run average cost curve is

  a the sum of the short-run average cost curves.
  b the lower boundary of the short-run average cost curves.
  c the upper boundary of the short-run average cost curves.
  d horizontal.
  e none of the above.

18 The long-run average cost curve

  a is unaffected by overhead costs.
  b may eventually slope up because of managerial problems.
  c always exhibits increasing returns to scale.
  d is always horizontal.
  e none of the above.

19 The concept of increasing returns to scale means that

  a it is more expensive to produce a variety of goods together than to produce them separately.
  b it is more expensive to produce a large quantity than a small quantity.
  c the average cost of production is lower when a larger quantity is produced.
  d the marginal cost curve is downward sloping.
  e none of the above.

20 The concept of economies of scope means that

  a it is less expensive to produce a variety of goods together than to produce them separately.
  b it is more expensive to produce a large quantity than a small quantity.
  c the average cost of production is lower when a larger quantity is produced.
  d the marginal cost curve is downward sloping.
  e none of the above.

Completion

1 The relationship between the inputs used in production and the level of output is called the _____.

2 The increase in output that results from using one more unit of an input is the _____.

3 The principle of _____ says that as more and more of one input is added, while other inputs remain unchanged, the marginal product of the added input diminishes.

4 Costs that do not depend upon output are called _____ or overhead costs.

5 The _____ is the extra cost of producing one more unit of output.

6 The marginal cost curve intersects the average cost curve at the _____ of the _____ cost curve.

7 If marginal costs are above average costs, then producing an additional unit will _____ the average.

8 An increase in the price of one input will lead a firm to substitute other inputs. This is a statement of the _____ of _____.

9 If the average cost is lower when the firm produces a larger quantity, then there are economies of _____.

10 If it is less expensive to produce a variety of goods together than to produce each good separately, then there are economies of _____.

Answers to Self-Test

True or False

1	t	4	t	7	f	10	f	13	t
2	t	5	t	8	t	11	t	14	t
3	f	6	t	9	t	12	t	15	f

Multiple Choice

1	b	6	a	11	a	16	c
2	e	7	a	12	a	17	b
3	c	8	d	13	e	18	b
4	b	9	a	14	b	19	c
5	b	10	b	15	b	20	a

Completion

1 production function
2 marginal product
3 diminishing returns
4 fixed
5 marginal cost
6 minimum, average
7 raise
8 principle of substitution
9 scale
10 scope

Doing Economics: Tools and Practice Problems

There is quite a bit of technical detail in this chapter, including production functions and a host of cost curves. First, we will explore the production function, calculating the marginal and average product and plotting the curves. It is important to understand how the shape of the production function exhibits diminishing, constant, or increasing returns. This is explained in Table 12.1. Next, we turn our attention to the cost curves; we calculate the various cost concepts and plot the curves. Again, it is important to understand the relationships between the curves and the economic meaning of the shapes of the curves.

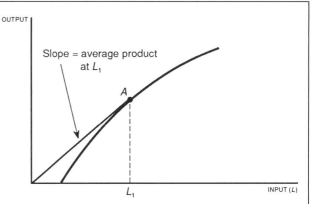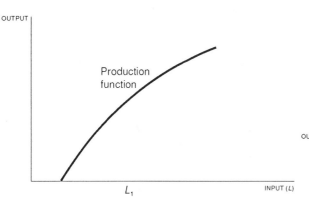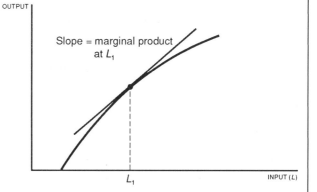

Tool Kit 12.1: Calculating Marginal
and Average Products

The production function summarizes the relationship between inputs and outputs. It is important to understand its relationship with the marginal and average products, which can be calculated from the information in the production function and also can be derived from the graph of the production function.

Step one: Identify and graph the production function.

Step two: Calculate the average product, which is output per unit of the input:

average product = output/input.

The average product is the slope of a line from the origin to the production function.

Step three: Calculate the marginal product, which is the extra output resulting from the use of one more unit of the input:

marginal product = change in output/change in input.

The marginal product equals the slope of the production function.

**Table 12.1
Production Function**

The marginal product is the slope of the production function:
marginal product = change in output/change in input.
The average product is the slope of a line from the origin to the production function:
average product = output/input.
If returns are diminishing,
the marginal product is decreasing.
the slope of the production function is becoming flatter.
If returns are constant,
the marginal product is constant.
the slope of the production function is constant.
If returns are increasing,
the marginal product is increasing.
the slope of the production function is becoming steeper.

1 (Worked problem: marginal and average products) Table 12.2 gives the production function for keyboards at Tek-Tek computer products.

Table 12.2

Number of workers	Output	Average product	Marginal product
1	80		
2	150		
3	210		
4	260		
5	300		

a Compute the average and marginal product, and fill in the table.
b Plot the production function. For each point, verify that the slope of the line from the origin to the

production function equals the average product.

   c Between each two adjacent points on the production function, verify that the slope equals the marginal product.

   d Does the production function exhibit diminishing, constant, or increasing returns?

Step-by-step solution

Step one (a): Identify and graph the production function. This is given in Table 2.2.

Step two: Calculate and graph the average product. The average product is output divided by the number of workers. If output is 80, the average product is 80/1 = 80. Enter this number. If output is 150, the average product is 150/2 = 75. Complete the average product column. The result is given in Table 12.3.

Table 12.3

Number of workers	Output	Average product	Marginal product
1	80	80	80
2	150	75	70
3	210	70	60
4	260	65	50
5	300	60	40

Step three: Calculate the marginal product. The marginal product is the extra output resulting from using one more input. The marginal product of the first worker is 80. Enter this number. When the second worker is used, output rises to 150. The marginal product of this worker is 150 − 80 = 70. Enter this number. Complete the marginal product column. Table 12.3 gives the result.

Step four (b): Plot the production function.

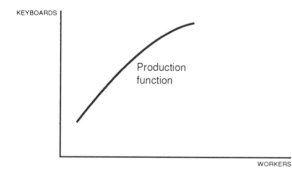

Step five: Choose a point on the production function, and verify that the slope of a line from the origin to that point is equal to the average product. Choose the point labelled *A*, where output is 210 and the number of workers is 3. Draw a line from the origin to point *A*. The slope is rise/run = 210/3 = 70, which is the average product.

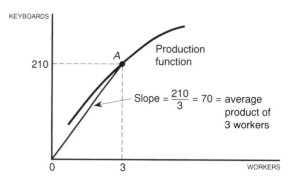

Step six (c): Verify that the slope of the production function is the marginal product. The slope of the production function between points *A* and *B*, where output is 300 and the number of workers is 5, is (300 − 260)/(5 − 4) = 40, which is the marginal product of the fourth worker.

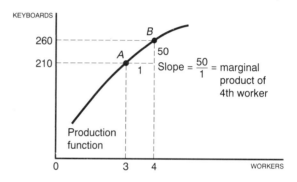

Step seven (d): The marginal product is decreasing; this indicates diminishing returns.

2 (Practice problem: marginal and average products) Table 12.4 gives the production function for the insect spray Nobeetle at Bugout Pesticide Company.

Table 12.4

Number of workers	Output	Average product	Marginal product
1	1,200		
2	2,200		
3	3,000		
4	3,600		
5	4,000		

   a Compute the average and marginal products, and fill in the table.

   b Plot the production function. For each point, verify that the slope of the line from the origin to the production function equals the average product.

   c Between each two adjacent points on the production function, verify that the slope equals the marginal product.

   d Does the production function exhibit diminishing, constant, or increasing returns?

Tool Kit 12.2: Calculating and Graphing Cost Measures

Ther are two sets of cost curves: the total curves (total cost, fixed cost, and variable cost) and the average-marginal curves (average cost, marginal cost). It is important to be able to calculate each of the cost concepts and also to recognize their relationships on the graphs.

Step one: Identify and graph the total cost curve.

Step two: Calculate and graph the variable cost curve:

variable cost = total cost − fixed cost

The variable cost curve is parallel to the total cost curve and lies below it by the amount of fixed costs.

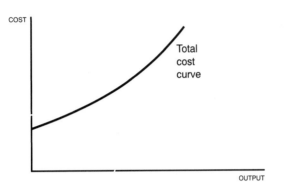

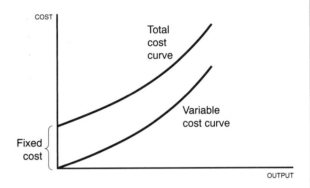

Step three: Calculate and graph the average cost curve: average cost = total cost/output.

Average cost equals the slope of a line from the origin to the total cost curve.

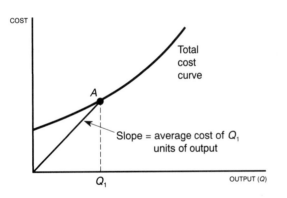

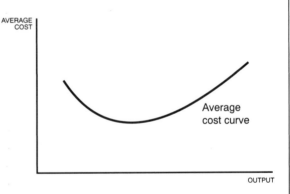

Step four: Calculate and graph the marginal cost curve: marginal cost = change in cost/change in output.

Marginal cost is the slope of the total cost curve.

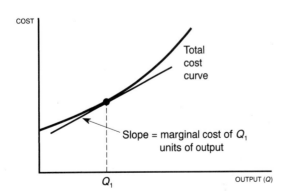

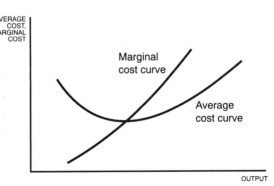

Table 12.5 summarizes the key information about cost curves.

Table 12.5
Cost Curves

Variable cost is parallel to the total cost curve, and below it by the amount of fixed cost:

variable cost = total cost − fixed cost.

Marginal cost is the slope of the total cost curve:

marginal cost = change in total cost/change in output.

Average cost is the slope of the line from the origin to the total cost curve:

average cost = total cost/output.

If returns are diminishing,
  the marginal cost is increasing.
  the slope of the total cost curve is becoming steeper.
If returns are constant,
  the marginal cost is constant.
  the slope of the total cost curve is constant.
If returns are increasing,
  the marginal cost is decreasing.
  the slope of the total cost curve is becoming flatter.
If marginal cost is below average cost,
  the average cost curve is decreasing.
If marginal cost equals average cost,
  the average cost curve is at its minimum.
If marginal cost is above average cost,
  the average cost curve is increasing.

3 (Practice problem: marginal and average products) For the following production functions, answer parts a through d in problem 2.

a Bedford Waterbeds

Number of workers	Output	Average product	Marginal product
1	24		
2	42		
3	57		
4	68		
5	75		

b Worry-Free Insurance

Number of sellers	Policies	Average product	Marginal product
10	200		
20	500		
30	700		
40	800		
50	850		

4 (Worked problem: cost curves) The total fixed costs at Stay-Brite Cleaning Company are $100,000. Table 12.6 gives their total costs for different levels of output measured in truckloads of Stay-Brite Cleaning Solution.

Table 12.6

Output	Total cost	Variable cost	Average cost	Marginal cost
1,000	$180,000			
2,000	$280,000			
3,000	$420,000			
4,000	$600,000			
5,000	$800,000			

a Compute variable, average, and marginal cost, and enter in the table.
b Plot the total cost and variable cost curves on one diagram, and verify the relationships given in Table 12.5.
c Plot the average cost and marginal cost curves, and verify the marginal-average relationship.
d Do the cost curves exhibit increasing, constant, or diminishing returns.

Step-by-step solution

Step one(a): Identify and graph the total cost curve.

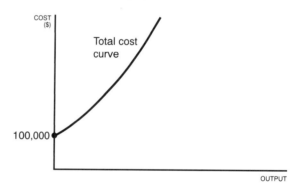

Step two: Calculate and graph the variable cost curve. Variable cost is just the difference between total cost and total fixed cost. The variable cost of 1,000 units is $180,000 − $100,000 = $80,000. Enter this number. Complete the variable cost column.

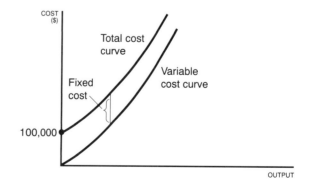

Step three: Calculate and graph the average cost curve. Average cost is total cost divided by output. The average cost of 1,000 units is $180,000/1,000 = $180. Enter this number. Complete the average cost column.

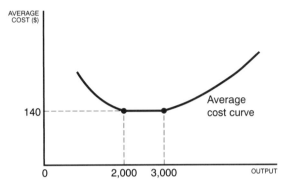

Step four: Calculate and graph the marginal cost curve. Marginal cost is the extra cost of producing one more unit. The marginal cost per unit for the first 1,000 units is $80,000/1,000 = $80. Enter this number, and continue to fill in the column. The complete information appears in Table 12.7.

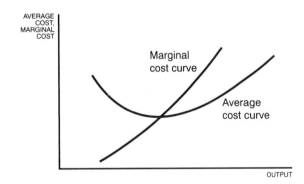

Table 12.7

Output	Total cost	Variable cost	Average cost	Marginal cost
1,000	$180,000	$ 80,000	$180	$ 80
2,000	$280,000	$180,000	$140	$100
3,000	$420,000	$320,000	$140	$140
4,000	$600,000	$500,000	$150	$180
5,000	$800,000	$700,000	$160	$200

Step five (b): Choose a point on the total cost curve, and verify the relationships.

Variable cost is parallel to total cost. For example, between *A* and *B*, the slope of the total cost curve is ($600,000 − $420,000)/(4,000 − 3,000) = 180. The slope of the variable cost curve for the same levels of output is ($500,000 − $320,000)/(4,000 − 3,000) = 180.

The variable cost curve lies below the total cost curve by the amount of the fixed cost. The difference all along the curves is $100,000, which is the fixed cost.

The slope of the total cost curve equals the marginal cost.

Between *A* and *B*, the slope is 180, which is the marginal cost at 4,000 workers.

The slope of a line from the origin to the total cost curve equals average cost. Between the origin and point *A*, the slope of the line is $420,000/3,000 = 140, which is the average cost.

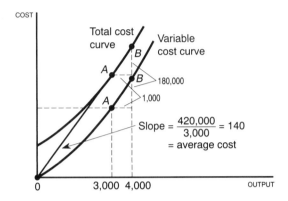

Step six (c): Plot the average and marginal cost curves, and verify the average-marginal relationship. As you can see, marginal cost is below average cost at *A*, where average cost is falling; they are equal at *B*, which is the minimum of average cost; and marginal cost is above average cost at *C*, where average cost is rising.

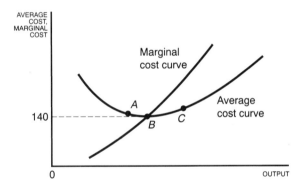

Step seven: The cost curves exhibit diminishing returns. Marginal cost is increasing, and total cost is becoming steeper.

5 (Practice problem: cost curves). The fixed costs at Pestle Mortar Company are $50,000. Table 12.8 gives their costs for different levels of output measured in mortars.

Table 12.8

Output	Total cost	Variable cost	Average cost	Marginal cost
1,000	$ 250,000			
2,000	$ 500,000			
3,000	$ 800,000			
4,000	$1,200,000			
5,000	$1,800,000			

a Compute variable, average, and marginal costs, and enter in the table.

b Plot the total cost and variable cost curves on one diagram, and verify the relationships given in Table 12.5.

c Plot the average cost and marginal cost curves, and verify the marginal-average relationship.

d Do the cost curves exhibit increasing, constant, or diminishing returns?

6 (Practice problem: cost curves) For the following cost data, answer parts a through d in question 5.

a Fixed costs are $1,000.

Output	Total cost	Variable cost	Average cost	Marginal cost
10	$1,500			
20	$2,200			
30	$3,000			
40	$4,000			
50	$6,000			

b Fixed costs are $0.

Output	Total cost	Variable cost	Average cost	Marginal cost
100	$1,000			
200	$1,800			
300	$2,400			
400	$2,800			
500	$3,200			
600	$3,600			

c Fixed costs are $80,000.

Output	Total cost	Variable cost	Average cost	Marginal cost
1	$140,000			
2	$180,000			
3	$220,000			
4	$260,000			
5	$300,000			
6	$340,000			

Answers to Problems

2 *a* The average and marginal products are given in Table 12.9.

Table 12.9

Number of workers	Output	Average product	Marginal product
1	1,200	1,200	1,200
2	2,200	1,100	1,000
3	3,000	1,000	800
4	3,600	900	600
5	4,000	800	400

b The production function is drawn in the figure. The average product for 3 workers, which is 1,000, is

shown as the slope of the line from the origin to point *B*.

c The marginal product of the fourth worker, which is 600, is shown as the slope between points *B* and *C*.

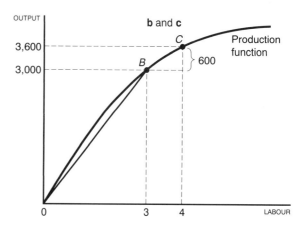

d The production function exhibits diminishing returns.

3 *a* Bedford Waterbeds—diminishing returns

Number of workers	Output	Average product	Marginal product
1	24	24	24
2	42	21	18
3	57	19	15
4	68	17	11
5	75	15	7

b Worry-Free Insurance—diminishing returns

Number of workers	Policies	Average product	Marginal product
10	200	20.0	20
20	500	25.0	30
30	700	23.3	20
40	800	20.0	10
50	850	17.0	5

5 *a* The completed table is given in Table 12.10.

Table 12.10

Output	Total cost	Variable cost	Average cost	Marginal cost
1,000	$ 250,000	$ 200,000	$250	$200
2,000	$ 500,000	$ 450,000	$250	$250
3,000	$ 800,000	$ 750,000	$267	$300
4,000	$1,200,000	$1,150,000	$300	$400
5,000	$1,800,000	$1,750,000	$360	$600

b The diagram shows the total cost and variable cost curves. The variable cost curve is parallel to the total cost curve and lies below it by $50,000, which is the amount of fixed cost.

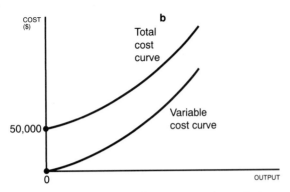

c   The diagram shows the average and marginal cost curves. Average and marginal costs are equal at $250, which is the minimum of the average cost curve. Average cost rises after this point, while marginal cost hovers above.

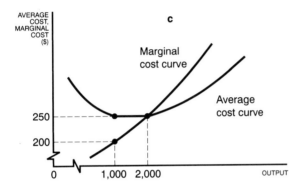

d   The cost curves exhibit diminishing returns.

6   The completed cost tables appear below.

a   These cost curves show diminishing returns.

Output	Total cost	Variable cost	Average cost	Marginal cost
10	$1,500	$ 500	$150	$ 50
20	$2,200	$1,200	$110	$ 70
30	$3,000	$2,000	$100	$ 80
40	$4,000	$3,000	$100	$100
50	$6,000	$5,000	$120	$200

b   These cost curves show increasing returns.

Output	Total cost	Variable cost	Average cost	Marginal cost
100	$1,000	$1,000	$10.00	$10
200	$1,800	$1,800	$ 9.00	$ 8
300	$2,400	$2,400	$ 8.00	$ 6
400	$2,800	$2,800	$ 7.00	$ 4
500	$3,200	$3,200	$ 6.50	$ 4
600	$3,600	$3,600	$ 6.00	$ 4

c   These cost curves show increasing returns until output equals 2, and constant returns thereafter.

Output	Total cost	Variable cost	Average cost	Marginal cost
1	$140,000	$ 60,000	$140,000	$60,000
2	$180,000	$100,000	$ 90,000	$40,000
3	$220,000	$140,000	$ 73,333	$40,000
4	$260,000	$180,000	$ 65,000	$40,000
5	$300,000	$220,000	$ 60,000	$40,000
6	$340,000	$260,000	$ 56,667	$40,000

Chapter 13

THE FIRM'S PRODUCTION DECISION

Chapter Review

This chapter moves the discussion from the firm's costs to decisions firms must make regarding production. In the process, it shows the role of the firm in the competitive model. The firm is a supplier in product markets and a demander in input markets, especially in labour markets. The chapter also explains why and when new firms will enter an industry and why and when existing firms will shut down. Each of these issues requires carefully distinguishing opportunity costs from sunk costs, and profits from rents. This close examination of the firm's production decision completes the discussion of all the individual parts of the basic competitive model that began in Chapter 8. What remains is to put them together and evaluate how the model works. This is done in Chapter 14.

ESSENTIAL CONCEPTS

1   Firms choose output to **maximize profits.** Profit is the difference between total revenue and total costs. The output decision can be illustrated in two ways. One way, shown in Figure 13.1A, is to draw the total revenue and total cost curves and find the quantity where the total revenue curve is above the total cost curve by the greatest amount. At this point, the curves are parallel and their slopes are equal. The second way, shown in panel B, uses the marginal revenue curve. The slope of the total revenue curve is marginal revenue, which for the competitive firm equals the price of its product. The slope of the total cost curve is marginal cost. Therefore, at this point, marginal revenue (price) equals marginal cost, and profit maximization can be shown by the intersection of these two curves.

2   If the market price for a good or service exceeds the minimum average cost, then it pays new firms to enter the market. In deciding whether to *exit* the market, however, a firm must pay attention to those costs it cannot recover. Costs that the firm must pay whether or not it leaves the market are called *sunk costs.* The firm should stay in the market whenever it can earn revenues greater than all the costs not sunk. If all the fixed costs are nonrecoverable sunk costs, then the firm will exit when price falls below the minimum of the average variable cost curve.

3   The *supply curve of the firm* is the marginal cost curve

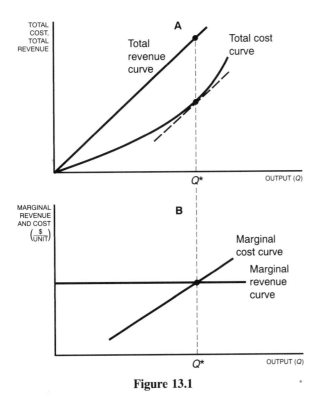

Figure 13.1

above the minimum price needed to keep the firm from exiting. The *market supply curve* is the sum of the quantities supplied by all firms in the market, and it takes into account both the adjustments made by existing firms and the new entrants attracted to the market as the price rises. This curve is more elastic in the long run than in the short run, because existing firms have time to adjust to the lowest-cost production techniques and new firms have time to enter the market and produce.

4   The firm's demand for inputs follows from its decision about how much to produce. More formally, the demand for an input is the **value of its marginal product (vmp),** which equals its marginal product (how much extra output the marginal input produces) times the product price (how much revenue the firm receives in selling the output). Again, the market demand is just the sum of the quantities demanded by all firms in the market. Because labour is by far the most important input in production, it is used as the main example of an input in the text. Nevertheless, the demand for any input is the value of its marginal product.

BEHIND THE ESSENTIAL CONCEPTS

1   It is important that cost include all opportunity costs of production borne by the firm. Not only are such explicit costs as wages, energy, raw materials, and in-

terest included, but also more subtle *opportunity costs* are taken into account, such as the value of the entrepreneur's time or the alternative earnings on the equity invested by the owners of the firm. These are considered opportunity costs because if the firm did not produce, the entrepreneur would devote time to some other activity, and the owners would take their investment capital elsewhere.

When a firm is making zero *economic* profits, its revenues are sufficient to cover all costs, including normal returns on the invested financial capital. An economist would say that the firm is making just enough to compensate the owners for the opportunity cost of putting their money into the firm. An accountant would view the situation differently, saying that a firm earning normal returns was actually making positive accounting profits.

2   Another difference between the way economists and accountants view profits concerns rent. **Rent** is the return to anything that is supplied inelastically. For example, suppose a firm's superior location enables it to earn 50 percent more than its competitors. An accountant would say that this firm's profits are 50 percent higher. An economist would call this extra return a rent, because the firm's earnings are higher than the minimum necessary to induce it to stay in its location. Although land is a good example, the concept of rent applies to any payment to a factor of production above the minimum necessary to bring the factor on to the market.

3   Sunk costs, overhead costs, and fixed costs are related to, but distinct from, each other. *Sunk costs* cannot be recovered no matter what the firm does. The firm can shut down production, sell off all its assets, and even go out of business, but it cannot recover its sunk costs. *Fixed costs* do not change as output changes, but they may be recoverable if the firm exits the industry. For example, the firm may own a plant, and the alternative earnings (the opportunity cost) of its plant do not depend on whether the firm produces a little or a great deal of output. If the firm can sell the factory when it exits the industry, then the costs of the plant are fixed but not sunk. Finally, a special type of fixed costs, also called **overhead costs,** are the costs necessary to start a business. Often overhead costs are also sunk costs, but not always. For example, to operate a taxi in New York City, the driver must buy a licence. This represents an overhead cost because the licence must be purchased to start the business, but it is not sunk, because the licence can be sold.

4   There is only one way to maximize profits. If the firm produces goods for the least cost and sets price equal to marginal cost, then it must set the input price equal to the value of the marginal product of that input. Thus, the profit-maximizing demand for labour is just the other side of the coin of the profit-maximizing supply of output. This fact is illustrated in Figure 13.2, where in panel A the firm sets the product price equal

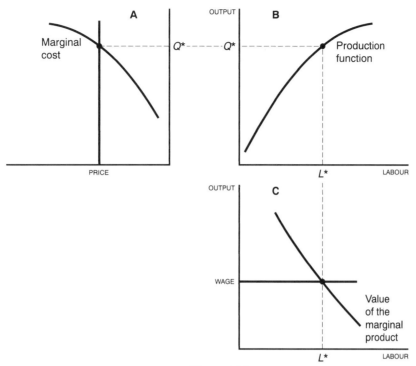

Figure 13.2

to marginal cost and produces Q^* units of output. (Note that this is the usual diagram turned on its side.) The production function, drawn in panel B, shows that this level of output requires L^* hours of labour. Finally, panel C shows that when the firm sets the wage equal to the value of the marginal product of labour, it chooses exactly L^* hours of labour.

5 The competitive firm has four basic decisions to make: when to enter, when to exit, how much to produce, and how many inputs to hire. Table 13.1 summarizes the decision rules.

Table 13.1

Entry	Enter when price > minimum average cost.
Exit	Exit when revenues < nonrecoverable costs.
Supply	Produce the quantity of output for which price equals marginal cost.
Demand	Hire the quantity of inputs for which the input price equals the value of the marginal product.

SELF-TEST

True or False

1 The firm is choosing the profit-maximizing level of output when price equals marginal cost.

2 The firm is choosing the profit-maximizing level of any input when the input price equals the value of the marginal product.

3 The value of the marginal product equals the marginal product divided by the wage.

4 In the competitive model, marginal revenue is less than price because increasing output leads to a fall in price.

5 All fixed costs are sunk, but not all sunk costs are fixed.

6 Accounting profits are always less than economic profits.

7 In the long run in a competitive industry, economic profits are zero for any potential entrant.

8 Firms exit the industry when price falls below the minimum of the average cost.

9 A firm will enter an industry if the price is above the minimum of the average variable cost curve.

10 Economic rent is any payment to an input in excess of that needed to keep the input in its current use.

11 Land is the only input that can earn economic rent.

12 The long-run supply is more elastic than the short-run supply for the industry but not for the individual firm.

13 The long-run supply curve is the sum of the supply curves of individual firms, including those that enter at high prices.

14 Even if a firm's supply curve is upward sloping in the short run, it may be perfectly elastic in the long run.

15 Correctly measured, total cost should include all opportunity costs of operating.

Multiple Choice

1 Marginal revenue

   a is less than price for the competitive firm because as it sells more output, it must lower the price.
   b equals price for the competitive firm.
   c is the revenue that the firm receives for selling its output.
   d is the extra profit that the firm receives from selling another unit of output, after accounting for all opportunity costs.
   e none of the above.

2 The firm supplies the profit-maximizing level of output when

   a marginal revenue equals price.
   b marginal revenue equals marginal cost.
   c economic profits are zero.
   d accounting profits are zero.
   e sunk costs equal fixed costs.

3 The extra cost of producing an additional unit of output is called

   a marginal cost.
   b fixed cost.
   c overhead cost.
   d sunk cost.
   e marginal revenue.

4 It pays a firm to enter a market whenever

   a the market price is greater than the minimum average cost at which the firm can produce.
   b the firm can earn revenues greater than any non-recoverable costs.
   c price is greater than the minimum of the average variable cost curve.
   d price equals marginal cost.
   e marginal revenue equals marginal cost.

5 The firm should exit the market whenever

   a it cannot earn revenues equal to at least its non-recoverable costs.
   b price is less than marginal cost.
   c price is less than the minimum of the average cost curve.
   d price is less than the minimum of the average variable cost curve.
   e none of the above.

6 Sunk costs are

   a costs that do not change when output changes.
   b the costs of starting the business.
   c nonrecoverable costs.
   d variable costs.
   e opportunity costs.

7 Which of the following is true?

   a Accounting costs are always greater than economic costs.
   b Economic costs are always greater than accounting costs.
   c Accounting profits are always greater than economic profits.
   d Economic profits are always greater than accounting profits.
   e None of the above.

8 Which of the following is not part of the firm's economic costs?

   a the opportunity cost of the time of the entrepreneur
   b the revenue that could be earned in alternative uses by the assets that the firm owns
   c the return on the equity invested in the firm by the owners
   d depreciation on company-owned buildings and machinery
   e none of the above

9 The long-run supply curve for the industry is

   a perfectly elastic.
   b more elastic than the short-run supply curve.
   c less elastic than the short-run supply curve.
   d the lower boundary of the short-run supply curve.
   e the sum of the short-run supply curves.

10 Economic rent refers to

   a economic profit minus sunk cost.
   b any payment to an input above the minimum needed to keep the input in its present use.
   c payments from tenants to landlords.
   d the wages of especially skilled labour.
   e revenues received by efficient firms.

11 In the basic competitive model, profits are driven to zero. This means that

   a revenues are just enough to cover all non-recoverable costs.
   b revenues are just enough to cover all costs, including the opportunity cost of invested financial capital.
   c price equals the minimum of the average variable cost curve.
   d accounting profits are equal to zero.
   e none of the above.

12 When price is greater than the minimum of the average variable cost curve, the firm

   a enters the market.
   b exits the market.
   c may continue or exit the market depending upon the magnitude of sunk costs.
   d shuts down production but does not exit.
   e enters the market only if overhead costs are zero.

13 The market supply curve

    a is the sum of the quantities of the supply curves of all the firms.

    b is less elastic than the supply curves of all the firms.

    c is the marginal cost curve of the last firm to enter the market.

    d is always horizontal.

    e none of the above.

14 The value to the firm of hiring one more worker is

    a equal to marginal cost.

    b equal to marginal revenue.

    c equal to the marginal product of labour.

    d equal to the marginal product of labour multiplied by the product price.

    e equal to the marginal product of labour multiplied by the wage.

15 The value of the marginal product is

    a the revenue that the firm receives for the last unit of output.

    b the revenue that the firm receives for entering the market.

    c the marginal product multiplied by the wage.

    d the marginal product multiplied by the product price.

    e none of the above.

16 The market demand for labour equals

    a the market supply of output.

    b the sum of the demands for labour of all the firms.

    c the wage.

    d the marginal product of labour.

    e none of the above.

17 If all of a firm's fixed costs are sunk, then it shuts down when

    a price is less than marginal cost.

    b price is less than the minimum of the average cost curve.

    c price is less than the minimum of the average variable cost curve.

    d accounting profits fall below zero.

    e economic profits fall below zero.

18 When renewable and nonrenewable resources are common property,

    a they will be excessively used.

    b they will be underused.

    c they will be optimally used.

    d they will not be used at all.

    e they will be used by everyone.

19 If a firm with a U-shaped short-run average cost curve doubles its output by doubling the number of plants and keeps its average cost the same, then the long-run supply is

    a perfectly elastic.

    b perfectly inelastic.

    c upward sloping.

    d downward sloping.

    e none of the above.

20 The real product wage is equal to

    a the value of the marginal product of labour.

    b the marginal cost.

    c the product price.

    d the wage divided by the marginal product of labour.

    e the wage divided by the product price.

Completion

1 The extra revenue that a firm receives for selling another unit of output is the _____.

2 In the basic competitive model, the marginal revenue equals the _____.

3 The extra cost that the firm bears for producing another unit of output is the _____.

4 The level of output that maximizes profits is found by setting _____ equal to _____.

5 The supply curve of the competitive firm is the same as the _____ curve when price is high enough to keep the firm in the market.

6 Costs that are not recoverable are called _____ costs.

7 Economic profits equal revenues received in excess of all _____ costs of operating the firm.

8 The demand for inputs is the _____ of the _____.

9 New firms enter the industry whenever price is greater than the minimum of the _____ curve.

10 The value of the marginal product is found by multiplying the _____ by the _____.

Answers to Self-Test

True or False

1	t	4	f	7	t	10	t	13	t
2	t	5	f	8	f	11	f	14	t
3	f	6	f	9	f	12	f	15	t

Multiple Choice

1	b	6	c	11	b	16	b
2	b	7	e	12	c	17	c
3	a	8	e	13	a	18	a
4	a	9	b	14	d	19	a
5	a	10	b	15	d	20	e

Completion

1 marginal revenue
2 price
3 marginal cost
4 price, marginal cost
5 marginal cost

6   sunk
7   unrecoverable
8   value, marginal product
9   average cost
10 marginal product, product price

Doing Economics: Tools and Practice Problems

The firm's decision of how much output to supply requires marginal benefit and marginal cost reasoning. So does the firm's demand for labour or any other input. In this section, we will do problems involving the profit-maximizing quantity of output and corresponding quantities of inputs. Next, we will investigate the entry and exit decisions, reviewing opportunity and sunk costs. A good understanding of costs allows us to derive the entire supply curve of output. Finally, we will tackle a capstone problem that integrates the production function, cost curves, entry decision, exit decision, supply curve, and demand curve for the competitive firm.

Tool Kit 13.1: Finding the Quantity of Output to Supply

The quantity of output that maximizes the firm's profits is found by setting marginal revenue equal to marginal cost. When the firm is a price taker, the marginal revenue equals the product price. The rule is then to find the quantity for which price equals marginal cost.

Step one: Calculate the marginal cost for each unit of output.

Step two: Identify the market price.

Step three: Find the greatest level of output for which price equals marginal cost. This is the quantity supplied.

---

1   (Worked problem: quantity supplied) Barbara's Carpet Cleaners has fixed costs of $100 per month and a total cost curve as given in Table 13.2. Output is the number of carpets cleaned.

Table 13.2

Output	Total cost
10	$ 200
20	$ 320
30	$ 460
40	$ 620
50	$ 800
60	$1,000

a   The current price for cleaning a carpet is $18. How many carpets must be cleaned to maximize

profits? What will the profit be?

b   Suppose that the price falls to $14. Calculate the profit-maximizing output and the total profits.

Step-by-step solution

Step one (a): Marginal cost is the extra cost of cleaning another carpet. When output is increased from 0 to 10, total costs increase by $200 – $100 = $100; therefore, the marginal cost is $100/10 = $10. Derive the marginal cost curve shown in Table 13.3.

Table 13.3

Output	Total cost	Marginal cost
10	$ 200	10
20	$ 320	12
30	$ 460	14
40	$ 620	16
50	$ 800	18
60	$1,000	20

Step two: Identify the market price. It is $18.

Step three: Find the greatest level of output for which price equals marginal cost. The $18 price equals marginal cost when output is 50.

Step four: Calculate profits. Profits equal revenues minus costs. Revenues equal $900 (50 × $18); profits equal $900 – $800 = $100. So the firm makes profits equal to $100.

Step five (b): If the price falls to $14, then price equals marginal cost at 30 units. Profits = (30 × $14) – $460 = –$40, and the firm loses $40.

2   (Practice problem: quantity supplied) The fixed cost for Martin Block, Inc., is $10,000. The company's cost curve is given in Table 13.4.

Table 13.4

Output	Total cost	Marginal cost
10,000	$21,000	
20,000	$32,100	
30,000	$43,300	
40,000	$54,600	
50,000	$66,000	
60,000	$77,500	

a   The current price for blocks is $1.12. Find the profit-maximizing quantity of blocks to produce. What will the profit be?

b   Suppose that the price rises to $1.15. Calculate the profit-maximizing output and the total profits.

3   (Practice problem: quantity supplied) For each of the following, find the profit-maximizing output level, and calculate total profits.

a   Fixed costs = $40,000; price = $600.

Output	Total cost	Marginal cost
100	$ 80,000	
200	$120,000	
300	$170,000	
400	$230,000	
500	$300,000	
600	$380,000	
700	$470,000	

b Fixed costs = $900; price = $3.00.

Output	Total cost	Marginal cost
1,000	$ 1,900	
2,000	$ 2,900	
3,000	$ 4,600	
4,000	$ 6,600	
5,000	$ 9,400	
6,000	$12,400	
7,000	$16,000	
8,000	$20,000	

c Fixed costs = $0; price = $80.

Output	Total cost	Marginal cost
1	$ 40	
2	$ 90	
3	$150	
4	$210	
5	$280	
6	$360	
7	$450	
8	$550	

Tool Kit 13.2: Finding the Quantity of an Input to Demand

Profits are always maximized by setting marginal revenue equal to marginal cost. When the firm is a price taker in both product and input markets, the marginal revenue from hiring another input is the value of the marginal product, which is the marginal product of that input multiplied by the product price. The marginal cost of hiring another input is the input price. In the case of labour, the input price is the wage.

Step one: Calculate the marginal product for each level of the input.

Step two: Identify the product price.

Step three: Compute the value of the marginal product by multiplying the marginal product by the product price for each level of the input:

value of the marginal product = marginal product × product price.

Step four: Identify the input price. (In the case of labour, this is the wage.)

Step five: Find the level of the input for which the value of the marginal product equals the input price. This is the quantity demanded.

---

4 (Worked problem: quantity demanded) The new company The Hair Cuttery is ready to start hiring. The price of haircuts is $8, and the production function is given in Table 13.5.

Table 13.5

Stylists	Haircuts per day	Marginal product	Value of the marginal product
1	8		
2	16		
3	23		
4	29		
5	34		
6	38		

a The wage paid to hair stylists is $40 per day. Find the profit-maximizing number of hair stylists to hire.
b Suppose that the wage rises to $64 per day. Find the number of hair stylists that maximizes profits.

Step-by-step solution

Step one (a): The marginal product is the extra output that results from hiring one more input. When the first hair stylist is hired, output rises from 0 to 8. The marginal product is 8. Enter this number. When the second hair stylist is hired, output rises from 8 to 16. The marginal product is 16 − 8 = 8; enter this number and continue. The marginal product column is given in Table 13.6.

Table 13.6

Stylists	Haircuts per day	Marginal product	Value of the marginal product
1	8	8	
2	16	8	
3	23	7	
4	29	6	
5	34	5	
6	38	4	

Step two: The product price is $8.

Step three: The value of the marginal product equals the product price multiplied by the marginal product. The value of the marginal product of the first worker is 8 × $8 = $64. Continue to enter the results in the appropriate column. The completed information is given in Table 13.7.

Table 13.7

Stylists	Haircuts per day	Marginal product	Value of the marginal product
1	8	8	$64
2	16	8	$64
3	23	7	$56
4	29	6	$48
5	34	5	$40
6	38	4	$32

Step four: The wage is $40 per day.

Step five: Profits are maximized when the wage is set equal to the value of the marginal product. The wage is $40, which equals the value of the marginal product when 5 hair stylists are hired.

Step six (b): When the wage is $64, it equals the value of the marginal product if 2 stylists are hired.

5 (Practice problem: quantity demanded) Moe's Lawn Service mows lawns for $20 each. Moe's production function is given in Table 13.8. Output is measured as the number of lawns mowed.

Table 13.8

Workers	Output per day	Marginal product	Value of the marginal product
1	5.0		
2	9.0		
3	13.0		
4	16.5		
5	19.5		
6	22.0		
7	24.0		

Moe pays his lawn mowers $40 per day.

a Find the profit-maximizing number of mowers to hire.
b Suppose that the wage rises to $70 per day. Find the profit-maximizing number of mowers to hire.

6 (Practice problem: quantity demanded) For each of the following, complete the table and find the profit-maximizing number of inputs.

a Product price = $10; wage = $100 per day

Workers	Output per day	Marginal product	Value of the marginal product
10	200		
30	360		
30	500		
40	620		
50	720		
60	800		

b Product price = $10,000; wage = $10,000 per month.

Workers	Output per month	Marginal product	Value of the marginal product
10	20		
20	40		
30	55		
40	65		
50	70		
60	70		

c Product price = $5; input price = $40.

Workers	Output	Marginal product	Value of the marginal product
1,000	10,000		
2,000	18,000		
3,000	25,500		
4,000	31,500		
5,000	36,000		
6,000	40,000		

Tool Kit 13.3: Determining Entry and Exit Prices

A firm should seize the opportunity and enter an industry whenever it can make positive (or at least zero) economic profits. This occurs when price is greater than the minimum of the average cost curve. A firm should give up and exit an industry whenever it can no longer earn revenues in excess of its nonrecoverable costs. If all fixed costs are recoverable, then the firm exits whenever price falls below the minimum of the average cost curve. If none of the fixed costs are recoverable, then the firm exits when price falls below the minimum of the average *variable* cost curve. If some costs are recoverable, the exit price lies somewhere in between. The next few problems explore this idea.

Step one: Calculate the average cost for each level of output.

Step two: Find the minimum average cost; this is the entry price. When the price is greater than or equal to the minimum average cost, then the firm should enter the market.

Step three: Identify all costs that are not sunk (nonrecoverable).

Step four: Calculate the average of the costs that are not sunk.

Step five: Find the minimum average nonsunk cost; this is the exit price. When the price falls below this level, the firm should exit the market.

7 (Worked problem: entry and exit prices) Let's return to Barbara's Carpet Cleaners in problem 1. The total cost curve is given in Table 13.9.

Table 13.9

Output	Total cost
10	$ 200
20	$ 320
30	$ 460
40	$ 620
50	$ 800
60	$1,000

a Find the entry price, which is the minimum price that will induce the firm to enter the market.

b Assume that all the fixed costs are sunk. Find the exit price, which is the maximum price that will induce the firm to exit the market.

c Now assume that $50 of the fixed cost is recoverable. Find the exit price.

Step-by-step solution

Step one (a): Calculate the average cost for each level of output, and enter in the table. The average cost at 10 carpets is $200/10 = $20. Continue to fill in the column as in Table 13.10.

Table 13.10

Output	Total cost	Average cost
10	$ 200	$20.00
20	$ 320	$16.00
30	$ 460	$15.33
40	$ 620	$15.50
50	$ 800	$16.00
60	$1,000	$16.66

Step two: The minimum of the average cost curve is $15.33, and this is the entry price. This is the answer to part a.

Step three (b): Identify the costs that are not sunk. If all fixed costs are sunk, then only the variable costs can be recovered. In this case, the exit price is the minimum of the average variable cost curve. First, compute variable cost by subtracting fixed costs from total cost. The variable cost for 10 units of output is $200 – $100 = $100. Continue to fill in this column as in Table 13.11.

Table 13.11

Output	Total cost	Variable cost
10	$ 200	$100
20	$ 320	$220
30	$ 460	$360
40	$ 620	$520
50	$ 800	$700
60	$1,000	$900

Step four: Compute average variable cost. For 10 carpets, the average variable cost is $100/10 = $10. Enter the results as given in Table 13.12.

Table 13.12

Output	Total cost	Variable cost	Average variable cost
10	$ 200	$100	$10
20	$ 320	$220	$11
30	$ 460	$360	$12
40	$ 620	$520	$13
50	$ 800	$700	$14
60	$1,000	$900	$15

Step five: The minimum of the average variable cost curve is $10; therefore, the firm should exit when the price falls below $10. This is the answer to part b.

Step six (c): Only $50 is sunk; thus, the firm exits when revenues fall below variable costs plus $50. To find the recoverable costs, simply add $50 to variable cost. Next, find the average of these numbers, and the minimum of these averages is the exit price. The results appear in Table 13.13.

Table 13.13

Output	Variable cost	Recoverable cost	Average recoverable cost
10	$100	$150	$15.00
20	$220	$270	$13.50
30	$360	$410	$13.66
40	$520	$570	$14.25
50	$700	$750	$15.00
60	$900	$950	$15.83

The minimum of the average recoverable cost column is $13.50, which is the exit price. When the price is $13.50, the firm loses $50, which means that revenues cover all but the nonrecoverable costs.

8 (Practice problem: entry and exit prices) Now let's return to Martin Block in problem 2. The total cost curve is reprinted in Table 13.14. Fixed costs equal $10,000.

Table 13.14

Output	Total cost
10,000	$21,000
20,000	$32,100
30,000	$43,300
40,000	$54,600
50,000	$66,000
60,000	$77,500

a Find the entry price, which is the minimum price that will induce the firm to enter the market.

b Assume that all the fixed costs are sunk. Find the exit price, which is the maximum price that will induce the firm to exit the market.

9 (Practice problem: entry and exit prices) Find the entry price and the exit price for the firms in problem 3. Assume that all the fixed costs are sunk.

10 (Worked problem: applications) The competitive firm is a price taker in product and input markets. It has a production function and a level of fixed costs. Given this information, we can derive all the firm's cost curves, its supply curve, its demand curve, and the price at which it will enter or exit the industry. Remo's Repos recovers the automobiles of delinquent borrowers. Local banks pay him $50 per car recovered. Remo hires agents at $100 per night to repossess the cars. He runs a low-budget operation with fixed costs of only $500. The production function is given in Table 13.15, where output is measured as the number of cars repossessed.

a Complete the table below, and calculate the profit-maximizing number of agents to hire.

Table 13.15

Agents	Output	Marginal product	Value of the marginal product
1	8		
2	15		
3	21		
4	26		
5	30		
6	33		
7	35		
8	36		
9	37		

b Complete the cost table below, and calculate the profit-maximizing number of automobiles to repossess.

Output	Total cost	Variable cost	Average cost	Average variable cost	Marginal cost

c Verify that the number of agents hired repossesses the quantity of output produced.

d Find the entry price.

e Assume that the fixed costs are sunk, and find the exit price.

Step-by-step solution

Step one (a): Follow along with the solution to problem 4, and complete the table given above. The results are given in Table 13.16.

Table 13.16

Agents	Output	Marginal product	Value of the marginal product
1	8	8	$400
2	15	7	$350
3	21	6	$300
4	26	5	$250
5	30	4	$200
6	33	3	$150
7	35	2	$100
8	36	1	$ 50
9	37	1	$ 50

Step two: Set the input price ($100) equal to the value of the marginal product, which is $100 when 7 agents are hired.

Step three (b): Compute the cost for each output level in the production function. For 8 cars repossessed, 1 agent is hired at $100 and fixed costs are $500; therefore, total costs equal $100 + $500 = $600. Enter this number. For 15 cars, 2 agents at $100 each added to the $500 gives a total cost of $700. Continue and complete the total cost column. The result is given in Table 13.17.

Table 13.17

Output	Total cost
8	$ 600
15	$ 700
21	$ 800
26	$ 900
30	$1,000
33	$1,100
35	$1,200
36	$1,300
37	$1,400

Step four: Follow the solution to problems 1 and 7, and complete the table. Be careful with marginal cost. For example, the marginal cost at 8 cars is ($600 − $500)/8 = $12.50. The marginal cost at 15 cars is ($700 − $600)/(15 − 8) = $14.29. The complete information is given in Table 13.18.

Table 13.18

Output	Total cost	Variable cost	Average cost	Average variable cost	Marginal cost
8	$ 600	$100	$75.00	$12.50	$ 12.50
15	$ 700	$200	$46.66	$13.33	$ 14.29
21	$ 800	$300	$38.09	$14.28	$ 16.66
26	$ 900	$400	$34.61	$15.38	$ 20.00
30	$1,000	$500	$33.33	$16.66	$ 25.00
33	$1,100	$600	$33.33	$18.18	$ 33.33
35	$1,200	$700	$34.28	$20.00	$ 50.00
36	$1,300	$800	$36.11	$22.22	$100.00
37	$1,400	$900	$37.83	$24.32	$100.00

Step five: Set price equal to marginal cost. The price is $50, which equals marginal cost when 35 cars are repossessed.

Step six (c): Check the production function to make sure that when 7 agents are hired, 35 cars are repossessed.

Step seven (d): The entry price is the minimum of the average cost curve, which is $33.33. Note that marginal cost equals average cost at the minimum of the average cost curve.

Step eight (e): The exit price for the case in which all fixed costs are sunk is the minimum of the average variable cost, which is $12.50. Again, note that at the minimum of average variable cost, it is equal to marginal cost.

11 (Practice problem: applications) Perry's Perfect Pet Place hires workers to give baths to dogs. Perry pays each worker $20 per day and charges the dogs $10 per bath. His fixed costs are $50. The production function is given in Table 13.19.

   a Complete the table below, and calculate the profit-maximizing number of workers to hire.

Table 13.19

Workers	Baths	Marginal product	Value of the marginal product
1	6		
2	11		
3	15		
4	18		
5	20		
6	21		

   b Complete the cost table below, and calculate the profit-maximizing number of baths.

Output	Total cost	Variable cost	Average cost	Average variable cost	Marginal cost

   c Verify that the number of workers hired does give the profit-maximizing number of baths.
   d Find the entry price.
   e Assume that the fixed costs are sunk, and find the exit price.

Answers to Problems

2 *a* The marginal cost is given in Table 13.20.

Table 13.20

Output	Total cost	Marginal cost
10,000	$21,000	—
20,000	$32,100	$1.11
30,000	$43,300	$1.12
40,000	$54,600	$1.13
50,000	$66,000	$1.14
60,000	$77,500	$1.15

When the price is $1.12, output is 30,000, and profits equal ($1.12 × 30,000) − $43,300 = −9,700.

   b When the price is $1.15, output is 60,000, and profits equal ($1.15 × 60,000) − $77,500 = −$8,500.

3 *a* The marginal cost is given in Table 13.21.

Table 13.21

Output	Total cost	Marginal cost
100	$ 80,000	$400
200	$120,000	$400
300	$170,000	$500
400	$230,000	$600
500	$300,000	$700
600	$380,000	$800
700	$470,000	$900

Output = 400;
profits = ($600 × 400) − $230,000 = $10,000.

   b The marginal cost is given in Table 13.22.

Table 13.22

Output	Total cost	Marginal cost
1,000	$ 1,900	$1.00
2,000	$ 2,900	$1.00
3,000	$ 4,600	$1.70
4,000	$ 6,600	$2.00
5,000	$ 9,400	$2.80
6,000	$12,400	$3.00
7,000	$16,000	$3.60
8,000	$20,000	$4.00

Output = 6,000;
profits = ($3.00 × 6,000) − $12,400 = $5,600.

   c The marginal cost is given in Table 13.23.

Table 13.23

Output	Total cost	Marginal cost
1	$ 40	$ 40
2	$ 90	$ 50
3	$150	$ 60
4	$210	$ 60
5	$280	$ 70
6	$360	$ 80
7	$450	$ 90
8	$550	$100

Output = 6; profits = (6 × $80) − $360 = $120.

5 The value of the marginal product is given in Table 13.24.

Table 13.24

Workers	Output per day	Marginal product	Value of the marginal product
1	5.0	5.0	$100
2	9.0	4.0	$ 80
3	13.0	4.0	$ 80
4	16.5	3.5	$ 70
5	19.5	3.0	$ 60
6	22.0	2.5	$ 50
7	24.0	2.0	$ 40

    a When the wage is $40, it equals the vmp if 7 are hired.

    b When the wage is $70, it equals the vmp if 4 are hired.

6 *a* The value of the marginal product is given in Table 13.25. The quantity demanded is 50 workers.

Table 13.25

Workers	Output per day	Marginal product	Value of the marginal product
10	200	20	$200
20	360	16	$160
30	500	14	$140
40	620	12	$120
50	720	10	$100
60	800	8	$ 80

    b The value of the marginal product is given in Table 13.26. The quantity demanded is 40 workers.

Table 13.26

Workers	Output per day	Marginal product	Value of the marginal product
10	20	2.0	$20,000
20	40	2.0	$20,000
30	55	1.5	$15,000
40	65	1.0	$10,000
50	70	0.5	$ 5,000
60	70	0	$ 0

    c The value of the marginal product is given in Table 13.27. The quantity demanded is 2,000 workers.

Table 13.27

Workers	Output per day	Marginal product	Value of the marginal product
1,000	10,000	10.0	$50.00
2,000	18,000	8.0	$40.00
3,000	25,500	7.5	$37.50
4,000	31,500	6.0	$30.00
5,000	36,000	4.5	$22.50
6,000	40,000	4.0	$20.00

8 The cost measures are given in Table 13.28.

Table 13.28

Output	Total cost	Average cost	Variable cost	Average variable cost
10,000	$21,000	$2.10	$11,000	$1.10
20,000	$32,100	$1.61	$22,100	$1.11
30,000	$43,300	$1.43	$33.300	$1.11
40,000	$54,600	$1.37	$44,600	$1.12
50,000	$66,000	$1.32	$56,000	$1.12
60,000	$77,500	$1.29	$67,500	$1.13

    a Entry price = $1.29.

    b Exit price = $1.10.

9 *a* The cost measures appear in Table 13.29.

Table 13.29

Output	Total cost	Average cost	Variable cost	Average variable cost
100	$ 80,000	$800	$ 40,000	$400
200	$120,000	$600	$ 80,000	$400
300	$170,000	$567	$130,000	$433
400	$230,000	$575	$190,000	$475
500	$300,000	$600	$260,000	$520
600	$380,000	$633	$340,000	$567
700	$470,000	$671	$430,000	$614

Entry price = $567; exit price = $400.

    b The cost measures appear in Table 13.30.

Table 13.30

Output	Total cost	Average cost	Variable cost	Average variable cost
1,000	$ 1,900	$1.90	$ 1,000	$1.00
2,000	$ 2,900	$1.45	$ 2,000	$1.00
3,000	$ 4,600	$1.53	$ 3,700	$1.23
4,000	$ 6,600	$1.65	$ 5,700	$1.43
5,000	$ 9,400	$1.88	$ 8,500	$1.70
6,000	$12,400	$2.07	$11,500	$1.92
7,000	$16,000	$2.29	$15,100	$2.16
8,000	$20,000	$2.50	$19,100	$2.39

Entry price = $1.45; exit price = $1.00.

c The cost measures appear in Table 13.31.

Table 13.31

Output	Total cost	Average cost	Variable cost	Average variable cost
1	$ 40	$40.00	$40	$40.00
2	$ 90	$45.00	$ 90	$45.00
3	$150	$50.00	$150	$50.00
4	$210	$52.50	$210	$52.50
5	$280	$56.00	$280	$56.00
6	$360	$60.00	$360	$60.00
7	$450	$64.29	$450	$64.29
8	$550	$68.75	$550	$68.75

Entry price = $40; exit price = $40.

11 a The complete information is given in Table 13.32.

Table 13.32

Workers	Baths	Marginal product	Value of the marginal product
1	6	6	$60
2	11	5	$50
3	15	4	$40
4	18	3	$30
5	20	2	$20
6	21	1	$10

Perry should hire 5 workers.

b The completed cost information appears in Table 13.33.

Table 13.33

Output	Total cost	Variable cost	Average cost	Average variable cost	Marginal cost
6	$ 70	$ 20	$11.67	$3.33	$ 3.33
11	$ 90	$ 40	$ 8.18	$3.64	$ 4.00
15	$110	$ 60	$ 7.33	$4.00	$ 5.00
18	$130	$ 80	$ 7.22	$4.44	$ 6.33
20	$150	$100	$ 7.50	$5.00	$10.00
21	$170	$120	$ 8.10	$5.71	$20.00

Perry should sell 20 baths.

c 5 workers give 20 baths.

d Entry price = $7.22.

e Exit price = $3.33.

COMPETITIVE EQUILIBRIUM

Chapter Review

The elements of the basic competitive model have been presented over the last six chapters of the text. In Chapter 14, these elements—from individuals and their decisions regarding consumption, savings, investment, and work to firms and their choices regarding production and costs—are brought together in the general equilibrium model. The focus of the model is on the interdependencies of the product, labour, and capital markets. Another major topic is a normative one: how well does the competitive economy perform? The notion of Pareto efficiency provides a tool with which economists can evaluate how well the market economy answers the basic economic questions. This chapter completes the presentation of the competitive model and closes Part Two. In Part Three, attention shifts to imperfect markets.

ESSENTIAL CONCEPTS

1 Partial equilibrium analysis looks at one market in isolation. This kind of analysis can be inappropriate if changes in the market under consideration cause disturbances in the rest of the economy, which then feed back in an important way to the original market. General equilibrium analysis takes into account the relationships among different markets and keeps track of the interactions.

2 The three-market model is a relatively simple general equilibrium model, and is very good for analyzing the interactions among markets. The three markets are the labour, capital, and product markets. They are interdependent in that as the price changes in one market, demand and supply curves shift in the others.

3 Another view of the general equilibrium of the economy is given by the circular flow model. The simple version given in Figure 14.1 shows that households supply labour and financial capital to firms and demand products. Firms demand labour and capital and supply products. The flows of funds balance. For example, the revenues that firms receive for the sale of their goods equal the payments to labour as wages and to capital as dividends and interest. The circular flow model can be expanded to keep track of flows between one country and the rest of the world and between the private sector and the government.

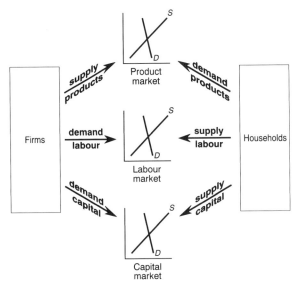

Figure 14.1

4 The concept of efficiency used by economists is called Pareto efficiency. An allocation of resources is Pareto efficient if there is no way to reallocate resources to make anyone better off without hurting someone else. The equilibrium of the competitive economy is Pareto efficient. There is exchange efficiency because the goods and services produced by the economy are distributed efficiently among individuals, production efficiency because the economy is on its production possibilities curve, and product-mix efficiency because the mix of goods matches consumers' tastes.

5 Although the equilibrium of the competitive economy allocates resources efficiently, there are no forces to ensure that it distributes them equally. How much of the economy's output any individual receives depends upon how the market values the individual's labour and how much capital the individual is endowed with. This process is not necessarily equal or fair. People often recommend that the government intervene in the economy to redistribute income. They should, however, be aware of the possible inefficiencies created by distorting the decisions of the market.

BEHIND THE ESSENTIAL CONCEPTS

1 The interdependencies of markets demonstrate another facet of the principle of substitution. When the price of one good rises, the demand for its substitutes rises, while the demand for its complement falls. When the price of one input rises, firms substitute other inputs. A change in the capital market affects the wealth of consumers and the costs of firms. The economy is a spider's web, and a movement in any one part reverberates throughout the whole.

2 Even though there are connections between all markets, in many cases the effects beyond a single market may be small. When this is true, it is sufficient to concentrate on the one market, that is, to employ partial equilibrium analysis, and ignore any general equilibrium repercussions. The art of economic analysis is to bring to light the important general equilibrium considerations and leave aside the portion of the economy that remains relatively unaffected.

3 If a firm produces several goods and there exists a way to rearrange its production and increase the output of one good without reducing the output of any other, an economist would say that this firm is inefficient. The firm is wasting inputs, because it is not getting the maximum output from the inputs. The output of the economy is the satisfaction (the utility) of its members. Therefore, if the economy is doing things one way, and there exists another way to do things that increases the utility of one individual (makes that individual better off) without reducing the utility of anyone else, then, just like the firm above, the economy is inefficient. Pareto efficiency is a natural definition of efficiency for the economy, the important output of which is ultimately not goods and services but human satisfaction.

SELF-TEST

True or False

1 A general equilibrium analysis takes into account all the important interactions between markets.

2 A partial equilibrium analysis focuses on one market only.

3 General equilibrium and partial equilibrium analyses always differ quite dramatically.

4 For the most part, in the capital market, firms are demanders and households are suppliers.

5 In the product market, firms are demanders and households are suppliers.

6 In the labour market, firms are demanders and households are suppliers.

7 The economy is in equilibrium when most of its markets clear.

8 In the circular flow model, the flows to households must equal the flows from households.

9 In the circular flow model, exports plus funds lent abroad must equal imports plus money borrowed from abroad.

10 The allocation of resources is Pareto efficient in competitive equilibrium.

11 The allocation of resources is equal in competitive equilibrium.

12 Pareto efficiency means that everyone can be made better off by some reallocation of resources.

13 All points along the utility possibilities curve are Pareto efficient.

14 All points along the production possibilities curve are Pareto efficient.

15 Pareto efficiency requires exchange efficiency, production efficiency, and product-mix efficiency.

Multiple Choice

1 When an analysis focuses on the interactions between markets, it is called

a partial equilibrium.
b interactive equilibrium.
c disequilibrium.
d general equilibrium.
e none of the above.

2 When an analysis looks only at the changes in one market, it is called

a partial equilibrium.
b interactive equilibrium.
c disequilibrium.
d general equilibrium.
e none of the above.

3 In a general equilibrium model, the supply of labour depends upon

a product prices alone.
b the wage rate alone.
c interest rates alone.
d product prices and the wage rate.
e product prices, the wage rate, and interest rates.

4 In a general equilibrium model, the supply of products depends upon the wage and interest rates because

a these input prices affect costs.
b household income is affected by changes in the wage and interest rates.
c households can substitute leisure or future consumption for current products.
d the demand for capital depends upon the wage rate.
e none of the above.

5 Which of the following is not necessarily true when the economy is in full, general equilibrium?

a The supply of labour equals the demand.
b The supply of products equals the demand.
c The supply of capital equals the demand.
d The distribution of income is fair.
e None of the above.

6 A restriction on immigration will

a shift the supply of labour to the left, and so increase wages, with no further effects.

b shift the supply of labour to the right, and so decrease wages, with no further effects.
c shift the supply of labour to the left, and so decrease wages, with no further effects.
d shift the supply of labour to the right, and so increase wages, with no further effects.
e shift the supply of labour initially to the left, and so increase wages, and also affect the demand for capital, and so possibly offset the increase in wages.

7 In general equilibrium, a tax on business profits will be paid by individuals through

a increases in product prices alone.
b decreases in wages alone.
c decreases in dividends alone.
d capital losses on stock ownership alone.
e all of the above.

8 An increase in the tax rate on commercial property will

a have no effect on the returns to other forms of capital investment.
b cause financial capital to flow from commercial property to other forms of capital investment, and so reduce the average return to capital.
c have no effect on the allocation of financial capital.
d have no effect on the returns to capital because all investments must be equally profitable in equilibrium.
e none of the above.

9 If the allocation of resources is Pareto efficient,

a the distribution of income is fair.
b there is a way to reallocate resources and make everyone better off.
c there is a way to reallocate resources and make some people better off without hurting others.
d there is no way to reallocate resources and make anyone better off without hurting some other person.
e none of the above.

10 In the basic circular flow model,

a households supply goods and services, labour, and financial capital, and firms demand goods and services, labour, and financial capital.
b households demand goods and services, labour, and financial capital, and firms supply goods and services, labour, and financial capital.
c households supply goods and services and demand labour and financial capital, and firms supply labour and financial capital and demand goods and services.
d households demand goods and services and supply labour and financial capital, and firms demand labour and financial capital and supply goods and services.
e none of the above.

11 The circular flow model shows that

 a some taxes are paid by businesses and some by households.

 b all taxes are paid by businesses through either lower product prices, higher wages, or higher costs of capital.

 c all taxes are paid by households through either higher product prices, lower wages, or lower returns to capital.

 d the government pays all taxes.

 e none of the above.

12 Which of the following probably does not require a general equilibrium analysis?

 a a corporate income tax.

 b a ban on foreign investment.

 c a national sales tax.

 d elimination of trade restrictions.

 e a tax on cigarettes.

13 Which of the following probably requires only a partial equilibrium analysis?

 a an increase in the supply of green beans.

 b stricter antipollution regulations.

 c a reduction in the size of the military by one-half.

 d an end to agricultural price supports.

 e none of the above.

14 According to the circular flow model, if the personal income tax is cut, then

 a government borrowing must increase.

 b some other tax must be increased.

 c government spending must decrease.

 d some other tax must increase or government spending must decrease.

 e some other tax must increase, government spending must decrease, government borrowing must increase, or a combination of all three.

15 When the allocation of resources is Pareto efficient,

 a the utility possibilities curve is a single point.

 b the economy is on the utility possibilities curve.

 c the economy is on or inside the utility possibilities curve.

 d each individual achieves the same level of utility.

 e individual utilities may differ, but the distribution of income is equitable.

16 The fact that the utility possibilities curve is downward sloping implies that

 a one person's gain is always another person's loss.

 b moving from one Pareto efficient allocation to another must make someone worse off.

 c the distribution of income is unequal when the economy is efficient.

 d all persons can be made better off.

 e none of the above.

17 Exchange efficiency means that

 a the distribution of the goods and services that the economy produces is efficient.

 b the distribution of the goods and services that the economy produces is equitable.

 c the economy is operating along its production possibilities curve.

 d nobody is exchanging anything.

 e none of the above.

18 Production efficiency means that

 a the mix of goods and services that the economy produces reflects the preferences of consumers.

 b the economy is operating along its production possibilities curve.

 c the distribution of what the economy produces is efficient.

 d the distribution of what the economy produces is equitable.

 e none of the above.

19 Which of the following is not implied by Pareto efficiency?

 a exchange efficiency

 b production efficiency

 c efficiency of the product mix

 d all individuals' sharing equally in the decisions that the economy takes

 e none of the above

20 Which of the following is not true when the competitive model is an accurate depiction of the economy?

 a The allocation of resources is Pareto efficient.

 b The distribution of income may be quite unequal.

 c The economy is operating on the production possibilities curve.

 d The economy is operating on the utility possibilities curve.

 e None of the above.

Completion

1 Focusing on a single market while ignoring any spillover effects on other markets is called _____ analysis.

2 _____ analysis takes into account all the interactions and interdependencies between various parts of the economy.

3 In the simple circular flow model of the economy, households _____ labour and savings (financial capital) to firms and _____ goods and services.

4 In the simple circular flow model of the economy, firms _____ labour and financial capital from households and _____ goods and services.

5 When there is no way to make anyone better off without hurting someone else, the allocation of resources is _____.

6 The curve giving the maximum level of utility that one individual can attain, given the level of utility attained by another individual, is called the _____ curve.

7 _____ requires that the economy's output of

goods and services be distributed efficiently among its consumers.

8 When the economy is productively efficient, it is operating on its _____ curve.

9 The competitive economy results in distributions of income that are _____.

10 Environmental degradation and unemployment are examples of _____.

Answers to Self-Test

True or False

1	t	4	t	7	f	10	t	13	t
2	t	5	f	8	t	11	f	14	f
3	f	6	t	9	f	12	f	15	t

Multiple Choice

1	d	6	e	11	c	16	b
2	a	7	e	12	e	17	a
3	e	8	b	13	a	18	b
4	a	9	d	14	e	19	d
5	d	10	d	15	b	20	e

Completion

1 partial equilibrium
2 General equilibrium
3 supply, demand
4 demand, supply
5 Pareto efficient
6 utility possibilities
7 Exchange efficiency
8 production possibilities
9 unequal
10 market failure

Doing Economics: Tools and Practice Problems

The skill in general equilibrium analysis lies in choosing which interdependencies are important and which can be left aside. In this problem set, we first use the three-market model to analyze the effects of major changes in the economy: the introduction of a national sales tax, an important technological advance, and an increase in savings. Finally, there are a few problems that focus on the connections between two markets. We consider corporate taxation, compensating differentials, and natural resource prices.

1 (Worked problem: general equilibrium analysis) There are three major markets: labour, capital, and product. They are interrelated in that the prices in other markets cause the demand curves and supply curves to shift. Because of this interdependence, there will be important second-round effects in the three-market model. Most European countries have a value-added tax, a national sales tax that is similar in some respects to the Goods and Services Tax.

   a Use the three-market model to evaluate the effects of a value-added tax.

   b Who pays the value-added tax?

Step-by-step solution

Step one (a): Identify the relevant markets. We will use the labour, capital, and product markets.

Step two: Start with an equilibrium in each market.

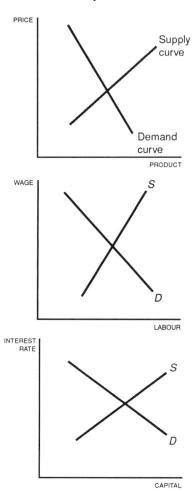

Step three: The value-added tax shifts the product market supply curve up by the amount of the tax. (This step is exactly like the analysis of the effects of taxes in Chapter 5.)

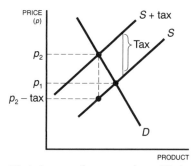

Step four: Find the new (temporary) equilibrium. Note that some of the tax is paid by consumers in the form of higher product prices. On the other hand, firms also receive less after the tax. This completes the first round.

Step five: Determine which curves shift as a result of the price changes observed in step four. The lower net of tax product prices observed in step four implies that the value of the marginal product of inputs is lower. This means that the

Tool Kit 14.1: Using General Equilibrium Analysis

When doing general equilibrium analysis, keep the following procedure in mind.

Step one: Identify the relevant markets.

Step two: Start with an equilibrium in each market, as in the figure.

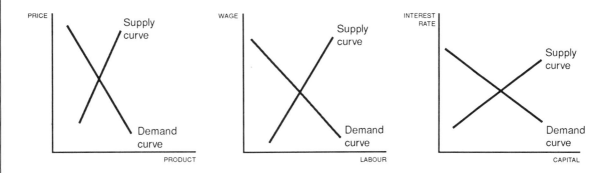

Step three: Identify a change, and determine which curves shift as a direct result of the change. In the second row of the figure, the demand for labour shifts outwards.

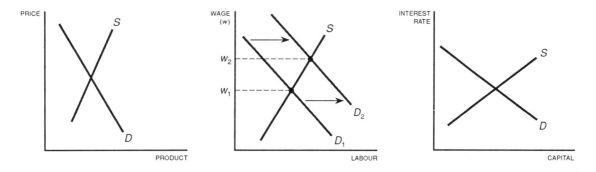

Step four: Shift the curves, and find the new equilibrium. In the general equilibrium model, this is only a temporary equilibrium because there are second-round effects to be accounted for. Observe which prices have changed. In the diagram, wages increase.

Step five: Determine which curves shift as a result of the price changes observed in step four.

Step six: Shift the curves, as shown here by lower supply in the product market and higher demand in the capital market, and find the new equilibrium.

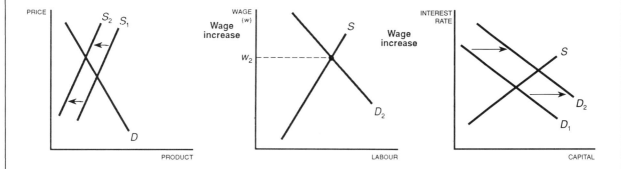

Step seven: Stop. Usually a second round is enough. Compare the new equilibrium with that in step two.

demand curve for labour and the demand curve for capital must shift to the left.

Step six: Shift the curves, and find the new equilibrium.

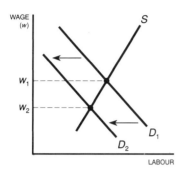

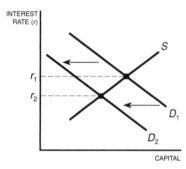

Step seven: Compare the new equilibrium with that in step two. We see that the wage and the interest rate are lower.

Step eight (b): The value-added tax is paid for in three ways. First, it is shifted forwards to consumers in the form of higher product prices. Second, it is shifted backwards to workers through lower wages. Third, it is shifted backwards to savers in terms of lower interest rates. A vital lesson of the general equilibrium approach is that all taxes are ultimately paid by individuals. A partial equilibrium treatment in the product market alone would imply that firms pay some of the tax. The full general equilibrium analysis reveals that the producers' share of the tax is passed backwards to workers and savers.

2   (Practice problem: general equilibrium analysis) A substantial part of the growth of developed countries is accounted for by technological advance, by improvements in how goods and services are produced, and by the introduction of new and better products. The hope

for continued economic progress rests on technological advance in production. Use the three-market model to analyze the effects of a major technological advance.

a   Start with an equilibrium in the three markets.
b   Better technology increases the marginal products of labour and capital. Which curves are shifted? (Hint: Remember the formula for the value of the marginal product and the relationship between marginal product and marginal cost.)
c   In the second round, how does the equilibrium change?

3   (Practice problem: general equilibrium analysis) Many people are concerned about relatively low savings rates. One cause for optimism is that the aging of the relatively large baby boom generation will lead to more savings. Suppose that households decrease their consumption and increase their savings. Trace through the effects using the three-market model.

4   (Worked problem: general equilibrium analysis) Often when a change occurs in one market, there is another market closely linked to the first. In these cases, both markets must be included in the analysis. Investors seeking the highest possible returns can choose to buy stock in corporations or to invest their money in other noncorporate businesses. If the returns were higher in the corporate sector of the economy, then no one would invest in the noncorporate sector. If the returns were higher in the noncorporate sector, all money would flow out of the corporate sector. In equilibrium, then, the rate of return must be equal in the two sectors.

a   Illustrate an equilibrium in the markets for corporate and noncorporate investment.
b   In Canada, corporations must pay taxes on their income. The corporate income tax is in addition to the taxes paid by investors on their dividend income. Show how a tax on corporate income affects the market for corporate investment.
c   Show how the noncorporate investment market will adjust to restore both markets to equilibrium.
d   Who pays the corporate income tax?

Step-by-step solution

Step one (a): Start with an equilibrium. In this case, not only must supply and demand be equal in each market, but also each market must pay the same returns.

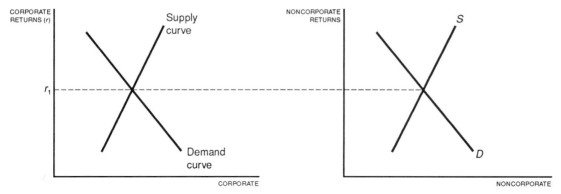

Step one

Step two (b): Determine which curve shifts. The corporate tax is paid by the demanders (corporations); therefore, the demand curve in the market for corporate investment shifts down.

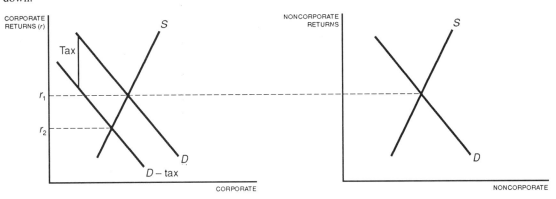

Step two

Step three: The (temporary) equilibrium in the market for corporate investment has a lower rate of return than in the market for noncorporate investment.

Step four (c): Determine the effects in the noncorporate investment market. Because they can earn higher after-tax returns in the noncorporate sector, corporate investors will move their money. The supply of corporate investment will shift left, and the supply of noncorporate investment will shift right, until the returns are equal.

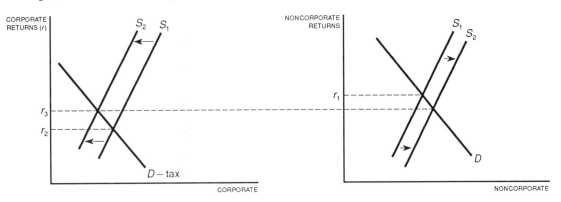

Step four

Step five (d): Find the new equilibrium and compare. In the new equilibrium, the returns are equal in each sector, but overall the returns are lower. We conclude that the corporate tax is paid by both noncorporate and corporate investors.

5   (Practice problem: general equilibrium analysis) Differences in wages that reflect differences in the characteristics of jobs are called compensating differentials. Truck drivers who haul freight over long distances are paid more than those who drive local routes. Suppose that the difference is $50 per week in equilibrium.

   a   Start with an equilibrium in the markets for local truck drivers and long-haul drivers. Be sure that the difference in wages is $50 per week.

   b   A new policy, agreed upon by both union and management, specifies that each driver must earn the same amount. Explain how the markets will adjust.

6   (Practice problem: general equilibrium analysis) Many people are concerned about the possible exhaustion of the limited supplies of natural resources, such as oil. To understand the economics of this issue, consider a two-period problem. Known reserves of oil equal 100,000 barrels. The oil can be sold now or be saved and sold in the future period. The discount rate is 50 percent over the time between the periods. The demand is the same now and in the future, and it is given in Table 14.1.

Table 14.1

Price	Quantity	Present discounted value of the future price
$50	20,000	
$45	30,000	
$40	40,000	
$35	55,000	
$30	70,000	
$25	80,000	
$20	90,000	
$10	100,000	

a Calculate the present discounted value of each of the prices for the future demand. This is the current value of waiting to sell at the future price.

b If the current price is greater than the present discounted value of the future price, all the oil will be sold today. If the reverse is true, the oil will be sold in the future. In equilibrium, current price must equal the present discounted value of the future price, and the total quantity sold in both periods must equal 100,000 barrels. Find the equilibrium price today, the price in the future, and the quantity sold in each period.

Answers to Problems

2 a The initial equilibrium price is p_1, the wage is w_1, and the interest rate is r_1.

b The technical advance shifts the demands for labour and capital to the right because both factors are made more productive, and it shifts the supply of products to the right because costs are lower. The product price falls to p_2, the wage rises to w_2, and the interest rate rises to r_2.

c In the second round, the supply curve for products shifts left (mitigating the effects of the original shift) because wages and interest rates are higher. The demand curves for labour and capital shift back to the left (offsetting somewhat the effects of the original shift) because product prices are lower. (Recall that the demand for a factor of production is the value of the marginal product, which is price

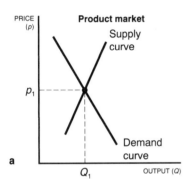

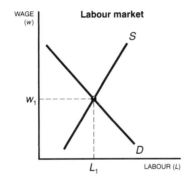

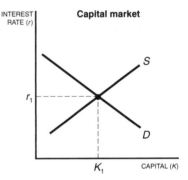

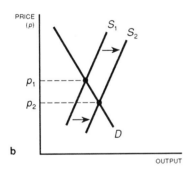

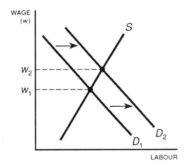

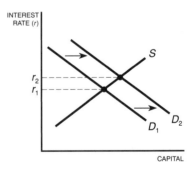

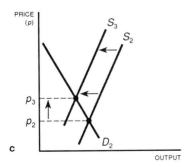

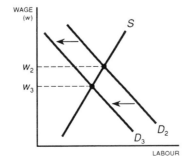

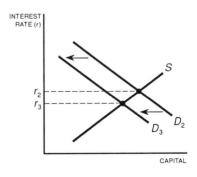

multiplied by marginal product.) The ultimate price is p_3, which is higher than p_1 but lower than p_2, because of the general equilibrium repercussions. Similarly, w_3 is greater than w_1 and r_3 is greater than r_1, but the changes are less great than a partial equilibrium analysis would imply.

3 *a* The initial equilibrium price is p_1, the wage is w_1, and the interest rate is r_1.

  b As people consume less, the demand for output falls. As they save more, the supply shifts to the right in the capital market. Product prices and interest rates fall as a result.

  c In the second round, the fall in interest rates shifts the supply of output to the right and further reduces product prices. The fall in product prices, observed in part b, reduces the demand for capital and leads to a further decrease in the interest rate. In the labour market, demand shifts up because of lower interest rates, but shifts down because of lower product prices. The ultimate impact on the wage is not certain.

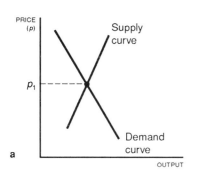
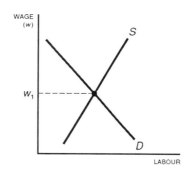
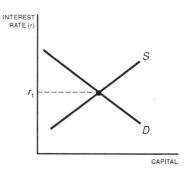

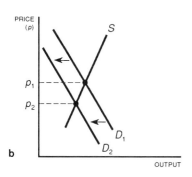
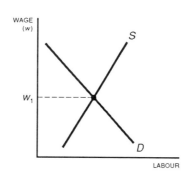
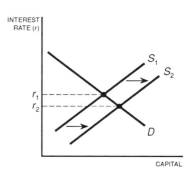

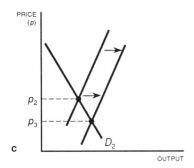
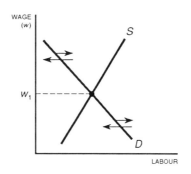
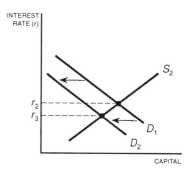

5 *a* In the initial equilibrium, both markets clear, and
       the weekly wage is $50 higher in the long-haul
       market.

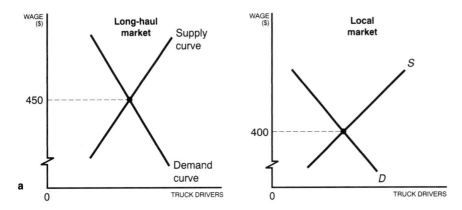

b When the same wage is paid in the two markets,
     there is a shortage of long-haul drivers, and a sur-
     plus of drivers in the local market.

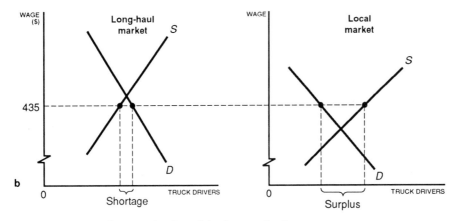

6 *a* The present discounted value of the future price is
       given in Table 14.2.

Table 14.2

Price	Quantity	Present discounted value of the future price
$50	20,000	$50/(1 + $.50) = $33.33
$45	30,000	$30.00
$40	40,000	$26.67
$35	55,000	$23.33
$30	70,000	$20.00
$25	80,000	$16.67
$20	90,000	$13.33
$10	100,000	$ 6.67

b The current price is $30, and 70,000 barrels are
     sold. The future price is $45, and 30,000 barrels
     are sold. The total is 70,000 + 30,000 = 100,000.
     The present discounted value of the future price is
     $30, which is the current price.

Part Three

Imperfect Markets

Chapter 15

MONOPOLIES AND IMPERFECT COMPETITION

Chapter Review

With the detailed study of perfect competition completed in Part Two, this chapter begins the study of imperfect competition. The real world differs from the basic competitive model in many important ways, and these differences shape the remainder of the text.

The first difference involves setting prices. While the competitive firm must accept the market price as a given fact, most firms in the real world have some control over their prices. How prices are set in monopolies, where there is only one seller, is the first topic taken up in the textbook chapter. The chapter then turns to a discussion of barriers to entry, which keep new firms from competing in an established industry, and competition among many firms producing similar but not identical products. Chapters 16, 17, 18, and parts of Chapter 20 consider related problems and build on this chapter's techniques for analyzing imperfect competition.

ESSENTIAL CONCEPTS

1   There are four important types of **market structure: perfect competition, monopoly, monopolistic competition**, and **oligopoly**, summarized in Table 15.1.

Table 15.1

Market structure	Firm's demand curve	Entry	Product differentiation	Examples
Perfect competition	Horizontal	Free entry	Homogenous products	Wheat, corn
Monopoly	Downward sloping	Barriers to entry	Only one firm	Major league baseball, holders of patents
Monopolistic competition	Downward sloping	Free entry	Differentiated products	Restaurants, designer clothing
Oligopoly	Downward sloping	Barriers to entry	Either homogenous or differentiated products	Steel manufacturers, automobiles

2   The last three market structures are called **imperfect competition.** In perfect competition, the demand curve facing the firm is horizontal; this indicates that the firm can sell all it wants at the market price. Because the market price does not change as the firm sells more, the *marginal revenue equals price in perfectly competitive industries.* In imperfect competition, the demand curve facing the firm slopes downwards; this indicates

that as the firm sells more, the price must fall. This implies that *marginal revenue is less than price in imperfectly competitive industries.* Finally, because all firms, whatever the market structure, maximize profits by setting marginal revenue equal to marginal cost, *price equals marginal cost in perfect competition and is above marginal cost in imperfect competition.*

3 An industry with a single seller is called a monopoly. Since a monopoly has no competitors, it need not worry about the reactions of other firms to its price policy. In monopolistic competition, enough firms are competing that any individual firm perceives itself to be so small that its rivals will neither notice nor care about its business strategy decisions. A few firms dominate the industry in oligopoly, and each firm must keep in mind how its rivals will choose their strategies when setting its own strategy. The extent of competition in the real world is measured with indexes of **concentration** and the degree of **production differentiation.**

4 The **market power** a firm exercises is revealed by how much the demand curve it faces slopes down. This in turn is influenced by the **product differentiation** in the industry. When products are less differentiated, they are closer substitutes, and firms' demands are more elastic (flatter). The characteristics of products, locations of the sellers, and the information and perceptions of buyers cause products to differ.

5 Factors that prevent entry into markets are called **barriers to entry.** Government policies such as licence requirements and patents create barriers to entry. The cost structure of the industry, specifically the fraction of market demand accounted for by the output at the minimum of the firm's average cost curve, can also be a barrier. If one firm can produce the entire market demand for less than it could if it shared the market, the structure is called a **natural monopoly.** A monopoly can be sustained if a firm has control over an essential resource or if the firm has information advantages. Finally, strategies of existing firms can create barriers if they can credibly convince potential competitors that entry would be met with fierce competition.

6 Monopolistic competition describes the market structure made up of many firms, each of which ignores the reactions of the others. The demand curves facing the firms slope down (thus, price is above marginal cost), but new firms enter when there are profit opportunities (thus, in equilibrium, price equals average cost). New entrants produce close substitutes for the products of existing firms. Each entry shifts the demand curves facing existing firms to the left, and so reduces their profits.

BEHIND THE ESSENTIAL CONCEPTS

1 One important idea in the theory of imperfect competition is the relationship between marginal revenue and price. Marginal revenue is the extra revenue that the

firm takes in when it sells another unit. In perfect competition, this amount is the price. But in imperfect competition, the price falls as more output is sold. Thus, there are two effects on revenue, shown in Figure 15.1. The firm is initially selling 10 units for $10 each. If it chooses to produce and sell 11 units, the price falls to $9.50. The first effect on revenue is that the firm sells more units at $9.50. This is shown as the area with pluses. If the demand curve facing the firm were horizontal, as under perfect competition, this would be the end of the story: the extra revenue would be price times the extra quantity sold. However, the downward-sloping demand curve makes the price drop in order to sell one extra unit. This is the second effect. It means that the firm loses revenue on all its existing sales (because the price is lower for all units). This effect is shown as the area with minuses, and it is this that makes marginal revenue less than price.

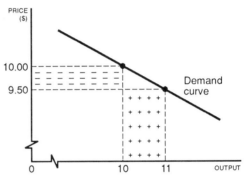

Figure 15.1

2 All imperfectly competitive firms face a downward-sloping demand curve. Thus, their profit-maximizing price is greater than marginal cost. In monopoly, there are barriers to entry, which allow monopolies to earn pure profits without attracting new competition. Monopoly prices are greater than average costs. In monopolistic competition, however, new entry drives economic profits to zero. When profits are zero, price equals average cost. To sum up,

a downward-sloping demand implies that price is greater than marginal cost.
b barriers to entry imply that price is greater than average cost.

3 Monopoly and monopolistic competition are similar in that each firm faces a downward-sloping demand curve and sets marginal revenue equal to marginal cost, which is less than price. The similarities stop here, however, because in a monopoly no new firm may enter even though a firm may earn pure profits. In monopolistically competitive industries, new firms enter, produce close substitutes, and capture customers. This entry shifts demand to the left until price equals average cost. The basic difference in the equilibria is that monopolies earn pure profits.

4 Monopolies are inefficient because price (which equals the marginal benefit of the good to consumers) is greater than marginal cost. Producing another unit would benefit customers more than it would cost. In monopolistic competition, things are not so simple. If all firms produce more goods, there are gains to both consumers and firms because, though price is greater than marginal cost, average cost falls. (Remember that the monopolistically competitive firm produces along the downward-sloping part of average cost.) On the other hand, the overall industry demand is only so large, and if the firms become bigger, there will be room for fewer firms. Fewer firms mean fewer types of goods, so there is a trade-off between costs and variety.

SELF-TEST

True or False

1 The demand curve facing the firm is downward sloping in perfect competition.

2 The demand curve facing the firm is downward sloping in monopolistic competition.

3 When the demand curve facing the firm is downward sloping, marginal revenue is less than price.

4 Marginal revenue is less than price because price must fall for output to increase.

5 An industry with a single seller is a monopoly.

6 The demand curve facing a monopolist is the same as the industry demand curve.

7 Price is greater than marginal cost in monopoly.

8 Price is greater than marginal cost in monopolistic competition.

9 Compared to perfect competition, monopolies produce more but charge higher prices.

10 If there is a barrier to entry, firms may continue to earn pure profits.

11 Product differentiation is caused by barriers to entry.

12 In a natural monopoly, one firm can produce at a lower average cost than it could if it shared the market with other firms.

13 In equilibrium in monopolistic competition, price is greater than average cost.

14 The extent of a firm's market power is measured by how steeply the industry demand curve slopes downwards.

15 The more elastic the monopolist's demand, the more price exceeds marginal cost.

Multiple Choice

1 Which of the following is not a characteristic of *only* the competitive model?

a Marginal revenue for the firm equals the market price.
b If the firm raises its price above that charged by its competitors, it will lose all its customers.
c The demand curve facing the firm is horizontal.
d The firm is a price taker.
e Price equals average cost.

2 If a single firm supplies the entire market, the market structure is

a perfect competition.
b oligopoly.
c monopoly.
d monopolistic competition.
e none of the above.

3 If the market is dominated by several firms, its market structure is

a perfect competition.
b oligopoly.
c monopoly.
d monopolistic competition.
e none of the above.

4 Monopolistic competition is distinguished from oligopoly by the fact that

a in monopolistic competition, firms do not worry about the reactions of their rivals.
b there is no competition in oligopoly.
c oligopoly is a form of imperfect competition.
d the demand curve facing the firm is downward sloping in monopolistic competition.
e price is above marginal cost in an oligopoly.

5 When there is imperfect competition, the demand curve facing the firm

a equals the market demand curve.
b is horizontal.
c is downward sloping.
d is upward sloping.
e is vertical.

6 When the demand curve facing the firm is downward sloping, marginal revenue is less than price

a because of the principle of diminishing returns.
b in the short run, but not in the long run.
c because as output increases, the price must fall on all units.
d because taxes must be paid.
e none of the above.

7 "Marginal cost equals price" is the rule for maximizing profits for firms in which of the following market structures?

a perfect competition.

b monopolistic competition.
c monopoly.
d oligopoly.
e none of the above.

8 Compared to competition, a monopoly

a charges a higher price but sells the same quantity of output.
b charges the same price but sells more output.
c charges a higher price but sells more output.
d charges the same price but sells less output.
e charges a higher price but sells less output.

9 The market demand curve is the same as the demand curve facing the firm when the market structure is

a perfect competition.
b monopoly.
c oligopoly.
d monopolistic competition.
e none of the above.

10 A monopoly increases price above marginal cost by a greater amount when the demand is

a more elastic.
b more inelastic.
c unitary elastic.
d perfectly elastic.
e none of the above.

11 Because they are single sellers, monopolies can earn

a pure economic profits.
b pure accounting profits.
c zero profits.
d the normal rate of return on invested capital.
e none of the above.

12 The measure of a firm's market power is

a the number of employees it has.
b the size of its capital stock.
c the market price of its stock shares.
d the extent to which the demand curve it faces is downward sloping.
e none of the above.

13 How much the demand curve facing the firm slopes downwards is determined by

a the number of firms in the industry and the extent to which its product is differentiated from those of its competitors.
b the number of potential entrants to the industry.
c the size of its capital stock.
d the minimum of its average cost curve.
e none of the above.

14 The four-firm concentration ratio measures

a the number of firms in the industry.
b the elasticity of industry demand.
c the extent to which production is concentrated among a few firms.
d the extent to which foreign firms dominate the industry.

e the average elasticity among the four largest firms.

15 Which of the following is not a characteristic of product differentiation?

a differences in characteristics of products produced by different firms.
b differences in the location of firms.
c perceived differences, often induced by advertising.
d imperfect information about price and availability.
e differences in tastes among consumers.

16 When the products sold in one industry are differentiated, if one firm raises its price,

a it will lose all of its customers.
b it will lose none of its customers.
c it will lose some but not all of its customers.
d it will go out of business.
e its profits will rise.

17 Barriers to entry

a are factors that prevent new firms from entering the market.
b are illegal.
c mean that firms do not need to engage in practices such as predatory pricing.
d imply that marginal revenue is greater than marginal cost.
e arise as a result of imperfect competition.

18 Which of the following is not true in equilibrium in the model of monopolistic competition?

a Firms make zero economic profits.
b Price equals average cost.
c Marginal revenue equals marginal cost.
d Price is greater than marginal cost.
e Price is greater than average cost.

19 The practice of charging different prices to different customers is called

a product differentiation.
b price discrimination.
c predatory pricing.
d limit pricing.
e natural monopoly.

20 Economies of scale refer to

a lower average cost as output is increased.
b charging different prices to different customers.
c any factor that erects barriers to the entry of new competitors.
d lower average cost as different goods are produced with the same plant and equipment.
e charging low prices for a limited time in order to drive competitors from the market.

Completion

1 The way in which an industry is organized is called its _____.

2 A few firms dominate an industry in _____.

3 An industry with a single seller is called _____.

4 In monopolistic competition, there are enough firms that each firm _____ the reactions of rivals.

5 In industries where the characteristics of products are different, there is said to be _____.

6 In imperfect competition, marginal revenue is _____ than price.

7 Any factor that prevents new firms from coming into an industry is called a _____.

8 If the market demand curve intersects the average cost curve for the firm at a point where it is decreasing, the industry is a _____.

9 In monopolistic competition, there is a trade-off between lower prices and more _____.

10 In equilibrium in monopolistic competition, price _____ average cost.

Answers to Self-Test

True or False

1	f	6	t	11	f
2	t	7	t	12	t
3	t	8	t	13	f
4	t	9	f	14	t
5	t	10	t	15	f

Multiple Choice

1	e	6	c	11	a	16	c
2	c	7	a	12	d	17	a
3	b	8	e	13	a	18	e
4	a	9	b	14	c	19	b
5	c	10	b	15	e	20	a

Completion

1 market structure
2 oligopoly
3 monopoly
4 ignores
5 product differentiation
6 less
7 barrier to entry
8 natural monopoly
9 variety
10 equals

Doing Economics: Tools and Practice Problems

In this section, we start with two basic topics and several applications. First, we calculate marginal revenue and find the profit-maximizing price and quantity for the monopolist. The second topic is price discrimination, the practice in which firms in imperfectly competitive markets charge different prices to different consumers in order to raise profits.

The applications that follow include the effects of taxes and price controls in monopoly markets and a couple of puzzles. Artists, entertainers, and authors are often paid a percentage of revenues. Also, they generally prefer lower prices than their producers and publishers. Two problems towards the end of this problem set show why this is true. Other problems explore the effects of taxes and price ceilings in monopoly markets and show that the monopolist always produces along the elastic portion of the demand curve.

Tool Kit 15.1: Calculating Marginal Revenue

The first step in solving the monopolist's problem is to calculate marginal revenue.

Step one: Make a table with four column headings: "Price," "Quantity," "Revenues," and "Marginal revenue." Enter the demand curve in the first two columns.

Price   Quantity   Revenues   Marginal revenue

Step two: Calculate revenues for each point on the demand curve, and enter the result in the table. Revenues are price multiplied by quantity:

$$revenues = price \times quantity.$$

Step three: Calculate marginal revenue for each interval along the demand curve, and enter the result in the table. Marginal revenue is the change in total revenue divided by the change in quantity:

marginal revenue =
    change in revenues/change in quantity.

After calculating marginal revenue, choose the price and quantity for which marginal revenue equals marginal cost.

---

1 (Worked problem: marginal revenue) As the only cement producer within 200 kilometres, Sam's Cement faces a downward-sloping demand curve, which is given in Table 15.2.

Table 15.2

Price	Quantity (tonnes)
$4.00	400
$3.50	800
$3.00	1,400
$2.50	2,800
$2.00	4,000

Sam's marginal cost is $2.00 per tonne, and he has fixed costs of $1,000.

a Calculate revenues and marginal revenue, and add these two columns to the table.

b Find the profit-maximizing price and quantity.

c Compute Sam's costs and profits at this price.

d Suppose that Sam's fixed costs fall to $500. What is his profit-maximizing price and quantity, and how much does he earn in profits?

e Illustrate your answer with a diagram.

Step-by-step solution

Step one (a): Make a table.

Price   Quantity   Revenues   Marginal revenue

Step two: Calculate revenues for each point on the demand curve. When the price is $4, revenues are $4 × 400 = $1,600. Continuing, we derive Table 15.3.

Table 15.3

Price	Quantity	Revenues	Marginal revenue
$4.00	400	$1,600	
$3.50	800	$2,800	
$2.50	2,800	$7,000	
$2.00	4,000	$8,000	

Step three: Calculate marginal revenue for each interval along the demand curve. For the first 400 units, revenue rises from $0 to $1,600. Thus, marginal revenue is $1,600/400 = $4. As output is increased to 800, total revenue grows from $1,600 to $2,800. Marginal revenue is ($2,800 − $1,600)/(800 − 400) = $3. Complete the marginal revenue column as shown in Table 15.4.

Table 15.4

Price	Quantity	Revenues	Marginal revenue
$4.00	400	$1,600	$4.00
$3.50	800	$2,800	$3.00
$3.00	1,400	$4,200	$2.33
$2.50	2,800	$7,000	$2.00
$2.00	4,000	$8,000	$0.83

Step four (b): To find the monopoly output and price, set marginal revenue equal to marginal cost. This occurs when the price is $2.50 and output is 2,800.

Step five (c): To find total costs, add fixed costs, which are $1,000, plus total variable costs. Each unit costs $2, and 2,800 units are produced. Total costs equal $1,000 + ($2 × 2,800) = $6,600. Profits equal revenues minus costs. Revenues are $7,000, so profits equal $7,000 − $6,600 = $400.

Step six (d): If fixed costs fall, marginal cost does not change. The profit-maximizing price is still $2.50, but total profits now equal $7,000 − ($500 + $5,600) = $900. Unless the firm decides to shut down, fixed costs do not affect the output and pricing decisions.

Step seven (e): The solution is illustrated in the diagram.

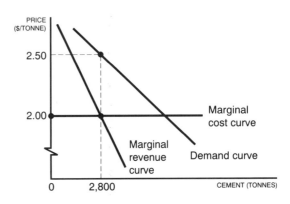

2 (Practice problem: marginal revenue) The Mudville Nine is the only professional baseball team within several hundred kilometres. The marginal cost of admitting another fan is $1. Fixed costs, which include player salaries, are $100,000. The demand curve is given in Table 15.5. The quantity column gives the season's attendance.

Table 15.5

Price	Quantity	Revenues	Marginal revenue
$8	100,000		
$7	150,000		
$6	200,000		
$5	250,000		
$4	300,000		
$3	350,000		
$2	400,000		

a Compute marginal revenue, and complete the column.

b Find the profit-maximizing price and quantity.

c Compute Mudville's costs and profits at this price.

d Suppose that the players win the right to negotiate with any team, and the increase in salaries raises fixed costs to $150,000. What is Mudville's profit-maximizing price and quantity, and how much profit does the team earn?

e Illustrate your answer with a diagram.

3 (Practice problem: marginal revenue) For each of the following firms, find the profit-maximizing price and quantity and total profits earned.

a Fixed costs = $0; marginal cost = $8.

Price	Quantity	Revenues	Marginal revenue
$10	1		
$ 9	2		
$ 8	3		
$ 7	4		
$ 6	5		
$ 5	6		
$ 4	7		

b Fixed costs = $50,000; marginal cost = $.10.

Price	Quantity	Revenues	Marginal revenue
$0.50	500,000		
$0.45	600,000		
$0.40	700,000		
$0.35	800,000		
$0.30	900,000		

c Compute marginal cost from the table.

Price	Quantity	Revenues	Marginal revenue	Total costs	Marginal cost
$20	400			$ 5,000	
$18	800			$ 7,000	
$16	1,200			$ 9,400	
$14	1,600			$12,600	
$12	2,000			$16,200	
$10	2,400			$21,000	

d Compute marginal cost from the table.

Price	Quantity	Revenues	Marginal revenue	Total costs	Marginal cost
$1.00	1,000			$ 200	
$0.90	2,000			$ 300	
$0.80	3,500			$ 450	
$0.70	5,500			$ 650	
$0.60	8,000			$ 900	
$0.50	11,000			$1,230	
$0.40	15,000			$1,730	
$0.30	20,000			$2,355	

4 (Worked problem: marginal revenue) When it is possible to do so, an imperfectly competitive firm can improve profits by charging different prices to different consumers. This is called price discrimination. This idea is to segment the markets and set marginal revenue equal to marginal cost in each market and charge the corresponding price. Although the sale of the product is illegal, a drug enterprise operates according to sound business practices. It sells addictive designer drugs to two types of customers: non-addicted experimenters and addicts (former experimenters). The demands for each type of customer are given in Table 15.6. The drug has no fixed costs and has marginal cost equal to $10 per dose.

Table 15.6

	Nonaddicts				Addicts		
Price	Quan-tity	Revenues	Marginal revenue	Price	Quan-tity	Revenues	Marginal revenue
$50	100			$50	500		
$40	300			$40	700		
$30	500			$30	1,050		
$20	1,000			$20	1,650		

a Calculate marginal revenue for each demand curve.

b Find the profit-maximizing price and quantity for each type of consumer.

c Calculate total profits.

Step-by-step solution

Step one (a): Follow the procedure outlined above to calculate marginal revenue. The result should look like Table 15.7.

Table 15.7

	Nonaddicts				Addicts		
Price	Quan-tity	Revenues	Marginal revenue	Price	Quan-tity	Revenues	Marginal revenue
$50	100	$ 5,000	$50	$50	500	$25,000	$50.00
$40	300	$12,000	$35	$40	700	$28,000	$15.00
$30	500	$15,000	$15	$30	1,050	$31,500	$10.00
$20	1,000	$20,000	$10	$20	1,650	$33,000	$ 2.50

Step two (b): Find the profit-maximizing price in each market. Marginal cost, which is $10, equals marginal revenue for nonaddicts at a price of $20 and a quantity of 1,000. For addicts, marginal revenue equals marginal cost at a price of $30 and a quantity of 1,050.

Step three (c): Calculate total profits. Revenues are $20,000 from the nonaddicts and $31,500 from the addicts. Costs are $10 × (1,000 + 1,050) = $20,500; so profits equal $51,500 – $20,500 = $31,000.

5 (Practice problem: marginal revenue) A common instance of price discrimination is dumping, which occurs when a firm faces less competition in its home market than abroad. In these cases, it will pay the company to charge different prices in the two markets. Opus Company sells carpet fibres in the foreign and domestic markets. Its marginal cost is $1 per spool, and it has fixed costs of $5,000. The domestic and foreign demands are given in Table 15.8.

Table 15.8

	Home market				Foreign market		
Price	Quan-tity	Revenues	Marginal revenue	Price	Quan-tity	Revenues	Marginal revenue
$10	2,000			$10	2,000		
$ 9	2,500			$ 9	3,000		
$ 8	3,000			$ 8	4,000		
$ 7	3,500			$ 7	5,000		
$ 6	4,000			$ 6	6,000		
$ 5	4,500			$ 5	7,000		
$ 4	5,000			$ 4	8,000		

a Calculate marginal revenue for each demand curve.

b Find the profit-maximizing price and quantity for each type of consumer.

c Calculate total profits.

6 (Practice problem: marginal revenue) Mark's Markets is one of the few chains that has not closed its inner-city stores. Mark's has expanded to the suburbs, but it faces more competition there. An example of a product it sells in both markets is hamburger, which has a marginal cost equal to $1. The space required to sell hamburger costs Mark's Markets about $100, and the demand curves in the suburbs and inner city are given in Table 15.9.

Table 15.9

	Suburbs			Inner city		
Price	Quantity	Revenues	Marginal revenue	Price	Quantity	Revenues	Marginal revenue
$4.00	200			$4.00	100		
$3.50	400			$3.50	120		
$3.00	600			$3.00	140		
$2.50	800			$2.50	160		
$2.00	1,000			$2.00	180		
$1.50	1,200			$1.50	200		

a Calculate marginal revenue for each demand curve.
b Find the profit-maximizing price and quantity for each type of consumer.
c Calculate total profits.

8 (Worked problem: marginal revenue) After the surprising success of her first novel, Imelda has negotiated a deal in which she receives 20 percent of the revenues from the sale of her second novel. The demand curve is given in Table 15.10. The publisher has fixed costs of $20,000, and the marginal cost of printing and distributing each book printed is $20.

Table 15.10

Price	Quantity	Revenues	Marginal revenue	Imelda's revenue
$40	10,000			
$35	20,000			
$30	30,000			
$25	40,000			
$20	50,000			

a Calculate marginal revenue, and enter in the table.
b Find the profit-maximizing price and quantity.
c Compute Imelda's revenue for each price, and enter in the table.
d What price maximizes Imelda's revenues?
e Draw a diagram illustrating your answer.

Step-by-step solution

Step one (a): Calculate marginal revenue. Follow the usual procedure. The answer is in Table 15.11.

Table 15.11

Price	Quantity	Revenues	Marginal revenue	Imelda's revenue
$40	10,000	$ 400,000	$40	
$35	20,000	$ 700,000	$30	
$30	30,000	$ 900,000	$20	
$25	40,000	$1,000,000	$10	
$20	50,000	$1,000,000	$ 0	

Step two (b): Find the profit-maximizing price and quantity. Marginal cost equals marginal revenue for the publisher at a price of $30, where the quantity sold is 30,000.

Step three (c): Calculate Imelda's revenue. She receives 20 percent of the total. At a price of $40, she receives .20 × $400,000 = $80,000. Continue to calculate, and enter the results. They are given in Table 15.12.

Table 15.12

Price	Quantity	Revenues	Marginal revenue	Imelda's revenue
$40	10,000	$ 400,000	$40	$ 80,000
$35	20,000	$ 700,000	$30	$140,000
$30	30,000	$ 900,000	$20	$180,000
$25	40,000	$1,000,000	$10	$200,000
$20	50,000	$1,000,000	$ 0	$200,000

Step four (d): Imelda prefers a price of $25 or $20, which earns her $200,000, more than the $180,000 that she earns at the publisher's preferred price.

Step five (e): Draw a diagram. Note that the publisher sets marginal revenue equal to marginal cost. Imelda is only concerned with revenues, so she prefers the point where marginal revenue equals zero.

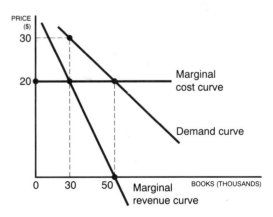

9 (Practice problem: marginal revenue) Magdalena, a budding female recording artist, has just completed her first album. She will receive 25 percent of the revenues. The record company reports that its demand curve is as given in Table 15.13, and its marginal costs are $6 per CD.

Table 15.13

Price	Quantity	Revenues	Marginal revenue	Magdalena's revenue
$20	20,000			
$18	25,000			
$16	30,000			
$14	35,000			
$12	40,000			
$10	48,000			

a Calculate marginal revenue, and enter in the table.
b Find the profit-maximizing price and quantity.
c Compute Magdalena's revenue for each price, and enter in the table.
d What price maximizes Magdalena's revenues?
e Draw a diagram illustrating your answer.

10 (Practice problem: marginal revenue) Like most cities, South Potato is a one-newspaper town. The *South Potato Truth* distributes its daily paper for a marginal cost of $0.10. The demand curve is given in Table 15.14.

Table 15.14

Price	Quantity	Revenues	Marginal revenue
$1.00	30,000		
$0.95	40,000		
$0.90	50,000		
$0.85	60,000		
$0.80	70,000		
$0.75	80,000		
$0.70	90,000		
$0.65	100,000		
$0.60	110,000		
$0.55	120,000		

a Calculate marginal revenue, and enter in the table.
b Find the profit-maximizing price and quantity.
c Suppose that a tax of $0.10 per paper is instituted. The tax will be paid by the newspaper company. Find the new profit-maximizing price and quantity.
d How much of the tax is paid by consumers?
e Draw a diagram illustrating your answer.

11 (Practice problem: marginal revenue) In competitive markets, price ceilings lower price and reduce the quantity sold. This is not true in monopoly markets. The demand for cable subscriptions in Motelville is given in Table 15.15. The marginal cost, including payments to the cable programming providers, is $15.

Table 15.15

Price	Quantity	Revenues	Marginal revenue
$45	60,000		
$40	80,000		
$35	100,000		
$30	120,000		
$25	140,000		

a Calculate marginal revenue, and enter in the table.
b Find the profit-maximizing price and quantity of subscriptions.
c Now suppose that the town sets a price ceiling equal to $25. How much will the company charge, and how many subscriptions will be sold?
d Draw a diagram illustrating your answer.

12 (Practice problem: marginal revenue) Because a monopoly is a single seller of a good, it has no competition. Since price elasticity is generally lower when consumers have little opportunity to find substitutes, you might think that the demand for the monopolist's product is always inelastic. Nevertheless, it is true that the monopolist always produces on the elastic portion of its demand curve. To see this, compute elasticity along the demand curve given in question 3a. Show that at the chosen price and quantity, the price elasticity of demand is greater than 1.

Answers to Problems

2 a Marginal revenue appears in Table 15.15.

Table 15.16

Price	Quantity	Revenues	Marginal revenue
$8	100,000	$ 800,000	—
$7	150,000	$1,050,000	$5
$6	200,000	$1,200,000	$3
$5	250,000	$1,250,000	$1
$4	300,000	$1,200,000	–$1
$3	350,000	$1,050,000	–$3
$2	400,000	$ 800,000	–$5

b Profits are maximized when the price is $5 and the number of fans is 250,000.
c Costs = $100,000 + (250,000 × $1) = $350,000; profits = $1,250,000 – $350,000 = $900,000.
d The price and quantity remain as in part a, but profits fall to $1,250,000 – $400,000 = $850,000.
e The solution is illustrated in the diagram.

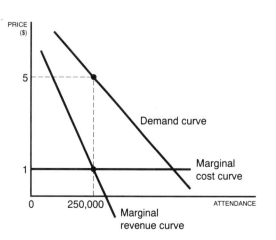

3 *a* Marginal revenue appears in Table 15.17.

Table 15.17

Price	Quantity	Revenues	Marginal revenue
$10	1	$10	—
$ 9	2	$18	$8
$ 8	3	$24	$6
$ 7	4	$28	$4
$ 6	5	$30	$2
$ 5	6	$30	$0
$ 4	7	$28	-$2

Price = $9; quantity = 2; profits = $18 – ($8 × 2) = $2.

b Marginal revenue appears in Table 15.18.

Table 15.18

Price	Quantity	Revenues	Marginal revenue
$0.50	500,000	$250,000	—
$0.45	600,000	$270,000	$0.20
$0.40	700,000	$280,000	$0.10
$0.35	800,000	$280,000	$0
$0.30	900,000	$270,000	-$0.10

Price = $0.40; quantity = 700,000; profits = $280,000 – [$50,000 + (700,000 × $0.10)] = $160,000.

c The complete table appears in Table 15.19.

Table 15.19

Price	Quantity	Revenues	Marginal revenue	Total costs	Marginal cost
$20	400	$ 8,000	—	$ 5,000	—
$18	800	$14,400	$16	$ 7,000	$ 5
$16	1,200	$19,200	$12	$ 9,400	$ 6
$14	1,600	$22,400	$ 8	$12,600	$ 8
$12	2,000	$24,000	$ 4	$16,200	$ 9
$10	2,400	$24,000	$ 0	$21,000	$12

Price = $14; quantity = 1,600; profits = $22,400 – $12,600 = $9,800.

d The completed table appears in Table 15.20.

Table 15.20

Price	Quantity	Revenues	Marginal revenue	Total costs	Marginal cost
$1.00	1,000	$1,000	—	$ 200	—
$0.90	2,000	$1,800	$0.80	$ 300	$0.10
$0.80	3,500	$2,800	$0.67	$ 450	$0.10
$0.70	5,500	$3,850	$0.52	$ 650	$0.10
$0.60	8,000	$4,800	$0.38	$ 900	$0.10
$0.50	11,000	$5,500	$0.23	$1,230	$0.11
$0.40	15,000	$6,000	$0.12	$1,730	$0.12
$0.30	20,000	$6,000	$0	$2,355	$0.14

Price = $0.40; quantity = 15,000; profits = $4,270.

5 *a* The marginal revenue figures appear in Table 15.21.

Table 15.21

	Home market				Foreign market		
Price	Quantity	Revenues	Marginal revenue	Price	Quantity	Revenues	Marginal revenue
$10	2,000	$20,000	—	$10	2,000	$20,000	—
$ 9	2,500	$22,500	$5	$ 9	3,000	$27,000	$7
$ 8	3,000	$24,000	$3	$ 8	4,000	$32,000	$5
$ 7	3,500	$24,500	$1	$ 7	5,000	$35,000	$3
$ 6	4,000	$24,000	-$1	$ 6	6,000	$36,000	$1
$ 5	4,500	$22,500	-$3	$ 5	7,000	$35,000	-$1
$ 4	5,000	$20,000	-$5	$ 4	8,000	$32,000	-$3

b Home market price = $7; quantity = 3,500. Foreign market price = $6; quantity = 6,000.

c Profits = $24,500 + $36,000 – [(3,500 + 6,000) × $1] – $5,000 = $46,000.

6 *a* The completed table appears in Table 15.22.

Table 15.22

	Suburbs				Inner city		
Price	Quantity	Revenues	Marginal revenue	Price	Quantity	Revenues	Marginal revenue
$4.00	200	$ 800	—	$4.00	100	$400	—
$3.50	400	$1,400	$3	$3.50	120	$420	$1
$3.00	600	$1,800	$2	$3.00	140	$420	$0
$2.50	800	$2,000	$1	$2.50	160	$400	-$1
$2.00	1,000	$2,000	$0	$2.00	180	$360	-$2
$1.50	1,200	$1,800	-$1	$1.50	200	$300	-$3

b Suburbs price = $2.50; quantity = 800. Inner city price = $3.50; quantity = 120.

c Profits = $2,000 + $420 – [(800 + 120) × $1] = $1,500.

9 *a,c* The marginal revenues and Magdalena's revenues are given in Table 15.23.

Table 15.23

Price	Quantity	Revenues	Marginal revenue	Magdalena's revenue
$20	20,000	$400,000	—	$100,000
$18	25,000	$450,000	$10	$112,500
$16	30,000	$480,000	$ 6	$120,000
$14	35,000	$490,000	$ 2	$122,500
$12	40,000	$480,000	-$ 2	$120,000
$10	48,000	$480,000	$ 0	$120,000

b,d The profix-maximizing price is $16 and the quantity is 30,000, but Magdalena's revenues are maximized at a price of $14, where 35,000 CDs are sold.

e The solution is illustrated in the diagram.

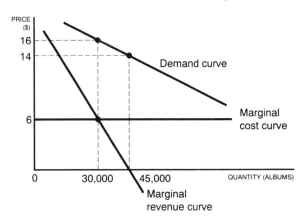

10 *a* Marginal revenue is given in Table 15.24.

Table 15.24

Price	Quantity	Revenues	Marginal revenue
$1.00	30,000	$30,000	—
$0.95	40,000	$38,000	$0.80
$0.90	50,000	$45,000	$0.70
$0.85	60,000	$51,000	$0.60
$0.80	70,000	$56,000	$0.50
$0.75	80,000	$60,000	$0.40
$0.70	90,000	$63,000	$0.30
$0.65	100,000	$65,000	$0.20
$0.60	110,000	$66,000	$0.10
$0.55	120,000	$66,000	$0

b Price = $0.60; quantity = 110,000.
c The tax increases marginal cost to $0.20. The price becomes $0.65 and the quantity, 100,000.
d Consumers pay $0.05 of the tax.
e The solution is illustrated in the diagram.

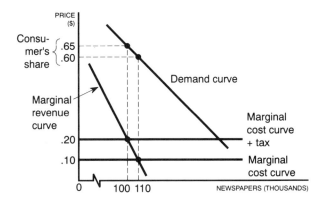

11 *a* Marginal revenue is given in Table 15.25.

Table 15.25

Price	Quantity	Revenues	Marginal revenue
$45	60,000	$2,700,000	—
$40	80,000	$3,200,000	$25
$35	100,000	$3,500,000	$15
$30	120,000	$3,600,000	$ 5
$25	140,000	$3,500,000	−$ 5

b Price = $35; quantity = 100,000.
c Price = $25; quantity = 140,000.
d The solution is illustrated in the diagram.

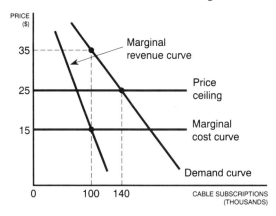

12 The elasticity for each point on the demand curve is given in Table 15.26.

Table 15.26

Price	Quantity	Revenues	Marginal revenue	Elasticity
$10	1	$10	—	—
$ 9	2	$18	$8	19/3
$ 8	3	$24	$6	17/5
$ 7	4	$28	$4	15/7
$ 6	5	$30	$2	13/9
$ 5	6	$30	$0	11/11
$ 4	7	$28	−$2	9/11

Along the elastic portion of the demand curve, which is where price exceeds $5, marginal revenue is positive. Marginal revenue equals marginal cost at a price of $9, which is on the elastic portion.

Chapter 16

OLIGOPOLIES

Chapter Review

Chapters 15 and 16 present the three imperfect competitive market structures: monopoly, monopolistic competition, and oligopoly. Chapter 15 dealt with the first two; this chapter rounds out the study with a look at oligopoly.

Oligopolies are industries in which only a few firms dominate. Each firm watches its competitors closely, because each firm's best price, output level, or strategy depends on what its rivals choose. The North American automobile industry is a perfect example of an oligopolistic market. Even today, with foreign firms competing in the Canadian market, it is still easy to see how the "big three" (General Motors, Ford, and Chrysler) respond to one another with competing rebate programs, lower prices, or cheap financing. The chapter introduces the Prisoner's Dilemma models to examine the possibilities and motives for collusion. Chapter 17 builds upon the insights of this chapter and Chapter 15 to explore government policy towards imperfect competition.

ESSENTIAL CONCEPTS

1 In **oligopolies**, a few firms dominate the industry. If any one firm changes its price, produces more, or adopts a new strategy, then the other firms in the oligopoly will notice the change and react to it. It is essential, then, that oligopolists pay careful attention and try to anticipate the reactions of rivals. This strategic interaction is the essential feature of oligopolies, and it makes the study of oligopolies both difficult and fascinating.

2 Because total profits are lower when firms compete, oligopolists have an incentive to form a cartel and to collude, fix prices, and share the market. This behaviour is not only illegal in Canada but is also difficult to sustain. First, individual firms are tempted to cheat and take advantage of the higher prices charged by others by undercutting their prices. Further, as demand and costs change over time, oligopolies have trouble renegotiating their tacit agreements. Finally, the pure profits earned by successful colluders attract entry and new competition.

3 The conflict between collusion and competition is at the heart of oligopoly. The combined profits of firms are highest if they collude. Collectively, their incentives are to fix prices and share the market. But each individual firm is tempted by its own self-interest. If the rivals keep their prices high, a firm can undercut

and capture the market. The **Prisoner's Dilemma** summarizes this conflict and shows how collusion might work. If the game is played only once and self-interest quickly takes over, all firms cheat and the equilibrium is competition. If the game is played repeatedly for an indefinite period of time, firms may be able to threaten cheaters with competitive price wars and motivate one another to collude.

4 Certain **restrictive practices** help sustain collusion. These include assigning exclusive territories to individual firms, requiring exclusive dealing at retail outlets, and insisting upon tie-in arrangements that force a customer who buys one product to buy an additional product. These practices can reduce competition by increasing the costs of capturing the customers of rival firms. Firms also facilitate cooperation through such practices as matching their rival's low-price offers.

5 Existing firms always face the problem of entry, and the threat can sometimes be so strong that it keeps prices close to production costs. When potential competition induces competitive prices, markets are called **contestable.** Costs of entry and exit must be relatively small, however, and the persistence of certain oligopolies through time suggests that significant barriers to entry exist in these industries, and hence that these particular markets are not contestable.

6 There are three important models of competition in oligopolies.

  a If firms are committed to producing a given amount of output, as is the case in industries where fixed costs are high and changing capacity is very expensive, there is quantity or **Cournot competition.** One such example is the steel industry. Setting up a factory to commence or expand production is very expensive, so the firm gets locked in at certain capacities. It tries to select capacities corresponding to a price where profits will be maximized. The equilibrium is given by the intersection of **reaction** functions, which indicate the quantity that one firm will produce for each possible quantity choice of its rivals.

  b If the costs of increasing capacity are low, then price or **Bertrand competition** reigns. An example of this is a particular route flown by an airline—for example, between Toronto and Montreal. Varying capacity is easy, and the airline selects a price corresponding to a quantity where profits will be maximized. The equilibrium is again given by the intersection of reaction functions; however, in this model, the reaction functions show the price that one firm will charge for each possible price of its rival.

  c The **kinked demand curve** model shows that if firms expect rivals to match a price cut but not price increases, then they are unlikely to change price or quantity.

BEHIND THE ESSENTIAL CONCEPTS

1 The world of perfect competition is simple and precise. The firm cannot affect the market of any competitor; it simply chooses its quantity to maximize profits. The world of oligopoly is rich and varied. Firms try to limit competition and promote collusion. They have a wealth of strategies to choose from: price and quantity, of course, but also such practices as matching offers of rivals and threatening price wars with new entrants or existing firms who cheat on tacit agreements to limit price competition. Oligopoly is an area in which economics has made much progress in the last 10 or 15 years.

2 As a group, firms in an oligopoly want to cooperate, charge high prices, and share monopoly profits, but they always run up against the problem of self-interest. Each individual firm would like to cheat while the others abide by the cooperative strategy. It is this noncooperative behaviour by individual firms that promotes economic efficiency, because it keeps the oligopolists from cooperating to gouge customers with high prices. It is ironic that if firms were more cooperative, the economy would not work so well.

3[1] The most important technique for studying oligopolies is the reaction function. The equilibrium in the industry is at the intersection of reaction functions, but the reasoning is not the same as in the supply and demand model. Because there are few firms, the profit-maximizing price, quantity, or other strategy depends upon what the other firms do. How is the individual firm to decide without actually knowing the choices of rivals? The reaction function shows what the choice would be for every possible choice by the rival. Putting the reaction functions of both firms together gives the equilibrium. At the intersection, each firm is choosing what is best for it in response to the actual choice of the rival. Since neither can improve matters unilaterally, there are no forces for change, and the market is in equilibrium.

SELF-TEST

True or False

1 In an oligopoly, firms must worry about the reactions of rivals.

2 In Cournot competition, oligopolists choose their quantity expecting that their rivals will produce the same quantity as they.

3 In Bertrand competition, firms choose their price expecting their rivals to keep price constant.

[1]This topic is covered in the appendix to Chapter 16.

4 In Bertrand competition, firms perceive a more elastic demand than in the Cournot model.

5 In Cournot competition, the quantity chosen is more than would be chosen in competition but less than would be chosen in monopoly.

6 If the firms' goods are perfect substitutes, the price in Bertrand competition is the monopoly price.

7 If the firm perceives a kinked demand curve, there is a jump in marginal revenue at the current output.

8 A cartel is a group of firms engaging in price competition.

9 Anti-combines laws allow cartels to negotiate openly to fix prices.

10 Offers to match prices charged by rivals result in more price competition.

11 A price leader can help a cartel adjust to changing conditions.

12 One difficulty that cartels have is that when they succeed in raising price, their members are tempted to undercut the cartel price.

13 If one firm offers to match a rival's prices, this encourages competitive pricing.

14 In contestable markets, charging higher prices discourages entry.

15 Resale price maintenance is an example of the form of restrictive practice referred to as a vertical price restraint.

Multiple Choice

1 Unlike firms operating in monopolistically competitive markets, oligopolists

   a face downward-sloping demand curves.
   b are price takers.
   c must worry about how rivals will react to their decisions.
   d set price above marginal cost.
   e none of the above.

2 A group of companies that act jointly to divide the industry and maximize profits is called

   a a monopoly.
   b a monopsony.
   c a cartel.
   d an anti-combine.
   e none of the above.

3 One difficulty cartels have is that individual firms may

   a charge more than the agreed-upon price and sell more than the agreed-upon quantity.
   b charge less than the agreed-upon price and sell less than the agreed-upon quantity.
   c charge more than the agreed-upon price and sell less than the agreed-upon quantity.

   d charge less than the agreed-upon price and sell more than the agreed-upon quantity.
   e none of the above.

4 In the Prisoner's Dilemma,

   a both prisoners act in their own self-interest; this leads to the best alternative from their combined standpoint.
   b both prisoners cooperate to bring about the best alternative.
   c acting in their own self-interest, the prisoners bring about the worst alternative.
   d it is impossible to say what happens because each prisoner must worry about the reactions of the other.
   e none of the above.

5 Which of the following is not true of a collusive agreement?

   a It is illegal.
   b It encourages firms to cheat on rival firms.
   c It is difficult to negotiate when demand and cost conditions are changing.
   d Cooperative arrangements among rival firms are a method of enforcement.
   e It will always break down eventually.

6 When oligopolists publicly offer to match any price charged by any other firm, there will be

   a more price competition.
   b the same amount of price competition.
   c less price competition.
   d trouble because matching offers are illegal.
   e none of the above.

7 In contestable markets,

   a firms can successfully collude to share monopoly profits.
   b firms are unable to collude because cartel members cheat on tacit agreements.
   c potential competition ensures competitive pricing.
   d price returns to the competitive level, but only after entry.
   e firms deter the entry of new competition by carrying excess capacity.

8 A tie-in is

   a a requirement that firms offer the same price as their rivals.
   b an agreement among cartel members to match price cuts but not price increases.
   c a requirement that any customer who buys one product must buy another.
   d a practice whereby the prices of the followers are tied to the leader's price.
   e a threat to meet new entry with resistance.

9 A firm that sets price below cost to drive a rival out of business is engaging in

   a predatory pricing.
   b limit pricing.

c contestable pricing.

d collusive pricing.

e none of the above.

10 A firm may use excess production capacity to

a deceive potential entrants into believing that business is bad.

b threaten potential entrants with increased production if they come into the market.

c confuse potential entrants about the cost of production.

d increase its rival's costs.

e none of the above.

11 An incumbent firm may lower its price to

a persuade potential entrants that its marginal costs are high.

b persuade potential entrants that its marginal costs are low.

c persuade potential entrants that its total costs are high.

d persuade potential entrants that its total costs are low.

e none of the above.

12 If collusion is not possible, restrictive practices that are used to restrict competition include

a vertical and horizontal restraints.

b exclusive dealing.

c resale price maintenance.

d price leadership.

e tied selling.

13 In Cournot competition, the firms

a compete by choosing quantity, given some conjecture about the quantity that the rival will produce.

b compete by choosing price, given some conjecture about the price that the rival will charge.

c match price cuts by rivals but not price increases.

d collude to fix prices and earn monopoly profits.

e divide the market in an orderly way.

14 In Bertrand competition, the firms

a compete by choosing quantity, given some conjecture about the quantity that the rival will produce.

b compete by choosing price, given some conjecture about the price that the rival will charge.

c match price cuts by rivals but not price increases.

d collude to fix prices and earn monopoly profits.

e divide the market in an orderly way.

15[2] In the Cournot model, the reaction function

a specifies the level of output of the firm given what it expects the other firm to produce.

b specifies the price the firm will charge given what it expects the other firm to charge.

c shows how the market will react to an increase in the profits of the firm.

d outlines how the firms in a cartel will react to cheating by one of the members.

e none of the above.

16 Equilibrium output in the Cournot model is

a more than in perfect competition.

b the same as in perfect competition.

c more than in monopoly.

d less than in monopoly.

e none of the above.

17 Marginal revenue for the firm with a kinked demand curve

a is greater than in monopoly.

b is less than in monopoly.

c is the same as in monopoly.

d has a jump at the level of current output.

e none of the above.

18 If the goods are not perfect substitutes, equilibrium price in the Bertrand model is

a higher than marginal cost.

b less than marginal cost.

c equal to marginal cost.

d the same as in monopoly.

e none of the above.

19 If the goods are perfect substitutes, equilibrium price in the Bertrand model is

a higher than marginal cost.

b less than marginal cost.

c equal to marginal cost.

d less than in monopoly.

e none of the above.

20 If rivals match price cuts but do not match price increases, the demand curve facing the firm

a is kinked at the current output level.

b has a jump at the current output level.

c is horizontal at the current price.

d is vertical at the current output level.

e none of the above.

Completion

1 In an oligopoly, there are so few firms that each must consider how its rival will _____ to any change in strategy.

2 A group of companies operating jointly as if they were a monopoly is called a _____.

3 Collusive behaviour is prohibited by _____ laws.

4 The _____ is a game that illustrates the problem cartels have in enforcing collusive behaviour.

5 Markets in which the threat of competition impels firms to charge the competitive price are called _____.

[2]This topic is covered in the appendix to Chapter 16.

6   A firm that insists that any other firm selling its products refrain from selling those of its rivals is engaging in _____.

7   Meeting competitors' prices is known as a _____.

8   Tied selling is a form of _____.

9   If a firm believes that its rivals will match its price cuts but not its price increases, then it will perceive its demand curve to be _____ at the current price.

10 Firms competing in price believe that they face _____ elastic demand curves than firms who compete through quantities.

Answers to Self-Test

True or False

1	t	6	f	11	t
2	f	7	t	12	t
3	t	8	f	13	f
4	t	9	f	14	f
5	f	10	f	15	t

Multiple Choice

1	c	6	c	11	b	16	c
2	c	7	c	12	d	17	d
3	d	8	c	13	a	18	a
4	c	9	a	14	b	19	c
5	e	10	b	15	a	20	a

Completion

1   react
2   cartel
3   anti-combines laws
4   Prisoner's Dilemma
5   contestable
6   exclusive dealing
7   facilitating practice
8   vertical restraint
9   kinked
10 more

Doing Economics: Tools and Practice Problems

This section looks at three issues pertaining to oligopoly. First, we consider collusion and the difficulty that cartels have in enforcing their tacit agreements. We see not only how two firms can divide a market and share monopoly profits but also how difficult it is to maintain a cartel. The cartel's success in restricting output and raising prices tempts each of the cartel members to cheat by producing more than their assigned amounts and undercutting the cartel's price. One way to lessen the incentives to cheat is to assign exclusive territories. We look at collusion and cheating in several problems before turning to some simple game theory

problems, using the Prisoner's Dilemma framework to investigate collusion.

Tool Kit 16.1: Organizing a Cartel of Many Price-Taking Firms

Step one: Identify and add up the supply curves of the individual firms. The result is the cartel's marginal cost curve.

Step two: Identify the market demand curve, and find its marginal revenue.

Step three: Find the profit-maximizing price and quantity for the cartel by setting marginal revenue equal to marginal cost.

Step four: Determine each firm's output by evenly dividing the cartel's output among its members.

---

1   (Worked problem: collusion and cheating) The Quebec Maple Syrup Board is a cartel of 1,000 maple syrup producers. The demand for maple syrup and the supply curve of one typical producer are given in Table 16.1. The quantity represents litres.

Table 16.1

Market demand		Firm's supply	
Price	*Quantity*	*Price*	*Quantity*
$10	10,000	$10	60
$ 9	15,000	$ 9	55
$ 8	20,000	$ 8	50
$ 7	25,000	$ 7	45
$ 6	30,000	$ 6	40
$ 5	35,000	$ 5	35
		$ 4	30
		$ 3	25
		$ 2	20

a   Find the profit-maximizing price for the cartel as a whole. How many litres will be sold at this price: How many must each firm produce to sustain this price?

b   If the cartel charges the price computed in part a, how many units would the individual firm like to produce?

c   Now suppose that all firms cheat and the market becomes competitive. Find the equilibrium price and quantity.

Step-by-step solution

Step one (a): Add up the individual supplies. Since there are 1,000 firms, the market supply is simply the quantity supplied by the firm multiplied by 1,000. The market supply is given in Table 16.2.

Table 16.2

Firm's supply		Market supply	
Price	Quantity	Price	Quantity
$10	60	$10	60,000
$ 9	55	$ 9	55,000
$ 8	50	$ 8	50,000
$ 7	45	$ 7	45,000
$ 6	40	$ 6	40,000
$ 5	35	$ 5	35,000
$ 4	30	$ 4	30,000
$ 3	25	$ 3	25,000
$ 2	20	$ 2	20,000

Step two: Derive marginal revenue. First find total revenue, and enter it in the appropriate column. Marginal revenue is the change in total revenue divided by the change in quantity. The answer is given in Table 16.3.

Table 16.3

Market demand		Total	Marginal
Price	Quantity	revenue	revenue
$10	10,000	$100,000	
$ 9	15,000	$135,000	$7
$ 8	20,000	$160,000	$5
$ 7	25,000	$175,000	$3
$ 6	30,000	$180,000	$1
$ 5	35,000	$175,000	−$1

Step three: Find the profit-maximizing price for the cartel. The market supply curve is the cartel's marginal cost. Marginal cost equals marginal revenue when the quantity is 25,000. The corresponding price is $7. Each firm produces 25 litres.

Step four (b): Find how much the firm would like to supply at the cartel price. At a price of $7, the firm would like to produce 45 units (this number is read off the firm's supply curve), which is 20 more than it is assigned.

Step five (c): If all firms cheat, then the market will become a competitive market and will clear at a price of $5, where each firm produces 35 litres.

2   (Practice problem: collusion and cheating) The 500 mail-order computer equipment suppliers are (discreetly) forming a cartel. The market demand curve and the supply curve of a typical equipment supplier are given in Table 16.4. The quantity represents the number of computers.

Table 16.4

Market demand		Total	Marginal
Price	Quantity	revenue	revenue
$1,000	300,000		
$ 900	400,000		
$ 800	500,000		
$ 700	600,000		
$ 600	700,000		
$ 500	800,000		
$ 400	900,000		
$ 300	1,000,000		

Firm's supply		Market supply	
Price	Quantity	Price	Quantity
$1,000	4,000		
$ 900	3,500		
$ 800	3,000		
$ 700	2,400		
$ 600	2,000		
$ 500	1,600		
$ 400	1,000		
$ 300	500		
$ 200	100		

a   Derive the marginal revenue for the computer equipment supplier market.

b   Add up the 500 individual firm supplies to derive the market supply.

c   Find the profit-maximizing price for the cartel as a whole. How many computers will be sold at this price? How many must each firm sell to sustain this price?

d   If the cartel charges the price computed in part c, how many units would the individual firm like to sell?

e   Now suppose that all firms cheat, and the market becomes competitive. Find the equilibrium price and quantity.

Tool Kit 16.2: Finding the Profit-Maximizing Output in Quantity Competition between Duopolists

In some industries, such as steel or aluminum, the fixed costs of plant and equipment are such a large share of total costs that firms have little discretion in changing output once the machinery is in place. In this case, the competition is over quantity, and the price will be whatever clears the market of the quantities that firms have collectively decided to produce.

Step one: Identify the market demand, marginal cost, and output of the opponent firm.

Step two: Subtract the output of the opponent firm from the market demand. The difference is called the **residual demand curve**:

residual demand =
market demand – opponent's output.

Step three: Find the marginal revenue for the residual demand curve.

Step four: Choose the output for which marginal revenue equals marginal cost.

---

3 (Worked problem: quantity competition) The New Chairs for Old Company shares the furniture-refinishing market in Southpoint with the Like New Company. Each uses enormous vats of chemicals, which are expensive to set up but cheap to operate. One vat will permit the refinishing of 10 pieces of furniture per day. The marginal cost for each firm is constant and equal to $4. Table 16.5 gives the market demand.

Table 16.5

Price	Quantity
$7.50	0
$7.00	10
$6.50	20
$6.00	30
$5.50	40
$5.00	50
$4.50	60
$4.00	70

a Suppose that the two firms try to operate as a cartel and share the market equally. Find the profit-maximizing quantity for each.

b Now look at the problem from the point of view of the owner of New Chairs for Old. The owner conjectures that the rival firm will commit to the quantity solved for in part a. Find the profit-maximizing quantity.

Step-by-step solution

Step one (a): We follow the usual procedure for the monopolist: find the marginal revenue and set marginal revenue equal to marginal cost. Table 16.6 gives the marginal revenue.

Table 16.6

Price	Quantity	Total revenue	Marginal revenue
$7.50	0	$ 0	—
$7.00	10	$ 70	$7
$6.50	20	$130	$6
$6.00	30	$180	$5
$5.50	40	$220	$4
$5.00	50	$250	$3
$4.50	60	$270	$2
$4.00	70	$280	$1

Marginal revenue equals marginal cost when the total quantity is 40. Each firm then buys two vats and refinishes 20 pieces of furniture.

Step two (b): Identify the market demand, marginal cost, and output of the opponent firm. The market demand is given in Table 16.5, the marginal cost is $4, and Like New is expected to produce 20.

Step three: Subtract the output of the opponent firm from the market demand, as shown in Table 16.7.

Table 16.7

Price	Quantity
$7.00	0
$6.50	20 – 20 = 0
$6.00	30 – 20 = 10
$5.50	40 – 20 = 20
$5.00	50 – 20 = 30
$4.50	60 – 20 = 40
$4.00	70 – 20 = 50

Step four: Find the marginal revenue for the residual demand curve, as given in Table 16.8.

Step five: Choose the output for which marginal revenue equals marginal cost. When output is 30, marginal revenue and marginal cost both equal $4.

Table 16.8

Price	Quantity	Total revenue	Marginal revenue
$7.00	0	0	—
$6.50	0	0	—
$6.00	10	$ 60	$6
$5.50	20	$110	$5
$5.00	30	$150	$4
$4.50	40	$180	$3
$4.00	50	$200	$2

4 (Practice problem: quantity competition) The Davis Lead Company competes with its rival Anderson Lead. Because the plant and equipment are so expensive and because marginal production costs are so low (only $5 per tonne) until capacity is reached, the two firms compete by choosing quantity. The market demand is given in Table 16.9.

Table 16.9

Price	Quantity (tonnes)
$22.50	0
$20.00	100
$17.50	200
$15.00	300
$12.50	400
$10.00	500
$ 7.50	600

a Suppose that the two firms try to operate as a cartel and share the market equally. Find the profit-maximizing quantity for each.

b Now look at the problem from the point of view of the owner of Davis. The owner conjectures that the rival firm will commit to the quantity solved for in part a. Find the profit-maximizing quantity.

5 (Worked problem: price competition) There are two dry-cleaning establishments in Mudville: Jay's Cleaners and Fay's Cleaners. Although they hate each other personally, the two owners have decided to form a cartel. This is illegal, of course, but they meet discreetly. Each faces a marginal cost of $1 per item. Consumers always patronize the lower-price establishment; therefore, either Jay or Fay can capture the entire market by pricing below the other. One additional fact is that in Mudville people only carry half dollars, so the price must be a multiple of $0.50. Table 16.10 gives the market demand.

Table 16.10

Price	Quantity
$3.00	1,500
$2.50	3,000
$2.00	4,500
$1.50	6,000
$1.00	7,500

a Derive marginal revenue, and enter in the table.

b Find the profit-maximizing price. If they divide the market equally, how many items will each clean?

c Compute the profits for each firm.

d Suppose that Fay decides to undercut Jay and capture the market. What price will Fay charge? How many will Fay sell? Compute Fay's profits.

Step-by-step solution

Step one (a): Derive marginal revenue. Follow the usual procedure, as in Table 16.11.

Table 16.11

Price	Quantity	Total revenue	Marginal revenue
$3.00	1,500	$4,500	$3
$2.50	3,000	$7,500	$2
$2.00	4,500	$9,000	$1
$1.50	6,000	$9,000	$0
$1.00	7,500	$7,500	–$1

Step two (b): Find the profit-maximizing price. Marginal cost equals marginal revenue at a price of $2.

Step three (c): At a price of $2, there are 4,500 items cleaned. If each does one-half, then each cleans 2,250. The profits for each are $2 – $1 = $1 per unit, so each earns $2,250.

Step four (d): Fay can capture the market by charging the next-lower price, which is $1.50. Fay will sell 6,000 units. Fay's profit will be $1.50 – $1.00 = $0.50 per unit for a total of $3,000. Fay gains $750 by cheating on their agreement.

6 (Practice problem: price competition) Yuppie Company and its rival Buppie Company sell dark green and gray rag wool sweaters through catalogues. They buy the sweaters from supplier firms for $10 each. The market demand is given in Table 16.12.

Table 16.12

Quantity (sweaters)	Price
$27.50	0
$25.00	100
$22.50	200
$20.00	300
$17.50	400
$15.00	500
$12.50	600

a Derive marginal revenue, and enter in the table.

b Find the profit-maximizing price. If the companies divide the market equally, how many items will each sell?

c Compute the profits for each firm.

d Suppose that Yuppie decides to undercut Buppie and capture the market. What price will it charge? How many will it sell? Compute its profits.

Tool Kit 16.3: Using the Prisoner's Dilemma

The Prisoner's Dilemma highlights the conflict between what is good for the cartel as a whole and what is best for the individual firm. The next few problems show how to represent this conflict as a game.

Step one: Draw a box with four cells, and label it as shown.

Step two: Identify the payoffs for each party if both cooperate, and enter in the appropriate cell.

		FIRM A	
		cooperate	compete
FIRM B	cooperate	A's profits = B's profits =	
	compete		

Step three: Identify the payoffs for each party if both compete, and enter in the appropriate cell.

		FIRM A	
		cooperate	compete
FIRM B	cooperate		
	compete		A's profits = B's profits =

Step four: Identify the payoffs for each party if one competes while the other cooperates, and enter in the corresponding cells.

		FIRM A	
		cooperate	compete
FIRM B	cooperate		A's profits = B's profits =
	compete	A's profits = B's profits =	

Step five: In the classic Prisoner's Dilemma, competing is always the best strategy, whatever the opponent chooses. Show that competition is the equilibrium.

7 (Worked problem: Prisoner's Dilemma) Chiaravelli and Fiegenshau are the only two dentists in Plainville. They have been colluding, sharing the market and earning monopoly profits of $100,000 each for several years. Fiegenshau is considering reducing the price. Fiegenshau estimates that if Chiaravelli keeps the price at current levels, Fiegenshau would earn $150,000, although Chiaravelli's earnings would fall to $25,000. There is also the possibility that Chiaravelli would compete against Fiegenshau. The resulting price war would reduce the earnings of each to $40,000.

  a Represent this market as a Prisoner's Dilemma game.
  b Explain why the equilibrium of both dentists competing might be the outcome.

Step-by-step solution

Step one (a): Draw a box with four cells, and label it as shown.

		CHIARAVELLI	
		cooperate	compete
FIEGENSHAU	cooperate		
	compete		

Step two: Identify the payoffs for each party if both co-operate, and enter in the appropriate cell. If both cooperate, they each earn $100,000.

		CHIARAVELLI	
		cooperate	compete
FIEGENSHAU	cooperate	C = $100,000 F = $100,000	
	compete		

Step three: Identify the payoffs for each party if both compete, and enter in the appropriate cell. If both compete, they each earn $40,000.

		CHIARAVELLI	
		cooperate	compete
FIEGENSHAU	cooperate	C = $100,000 F = $100,000	
	compete		C = $40,000 F = $40,000

Step four: Identify the payoffs for each party if one competes while the other cooperates, and enter in the corresponding cells. In this case, the dentist who competes earns $150,000, and the other is left with $25,000.

		CHIARAVELLI	
		cooperate	compete
FIEGENSHAU	cooperate	C = $100,000 F = $100,000	C = $150,000 F = $25,000
	compete	C = $25,000 F = $150,000	C = $40,000 F = $40,000

Step five (b): Show that competition is the equilibrium. For each party, competition is always the best alternative. If Chiavarelli cooperates, then Fiegenshau can earn more by competing ($150,000 > $100,000). If Chiavarelli competes, again Fiegenshau earns more by competing ($40,000 > $25,000). The same is true for Chiavarelli, and both choose to compete.

8 (Practice problem: Prisoner's Dilemma) Upper Peninsula Airlines and Northern Airways share the market from Toronto to the winter resorts in the South. If they cooperate, they can extract enough monopoly profits to earn $400,000 each, but unbridled competition would reduce profits to $50,000 each. If one is foolish enough

to cooperate in its pricing policy while the other under-cuts it, the cooperating firm would earn $0, and the competing firm would earn $800,000.

  a Represent this market as a Prisoner's Dilemma game.
  b Explain why the equilibrium might be that both firms choose a competitive strategy.

9 (Practice problem: Prisoner's Dilemma) Hill College and Allan College are the best private schools in the city. Each also prides itself on its lacrosse team. If neither offers scholarships for promising players, then obviously the cost of scholarships will be zero. For $20,000 in scholarships, either could attract the best players (if the other did not offer scholarships), win the provincial championship, and attract at least $50,000 in new donations. In this case, however, do-nations at the losing school would fall by $30,000. On the other hand, if both offered scholarships, there would be no advantage, no extra donations, and each would have spent the $20,000 for nothing.

  a Represent this market as a Prisoner's Dilemma game.
  b Explain why the equilibrium might be that both schools compete.

10 (Worked problem: facilitating and restrictive prac-tices) This problem builds upon problem 3. Having accumulated several years of experience with the un-pleasant results of competition, the owners of South-point's two furniture-refinishing firms decide to try a new method of collusion. Henceforth, the New Chairs for Old Company will specialize in refinishing chairs, and the Like New Company will take care of the ta-ble share of the market. It so happens in Southpoint that exactly half the business involves tables and half involves chairs. Their marginal costs remain at $4.

  a Compute the profit-maximizing quantity of chairs and tables and the corresponding prices for both companies.
  b Compare the answer to the answer to part a of problem 3.

Step-by-step solution

Step one (a): Divide the market into chair and table markets. The result is given in Table 16.13.

Table 16.13

Price	Quantity of chairs	Quantity of tables
$7.50	0	0
$7.00	5	5
$6.50	10	10
$6.00	15	15
$5.50	20	20
$5.00	25	25
$4.50	30	30
$4.00	35	35

Step two: Compute the marginal revenue for each firm. These are shown in Table 16.14. Note that since the demands are exactly the same, so are the marginal revenues. Only one is shown.

Table 16.14

Price	Quantity of chairs	Quantity of tables	Total revenue	Marginal revenue
$7.50	0	0	$ 0	—
$7.00	5	5	$ 35	$7
$6.50	10	10	$ 65	$6
$6.00	15	15	$ 90	$5
$5.50	20	20	$110	$4
$5.00	25	25	$125	$3
$4.50	30	30	$135	$2
$4.00	35	35	$140	$1

Step three (b): Marginal revenue equals marginal cost at a quantity of 20 for each. The market price will be $5.50, which is exactly the outcome that was solved for in part a of problem 3. Dividing the market promotes collusion.

11 (Practice problem: facilitating and restrictive prac-tices) This problem builds upon problem 4. The Da-vis and Anderson Companies have come up with a scheme to promote collusion. From now on, Davis will advertise and take orders from customers in the West and leave the eastern half of the market to An-derson. They divide the territories so that exactly half the customers will go to each firm. The marginal cost remains at $5 per tonne, and the market demand is as given in Table 16.9.

  a Compute the profit-maximizing quantity and price for each firm.
  b Compare with the collusive price and quantity solved for in part a of problem 4.

12 (Worked problem: facilitating and restrictive prac-tices) Let's return to Mudville and problem 5, where Fay is considering undercutting Jay.

  a Compute profits if Fay reduces the price by $50 be-low the collusive price and Jay matches the price cut. Assume that customers divide themselves equally between the firms charging the same price.
  b Derive Fay's demand curve under the assumption that Jay will match any price cuts but not price in-creases. Draw a diagram illustrating your answer.

Step-by-step solution

Step one (a): The collusive price is $2.00, and Fay's profits are $2,250. If Fay cuts price to $1.50 and Jay matches the cut, then the quantity demanded is 6,000, and Fay will clear 3,000 items.

Step two: Fay earns ($1.50 − $1.00) × 3,000 = $1,500. Be-cause this number is less than collusive profits, the offer to match price cuts by Jay will deter Fay from undercutting.

Step three (b): To find the demand if Jay matches price cuts (below $2) but not price increases, simply divide the market evenly at prices of $2 or below, and give all the customers to Jay for higher prices. Table 16.15 gives the result. Notice the kink at a price of $2.

Table 16.15

Price	Quantity
$3.00	0
$2.50	0
$2.00	2,250
$1.50	3,000
$1.00	3,750

13 (Practice problem: facilitating and restrictive practices) Return to problem 6 and the competition between Yuppie and Buppie. Suppose that each agrees to match price offers of the other.

a   Compute Yuppie's profits if it cuts price by $2.50 below the collusive price and its cut is matched by Buppie. Assume that customers divide themselves equally between firms charging the same price.

b   Derive Yuppie's demand curve assuming that Buppie will match price cuts (below the collusive price) but not price increases.

Answers to Problems

2   *a,b* The marginal revenue and the market supply appear in Table 16.16.

Table 16.16

Market demand		Total revenue	Marginal revenue
Price	Quantity		
$1,000	300,000	$300,000,000	—
$ 900	400,000	$360,000,000	$600
$ 800	500,000	$400,000,000	$400
$ 700	600,000	$420,000,000	$200
$ 600	700,000	$420,000,000	$ 0
$ 500	800,000	$400,000,000	–$200
$ 400	900,000	$360,000,000	–$400
$ 300	1,000,000	$300,000,000	–$600

Firm's supply		Market supply	
Price	Quantity	Price	Quantity
$1,000	4,000	$1,000	2,000,000
$ 900	3,500	$ 900	1,750,000
$ 800	3,000	$ 800	1,500,000
$ 700	2,400	$ 700	1,200,000
$ 600	2,000	$ 600	1,000,000
$ 500	1,600	$ 500	800,000
$ 400	1,000	$ 400	500,000
$ 300	500	$ 300	250,000
$ 200	100	$ 200	50,000

c   Cartel price = $800; market quantity = 500,000; each firm's quantity = 1,000.
d   3,000.
e   Price = $500; quantity = 800,000.

4   a   Marginal revenue for the market demand is given in Table 16.17.

Table 16.17

Price	Quantity (tonnes)	Revenues	Marginal revenue
$22.50	0	$ 0	
$20.00	100	$2,000	$20
$17.50	200	$3,500	$15
$15.00	300	$4,500	$10
$12.50	400	$5,000	$ 5
$10.00	500	$5,000	$ 0
$ 7.50	600	$4,500	–$ 5

Price = $12.50; market quantity = 400; each firm sells 200 tonnes.

b   The residual demand is found by subtracting 200 from the market demand. This and marginal revenue appear in Table 16.18.

Table 16.18

Price	Quantity (tonnes)	Revenues	Marginal revenue
$22.50	0	$ 0	
$20.00	0	$ 0	
$17.50	0	$ 0	
$15.00	100	$1,500	$15
$12.50	200	$2,500	$10
$10.00	300	$3,000	$ 5
$ 7.50	400	$3,000	$ 0

Davis will produce 300. The market quantity will be 200 + 300 = 500, and the price will be $10 per tonne.

6   a   Marginal revenue for the market demand is given in Table 16.19.

Table 16.19

Price	Quantity (sweaters)	Revenues	Marginal revenue
$27.50	0	$ 0	—
$25.00	100	$2,500	$25
$22.50	200	$4,500	$20
$20.00	300	$6,000	$15
$17.50	400	$7,000	$10
$15.00	500	$7,500	$ 5
$12.50	600	$7,500	$ 0

b   Cartel price = $17.50; market quantity = 400; each firm sells 200.
c   Profits = (200 × $17.50) – (200 × $10) = $1,500.
d   Yuppie's price = $15; quantity = 500; profits = ($15 × 500) – ($10 × 500) = $2,500.

8 *a*

	Upper Peninsula	
	cooperate	compete

		Upper Peninsula	
		cooperate	compete
Northern	cooperate	UP = $400,000 N = $400,000	UP = $800,000 N = $0
	compete	UP = $0 N = $800,000	UP = $50,000 N = $50,000

b If Northern competes, UP prefers to compete ($800,000 > $400,000). If Northern cooperates, UP still prefers to compete ($50,000 > $0). If UP competes, Northern prefers to compete ($800,000 > $400,000). If UP cooperates, Northern still prefers to compete ($50,000 > $0) Since both always prefer competition, the equilibrium is that both compete and profits are $50,000 each.

9 *a*

		Allan	
		cooperate	compete
Northern	cooperate	A = $0 H = $0	A = +$30,000 H = −$30,000
	compete	A = −$30,000 H = +$30,000	A = −$20,000 H = −$20,000

b If Hill cooperates and does not offer scholarships, Allan prefers to compete and offer them because the return by doing so when Hill cooperates, which is $30,000, exceeds the return of $0 if Allan cooperates too. If Hill competes and offers scholarships, Allan is better off offering them (−$20,000) than not offering them (−$30,000). If Allan cooperates and does not offer scholarships, Hill prefers to offer them ($30,000 > $0). If Allan competes and offers scholarships, Hill still prefers to offer them (−$20,000 > −$30,000). Since each prefers to compete and offer scholarships, regardless of the actions of the other, the equilibrium is that both compete.

11 The demand for each firm's share of the market and the corresponding marginal revenue appear in Table 16.20.

Table 16.20

Price	Quantity (tonnes)	Revenues	Marginal revenue
$22.50	0	$ 0	—
$20.00	50	$1,000	$20
$17.50	100	$1,750	$15
$15.00	150	$2,250	$10
$12.50	200	$2,500	$ 5
$10.00	250	$2,500	$ 0
$ 7.50	300	$2,250	−$ 5

a Each firm charges $12.50 and sells 200.
b The price and quantity are the same as under monopoly.

13 *a* If both reduce price by $2.50 to $15.00, the market quantity will equal 500, which implies that each will sell 250. Profits will equal ($15 × 250) − ($10 × 250) = $1,250, which is less than the $1,500 they earn by charging $17.50.
b Yuppie's demand curve if price cuts below $17.50 are matched but price increases are not is given in Table 16.21.

Table 16.21

Price	Quantity (sweaters)
$27.50	0
$25.00	0
$22.50	0
$20.00	0
$17.50	200
$15.00	250
$12.50	300

Chapter 17

GOVERNMENT POLICIES TOWARDS COMPETITION

Chapter Review

Monopolies and oligopolies, explored in Chapters 15 and 16, produce too little output and charge inefficiently high prices. This chapter of the text returns to the role government plays in the economy, but this time examines government policies to promote competition. Another important topic is government responses to natural monopolies. Natural monopolies occur when a single firm can produce the good more cheaply than multiple firms. In Chapter 18, the focus shifts to how firms compete to introduce new products and discover better ways of producing.

ESSENTIAL CONCEPTS

1   Competitive industries allocate resources efficiently. Monopolies and other imperfectly competitive industries, however, often operate inefficiently. Economists study four types of inefficiency.

    a Monopolies restrict output below what it would be if the industry were competitive. The lower output results in higher prices and a transfer of wealth from consumers to the monopoly. There is an additional loss in consumer surplus, because output is below the level at which all gains from trade are realized. This loss is called the deadweight loss of monopoly.

    b Although monopoly profits are higher when their costs are lower, monopolies are not forced to produce at the lowest cost. There is some room for **managerial slack**, which allows monopolies to be inefficient.

    c Although there are examples of monopolies that engage in effective **research and development**, the incentives are less under monopoly.

    d Because monopolies earn rents (profits above the level necessary to compensate investors), resources are expended to acquire and retain these existing rents. This type of activity is called **rent seeking** and is socially wasteful.

2   In some industries, where there are high fixed and low marginal costs, lowest cost of production occurs when there is only one firm. Such an industry is called a **natural monopoly**. Figure 17.1 shows that the average cost curve for a natural monopoly is falling and that marginal cost always lies below average cost. Govern-

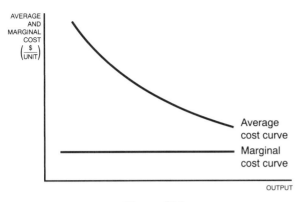

Figure 17.1

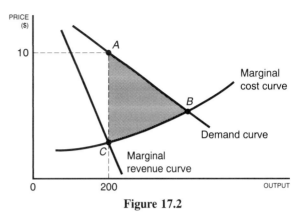

Figure 17.2

ments sometimes nationalize and operate natural monopolies, but more often governments regulate them. A regulatory agency sets prices designed to limit the firm to a normal rate of return. This policy in turn motivates firms to overinvest. Also, because in both the nationalized and regulated cases the pricing decisions are made politically, products may be sold below cost in some markets and above cost in others. This practice is called **cross subsidization.**

3 A final way of dealing with natural monopolies is to increase competition. Examples in Canada include the deregulation of long-distance telephone service and of the trucking and airline industries. Competition provides firms with incentives to innovate and reduce costs, and it eliminates cross subsidization. On the other hand, with more firms in the industry, each firm produces less, that is, chooses a point higher up on the average cost curve.

4 The various ways in which the government attempts to promote competition were referred to historically as anti-combines legislation. More recently, the Competition Act of 1986 replaced the Combines Investigation Act. It set up a Competition Tribunal to investigate the effect of large corporate mergers according to seven factors. Additionally, it defined "abuse of a dominant position" as constituting various types of "anticompetitive acts," rather than declaring monopoly itself as an offence. The Competition Act also prohibited certain restrictive practices where it can be proved that they do economic harm.

BEHIND THE ESSENTIAL CONCEPTS

1 The problem of deadweight loss lies at the heart of economic arguments about making exchange efficient. As an example, look at Figure 17.2, which shows a monopoly output equal to 200. The firm sets the price at $10 and maximizes its profits. Notice, however, that at this point the marginal benefit to consumers of one or more unit (measured, as usual, by the price they're

willing to pay) is greater than the marginal cost. This means that producing and selling additional units would create value; there would be gains from trade. The total possible additional gains equal the area of the triangle *ABC*. But these gains are not realized, and therefore they are called the deadweight loss of monopoly.

The idea that exchange creates value and that any reduction in the amount of exchange below the competitive level leads to a deadweight loss (as seen in Figure 17.2) is very important in economics.

2 Firms desiring greater profits seek them in two ways. First, they offer better products or devise better ways of producing and doing business. These activities do make profits, and they create value and enhance efficiency as well. Second, firms try to convince the government to protect them against competition or devise strategies to deter entry. Practices of this type do not create anything; they only redistribute money and reduce economic efficiency. Such behaviour is called rent seeking.

3 In competitive industries, firms are forced to produce at the lowest possible cost. If they do not, new firms will enter the market, undercut the price, and drive existing firms out. In a monopoly, however, whether it is private, nationalized, or regulated, the firm can get away with some slack. It can pay its workers a little more than the going wage, it can postpone adopting the most efficient production techniques, or it can overlook the low-cost suppliers. You can probably see how this could happen in an unregulated monopoly, where there are extra profits, or in a nationalized industry, where the government makes up any losses, but it is also possible in a regulated monopoly because regulators do not always know the lowest cost. The firm has an incentive and the ability to make the regulators believe that it is more costly to do business than it really is. Regulators can prevent fraud, but it is very difficult to find and eliminate waste.

4 In order to determine whether a merger will inhibit competition, the number of firms in an industry and their size relative to the market needs to be deter-

mined. The geographical size of the market should be considered, as some industries are local, while many have become international. For example, the gold market is a world market. The cement industry, on the other hand, is local. The product is very expensive to transport, and only nearby firms could merge. The similarity of the products also needs to be considered. Is plastic wrap in the same industry as aluminum foil? If so, does a single producer of plastic wrap have a monopoly, or is it simply another firm in the food-wrapping industry? Economists look at the cross-price effect to determine the extent to which firms are competing. How much does a price decrease by one firm reduce another's demand?

SELF-TEST

True or False

1 Monopolies produce less output than would be produced if the industry were competitive.

2 Monopolies must produce at the lowest cost.

3 Rent seeking refers to anything done in pursuit of monopoly profits.

4 Monopolies have stronger incentives to undertake research and development than do competitive firms.

5 In a natural monopoly, the cost of production is higher because of the lack of competition.

6 Cross subsidization refers to the practice of selling below cost in one market and above cost in another.

7 Regulated natural monopolies are usually forced to charge a price equal to marginal cost.

8 Subjecting a natural monopolist to competition can be an effective strategy if the average cost curve is not too steep.

9 In a horizontal agreement, a firm colludes with an upstream supplier.

10 The vertical agreement known as resale price maintenance is illegal per se, not just if competition is restricted.

11 In 1985, at the time of the introduction of the Competition Act, Canadian industries were much more concentrated than in 1970.

12 Anticompetitive behaviour can sometimes be successfully defended by claiming that the behaviour also enhances economic efficiency.

13 Collusive agreements are examples of vertical agreements.

14 The liberalization of trade between Canada and other countries through the Free Trade Agreement (FTA), the North American Free Trade Agreement (NAFTA), and the General Agreement on Tariffs and Trade (GATT)

reduces domestic firms' market power, and hence their tendency to indulge in anticompetitive behaviour.

15 A natural monopoly can only be prevented from taking advantage of its market power by nationalization.

Multiple Choice

1 Monopolists set the price

a equal to marginal cost.
b equal to average cost.
c above marginal cost.
d below marginal cost.
e below average cost.

2 Monopoly output is

a the same as competitive output.
b less than competitive output.
c more than competitive output.
d sometimes more and sometimes less than competitive output.
e determined by setting marginal cost equal to price.

3 The deadweight loss caused by monopoly is

a the difference between consumer surplus under the monopoly and what consumer surplus would have been if the industry were competitive.
b the amount of monopoly profits.
c the increase in cost brought about by managerial slack.
d the total of rent-seeking expenditures.
e the loss of consumer surplus due to monopoly minus the transfer from consumers to the monopolist.

4 Managerial slack refers to

a the lack of efficiency in some monopolies.
b activities designed to protect a monopoly position.
c the loss in consumer surplus as a result of restricted output.
d the lessened incentives for research and development under monopoly.
e the failure of competition policy.

5 The problems of monopolies include

a restricted output.
b managerial slack.
c reduced incentives for research and development.
d rent seeking to protect the monopoly position.
e setting price equal to marginal cost.

6 Which of the following is not a type of rent seeking?

a research aimed at reducing the cost of production
b lobbying the legislature for protection against foreign competition
c contributions to political campaigns for candidates who support regulations favoured by the monopoly
d entry-deterring activities
e designing the product to be incompatible with competitors' products

7 If the cost of production is lowest when there is only one firm, then the industry is a

a trust.
b natural oligopoly.
c natural monopoly.
d horizontal agreement.
e vertical agreement.

8 In a natural monopoly, marginal cost

a equals price.
b equals average cost.
c is less than average cost.
d is greater than average cost.
e is greater than price.

9 Cross subsidization involves

a selling at below cost in some markets and above cost in others.
b selling at cost in all markets.
c selling above cost in each market.
d selling below cost in each market.
e none of the above.

10 Cross subsidization

a occurs in nationalized monopolies but not in regulated monopolies.
b occurs in regulated monopolies but not in nationalized monopolies.
c occurs in neither regulated nor nationalized monopolies.
d occurs in both regulated and nationalized monopolies.
e never occurs.

11 Natural monopoly regulation usually sets price equal to

a marginal revenue.
b marginal cost.
c average revenue.
d average cost.
e average variable cost.

12 Regulated natural monopolies often

a invest too much.
b invest too little.
c hire too much labour.
d hire too few workers.
e sell too much output.

13 Government policies to promote competition were historically called

a anti-combines.
b rent seeking.
c managerial slack.
d natural monopoly.
e horizontal agreements.

14 Which of the following is an example of a horizontal agreement?

a One steel producer colludes with another steel producer.

b A meat-packing firm colludes with a large cattle ranch.
c A maker of chalk colludes with a pizza delivery firm.
d A Canadian company colludes with a U.S. company.
e A U.S. company colludes with a Canadian company.

15 Which of the following is an example of a vertical agreement?

a One steel producer colludes with another steel producer.
b A meat-packing firm colludes with a large cattle ranch.
c A maker of chalk colludes with a pizza delivery firm.
d A Canadian company colludes with a U.S. company.
e A U.S. company colludes with a Canadian company.

16 Based on figures for the percentage of shipments accounted for by the four leading firms in the industry, the least competitive manufacturing industry in Canada is

a motor vehicle manufacturing.
b pharmaceutical medicines.
c brewing.
d iron and steel mills.
e aircraft and aircraft parts manufacturing.

17 The Canadian Competition Tribunal

a determines whether foreign firms are engaging in dumping.
b is responsible for the legislation that makes monopolies illegal.
c investigates, but cannot prosecute, firms engaging in behaviour that prevents or lessens competition.
d measures the degree of competition in sectors of Canadian industry and reports the findings to the government, which decides whether any action should be taken.
e investigates and prosecutes firms engaging in behaviour that prevents or lessens competition.

18 Restrictive practices can be classified as horizontal or vertical agreements. All the following are vertical agreements except one. Which one?

a bid-rigging.
b resale price maintenance.
c tied selling.
d exclusive dealing.
e market restrictions (exclusive territories).

19 The hypothesis that regulators eventually serve the interests of the industry that they regulate and not the customers is called the

a anti-combines hypothesis.
b rent-seeking hypothesis.
c regulatory capture hypothesis.

d natural monopoly hypothesis.

e none of the above.

20 A per se offence against the Competition Act is one that

    a is judged to be anticompetitive only if does not provide offsetting gains in economic efficiency.

    b does not require investigation by the Competition Tribunal.

    c is not conditional on the restriction of competition.

    d is conditional on the restriction of competition.

    e is not described in any of the above.

Completion

1 Monopolies restrict output and cause a loss in consumer surplus, part of which is a transfer to the monopolist, and the remainder is called the _____.

2 The fact that, shielded from competition, monopolists may not produce for the lowest costs is called _____.

3 Political contributions and lobbying expenses for the purpose of winning regulations to restrict competition are examples of _____.

4 Regulated or nationalized firms may sell below cost in some markets and above cost in others, a practice known as _____.

5 In a _____, the cost of production is lowest if there is only one firm in the industry.

6 Before 1986, government efforts to promote competition by restricting anticompetitive tactics or opposing mergers were called _____ legislation.

7 When a firm buys a competitor that was producing a competing product, it is called a _____.

8 The purchase by one firm of an upstream supplier or downstream distributor is called a _____.

9 Collusion was made illegal by the _____.

10 The _____ investigates and proscribes unfair trade practices.

Answers to Self-Test

True or False

1	t	6	t	11	t
2	f	7	f	12	t
3	f	8	t	13	f
4	f	9	f	14	t
5	f	10	t	15	f

Multiple Choice

1	c	6	a	11	d	16	c
2	b	7	c	12	a	17	e
3	e	8	c	13	a	18	a
4	a	9	a	14	a	19	c
5	e	10	d	15	b	20	c

Completion

1 deadweight loss
2 managerial slack
3 rent seeking
4 cross subsidization
5 natural monopoly
6 anti-combines
7 horizontal merger
8 vertical merger
9 Competition Act
10 Competition Tribunal

Doing Economics: Tools and Practice Problems

One of the important costs that monopolies impose on the economy is the deadweight loss, which reflects the losses resulting from the fact that monopolies restrict output. Here, we study how to compute the deadweight loss and then move on to consider the regulation of natural monopolies.

Tool Kit 17.1: Finding the Deadweight Loss of Monopoly

When a monopoly controls an industry, it can increase its profits by restricting output below the level where price equals marginal cost. By doing so, the monopoly reduces the number of mutually beneficial trades. Because these trades do not occur, there is a loss in consumer surplus, and this loss is called the deadweight burden. (Consumer surplus falls still further because of the higher price that the monopoly charges, but this loss in consumer surplus is only a transfer from consumers to the monopolist and is not part of the deadweight loss.)

Step one: Identify the demand and marginal cost curves.

Step two: Calculate marginal revenue.

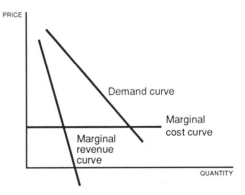

Step three: Find the monopoly output (Q_m) and price (p_m) by choosing the quantity for which marginal revenue equals marginal cost (MC_m).

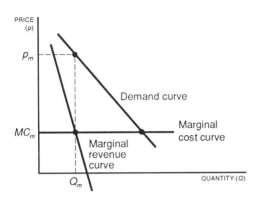

Step four: Find the "competitive" quantity (Q_c) by choosing the quantity for which demand equals marginal cost.

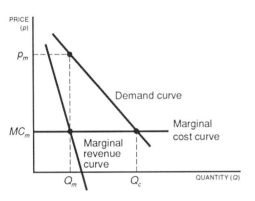

Step five: Compute the deadweight loss as the area between the demand and marginal cost curves:

deadweight loss = ½ $(Q_c - Q_m) \times (p_m - MC_m)$.

(This formula exactly measures the area only when demand is a straight line.)

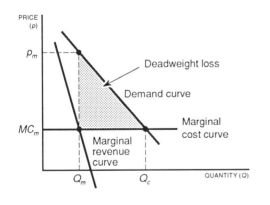

1 (Worked problem: deadweight loss) The West India Tea Company has been granted the sole franchise to sell green tea in Greenville. Its marginal cost is $5 per box. Demand is given in Table 17.1. Solve for its output and price and the deadweight loss.

Table 17.1

Price	Quantity
$10	10,000
$ 9	15,000
$ 8	20,000
$ 7	25,000
$ 6	30,000
$ 5	35,000

Step-by-step solution

Step one: Identify the demand and marginal cost curves. The demand curve is given in Table 17.1; marginal cost is constant and equal to $5.

Step two: Calculate marginal revenue. Follow the usual procedure outlined in Tool Kit 15.1. The marginal revenue for the West India Tea Company is given in Table 17.2.

Table 17.2

Price	Quantity	Total revenue	Marginal revenue
$10	10,000	$100,000	—
$ 9	15,000	$135,000	$7
$ 8	20,000	$160,000	$5
$ 7	25,000	$175,000	$3
$ 6	30,000	$180,000	$1
$ 5	35,000	$175,000	–$1

Step three: Find the monopoly output by choosing the quantity for which marginal revenue equals marginal cost. Marginal revenue equals marginal cost when price is $8 and 20,000 boxes are sold.

Step four: Find the competitive quantity by choosing the quantity for which demand equals marginal cost. The competitive price is $5, and the quantity is 35,000.

Step five: Compute the deadweight loss as the area between the demand and marginal cost curves.

Deadweight loss = ½ $(Q_c - Q_m) \times (p_m - MC_m)$

= ½ (35,000 – 20,000) × ($8 – $5)

= $22,500.

2 (Practice problem: deadweight loss) Although its marginal cost is only $4 for each ride, the Calloway Cab Company has bribed the city council in Venal City to grant it monopoly status at the local airport. The demand for rides is given in Table 17.3.

Table 17.3

Price	Quantity
$7.50	0
$7.00	10
$6.50	20
$6.00	30
$5.50	40
$5.00	50
$4.50	60
$4.00	70

Solve for the company's output and price and the deadweight loss.

3   (Practice problem: deadweight loss) As all baseball fans know, there is only one team in Mudville. The marginal cost of another fan in the park is $1, and the demand is given in Table 17.4.

Table 17.4

Price	Quantity
$3.00	1,500
$2.50	3,000
$2.00	4,500
$1.50	6,000
$1.00	7,500

Solve for the team's output and price and the deadweight loss.

Tool Kit 17.2: Finding the Price for a Regulated Natural Monopoly

Natural monopolies are industries with high fixed and low marginal costs. Costs in these industries are lowest when there is only one firm. Many so-called natural monopolies, such as public utilities, cable television companies, and phone companies, are regulated by a public commission that prevents the entry of competitors and sets prices just high enough to allow the firms to earn a normal rate of return. This practice mandates that price equal average cost.

Step one: Identify the demand curve, marginal cost, and fixed costs.

Step two: Compute the average cost by dividing total cost by quantity:

average cost = total cost/quantity.

Step three: Find the price for which average cost crosses the demand curve. This is the price for a regulated natural monopoly.

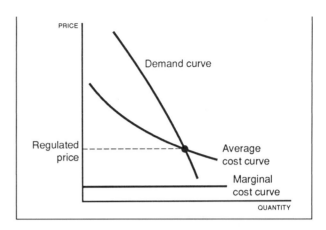

4   (Worked problem: natural monopoly) Cutthroat Co-Axial Cable Company is the only provider of cable television services in Kings. Most of its costs are access fees and maintenance expenses, and these fixed costs, which do not vary with the number of customers, total $760,000 monthly. The marginal cost of another subscriber is only $1 per month. The company's demand curve is given in Table 17.5.

Table 17.5

Price (per month)	Number of subscribers
$50	10,000
$40	20,000
$30	30,000
$20	40,000
$10	50,000
$ 1	100,000

The Kings Telecommunications Commission regulates the price of cable service and wants to set the price so that Cutthroat makes a normal rate of return. What price should it mandate?

Step-by-step solution

Step one: Identify the demand curve, marginal cost, and fixed costs. Demand is given in Table 17.5; marginal cost is $1, and fixed costs are $760,000.

Step two: Compute average cost. When price is $50, there are 10,000 subscribers, and total costs are $760,000 + (10,000 × $1) = $770,000. Average cost is $770,000/10,000 = $77. Continuing this procedure, we derive Table 17.6.

Table 17.6

Price	Number of subscribers	Total cost	Average cost
$50	10,000	$770,000	$77.00
$40	20,000	$780,000	$39.00
$30	30,000	$790,000	$26.33
$20	40,000	$800,000	$20.00
$10	50,000	$810,000	$16.20
$ 1	100,000	$860,000	$ 8.60

Step three: Find the price for which average cost crosses the demand curve. This price is $20, and it is the price that the public utility commission will choose.

5 (Practice problem: natural monopoly) The new big-cat exhibit at the Potter Park Zoo is bringing in the public. Demand is given in Table 17.7. The zoo costs the park service only $1 per visitor, but its fixed costs equal $12,000. Governor Scissorhands has declared that no public funds will be used to support zoos, so Potter Park must charge a price just high enough to cover its costs. What price will solve this problem?

Table 17.7

Price	Number of visitors
$8	1,000
$7	2,000
$6	3,000
$5	4,000
$4	5,000
$3	6,000
$2	7,000
$1	8,000

6 (Practice problem: natural monopoly) Country Line Commuter Service runs from rural areas into the city. It has fixed costs of $20,400 and a marginal cost of $10 per commuter. Demand is given in Table 17.8. The Metro Transportation Commission sets the monthly price for a pass on Country Line, and it wants to allow the firm to earn a normal rate of return. Find the price that allows the service to cover its costs.

Table 17.8

Price (per month)	Number of commuters
$200	100
$180	120
$160	140
$140	160
$120	180
$100	200

Answers to Problems

2 The marginal revenue is given in Table 17.9.

Table 17.9

Price	Quantity	Revenues	Marginal revenue
$7.50	0	$ 0	—
$7.00	10	$ 70	$7
$6.50	20	$130	$6
$6.00	30	$180	$5
$5.50	40	$220	$4
$5.00	50	$250	$3
$4.50	60	$270	$2
$4.00	70	$280	$1

The monopoly output and price are 40 and $5.50, respectively. The competitive output and price would be 70 and $4, respectively. The deadweight loss is

½(70 − 40) × ($5.50 − $4.00) = $22.50.

3 The marginal revenue is given in Table 17.10.

Table 17.10

Price	Quantity	Revenues	Marginal revenue
$3.00	1,500	$4,500	$3
$2.50	3,000	$7,500	$2
$2.00	4,500	$9,000	$1
$1.50	6,000	$9,000	$0
$1.00	7,500	$7,500	−$1

The monopoly price and output are $2 and 4,500, respectively. The competitive price and output would be $1 and 7,500, respectively. The deadweight loss is

½(7,500 − 4,500) × ($2 − $1) = $1,500.

5 Average cost is given in Table 17.11.

Table 17.11

Price	Number of visitors	Total cost	Average cost
$8	1,000	$13,000	$13.00
$7	2,000	$14,000	$ 7.00
$6	3,000	$15,000	$ 5.00
$5	4,000	$16,000	$ 4.00
$4	5,000	$17,000	$ 3.40
$3	6,000	$18,000	$ 3.00
$2	7,000	$19,000	$ 2.70
$1	8,000	$20,000	$ 2.50

The price that allows Potter Park to cover its costs is $3.

6   Average cost is given in Table 17.12.

Table 17.12

Price	Number of commuters	Total cost	Average cost
$200	100	$21,400	$214
$180	120	$21,600	$180
$160	140	$21,800	$156
$140	160	$22,000	$138
$120	180	$22,200	$123
$100	200	$22,400	$112

Average cost equals price when price is $180. The commission should choose this price.

Chapter 18

TECHNOLOGICAL CHANGE

Chapter Review

Think back once again to the history of the automobile in Chapter 1. At the beginning of this century, the automobile had not been invented, much less produced in any quantity or in the form we know it today. The enormous technological change in the automobile industry during this century is astounding. Yet the basic model of perfect competition assumes that the goods produced and the technology used to produce them does not change. In this chapter, the emphasis shifts to firms as they actively compete to discover new products and new ways of producing. Although many firms may be involved, the race for new ideas brings with it many of the aspects of imperfect competition covered in Chapters 15 to 17.

The most important point made in this chapter is that imperfect competition is not all bad. It brings with it the positive benefits of technological advance. Government policy to promote technological change includes granting patents, subsidizing research and development, and occasionally protecting infant industries.

ESSENTIAL CONCEPTS

1 In the basic competitive model, there is one lowest-cost way of producing, and all firms adopt this technology. The entry of new firms into the market soon drives away any profits, and all firms settle down to produce at the minimum of the average cost curve. The world of **technological change**, however, is vastly different. Firms compete aggressively to develop new products or production processes so that they can earn monopoly profits, at least for a while. For various reasons, the study of technological change must focus on imperfect competition.

2 A **patent** is a property right to an idea, and it gives the owner monopoly status and the opportunity to earn monopoly profits for the duration of the patent. Firms compete in **patent races**, a winner-take-all system in which the first firm with a discovery is awarded that patent, and its competitors get nothing. Because not all ideas are patentable and because to obtain a patent the firm must disclose details of the idea, firms sometimes forgo applying for one and keep the idea a **trade secret.** In this case, the firm earns monopoly profits until its competitors discover the idea or a better one.

3 Patent policy involves two types of trade-offs:

  a The first issue is the **length** of the patent. Longer patents offer greater rewards for winning the race, and at the same time they promote research and development. On the other hand, for the duration of the patent, the firm sells at the monopoly price, which is above marginal cost, and so causes short-run deadweight losses.

 b The second issue is the **breadth** of the patent. Should patents be given for the narrowly defined idea or something more general? More broadly defined patents increase the rewards for R & D; however, access to the idea is restricted, and this restriction inhibits any subsequent innovative activity that might build on the patented idea.

4 Several features of research and development encourage large-sized firms.

 a First, R & D is a *fixed cost*, in the sense that once discovered, an idea can be used many times without additional cost. Fixed costs increase the efficient scale of the firm.

 b Second, the **learning curve** shows that costs fall with experience. The more the firm learns, the more it produces, and thus learning by doing encourages firms to increase their size.

 c Third, firms have difficulty borrowing to finance R & D. Larger firms with more retained earnings can finance more of their own research.

5 **Basic research** on the nature of fundamental ideas generates such widespread external benefits that it has the two characteristics of **public goods:** basic research produces knowledge, and it is difficult (not to mention undesirable) to exclude others from learning and taking advantage of new knowledge. Also, the marginal costs of giving another user access to new knowledge is certainly zero. Because basic research has the characteristic features of public goods, the government has an important role to play in providing funding for such work.

6 Because R & D creates external benefits not captured through patents, most economists advocate additional government policies to encourage it. Tax credits for R & D spending are one form of subsidy used in Canada. Also, the **infant industry argument** for protection says that new industries require protection against foreign competition until they move down the learning curve and acquire sufficient expertise to compete effectively. Further, anti-combines laws can be relaxed to allow for joint ventures.

BEHIND THE ESSENTIAL CONCEPTS

1 Most of microeconomics sings the praises of perfect competition, especially to the extent that it allocates resources efficiently given the existing production technology. But does a perfectly competitive economy always find the best way to generate more advanced technologies of production, better products, and new ways of doing things? This chapter suggests that the answer is no. In order to encourage R & D, the government set up the patent system to motivate firms towards innovation by rewarding the winner with a period of freedom from competition. Perhaps paradoxically, government creates monopoly to encourage competition.

2 Technological advance is a vital engine of economic growth. Because it is so important, government promotes it with a wide range of complementary policies. Longer-lived and more broadly defined patents increase the rewards for R & D, while tax subsidies reduce the cost. Government also provides direct funding for basic research.

3 Economists consider the infant industry argument for protection to be valid but dangerous. Sometimes the protected industry gains expertise through experience and becomes a world-class competitor; other times the industry becomes inefficient and requires constant government support to survive. The difficulty is determining which industries will thrive and which will not.

4 You learned the basic logic of externalities in Chapter 7: whenever costs or benefits of some decision are not borne entirely by the decision maker, there is inefficiency. Most important to note in this chapter are the external benefits not captured by the firm that invests in R & D. These positive externalities include the fruits of subsequent R & D following an initial discovery, the gains after the expiration of the patent, and the consumer surplus arising from the application of the new idea. The firm ignores these externalities and thus undervalues the true social benefit of the R & D. Government policy can improve matters by promoting additional research efforts.

SELF-TEST

True or False

1 Firms engage in R & D expenditures so that they can participate in competitive markets.

2 A patent confers the exclusive right to produce and market an innovation for a limited period of time.

3 Patents and copyrights are forms of intellectual property.

4 The firm that finishes second in a patent race wins nothing.

5 Holders of patents set the price of their goods equal to marginal cost.

6 Patents promote dynamic efficiency at the expense of static inefficiency.

7 The length of patents is set to balance the costs of monopoly pricing by patent holders against the incentives to innovate.

8 Defining a patent more broadly might reduce the rate of innovation by denying access to previous innovations.

9 Any firm eligible for a patent will surely apply for one.

10 R & D is a variable cost of production.

11 The learning curve shows how fixed costs decline with experience.

12 One advantage that smaller firms have in R & D is their better access to capital markets.

13 Venture capital firms specialize in assessing the prospects of R & D ventures and providing capital to innovating firms.

14 The market is unlikely to provide enough basic research because basic research is a public good.

15 The anti-combines laws inhibit firms from engaging in joint ventures.

Multiple Choice

1 Capitalism is a process of

a steady and smooth growth in the living standards of every individual.
b stagnation, in which the same goods are produced in the same way and distributed to the same people.
c creative destruction, in which new products and technologies continually destroy existing jobs, firms, and even entire industries.
d efficient allocation of resources in the short run, without any incentives for technological advance.
e none of the above.

2 Firms engage in research and development expenditures in order to

a destroy their rivals.
b provide beneficial externalities to society.
c advance knowledge, which is a public good.
d gain market power and charge prices above costs.
e promote perfect competition.

3 Research and development refers to expenditures intended to

a discover new ideas, products, and technologies.
b discover new markets for existing products.
c devise better marketing for existing products.
d subsidize universities.
e none of the above.

4 A patent is

a the exclusive right to use an improvement in existing methods of production for a limited time.
b the exclusive right to use an improvement in existing methods of production for all time.
c the exclusive right to produce and sell an invention for a limited time.

d the exclusive right to produce and sell an invention for all time.
e none of the above.

5 Patents

a promote short-run efficiency by encouraging firms to set price equal to marginal cost.
b stimulate research and innovation and promote dynamic efficiency.
c are awarded to the firm that has devoted the most resources to researching and developing the idea.
d are given for advances in basic knowledge.
e none of the above.

6 The typical patent life involves a trade-off between

a short-run inefficiency and incentives to innovate.
b greater incentives to innovate and stimulation of subsequent innovation through greater access to past innovations.
c promoting research and fostering new product development.
d the profits of innovators and those of rivals.
e none of the above.

7 The breadth of patent coverage involves a trade-off between

a short-run inefficiency and incentives to innovate.
b greater incentives to innovate and stimulation of subsequent innovation through greater access to past innovations.
c promoting research and fostering new product development.
d the profits of innovators and those of rivals.
e none of the above.

8 Direct rewards from R & D are given

a in proportion to R & D expenditures.
b in proportion to market share.
c based on how many positive externalities are generated.
d on a winner-take-all basis.
e equally to all who entered the race.

9 A patent might not be awarded for an innovation if

a the innovator, preferring to hide the advance as a trade secret, chose not to apply for the patent.
b other firms were on the verge of perfecting the same innovation.
c other firms had tried harder to find this particular innovation.
d too many jobs would be destroyed if the patent were awarded.
e none of the above.

10 Intellectual property includes

a patents and copyrights.
b a university professor's furniture.
c basic research, which is a public good.
d the externalities generated by innovation.
e none of the above.

11 R & D expenditures are

    a variable costs.
    b fixed costs.
    c marginal costs.
    d U-shaped average costs.
    e none of the above.

12 Which of the following is true?

    a Small firms have advantages in R & D because they may have better access to capital markets.
    b Large firms have advantages in R & D because they can reap the cost savings on sales of more units.
    c Large firms have advantages in R & D because of the bureaucratic environment in large corporations.
    d Small firms have advantages in R & D because the costs of innovating, which vary with the scale of production, are smaller.
    e None of the above.

13 Learning by doing refers to

    a the fact that education only signals higher productivity; it does not increase productivity.
    b the idea that as firms gain experience from production, their costs fall.
    c the fact that R & D is wasteful because firms must produce products before they can innovate.
    d the fact that R & D is the only way to lower costs.
    e none of the above.

14 The learning curve

    a shows the trade-off between short-run and dynamic efficiency.
    b shows the trade-off between providing incentives to innovate and allowing access to previous innovations.
    c shows that patents lead to monopoly profits.
    d shows how marginal cost declines as cumulative experience increases.
    e disproves the infant industry argument.

15 According to the infant industry argument,

    a firms that have higher costs than their foreign rivals should be protected in order to save jobs.
    b firms should be protected if foreign labour costs are so low that the domestic firm cannot compete.
    c firms that have higher costs than their foreign rivals should be protected until they move down the learning curve.
    d free trade is efficient.
    e none of the above.

16 Which of the following is not true?

    a Competition drives firms that do not innovate from the market.
    b Competition inhibits innovation by eliminating profits that could be used to finance R & D.
    c Competition leads firms to imitate innovations, and so erodes returns.

    d Competition spurs R & D by making it clear that the principal way to earn profits is to innovate and capture market power.
    e None of the above.

17 The market will not supply enough R & D because

    a firms that win patent races do not have to pay for the patents.
    b the benefits of R & D spill over to others not directly involved.
    c firms that lose patent races cannot market the innovation.
    d firms that win patent races set price higher than marginal cost.
    e none of the above.

18 Which of the following is not a property of public goods?

    a It is difficult to exclude anyone from the benefits.
    b The marginal cost of an additional user is close to zero.
    c The market is likely to supply too few public goods.
    d Private-sector research on and development of them will be sufficient from society's viewpoint.
    e None of the above.

19 Which of the following types of R & D is most likely to be a public good?

    a basic research.
    b product development.
    c applied research.
    d the costs of marketing new goods and services.
    e none of the above.

20 Selling goods below cost in foreign markets is called

    a invention.
    b subsidization.
    c dumping.
    d protection.
    e none of the above.

Completion

1 As new products and technologies drive older jobs, technologies, and industries from the market, capitalism, in the words of Joseph Schumpeter, is a process of _____.

2 Expenditures designed to discover new ideas, products, and technologies and bring them to market are called _____.

3 The exclusive right to produce and sell an invention or innovation is a _____.

4 The fact that the rewards of research and development are given on a winner-take-all basis makes R & D a _____.

5 Rather than seek a patent, an innovator may try to hide the new knowledge as a _____.

6 _____ refers to the idea that as firms gain experience, their costs fall.

7 The curve showing how marginal costs of production decline as total experience increases is called the _____ .

8 The benefits of research and development spill over to others not directly involved and generate positive _____ .

9 Basic research produces knowledge from which it is difficult to exclude potential users and which can be used by others at no cost to the producers; therefore, it is an example of a _____ .

10 The hope that an industry not currently able to compete with foreign firms may in time acquire the experience to move down the learning curve is called the _____ argument for protection.

Answers to Self-Test

True or False

1	f	6	t	11	f
2	t	7	t	12	f
3	t	8	t	13	t
4	t	9	f	14	t
5	f	10	f	15	t

Multiple Choice

1	c	6	a	11	b	16	e
2	d	7	b	12	b	17	b
3	a	8	d	13	b	18	d
4	c	9	a	14	d	19	a
5	b	10	e	15	c	20	c

Completion

1 creative destruction
2 research and development
3 patent
4 patent race
5 trade secret
6 Learning by doing
7 learning curve
8 externalities
9 public good
10 infant industry

Doing Economics: Tools and Practice Problems

Firms undertake research and development in order to market new products or to find new and less costly ways of producing. They compete to win patents or secure trade secrets that will allow them to enjoy some protection against competition and to earn above-normal profits. In this section we study the rewards that motivate R & D. First, several problems explore the value of new product patents and trade secrets. Next, we study innovations that result in lower production costs and consider whether incumbent monopolies have as much incentive to innovate as do potential entrants.

Tool Kit 18.1: Calculating the Value of a Patent

The developer of a new product may be able to win a patent, which grants the exclusive right to market the product for 20 years. The value of the patent is then the present discounted value of monopoly profits for the duration of the patent.

Step one: Compute monopoly profits resulting from the patent.

Step two: Find the present discounted value of 20 years of profits. This number is the value of the patent:

value of the patent = profits + [(profits)] $\times$ 1(1 + r)^1]

$\qquad$ + [(profits) $\times$ 1/(1 + r)^2] + . . .

$\qquad$ + [(profits) $\times$ 1/(1 + r)^{19}].

(The variable r stands for the real rate of interest. In the problems below, we will set r equal to 3 percent. A shortcut for step two is to multiply profits by 15.32.)

---

1 (Worked problem: patents) Nu Products, Inc., has come up with another winning idea—a rubberized surface for premium, no-injury waterslide parks. The company wins the patent. Demand for resurfacings is given in Table 18.1, and costs are $20,000 per park. Calculate the value of the patent.

Table 18.1

Price	Parks resurfaced
$60,000	10
$50,000	20
$40,000	30
$30,000	40
$20,000	50

Step-by-step solution

Step one: Compute the monopoly profits resulting from the patent. Table 18.2 gives the marginal revenue for resurfacings.

Table 18.2

Price	Parks resurfaced	Revenues	Marginal revenue
$60,000	10	$ 600,000	$60,000
$50,000	20	$1,000,000	$40,000
$40,000	30	$1,200,000	$20,000
$30,000	40	$1,200,000	$ 0
$20,000	50	$1,000,000	–$20,000

Marginal cost equals marginal revenue when price is $40,000 and 30 parks are resurfaced. Profits then equal ($40,000 × 30) – ($20,000 × 30) = $600,000.

Step two: Find the present discounted value of 20 years of profits. This number is the value of the patent.

Value of the patent = $600,000 + [($600,000) \times 1/(1 + r)^1]$
$$+ [(\$600,000) \times 1/(1 + r)^2] + \ldots$$
$$+ [(\$600,000) \times 1/(1 + r)^{19}]$$
$$= \$600,000 \times 15.32 = \$9,192,000.$$

2 (Practice problem: patents) Bugout Pesticide has discovered a new product that kills potato bugs. It wins the patent. The firm's economics department computes that it can expect to earn $100,000 for the length of the patent. Compute the value of the patent.

3 (Practice problem: patents) Nip and Tuck Bodyshapers have developed a new procedure for smoothing those wrinkles that trouble the after-40 generation. They have decided not to apply for a patent, but rather to keep the technique secret. They expect that others will be able to duplicate the procedure in 4 years and that the resulting competition will allow only a normal rate of return thereafter. Their costs are $5,000 per face, and they estimate that the demand curve is as given in Table 18.3.

Table 18.3

Price	Quantity
$30,000	20
$25,000	30
$20,000	40
$15,000	50
$10,000	60
$ 5,000	70

The real interest rate is expected to remain at 5 percent over the period. Find the value of the trade secret.

Tool Kit 18.2: Finding Equilibrium with an Incumbent Monopolist and a Potential Entrant

A firm that discovers and patents a new, lower-cost production technique will be able to earn above-normal profits for the duration of the patent. If the firm is already a monopoly, then it merely takes advantage of the lower costs. If the firm is a potential entrant, it can undercut the existing firm, drive it from the market, and take its place as the incumbent monopolist. Here, we compare the incentives that incumbent and entrant firms have to innovate, and demonstrate that monopolists do have lower incentives to innovate, as we learned in Chapter 17.

Step one: Identify the incumbent's costs, the potential entrant's costs, and the demand curve.

Step two: Find the equilibrium. The incumbent sets price equal to the entrant's average cost and captures the entire market. (Actually, the price must be 1 cent less than the average cost of the entrant, but we will round up in the problems below.)

---

4 (Worked problem: monopolist and potential entrant) Dentalcomp has had the monopoly in the market for computerizing dental offices in Roseville. While other firms could set up a computer system for $20,000, Dentalcomp's costs are only $15,000. Demand is given in Table 18.4.

Table 18.4

Price	Offices computerized
$30,000	20
$25,000	30
$20,000	40
$15,000	50
$10,000	60

a Find the equilibrium.
b Suppose that a new innovation in programming would lower costs to $10,000. Assume that the incumbent, Dentalcomp, discovers and patents the innovation first. Find the new equilibrium and the incumbent's profits. How much is the innovation worth to Dentalcomp?
c Now assume that a potential entrant discovers and patents the innovation first. Find the new equilibrium and the entrant's profits.
d Who has stronger incentives to innovate?

Step-by-step solution

Step one (a): Identify the incumbent's costs, the potential entrant's costs, and the demand curve. The incumbent, Dentalcomp, has an average cost of $15,000; the entrant has an average cost of $20,000. The demand appears in Table 18.4.

Step two: Find the equilibrium. The incumbent sets price equal to the entrant's average cost, which is $20,000, and captures the entire market of 40 offices. Its profits are ($20,000 \times 40) – ($15,000 \times 40) = $200,000.

Step three (b): If it discovers the innovation and wins the patent, Dentalcomp is still the low-cost firm. It captures the entire market with the same price of $20,000 and earns profits of ($20,000 \times 40) – ($10,000 \times 40) = $400,000.

Step four (c): If a potential entrant discovers the patent first, it becomes the low-price firm. It sets price equal to Dentalcomp's average cost, which is $15,000, and captures the entire market of 50 offices. Its profits are ($15,000 \times 50) – ($10,000 \times 50) = $250,000.

Step five (d): The gain to innovation for Dentalcomp is the difference between its profits before and after the innovation, which equals $400,000 − $200,000 = $200,000. The entrant gains $250,000 by innovating and thus has stronger incentives.

5 (Practice problem: monopolist and potential entrant) Blackdare has patented its unique process for extinguishing oil fires. It can put out a typical well fire for $150,000, but its competitors, without access to the patented process, have average costs equal to $200,000. The demand for extinguishing oil fires is given in Table 18.5.

Table 18.5

Price	Fires
$400,000	10
$350,000	12
$300,000	14
$250,000	16
$200,000	18
$150,000	20
$100,000	22

a Find the equilibrium price and quantity and profits.
b Suppose that a new innovation in firefighting would lower costs to $100,000. Assume that the incumbent, Blackdare, discovers and patents the innovation first. Find the new equilibrium and the incumbent's profits. How much is the innovation worth to Blackdare?
c Now assume that a potential entrant discovers and patents the innovation first. Find the new equilibrium and the entrant's profits.
d Who has the stronger incentives to innovate?

6 (Practice problem: monopolist and potential entrant) PhXXX Pharmaceuticals has a monopoly on the treatment of Rubinksi's Trauma, an obscure ailment of the saliva glands. The average cost of curing a patient is $2,000 for PhXXX. The only other treatment available costs $5,000. Demand for the treatment of Rubinski's Trauma is given in Table 18.6.

Table 18.6

Price	Treatments
$8,000	100
$7,000	200
$6,000	300
$5,000	400
$4,000	500
$3,000	600
$2,000	700
$1,000	800

a Find the equilibrium price and quantity.
b Suppose that a new genetically engineered drug would lower treatment costs to $1,000. Assume that the incumbent, PhXXX, discovers and patents the new drug first. Find the new equilibrium and the incumbent's profits. How much is the innovation worth to PhXXX?
c Now assume that a potential entrant discovers and patents the innovation first. Find the new equilibrium and the entrant's profits.
d Who has the stronger incentives to innovate?

Answers to Problems

2 Value of patent = $100,000 × 15.32 = $1,532,000.

3 Marginal revenue is given in Table 18.7.

Table 18.7

Price	Quantity	Revenues	Marginal revenue
$30,000	20	$600,000	—
$25,000	30	$750,000	$15,000
$20,000	40	$800,000	$ 5,000
$15,000	50	$750,000	−$ 5,000
$10,000	60	$600,000	−$15,000
$ 5,000	70	$350,000	−$25,000

Marginal revenue equals marginal cost at a price of $20,000, where 40 faces are smoothed. Profits = ($20,000 × 40) − ($5,000 × 40) = $600,000. The value of the trade secret is $600,000 + [($600,000) × 1/(1.05)] + [($600,000) × 1/(1.05)^2] + [($600,000) × 1/(1.05)^3] = $2,233,949.

5 a Price = $200,000; quantity = 18; profits = $900,000.
  b Price = $200,000; quantity = 18; profits = $1,800,000.
  c Price = $150,000; quantity = 20; profits = $1,000,000.
  d The entrant would gain $1,000,000, while Blackdare would only gain $1,800,000 − $900,000 = $900,000. The entrant has stronger incentives.

6 a Price = $5,000; quantity = 400; profits = $1,200,000.
  b Price = $5,000; quantity = 400; profits = $1,600,000.
  c Price = $2,000; quantity = 700; profits = $700,000.
  d The entrant would gain $700,000, while PhXXX would only gain $1,600,000 − $1,200,000 = $400,000. The entrant has stronger incentives.

IMPERFECT INFORMATION IN THE PRODUCT MARKET

Chapter Review

Chapter 19 begins the exploration of the economics of information with a look at information problems in the product market. Why can't customers always be sure of the quality of a good? Why do customers sometimes pay a higher price for a good than the good is worth? This chapter explains the various ways in which the economy attempts to solve these problems. In doing so, the chapter deviates from the basic competitive model to introduce a fascinating world of signalling, reputation, search, and advertising. Imperfect information causes markets to look a lot like the imperfect competition models discussed in Chapters 15 to 17 (on monopoly and oligopoly). Chapters 20 and 21 will take up imperfect information in the labour and capital markets.

ESSENTIAL CONCEPTS

1 The basic competitive model assumes that information is perfect, that households are well-informed about the prices, quality, and availability of goods and services,

and that firms know all input and output prices and the best available technology. Economists now believe that there are important aspects of the economy's performance that are the result of **imperfect information.** For instance, car manufacturers now commonly offer long-term guarantees on their products. These guarantees would not be necessary if car buyers had perfect information (and cars were perfectly reliable).

If there were such a thing as a market for information, it would not solve the problem. There would be no way for a customer to evaluate information before buying it, and if the customer already had the information, there would be no need to buy it.

2 **Asymmetric information** exists when one side of the market knows something that the other does not. For example, the seller of a used car may know more about its reliability than the buyer. Asymmetric information can cause the demand curve to be upward sloping, because buyers reason that only low-quality cars would be sold at low prices and that quality increases with price. This odd situation can lead to more than one possible equilibrium and can cause markets to be thin or nonexistent in spite of potential gains from trade.

3 One way to send buyers a message in a market with asymmetric information is called **signalling.** For example, a seller of quality used cars can distinguish the product by offering warranties or by building expensive showrooms. Buyers will reason that a seller of lemons could not afford the expenses of honouring the warranty and will conclude that this seller's used cars are reliable. The seller can also charge higher prices, another potentially informative signal. Buyers understand that only lemons would be sold at low prices, and thus they judge the quality according to the price.

4 If buyers can observe the quality of what is sold, then they can provide sellers with good incentives by basing pay on quality. For example, an employer can pay a typist according to the number of errors made. When buyers do not know the quality of goods before purchasing them, markets do not provide built-in incentives for firms to produce high-quality merchandise. Two possible solutions to this incentive problem are **contracts** and **reputations.**

   a Contracts typically include **contingency clauses**, which make payment depend on the quality of the service. For example, a contract might specify that the service must be performed by a certain date unless there is a strike or bad weather. Spelling out contingencies provides incentives and shares the risk, but it makes contracts complicated. When the terms of a contract are violated, one party is said to be in breach, but if the reasons for the breach are ambiguous, contract enforcement becomes an issue. Certainly, contracts help, but they provide only an imperfect solution to the incentive problems accompanying trade in the presence of asymmetric information.

   b By repeatedly providing quality goods and service, a firm establishes a reputation, which enables it to earn extra profits, called **reputation rents.** To preserve its valuable reputation, the firm must continue to provide quality. Reputations thus provide firms with incentives to perform well.

5 Because quality is uncertain and also because the same good may be sold at different prices in different locations (**price dispersion**), customers spend time and money in **search.** Rational search balances the benefits (finding better goods at lower prices) against the costs. Customers usually stop searching even though there is more to learn. **Information intermediaries** are firms that gather information to make customer search easier and more effective. Department stores and travel agents are examples of information intermediaries.

6 Firms try to influence customers' purchasing decisions through **informative** and **persuasive advertising.** The goal of advertising is to shift the demand curve to the right, and so enable the firm to raise prices and sell more goods. Advertising may also serve as a signal. Customers may reason that only a high-quality product with good sales would justify a large expenditure on advertising.

7 Concern for poorly informed consumers and deceptive advertising has led to **consumer protection legislation**, which attempts to stop false advertising. Such legislation includes truth-in-lending regulations, which require lenders to disclose the true interest rate. Even so, distinguishing between illegal, false advertising and its legal counterparts (confusing and persuasive advertising) is difficult.

BEHIND THE ESSENTIAL CONCEPTS

1 Markets do not necessarily fail when information is imperfect. The market for assets is an example of a very efficient market. Uncertainty in these markets exists, but the uncertainty is symmetric. Neither side knows the ultimate value of the assets they are trading. Efficiency problems arise, however, when information is asymmetric, that is, when one side of the market knows something that the other does not. Many mutually beneficial exchanges do not take place because buyers cannot be sure about quality, and they fear that sellers may exploit their informational advantage and sell lemons.

2 In the basic competitive model, customers ask simple questions such as, "Is the good worth its price?" In the presence of asymmetric information, and, especially signalling, customers must be more sophisticated. The seller of a quality item wants to signal that the goods offered have value. The seller could just say, "My goods are great!" but few customers would believe this. If the seller provides a guarantee and builds an expensive shop, customers may be more confident that the guarantee would be honoured should the product fail. The customer infers from the warranty and the shop that the seller's goods are high-quality goods.

3 The information problems discussed in this chapter lead the market structure away from perfect competition and create two possible situations: **barriers to entry** and firms with **downward-sloping demand curves.**

   a Customers who cannot know the quality of goods buy from businesses with good reputations. Because a reputation is built up over time, firms that would otherwise enter an industry will not be able to justify the investment necessary to establish a good reputation. In this scenario, reputation becomes a barrier to entry and results in less competition.

   b Because customers must search to learn about price and quality, it becomes cheaper for them to shop at familiar stores. Although the goods themselves may be identical, the stores are different in the eyes of the customer because the customer knows about some stores and is ignorant of others. Thus, a firm faces a downward-sloping demand curve, where high demanders are those who have information about the firm and lower demanders do not as yet.

4 Information problems in the product market run parallel to the problems in the insurance market discussed in Chapter 6. Again, there are two types of information problems.

    a In the insurance market, when the price of insurance is high, only the risky customers buy insurance. The mix of customers is adversely selected when the price rises. Adverse selection also appears in the market for lemons. Customers reason that as the price rises, more quality cars are offered for sale, and the fraction of lemons declines. In other words, there is *adverse selection* in the average quality of used cars when the price falls.

    b *Moral hazard* troubles the insurance market because people who have insurance tend to be less cautious. They lose their incentives to be careful when they are protected against loss. Similarly, in this chapter, we see that suppliers must be given incentives to live up to the terms of their contracts. There is a moral hazard that the other parties may not fulfill their promises and instead give some excuses that cannot be verified.

5 Although this chapter is about information problems, you should also keep in mind that markets do economize on the need for gathering information. In deciding what to produce and in what quantities and the method of production, firms do not need to know the preferences or incomes of households, the production techniques of other firms, or the overall quantities of inputs available. They only need to know the price. Similarly, households do not need to know others' tastes or anything about firms. Price conveys all relevant information—a great advantage of markets.

SELF-TEST

True or False

1 In the basic competitive model, individuals know their opportunity sets.

2 In the basic competitive model, firms know the opportunity sets of individuals.

3 Markets for information do not work well because once the consumer has enough information to evaluate the worth of the information, the customer no longer has the incentive to pay for it.

4 In the lemons model, demand may slope upwards if average quality increases as price increases.

5 Supply and demand may cross more than once if customers do not know the quality of the goods they are asked to buy.

6 Lemons markets have adverse selection in that as the price falls, the mix of goods offered for sale contains more low-quality goods.

7 Customers may believe that a product that carries a warranty is reliable because if the product were not reliable, the firm would incur costs honouring the warranty.

8 Even if customers judge the quality of goods by their price, the market clears in equilibrium.

9 In the rental car market, there is an incentive problem because customers have less reason to drive carefully.

10 Contracts attempt to provide incentives through contingency clauses that specify what each party agrees to do in different situations.

11 Problems of specifying and enforcing quality make it difficult to overcome the incentive problems with contracts.

12 The reputation of a firm may persuade customers that its goods are of high quality because if the firm were to lose its reputation, its profits would fall.

13 The reputations of existing firms attract new competitors to the market because these firms earn reputation rents.

14 Markets where customers must search to learn price are characterized by perfect competition.

15 Information intermediaries reduce the search costs of firms and customers.

Multiple Choice

1 In the basic competitive model, there is no need for an assumption that households know

    a their opportunity set.
    b the prices of all goods and services offered for sale.
    c the characteristics of all goods and services.
    d their preferences.
    e the firms' production techniques.

2 In the basic competitive model, there is no need for an assumption that firms know

    a the best available technology.
    b the productivity of each job applicant.
    c all input prices from every possible supplier.
    d the present and future prices for their outputs.
    e the households' preferences.

3 In the basic competitive model, firms are assumed to know

    a the preferences of individual consumers.
    b the costs of production for their suppliers.
    c the overall quantities of available inputs.
    d the production techniques of their competitors.
    e none of the above.

4 Markets for information do not work well because

    a no firm would be willing to sell information.
    b consumers are not willing to pay for information.

c consumers cannot know what they are buying before they actually buy the information.

d markets only work to allocate material goods.

e none of the above.

5 In the lemons model,

a customers know the quality of the goods, but sellers do not.

b sellers know the quality of the goods, but customers do not.

c neither customers nor sellers know the quality of the goods.

d both customers and sellers know that the quality of the goods is low.

e none of the above.

6 In the lemons model,

a average quality rises as price falls.

b average quality falls as price falls because sellers know the quality, and owners of lower-quality goods are willing to sell at lower prices.

c average quality does not change as price falls because consumers know quality and will not buy lower-quality goods.

d average quality may rise or fall as price falls.

e none of the above.

7 In the lemons model,

a demand is downward sloping.

b supply is downward sloping.

c demand may slope up or down.

d supply may slope up or down.

e none of the above.

8 Which of the following involves adverse selection?

a Consumers sometimes make mistakes and select inferior products.

b Consumers may not be able to find the lowest-price supplier.

c As the price rises, the fraction of used cars that are lemons increases.

d As the automobile insurance premium is increased, those least likely to have an accident drop out of the market.

e None of the above.

9 In markets with imperfect information,

a firms are price takers.

b firms set prices, taking into account the effect that price has as a signal of quality.

c price plays no role because consumers are uncertain about quality.

d markets clear for the usual reasons.

e there is a uniform market price per unit of quality, but the goods of different firms sell for different prices.

10 Which of the following are examples of informative signals?

a The seller claims that the goods offered are high quality.

b The seller does not offer a warranty.

c The seller constructs an expensive showroom.

d The seller claims competitors' goods are low quality.

e None of the above.

11 In markets with imperfect information, the incentive problem arises because

a firms have limited incentive to produce good-quality items if they cannot convince consumers.

b firms have no incentive to pay lower prices because they do not know the quality.

c firms can raise price above the consumer's willingness to pay.

d firms have no incentive to produce quality items unless they can be patented.

e firms have no incentive to build reputations.

12 Agreements with contracts that specify what each of the parties must do in certain situations are called

a signals.

b adverse selection.

c contingency clauses.

d reputations.

e none of the above.

13 Which of the following does not undermine the ability of contracts to solve the incentive problem for buyers and sellers?

a If the contract provides better incentives, the supplier will bear more risk and demand a higher price.

b Specifying and enforcing quality is difficult.

c Writing a clause for every possible contingency is expensive.

d Buyers do not know the quality of goods before purchasing them.

e None of the above.

14 In some markets, the reputations of firms help persuade customers that their products are high quality. In these markets, which of the following is not true?

a Price remains above the cost of production.

b Firms earn reputation rents.

c The reputations of existing firms act as a barrier to the entry of new competitors.

d Marginal revenue equals marginal cost.

e Price equals marginal cost.

15 A firm with a reputation for high-quality goods might not cut its price because

a cutting price would attract more customers.

b customers might infer that at the low price, the firm will not have enough incentive to maintain its reputation.

c lower prices would attract new competitors.

d the firm cannot set its price; it must be a price taker.

e none of the above.

16 When customers do not have perfect information about price, there may be price dispersion, which means

a the same good is sold at different prices and customers will search for the best value.

b the expenses of searching eliminate the gains from trade.

c price equals marginal revenue.

d competing goods differ in quality.

e none of the above.

17 When search is costly for customers,

a the demand curves for a firm's products will be downward sloping.

b firms will be price takers.

c the firm will lose all its customers if it raises its price above the prices of its competitors.

d the firm will gain all its competitors' business if it charges lower prices.

e none of the above.

18 Markets in which customers must search to learn prices and qualities are best described by the

a competitive model.

b pure monopoly model.

c monopolistic competition model.

d oligopoly model.

e none of the above.

19 An information intermediary

a helps bring together buyers and sellers.

b cannot make money because markets for information do not work well.

c writes contracts for buyers and sellers.

d eliminates the need for advertising.

e none of the above.

20 Advertising is not designed to

a provide price information to potential customers.

b inform customers about which products are available.

c persuade customers to buy certain products.

d make it easy to determine whether it is informative or persuasive.

e none of the above.

Completion

1 In the market for _____, customers do not know the quality of the goods being sold.

2 Actions taken by sellers to convince buyers of the high quality of their goods are called _____.

3 The _____ arises when the individual is not rewarded for what he or she does or when the individual does not have to pay the full costs of what he or she does.

4 Clauses in contracts that make the payment depend on precisely how the service is performed are called _____.

5 Profits accruing to firms with reputations of high quality are called _____.

6 The reputations of existing firms act as a _____ against new competition.

7 When the same good is sold at different prices, there is _____.

8 When customers must search for price and quality information, competition is _____.

9 Advertising that conveys information about price, product availability, and quality is called _____ advertising.

10 Advertising may _____ to customers that the product is of high quality because if the quality were poor, the firm would soon lose its new customers and would have wasted its advertising expenses.

Answers to Self-Test

True or False

1	t	6	t	11	t
2	f	7	t	12	t
3	t	8	f	13	f
4	t	9	t	14	f
5	t	10	t	15	t

Multiple Choice

1	e	6	b	11	a	16	a
2	e	7	c	12	c	17	a
3	e	8	d	13	d	18	c
4	c	9	b	14	e	19	a
5	b	10	c	15	b	20	e

Completion

1 lemons
2 signals
3 incentive problem
4 contingency clauses
5 reputation rents
6 barrier to entry
7 price dispersion
8 imperfect
9 informative
10 signal

Doing Economics: Tools and Practice Problems

Three topics are discussed in this section. First, we look at the important **lemons model**, where average quality is higher as price increases. In this situation, we may see upward-sloping demand curves, which may cause markets to fail to exist or may create the possibility of more than one equilibrium. Also, when firms are able to set prices in this model, there is the possibility of excess supply. Second, we turn to price dispersion and search. We explore the benefits and costs of searching and see why the consumer will likely stop searching before the lowest price is found. Finally, we study how advertising increases profits.

Tool Kit 19.1: Deriving the Demand Curve When Consumers Do Not Know the Quality of the Good

When consumers do not know the quality of a good until after they make the purchase, there is asymmetric information in the product market. Firms that produce low-quality goods (lemons) can sell their goods in the high-quality market. If information were perfect, there would be two markets; now there is one. In figuring out their own demand, consumers must estimate how average quality changes as the market expands. We see how to derive the demand curve under these circumstances and find that it may slope upwards.

Step one: Add the supplies of low- and high-quality goods to find the market supply curve.

Price	Quantity supplied
p_1	$Q_{\text{low}} + Q_{\text{high}}$
p_2	$Q_{\text{low}} + Q_{\text{high}}$
etc.	

Step two: Find the fractions of high- and low-quality goods at each point on the supply curve.

Fraction of high-quality goods = $Q_{\text{high}}/(Q_{\text{low}} + Q_{\text{high}})$.

Fraction of low-quality goods = $Q_{\text{low}}/(Q_{\text{low}} + Q_{\text{high}})$.

Step three: Find the average value at each point. This number is what consumers are willing to pay; therefore, it is the demand price.

Average value = demand price
= (fraction of high quality × value of high quality)
+ (fraction of low quality × value of low quality).

Step four: Construct the demand curve.

Price =
average value | Quantity demanded

p_1	$Q_{\text{low}} + Q_{\text{high}}$
p_2	$Q_{\text{low}} + Q_{\text{high}}$
etc.	

1 (Worked problem: asymmetric information) Many firms sell 50-pound packages of meat at the local farmers' market. Customers place a value of $20 on fatty, low-quality beef, and they place a value of $50 on lean, good-quality beef. The beef is wrapped and frozen, so at the time of purchase, customers cannot distinguish the quality of beef they are buying. The supply curves for low- and high-quality beef appear in Table 19.1.

Table 19.1

Low quality		High quality	
Price	Quantity	Price	Quantity
$15	1,000	$15	0
$20	2,000	$20	0
$25	3,000	$25	1,000
$30	4,000	$30	4,000
$35	5,000	$35	10,000
$40	6,000	$40	12,000
$45	7,000	$45	14,000
$50	8,000	$50	16,000

a Derive the demand curve for beef.
b Find the market-clearing price (or prices) and quantity (or quantities).
c For purposes of comparison, suppose that consumers could tell the difference and that there were separate markets for the two types of beef. Find the equilibrium price and quantity for each type of beef. How does the asymmetric information about quality affect the market for high-quality beef?

Step-by-step solution

Step one (a): Add the supplies to find the market supply. For example, if the price is $35, there will be 5,000 low-quality packages of beef and 10,000 high-quality packages for a total of 15,000. Proceeding in this way gives the market supply as shown in Table 19.2.

Table 19.2

	Market supply
Price	Quantity both high (and low quality)
$15	1,000
$20	2,000
$25	4,000
$30	8,000
$35	15,000
$40	18,000
$45	21,000
$50	24,000

Step two: Find the fractions of the total that are high and low quality at each point. For example, if the price is $35, there are 10,000 high-quality packages. The total number of packages is 15,000. The fraction is (10,000/15,000) = 2/3. Enter the number and continue. The corresponding fraction of low-quality goods is then 1/3. The complete information appears in Table 19.3.

Table 19.3

Price	Low-quality quantity	High-quality quantity	Fraction high	Fraction low
$15	1,000	0	0	1
$20	2,000	0	0	1
$25	3,000	1,000	1/4	3/4
$30	4,000	4,000	1/2	1/2
$35	5,000	10,000	2/3	1/3
$40	6,000	12,000	2/3	1/3
$45	7,000	14,000	2/3	1/3
$50	8,000	16,000	2/3	1/3

Step three: Compute the average value for each price. For example, when the price is $35, there are 5,000 packages valued at $20 and 10,000 valued at $50. The average value is [($20 × 5,000) + ($50 × 10,000)]/15,000 = $40. Continue and complete the table as shown in Table 19.4. Note that average value increases with price. This is because at a higher price, the percentage of packages that are high quality is greater.

Table 19.4

Price	Low-quality quantity	High-quality quantity	Fraction high	Average value
$15	1,000	0	0	$20.00
$20	2,000	0	0	$20.00
$25	3,000	1,000	1/4	$27.50
$30	4,000	4,000	1/2	$35.00
$35	5,000	10,000	2/3	$40.00
$40	6,000	12,000	2/3	$40.00
$45	7,000	14,000	2/3	$40.00
$50	8,000	16,000	2/3	$40.00

Step four: Construct the demand curve. It is given in Table 19.5 and drawn in the diagram. The price column is the average value, and the quantity column is the sum of the low- and high-quality quantities.

Table 19.5

Market demand	
Price	Quantity
$20.00	1,000
$20.00	2,000
$27.50	4,000
$35.00	8,000
$40.00	15,000
$40.00	18,000
$40.00	21,000
$40.00	24,000

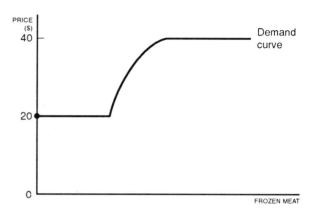

Step five (b): Find the market-clearing prices and quantities. The market clears at a price of $20, where the quantity demanded equals the quantity supplied at 2,000. At this equilibrium, there are no high-quality packages sold. Also, the market clears at a price of $40, where the quantity demanded and the quantity supplied equal 18,000. At this equilibrium, there are 6,000 low-quality and 12,000 high-quality packages. The two equilibria are shown in the diagram.

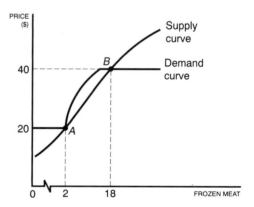

Step six (c): If consumers had perfect information about quality, then there would be a separate low-quality market with 2,000 sold at a price of $20 and a high-quality market with a price of $50 and 16,000 units sold. With asymmetric information, the high-quality market is destroyed at equilibrium A. In equilibrium B, the high-quality market survives, but the quantity is smaller than it would be with perfect information.

2 (Practice problem: asymmetric information) Trying to appear better educated, many Canadians are buying abbreviated guides to culture—lists of novels, operas, and works of art an educated person should know. The guides also include a paragraph or two of witty things to say. The consumers of these books, obviously, cannot judge the quality until they say the wrong thing at the next important social function. The supply curves of low- and high-quality guides are given in Table 19.6. The value of a high-quality guide (complete with video tapes and workbooks) is $300. Low-quality guides are worthless.

Table 19.6

Price	Low-quality guides	High-quality guides
$ 50	1,000	0
$100	2,000	1,000
$150	4,000	6,000
$200	8,000	16,000
$250	12,000	36,000
$300	16,000	48,000

a Derive the demand curve for guides.

b Find the market-clearing price (or prices) and quantity (or quantities).

c For the purposes of comparison, suppose that consumers could tell the difference and that there were separate markets for the two types of guides. Find the equilibrium price and quantity for each type of guide. How does the asymmetric information about quality affect the market for high-quality guides?

3 (Practice problem: asymmetric information) Several new varieties of tomatoes are coming onto the market. Each promises tasty tomatoes with long shelf lives, and a tomato plant that fulfilled this promise would be worth $4. Consumers cannot observe the quality until the end of the growing season, but they suspect that the new hybrids are no better or worse than existing ones valued at $1 per plant. The supply curves of low- and high-quality tomato plants are given in Table 19.7.

Table 19.7

Price	Low-quality tomato plants	High-quality tomato plants
$1.00	10,000	0
$1.50	20,000	5,000
$2.00	30,000	20,000
$2.50	40,000	60,000
$3.00	50,000	100,000
$3.50	60,000	300,000
$4.00	70,000	500,000

a Derive the demand curve for tomato plants.

b Find the market-clearing price (or prices) and quantity (or quantities).

c For the purposes of comparison, suppose that consumers could tell the difference and that there were separate markets for each of the two types of plants. Find the equilibrium price and quantity for each type of plant. How does the asymmetric information about quality affect the market for high-quality plants?

Tool Kit 19.2: Finding the Price That Maximizes Quality per Dollar

Because it is more expensive to produce high-quality goods than low, consumers may reason that at low prices only the poor-quality items are offered for sale, and that as price increases, so does average quality. If firms understand this sort of reasoning, they will set price so that quality per dollar is as high as possible, even though this price may not be the market-clearing price. It is possible that shortages will occur, and yet no firm will reduce its price because it knows that it will not gain customers, who believe that lower prices imply lower quality. This is a profound result. In normal competitive markets, the role of prices is only to clear the market. In markets where customers do not know quality, however, price acts as a signal of quality. The price that does the best job of signalling quality may not clear the market.

Step one: Identify and plot the relationship between quality and price.

Step two: For each price, find the quality-price ratio: quality-price ratio = quality/price.

Step three: Choose the highest quality-price ratio. Label this point *A*.

QUALITY

Quality-price
relation

A

Tangent at A

PRICE

Step four: Draw a line from the origin to point A. It should be tangent to the quality-price curve, and its slope equals the maximum quality-price ratio.

4 (Worked problem: quality and price) Consumers of 12-litre fire extinguishers care deeply about the quality of the item, but they cannot distinguish effective and ineffective goods at the time of purchase. The quality of a fire extinguisher only matters if and when it is used. Consumers may reason that at low prices, firms could not afford the quality-control procedures necessary to ensure effective operation. Suppose consumers believe that the relationship between quality and price is as given in Table 19.8.

Table 19.8

Price	Quality (litres of fire retardant released)
$ 5	0
$10	1.0
$15	4.5
$20	7.0
$25	10.0
$30	11.0
$35	12.0
$40	12.0

a Find the price that maximizes quality per dollar.
b Suppose that demand and supply are as given in Table 19.9. Find the equilibrium price. Does it clear the market? Why or why not?

Table 19.9

Price	Demand	Supply
$40	10,000	28,000
$35	12,000	25,000
$30	14,000	21,000
$25	16,000	20,000
$20	17,000	19,000
$15	19,000	17,000
$10	21,000	11,000

Step-by-step solution

Step one (a): Identify and plot the relationship between quality and price. It is given in Table 19.8 and drawn in the diagram.

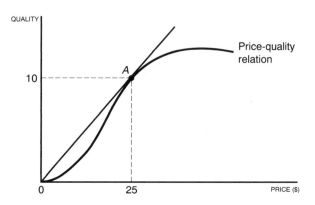

QUALITY

10

A

Price-quality
relation

0   25   PRICE ($)

Step two: For each price, find the quality-price ratio. When the price is $40, the quality-price ratio is 12/40 = 0.30. Continuing, we derive Table 19.10.

Table 19.10

Price	Quality	Quality-price ratio
$ 5	0	—
$10	1.0	0.10
$15	4.5	0.30
$20	7.0	0.35
$25	10.0	0.40
$30	11.0	0.37
$35	12.0	0.34
$40	12.0	0.30

Step three: Choose the highest quality-price ratio. It is 0.40, which occurs at a price of $25.

Step four: Draw a line from the origin to point A. It should be tangent to the quality-price curve, and its slope should equal the maximum quality-price ratio, as shown in the diagram.

Step five (b): At a price of $25, the quantity demanded is 16,000, and the quantity supplied is 20,000. Even though there is a surplus of 4,000, firms do not reduce the price. They know that customers would interpret the lower price as a signal of lower quality.

5 (Practice problem: quality and price) Tourists come to San Gordo for the shrimp. Dozens of small establishments offer shrimp, but tourists have little ability to judge the quality before eating. They reason, however, that at low prices the firms cannot afford to ensure that the shrimp are tasty. Suppose consumers believe that the relationship between quality and price is as given in Table 19.11.

Table 19.11

Price (dozen shrimp)	Quality (percentage of tasty shrimp)
$1	10
$2	30
$3	60
$4	70
$5	80
$6	85

a Find the price that maximizes quality per dollar.
b Suppose that demand and supply are as given in Table 19.12. Find the equilibrium price. Does it clear the market? Why or why not?

Table 19.12

Price	Demand	Supply
$6	2,000	6,000
$5	2,500	5,500
$4	3,000	5,000
$3	3,500	4,500
$2	4,000	4,000
$1	6,000	3,000

6 (Practice problem: quality and price) The boom in home exercise equipment continues, but there are many purchasers who have given up the quest for the perfect body. These purchasers offer their used equipment for sale. The market also includes those who are selling used lemons, worthless devices that do not perform as advertised. Consumers of used exercise equipment judge that the relationship between price and quality is as given in Table 19.13.

Table 19.13

Price	Quality (calories burned per hour)
$100	100
$200	500
$300	1,100
$400	1,600
$500	1,750

Find the price that maximizes quality per dollar.

Tool Kit 19.3: Searching for Lower Prices

In imperfectly competitive markets, different firms may offer the same good for sale at different prices. This situation, called price dispersion, means that consumers must not only decide which goods to purchase, they also must expend time and effort to locate lower price offers and decide which offer to accept. The optimal amount to search is the subject of these problems. As usual, the solution involves carefully balancing benefits and costs.

Step one: Identify the marginal cost of search and the relationship between search effort and price.

Step two: Calculate the marginal benefits of search:

marginal benefit =
    change in lowest price/change in search effort.

Step three: Find the amount of search for which the marginal benefits equal the marginal cost.

Step four: Draw a diagram illustrating the solution.

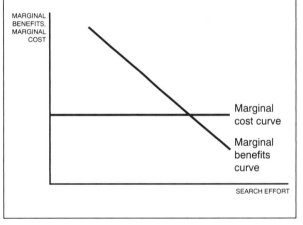

7 (Worked problem: search) Jennifer would like to build a deck behind her new condominium. She has in mind the type she would like and is considering sending away for catalogues offering deck kits. Each catalogue costs $5. The relationship between the lowest appropriate deck kit price and the number of catalogues is given in Table 19.14.

Table 19.14

Number of catalogues ordered	Lowest price found	Marginal benefit
1	$250	
2	$225	
3	$210	
4	$205	
5	$202	
6	$200	

a What is the optimal number of catalogues for Jennifer to order?

b What price does she expect to pay for a deck kit?

c Draw a diagram illustrating your solution.

Step-by-step solution

Step one (a): Identify the marginal cost of search and the relationship between search effort and price. The marginal cost is $5, and the relationship appears in Table 19.14.

Step two: Calculate the marginal benefit of search. The expected price is $250 from the first catalogue and $225 from the second. The marginal benefit is thus $25. Continuing, we derive the marginal benefits as shown in Table 19.15.

Table 19.15

Number of catalogues ordered	Lowest price found	Marginal benefit
1	$250	—
2	$225	$25
3	$210	$15
4	$205	$ 5
5	$202	$ 3
6	$200	$ 2

Step three: Find the amount of search for which the marginal benefit equals the marginal cost. This is 4 catalogues, which is the answer to part a.

Step four (b): The expected lowest price is $205, when she buys 4 catalogues.

Step five (c): The solution appears in the diagram.

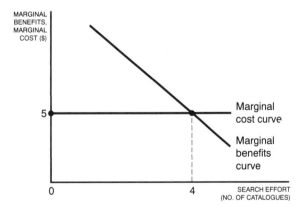

8 (Practice problem: search) Raul wants to refinish his floors. This type of home improvement project is very popular in his neighbourhood, and appointments for estimates must be made and paid for weeks in advance. Estimates cost $25, and Raul guesses that the relationship between the number of estimates and the lowest price is as given in Table 19.16.

Table 19.16

Number of estimates	Expected lowest price
1	$800
2	$650
3	$550
4	$500
5	$475
6	$465
7	$460

a What is the optimal number of estimates for Raul to schedule?

b What price does he expect to pay for refinishing his floors?

c Draw a diagram illustrating your solution.

9 (Practice problem: search) The Melling Forging Company needs a new robotic lathe. Several companies offer the lathes, but Melling's management feels there is enough variety that an on-site inspection is needed for each. Time is short, so the company plans to send engineers simultaneously to the plants of some of the firms that sell robotic lathes. The company would like to visit all robotic lathe producers, but a plant visit costs the company $1,000. The relationship between the number of visits and the profits that the new system will earn is given in Table 19.17.

Table 19.17

Number of visits	Expected maximum profitability
1	$18,000
2	$23,000
3	$26,000
4	$27,000
5	$27,500

How many engineers should Melling send?

10 (Practice problem: advertising) Advertising is designed to shift the demand curve to the right. This allows a firm to charge higher prices on the goods that it sells and to adjust the quantity to the profit-maximizing level along the new demand curve. To see how profits change with a successful advertising program, simply follow the procedure outlined in Chapter 15 for deriving marginal revenue and finding the monopoly price and quantity.

Fay's Cleaners has been advertising its new service, which offers customers the opportunity to leave and pick up their dry cleaning at the commuter train station. The demand curves before and after the advertising campaign are given in Table 19.18. Quantity measures suits cleaned and pressed. The marginal cost of each item is $1. Fixed costs equal $1,000.

Table 19.18

Before		After	
Price	Quantity	Price	Quantity
$5.00	100	$5.00	500
$4.50	200	$4.50	1,000
$4.00	300	$4.00	1,500
$3.50	400	$3.50	2,000
$3.00	500	$3.00	2,500
$2.50	600	$2.50	3,000
$2.00	700	$2.00	3,500

a Find the profit-maximizing price and quantity and level of profits before the advertising campaign.

b Find the profit-maximizing price and quantity and level of profits after the advertising campaign.

c How much is the advertising campaign worth to Fay's Cleaners?

11 (Practice problem: advertising) The Vancouver Vermin, a minor league franchise in the A league, is evaluating its advertising program. The demand curves before and after the advertising campaign are given in Table 19.19. Quantity measures the attendance. The marginal cost of another customer in the park is $0.50. Fixed costs are $50,000.

Table 19.19

Before		After	
Price	Quantity	Price	Quantity
$10.00	15,000	$10.00	20,000
$ 9.50	17,500	$ 9.50	30,000
$ 9.00	20,000	$ 9.00	40,000
$ 8.50	22,500	$ 8.50	50,000
$ 8.00	25,000	$ 8.00	60,000
$ 7.50	27,500	$ 7.50	70,000
$ 7.00	30,000	$ 7.00	80,000
$ 6.50	32,500	$ 6.50	90,000
$ 6.00	35,000	$ 6.00	100,000
$ 5.50	37,500	$ 5.50	110,000

a Find the profit-maximizing price and quantity and level of profits before the advertising campaign.

b Find the profit-maximizing price and quantity and level of profits after the advertising campaign.

c How much is the advertising campaign worth to the Vancouver Vermin?

Answers to Problems

2 a The market demand and supply curves appear in Table 19.20.

Table 19.20

Price	Low-quality guides	High-quality guides	Total market quantity	Demand price
$ 50	1,000	0	1,000	$ 0
$100	2,000	1,000	3,000	$100
$150	4,000	6,000	10,000	$180
$200	8,000	16,000	24,000	$200
$250	12,000	36,000	48,000	$225
$300	16,000	48,000	64,000	$225

b The market clears at a price of $100, with 1,000 high- and 2,000 low-quality guides. Another market-clearing price is $200, where high-quality guides number 16,000 and low-quality, 8,000.

c If there were perfect information, there would be no low-quality guides, 48,000 high-quality guides, and an equilibrium price equal to $300.

3 a The market demand and supply curves appear in Table 19.21.

Table 19.21

Price	Low-quality tomato plants	High-quality tomato plants	Total market quantity	Demand price
$1.00	10,000	0	10,000	$1.00
$1.50	20,000	5,000	25,000	$1.60
$2.00	30,000	20,000	50,000	$2.20
$2.50	40,000	60,000	100,000	$2.80
$3.00	50,000	100,000	150,000	$3.00
$3.50	60,000	300,000	360,000	$3.50
$4.00	70,000	500,000	570,000	$3.63

a The market clears at a price of $1.00 where 10,000 low-quality plants are sold and also at a price of $3.00 where 50,000 low-quality and 100,000 high-quality plants are sold.

c The equilibrium price of low-quality plants would be $1.00 with 10,000 sold. In the high-quality market, the price would equal $4.00, and 500,000 would be sold.

5 a The quality-price ratio appears in Table 19.22.

Table 19.22

Price	Quality	Quality-price ratio
$1	10	10.0
$2	30	15.0
$3	60	20.0
$4	70	17.5
$5	80	16.0
$6	85	14.2

Firms choose a price of $3.

b This results in a surplus of 4,500 − 3,500 = 1,000.

6   The quality-price ratio appears in Table 19.23.

Table 19.23

Price	Quality	Quality-price ratio
$100	100	1.00
$200	500	2.50
$300	1,100	3.67
$400	1,600	4.00
$500	1,750	3.50

8   The marginal benefits of searching appear in Table 19.24.

Table 19.24

Number of estimates	Expected lowest price	Marginal benefits
1	$800	—
2	$650	$150
3	$550	$100
4	$500	$ 50
5	$475	$ 25
6	$465	$ 10
7	$460	$ 5

a   Raul should get 5 estimates.
b   He expects to pay $475.
c

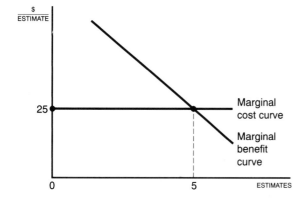

9   The marginal benefits of search appear in Table 19.25.

Table 19.25

Number of visits	Expected maximum profitability	Marginal benefits
1	$18,000	—
2	$23,000	$5,000
3	$26,000	$3,000
4	$27,000	$1,000
5	$27,500	$ 500

The company should send 4 engineers and expect to earn $27,000.

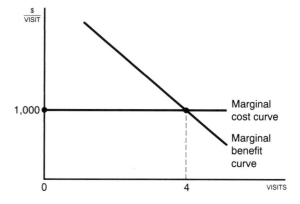

10   *a*   Price = $3; quantity = 500; profits = ($3 × 500) − ($1 × 500) − $1,000 − $0.
      b   Price = $3; quantity = 2,500; profits = ($3 × 2,500) − ($1 × 2,500) − $1,000 = $4,000.
      c   The advertising campaign increases profits by $4,000 − $0 = $4,000.

11   *a*   Price = $6; quantity = 32,500; profits = ($7 × 30,000) − ($0.50 × 30,000) − $50,000 = $145,000.
      b   Price = $5.50; quantity = 110,000; profits = ($5.50 × 110,000) − ($0.50 × 110,000) − $50,000 = $500,000.
      c   The advertising campaign increases profits by $500,000 − $145,000 = $355,000.

Chapter 20

IMPERFECTIONS IN THE LABOUR MARKET

Chapter Review

This chapter of the text returns to the labour market and applies the lessons of imperfect competition from Chapter 15 and imperfect information from Chapter 19. The chapter first explores labour unions and compares them to monopolies in the context of the labour they supply to the firm. Next the chapter examines reasons for wage differences. Finally, it takes up the problems of motivating and selecting employees. Particular attention is paid to how different compensation schemes affect incentives. Chapter 21 moves on to explore the capital market from the perspective of imperfect information, but much of the material in this chapter will reappear when the focus shifts back to the management of the firm in Chapter 22.

ESSENTIAL CONCEPTS

1   Employees band together in **unions** to negotiate better working conditions and higher wages. The unionized share of nonagricultural employment in Canada rose from about 25 percent at the start of the 1950s to a little over 35 percent by the mid-1970s, and has stayed at that level subsequently. This increase masks a fall in private-sector unionism and a dramatic rise in the proportion of workers in the public sector who belong to a union. The overall increase in union membership reflects also the growth in the size of the public sector in Canada.

2   The decline in unionization in the private sector is even more pronounced in the United States than it is in Canada. The reasons for the declining importance of unions in the private sector in both countries include improved working conditions generally, a major transfer of employment from manufacturing industries to service industries, and increased competition in product markets as barriers to international trade have been reduced.

3   Unions can be thought of as *monopolies* in the supply of labour to the firm. As such, they raise the wage and allow employment to fall. When the employer firm makes monopoly profits in its own product market, however, it is possible for unions to secure higher wages without reduced employment, at least for a while. Overall, higher union wages probably result in

somewhat higher product prices and lower wages for nonunion workers.

4 Because of imperfect information and other factors, labour is somewhat immobile, and wage differentials exist. Wage differentials may be caused by several factors:

  a **Compensating differentials** are wage differences that reflect characteristics of the job. For example, a police officer may earn more than a firefighter; this reflects the greater danger of police work.

  b **Information-based differentials** reflect a worker's imperfect information. Workers must search for job offers. A worker currently receiving a low wage may not be able to convince another employer to offer a higher wage because the prospective employer will not know the quality of the worker. This is the lemons model from Chapter 19 applied to the labour market. The difficulty that workers have in moving from job to job gives firms some market power and leads to lower wages.

  c **Productivity wage differentials** simply account for differences in abilities to produce output.

5 **Discrimination** reduces the wages of certain groups. This may involve outright prejudice or just **statistical discrimination**, which results from the use of screening devices (such as degrees from well-established schools) that unintentionally sort out certain classes of workers from the hiring pool. **Affirmative action** requires that firms must actively seek out minorities and women and include them in the applicant pool.

6 Employers must **motivate** workers to perform the task for which they were hired. When the marginal product of a worker is observable, a firm can base pay on output. Thus, **piece-work compensation** schemes provide strong incentives to workers but can subject them to substantial risk. Again, there is a risk-incentive trade-off.

7 Especially when a worker's output is difficult for the employer to observe, the employer may want to **monitor** workers. Also, paying relatively high **efficiency wages** gives workers incentives to work hard and be more productive. Employers can reduce turnover (and training costs) by letting pay and fringe benefits increase with seniority.

8 Sometimes the employer may not know whether output is high because the employees are working hard and well or because the demand for the product is high. In this case, one option is to set up **contests** where workers are paid according to how well they do relative to their peers.

9 Employers must select and promote without knowing how things will work out. High-quality, hardworking workers may want to signal their abilities by acquiring credentials, working long hours, or speaking and acting in certain ways. Firms may offer **self-selection devices**, such as alternative salary structures or career paths, that allow workers to demonstrate commitment by choosing. This policy can help firms assign workers to the appropriate tasks.

BEHIND THE ESSENTIAL CONCEPTS

1 The most important idea to keep in mind when thinking about the labour market is that it is a market. Many of the same models that explained aspects of imperfect product markets appear here in the labour market. Consider the following.

  a Just as the firm may be a monopoly in the product market, a union has monopoly power over the labour supply to the firm. In each case, the price (wage) is set above marginal cost (supply curve of labour), and the quantity (employment) is less.

  b Consumers must search for price and quality information, while workers must search for job offers. In each case, the firm reaps some market power. In the product market, prices are somewhat higher; in the labour market, wages are lower.

  c Consumers who are uncertain of the quality of the product are reluctant to buy. Employers who are uncertain of the abilities and character of the workers are reluctant to hire. In each case, lowering the price (the wage) leads to adverse selection—more low-quality products or workers.

  d Firms need incentives to produce quality products just as workers need incentives to be productive. There is always the risk-incentive trade-off. Contracts and reputations create incentives in product markets. Monitoring, efficiency wages, seniority benefits, contests, and team rewards create incentives in labour markets.

  e Firms may want to signal that their products are of high quality and offer warranties, set up elaborate showrooms, advertise, or protect a reputation. Likewise, workers can signal high productivity with credentials, education, long hours, and certain kinds of behaviour.

2 Not only is information imperfect, but exactly what the employer does not know is important. Based upon what is not known, the employer must choose a means of selecting and motivating workers. For example:

  a If the productivity of a job applicant is not known, the employer may rely on signals. A low wage in the current job may indicate low productivity. A university degree may indicate innate abilities.

  b If the employer can observe the marginal productivity of workers, then the employer may offer a piece-rate schedule of wages, but this scheme may expose the employee to substantial risk.

  c If the employer cannot observe the effort of the workers, the employer can monitor them and pay above-market efficiency wages. High wages make the job valuable and make the possibility of losing the job something to motivate the worker.

d If the employer thinks that the worker might have other employment opportunities, the employer may offer higher wages and better working conditions to discourage more senior workers from quitting. This becomes especially important if the employer must pay to train new workers.

e If the employer does not know whether the output of workers is due to their productivity or due to market conditions, the employer may set up contests and pay more to workers who do relatively better.

f If the employer cannot observe the productivity of employees but thinks that the employees are aware of one another's productivity, the employer can reward good performance by a team; this induces employees to motivate one another.

SELF-TEST

True or False

1 Public-sector workers now form the majority of all unionized workers in Canada.

2 Labour relations in Canada are primarily governed by provincial legislation.

3 One reason for the decline in the percent of the work force in the private sector that belongs to unions is that consumers have shifted their demand towards more manufacturing and fewer services.

4 Unions act like monopolies in the supply of labour to the firm.

5 Unions usually support innovation even though it might reduce the demand for the services of their members.

6 Wage differentials resulting from differences in job characteristics are called compensating differentials.

7 Imperfect information will not lead to wage differentials if workers search for job opportunities.

8 Employers may be reluctant to offer jobs to workers who currently earn low wages, if they believe that current wages signal low productivity.

9 Statistical discrimination results from overt prejudice.

10 Affirmative action is designed to eliminate union shops.

11 Under a piece-rate system, workers are insured against any risk related to the overall success of the business.

12 Piece-rate systems do not work well if the firm cannot easily and accurately measure the marginal product of workers.

13 Paying higher efficiency wages may motivate workers to be more productive because they perceive that the high-wage job is worth keeping.

14 Firms that are unsure about whether their workers' productivity is due to luck or effort can motivate workers by using contests.

15 The only reason why a firm might pay more to an educated worker is that the firm believes the education makes the worker more productive.

Multiple Choice

1 Since World War II,

a unionization has increased, with increases in both the private and public sectors.
b unionization has declined, with declines in both the private and public sectors.
c unionization has increased, because the increase in the public sector outweighed the decline in the private sector.
d unionization has decreased, because the decline in the private sector outweighed the increase in the public sector.
e unionization has increased, because the increase in the private sector outweighed the decline in the public sector.

2 A majority of the unionized workers in Canada are employed in

a service industries.
b the public sector.
c manufacturing industries.
d the construction industry.
e none of the above.

3 Which of the following does not provide part of the explanation for the decline in the percentage of the work force in the private sector belonging to unions?

a An overall improvement in working conditions has reduced the demand of workers for unions.
b Consumer demand has shifted towards the relatively less unionized sectors, such as services.
c Increasingly competitive markets have limited the power of unions to negotiate increased wages.
d the size of the public sector has increased.
e none of the above.

4 In negotiating wages with firms, unions are most like

a monopolies.
b monopsonies.
c competitive firms.
d individual consumers.
e none of the above.

5 Unless the firm is making monopoly profits in its product market, the higher wages negotiated by a union must

a increase the level of employment at the firm.
b have no effect on the level of employment at the firm.
c reduce the level of employment at the firm.
d lead the firm to substitute labour for capital.
e none of the above.

6   Higher wages for union labour

   a   decrease the supply of nonunion labour.
   b   increase the supply of nonunion labour.
   c   increase wages received by nonunion labour.
   d   increase the supply of union labour.
   e   none of the above.

7   In a labour-management negotiation, the bargaining surplus refers to

   a   the fact that although the firm can hire other workers and workers can find other jobs, both sides can gain by reaching agreement.
   b   the costs of negotiation in lawyers' and arbitrators' salaries.
   c   the strike funds built up by the firm and union in anticipation of possible work stoppages.
   d   the extra workers that the union forces management to hire.
   e   none of the above.

8   Compensating differentials are wage differences resulting from

   a   the fact that workers must search to find job offers and learn of alternative wages.
   b   the fact that employers are unlikely to make offers to workers who currently earn low wages, inferring that these workers may be less productive.
   c   differences in job characteristics.
   d   wage differences that compensate for differences in productivity.
   e   none of the above.

9   Jobs that are similar in all respects

   a   must pay the same wage, because no worker would take the lower-paying job when higher-paying ones are available.
   b   can have different wages according to the theory of compensating differentials.
   c   may pay different wages, because employers can pay whatever they want and workers must accept.
   d   may pay different wages if it takes time and effort for workers to learn about the alternative job possibilities.
   e   none of the above.

10   Wage differences that are due to differences in ability to produce output are called

   a   compensating differentials.
   b   information-based differentials.
   c   statistical discrimination.
   d   affirmative action.
   e   productivity differentials.

11   When workers are not aware of alternative job possibilities,

   a   firms may take advantage of their information-based market power and raise wages.

   b   firms may take advantage of their information-based monopsony power and lower wages.
   c   workers can earn compensating differentials.
   d   all similar workers must earn the same wage for jobs with the same characteristics.
   e   none of the above.

12   Statistical discrimination refers to

   a   wage differences based on statistical measures of productivity differentials.
   b   requirements that firms keep statistics on the numbers of employees in each ethnic group.
   c   requirements that firms actively seek out women and minorities for hiring and promotion.
   d   the use of screening devices that unintentionally sort out members of certain groups.
   e   paying lower wages to workers who have little statistical information about the labour market and alternative job possibilities.

13   The system of payment in which a worker is paid for each item produced is called

   a   a compensating differential system.
   b   an adverse selection system.
   c   a signalling system.
   d   monopsony.
   e   a piece-rate system.

14   One difficulty with basing workers' pay on their output is that

   a   although workers are given appropriate incentives to work hard, they bear considerable risk.
   b   although they bear the appropriate amount of risk, workers are given little incentive to work hard.
   c   piece-rate schemes are illegal.
   d   workers produce too much.
   e   none of the above.

15   Most workers are not paid on a piece-rate basis, because

   a   piece-rate pay is illegal.
   b   workers are risk lovers.
   c   it is often difficult to measure the quantity and quality of an individual worker's output.
   d   workers produce too much.
   e   none of the above.

16   If the employer cannot observe the contribution to output of each worker, the employer can

   a   charge higher wages to offset the costs of the shirking that is believed to be taking place.
   b   pay higher wages to increase the cost to the worker of being fired.
   c   set up a piece-work system.
   d   require the workers to work longer hours to offset the costs of the shirking that is believed to be taking place.
   e   none of the above.

17   Setting up a compensation system where pay and promotion possibilities increase with seniority

a reduces turnover and saves on the costs of training new workers.

b is illegal.

c is legal in union shops but not elsewhere.

d only makes sense when piece-rate systems do not work.

e bases pay on relative performance.

18 When workers are paid on the basis of relative performance, as in contests,

a they are given incentives to be productive, even though management does not know whether their good performance is due to luck or effort.

b workers are better off because they bear less risk.

c workers receive efficiency wages and thus work hard.

d turnover is reduced.

e none of the above.

19 Firms may infer applicants' productivity from information such as their education level, demeanour, or dress. This is called

a adverse selection.

b signalling.

c compensating differentials.

d contests.

e self-selection.

20 A firm may promote only those workers who work long hours, believing that these people like the job and are unlikely to leave. This is an example of

a a self-selection device.

b an information differential.

c monopsony.

d a union shop.

e a piece-rate system.

Completion

1 In _____, all labourers at unionized establishments must join the union.

2 Unions can raise wages because they have a _____ on the supply of labour to the firm.

3 _____ are differences in wages that reflect different job characteristics, such as working conditions or advancement possibilities.

4 _____ results from firms using screening devices that unintentionally sort out members of certain groups from the applicant pool.

5 The system of payment in which a worker is paid for each item produced or each task performed is called a _____ system.

6 The theory that paying higher wages leads to a more productive work force is called _____ theory.

7 Employers can discourage quitting and save costs of retraining replacements by offering compensation schemes that pay more on the basis of _____.

8 Some compensation schemes, such as bonuses for the top sales representatives, base pay on _____ performance.

9 Employers who do not know the abilities of job applicants may look for _____ such as education or other credentials.

10 An employer who offers a choice of contracts to workers, and so allows the workers to signal that they have qualities valuable to the employer by selecting a particular contract, is using a _____.

Answers to Self-Test

True or False

1	f	6	t	11	f
2	t	7	f	12	t
3	f	8	t	13	t
4	t	9	f	14	t
5	f	10	f	15	f

Multiple Choice

1	c	6	b	11	b	16	b
2	a	7	a	12	d	17	a
3	d	8	c	13	e	18	a
4	a	9	d	14	a	19	b
5	c	10	e	15	c	20	a

Completion

1 union shops
2 monopoly
3 Compensating differentials
4 Statistical discrimination
5 piece-rate
6 efficiency wage
7 seniority
8 relative
9 signals
10 self-selection device

Doing Economics: Tools and Practice Problems

A successful union forms a monopoly in the supply of labour to a firm or industry. We apply the tools of monopoly to study the behaviour of unions in several problems in this section. Then we move to compensating differentials, an important source of wage differences among workers. In accepting a job offer, a worker also buys a list of job characteristics, such as safety, advancement potential, training, and the aesthetics of the workplace. We use the budget constraint to show how the labour market offers a choice among job characteristics and establishes an implicit market price for them.

1 (Worked problem: unions) The miners of Davis Lead are represented by the Lead Workers Union, which is considering its stance for the upcoming contract nego-

tiations. The union's economist has estimated a production function for lead, as given in Table 20.1. Its current price is $10 per tonne.

Tool Kit 20.1: Constructing the Union's Trade-off between Wages and Employment

If a union is able to force the signing of a contract, guaranteeing that only union members will be hired, it is in the position of a monopolist in the supply of labour. Unions may control the supply of labour to an industry, a craft, or an individual firm. The problems here focus on the latter case. Usually unions set wages and let management choose the quantity of labour to hire. In this case, the firm's demand for labour, which is the marginal revenue product, includes all the combinations of wages and employment that the union can achieve. These combinations, in turn, show the trade-off faced by the union. We study how to construct the demand for labour and some possible choices that a union might make.

Step one: Identify the production function and the price of the product, and set up a table as follows.

Workers	Output	Revenues	Marginal revenue product

Step two: Find the revenue corresponding to each level of labour use by multiplying the output level by price, and enter the results in the table:

$$\text{revenues} = \text{output} \times \text{price}.$$

Step three: Compute the marginal revenue product, which is the change in revenue divided by the change in labour, and enter the results in the table:

$$\text{marginal revenue product} =$$
$$\text{change in revenues/change in output}.$$

Step four: Plot the marginal revenue product. This curve is the schedule of possible wage and employment levels.

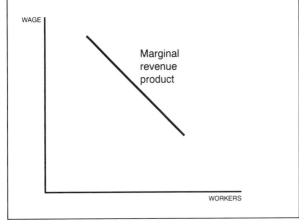

Table 20.1

Workers	Output (tonnes per month)
10	20,000
20	40,000
30	60,000
40	75,000
50	85,000
60	90,000
70	90,000

a Calculate the marginal revenue product, plot it, and interpret it as a schedule of wage and employment possibilities.

b What is the maximum wage? How much employment would result at this wage?

c Workers can earn $5,000 elsewhere. What is the maximum level of employment?

Step-by-step solution

Step one (a): Identify the production function and the price of the product. The production function is given in Table 20.1, and the price of lead is $10 per tonne.

Step two: Find the revenue corresponding to each level of labour use. We multiply output by $10, which is the price of lead. When there are 10 workers, output is 20,000, and revenue is 20,000 × $10 = $200,000. Continuing, we derive Table 20.2.

Table 20.2

Workers	Output	Revenues
10	20,000	$200,000
20	40,000	$400,000
30	60,000	$600,000
40	75,000	$750,000
50	85,000	$850,000
60	90,000	$900,000
70	90,000	$900,000

Step three: Compute the marginal revenue product, which is the change in revenue divided by the change in labour. The marginal revenue product for the first 10 workers is $200,000/10 = $20,000. Continuing, we derive Table 20.3.

Table 20.3

Workers	Output	Revenues	Marginal revenue product
10	20,000	$200,000	$20,000
20	40,000	$400,000	$20,000
30	60,000	$600,000	$20,000
40	75,000	$750,000	$15,000
50	85,000	$850,000	$10,000
60	90,000	$900,000	$ 5,000
70	90,000	$900,000	$ 0

Step four: Plot the marginal revenue product.

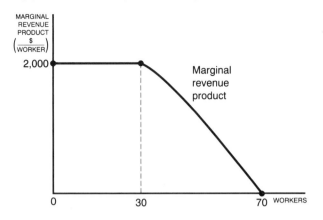

Step five (b): The maximum possible wage is $20,000 per month, and 30 workers will have jobs at this wage.

Step six (c): If the company pays $5,000, which is the alternative wage, there will be 60 workers hired.

2   (Practice problem: unions) North Dundas Provincial (NDP) University's faculty has voted to join the Canadian Union of Educational Workers to win higher wages from the administration. Its economics department has estimated the production function, which is given in Table 20.4. Tuition nets NDP University a profit of $1,000 per student after all expenses (except salaries for professors) are deducted.

Table 20.4

Faculty	Students
20	100
30	600
40	1,000
50	1,300
60	1,500
70	1,600
80	1,600

a   Calculate and plot the marginal revenue product schedule. Interpret it as a schedule of salary and employment possibilities.
b   What is the maximum salary that the union could negotiate? Keep in mind that with its enormous endowment, NDP would not shut down even if it lost money.
c   The alternative salary for a typical NDP professor is $20,000. What is the maximum level of employment?

3   (Practice problem: unions) The cherry pickers at Bingo's Cherry Orchard have won an agreement that the owner will only hire union workers. The production function is given in Table 20.5, and cherries sell for $2 per bushel.

Table 20.5

Pickers	Cherries (bushels per day)
1	24
2	64
3	96
4	120
5	136
6	144
7	148
8	150

a   Calculate and plot the marginal revenue product. Interpret it as a schedule of wage and employment possibilities.
b   What is the maximum wage? Will the orchard shut down if labour is its only nonsunk cost?
c   The workers have an alternative wage of $16 per day. What is the maximum level of employment?

Tool Kit 20.2: Using Budget Constraints to Analyze Compensating Differentials

A job offer brings with it a promised wage and a bundle of job characteristics. Workers may not accept the highest-paying job, preferring a lower wage alternative if it offers more attractive nonwage benefits. The additional wage that accompanies a job with some undesirable nonwage aspect is called the compensating differential. The budget constraint allows us to identify and study the trade-off between wages and job characteristics.

Step one: Draw a set of axes with the wage measured on the vertical axis and the nonwage characteristic on the horizontal.

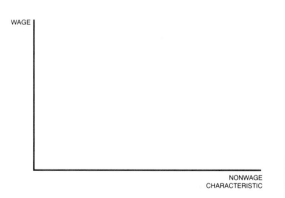

Step two: Plot a point corresponding to each job offer.

Step three: Cancel the "dominated" offers. The dominated offers represent jobs with both lower wages and less-attractive job characteristics.

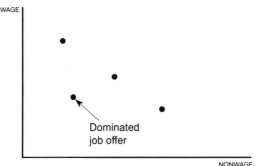

Step four: Draw a smooth curve through the undominated job offers. These are the ones that include higher wages and/or more attractive job characteristics. This curve is the budget constraint, reflecting the alternative combinations of wages and job characteristics available to the worker.

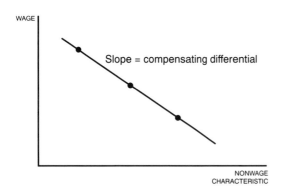

Step five: Identify the trade-off between several points on the budget constraint. The slope is the compensating differential.

4 (Worked problem: compensating differentials) Many parents in two-earner families worry about day care for infants. Recognizing this concern, some progressive companies offer on-site day care, although the facilities

vary greatly in quality. Table 20.6 lists some local firms, the entry-level salaries for management trainees, and the expenditure per child for the day care facility.

Table 20.6

Firm	Salary	Expenditure per child
ALX Corp.	$30,000	$5,000
ABX Corp.	$35,000	$3,000
PBX Corp.	$37,000	$4,000
APX Corp.	$46,000	$ 0
AXX Corp.	$40,000	$1,000

a Represent the salaries and day care expenditures as an opportunity set.
b Are there any dominated offers?
c What is the compensating differential for reducing day care expenditures from $5,000 to $4,000? From $1,000 to $0?

Step-by-step solution

Step one (a): Draw a set of axes.

Step two: Plot a point corresponding to each job offer.

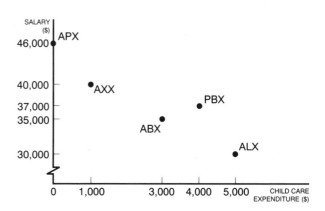

Step three (b): Cancel the dominated offers. The ABX offer, which entails less money and child care expenditure, is dominated by the PBX offer.

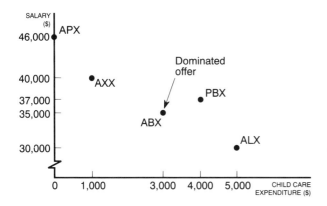

Step four: Draw a smooth curve through the undominated job offers.

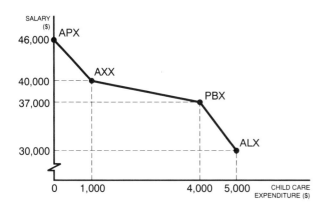

Step five (c): Identify the trade-offs between several points on the budget constraint. As the day care expenditure falls from $5,000 to $4,000, salary rises by $37,000 − $30,000 = $7,000. The compensating differential for a decrease from $1,000 to $0 is $46,000 − $40,000 = $6,000.

5 (Practice problem: compensating differentials) Sylvester Stallion is looking for a job. The alternatives, the corresponding annual salaries, and some data on accidental deaths are given in Table 20.7. Sylvester has offers for each type of job, he is qualified for each, and he considers them equally satisfying except for the risk of death.

Table 20.7

Job	Salary	Deaths per 100,000
Night guard	$16,000	2
Shoe seller	$15,000	1 (irate customer)
Clerk in convenience store	$24,000	5
Cab driver	$19,000	6
Armed guard	$22,000	3

a Represent the job offers as an opportunity set.

b Without knowing anything about Stallion's willingness to risk death, can you say if there is a job offer he will definitely refuse? Explain.
c What is the compensating differential for increasing the annual death risk from 1 to 2 deaths per 100,000 workers? What is the compensating differential for increasing the annual death risk from 3 to 5 deaths per 100,000 workers?

6 (Practice problem: compensating differentials) The banking industry in Gotham offers a wide variety of salaries and vacation days. Table 20.8 gives entry salaries and vacation time offered to new hires.

Table 20.8

Bank	Salary	Vacation days
First One	$20,000	5
Bank One	$25,000	8
First Bank	$32,000	5
Premier Bank	$30,000	6
Second Bank	$28,000	7

a Represent the salaries and vacation days as an opportunity set.
b Are there any dominated offers?
c What is the compensating differential for reducing vacation days from 8 to 7? From 6 to 5?

Answers to Problems

2 a The marginal revenue product schedule is given in Table 20.9.

Table 20.9

Faculty	Students	Revenues	Marginal revenue product
20	100	$ 100,000	—
30	600	$ 600,000	$50,000
40	1,000	$1,000,000	$40,000
50	1,300	$1,300,000	$30,000
60	1,500	$1,500,000	$20,000
70	1,600	$1,600,000	$10,000
80	1,600	$1,600,000	$ 0

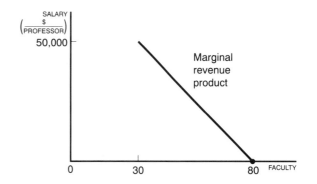

b The maximum wage is $50,000, at which 30 faculty will be hired.

c The maximum employment occurs at a wage of $20,000, with 60 faculty.

3 *a* The marginal revenue product schedule is given in Table 20.10.

Table 20.10

Pickers	Cherries	Revenues	Marginal revenue product
1	24	$ 48	$48
2	64	$128	$80
3	96	$192	$64
4	120	$240	$48
5	136	$272	$32
6	144	$288	$16
7	148	$296	$ 8
8	150	$300	$ 4

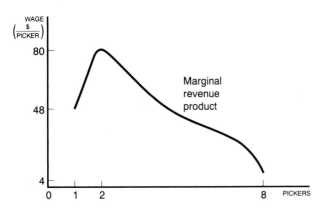

b The maximum wage is $80, at which there will be 2 pickers.

c The maximum employment is 6, where the wage equals $16.

5 *a*

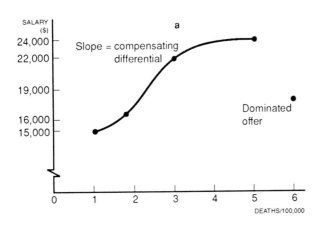

b Stallion will refuse the cab driver offer, which is dominated by the job of clerk in a convenience store.

c $1,000, $2,000.

6 *a*

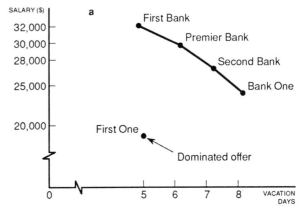

b First One.

c $3,000, $2,000.

Chapter 21

FINANCING AND CONTROLLING THE FIRM

Chapter Review

Information problems pervade the entire economy. This chapter continues the discussion of information problems in markets by turning to the market for financial capital. The same problems caused by asymmetric information in product markets (Chapter 19) and labour markets (Chapter 20) reappear in this chapter, when we consider how the firm is financed, how it is managed, and who owns it. A more detailed treatment of the firm's management follows in Chapter 22.

ESSENTIAL CONCEPTS

1 There are three legal forms for businesses in Canada. A single-owner firm is called a **proprietorship.** A firm with two or more owners is a **partnership.** Ownership of **corporations** is divided into shares, and each owner of a share has voting rights in management elections. The most important feature of the corporate form, however, is **limited liability**. Each owner can lose no more than his or her original investment. In contrast, if a partnership incurs large losses, each partner is fully liable for all the debts.

2 Corporations can finance their investments by borrowing, either from banks or by selling bonds, by issuing new shares of stock (equity finance), or from retained earnings, which are accounting profits not paid out as dividends to owners. If corporate managers act in the interest of the owners, they will maximize the market value of the firm. Surprisingly, the **Modigliani-Miller theorem** states that the mix of debt and equity finance makes no difference to the market value of the firm.

3 The Modigliani-Miller theorem is the starting point for the analysis of the financial structure of corporations. Nevertheless, there are certain features of real-world corporations that make the level of debt important.

   a A heavy debt load raises the probability of a costly **bankruptcy.** Banks are reluctant to let a firm's indebtedness grow too large without charging higher interest rates as a risk premium in case of default.

   b The tax system encourages debt because interest payments by firms are tax deductible, but dividends are not. For individuals, however, capital gains and dividends are favoured by the tax system, which offsets some of the tilt towards debt finance.

c Higher debt loads force managers to keep costs low and profits high to stave off bankruptcy. Equity finance, on the other hand, may allow managers some freedom to pursue goals other than maximizing the market value.

d Markets may perceive a firm's issuing debt as a *signal* that managers have confidence in the prospects for the profitability of the firm. This perception will drive up the market value of the firm.

e Firms that borrow may have to cede substantial *control* to banks or bondholders. This can provide management with different incentives, because shareholders lack information about what management is doing and why.

4 If lenders had perfect information about the default risk of borrowers, then the interest rate would adjust to clear the market for loans. In the real world, however, lenders do not know how risky each borrower is; thus, they give each borrower incentives to pay the loans back. Furthermore, charging higher interest rates attracts especially risky borrowers and motivates borrowers to take on extra risks to earn enough to repay the interest. Rather than raise the interest rate, lenders may ration loans. This phenomenon is known as **credit rationing.**

5 Issuing new shares is one way firms can raise new capital, but this practice may also pose problems. Prospective buyers of shares may reason that managers believe that the firm is overvalued or that it has been turned down on previous loan applications. Such expectations will cause the stock price to fall when new shares are issued. When the price of a stock falls significantly in response to the issuing of new shares, economists say that the firm is **equity rationed.** Few firms raise capital through equity finance in modern economies.

6 Inefficient management lowers the market value of a firm, but shareholders often do not have good enough information to monitor the managers. Other investors may buy up a majority voting share, replace the inefficient managers, and make profits. In this way, the **market for takeovers** can promote efficient management. Some economists have reservations about the effects of hostile takeovers, noting that takeovers are usually financed with additional debt and that the increased indebtedness injures other bondholders. Another important criticism is that the takeover firm may be managed inefficiently itself and may be pursuing the takeover for reasons other than the well-being of the shareholders. These criticisms have led to proposals to limit takeovers, but most economists favour leaving the control of firms to markets.

BEHIND THE ESSENTIAL CONCEPTS

1 Over and over again, economists approach a problem by first understanding a simple situation and then moving on to more realistic complications. When studying corporate finance, the simple starting point is the Modigliani-Miller theorem. This theorem says that the method of corporate finance makes no difference to the market value of the firm. It is important for you to understand both the logic of this theorem and why the real world of corporate finance is different.

a How does the market adjust when the firm uses borrowing rather than new shares to finance new investment? First, what the firm does with the money is unaffected by the means of raising it. Second, a higher debt load makes the stock riskier and lowers its price. The lower price is just enough to keep the market value of the firm the same under debt and equity finance.

b What is missing from this story? In the real world of corporate finance, firms must worry about the high costs of bankruptcy, and they must consider the tax consequences of debt and equity. Managerial incentives, market perceptions of value based on these incentives, and the ultimate control of the firm's decisions may all be affected by the financial structure of the firm.

2 If a firm raises money by borrowing, the lenders receive interest payments. If it raises money through new equity, then the investors receive dividends and capital gains as the stock price rises. The Canadian tax system affects the firm's decision in the following way: the system encourages borrowing and discourages equity finance because interest paid is a tax-deductible expense for the firm but dividends are not. Offsetting this to some extent is the more favourable treatment afforded individuals who receive capital gains and dividends. The net effect is that the Canadian tax system encourages borrowing to some extent.

3 Whenever one side of the market knows something that the other side does not, there is asymmetric information. In the corporate world, an important example of this is that the owners of the firms (shareholders) will not know everything that management is doing and will not be able to judge whether management's decisions are the right ones. Management may be able to get away with activities that lower profits without the owners knowing. There remains, however, the threat of takeovers. Inefficient management risks being discovered not so much by owners as by other investors, who can purchase the outstanding stock, acquire majority voting status, and replace the laggards.

4 Asymmetric information is also important when the firm goes to the market for loanable funds in search of capital to finance investments. Suppose you are thinking of providing some of this capital by purchasing a corporate bond. You do not know as much about the default risk as the firm issuing the bond, and you

should therefore be suspicious about bonds that pay very high interest rates. After all, why would a firm pay high interest rates unless it is selling a risky bond? Other investors reason as you do, and therefore the interest rate does not rise to clear the market for bonds. Firms are credit rationed because of asymmetric information in credit markets.

5 Chapter 10 focused on the efficiency of capital markets. Because each investor seeks the highest rate of return, it will be impossible to beat the market consistently. The credit market problems discussed in this chapter (credit and equity rationing) pertain to the inability of borrowers to obtain loans or raise capital even though they are willing to pay the going rate of return. The conclusion is that capital markets are efficient in valuing different assets, but not efficient in that the market for loanable funds does not clear.

SELF-TEST

True or False

1 A proprietorship is a firm owned by two or more proprietors.

2 Partnerships offer each partner limited liability in case of bankruptcy.

3 One risk of owning shares of a corporation is that should the firm go out of business, each shareholder is liable for all the debts.

4 The market value of the firm is the total value of the firm's outstanding shares and debt.

5 The Modigliani-Miller theorem states that the market value of the firm is higher if it has less debt.

6 If a firm has a heavy debt load, it can only issue new debt at high rates of interest.

7 Dividends are tax deductible for firms, because individuals must pay income tax on their dividend earnings.

8 If a firm cannot afford the interest rate charged by banks for loans, then it is credit rationed.

9 Credit rationing occurs because banks and other lenders do not have as much information about default risks as borrowers.

10 Because of credit rationing, the supply of loans exceeds the demand.

11 Investors may infer that the managers of a firm issuing new shares feel that the firm is overvalued by the market.

12 When issuing new shares causes the price of shares to fall substantially, there is credit rationing.

13 The market for takeovers may motivate managers to work hard to increase profits.

14 Most takeovers are financed through the issuing of new shares.

15 Actions taken by a company to discourage takeovers are called greenmail.

Multiple Choice

1 A business with two or more owners, each fully responsible for the liabilities, is called a

a proprietorship.
b partnership.
c limited partnership.
d corporation.
e none of the above.

2 Under the partnership form of business,

a each partner is liable for no more than the amount invested.
b Each partner is liable for his or her share of the debts.
c each partner is fully responsible for all the liabilities of the business.
d neither partner has any liability.
e none of the above.

3 If there is a single owner, the business is called a

a monopsony.
b monopoly.
c partnership.
d proprietorship.
e corporation.

4 Because of limited liability, the owners of corporations

a are exempt from taxes on capital gains that are due to inflation.
b are not taxed on their share of the retained earnings of the firm.
c have only a limited say in the operation of the corporation.
d can lose no more than the amount they invest.
e none of the above.

5 Retained earnings equal

a revenues minus expenses minus debt payments minus dividend distributions.
b revenues minus expenses.
c revenues minus debt and dividend distributions.
d revenues minus expenses and interest.
e revenues.

6 A firm will be forced to pay a high rate of interest on new debt if

a the company union has a representative on the board.
b its outstanding debt is large relative to the value of the firm.
c its equity is large relative to the value of the firm.
d its retained earnings are large relative to the value of the firm.
e none of the above.

7 If it is feasible, most firms find it better to finance new investments with

a retained earnings.
b bonds.
c loans.
d equity.
e barter.

8 The Modigliani-Miller theorem says that

a debt is riskier than equity finance.
b retained earnings are always the best way to finance new investment.
c the value of the firm is independent of the way in which it is financed.
d the market perceives highly leveraged firms to be a bad risk.
e market prices reflect the belief that when the level of debt is low, management is not sufficiently motivated to be profitable.

9 The Modigliani-Miller theorem

a is an accurate description of corporate finance.
b would be true if corporate managers understood economics.
c does not accurately describe the world of corporate finance.
d is true only in monopolistic product markets.
e would be true in the absence of government involvement in capital markets.

10 Because increased debt imposes a greater risk of bankruptcy on the corporation,

a the price of the firm's shares falls, and hence there is no change in the market value of the firm.
b banks that are willing to lend require higher interest rates to compensate them for the risk of bankruptcy.
c there is no effect on borrowing and lending incentives because the value of the firm does not depend upon the debt-to-equity ratio.
d there is no effect on borrowing and lending because the financial capital market always clears, and any firm seeking a loan at the going rate can secure one.
e none of the above.

11 Overall, the tax structure

a treats debt and equity finance equally.
b favours debt finance because interest is deductible but dividends are not.
c favours debt finance because stockholders must pay taxes on dividend income, and this affects their willingness to supply capital.
d favours debt because capital gains receive some tax advantages.
e none of the above.

12 The backs-to-the-wall theory of corporate finance holds that

a firms should be encouraged to borrow so that managers are forced to work hard to avoid bankruptcy.
b firms should be discouraged from borrowing because while stockholders oversee the operation of the firm, bondholders do not.
c the value of the firm does not depend on the debt-to-equity ratio.
d because of bankruptcy fears, the market is unwilling to buy firms with large debts.
e firms with large debts must cede some control over day-to-day operations to creditors.

13 Markets may perceive that a heavy debt position

a indicates that managers have confidence in the prospects of the firm.
b has no effect on managerial incentives.
c indicates that managers have little confidence in the prospects of the firm.
d indicates nothing because of the Modigliani-Miller theorem.
e none of the above.

14 In large corporations that are not closely held,

a stockholders effectively supervise business operations.
b while all stockholders would benefit from better management, none has enough incentive to learn how to judge the managers.
c bondholders and banks receive interest but have no control over management.
d bondholders have more effective control than banks.
e none of the above.

15 Credit rationing refers to

a the means by which prospective borrowers are allocated to banks.
b the fact that there is a limited number of seats on stock exchanges.
c the policy that firms must first go to domestic banks before seeking foreign funds.
d any situation where individuals or firms cannot obtain funds at the going rate for borrowers of similar risk.
e the fact that issuing new shares of stock may cause the stock price to fall.

16 Information in the market for loanable funds is imperfect because

a borrowers cannot know the going interest rate.
b lenders and borrowers cannot find each other.
c good banks are hard to find.
d lenders cannot monitor a borrower to ensure that enough care is being taken to prevent default.
e none of the above.

17 The idea of credit rationing says that if the lender is unsure of the likelihood of default by a certain class of borrowers, the lender will likely

a raise the interest rate to compensate for added risk.

b not be willing to raise the interest rate because higher rates may attract a relatively riskier mix of borrowers.

c charge an interest rate that clears the market for funds.

d not lend to anyone.

e none of the above.

18 If a firm issues more shares, the stock price

    a should not change because the stock market is an example of a competitive market.

    b should increase because investors will interpret the sale as a signal of confidence in the future.

    c should decrease because investors will infer that a confident firm would have sought funds from banks.

    d should not change because of the Modigliani-Miller theorem.

    e none of the above.

19 Takeovers of corporations by others

    a are never justified because stockholders can oversee the operation of the firm and motivate managers to be efficient.

    b are never justified because banks and stockholders can oversee the operation of the firm and motivate managers to be efficient.

    c can be important because other methods of controlling managers are relatively ineffective.

    d reduce the wealth of shareholders.

    e none of the above.

20 A Canadian firm may make itself an unattractive takeover target by doing all of the following except

    a making itself more efficient.

    b taking on more debt.

    c reducing the value of its assets by tying them up in bad investments.

    d creating a poison pill.

    e greenmail.

Completion

1 A business with a single owner is called a _____.

2 Two or more individuals owning a business together form a _____.

3 The key distinguishing characteristic of corporations is that their owners have _____.

4 Cash left over after expenses, debt payment, and dividend distributions is called _____.

5 According to the Modigliani-Miller theorem, the method of financing the corporation makes no difference to the _____ of the firm.

6 Overall the Canadian tax structure favours _____ finance.

7 When individuals or firms cannot borrow all they desire at the going interest rate, they are subject to _____.

8 There is an adverse selection effect in the credit market if higher interest rates _____ the expected return to a loan.

9 If firms are reluctant to issue new shares of stock because the market may perceive this action as a signal that management does not have enough confidence in the business to borrow, then firms are said to be _____.

10 A _____ occurs when one company buys enough shares of the stock of another company to seize control.

Answers to Self-Test

True or False

1	f	6	t	11	t
2	f	7	f	12	f
3	f	8	f	13	t
4	t	9	t	14	f
5	f	10	f	15	f

Multiple Choice

1	b	6	b	11	b	16	d
2	c	7	a	12	a	17	b
3	d	8	c	13	a	18	c
4	d	9	c	14	b	19	c
5	a	10	b	15	d	20	d

Completion

1 proprietorship
2 partnership
3 limited liability
4 retained earnings
5 market value
6 debt
7 credit rationing
8 reduce
9 equity rationed
10 takeover

Doing Economics: Tools and Practice Problems

Credit rationing is a reason why firms may not be able to obtain loans even when they are willing to pay the going interest rate. As in the lemon and efficiency wage models, the price (the interest rate in the loanable funds market) has two jobs: it balances supply and demand and influences the riskiness of loan applicants. The latter job refers to the fact that at higher rates of interest, firms may seek funds for riskier projects with greater default rates. Because the interest rate that maximizes the expected rate of return on loans encourages a high percentage of safe loan applicants, it may be too low to clear the market. In this case, supply is less than demand, and there is credit rationing.

228 • CHAPTER 21

Tool Kit 21.1: Credit Rationing

Step one: Identify and plot the relationship between the interest rate and the expected rate of return on loans. Also, identify the supply and demand for loans. Note that the demand depends on the interest rate actually charged by banks, but the supply depends on the expected rate of return.

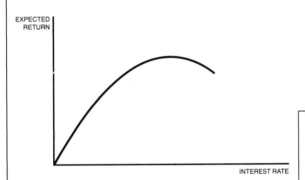

Step two: Find the interest rate that maximizes the expected rate of return. This will be the equilibrium interest rate.

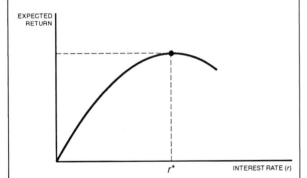

Step three: Find the quantity supplied by substituting the maximum expected rate of return into the supply curve.

Step four: Find the quantity demanded by substituting the equilibrium interest rate (found in step two) into the demand curve.

Step five: Find the amount of credit rationing by subtracting the loans supplied from the loans demanded:

credit rationing = loans demanded – loans supplied.

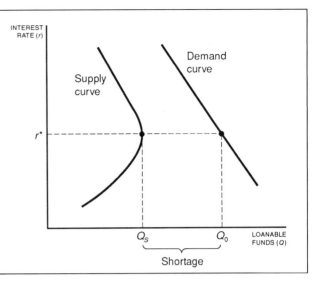

1 (Worked problem: credit rationing) Banks in North End realize that at high interest rates, the pool of loan applicants will include relatively more firms with high default rates. They calculate that the relationship between the interest rate and the expected returns is as given in Table 21.1. The table also gives the supply and demand for new loans. Note that the demand depends on the interest rate actually charged by banks, but the supply depends on the expected rate of return. Find the equilibrium interest rate and the level of credit rationing.

Table 21.1

Interest rate	Expected rate of return
4.0%	4.0%
4.5%	4.4%
5.0%	4.8%
5.5%	5.2%
6.0%	5.0%
6.5%	4.8%
7.0%	4.0%

Demand for loans		Supply of loans	
Interest rate	Value (thousands)	Expected rate of return	Value (thousands)
4.0%	$2,500	4.0%	$ 300
4.5%	$1,900	4.4%	$ 400
5.0%	$1,500	4.8%	$ 600
5.5%	$1,200	5.0%	$ 800
6.0%	$1,000	5.2%	$1,000
6.5%	$ 700		
7.0%	$ 400		

Step-by-step solution

Step one: Identify the relationship between the interest rate and the expected rate of return on loans, and the supply and demand for loans. They are given in Table 21.1.

Step two: Find the interest rate that maximizes the expected rate of return. The expected rate of return reaches its maximum of 5.2 percent when the interest rate is 5.5 percent.

Step three: Find the quantity supplied by substituting the maximum expected rate of return into the supply curve; $1,000,000 is supplied when the expected rate of return is 5.2 percent.

Step four: Find the quantity demanded by substituting the equilibrium interest rate into the demand curve; $1,200,000 is supplied when the interest rate is 5.5 percent.

Step five: Find the amount of credit rationing. It is $1,200,000 – $1,000,000 = $200,000. Although there is a shortage, banks will not raise the interest rate because higher interest rates bring about more defaults and a lower expected rate of return.

2 (Practice problem: credit rationing) The relationship between the interest rate and the expected rate of return is given in Table 21.2, which also gives the supply and demand curves for university loans in Gotham. Find the equilibrium interest rate and the amount of credit rationing.

Table 21.2

Interest rate	Expected rate of return
6.0%	5.8%
6.5%	6.0%
7.0%	6.2%
7.5%	6.3%
8.0%	6.2%
8.5%	6.0%
9.0%	5.0%

Demand for loans		Supply of loans	
Interest rate	Value (thousands)	Expected rate of return	Value (thousands)
6.0%	$8,000	5.0%	$1,000
6.5%	$7,000	5.8%	$1,500
7.0%	$6,000	6.0%	$2,000
7.5%	$5,000	6.2%	$2,500
8.0%	$4,000	6.3%	$3,000
8.5%	$3,000		
9.0%	$2,000		

3 (Practice problem: credit rationing) The relationship between the interest rate and the expected rate of return is given in Table 21.3, which also gives the supply and demand curves for small-business loans in Eastpointe. Find the equilibrium interest rate and the amount of credit rationing.

Table 21.3

Interest rate	Expected rate of return
6.0%	5.0%
6.5%	6.0%
7.0%	6.1%
7.5%	6.0%
8.0%	5.5%
8.5%	5.0%
9.0%	5.0%

Demand for loans		Supply of loans	
Interest rate	Value (thousands)	Expected rate of return	Value (thousands)
6.0%	$17,000	5.0%	$6,000
6.5%	$15,000	5.5%	$7,000
7.0%	$13,000	6.0%	$8,000
7.5%	$11,000	6.1%	$9,000
8.0%	$ 9,000		
8.5%	$ 7,000		
9.0%	$ 5,000		

Answers to Problems

2 Equilibrium interest rate = 7.5%; expected return = 6.3%; credit rationing = $5,000,000 – $3,000,000 = $2,000,000.

3 Equilibrium interest rate = 7%; expected return = 6.1%; credit rationing = $13,000,000 – $9,000,000 = $4,000,000.

Chapter 22

MANAGING THE FIRM

Chapter Review

This chapter of the text looks inside the firm to examine its economic functions and its problems. To run efficiently and turn a profit, a firm must divide tasks among its employees, motivate them to work hard, account for their outputs, and decide on a structure and size that suits its needs. In each of these decisions, the information problems that dominated the product, labour, and capital markets in Chapters 19 to 21 reappear. This chapter completes the detailed exploration of imperfect information. Two other market failures, externalities and inequality, are the subjects of the remaining chapters (23 and 24) of this part of the text.

ESSENTIAL CONCEPTS

1 Executives in large organizations do not have the time or the information to perform all the tasks that the organization needs done. They must **delegate** tasks to others in the organization. Delegation presents three fundamental problems. First, the persons who are to perform the tasks must be **selected**. Second, because the employees may not always have the same interests as the organization, they must be **motivated** to perform the tasks well. Finally, the organization must **monitor** and keep track of the performance of its employees.

2 Managers must select workers to perform tasks, but selecting the best workers is difficult because managers may have only limited information about the capabilities and motivation of the candidates. Most job selections and promotions are based on **relative performance**—one worker's performance compared with that of the worker's colleagues. This has the advantage of providing employees with incentives to work hard in the hope of being selected for a better position, but it can also have the disadvantages of possibly impeding cooperation and encouraging unprofitable activities that enhance promotion possibilities.

3 The **principal-agent problem** summarizes the difficulty of providing good incentives to employees. One important example is the case in which the owners of a firm are the principals and the managers are their agents. The owners (the shareholders) want managers to act in the best interest of the firm. The managers, however, may have other interests, and it is

difficult for the owners to judge whether a manager takes appropriate actions. The problem for the principal is to design incentives to motivate the managers to work hard and to take the appropriate risks in order to further its own interests.

4 One approach to solving the principal-agent problem is for the manager to buy a share of the enterprise. As an *owner*, the manager has the appropriate incentives. Another approach to solving the principal-agent problem involves **incentive pay**, such as sales commissions or stock options, which give the manager the right to buy a number of shares at a given price. If the manager can increase the market value of the firm, the manager can profit.

5 Managing a large corporation requires detailed information about the profitability of its components. **Accounting** provides this information, but accountants face two major problems. They must correctly determine the true opportunity costs and values of the firm's outputs that are not sold in markets, and they must allocate the fixed or overhead costs among the firm's departments.

6 Another interesting issue for accounting is the different objectives for which the data are gathered. Accounting information is used by the firm to manage its affairs more profitably, by the capital market to assess the value and riskiness of the firm and its offerings, and by the government for tax purposes. Firms may have conflicting objectives: they want to appear profitable to the capital market but unprofitable to Revenue Canada.

7 Firms confront uncertainty when making decisions. The profitability of certain actions may depend on events that are unpredictable. Firms can construct a **decision tree** to help them identify the sources of uncertainty and the consequences of different decisions. The decision tree will often show alternatives that allow the firm to keep its options open and postpone risky decisions until more information arrives.

8 A fundamental issue in the structure of a large organization is the degree of **centralization.** A centralized, top-down structure has many layers of decision making and review. Its advantages include the approval of fewer bad projects, coordination to account for interdependencies and externalities within the organization, and a lack of duplication. A decentralized structure grants more autonomy to the individual units within the organization; it usually approves more good projects and acts more quickly with more diversity and experimentation; and it allows management to compare the performance of the units and decide how to allocate resources within the firm.

9 The issue of how large the firm should be involves how many activities it will do in-house, how many it will contract out, and whether it should **vertically** integrate with its suppliers or its customer firms. If **transactions costs**, which are the extra costs over and above the price of purchasing an item on the market,

are high, it may be less costly to do the activities within the firm. One problem with outside contracting may occur if the outside firm must make specialized investments and thereby risk becoming dependent. This is known as a "hold-up problem." Usually the threat of dependency results in higher costs. Generally, it is more efficient to produce some services in-house and purchase others outside.

BEHIND THE ESSENTIAL CONCEPTS

1 This chapter goes a long way beyond the firm in the basic competitive model. The competitive firm has two simple problems to solve: how much should it produce and by what means. Competitive firms hardly need managers. The firms in this chapter are much more realistic and, naturally, more complicated. In addition to the problems of competitive firms, these firms must select employees for tasks, motivate them, monitor their efforts, and account for their outputs. Further, they must deal with uncertainty, determine the degree of centralization, and decide on the number of activities to produce in-house and contract out. It is in solving these problems that real-world managers earn their salaries.

2 As an organization grows, the level of direct control owners exercise diminishes and the problem of providing incentives arises. When incentives are the issue, the usual suspects appear: asymmetric information in that the principal (the owner) cannot observe and evaluate the activities of employees (the agents), and moral hazard in that the agents may pursue their own interests and not those of the principal. Solutions to the problem involve the risk-incentive trade-off. For example, basing pay on performance or tying pay to profitability provides stronger incentives but also subjects the agents to more risk. These are fundamental problems within any organization. An understanding of their source and nature, however, may enable you to manage better in any organization that you work for or join.

3 Centralization versus decentralization is a question raised in organizations such as business firms, nonprofit organizations, and government. It is also a fundamental question about the economic system itself. Socialism can be seen as a more centralized system, in which the state makes more economic decisions. Market economies are more decentralized; that is they leave more decisions to individuals and firms. The debate between socialists and advocates of markets has taken place over the same issues that are discussed in this chapter. Adherents of socialism claim that fewer bad projects are adopted, activities are coordinated better, and there is less duplication. Advocates of market economies point to the abundance of good projects and the diversity, experimentation, and incentives that market economies provide.

4 Transactions costs do not include the purchase price, but rather all those costs in addition to the price. Transactions costs are the costs of using the market: the time, effort, and expense involved in searching the market to find high quality at a good price. Contracts must then be drawn up (at least implicitly) to specify the terms. If it were always easy, reliable, and cheap to use the market, then firms could be quite small and simply buy and sell what they needed among themselves. Often transactions costs are high, and it is cheaper to integrate an activity within the firm even though the added size brings about the problems discussed above.

SELF-TEST

True or False

1 Assigning tasks to others is called delegating.

2 Most job selections and promotions are made on the basis of relative performance.

3 The principal-agent problem refers to the difficulty in providing incentives within organizations.

4 Stock options are rights to buy shares at the market price.

5 An example of the principal-agent problem is the difficulty that managers have in motivating their owners to agree to issue new shares of stock.

6 The principal-agent problem grows worse in long-term relationships between principals and agents.

7 Accounting tracks profits and losses of various components of firms.

8 One problem faced by accountants is how to allocate the marginal costs among the various activities of the firm.

9 Although accounting data are used by several institutions, there is little discretion in how firms can keep their accounts.

10 When there is a great deal of uncertainty, firms usually do better if they plunge ahead rather than waiting to keep their options open.

11 Centralized decision making provides strong incentives because the directives come from the top.

12 Decentralized decision making leads to the acceptance of more good projects and more bad projects.

13 Vertical integration occurs when two firms that sell the same products merge.

14 Transactions costs involve both the purchase price and the other costs of using the market.

15 When transactions costs are high, firms usually will decide to contract out for the service.

Multiple Choice

1 An individual who both owns and manages a firm will

a have to deal with the principal-agent problem just like any other owner.
b always maximize profits.
c balance the extra profits against the extra effort required to earn them.
d make the same decisions that would be made by a manager hired by the owner.
e none of the above.

2 Which of the following is not true of assigning the responsibility for a task to another?

a It is a poor choice, because "if you want something done right, you should do it yourself."
b It is necessary because executives lack the time or information necessary to do all tasks.
c It can be efficient because the person to whom the task is delegated may have a comparative advantage.
d It leads to the principal-agent problem.
e It requires due consideration of providing appropriate incentives to the employee.

3 Which of the following is not a problem faced by the owner or manager who delegates?

a selecting the agent to perform the task
b motivating the agent to perform the task
c monitoring the performance of the agent
d determining whether the performance of the agent is in the best interests of the firm
e none of the above

4 Evaluating the performance of an agent is difficult because

a the principal often cannot tell whether success is a result of effort, ability, or simply luck.
b the agent's interests are often different from the manager's.
c basing pay on performance imposes risk upon the agent.
d offering incentives to the agent changes the agent's behaviour.
e none of the above.

5 Firms often make job selections and promotions based on relative performance

a to foster team spirit.
b to motivate employees to do their jobs especially well.
c to encourage employees to hold meetings.
d to prevent destructive competition among employees.
e none of the above.

6 Basing pay exclusively on piece-work measures of performance, such as sales figures or profits,

a leads to bad-mouthing of employees by their fellow employees.

b   motivates employees to work too hard.

c   gives employees incentives to hold too many meetings.

d   imposes risk on employees.

e   none of the above.

7   Suppose the owner of the firm wants to motivate the manager to make the decision that the owner would make in the same situation but does not have the information necessary to evaluate the decisions made by the manager. This is an example of

a   comparative advantage.

b   diminishing returns.

c   the principal-agent problem.

d   adverse selection.

e   none of the above.

8   In the principal-agent problem,

a   the interests of the principal and agent coincide.

b   the principal cannot judge whether the agent takes the appropriate action by looking at the results.

c   the agent cannot judge whether the principal takes the appropriate action by looking at the results.

d   the principal and the agent work together to solve a problem.

e   none of the above.

9   In the principal-agent problem,

a   the agent wants to motivate the principal to take the appropriate risks.

b   the principal wants to motivate the agents to take the appropriate risks.

c   the agent wants to motivate the principal to work hard.

d   each wants to motivate the other to work hard.

e   none of the above.

10   Corporations use stock options to motivate their managers, because

a   there are tax advantages to this type of payment.

b   they encourage the managers to take actions that increase the market value of the firm.

c   they are a relatively inexpensive form of compensation.

d   they motivate the managers to focus on the true value of the firms, not their market values.

e   the owners bear less risk because they always have the option of substituting shares of stock for cash payments.

11   Which of the following is not a problem associated with accounting?

a   It is difficult to measure the value of outputs not traded in markets.

b   Accounting data are used by different audiences for different purposes.

c   Firms that make specialized investments may become dependent on their customer firms.

d   Fixed costs must be allocated among the firm's departments.

e   None of the above.

12   The diagram that shows how decisions are linked and identifies the possible consequences is the

a   production possibilities curve.

b   budget constraint.

c   demand curve.

d   decision tree.

e   principal-agent problem.

13   Which of the following is not an advantage of centralized decision making?

a   Fewer bad projects are accepted.

b   There is better coordination.

c   There is less duplication.

d   There is more experimentation.

e   Externalities within the organization are accounted for.

14   Which of the following is not an advantage of decentralized decision making?

a   More good projects are accepted.

b   There is less duplication.

c   Decisions are made and implemented more quickly.

d   There is greater diversity and experimentation.

e   Incentives are stronger.

15   Vertical integration occurs when

a   a firm combines with its supplier.

b   two firms selling the same goods merge.

c   two firms selling different goods merge.

d   a firm contracts out for accounting services.

e   the Competition Tribunal orders the breakup of a large firm.

16   Which of the following is not a component of transactions costs?

a   the purchase price

b   the time and effort involved in searching the market

c   the expense of drawing up contracts

d   the risk that the supplier will place a low priority on the firm's business

e   none of the above

17   The possibility that a firm might become dependent on its customer firm after it makes investments specifically designed for that firm's business is called

a   transactions costs.

b   the hold-up problem.

c   the principal-agent problem.

d   the accounting problem.

e   adverse selection.

18   Accounting for externalities within an organization is an advantage of

a   decentralized decision making.

b   centralized decision making.

c   horizontal integration.

d   vertical integration.

e   the principal-agent problem.

19 Which of the following is not true?

   a Corporate management uses accounting data to help in allocating resources more efficiently.

   b Capital markets use accounting data to help in assessing the value of the firm.

   c Corporate management uses accounting data to help in allocating fixed costs to the various units of the corporation.

   d Governments use accounting data for tax purposes.

   e Corporate management uses accounting data to decide whether its accountants are doing a good job.

20 Greater diversity, experimentation, and incentives are advantages of

   a decentralized decision making.

   b centralized decision making.

   c horizontal integration.

   d vertical integration.

   e the principal-agent problem.

Completion

1 Job selections and promotions are generally made on the basis of _____.

2 Basing pay on a piece-work measure of performance provides strong incentives but imposes _____ on employees.

3 The difficulty that owners have in motivating managers to act in the interest of ownership is an example of the _____.

4 The right to purchase a specified number of shares of stock at a certain price is called a _____.

5 One way to lessen the principal-agent problem is to _____ employees and keep track of their actions.

6 Tracking the profits and losses of the various components of the firm is called _____.

7 A diagram that identifies the sources of uncertainty, specifies the consequences, and evaluates the likelihood of the various consequences is called a

   _____.

8 A firm using _____ decision making usually has a hierarchical structure with a well-defined set of approval layers.

9 Considerable autonomy is granted to units within a firm using _____ decision making.

10 _____ decision making has the advantage of allowing fewer bad projects, while _____ decision making has the advantage of rejecting fewer good projects.

Answers to Self-Test

True or False

1	t	6	f	11	f
2	t	7	t	12	t
3	t	8	f	13	f
4	f	9	f	14	f
5	f	10	f	15	f

Multiple Choice

1	c	6	d	11	c	16	a
2	a	7	c	12	d	17	b
3	e	8	b	13	d	18	b
4	a	9	d	14	b	19	e
5	b	10	b	15	a	20	a

Completion

1 relative performance
2 risk
3 principal-agent problem
4 stock option
5 monitor
6 accounting
7 decision tree
8 centralized
9 decentralized
10 Centralized, decentralized

Doing Economics: Tools and Practice Problems

Organizations face information problems that stand in the way of their goals. Two difficulties are illustrated in this section: selecting which resource to assign to each task, and providing incentives.

With many different resources at its command, an organization (just like a country) has a production possibilities curve. To construct the production possibilities curve, however, the organization must assign each resource to the task in which it has a comparative advantage. This is easier said than done. We show the costs of not solving the selection problem correctly by returning to the topic of the production possibilities curve when resources are different, which you learned in Chapter 3. Specifically, we will do problems 6, 7, and 8 of Chapter 3 *incorrectly* to see the consequences of failing to distinguish comparative advantage when selecting who or what resource to assign to each task.

1 (Worked problem: selection) Harrigan and her daughter have formed a two-person firm. They do business incorporations and real estate transactions. The hours required for each type of task are given below. Each works 48 hours every week.

Lawyer	Hours required to perform each incorporation	Hours required to complete each transaction
Harrigan	4	8
Daughter	8	24

a Plot their weekly production possibilities curve.

b Now suppose that Harrigan and her daughter are not able to determine the comparative advantage and assign tasks incorrectly. Harrigan does the incorporations and her daughter does the real estate transactions when necessary. On the same diagram, plot their production possibilities curve with the mistaken assignments.

c Shade the area between the two production possibilities curves. This area indicates the combinations of outputs that are not feasible unless the selection problem is solved correctly.

Step-by-step solution:

Step one (a): Plot the production possibilities curve. Step-by-step instructions for this are given in problem 6 of Chapter 3.

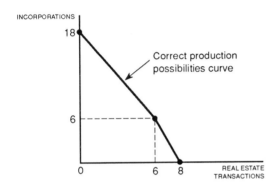

Step two (b): Plot the production possibilities curve with Harrigan doing the incorporations and her daughter doing the real estate transactions.

Step three: Plot the maximum quantities of each output. The Harrigans can still produce 18 incorporations if both devote all their time to that task or 8 real estate transactions if both specialize in that task. Plot the points (0,18) and (8,0).

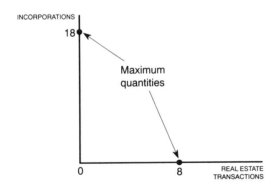

Step four: Select Harrigan to do the incorporations, where her total is 12. Select her daughter to do the real estate transactions, where her total is only 2. Plot the point (2, 12).

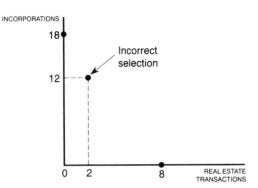

Step five: Draw the production possibilities curve by connecting the three points, and notice that it bows inwards.

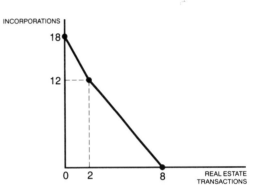

Step six (c): Shade the area between the two production possibilities curves. Overlaying the correct and incorrect curves shows what is lost when the selection problem is not solved correctly. The shaded area indicates reduced efficiency.

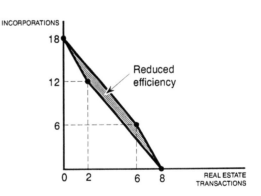

2 (Practice problem: selection) A farmer has 3 hectares of land. Owing to various characteristics of the land, the farmer's ability to produce two cash crops (corn and soybeans) differs on each hectare. The technology of production is given in the table below.

Maximum outputs of each crop
per hectare (bushels)

	Hectare #1	Hectare #2	Hectare #3
Corn	200	200	100
Soybeans	400	200	50

These figures represent the maximum output of each crop assuming that only that crop is grown on that hectare. That is, hectare #1 can produce either 200 bushels of corn or 400 bushels of soybeans. Of course, the farmer can also divide the hectare into one part corn and one part soybeans. For example, the farmer can grow 100 bushels of corn and 200 bushels of soybeans on hectare #1.

a   Plot the production possibilities curve.

b   Now assign the hectares incorrectly (not according to comparative advantage) and plot the resulting production possibilities curve.

c   Shade the area between the two curves. This area indicates the combinations of outputs not feasible unless the selection problem is solved correctly.

3   (Practice problem: selection) Plot the following production possibilities curves incorrectly. That is, make the selections on the basis of comparative *disadvantage*. Compare the answers with the correctly drawn production possibilities curves in problem 8 of Chapter 3.

a

	Maximum harvest of each type of fish per trawler (tonnes)		
	Trawler #1	Trawler #2	Trawler #3
Salmon	2	3	4
Tuna	2	6	6

b

	Maximum amounts of pollutants removed (ppm)	
	Smokestack scrubbers	Coal treatment
Sulphur	100	50
Particulates	500	100

4   (Worked problem: incentives) Once individuals have been assigned to tasks within an organization, they must be given incentives to perform the tasks in a manner that furthers the goals of the organization. We will look at two aspects of the incentive problem. First, how does the absence of prices within organizations lead to inefficiency? Second, what are the incentive problems associated with sharing the profits? The Add advertising agency has several creative teams in its employ, and for years each team has been given a budget of $10,000 for any services that their work requires. The team hires outside contractors to do layouts and printing. The price of each service is $200 per day.

a   Plot the budget constraint for the typical creative team.

b   The typical team has spent half its budget on each service. Plot the point that corresponds to this choice.

c   Following the recommendation of a consultant, the agency decides to do all its printing in-house. Now the creative teams purchase only layout services from outside the agency. Since they can have their printing services performed at the agency and do not need to purchase printing, their budgets are cut to $5,000. Plot the budget constraint.

d   The agency finds that the print shop is always overcrowded. Why?

Step-by-step solution

Step one (a): Draw coordinate axes, and label the horizontal one "Printing services" and the vertical one "Layout services."

Step two: If the team spends all its budget on printing, it can purchase $10,000/$200 = 50 days. Plot this point along the horizontal axis.

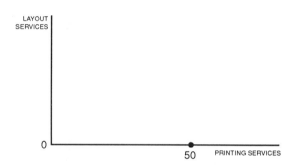

Step three: If the team spends all its budget on layouts, it can purchase $10,000/$200 = 50 days. Plot this point along the vertical axis.

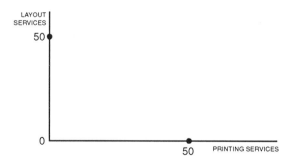

Step four (b): The team spends $5,000 on each service and buys $5,000/$200 = 25 days of each. Plot the point (25, 25) and label it *A*.

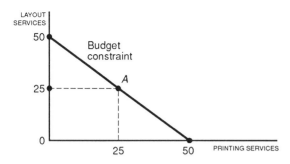

Step five (c): The team has a budget of $5,000. The price of layout service is still $200 per day, but printing is free. The team can still purchase 25 days of layout services, and it can have all of the printing that it wants. The budget constraint is a horizontal line intersecting the vertical axis at 25.

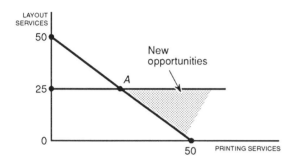

Step six (d): The new way of doing things at the agency allows teams to use printing services without paying for them. In terms of the budget constraint, the teams now can choose all the combinations to the right of point *A*. As long as printing has any value to the team, they will buy more and the shop will be overcrowded.

5 (practice problem: incentives) Betty and Wilma are copy editors. They pore over manuscripts looking for typographical, grammatical, and other errors. Betty is self-employed and receives $2 per page. Wilma works for Meglith Publishers and receives a straight salary of $800 each week. Each can edit 10 pages an hour, and each has 60 hours available every week. They both like to goof off, and they both like money.

a Plot Betty's budget constraint. Put income on the vertical axis and time spent goofing off on the horizontal. What is the slope of her budget constraint?

b Plot Wilma's budget constraint. What is its slope?

c Which editor has the greater incentive to goof off? Why?

6 (Worked problem: incentives) Michael and Eliot have part-time jobs as Mexway distributors; they sell soap. The amount that each can sell depends on the time that he puts in knocking on doors. The relationship is given in Table 22.1.

Table 22.1

Time (hours)	Revenues
1	$ 40
2	$ 70
3	$ 90
4	$100
5	$105
6	$106

Both Michael and Eliot place a value of $10 on 1 hour of their time.

a Complete the marginal benefit column.

b How many hours will each work? How much revenue will each earn?

c Now suppose that Michael and Eliot form a business to sell soap. They agree to share the revenues. If Michael works 1 hour, he brings in $40, but he gives $20 to Eliot. Michael's personal reward is only $20. Revise the table above to reflect the agreement that revenues are shared.

d Complete a marginal benefit column for the revised revenue numbers.

e How many hours will each work now?

Step-by-step solution

Step one (a): Complete the marginal benefit column. If Michael works 1 hour, he earns $40, which is the marginal benefit. If he works 2 hours, his revenues rise from $40 to $70, which is a marginal benefit of $30. The results are given in Table 22.2.

Table 22.2

Time (hours)	Revenues	Marginal benefit
1	$ 40	$40
2	$ 70	$30
3	$ 90	$20
4	$100	$10
5	$105	$ 5
6	$106	$ 1

Step two (b): The marginal cost of an hour is $10. Setting marginal cost equal to marginal benefit implies 4 hours of work, which brings in $100.

Step three (c): Accounting for the sharing of revenues means that the relationship between time spent selling and the revenues that each gets to keep for himself are in Table 22.3.

Table 22.3

Time (hours)	Revenues
1	$20.00
2	$35.00
3	$45.00
4	$50.00
5	$52.50
6	$53.00

Step four (d): Now the marginal benefit is half what it was before, as shown in Table 22.4.

Table 22.4

Time (hours)	Revenues	Marginal benefit
1	$20.00	$20.00
2	$35.00	$15.00
3	$45.00	$10.00
4	$50.00	$ 5.00
5	$52.50	$ 2.50
6	$53.00	$ 0.50

Step five (e): Now marginal benefit equals marginal cost at 3 hours worked, which brings in only $45. Sharing the profits means that neither person receives the full benefits of his time and effort. This is the classic incentive problem. Because of bad incentives, each is led to work less.

7 (Practice problem: incentives) Mr. Davis is a sharecropper on a farm owned by Miss Tilly. He gives her one-third of his revenues from farming her 20 hectares in rural Mississauga. Table 22.5 gives the relationship between his effort and the revenues from the farm.

Table 22.5

Time (hours)	Total revenues	Mr. Davis' revenues	Marginal benefit
1	$18		
2	$33		
3	$45		
4	$54		
5	$60		
6	$63		

Mr. Davis, when not sharecropping, can work in town and make $6 per hour.

a Complete the table.
b How much does Mr. Davis choose to work on the farm?
c If he owned the farm himself and did not share revenues with Miss Tilly, how much would he work on the farm?

Answers to Problems

2

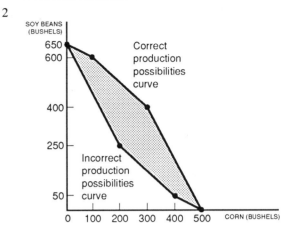

3

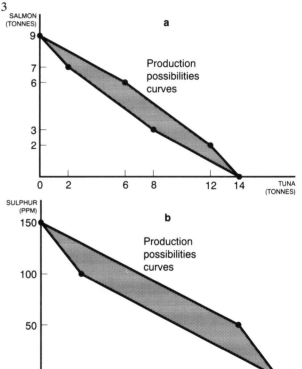

5 *a,b*

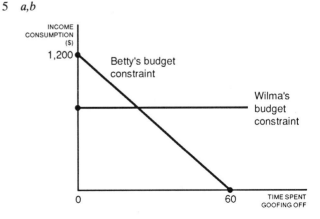

c Wilma has more opportunities that involve less work; thus, she has more incentive to goof off.

7 *a* The completed information is given in Table 22.6.

Table 22.6

Time (hours)	Total revenues	Mr. Davis' revenues	Marginal benefit
1	$18	$12	$12
2	$33	$22	$10
3	$45	$30	$ 8
4	$54	$36	$ 6
5	$60	$40	$ 4
6	$63	$42	$ 2

b He works 4 hours, where the marginal benefit equals marginal cost, which is $6 per hour.

c If he owned the farm, the marginal benefit would be as given in Table 22.7.

Table 22.7

Time (hours)	Total revenues	Marginal benefit
1	$18	$18
2	$33	$15
3	$45	$12
4	$54	$ 9
5	$60	$ 6
6	$63	$ 3

Mr. Davis would work 5 hours.

Chapter 23

EXTERNALITIES, MERIT GOODS, AND PUBLIC DECISION MAKING

Chapter Review

Of the three major economic players—individuals, firms, and government—the first two have been centre stage so far in the text, while the third has mainly stood silently at the side. Government has been the central focus only of Chapters 7 and 17. This is appropriate, because the critical points for you to understand are where markets succeed at answering the main economic questions, where they fail, and how.

Where markets fail, government may have an economic role to play. This chapter completes the discussion of government's role in cases of market failure. You have already seen problems of competition, information, and technological change that interfere when private markets are used to answer economic questions. Another major category of market failure is externalities, a concept first introduced in Chapter 7. As you may remember, externalities can be positive or negative. The distinguishing characteristic of externalities is that, positive or negative, they are not captured in the market price. The main example studied in Chapter 23 is pollution, a negative externality, which results in a cost that is not reflected in the market price of the good produced by the firm causing the pollution. The chapter also considers merit goods, for which the government wishes to mandate consumption or abstinence. Inoculations against disease required

of students entering grade school are an example of mandated consumption; the outlawing of certain recreational drugs is an example of mandated abstinence. In both cases, the government simply overrides the principle of consumer sovereignty.

An important theme of economics is that the intervention of governments when markets fail does not mean the situation is necessarily improved. In fact, economists have identified characteristics of government that interfere with the rational pursuit of the public interest. In the final major section, the chapter looks at the performance of government from an economic perspective. Chapter 24 completes Part Three with a discussion of economic inequality and redistribution.

ESSENTIAL CONCEPTS

1 A market transaction is a voluntary exchange between two parties. Any costs or benefits not captured by market transactions are called **externalities. Positive externalities** are benefits received by others. Markets produce too few activities that generate positive ex-

ternalities, such as research and development or on-the-job training. Other activities, such as pollution, noise, or congestion, confer costs on others that often do not figure into the market price. Markets create too many of these **negative externalities.**

2 Markets require clearly defined **property rights** in order to allocate resources efficiently. The **Coase theorem** says that any externality problem could be solved if the government assigned property rights for the externalities. For example, direct pollution of a privately owned lake would not occur unless the owner judged that the benefits exceeded the costs. General environmental pollution is a serious problem because the environment is commonly, not privately, owned.

3 Externalities lead to **market failure** because resources are not allocated efficiently. Individuals consider only their private costs and benefits and ignore the larger social costs and benefits. Potential governmental solutions to the problems fall into two categories: **command and control regulations** and marketlike devices such as taxes, subsidies, and **marketable permits.** For example, in the case of pollution, governments can issue regulations requiring pollution-control equipment or banning the use of hazardous materials. Alternatively, they can employ more market-oriented policies, such as taxes on pollution emissions, subsidies for pollution abatement, or even the creation of a market for pollution permits.

4 The idea that individuals know what is in their interest and can best make their own choices about economic activities is called **consumer sovereignty. Paternalism**, in contrast, supposes that government can make better choices in some cases. Government mandates consumption of certain **merit goods**, such as education for children, and bans other **merit bads**, such as cocaine, on paternalistic grounds.

5 Although market failures, such as externalities, provide an argument for government intervention, the government may not be efficient at correcting the market's problems. The government may have limited and imperfect information about the costs and benefits of activities as well. And, like private firms, the government must provide incentives for its employees to design, carry out, and enforce efficient policies. Finally, there is the difficult task of foreseeing the relevant side effects of the government's actions. Any reform proposal should specify not only why the market fails but also how the government can succeed in making things better.

6 Government is not a coordinated, benign decision-maker, but rather a collection of individuals playing a variety of roles. While government should represent voters, the **voting paradox** illustrates that a majority of the electorate may not hold consistent views about desirable policies. When it comes to such matters as deciding how much to spend on fire protection, the **median voter model** demonstrates that government responds to the preferences of the voter whose position

on the amount of spending that should be undertaken divides the rest of the population such that the number of people desiring more spending than the voter equals the number of people desiring less spending. **Rent-seeking** activities of interest groups may lead to inefficient policies that benefit their own members. Finally, once a policy is set, there is the **principal-agent problem**, which inhibits the ability to motivate bureaucrats to act in the public interest.

BEHIND THE ESSENTIAL CONCEPTS

1 Individuals and firms make efficient decisions when they bear the full costs and benefits of their choice. When externalities are present, some benefit or cost is ignored, and the decision becomes inefficient. The missing ingredient is property rights. The Coase theorem says that if property rights are clearly assigned, decisions will be efficient. The logic can best be understood with an example.

Suppose that your neighbour likes to play the stereo very loudly each evening while you are reading this book. Clearly, there is an externality. You complain to the building manager, and there are two possible reactions. The manager might say that playing the stereo is a right of all tenants, and in effect give the property right (to make noise) to your neighbour. Or the manager may insist on quiet and give the property right (to silence) to you. According to the Coase theorem, either way of assigning property rights will do. If your neighbour has the right, then you can buy the right to silence by paying your neighbour to be quiet. If you have the right, your neighbour must buy your permission to play the music. Of course, you would prefer the latter; nevertheless, in either case, the externality is eliminated and replaced by a market transaction. (Any reader who lives in a university residence can judge how realistic it is to expect the Coase theorem to work.)

2 Pollution is an example of a negative externality. It is a cost ignored by the polluter and borne by others. The inefficiency can be corrected by raising the polluter's private marginal opportunity cost of pollution to the level of the social marginal cost. There are three marketlike ways to do this: taxes on pollution, subsidies for pollution abatement, and marketable pollution permits. Here is how they work.

a Suppose that the firm must pay a *tax* of $10 per unit of pollution. Clearly, any pollution now has a private marginal cost of $10, because the tax must be paid.

b Suppose that the government pays a *subsidy* of $10 per unit of pollution abatement. Again, the marginal opportunity cost of the pollution is $10, because if the pollution is emitted, it is not abated, and the subsidy is not received.

c Under the marketable permits scheme, pollution requires a permit, which must be purchased. The purchase price of the permit is the marginal cost of the pollution. All three marketlike policies put a price on pollution and encourage polluters to find economical ways to reduce emissions.

3 Whether we are using our limited natural resources efficiently and whether we are likely to run out of these resources are important economic questions. The key aspects in the answers to these questions are property rights and markets.

a For those resources, such as oil, minerals, and arable farmland, that are *privately owned*, markets provide good incentives for conservation. Future shortages mean high prices in the future. The profit opportunities from future sales motivate owners to conserve resources for the future.

b For those resources, such as the ozone layer and endangered species, that are not privately owned, there is no reason for optimism. Since there are *no markets* for these resources, there is no financial incentive to conserve.

4 The voting paradox shows that a majority of voters may make choices that are not consistent. It does not say that the choices must always be inconsistent, only that such cases may occur. One case in which voters *will* be consistent is described by the median voter model, but the outcome may not be *efficient*. The reason is that only the median voter's preferences affect the decision. Regardless of how strongly you feel about an issue, you cannot affect the outcome unless you can influence the median voter.

5 The government is a large organization; so it should not be surprising that it is troubled by all the problems involved in managing a firm (Chapter 22). One example is the principal-agent problem. Elected officials (the principals) delegate to **bureaucrats** (the agents) the task of writing and enforcing regulations. The bureaucrats may be concerned not only with the goal of the regulations, but also with their careers. They may act in a risk-averse manner, perhaps being overly cautious or "bureaucratic" in their approach. This is one reason why even though there is market failure, the government may not be able to do any better.

SELF-TEST

True or False

1 When there is no government interference, markets will always produce efficient outcomes.

2 The market failures approach assigns to government the task of improving matters when markets allocate resources inefficiently.

F 3 Markets fail because too many people are motivated by greed.

F 4 The market will supply too many goods for which there are positive externalities.

5 The social marginal cost is greater than the private marginal cost for a good that generates negative externalities.

6 The Coase theorem contends that externality problems are due to the voting paradox.

7 Reassigning property rights can sometimes correct a market failure.

F 8 Because pollution is an example of a negative externality, economists recommend taxing pollution abatement.

9 Goods for which there are negative externalities should be taxed so that the price captures more of the social costs.

10 Public goods are nonrivalrous in consumption in that, once provided, any number of people can enjoy them.

11 We are using up our limited supply of natural resources because they are sold without concern for the needs of future users.

12 Paternalistic governments mandate consumption of merit goods as an exception to the principle of consumer sovereignty.

F 13 Imperfect information is a reason for market failure, not public failure.

F 14 The voting paradox implies that political parties will reflect the preferences of the median voter.

15 When landlords advertise office space for lease, they are engaging in rent seeking.

Multiple Choice

1 Government's role in the economy includes

a stepping in when markets fail to produce inefficient outcomes.
b allocating most goods and services.
c determining the levels of prices and wages.
d stepping in when markets fail to produce efficient outcomes.
e none of the above.

2 Which of the following does not represent an example of market failure?

a increased oil prices during the Gulf War.
b a lack of sufficient competition.
c information problems.
d insufficient technological innovation.
e externalities.

3 The costs of environmental pollution are examples of

a positive externalities.
b public goods.

c negative externalities.
d private costs.
e diminishing returns.

4 Social marginal cost includes

a all marginal costs borne by all individuals in the economy.
b only those marginal costs not included in private marginal costs.
c only those marginal costs included in private marginal cost.
d total revenues minus total private costs.
e marginal revenue minus marginal cost.

5 The Coase theorem claims that

a market outcomes are always efficient.
b when markets fail to produce efficient outcomes, government should allocate resources.
c negative externalities should be subsidized.
d reassigning property rights can solve externality problems.
e the decisions made by a majority of voters may be inconsistent.

6 Which of the following is not a characteristic of public goods?

a They can be enjoyed by almost everyone, once they are provided.
b They are goods for which it is difficult to exclude anyone from enjoying.
c They are the most extreme form of externality.
d They are goods that are produced or grown on publicly owned land.
e None of the above.

7 Which of the following is an example of command and control regulations?

a subsidies for the production of goods with positive externalities
b taxation of goods with negative externalities
c regulations limiting the allowable level of pollution emissions
d assigning property rights to victims of environmental pollution
e nonrivalrous consumption

8 To reduce emissions of pollution, the government can

a tax pollution abatement.
b subsidize pollution abatement.
c subsidize the sale of polluting goods, such as steel and chemicals.
d reassign to polluters the property rights to pollute.
e take over the production facilities of firms.

9 Under the marketable permits approach to curbing pollution, which of the following is false?

a Firms purchase permits from the government.
b Permits allow firms to emit a certain amount of pollution.
c A market for pollution permits exists for firms to buy and sell the permits.

d Firms have strong incentives to reduce pollution.
e None of the above.

10 The market system encourages conservation because

a the price of a natural resource, such as an oil well, equals the present discounted value of potential future uses.
b wasteful exploitation is punished by fines or imprisonment.
c markets always allocate resources efficiently.
d permits from the government are required before natural resources may be sold.
e there is such an abundance of natural resources.

11 Which of the following is not a reason why private owners may undervalue future demand for natural resources?

a There are negative externalities associated with the use of the resource.
b There are positive externalities associated with the use of the resource.
c Property rights are not secure.
d Owners may face limited borrowing opportunities.
e None of the above.

12 The view that government can make better choices than individuals in some matters is called

a diminishing returns.
b paternalism.
c consumer sovereignty.
d nonrivalrous consumption.
e market failure.

13 When the government paternalistically mandates consumption of some good, that good is called a

a positive externality.
b merit good.
c subsidy.
d public good.
e merit bad.

14 In cases where the market fails to produce efficient outcomes,

a the government can possibly improve matters, but attention must be paid to the potential sources of public failures.
b a reassignment of property rights will always bring about efficiency.
c there is no scope for improvement because markets always bring about the maximum possible efficiency.
d the government should take over all resource allocation decisions.
e resource allocation decisions should be made by the median voter.

15 On issues such as school finance, where people have different views about the desirable level of public support, the median voter theory predicts that the majority vote will result in

a inconsistent decisions.

b no money allocated to schools because everyone cannot agree.

c the preferences of the median voter determining the level of funding.

d property rights being reassigned.

e inefficient public decisions as a result of imperfect information.

16 Consider a majority vote to decide how much land to set aside for a local park. The median voter

a earns the average level of income.

b desires less park land than half the voters, but also more park land than half the voters.

c lives an average distance from the park.

d neither likes nor dislikes parks.

e is an example of the voting paradox.

17 Activities devoted to securing returns above those required to bring a factor of production onto the market are called

a nonrivalrous consumption.

b command and control.

c negative externalities.

d subsidies.

e rent seeking.

18 The voting paradox refers to the

a tendency of democratic governments to make inconsistent choices.

b reasons for market failure.

c reasons for public failure.

d principle that political parties gravitate towards the political centre.

e principal-agent problem as applied to motivating bureaucrats.

19 The production of too many goods with negative externalities is an example of

a paternalism.

b consumer sovereignty.

c public failure.

d market failure.

e the voting paradox.

20 Student loan programs have cost much more than originally projected because many recent graduates declared bankruptcy soon after completing their education. This is an example of

a paternalism.

b consumer sovereignty.

c public failure.

d market failure.

e the voting paradox.

Completion

1 The _mkt failure_ approach to the role of government calls upon the government when markets fail to produce efficient outcomes.

2 The extra costs and benefits not captured by market transactions are called _externalities_

3 The _private_ cost of pollution is borne entirely by the polluter, while the _social_ cost includes all costs borne by individuals in the economy.

4 _The Coase theory_ claims that externality problems can be solved by reassigning property rights.

5 Regulatory measures that set limits on pollution emissions and mandate the use of specific types of pollution-control technologies are examples of the _command control_ approach.

6 The _marketable permits_ approach issues to firms permits, which allow them to emit a certain amount of pollution and which can be traded.

7 The view that individuals can make the best choice among their available options is called _Consumer sovereignty_.

8 In the case of _merit goods_, the government adopts a paternalistic approach and mandates increased consumption.

9 The _voting paradox_ illustrates the tendency for public decisions to be inconsistent.

10 Activities devoted to securing returns for a factor of production beyond those required to elicit its supply are called _rent seeking_

Answers to Self-Test

True or False

1	f	6	f	11	f
2	t	7	t	12	t
3	f	8	f	13	f
4	f	9	t	14	f
5	t	10	t	15	f

Multiple Choice

1	d	6	d	11	a	16	b
2	a	7	c	12	b	17	e
3	c	8	b	13	b	18	a
4	a	9	e	14	a	19	d
5	d	10	a	15	c	20	c

Completion

1 market failure
2 externalities
3 private, social
4 The Coase theorem
5 command and control
6 marketable permits
7 consumer sovereignty
8 merit goods
9 voting paradox
10 rent seeking

Doing Economics: Tools and Practice Problems

The first topic of this section is how taxes and subsidies can be used to encourage an activity for which there are positive externalities. We see how firms can be induced to emit less pollution by engaging in pollution abatement. Next, we turn to markets for goods that generate negative externalities such as noise, congestion, and pollution. A few problems show situations in which market equilibrium levels are too high and investigate how taxes can be used to make the market more efficient. The last topic focuses directly on the market for pollution and the way in which the marketable permits system brings about efficient use of the environment.

1 (Worked problem: pollution abatement) Runoff from the Quarta Lead Mine has raised lead levels in the Maumee River. The current level of lead effluent is 10 kilograms per month. A filtering technology would enable the company to reduce its effluent. The abatement costs are given in Table 23.1.

Table 23.1

Pollution emitted (kilograms/month)	Pollution abated (kilograms/month)	Total cost	Marginal cost
10	0	$ 0	—$40
9	1	$ 10	
8	2	$ 25	
7	3	$ 45	
6	4	$ 70	
5	5	$100	
4	6	$135	
3	7	$175	
2	8	$225	
1	9	$290	
0	10	$400	

a Suppose that a pollution tax (or fine) of $40 is assessed per kilogram of lead emitted. How much will the company emit? What quantity of pollution will be abated?

b Suppose that rather than a tax, a subsidy of $40 is given per unit of pollution abated. How much will the company emit? What quantity of pollution will be abated?

c The firm's profits from the production and sale of lead total $10,000. Compare its profits under the tax and the subsidy plan.

Step-by-step solution

Step one (a): The cost of pollution emission and abatement is given in Table 23.1.

Step two: Calculate the marginal abatement cost. The marginal abatement cost is the extra cost incurred in reducing pollution emissions by 1 more unit. For example, reducing pollution from 10 to 9 units raises costs from $0 to $10; therefore, the marginal abatement cost is $10 for the first unit. The remainder of the schedule is given in Table 23.2.

Tool Kit 23.1: Determining the Level of Pollution Abatement

Like other decisions made by firms, the question of the level of pollution abatement involves marginal benefit and cost reasoning. If the government taxes pollution emissions, then abating pollution saves the tax. If the government subsidizes pollution abatement, then abating pollution earns the subsidy. In each case, the marginal benefit of pollution abatement is determined by the government's policy.

Step one: Identify the cost of pollution emission and abatement.

Step two: Calculate the marginal abatement costs:

marginal abatement cost = change in cost/change in level of pollution abatement.

Step three: Determine the marginal benefit of abatement.

Step four: Set the marginal benefit of pollution abatement equal to its marginal cost.

Table 23.2

Pollution emitted	Pollution abated	Total cost	Marginal cost
10	0	$ 0	—
9	1	$ 10	$ 10
8	2	$ 25	$ 15
7	3	$ 45	$ 20
6	4	$ 70	$ 25
5	5	$100	$ 30
4	6	$135	$ 35
3	7	$175	$ 40
2	8	$225	$ 50
1	9	$290	$ 65
0	10	$400	$110

Step three: Determine the marginal benefit of abatement. Each unit of pollution emitted incurs a tax of $40; thus, the marginal benefit of abatement is $40.

Step four: Set the marginal benefit of pollution abatement equal to its marginal cost. This results in 3 kilograms of lead emitted and 7 kilograms abated.

Step five (b): When the policy is to subsidize abatement, the marginal benefit is the subsidy, which is $40. Setting $40 equal to the marginal abatement cost again gives 3 kilograms of lead emitted and 7 kilograms abated. The answer is the same as for part a. Notice that under the subsidy scheme, each unit emitted still costs the firm $40, in the sense that any unit emitted is a unit not abated and a subsidy not received.

Step six (c): Profits under the tax equal $10,000 less the abatement cost and the tax, or

profits = $10,000 − $175 − $40 (3) = $9,705.

Under the subsidy, however,

profits = $10,000 − $175 + $40 (7) = $10,105.

Notice that the difference in profits is $10,105 − $9,705 = $400, which is the magnitude of the tax/subsidy multiplied by the number of units that the firm emits with no regulation. It is the total value of the property right to pollute.

2 (Practice problem: pollution abatement) Avenger of the Sea Tuna kills 20 dolphins during an average harvest. It has various options for reducing the dolphin kill, and the costs are given in Table 23.3.

Table 23.3

Dolphins killed	Dolphins saved	Total cost	Marginal cost
20	0	$ 0	—
18	2	$ 100	
16	4	$ 240	
14	6	$ 400	
12	8	$ 600	
10	10	$ 1,000	
8	12	$ 1,500	
6	14	$ 2,200	
4	16	$ 3,000	
2	18	$ 5,000	
0	20	$10,000	

a Suppose that a tax (or fine) of $100 is assessed per dolphin killed. How many dolphins will be killed? What number of dolphins will be saved?

b Suppose that rather than a tax, a subsidy of $100 per dolphin is granted for reductions in the dolphin kill. How many will the company kill? How many will be saved?

c With no tax or subsidy, the company's profits are $10,000. Compute its profits with the tax and with the subsidy.

3 (Practice problem: pollution abatement) Flying Turkey Air Transport has its hub in Thanksgiving. Dozens of planes land and take off each night and cause considerable noise. By muffling engines or other more advanced techniques, the company can reduce its noise. The costs are given in Table 23.4.

Table 23.4

Average level of noise (decibels)	Total cost	Marginal cost
1,000	$ 0	—
900	$ 50	
800	$ 150	
700	$ 300	
600	$ 500	
500	$ 750	
400	$1,100	

a Suppose that a pollution tax (or fine) of $2.50 is assessed per decibel of noise created. How much will the company create? What quantity of noise will be abated?

b Suppose that rather than a tax, a subsidy of $2.50 is granted per unit of noise abated. How much will the company create? What quantity of noise will be abated?

c With no tax or subsidy, the company's profits are $5,000. Compute its profits with the tax and with the subsidy.

Tool Kit 23.2: Finding the Efficient Quantity in Markets with Negative Externalities

The production and consumption of many goods causes negative externalities, such as pollution, noise, and congestion. In these cases, markets bring about too much production and consumption.

Step one: Determine the market equilibrium at the intersection of the supply and demand curves.

Step two: Add the marginal external cost to the supply curve, which is the private marginal cost, to determine the social marginal cost curve.

Step three: Find the efficient quantity at the intersection of the demand curve and the social marginal cost curve.

Step four: Compare the market equilibrium and efficient quantities.

---

4 (Worked problem: negative externalities) Runoff from local feedlots is polluting the Red Cedar River. The negative externality per steer is $100. The demand and supply curves for steer are given in Table 23.5.

Table 23.5

Demand		Supply	
Price	Quantity	Price	Quantity
$200	350	$200	1,100
$180	500	$180	1,000
$160	650	$160	900
$140	800	$140	800
$120	950	$120	700
$100	1,100	$100	600
$ 80	1,300	$ 80	500

a Find the market equilibrium quantity and price.

b Calculate the social marginal cost, and determine the efficient quantity of steers.

Step-by-step solution

Step one (a): Find the market equilibrium quantity and price. At a price of $140, the market clears with 800 sold.

Step two (b): Find the social marginal cost curve. We add the marginal external cost, which is $100, to the supply curve, which is the private marginal cost. Table 23.6 gives the solution.

Table 23.6

Quantity	Social marginal cost
500	$180
600	$200
700	$220
800	$240
900	$260
1,000	$280
1,100	$300

Step three: Find the efficient quantity at the intersection of the demand curve and the social marginal cost curve. This occurs at a quantity of 500 and a price of $180.

Step four: Compare the market equilibrium and efficient quantities. Notice that the efficient quantity is only 500, while the market produces 800. Incorporating the external cost into the supply curve would raise the price and reduce the quantity to the efficient level.

5 (Practice problem: negative externalities) The private flying lessons at Daredevil Airport cause noise that disturbs local residents. The residents are also uneasy about the periodic crashes. One estimate of the magnitude of the negative externalities is $15 per flight. The market supply and demand curves for flight lessons are given in Table 23.7.

Table 23.7

Demand		Supply	
Price	Quantity	Price	Quantity
$75	10	$75	100
$70	20	$70	80
$65	30	$65	60
$60	40	$60	40
$55	50	$55	20
$50	60	$50	0

a Find the market equilibrium price and quantity.
b Calculate the social marginal cost, and find the efficient quantity.

6 (Practice problem: negative externalities) New developments of townhouses are springing up in the once-rural community of Outland. The supply and demand curves for new townhouses are given in Table 23.8.

Table 23.8

Demand		Supply	
Price	Quantity	Price	Quantity
$140,000	100	$140,000	900
$130,000	200	$130,000	800
$120,000	300	$120,000	700
$110,000	400	$110,000	600
$100,000	500	$100,000	500
$ 90,000	600	$ 90,000	400
$ 80,000	700	$ 80,000	300

a Find the market equilibrium quantity of townhouses and the corresponding price.
b The new developments impose costs on other current residents for sewage, transportation, and congestion. An estimate of the magnitude of these negative externalities is $20,000 per townhouse. Find the efficient level of townhouse production and the corresponding price.

Tool Kit 23.3: Using Marketable Permits to Bring about the Efficient Level of Pollution

The problem of pollution (and other negative externalities) can be attacked more directly by considering the "market" for pollution itself. The polluters are the demanders for pollution, and their demand curve is just the marginal abatement cost curve. If it costs a firm $40 to clean up a tonne of sludge from its emissions, then that firm is willing to pay $40 to be given the right to emit the sludge. The efficient level of pollution occurs where the demand curve intersects the social marginal cost curve, which is the marginal damage done by the pollution. These problems explore the issue of the efficient level of pollution and how a marketable permit scheme can bring about this outcome.

Step one: Identify the demand for pollution (the sum of all the marginal abatement cost curves) and the social marginal cost curve.

Step two: Find the efficient level of pollution, which is at the intersection of the demand for pollution and the marginal abatement cost curve.

Step three: Determine how many permits to sell. This quantity is the efficient level of pollution found in step two.

Step four: Find the market price for the permits. Read this price off the demand curve.

7 (Worked problem: marketable permits) Discharges from factories, runoff from farmlands, and many other activities pollute the Metatarsal Lakes. The pollution could be reduced, but any reduction would involve expensive abatement procedures. The marginal abatement

cost schedule is given in Table 23.9 along with the social marginal cost of the pollution.

Table 23.9

Pollution (parts/million)	Marginal abatement cost	Social marginal cost
100	$1,200	$ 0
200	$1,000	$ 0
300	$ 900	$ 150
400	$ 800	$ 300
500	$ 700	$ 450
600	$ 600	$ 600
700	$ 500	$ 800
800	$ 300	$1,000

Find the efficient level of pollution, and explain how a marketable permits scheme can achieve an efficient outcome.

Step-by-step solution

Step one: Identify the demand for pollution and the social marginal cost curve. The demand is the marginal abatement cost curve given in Table 23.9, which also includes the social marginal cost curve.

Step two: Find the efficient level of pollution. The intersection of the demand for pollution and the marginal abatement cost curve occurs at 600 parts/million.

Step three: Determine how many permits to sell. This number is 600, and each permit entitles the holder to emit 1 part/million of pollution.

Step four: Find the market price for the permits. If 600 permits are offered for sale, their market price will be $600. This price is read off the marginal abatement cost curve at 600 units.

8   (Practice problem: marketable permits) The marginal abatement cost and social marginal cost of pollution in the Northwest Air Shed are given in Table 20.10. Find the efficient level of pollution, and explain how a marketable permits scheme can achieve an efficient outcome. Pollution is measured as metric tonnes of sulphur oxide.

Table 23.10

Pollution	Marginal abatement cost	Social marginal cost
10	$100	$ 0
20	$ 80	$ 0
30	$ 60	$ 5
40	$ 50	$ 10
50	$ 40	$ 20
60	$ 30	$ 30
70	$ 15	$ 50

9   (Practice problem: marketable permits) Pesticides, engine oil, chemicals, and other pollutants are finding their way into the groundwater. Abatement is possible but expensive. The marginal abatement cost and social marginal cost of this type of pollution for the Alago Aquafier are given in Table 23.11. Find the efficient level of pollution, and explain how a marketable permits scheme can achieve it.

Table 23.11

Pollution	Marginal abatement cost	Social marginal cost
100	$10,000	$ 10
150	$ 8,000	$ 100
200	$ 6,000	$ 1,000
250	$ 5,000	$ 5,000
300	$ 4,000	$ 10,000
350	$ 3,000	$ 20,000

Answers to Problems

2   The marginal abatement cost for reducing the dolphin kill is given in Table 23.12.

Table 23.12

Dolphins killed	Dolphins saved	Total cost	Marginal cost
20	0	$ 0	—
18	2	$ 100	$ 50
16	4	$ 240	$ 70
14	6	$ 400	$ 80
12	8	$ 600	$ 100
10	10	$ 1,000	$ 200
8	12	$ 1,500	$ 250
6	14	$ 2,200	$ 350
4	16	$ 3,000	$ 400
2	18	$ 5,000	$ 1,000
0	20	$ 10,000	$ 2,500

a   The firm reduces its dolphin kill by 8 for a total of 12 killed.

b   Again, the firm reduces its dolphin kill by 8 for a total of 12 killed.

c   Profits under the tax = $10,000 − (12 × $100) = $8,800; profits under the subsidy = $10,000 + (8 × $100) = $10,800.

3   The marginal abatement cost for noise is given in Table 23.13.

Table 23.13

Average level of noise	Total cost	Marginal cost
1,000	$ 0	—
900	$ 50	$0.50
800	$ 150	$1.00
700	$ 300	$1.50
600	$ 500	$2.00
500	$ 750	$2.50
400	$1,100	$3.50

   a The firm will emit 500 decibels (abating 500).
   b The firm will abate 500 decibels (emitting 500).
   c Profits under tax = $5,000 − (500 × $2.50) = $3,750; profits under subsidy = $5,000 + (500 × $2.50) = $6,250.

5 *a* Market equilibrium quantity = 40; price = $60.
   b The social marginal cost is given in Table 23.14.

Table 23.14

Quantity	Social marginal cost
0	$65
20	$70
40	$75
60	$80
80	$85
100	$90

Efficient quantity = 20; price = $70.

6 *a* Market equilibrium quantity = 500; price = $100,000.
   b The social marginal cost is given in Table 23.15.

Table 23.15

Quantity	Social marginal cost
300	$100,000
400	$110,000
500	$120,000
600	$130,000
700	$140,000
800	$150,000
900	$160,000

Efficient quantity = 400; price = $110,000.

8 Efficient level = 60. If 60 permits are sold, the market price will be $30 each, 60 permits will be purchased, and the level of pollution will be 60.

9 Efficient level = 250. If 250 permits are sold, the market price will be $5,000 each, 250 permits will be purchased, and the level of pollution will be 250.

TAXATION, REDISTRIBUTION, AND SOCIAL INSURANCE

Chapter Review

Chapter 24 is about why governments redistribute income and how they do so. It begins with the basic argument of why markets may not provide a satisfactory answer to the question of for whom goods are produced. It looks separately at the tax and transfer system and at social insurance and asks how each promotes a more equitable distribution of the economy's output. The chapter examines the fundamental trade-off between efficiency and equality and discusses various current public-policy controversies.

ESSENTIAL CONCEPTS

1   Though the idea of market failure justifies many government policies aimed at improving the efficiency of the economy, the case for **redistribution** of the economy's output depends on overriding social values relating to equality. Markets allocate too small a share of output to those at the lower end of the economic spectrum and too much to those at the upper end. Programs such as welfare assistance and Unemployment In-

surance redistribute income directly to the poor and unemployed. Also, the wide variety of taxes, from individual to corporate income taxes to sales and luxury taxes, affect the distribution of income.

2   A good tax system has five important characteristics, the first of which is **fairness**. Economists have emphasized two principles of fairness. **Horizontal equity** says that individuals in the same circumstances should pay the same tax, and **vertical equity** says that taxes should be based on ability to pay. By the standard of vertical equity, the tax system should be **progressive**, which means that the fraction of income paid in taxes should be larger for those with more income.

3   The second characteristic of a good tax system is **efficiency**. The system should change the economy's resource allocation decisions as little as possible and also impose few extra costs on taxpayers. The Canadian tax system often encourages more consumption and production of some goods with special tax provisions called **tax subsidies**. These reduce taxes for those who engage in the favoured activity and result in lower tax revenues for the government. The lost tax revenue is called a **tax expenditure.** Other characteristics of a good tax system include **administrative**

simplicity, flexibility, and transparency, which means that it should be clear who is paying how much of each tax.

4 Government programs for alleviating poverty target the unemployed through Unemployment Insurance, job-retraining programs, and the overall commitment to full employment. Attempts to raise the income of the employed include controversial minimum wage legislation and refundable tax credits. Old Age Security and the Guaranteed Income Supplement provide federal support for the aged and disabled, which is supplemented in some cases by provincial programs. Welfare assistance programs are operated by each province to direct money to those nonworking low-income families that are not eligible for Unemployment Insurance. These programs are designed to provide the poor with a minimal level of basic necessities.

5 Among current public-policy issues are the questions of whether to require welfare recipients to work, whether to continue with **categorical assistance** programs that direct support to particular groups or move to more **general assistance** for the poor, and whether to replace **assistance in kind** programs, such as housing subsidies, with cash grants. An alternative approach would direct attention towards the root causes of poverty by attacking discrimination and improving job skills (human capital).

6 Many social insurance programs, such as Old Age Security, Unemployment Insurance, disability insurance, and Medicare, benefit the middle class. They are financed by payroll taxes, but the ultimate burden—the economic **incidence**—is in the form of lower wages. Although they are called insurance programs, the provisions of each cause some income to be redistributed.

7 Any program or tax provision that promotes equality inevitably reduces efficiency. This basic **equity-efficiency trade-off** must be faced in making choices about social programs and tax reforms. Overall, income equality in Canada, as shown by the **Lorenz curve**, is significantly more unequal than in other developed countries.

BEHIND THE ESSENTIAL CONCEPTS

1 You can judge the Canadian tax system on how well it meets the five criteria outlined in the text. The following are some arguments.

   a Fairness: The marginal tax rate, which is the tax paid out of the extra dollar of income, is higher for higher incomes. This aspect and refundable tax credits combine to make the income tax system mildly progressive, although the progressivity is offset somewhat by a variety of special provisions that help higher-income households, such as deduc-

tions for Registered Retirement Savings Plan (RRSP) and Registered Pension Plan (RPP) contributions, and capital gains exclusions. Payroll taxes and federal and provincial sales taxes are regressive, however, and in sum, the total tax system is probably at best only slightly progressive.

   b Efficiency: Although the reform of the federal tax system—the reduction of marginal income tax rates in 1988 and the introduction of the Goods and Services Tax (GST) in 1991—improved the efficiency of the income tax system, many special provisions remain.

   c Administrative simplicity: An important source of administrative simplicity in the Canadian tax system is the extent to which the income taxes collected by the federal and provincial governments are harmonized. Also, the income tax reform of 1988 simplified the administration of the tax system, for example, by making it less profitable for taxpayers to search for loopholes to enable them to avoid paying taxes. The introduction of the GST in 1991, however, probably worked in the opposite direction, in part because provinces have been reluctant to harmonize their sales taxes with the GST.

   d Flexibility: The Canadian tax system is reasonably flexible, as compared to that of the United States. In Canada, the government simply announces the tax schedule in its annual budget. By contrast, any proposed tax change seems to open up debate on all aspects of the U.S. tax code.

   e Transparency: For some taxes, such as the corporation income tax and sales taxes, it is difficult to determine the actual tax burden.

2 The equity-efficiency trade-off is similar to the risk-incentive trade-off you studied in earlier chapters. You learned that an employer who pays commissions, for example, will provide stronger incentives to the sales force than another who pays a straight salary. The result of the strong incentives, however, is risk for the employees. The risk is not only that incomes may be high in some months and low in others, but also that some employees may earn more than others. Just as an employer can have strong incentives at a cost of risk for the employees, an economy can have efficiency at a cost of inequality. Social programs that alleviate poverty also reduce the incentives to earn income. Similarly, progressive income taxation pays for social programs, but discourages effort.

SELF-TEST

True or False

1 Redistribution is necessary to promote a more efficient allocation of resources than the market provides.

F 2 Horizontal equity says that upper-income individuals should pay a larger fraction of income in taxes.

F 3 Vertical equity says that people in similar situations should pay the same tax.

T 4 A tax system is progressive if upper-income individuals pay a larger fraction of income in taxes.

F 5 The payroll tax is an example of a progressive tax.

6 The Canadian income tax system is quite flexible and able to respond quickly to changes in economic circumstances, at least by comparison to the U.S. tax code.

T 7 The 1988 tax reform reduced administrative complexity somewhat by reducing marginal tax rates.

F 8 The corporate income tax is an example of a transparent tax in that it is easy to see how much each person effectively pays.

T 9 Refundable tax credits increase the after-tax income of the working poor.

T 10 Tax expenditures refer to the lost revenue from tax subsidies, such as the deduction for RRSP combinations.

T 11 Housing subsidies are examples of assistance in kind.

T 12 Categorical assistance provides support to specific classes of individuals, such as the disabled.

T 13 Medicare is an example of a middle-class entitlement program.

F 14 The Lorenz curve illustrates the efficiency of the economy.

F 15 Canada has a more equal distribution of economic goods than most other developed economies.

Multiple Choice

1 Which of the following is not an excise tax?

 a cigarette tax
 b tax on alcohol
 c gasoline tax
 d tax on air travel
 e corporate income tax

2 Horizontal equity means that

 a people in the same economic situation should pay the same amount in tax.
 b richer individuals should pay a larger fraction of their income in taxes.
 c richer individuals should pay a larger monetary amount in taxes.
 d the marginal tax rate should be higher for higher-income individuals.
 e the tax schedule should be flat.

3 Vertical equity means that

 a people in the same economic situation should pay the same amount in taxes.
 b richer individuals should pay a larger fraction of their income in taxes.
 c richer individuals should pay a larger monetary amount in taxes.
 d the marginal tax rate should be higher for higher-income individuals.
 e the tax schedule should be flat.

4 If lower-income individuals pay a larger fraction of their income in tax, the system is

 a progressive.
 b regressive.
 c transparent.
 d efficient.
 e flexible.

5 If the income tax allows a tax credit for any money spent on some item, then there is said to be a

 a tax subsidy.
 b tax incidence.
 c excise tax.
 d tax burden.
 e refundable income tax credit.

6 The marginal tax rate is the

 a extra tax owed on an additional dollar of income.
 b amount of tax expenditure on an additional dollar of income.
 c amount of tax subsidy on an additional dollar of income.
 d ratio of taxes to taxable income.
 e tax rate at which the earned-income credit no longer applies.

7 The incidence of a tax refers to

 a how many people must pay it.
 b how difficult it is to determine how much is paid.
 c who really bears the burden of the tax, taking into account its economic repercussions.
 d who actually sends the money to the tax authority.
 e how much the tax distorts economic decisions.

8 An efficient tax system

 a distorts economic decisions as little as possible.
 b pays no attention to the cost of tax collection from taxpayers.
 c is flexible.
 d has redistribution as its primary objective.
 e is simple to administer.

9 Which of the following is not an attribute of a good tax system?

 a efficiency
 b vertical equity
 c horizontal equity
 d transparency
 e none of the above

10 Unemployment Insurance pays benefits to

 a all unemployed.

b those who are temporarily unemployed while looking for the first job.

c those who have been unemployed for a short time since leaving their last job involuntarily.

d the long-term unemployed.

e those who cannot work because of age or disability.

11 Which of the following groups is not included among the very poor?

a those who cannot work because of age or disability

b those who cannot find work

c those who choose not to work

d those whose work pays a very low wage

e those whose marginal rate of income tax is very high b/c of high incomes

12 Which of the following is not a reason for low wages?

a lack of skills or human capital

b racial discrimination

c discrimination against women

d voluntary choice of low-wage, part-time jobs

e none of the above

13 A subsidy that the tax system currently provides to low-wage workers is

a Unemployment Insurance.

b the refundable income tax credit.

c minimum wage laws.

d the negative income tax.

e none of the above.

14 Which of the following groups never bears the ultimate burden of the corporation income tax?

a the corporations' workers.

b consumers who buy the corporations' products.

c investors in the corporations.

d the corporations themselves.

e none of the above.

15 Which of the following is not a qualifying condition for workfare programs?

a joining a job-training program

b attending school

c looking for a job

d working already

e none of the above

16 Which of the following is not a social insurance program?

a Old Age Security

b Unemployment Insurance

c Guaranteed Income Supplement

d public health insurance

e disability insurance

17 Assistance targetted to particular groups is called

a categorical assistance.

b negative income tax.

c in-kind assistance.

d workfare.

e social insurance.

18 Which of the following is not an example of assistance in kind?

a public day care

b minimum wages

c Medicare

d public housing

e none of the above

19 The incidence of the payroll tax almost surely falls

a evenly between the employer and the employee.

b entirely on the employee.

c entirely on the employer.

d on upper-income salaried workers.

e on the self-employed.

20 The government's role in redistribution is primarily motivated by

a market failure.

b social values concerning those unable to sustain a minimum standard of living.

c imperfect information.

d distrust of consumer sovereignty.

e noncompetitive markets.

Completion

1 The idea that individuals who are in identical situations should pay the same tax is called _horizontal equity_

2 The idea that people who have more income or wealth should pay more tax is called _vertical equity_

3 A tax system in which individuals pay a larger fraction of income as income increases is called _progressive_

4 The term _tax expenditure_ refers to the revenue lost as a result of tax credits and deductions.

5 A good tax system has the characteristics of _transparency_ which means that it is clear what each person is paying in taxes.

6 The tax owed on an additional dollar of income is the _marginal tax rate_

7 The _incidence_ of a tax refers to who actually bears its economic burden.

8 Under the _negative income tax_ plan, those with low incomes would receive money from the government.

9 Housing subsidies are an example of an assistance _in kind_ program.

10 The _Lorenz curve_ shows the fraction of income earned by the poorest 10 percent, 20 percent, etc.

Answers to Self-Test

True or False

1	f	6	t	11	t
2	f	7	t	12	t
3	f	8	f	13	t
4	t	9	t	14	f
5	f	10	t	15	f

Multiple Choice

1	e	6	a	11	e	16	c
2	a	7	c	12	e	17	a
3	b	8	a	13	b	18	b
4	b	9	e	14	d	19	b
5	a	10	c	15	d	20	b

Completion

1 horizontal equity
2 vertical equity
3 progressive
4 tax expenditure
5 transparency

6 marginal tax rate
7 incidence
8 negative income tax
9 in-kind
10 Lorenz curve

Doing Economics: Tools and Practice Problems

Although a market system produces much inequality, government can reduce the inequality through tax and expenditure programs. The fundamental trade-off, however, involves the disincentive effects that accompany programs that redistribute income. We consider progressive income taxation and the negative income tax, general assistance program designed to merge the welfare system into the income tax system. Finally, we look at how to measure income inequality with the Lorenz curve.

Tool Kit 24.1: Plotting the Budget Constraint with Progressive Income Taxes

A progressive income tax system promotes equality by taxing higher-income individuals more than lower-income individuals. There are disincentives, however, and we explore how progressive taxation reduces work effort below what it would be under a proportional tax system (flat tax) that realizes the same revenue.

Step one: Identify the wage, the time available, and the tax schedule. Also, note the notches in the tax schedule, which are the income levels at which the tax rate changes.

Step two: Draw coordinate axes, labelling the horizontal one "Leisure" and the vertical one "Consumption."

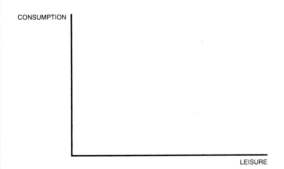

Step three: Plot the no-work point.

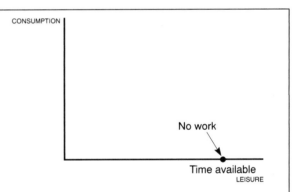

Step four: Identify the lowest level of income at which the tax rate changes. Determine how much time is needed to earn this level of income and the corresponding after-tax income:

time needed =
  income at which tax rate changes/wage;
after-tax income = income − (tax rate × income).

Plot this point.

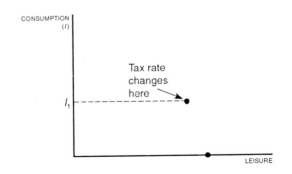

Step five: Identify the next lowest level of income at which the tax rate changes, and repeat step four. Continue.

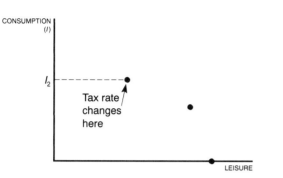

Step six: Draw line segments connecting the points. This is the budget constraint.

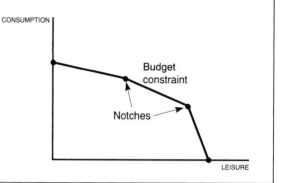

Tool Kit 24.2: Comparing Progressive and Flat Income Tax Systems

Step one: Plot the budget constraint with the progressive tax schedule.

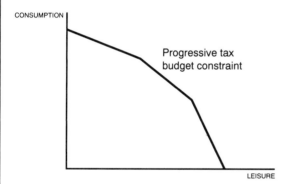

Step two: Choose a point on the budget constraint. Label it *A*.

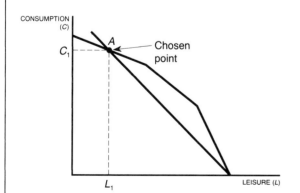

Step three: Draw a line segment from the no-work point through *A* to the vertical axis. This is the proportional tax (flat tax) budget constraint, which raises the same tax revenue as paid under the proportional tax system.

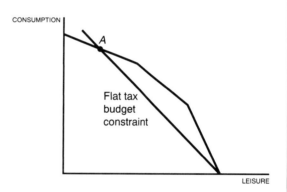

Step four: Darken the portion of the progressive tax budget constraint that lies outside the proportional tax budget constraint. These points are possible under the progressive system but not under the equivalent proportional tax system. Note that they involve less work.

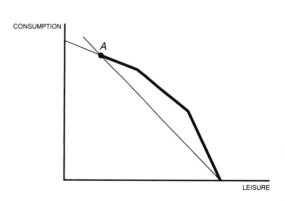

1 (Worked problem: comparing tax systems) Mary Beth
earns $200 per day as a design consultant and can
work 300 days each year. The income tax schedule is
given in the table. She has no nonwage income.

Annual income	Tax rate
$0–$10,000	0%
$10,000–$50,000	20%
$50,000 and up	40%

a Plot her budget constraint.
b Suppose that she chooses to work 150 days. Compute her average tax rate.
c Compare her budget constraint drawn in part a with the budget constraint if she paid the flat tax rate computed in part b.

Step-by-step solution

Step one (a): Plot the budget constraint with the progressive tax schedule. Identify the wage, the time available, and the tax schedule. Also, note the notches in the tax schedule, which are the income levels at which the tax rate changes. The wage is $200 per day. There are 300 days available, and the notches occur at $10,000 and $50,000.

Step two: Draw coordinate axes, labelling the horizontal one "Leisure" and the vertical one "Consumption."

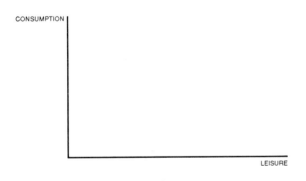

Step three: Plot the no-work point.

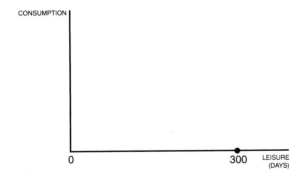

Step four: Identify the lowest level of income at which the tax rate changes. This is $10,000. Determine how much time is needed to earn this level of income and the corresponding after-tax income:

time needed = $10,000/$200 = 50 days.
after-tax income = $10,000 − (.0 × $10,000) = $10,000.

Plot this point.

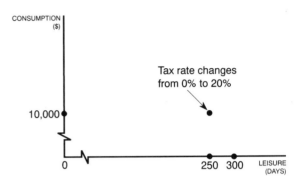

Step five: Identify the next lowest level of income at which the tax rate changes, and repeat step four. This point is 250 days, and $10,000 + $40,000 − (.20 × $40,000) = $42,000. Finally, if she works all 300 days, she earns $42,000 + $18,000 − (.4 × $18,000) = $52,800.

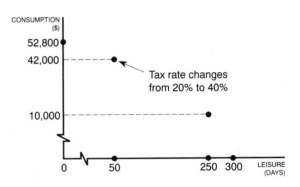

Step six: Draw line segments connecting the points. This is the budget constraint.

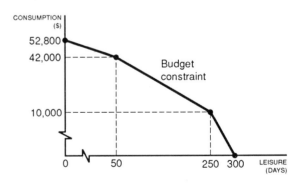

Step seven (b): Compute Mary Beth's average tax rate. She works 150 days and earns $30,000. She pays zero dollars on the first $10,000 and .20 × $20,000 = $4,000 on the remainder. Her average tax rate is $4,000/$30,000 = 13.3 percent.

Step eight (c): Compare progressive and proportional tax systems on her budget constraint. Plot the budget constraint with the progressive tax schedule.

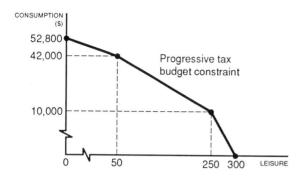

Step nine: Choose a point on the budget constraint.

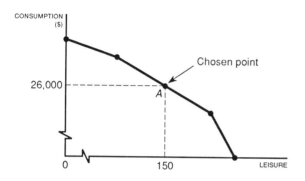

Step ten: Draw a line segment from the no-work point through *A* to the vertical axis. This is the proportional tax (flat tax = 13.3 percent) budget constraint, which raises the same tax revenue as paid under the proportional tax system.

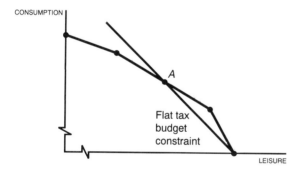

Step eleven: Darken the portion of the progressive tax budget constraint that lies outside the proportional tax budget constraint. Note that Mary Beth's incentives to work more days are weaker under the progressive tax. The two budget constraints illustrate the disincentive effects of progressive taxation.

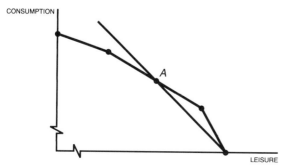

2 (Practice problem: comparing tax systems) Sara earns $100 per day and can work only 200 days each year.

   a Plot her budget constraint under the tax system given in problem 1.

   b Suppose that she chooses to work 150 days. Compute her average tax rate.

   c Compare her budget constraint drawn in part a with the budget constraint if she paid the flat tax rate computed in part b.

3 (Practice problem: comparing tax systems) Return to problem 1 and answers to parts a, b, and c under the following tax system.

Annual income	Tax rate
$0–$20,000	0%
$20,000 and up	40%

Is this tax system progressive?

Tool Kit 24.3: Analyzing the Negative Income Tax

A general assistance plan often favoured by economists is the negative income tax. Under this plan, each person receives a fixed payment from the tax authority but pays a fixed percentage of income in taxes.

Step one: Draw coordinate axes. Label the horizontal one "Leisure" and the vertical one "Consumption."

Step two: Plot the budget constraint with no negative income tax.

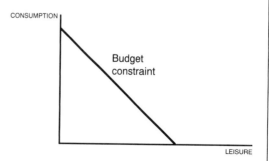

Step three: Plot the no-work point under the negative income tax. The level of consumption at this point is the amount of the fixed payment.

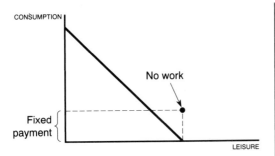

Step four: Plot the no-leisure point. Consumption is the fixed payment plus after-tax income if all time is spent working.

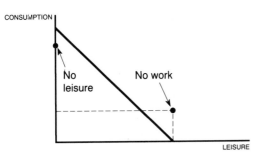

Step five: Draw a line segment connecting the two points. This is the budget constraint for the negative income tax.

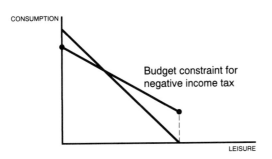

Step six: Identify the break-even point. This is where the two budget constraints cross. It indicates the point where the tax payment exactly equals the fixed payment, and the individual neither pays nor receives taxes.

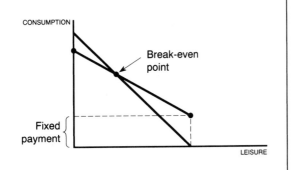

4 (Worked problem: negative income tax) John earns $200 per day and can work a total of 200 days each year. He has no nonwage income. His member of parliament proposes a negative income tax with a fixed payment of $5,000 and a 25 percent tax rate. Analyze how this plan affects John's budget constraint.

Step-by-step solution

Step one: Draw coordinate axes. Label the horizontal one "Leisure" and the vertical one "Consumption."

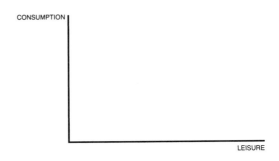

Step two: Plot the budget constraint with no negative income tax.

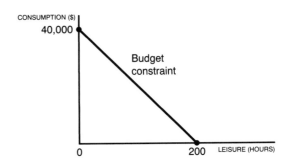

Step three: Plot the no-work point under the negative income tax. The level of consumption at this point is the amount of the fixed payment.

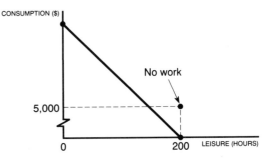

Step four: Plot the no-leisure point. Consumption is the fixed payment plus after-tax income if all time is spent working.

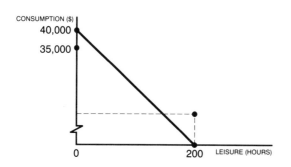

Step five: Draw a line segment connecting the two points. This is the budget constraint for the negative income tax.

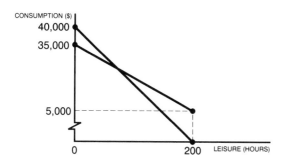

Step six: Identify the break-even point. John breaks even when he works 100 days and earns $20,000. He owes .25 × $20,000 = $5,000, which exactly offsets the fixed payment.

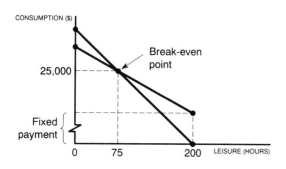

5 (Practice problem: negative income tax) Lucinda earns $200 per day as a private investigator, and she can work 100 days each year. Analyze a negative income tax system with a fixed payment of $8,000 and a 40 percent marginal tax rate. Draw Lucinda's budget constraint with and without the negative income tax. How many days must she work to break even?

6 (Practice problem: negative income tax) Stanislav can earn $12 per hour as a taxicab driver. He can work 80 hours each week. Analyze a negative income tax system with a fixed payment of $100 per week and a 33 percent tax rate. Plot his budget constraint without and with the negative income tax. How many hours must he work to break even?

Tool Kit 24.4: Plotting the Lorenz Curve

The Lorenz curve is a convenient way to represent graphically the inequality in income (or any other economic variable). It shows what percentage of income is earned by the lowest 10 percent of the population, the lowest 20 percent, etc. If you know the income earned by each group, then you can construct the Lorenz curve.

Step one: Order the groups from lowest income to highest.

Step two: Make a table with headings as follows.

Group	% population	Cumulative % population	% income	Cumulative % income

Step three: Compute the percentage of income for each group, and enter in the table.

Step four: Compute the percentage of the population for each group, and enter in the table.

Step five: Compute the cumulative percentage of income for each group by adding its percentage to all percentages of the lower-income groups, and enter in the table.

Step six: Compute the cumulative percentage of the population for each group by adding its percentage to all percentages of the lower-income groups, and enter in the table.

Step seven: Draw coordinate axes. Label the horizontal one "Cumulative percentage of population" and the vertical one "Cumulative percentage of income."

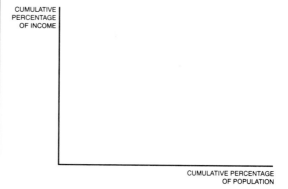

Step eight: Plot points corresponding to each group.

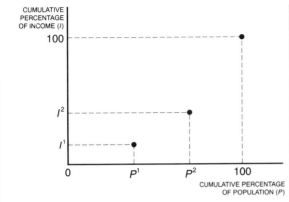

Step nine: Draw a curve connecting the points. This curve is the Lorenz curve.

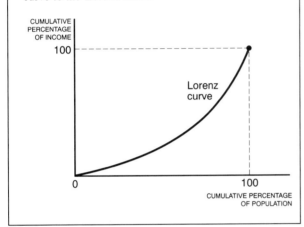

7   (Worked problem: Lorenz curve) In Costa Guano, there are four types of households: peasant farmers, ranchers, shopkeepers, and business owners. The population of each group (in millions) and the income (in Canadian dollar equivalent) of each are given in Table 24.1.

Table 24.1

	Income	Population (millions)
Peasant farmers	$ 5,000	40
Ranchers	$50,000	20
Shopkeepers	$10,000	30
Business owners	$80,000	10

Plot the Lorenz curve.

Step-by-step solution

Step one: Order the groups from lowest income to highest.

Peasant farmers	$ 5,000	40
Shopkeepers	$10,000	30
Ranchers	$50,000	20
Business owners	$80,000	10

Step two: Make a table.

Group	% population	Cumulative % population	% income	Cumulative % income
Peasant farmers				
Shopkeepers				
Ranchers				
Business owners				

Step three: Compute the percentage of income for each group, and enter in the table. For peasant farmers, it is {40 × $5,000/[(40 × $5,000) + (30 × $10,000) + (20 × $50,000) + (10 × $80,000)]} × 100 = 9 percent (this is rounded to the nearest whole percentage point). The completed column is given in Table 24.2.

Step four: Compute the percentage of the population for each group, and enter in the table. For peasant farmers, it is 40/(40 + 30 + 20 + 10) = 40 percent. Continue, and complete the column, which is given in Table 24.2.

Table 24.2

Group	% population	Cumulative % population	% income	Cumulative % income
Peasant farmers	40		9	
Shopkeepers	30		13	
Ranchers	20		43	
Business owners	10		35	

Step five: Compute the cumulative percentage of income for each group by adding its percentages to all percentages of the lower income groups, and enter in the table. For peasant farmers, it is simply 9 percent. For shopkeepers, it is 9 + 13 = 22 percent. Continue.

Step six: Compute the cumulative percentage of the population for each group by adding its percentage to all percentages of the lower income groups, and enter in the table. For peasant farmers, it is simply 40 percent. For shopkeepers, it is 40 + 30 = 70 percent. Continue. The complete information appears in Table 24.3.

Table 24.3

Group	% population	Cumulative % population	% income	Cumulative % income
Peasant farmers	40	40	9	9
Shopkeepers	30	70	13	22
Ranchers	20	90	43	65
Business owners	10	100	35	100

Step seven: Draw coordinate axes. Label the horizontal one "Cumulative percentage of population" and the vertical one "Cumulative percentage of income."

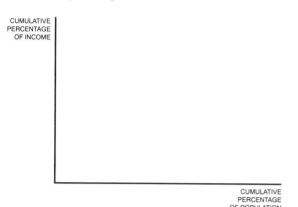

Step eight: Plot points corresponding to each group.

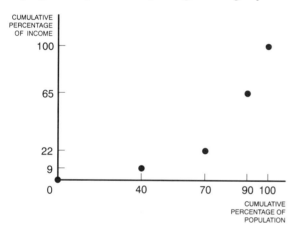

Step nine: Draw a curve connecting the points. This curve is the Lorenz curve.

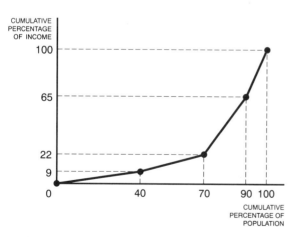

8 (Practice problem: Lorenz curve) North Dundas Provincial University is reconsidering the equity of its pay structure. All professors within a department receive the same salary, but salaries differ across departments. The number of professors in each department and the salary of each professor in the department are given in Table 24.4.

Table 24.4

Department	Number of professors	Salary
Sociology	8	$50,000
Economics	10	$60,000
Marketing	2	$80,000
Literature	16	$30,000
Philosophy	4	$40,000

a Plot the Lorenz curve.
b An organization of faculty members proposes paying each professor $50,000. Plot the Lorenz curve for the faculty if this proposal were adopted.
c What would the Lorenz curve look like if each professor were paid $80,000?

9 (Practice problem: Lorenz curve) Exurbia, a pleasant town outside Gotham City, is populated by factory workers, bureaucrats, professionals, and retirees. All members of a particular group receive the same income and hold the same level of wealth, but incomes and levels of wealth differ across groups. The number of individuals in each group and the income and wealth of each individual in the group are given in Table 24.5.

Table 24.5

Career	Number	Income	Wealth
Factory workers	100	$30,000	$ 30,000
Bureaucrats	100	$40,000	$ 40,000
Professionals	100	$80,000	$ 80,000
Retirees	100	$50,000	$350,000

a Plot the Lorenz curve for income.
b Plot the Lorenz curve for wealth.
c Compare the two. Is there more inequality in income or in wealth?

Answers to Problems

2 *a,c*

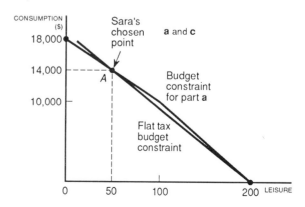

b Tax = ($15,000 – $10,000) × .2 = $1,000; average tax rate = $1,000/$15,000 = 7 percent.

3 *a,b*

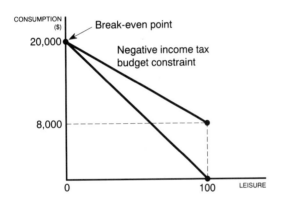

c Tax = ($30,000 − $20,000) × .4 = $4,000; average tax rate = $4,000/$30,000 = 13.3 percent. Yes, it is progressive.

5 Her break-even income is $8,000/0.4 = $20,000, which requires 100 days of work.

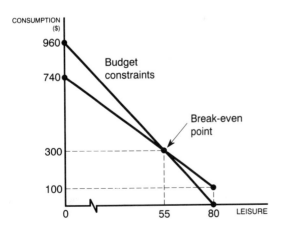

6 His break-even income is $300, which requires 25 hours each week.

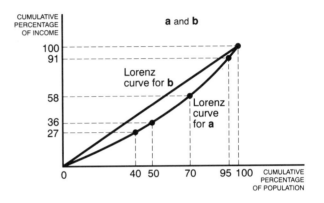

8 *a* The Lorenz curve appears in Table 24.6 and the diagram.

Table 24.6

	%	Cumulative %	%	Cumulative %
Department	population	population	income	income
Literature	40	40	27	27
Philosophy	10	50	9	36
Sociology	20	70	22	58
Economics	25	95	33	91
Marketing	5	100	9	100

b The complete information is given in Table 24.7. The Lorenz curve is the 45-degree line if there is equality.

Table 24.7

	%	Cumulative %	%	Cumulative %
Department	population	population	income	income
Literature	40	40	40	40
Philosophy	10	50	10	50
Sociology	20	70	20	70
Economics	25	95	25	95
Marketing	5	100	5	100

c The answer does not depend on the magnitude of income, only on its distribution. The answer is the same as for part b.

9 *a* The Lorenz curve for income is given in Table 24.8 and the diagram.

Table 24.8

Career	% population	Cumulative % population	% income	Cumulative % income
Factory workers	25	25	15	15
Bureaucrats	25	50	20	35
Retirees	25	75	25	60
Professionals	25	100	40	100

Table 24.9

Career	% population	Cumulative % population	% income	Cumulative % income
Factory workers	25	25	6	6
Bureaucrats	25	50	8	14
Retirees	25	75	16	30
Professionals	25	100	70	100

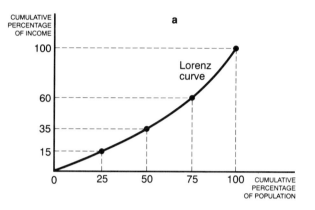

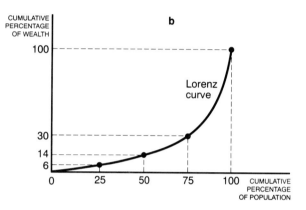

b The Lorenz curve for wealth is given in Table 24.9 and the diagram.

c Wealth is distributed more unequally than income. The Lorenz curve for wealth is further from the diagonal (45-degree line) than is the Lorenz curve for income.

Part Four

Aggregate Markets

Chapter 25

MACROECONOMIC GOALS AND MEASURES

Chapter Review

Macroeconomics is concerned with the characteristics of the economy as a whole. This chapter of the text introduces three central macroeconomic variables: the unemployment rate, the inflation rate, and gross domestic product, which is the standard measure of the economy's output. We learn how to measure each variable and discover how each is related to the major goals for the performance of the economy. Chapter 26 gives an overview of how macroeconomic theory explains the levels of and changes in unemployment, inflation, and output.

ESSENTIAL CONCEPTS

1   **Macroeconomics** is concerned with the performance of the economy as a whole. Three important indicators of overall macroeconomic performance are the level of unemployment, the inflation rate, and the rate of growth in output. The corresponding goals of macro-economic policy are to achieve full employment, price stability, and a high rate of economic growth. To see how the economy is doing in pursuit of these goals, economists have devised measures corresponding to each: the unemployment rate, the price index, and the gross domestic product.

2   The **labour force** includes those individuals who are either employed or actively seeking employment. The fraction of the labour force that is without work is called the **unemployment rate.** Unemployment is a persistent phenomenon in Canada: an average of 9.3 percent of the labour force was unemployed in the 1980s. This represents an enormous waste of resources, and it can be devastating personally for the un-employed and also for communities with high un-employment.

3   Economists distinguish among four types of unemploy-ment. **Seasonal unemployment** occurs when the jobs are available for only part of the year. People who are between jobs make up **frictional unemployment.** **Structural unemployment**, which is more long term, arises because the skills of the current labour force do not match the skills required by the available jobs. Fi-nally, **cyclical unemployment** is due to a slowdown in the overall level of economic activity. One of the im-portant tasks of macroeconomics is to understand and reduce cyclical unemployment.

4 The **inflation rate** is the rate of increase in the general level of prices. It is measured using **price indices** such as the consumer price index, or CPI. The annual percentage change in the CPI indicates the increase in the cost of living from one year to the next. Inflation averaged 5.5 percent and ranged from 4 to 13 percent in the 1980s. Inflation hurts people on fixed incomes because it erodes their purchasing power. When variable, inflation makes borrowing and lending riskier, and it is generally disruptive to the economy.

5 The **gross domestic product** or **GDP** measures the output of the economy. It is the money value of the goods and services produced within a country in a year. Adjusting the number for inflation gives **real GDP**. GDP can be measured in three equivalent ways. The **final goods approach** computes the market value of goods sold to their ultimate consumers. The **value-added approach** adds up the additional market value created at each step in the process from production to market. Finally, the **income approach** adds the total income received by all individuals.

6 The rate of increase in GDP is the primary measure of economic growth. Although the rate has averaged slightly over 3 percent in Canada during the 1980s, it fluctuates. During recessions, the rate of increase falls below **potential GDP**, which is the output the economy can produce with normal levels of unemployment and idle productive capacity. During economic booms, real GDP can temporarily exceed potential GDP.

BEHIND THE ESSENTIAL CONCEPTS

1 If you have a job or are looking for one, then economists count you as a member of the labour force. The unemployment rate is the fraction of the labour force that does not have a job. But the unemployment rate may not measure how hard it is to find work, for several reasons. First, you would be counted as unemployed even if you were only claiming to look for work in order to be eligible for unemployment insurance or if you were holding out for an unrealistic offer. On the other hand, if, during a recession, you realistically gave up hope of finding a job and stopped looking, you would not be counted as unemployed, but rather as out of the labour force.

2 Economists use the price index, which is constructed by comparing the costs of a particular basket of goods in different years, to measure inflation. The consumer price index measures your cost of living only if you consume exactly what is in the market basket.

3 Similarly, GDP does not quite measure all the output in the economy. It ignores nonmarketed goods, such as the services of unpaid spouses, and it can only be adjusted imperfectly to capture changes in the quality of

goods and the value of nonmarketed government services.

SELF-TEST

True or False

T 1 Inflation refers to a rise in the general price level.

F 2 The unemployment rate measures the percentage of the working-age population that is unemployed.

F 3 The labour force includes the entire working-age population.

T 4 Structural unemployment includes those unemployed who have skills that do not match the skills required for currently available jobs.

T 5 When the economy is on an upswing, cyclical unemployment declines.

T 6 The price index for the base year equals 100.

T 7 The wholesale price index is based upon a market basket of goods sold by wholesalers to retailers.

F 8 The producer price index is based upon a market basket of goods sold by wholesalers to producers.

T 9 Inflation reduces the purchasing power of people living on fixed incomes.

T 10 Variable rates of inflation increase the riskiness of borrowing and lending.

T 11 The gross domestic product measures the money value of goods and services produced within a country during a specific time period.

T 12 The gross national product includes income that residents of a country receive from abroad.

T 13 Value added is computed by subtracting a firm's purchases of inputs from its revenues.

T 14 There are three equally valid ways to compute gross domestic product: final goods, value added, and income.

T 15 Nominal GDP is real GDP adjusted for inflation.

Multiple Choice

1 Which of the following is *not* an important macroeconomic goal?

   a price stability
   b full employment
   c perfect competition
   d rapid growth
   e none of the above

2 The total labour force comprises all

   a individuals of working age who are employed.
   b individuals of working age who are unemployed.

c individuals of working age.

d heads of household.

e individuals of working age who are either employed or unemployed.

3 Which of the following cannot be counted as a cost of unemployment?

a underutilization of the economy's resources

b personal difficulties for unemployed individuals

c financial troubles for communities with high unemployment

d exacerbated racial and ethnic divisions

e higher output prices

4 The unemployment rate is the ratio of the number of unemployed to the

a number of employed.

b total labour force.

c inflation rate.

d gross domestic product.

e adult working-age population.

5 The Statistics Canada data on the unemployment rate are affected by discouraged workers who have given up hope of finding work and by those individuals who say they are looking for work but are not. The effect is that

a the first tends to overestimate the unemployment rate and the second tends to underestimate it.

b the first tends to underestimate the unemployment rate and the second tends to overestimate it.

c both tend to overestimate the unemployment rate.

d both tend to underestimate the unemployment rate.

e they cancel each other out.

6 Those individuals who are unemployed because they work in seasonal jobs are subject to

a seasonal unemployment.

b frictional unemployment.

c structural unemployment.

d cyclical unemployment.

e discouraged-worker unemployment.

7 Those individuals who are temporarily between jobs are subject to

a seasonal unemployment.

b frictional unemployment.

c structural unemployment.

d cyclical unemployment.

e discouraged-worker unemployment.

8 When the skills required by available jobs are not the same as the skills of the unemployed, there is

a seasonal unemployment.

b frictional unemployment.

c structural unemployment.

d cyclical unemployment.

e discouraged-worker unemployment.

9 In recessions, the level of economic activity declines and there is an increase in

a seasonal unemployment.

b frictional unemployment.

c structural unemployment.

d cyclical unemployment.

e discouraged-worker unemployment.

10 If prices and wages rise at the same rate, the purchasing power of typical workers

a increases.

b decreases.

c remains the same.

d doubles.

e falls to zero.

11 When the inflation rate rises and falls unpredictably,

a lenders gain at the expense of borrowers.

b borrowers gain at the expense of lenders.

c there is no appreciable impact on borrowing and lending.

d borrowing and lending become riskier.

e lending increases, but borrowing falls.

12 The wholesale price index includes in its market basket a representative bundle of goods

a purchased by consumers.

b sold by wholesalers to retailers.

c sold by producers to wholesalers.

d purchased by government.

e sold by wholesalers to consumers.

13 The money value of all goods and services produced within a country in a year is the

a gross national product.

b gross domestic product.

c net domestic product.

d depreciation index.

e producer price index.

14 Inflation-adjusted gross domestic product is called

a gross national product.

b net domestic product.

c nominal gross domestic product.

d real gross domestic product.

e nominal gross national product.

15 If the price level has risen recently, then the real GDP is

a greater than the nominal GDP.

b less than the nominal GDP.

c equal to the nominal GDP.

d greater than the GNP.

e less than the GNP.

16 During recessions, the GDP

a is less than potential GDP.

b is greater than potential GDP.

c is equal to potential GDP.

d bears no predictable relationship to potential GDP.

e rises at a decreasing rate.

17 The final goods approach to GDP

   a adds the differences between the revenues and costs of intermediate goods.

   b adds all income received by individuals and governments in the economy.

   c subtracts the inflation rate from the nominal GDP.

   d adds the value of goods, services, and the environment.

   e adds the total money value of goods and services purchased by their ultimate users.

18 The value-added approach to GDP

   a adds the differences between the revenues and costs of intermediate goods.

   b adds all income received by individuals and governments in the economy.

   c substracts the inflation rate from the nominal GDP.

   d adds the value of goods, services, and the environment.

   e adds the total money value of goods and services purchased by their ultimate users.

19 Money earned abroad and remitted to residents of a country is

   a included in GNP.

   b included in GDP.

   c included in GNP and GDP.

   d excluded from GNP and GDP.

   e accounted for in the value-added but not in the final goods approach to calculating GDP.

20 Gross domestic product divided by the number of hours worked equals

   a net domestic product.

   b real GNP.

   c real GDP.

   d productivity.

   e NDP.

Completion

1 The unemployment rate is the ratio of the number of unemployed to the _labour force_

2 People who are temporarily between jobs are part of _frictional_ unemployment.

3 _Structural_ unemployment is due to a mismatch between the skills of those without jobs and the skills needed to perform the available jobs.

4 The percentage increase in the price level from one year to the next is called the _inflation rate_

5 The money value of all final goods and services produced within the country in a year is called the _GDP_ .

6 Dividing nominal GDP by the price level gives _real GDP_ .

7 The measure of what the economy could produce given normal levels of frictional unemployment and idle productive capacity is called _potential GDP_

8 A firm's revenues minus the cost of intermediate goods equal its _value added_

9 _GDP_ differs from gross national product in that it ignores payments made by residents of a country to those abroad and income that residents receive from foreign sources.

10 _Productivity_ is calculated by dividing GDP by the number of hours worked.

Answers to Self-Test

True or False

1	t	6	t	11	t
2	f	7	t	12	t
3	f	8	f	13	t
4	t	9	t	14	t
5	t	10	t	15	f

Multiple Choice

1	c	6	a	11	d	16	a
2	e	7	b	12	b	17	e
3	e	8	c	13	b	18	a
4	b	9	d	14	d	19	a
5	b	10	c	15	b	20	d

Completion

1 labour force
2 frictional
3 Structural
4 inflation rate
5 gross domestic product
6 real GDP
7 potential GDP
8 value added
9 Gross domestic product
10 Productivity

Doing Economics: Tools and Practice Problems

In this section, we will explore how economists measure economic performance. After learning how to calculate the rate of inflation, we use this technique to construct the price index and to distinguish real and nominal GDP. Finally, we calculate GDP by the final goods, value-added, and income approaches and verify that the three techniques give equivalent answers. Although the examples are simplified, you should realize that the government agencies responsible for computing inflation and GDP perform their calculations in the same way.

Tool Box 25.1: Calculating the Inflation Rate

The inflation rate is the percentage increase in the cost of purchasing a predetermined basket of goods. Follow this procedure to calculate the inflation rate.

Step one: Identify the quantities of each good in the market basket:

quantity of good 1 =
quantity of good 2 =
quantity of good 3 =

Step two: Calculate the cost of purchasing the quantities in the market basket at year 1 prices:

  (quantity of good 1 × price in year 1)
+ (quantity of good 2 × price in year 1)
+ (quantity of good 3 × price in year 1)
= cost of living at year 1 prices.

Step three: Calculate the cost of purchasing the quantities in the market basket at year 2 prices:

  (quantity of good 1 × price in year 2)
+ (quantity of good 2 × price in year 2)
+ (quantity of good 3 × price in year 2)
= cost of living at year 2 prices.

Step Four: Find the percentage change in the two costs of living by using the following formula:

$$\left[\left(\frac{\text{cost of living at year 2 prices}}{\text{cost of living at year 1 prices}}\right) - 1\right] \times 100 = \text{inflation rate.}$$

1 (Worked problem: inflation rate) There are three goods consumed in Euthanasia: fast cars, parachute jumps, and hang gliders. The quantities and prices for each in 1990 and the prices in 1991 are given below.

Goods	Quantities	1990 prices	1991 prices
Fast cars	20	$20,000	$30,000
Parachute jumps	2,500	$ 100	$ 80
Hang gliders	400	$ 500	$ 800

The market basket is defined by the quantities indicated in the table.

Calculate the inflation rate.

Step-by-step solution:

Step one: Identify the quantities in the market basket. There are 20 fast cars, 2,500 parachute jumps, and 400 hang gliders.

Step two: Calculate the cost of purchasing the market basket at 1990 prices:

($20,000 × 20) + ($100 × 2,500) + ($500 × 400) = $850,000.

Step three: Calculate the cost of purchasing the market basket at 1991 prices:

($30,000 × 20) × ($80 × 2,500) + ($800 × 400) = $1,120,000.

Step four: Find the percentage change:

($1,120,000/$850,000 − 1) × 100 = 32 percent.

The inflation rate is 32 percent.

2 (Practice problem: inflation rate) In order to determine how to adjust stipends for disabled workers, the Paper Profits Company wants to compute the inflation rate. It has identified a market basket for stipend recipients. This is given below, along with the prices in 1980 (the year of the last adjustment) and in 1990.

Good or service	Quantities	1980 prices	1990 prices
Prepared meals	7	$ 5	$ 6
Housecleaning	1	$25	$30
Physical therapy	3	$50	$75
Compact discs	4	$10	$10

Compute the inflation rate.

3 (Practice problem: inflation rate) A recent graduate of NDP University, Lamont has dozens of job offers. He has narrowed his search to jobs in two cities: Gotham and Smallville. In order to compare the offers, he must compute the relative cost of living in the two cities. His market basket and prices are given below.

Good or service	Quantity	Gotham price	Smallville price
2-bedroom apartment	1	$1,500	$300
Pickup truck	1	$ 600	$400
Meals	90	$ 10	$ 5

How much more expensive (in percent) is the cost of living in Gotham than in Smallville?

Tool Kit 25.2: Adjusting for Inflation

The money value of all goods and services purchased during a year is the nominal GDP. To get a better idea of how actual output changes from year to year, it is important to adjust this number for inflation. Real GDP is nominal GDP adjusted for inflation, and it gives the value of output measured in base year dollars. Follow this procedure to calculate real GDP.

Step one: Calculate this year's price index. Multiply last year's price index by 1 plus the inflation rate (where the inflation rate is expressed as a proportion; for example, 10 percent equals 0.10):

last year's price index × (1 + inflation rate) = current year's price index.

Step two: Calculate this year's real GDP. Divide current nominal GDP by the price index and multiply by 100. The result is current real GDP expressed in base year dollars:

(nominal GDP/price index) × 100 = real GDP.

To express real GDP in any other year's dollars, simply multiply by the price index in the desired year and divide by 100.

4 (Worked problem: adjusting for inflation) The nominal GDP in Monrovia was $2 billion during 1992. The price index for 1991 was 210, and 1992 saw an inflation rate of 30 percent.

 a Calculate the price index in 1992.
 b Calculate real GDP for 1992. Express it in base year dollars.
 c Express real GDP in 1991 dollars.

Step-by-step solution

Step one (a): Calculate the price index for the current year (1992). The price index for 1991 was 210. The inflation rate was 30 percent. The price index for 1992 is

$$210 \times 1.30 = 273.$$

Step two (b): Calculate this year's real GDP. The current nominal GDP is $2 billion. The 1992 real GDP is

$$(\$2 \text{ billion}/273) \times 100 = \$732.6 \text{ million}.$$

Step three (c): Real GDP in 1991 dollars is

$$(\$732.6 \times 210)/100 = \$1,538 \text{ million}.$$

5 (Practice problem: adjusting for inflation) Suppose that the nominal GDP in 1992 is $4 trillion, the 1991 price index is 352, and the 1992 inflation rate is 95 percent.

 a Calculate the price index in 1992.
 b Calculate real GDP for 1992. Express it in base year dollars.
 c Express real GDP in 1991 dollars.

6 (Practice problem: adjusting for inflation) Suppose that sales of new homes total $30 billion in 1992. The 1992 price index is 222. Express the total sales of new homes in base year dollars.

Tool Kit 25.3: Calculating GDP

Gross domestic product is the money value of all goods and services as purchased by their ultimate users. It can be calculated by adding the money value of all final products, by summing the values added by all firms, or by adding the incomes received by all individuals.

Final goods approach

Step one: Determine which goods are purchased by their ultimate users.

Step two: Add the money values (price × quantity) of these goods:

GDP = money value of good 1 +
       money value of good 2 + . . .

Value-added approach

Step one: For each firm, compute the value added by subtracting any payments to other firms from its receipts:

  value added = receipts − purchases from other firms.

Step two: Sum the values added of each firm:

GDP = value added at firm 1 +
      value added at firm 2 + . . .

Income approach

Step one: Find the total wages, total dividends, total interest, and any other form of income for all individuals in the economy.

Step two: Add the totals of each kind of income:

    GDP = wages + dividends + interest.

---

7 (Worked problem: calculating GDP) Suppose that the economy produces three goods: wheat, flour, and bread. All the wheat is sold to millers. All the flour is sold to bakers. Consumers buy the bread from the bakers. The income and expenditure accounts for each of the three industries are given in Table 25.1.

Table 25.1

	Expenditures (billions)	Receipts (billions)
Wheat industry		
Wages	$ 40	$ 50
Dividends	$ 0	
Interest	$ 10	
Flour industry		
Wages	$ 30	$110
Purchases of wheat	$ 50	
Dividends	$ 15	
Interest	$ 15	
Bread industry		
Wages	$ 60	$200
Purchases of flour	$110	
Dividends	$ 30	
Interest	$ 0	

 a Calculate (nominal) GDP using the final goods approach.
 b Calculate (nominal) GDP using the value-added approach.
 c Calculate (nominal) GDP using the income approach.
 d Compare the three answers.

Step-by-step solution

Step one (a): Determine which goods are purchased by their ultimate users. Only bread is a final output.

Step two: Add the money value of these goods. The value of bread is $200. The GDP thus equals $200.

Step three (b): Find the value added for each firm or industry.

value added in wheat = $50 − $0 = $50.
value added in flour = $110 − $50 = $60.
value added in bread = $200 − $110 = $90.

Step four: Sum the value-added numbers.

GDP = $50 + $60 + $90 = $200.

Step five (c): Find the total wages, dividends, and interest.

total wages = $40 + $30 + $60 = $130.
total dividends = $0 + $15 + $30 = $45.
total interest = $10 + $15 + $0 = $25.

Step six: Add the totals of each income type.

GDP = $130 + $45 + $25 = $200.

Step seven (d): Compare. Note that the GDP equals $200 billion according to each method.

8 (Practice problem: calculating GDP) The economy of Literaria cuts down trees in order to make paper and uses all its paper for books. The expenditure and income accounts for each of the three industries are given in Table 25.2.

Table 25.2

	Expenditures (billions)	Receipts (billions)
Tree industry		
Wages	$ 80	$100
Dividends	$ 20	
Interest	$ 0	
Paper industry		
Wages	$100	$250
Purchases of trees	$100	
Dividends	$ 40	
Interest	$ 10	
Book industry		
Wages	$150	$500
Purchases of paper	$250	
Dividends	$ 50	
Interest	$ 50	

 a Calculate (nominal) GDP using the final goods approach.
 b Calculate (nominal) GDP using the value-added approach.
 c Calculate (nominal) GDP using the income approach.
 d Compare the three answers.

9 (Practice problem: calculating GDP) in Computavia, they produce chips, all of which are used in the production of computer hardware. Half the hardware is purchased by consumers, and half is sold to the software industry. Consumers purchase all the software. The expenditure and income accounts for each of the three industries are given in Table 25.3.

Table 25.3

	Expenditures (billions)	Receipts (billions)
Chip industry		
Wages	$ 600	$1,000
Dividends	$ 400	
Interest	$ 0	
Hardware industry		
Wages	$ 600	$2,000
Purchases of chips	$1,000	
Dividends	$ 200	
Interest	$ 200	
Software industry		
Wages	$ 600	$2,000
Purchases of hardware	$1,000	
Dividends	$ 0	
Interest	$ 400	

 a Calculate (nominal) GDP using the final goods approach.
 b Calculate (nominal) GDP using the value-added approach.
 c Calculate (nominal) GDP using the income approach.
 d Compare the three answers.

Answers to Problems

2 {[(42 + 30 + 225 + 40)/(35 + 25 + 150 + 40)] − 1} × 100 = 34.8 percent.

3 {[(1,500 + 600 + 900)/(300 + 400 + 450)] − 1} × 100 = 160.9 percent.

5 a 1992 price index = 352 × 1.95 = 686.4.
  b 1992 real GDP (base year dollars) = (4/686.4) × 100 = $0.58 trillion.
  c 1992 real GDP (1991 dollars) = (0.58 × 352)/100 = $2.042 trillion.

6 (30/222) × 100 = $14 billion.

8 a $500 (books).
  b value added in tree industry = $100 − 0 = $100.
    value added in paper industry = $250 − $100 = $150.
    value added in book industry = $500 − $250 = $250.
    total value added = $100 + $150 + $250 = $500.
  c wages = $80 + $100 + $150 = $330.
    dividends = $20 + $40 + $50 = $110.
    interest = $0 + $10 + $50 = $60.
    total income = $330 + $110 + $60 = $500.
  d Each answer is $500, which is the GDP.

9 a hardware purchased by consumers = $2,000/2 = $1,000.
    software purchased by consumers = $2,000.
    total final goods = $1,000 + $2,000 = $3,000.

b value added in chip industry = $1,000 − $0 = $1,000.
value added in hardware industry = $2,000 − $1,000 = $1,000.
value added in software industry = $2,000 − $1,000 = $1,000.
total value added = $1,000 + $1,000 + $1,000 = $3,000.

c wages = $600 + $600 + $600 = $1,800.
dividends = $400 + $200 + $0 = $600.
interest = $0 + $200 + $400 = $600.
total income = $1,800 + $600 + $600 = $3,000.

d each answer is $3,000, which is the GDP.

AN OVERVIEW OF MACROECONOMICS

Chapter Review

The major macroeconomic issues presented in Chapter 25—unemployment, inflation, and growth—remain central concerns to Chapter 26. The emphasis shifts from measuring these variables to explaining how they move. This chapter provides an overview of the models used for the three major markets—labour, product, and capital—and succeeding chapters examine each market in depth. Chapter 27 takes up the labour market, Chapters 28 to 32 explore the product market, and Chapters 33 to 36 study the capital market and the role of money.

ESSENTIAL CONCEPTS

1 The concerns of modern macroeconomics are rooted in events in economic history: the Great Depression, post–World War II business cycles, the high inflation of the 1970s, and growth and persistent unemployment. Two rival schools of thought dominate the scene. **New Keynesian economists** believe that the economy periodically settles into states of low output and high unemployment, and thus see government in-tervention as an important solution. **New classical economists** view the economy as a system that regulates itself; they see a limited need for government intervention.

2 The aggregate *labour market* includes all the workers and jobs in the economy. If the wage settles at the market-clearing level, the economy is at full employment. Anyone willing to work at the going wage can find a job. In reality, this is not the case, because wages are somewhat inflexible. When the demand for labour shifts to the left (or when supply shifts to the right) and the wage fails to adjust downwards, un-employment exists. The key to understanding un-employment is to know two things: what causes shifts in the demand and supply for labour, and why wages do not adjust to these shifts.

3 The *product market* explains the forces that determine the economy's output of all goods and services—the gross domestic product. The aggregate supply curve shows the output that all firms are willing to supply at each price level. The aggregate demand curve shows the total demand of households, businesses, and gov-ernment at each price level. Product market equilib-rium occurs at the intersection of the two curves.

4 The **aggregate supply curve**, as shown in Figure 26.1, is flat at relatively low output levels, upward sloping at intermediate output levels, and steep at high output levels. Fluctuations in the economy are explained by shifts in aggregate demand and aggregate supply, but the effects of these shifts on output and the price level depend on whether the intersection lies on the flat, upward-sloping, or steep part of the aggregate supply curve. Important product market issues include the causes of shifts in aggregate demand supply, where the intersection of the curves lies, and whether disequilibrium can occur in the product market.

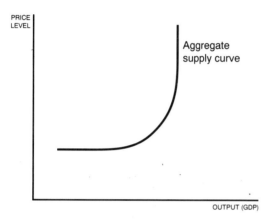

Figure 26.1

5 The **capital market** determines the level of investment in the economy. In the short run, investment is an important component of aggregate demand; the capital market therefore affects the product and labour markets. In the longer run, investment increases the productive capacity of the economy; it shifts aggregate supply to the right, expands the production possibilities curve, and generates growth. The effect of government monetary policies on the capital market, investment, and growth is an important issue in capital market theory.

BEHIND THE ESSENTIAL CONCEPTS

1 You should keep in mind two aspects of wage adjustment. The first is the question of whether wages will adjust to clear the market if labour demand and supply remain stable for a substantial period of time. In other words, is the wage at the intersection of supply and demand? If it is not, then high wages are part of the reason for unemployment. The second issue concerns how quickly wages change when supply or demand shifts. They seem to change rather slowly, and this slow adjustment helps explain why unemployment rises during economic downturns and remains high for significant periods of time. Chapter 27 takes up this topic in greater detail.

2 The supply of labour is quite inelastic, but not perfectly so. If the wage rises, more people are willing to work. If the wage that you could currently earn rose high enough, you might get a part-time job, increase the hours at the part-time job you already have, or even drop out of university to get a full-time job. It follows that if the wage falls, individuals voluntarily leave the labour force. Involuntary unemployment, however, differs from voluntary unemployment. If the wage is stuck above the market-clearing level, there is an excess supply of workers, each of whom would like a job at the going wage. Because there is a shortage of jobs, these individuals are involuntarily unemployed.

3 In the aggregate product market, the shape of the aggregate supply curve and the reasons behind its shape are important to understand. At low levels of output, the aggregate supply curve is quite flat. The economy is producing well below its capacity; there are idle plants and equipment and unemployed workers. It is easy to expand output, and so a small increase in the price level brings about large increases in output. At high levels of output, the aggregate supply curve is vertical. Here the economy is producing virtually all that it can; most plants are operating near their maximum and most individuals who want work can find it. Firms cannot expand output as prices rise.

SELF-TEST

True or False

1 The classical economists believed in a policy of *laissez-faire*.

2 According to real business-cycle theory, the economy occasionally gets mired in situations of high unemployment for extended periods.

3 Macroeconomics is concerned with business cycles and long-term growth.

4 Although the new classical economists base their theories on firm microeconomic principles, the new Keynesian economists do not see the need.

5 The basic model of the labour market assumes that product prices are fixed.

6 By definition, when the labour market clears, there is full employment.

7 Involuntary unemployment results when the demand for labour shifts to the right and wages fail to adjust.

8 The aggregate supply curve is vertical.

9 The aggregate supply curve is flat at relatively low levels of output and steeper at relatively high levels.

10 If aggregate demand and aggregate supply intersect along the flat section of aggregate supply, then a shift to the left in aggregate demand reduces output without reducing the price level. *(little or no change)*

11 The tax cut in Canada in 1965 shifted aggregate supply to the right and a recession was avoided.

12 U.S. President Johnson's policy of paying for the war in Vietnam without a tax increase shifted aggregate demand to the right and caused higher inflation.

13 The oil price shock of the early 1970s shifted aggregate demand to the left and caused a recession.

14 U.S. Federal Reserve Board chairman Paul Volcker's restrictive monetary policies in the early 1980s shifted aggregate demand to the left in the United States; this contributed to the recession in Canada.

15 In the model of the product market, product prices are assumed to be fixed.

Multiple Choice

1 Modern macroeconomics began

a in the 1930s, at the time of the Great Depression.
b in the 1940s, at the time of World War II.
c in the 1960s, at the time of expansionary fiscal policy in Canada and the United States.
d in the 1970s, at the time of the OPEC oil price shock.
e in the 1980s, at the time of U.S. President Ronald Reagan's attempts at supply-side economics.

2 The classical economists did not subscribe to the view that

a the economy might have short bouts of unemployment but would quickly return to full employment.
b prices and wages were flexible.
c markets were in equilibrium most of the time.
d the best economic policy was *laissez-faire.*
e fiscal policy was necessary to maintain full employment.

3 John Maynard Keynes did not subscribe to the view that

a the economy might experience high unemployment and low output for an extended period of time.
b increased government expenditures and reduced taxes were necessary to bring the economy back to full employment.
c markets were often persistently out of equilibrium.
d the best economic policy was *laissez-faire.*
e none of the above.

4 In the 1970s, monetarists argued that inflation was the result of

a government *laissez-faire* policies.
b the failure of markets to be in equilibrium most of the time.
c government fiscal and monetary policies.

d the tendency of the economy to get stuck in situations of high unemployment and low output.
e none of the above.

5 According to real business-cycle theory, fluctuations in the economy

a do not happen.
b are the result of government monetary policies.
c are the result of shocks, such as innovations and natural disasters.
d lead to extended periods of high unemployment and low output.
e are the result of government taxes and expenditures.

6 The leading schools of macroeconomics today are the

a new classical and real business-cycle schools.
b monetarist and Keynesian schools.
c new Keynesian and monetarist schools.
d new classical and new Keynesian schools.
e classical and new classical schools.

7 The basic model of the labour market in this chapter is based on the assumption that

a wages are fixed.
b only product prices are fixed.
c interest rates and product prices are fixed.
d wages and product prices are fixed.
e wages, interest rates, and product prices are fixed.

8 In modern economies, the labour supply curve is

a perfectly elastic.
b relatively flat.
c horizontal.
d relatively inelastic.
e downward sloping.

9 Suppose that the demand for labour increases. If the supply of labour is perfectly inelastic, then

a wages increase.
b employment increases.
c both wages and employment increase.
d wages decrease.
e both wages and employment decrease.

10 One problem with using basic supply and demand analysis to study the labour market is that

a basic supply and demand do not allow for unemployment.
b the supply of labour is relatively inelastic.
c the demand for labour is not always downward sloping.
d the supply of labour is relatively flat at low levels of employment and relatively steep at high levels.
e the demand for labour is relatively flat at low levels of employment and relatively steep at high levels.

11 If the wage is the market-clearing wage, then

a any unemployment is involuntary.
b any unemployment is voluntary.

c unemployment is voluntary at low wages and voluntary at high wages.

d the supply of labour is relatively elastic.

e none of the above.

12 If every worker who wants a job at prevailing wages has one, then there is

a full employment.

b no voluntary unemployment.

c no inflation.

d stagflation

e none of the above.

13 Suppose the demand curve for labour shifts to the left. Then

a there is full employment if wages are inflexible.

b if wages are inflexible, there is involuntary unemployment.

c there is unemployment if the supply of labour is relatively inelastic.

d the supply of labour will also shift to the left.

e none of the above.

14 Suppose the demand curve for labour shifts to the left. If wages are sticky, then

a most workers work fewer hours.

b wages rise.

c most workers work more hours.

d most workers work the same number of hours, but some individuals will not be able to find employment.

e most workers work more hours, but some job vacancies will not be filled.

15 The aggregate supply curve is

a downward sloping.

b relatively flat at low levels of output but relatively steep at higher levels of output.

c relatively steep at low levels of output but relatively flat at higher levels of output.

d relatively inelastic.

e horizontal.

16 The aggregate demand and supply model of the product market presented in this chapter is based on the assumption that

a wages are fixed.

b product prices are fixed.

c interest rates and product prices are fixed.

d wages and product prices are fixed.

e wages, interest rates, and product prices are fixed.

17 Suppose that the aggregate demand curve shifts to the right. If the intersection with aggregate supply lies along the flat portion of the aggregate supply curve, then

a wages increase.

b product prices increase.

c output increases.

d output and product prices increase.

e wages, output, and product prices increase.

18 The 1965 tax cut caused

a aggregate demand to shift to the left.

b aggregate supply to shift to the left.

c aggregate demand to shift to the right.

d aggregate supply to shift to the right.

e no change in either aggregate supply or demand.

19 The oil price shocks of the early 1970s caused

a aggregate demand to shift to the left.

b aggregate supply to shift to the left.

c aggregate demand to shift to the right.

d aggregate supply to shift to the right.

e no change in either aggregate supply or demand.

20 In late 1979 and 1980, aggregate demand shifted to the left; this started a severe recession and reduced inflation dramatically. These events can be partially attributed to

a the Reagan program of tax cuts and increased military spending.

b the monetary policies of the U.S. Federal Reserve Board under Paul Volcker.

c unanticipated shocks to the Canadian economy.

d a series of droughts and other natural disasters.

e several prolonged strikes at major manufacturing plants.

Completion

1 Modern macroeconomics began with the publication in 1936 of *The General Theory of Employment, Interest, and Money* by ___Keynes___.

2 The two leading schools of macroeconomic thought today are the ___Keynesian___ and ___new classical___ schools.

3 When employers pay the market-clearing wage, any unemployment is ___voluntary___.

4 If the demand for labour shifts to the left and there is no adjustment in wages, unemployment ___↑___.

5 When output is low, the aggregate supply curve is relatively ___flat___; when output is high, it is ___steep (vertical)___

6 If the price level is greater than the level at which aggregate demand equals aggregate supply, then there is an excess ___supply___ of goods.

7 The 1965 tax cut shifted the aggregate ___demand___ curve to the ___right___.

8 The oil price shocks of the early 1970s shifted the aggregate ___supply___ curve to the ___left___.

9 In the early 1980s, the U.S. Federal Reserve Board took actions that caused the aggregate ___demand___ curve to shift to the ___left___, and led to both a recession and a reduction in inflation in the United States.

10 Over time, investment increases the productive capacity of the economy and shifts the aggregate ___supply___ curve to the ___right___.

AN OVERVIEW OF MACROECONOMICS • 279

Answers to Self-Test

True or False

1	t	6	t	11	f
2	f	7	f	12	t
3	t	8	f	13	f
4	f	9	t	14	t
5	t	10	t	15	f

Multiple Choice

1	a	6	d	11	b	16	a
2	e	7	c	12	a	17	c
3	d	8	d	13	b	18	c
4	c	9	a	14	d	19	b
5	c	10	a	15	b	20	b

Completion

1 John Maynard Keynes
2 New Keynesian, new classical
3 voluntary
4 increases
5 flat, vertical
6 supply
7 demand, right
8 supply, left
9 demand, left
10 supply, right

Doing Economics: Tools and Practice Problems

In the aggregate labour market, the economy's levels of employment, unemployment, and real wages are determined. Unemployment results from the failure of wages to adjust to the market-clearing level, and several problems explore this relationship between sticky wages and unemployment. The output of the economy is determined in the product market. The key to analyzing how low output is affected by changes in the economy is to find out whether the initial equilibrium lies on the horizontal, upward-sloping, or vertical section of the aggregate supply curve. Several problems study this issue.

Tool Kit 26.1: Determining the Unemployment Rate

When real wages remain stuck above market-clearing levels, the number of workers willing to work at the going wage exceeds the number of jobs available. This excess supply of labour is involuntary unemployment and is part of the overall unemployment rate.

Step one: Identify the demand curve, the supply curve, and the nominal wage and price level.

Step two: Find the real wage by adjusting the nominal wage for inflation:

real wage = (nominal wage/price index) × 100.

Step three: Substitute the real wage into the demand curve and find the quantity demanded. This is the number of jobs available.

Step four: Substitute the real wage into the supply curve and find the quantity supplied. This is the number of workers willing to work at the going wage.

Step five: Find the quantity of unemployment by subtracting the quantity demanded from the quantity supplied:

unemployment =
   quantity supplied – quantity demanded.

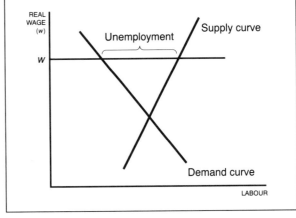

1 (Worked problem: unemployment rate) The nominal wage level equals $2,400 per month, and the price index equals 120. Table 26.1 gives the demand and supply of labour. Find the level of unemployment.

Table 26.1

Real wage	Demand	Supply
$2,400	6,000	18,000
$2,200	7,000	16,000
$2,000	8,000	14,000
$1,800	9,000	12,000
$1,600	10,000	10,000
$1,400	11,000	8,000
$1,200	12,000	6,000

Step-by-step solution

Step one: Identify the demand curve, the supply curve, and the nominal wage and price level. The demand and supply are given in Table 26.1, the nominal wage is $2,400, and the price index equals 120.

Step two: Find the real wage by adjusting the nominal wage for inflation:

real wage = ($2,400/120) × 100 = $2,000.

Step three: Substitute the real wage into the demand curve, and find the quantity demanded. It is 8,000.

Step four: Substitute the real wage into the supply curve, and find the quantity supplied. It is 14,000.

Step five: Find the quantity of unemployment by subtracting the quantity demanded from the quantity supplied:

unemployment = 14,000 − 8,000 = 6,000.

2 (Practice problem: unemployment rate) Suppose that the nominal wage level remains at $2,400, as in problem 1, and the demand and supply curves remain as in Table 26.1 but the price level increases to 150. Find the new level of unemployment.

3 (Practice problem: unemployment rate) Suppose that the nominal wage is $3,300, the price index is 150, and the demand and supply curves are as given in Table 26.1. Find the level of unemployment.

4 (Practice problem: unemployment rate) For each of the following, find the level of unemployment given the demand and supply of labour shown in Table 26.2.

a Nominal wage = $50,000; price level = 100.
b Nominal wage = $50,000; price level = 125.
c Nominal wage = $50,000; price level = 167.
d Nominal wage = $60,000; price level = 120.

Table 26.2

Real wage	Demand	Supply
$60,000	8,000	26,000
$55,000	10,000	25,000
$50,000	12,000	24,000
$45,000	14,000	23,000
$40,000	16,000	22,000
$35,000	18,000	21,000
$30,000	20,000	20,000
$25,000	22,000	19,000

Tool Kit 26.2: Sticky Real Wages and Unemployment

When either the demand or supply of labour shifts and wages fail to adjust to the market-clearing level, there is unemployment. In modern economies, wages exhibit downward rigidity, although they do adjust upwards when conditions warrant it.

Step one: Start with a market-clearing equilibrium in the labour market.

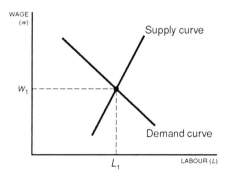

Step two: Identify a cause, and determine which curve shifts.

Step three: Shift the supply or demand curve.

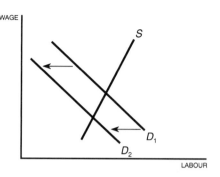

Step four: Find the new equilibrium. If there is excess demand, increase the real wage to the market-clearing level. If there is excess supply, keep the real wage constant.

Step five: Show the level of unemployment as the difference between quantity demanded and quantity supplied.

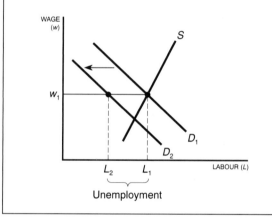

5 (Worked problem: sticky wages) Suppose a deep recession strikes the economy. Show the effect on real wages, unemployment, and the labour market.

Step-by-step solution

Step one: Start with an equilibrium.

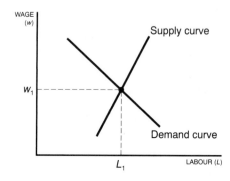

Step two: Identify a cause, and determine which curve shifts. The economy's output falls in a recession, and this reduces the demand for labour.

Step three: Shift the demand curve. It shifts left.

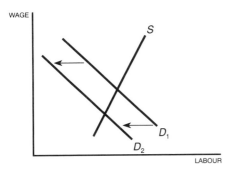

Step four: Find the new equilibrium. Although there is an excess supply of labour, wages do not adjust downwards, because they are assumed sticky.

Step five: Show the level of unemployment.

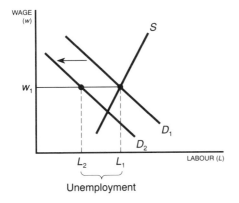

6 (Practice problem: sticky wages) Strife abroad leads to a wave of new immigration. Show the effect on real wages, unemployment, and the labour market.

7 (Practice problem: sticky wages) For each of the following, show the effect on real wages, unemployment, and the labour market.

   a The economy booms, and its output increases.
   b As barriers fall, millions of women enter the labour market.
   c The demand for Canadian exports soars, and the economy's output expands to meet the demand.
   d The baby bust generation reaches working age, and the number of new entrants declines.
   e Recession overseas reduces the demand for Canadian exports, and the economy falls into a recession.

Tool Kit 26.3: Using Aggregate Demand and Supply

The economy's equilibrium output and price level are determined in the product market at the intersection of aggregate demand and aggregate supply. The aggregate supply curve is flat at low levels of output, upward sloping at intermediate levels, and nearly vertical at high levels where the economy approaches its capacity. Factors that shift either aggregate demand or aggregate supply change the levels of output and prices. The impact of these shifts depends on where the initial equilibrium lies on the aggregate supply curve. Table 26.3 summarizes the factors that shift aggregate demand and supply.

Table 26.3

Shifts in aggregate demand: changes in consumption, investment, government spending, or net exports.

Shifts in aggregate supply: increases in capacity (aggregate supply shifts right) or changes in import prices (aggregate supply shifts up or down).

Step one: Start with an equilibrium. This will be on the flat, upward-sloping, or vertical portion of the aggregate supply curve.

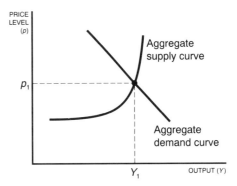

Step two: Identify a cause, and determine which curve shifts and in what direction.

Step three: Shift the curve.

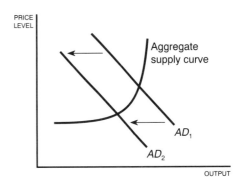

Step four: Find the new equilibrium, and compare the output and price levels.

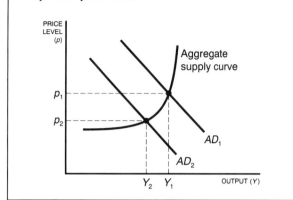

8 (Worked problem: aggregate demand and supply) The economy is in deep recession with high unemployment and a great deal of excess capacity. The government grants an investment tax credit, and firms respond with larger levels of private investment. Show the effect on equilibrium output and the price level.

Step-by-step solution

Step one: Start with an equilibrium. Because the economy is in deep recession, this will be on the flat portion of the aggregate supply curve.

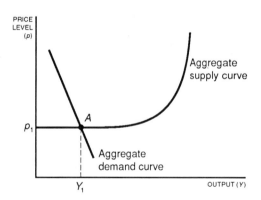

Step two: Identify a cause, and determine which curve shifts and in what direction. The increase in investment shifts aggregate demand to the right.

Step three: Shift the curve.

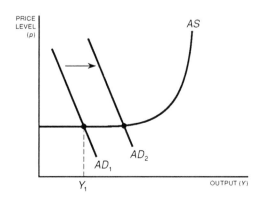

Step four: Find the new equilibrium, and compare the output and price levels. Output increases with little or no change in the price level.

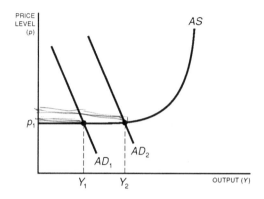

9 (Practice problem: aggregate demand and supply) The economy is brimming with activity. Although unemployment and idle production capacity are at 10-year lows, foreign demand for Canadian exports surges still higher. Show the effect on equilibrium output and the price level.

10 (Problem: aggregate demand and supply) For each of the following, show the effect on equilibrium output and the price level.

  a The economy is in equilibrium along the upward-sloping portion of aggregate supply. Tight monetary policy raises interest rates, and this causes a dramatic decline in new investment.
  b The economy is in deep recession, and the government stimulates private consumption with a tax cut.
  c The economy is at maximum capacity, and the government increases its spending.
  d The economy is in equilibrium along the upward-sloping portion of aggregate supply. The government increases income taxes.
  e The economy is in deep recession, and foreign demand for exports falls still further.
  f The economy is in equilibrium along the upward-sloping portion of aggregate supply. The price of imported oil rises by 50 percent.
  g The economy is in deep recession, and the price of imported oil rises by 50 percent.
  h The economy is at maximum capacity. Capacity expands.

Answers to Problems

2 Real wage = ($2,400/150) × 100 = $1,600; unemployment = 10,000 − 10,000 = 0.

3 Real wage = ($3,300/150) × 100 = $2,200; unemployment = 16,000 − 7,000 = 9,000.

4 *a* Real wage = ($50,000/100) × 100 = $50,000; unemployment = 24,000 − 12,000 = 12,000.
   b Real wage = ($50,000/125) × 100 = $40,000; unemployment = 22,000 − 16,000 = 6,000.

c Real wage = ($50,000/167) × 100 = $30,000; unemployment = 20,000 − 20,000 = 0.

d Real wage = ($60,000/120) × 100 = $50,000; unemployment = 24,000 − 12,000 = 12,000.

6 The supply curve shifts to the right, and the wage fails to adjust downwards; this results in unemployment equal to $L_s - L_1$.

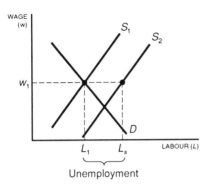

7 *a* The demand curve shifts to the right, and wages adjust upwards to clear the market.

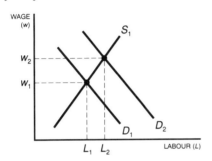

b The supply curve shifts to the right, and the wage falls to adjust downwards; this results in unemployment equal to $L_s - L_1$.

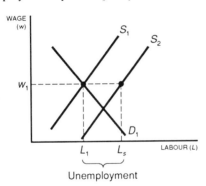

c The demand curve shifts to the right, and wages adjusts upwards to clear the market.

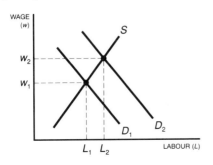

d The supply curve shifts to the left, and the wage adjust upwards to clear the market.

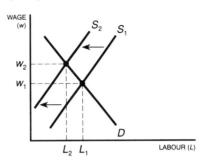

e The demand curve shifts to the left, and the wage fails to adjust downwards; this results in unemployment equal to $L_1 - L_s$.

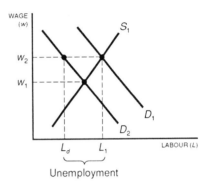

9 Aggregate demand shifts to the right; this increases the price level and leaves output unchanged.

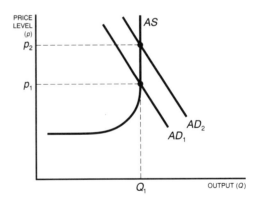

10 *a* Aggregate demand shifts to the left and decreases output and the price level.

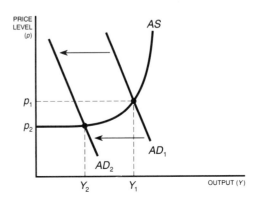

b Aggregate demand shifts to the right; this increases output and leaves the price level unchanged.

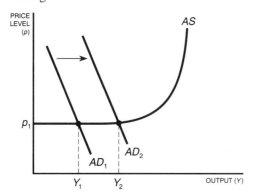

c Aggregate demand shifts to the right; this increases the price level and leaves output unchanged.

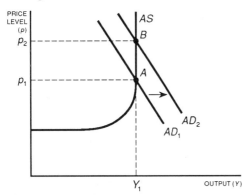

d Aggregate demand shifts to the left and decreases output and the price level.

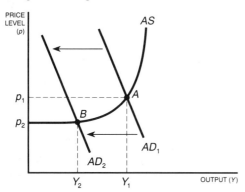

e Aggregate demand shifts to the left; this decreases output and leaves the price level unchanged.

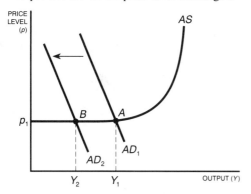

f Aggregate supply shifts to the left; this increases the price level and decreases output.

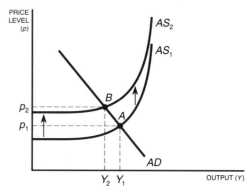

g Aggregate supply shifts to the left; this increases the price level and decreases output.

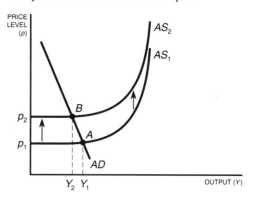

h Aggregate supply shifts to the right; this decreases the price level and increases output.

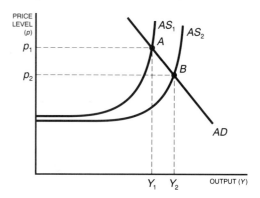

Chapter 27

THE AGGREGATE LABOUR MARKET

Chapter Review

In Chapter 26, we saw how macroeconomics analyzes and explains the economy in terms of three markets: labour, product, and capital. This chapter focuses on the labour market to examine the causes of unemployment more closely. The key issues of this chapter are the causes of shifts in demand and supply in the labour market and why wages do not adjust to clear the market and bring about full employment. Much of the remainder of the book is devoted to the macroeconomic analysis of the other two major markets: the product market and the capital market.

ESSENTIAL CONCEPTS

1   In the labour market, the demanders are firms, which hire workers, and the suppliers are individuals, who offer themselves for work. But many workers are unemployed. The central question here is why the real wage does not adjust to clear the market. Because wages are rigid, they remain at levels where the quantity of workers supplied exceeds the quantity demanded. Thus, the extra workers who cannot find jobs are involuntarily unemployed.

2   Wages may not adjust to bring about full employment for several reasons.

   a   **Union contracts** may specify wages above the market-clearing level. If the demand for labour falls, the union may not agree to accept lower wages.
   b   Firms may have informal agreements, or **implicit contracts**, with their risk-averse workers to provide fixed wages as a kind of insurance against economic downturns.
   c   **Insider-outsider theory** suggests that because existing workers must train new hires, the current work force may be unwilling to provide training to newly hired workers unless the new workers are paid the same wage as existing workers.
   d   **Minimum wage laws** mandate a price floor in the labour market.
   e   **Efficiency wage theory** shows how firms may make higher profits by paying wages that are above the market-clearing level, because workers have incentives to work harder and be more productive.
   f   When the wage level in the economy falls, product prices may also fall; this results in a (relatively) **constant real wage**.

3 There are three reasons why firms can increase the productivity of their workers by paying the higher efficiency wage rather than the market wage.

    a When a firm cuts its wage, some workers leave. These workers are likely to be the firm's most productive workers who will have good alternatives elsewhere. The pool of the firm's new hires will be of lower quality when the wage offer is less. Thus, the overall quality of the work force is poorer at lower wages. This phenomenon is called adverse selection.

    b Workers may put forth greater effort on a job that pays more than alternative jobs. In effect, the higher wage makes the job more valuable and motivates the worker to work harder for fear of losing the high-paying job.

    c By paying higher wages, firms can reduce the rate at which workers quit—the labour turnover rate. Because it is costly to hire and train new workers, a firm's profits may be higher than they would be if the firm paid lower wages.

4 The **risk-incentive trade-off** illustrates the fact that when workers are protected from risk, they lose incentives to put forth effort. Two examples of this trade-off are **profit sharing** and **unemployment insurance**.

    a If workers receive more of their wages in the form of profit sharing, their earnings become more flexible; they rise in booms and fall in recessions. Such a policy reduces the risk of unemployment, yet increases the risk of income loss during economic downturns.

    b Unemployment insurance protects workers against income loss if they are laid off, yet it reduces their incentives to find and accept new jobs.

BEHIND THE ESSENTIAL CONCEPTS

1 While each of the reasons for wage rigidity listed above has some validity, the efficiency wage theory is the most satisfactory explanation. Economists favour efficiency wage theory because it explains three important facts about the labour market: the failure of wages to adjust to market-clearing levels, the fact that firms lay off excess workers during downturns rather than share the available work equally among the firm's total labour demand, and the fact that wages adjust slowly when economic conditions change.

2 The efficiency wage theory explains rigid wages in the following way. Suppose you are an employer. You need quality workers who put forth a lot of effort and remain loyal to your firm. Your problem is how to keep and motivate your good workers. If you pay the market-clearing wage, jobs with your firm will be worth no more than those with other firms. Your workers will know that they can quickly find work elsewhere at the going wage. The efficiency wage solves the problem in a very clever way. It is part carrot and part stick. You offer the carrot of higher wages, and gain influence over your workers with the stick, which is the threat to take away the job. Your workers have good incentives to stay, because the job is now worth more than their alternatives.

3 Once you understand why one firm gains by paying its workers wages above market-clearing levels, you can then see that other firms will do the same. It might seem to you that if all firms pay higher wages, then no firm offers anything special. But because all wages are higher than the market-clearing level, there remains a surplus of unemployed workers and not enough jobs to go around. Losing a valuable job represents a substantial cost to your workers, not because other jobs pay less, but because workers without jobs face a considerable time of unemployment.

4 Unemployment is a surplus of labour, or workers. You might ask, "Why don't the unemployed offer to work for less?" After all, the usual explanation for why the price of anything adjusts down to the market-clearing level is that the suppliers who cannot find buyers offer to sell at lower prices. In the efficiency wage world, however, if the unemployed offer to work at lower wages, the manager of the firm will conclude that they are either low-quality workers who will not make the required effort or that they will soon look for other employment. Remember that the efficiency wage is just high enough to attract, motivate, and keep high-quality workers. Any offer to do high-quality work for less is simply not credible.

5 When the demand for labour falls during economic downturns, firms use layoffs to reduce the size of the work force rather than share the available work among their workers. Why? According to the efficiency wage view, sharing work lowers average earnings in the same way that cutting wages does. If you let your employees share the work, you will lose your high-quality workers and have difficulty motivating those who stay. It is better to use layoffs.

6 A final implication of the efficiency wage theory is that wages adjust slowly. Put yourself again in the shoes of an employer. If business falls off, you may want to cut wages, but first you must see whether your competitors will reduce *their* wages. If you move too soon, you may lose your best workers. Efficiency wage theory counsels waiting, perhaps spending a few dollars more in labour costs.

SELF-TEST

True or False

T 1 The model of the total labour market studied in this chapter is based on the assumption that product prices are fixed.

F 2 Seasonally unemployed workers are involuntarily unemployed.

3 Skilled unemployed workers may not accept temporary employment at low-wage jobs because potential employers may infer from their low wages a lack of confidence in ability. *T*

T (4) Employment levels fluctuate quite dramatically; nevertheless, real wages are rather stable.

(5) Most union contracts contain provisions for adjusting wages downwards when the firm's demand for labour shifts. *F*

T (6) Cost-of-living adjustment provisions (COLAs) prevent real wages from falling even if inflation increases.

7 An implicit contract is an informal arrangement between workers and firms, often involving the firm's paying constant wages even as the wages its workers could receive elsewhere change. *T*

F (8) Implicit contract theory explains why real wages of job seekers do not decline significantly during recessions.

9 Insider-outsider theory argues that a firm's current workers refuse to train new hires unless the new hires receive the same wage as existing workers. *T*

10 The minimum wage is a price ceiling in the market for unskilled labour. *floor* *F*

T (11) According to efficiency wage theory, the firm can make higher profits by paying higher wages.

(12) One reason firms may not wish to pay lower wages is the adverse selection effect, whereby the average quality of the pool of workers willing to accept a job with a firm depends upon the wage offered. *T*

F 13 As a general rule, the efficiency wage is *less* than the market-clearing wage. *more*

14 Efficiency wage theory implies that wages will adjust slowly because firms are reluctant to change wages before their competitors do. *T*

F 15 Unemployment affects most demographic groups *unequally*.

Multiple Choice

16/20

1 The demand curve for labour studied in this chapter

a shows the total amount of labour demanded by all firms in the economy at each wage.
b is drawn assuming that product prices can vary.
c may shift to the right but never shifts to the left.
d is upward sloping, according to efficiency wage theory.
e is perfectly elastic.

2 Unemployed workers may not seek temporary employment at low-wage jobs because

a low-wage jobs are reserved for recent immigrants.
b taking a low-wage job may suggest to potential employers that the individual does not need a job.
c taking a low-wage job may suggest to potential employers that the individual lacks confidence in his or her abilities.

d low-wage jobs are reserved for teenagers.
e none of the above.

3 Which of the following is not a possible explanation for wage rigidity? — wages same

a The supply curve of labour is horizontal (perfectly elastic).
b The labour supply curve shifts whenever the labour demand curve shifts.
c The demand curve for labour is perfectly inelastic.
d Union contracts restrict wage adjustment.
e Some firms have implicit contracts with their risk-averse workers to provide insurance by paying the same wage even as the market wage varies.

4 Unemployment results if

a the demand for labour shifts to the left, or the supply of labour shifts to the right, and the wage fails to rise.
b the demand for labour shifts to the left, or the supply of labour shifts to the right, and the wage fails to fall.
c the demand for labour shifts to the right, or the supply of labour shifts to the left, and the wage fails to rise.
d the demand for labour shifts to the right, or the supply of labour shifts to the left, and the wage fails to fall.
e none of the above.

5 If the supply of labour is upward sloping and demand shifts to the right, then

a if wages adjust to the market-clearing level, anyone willing to work at the going wage can eventually find a job.
b if wages adjust to the market-clearing level, any unemployment will be involuntary.
c if wages adjust to the market-clearing level, employment will decrease.
d if wages do not adjust to the market-clearing level, any unemployment will be involuntary.
e if wages do not adjust to the market-clearing level, the supply of labour will shift to the right.

6 In modern economies, when the demand for labour falls,

a the real wage always falls to clear the market.
b the real wage does not change, but workers share the available jobs by each working fewer hours.
c the real wage does not change, but workers share the available jobs by rotating between full time and unemployment.
d the real wage does not change, and some workers are laid off while others retain employment.
e none of the above.

7 Which of the following is not an explanation of the failure of real wages to adjust to changes in the demand and supply of labour?

a union contracts.
b implicit contracts.

- c   insider-outsider theory.
- d   efficiency wage theory.
- e   none of the above.

8   The minimum wage is a

- a   price floor in the labour market, causing the quantity of workers demanded to exceed the quantity supplied.
- b   price floor in the labour market, causing the quantity of workers demanded to be less than the quantity supplied.
- c   price ceiling in the labour market, causing the quantity of workers demanded to exceed the quantity supplied.
- d   price ceiling in the labour market, causing the quantity of workers demanded to be less than the quantity supplied.
- e   none of the above.

9   The theory that argues that firms have an informal agreement to protect risk-averse workers from variations in their incomes by paying the same wage even though their alternative wage changes is called

- a   efficiency wage theory.
- b   implicit contract theory.
- c   insider-outsider theory.
- d   minimum wage theory.
- e   none of the above.

10   The theory that points out that it is not in the interests of the firm's workers to train newcomers if the new hires receive lower wages is

- a   efficiency wage theory.
- b   implicit contract theory.
- c   insider-outsider theory.
- d   minimum wage theory.
- e   none of the above.

11   The theory that says that wages above market-clearing wages motivate workers to put forth greater effort to remain with the high-paying firm is

- a   efficiency wage theory.
- b   implicit contract theory.
- c   insider-outsider theory.
- d   minimum wage theory.
- e   none of the above.

12   Typically, when the firm's demand for labour falls, it

- a   immediately cuts wages for all workers.
- b   shares the available work among all its workers.
- c   reduces the size of its labour force through layoffs.
- d   leaves some of its capital stock idle in order to keep its workers busy.
- e   retains its entire work force at current wages, hoping that business will return.

13   Which of the following is not true? Efficiency wages

- a   motivate workers.
- b   retain high-quality workers.
- c   attract high-quality job applicants.
- d   reduce turnover.
- e   encourage the labour market to clear.

14   Unemployment typically

- a   affects different groups in the economy equally.
- b   affects high-skilled, high-wage workers more because employers can save more in labour costs by laying them off.
- c   affects lower-skilled and part-time workers more.
- d   affects only those paid on a piece-rate basis.
- e   none of the above.

15   The system under which workers are paid on the basis of what they produce is called

- a   efficiency wages.
- b   implicit contracts.
- c   the insider-outsider system.
- d   minimum wages.
- e   piece work.

16   If wages and prices fall in the same proportion, then real wages

- a   increase.
- b   decrease.
- c   stay the same.
- d   may increase or decrease depending on the absolute level of the real wage.
- e   may increase or decrease depending on the absolute level of the nominal wage.

17   Firms that keep their best workers on the payroll hoping that business will pick up are engaging in

- a   piece work.
- b   labour hoarding.
- c   profit sharing.
- d   layoffs.
- e   union busting.

18   Okun's law asserts that

- a   for every 1 percent increase in output, employment increases by 1 percent.
- b   for every 1 percent increase in employment, output increases by 3 percent.
- c   for every 1 percent increase in employment, output increases by less than 1 percent.
- d   for every 1 percent increase in output, employment increases 3 percent.
- e   for every 1 percent increase in output, employment increases by less than 1 percent.

19   If workers received some of their compensation in the form of bonuses tied to the profit level, which of the following would not occur?

- a   more flexible wages
- b   a greater risk of income fluctuations for workers
- c   a lower rate of unemployment
- d   a lower rate of employment
- e   none of the above

20   Unemployment compensation

- a   increases the risk of income fluctuations for workers.

b reduces unemployment.

c gives unemployed workers more incentive to look for and accept job offers.

d increases both risk and incentives to look for work.

e decreases both risk and incentives to look for work.

Completion

1 Wage rigidities refers to the failure of wages to adjust sufficiently to changes in the demand or supply curve of labour.

2 An understanding between a firm and its workers that requires the payment of constant wages is called an implicit contract

3 According to insider-outsider theory, the current employees of a firm refuse to train new hires unless the new hires receive wages that are comparable to those of existing workers.

4 The minimum wage is a government-mandated price floor in the labour market.

5 According to efficiency wage theory, firms can make higher/ more profits by paying more than the wage that would clear the market.

6 Paying higher wages can increase productivity by attracting more qualified workers, increasing effort, and reducing turnover.

7 The wage that minimizes total labour costs is called the efficiency wage.

8 Because it is expensive to hire and fire workers, firms may hoard employees during recessions.

9 Making wages more flexible by substituting some form of profit sharing may be unattractive to workers who are relatively risk-averse

10 Unemployment insurance reduces the risk associated with unemployment, but it also reduces the incentives of the unemployed to search for work.

Answers to Self-Test

True or False

1	t	6	t	11	t
2	f	7	t	12	t
3	t	8	f	13	f
4	t	9	t	14	t
5	f	10	f	15	f

Multiple Choice

1	a	6	d	11	a	16	c
2	d	7	e	12	c	17	b
3	c	8	b	13	e	18	b
4	b	9	b	14	c	19	d
5	a	10	c	15	e	20	e

Completion

1 rigidity
2 implicit contract

3 insider-outsider
4 floor
5 higher
6 productivity
7 efficiency
8 hoard
9 risk averse
10 incentives

Doing Economics: Tools and Practice Problems

Involuntary unemployment results when the wage does not adjust to clear the market. Efficiency wage theory explains the failure of wages to bring about full employment. It also implies that firms will use layoffs (rather than job sharing) to reduce the work force when the demand for labour is low, and wages will adjust slowly as conditions change. In this section, we learn how to determine the efficiency wage.

Tool Kit 27.1: Determining the Efficiency Wage

Firms perceive that the productivity of their workers depends upon the wage. Higher wages motivate workers to put forth effort, attract a high-quality pool of applicants, and reduce turnover. When productivity depends on the wage, the profit-maximizing strategy for the firm is to set the wage at the level that attains the highest output per dollar. This level is achieved when the ratio of productivity (output per hour) to the wage rate is maximized.

Step one: Identify and graph the wage-productivity relationship.

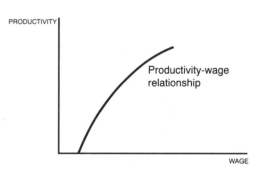

Step two: Calculate the ratio of productivity to the wage for each wage level. This ratio gives output per dollar spent on labour:

output per dollar = productivity/wage.

Step three: Choose the wage for which the corresponding productivity-wage ratio is the highest. Label this point *A* on the graph of the wage-productivity relationship.

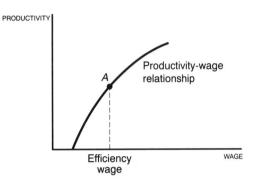

Step four: Draw a line from the origin to *A*. The slope of this line is the productivity-wage ratio. The line should be tangent, and so indicates that output per dollar is maximized.

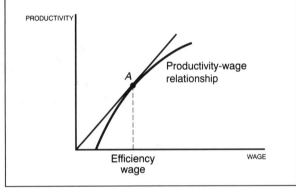

1 (Worked problem: efficiency wage) Murray's Auto Parts has had trouble with labour turnover. Once its workers are trained, they leave. A consultant points out that productivity would be higher if the firm could keep its workers and that one way to discourage quitting is to pay higher wages. The consultant estimates that the relationship between productivity and wages is as shown in Table 27.1.

Table 27.1

Wage (per hour)	Productivity (sales per hour)
$4	8.00
$5	12.50
$6	18.00
$7	24.50
$8	26.00
$9	27.00

Determine the efficiency wage for Murray's.

Step-by-step solution

Step one: Identify and graph the wage-productivity relationship.

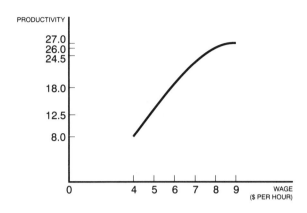

Step two: Calculate the ratio of productivity to the wage for each wage level. This ratio is shown in Table 27.2.

Table 27.2

Wage ($ per hour)	Productivity (sales per hour)	Productivity/wage
$4	8.00	2.00
$5	12.50	2.50
$6	18.00	3.00
$7	24.50	3.50
$8	26.00	3.25
$9	27.00	3.00

Step three: Choose the wage for which the corresponding productivity-wage ratio is the highest. The efficiency wage is $7 per hour and is shown as point *A*.

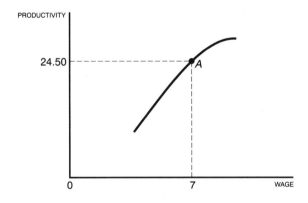

Step four: Draw a line from the origin to *A*. The slope of this line is the productivity-wage ratio, which is 3.5. The line is tangent; this indicates that output per dollar is maximized.

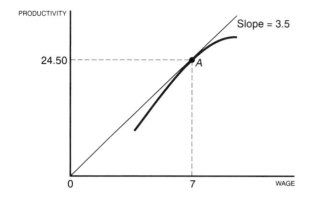

2 (Practice problem: efficiency wage) Moe's Lawn Care has plenty of customers, but Moe is having difficulty getting his mowers to work hard. He cannot monitor each worker all the time and suspects that there is considerable shirking on the job. His brother-in-law, always ready with helpful advice, suggests that if wages were higher, his workers would put forth more effort for fear of losing a well-paying job. Moe considers this and estimates that the relationship between wages and productivity is as appears in Table 27.3.

Table 27.3

Wage (per month)	Productivity (hectares mowed per month)
$ 900	800
$1,000	1,000
$1,100	1,320
$1,200	1,680
$1,300	1,950
$1,400	1,960

Determine the efficiency wage for Moe's business.

3 (Practice problem: efficiency wage) Luke's Warm and Now food delivery business needs good drivers. He thinks that he may get a better pool of applicants if he offers higher wages. Table 27.4 shows the relationship between the wage and productivity.

Table 27.4

Wage (per week)	Productivity (deliveries per week)
$200	110
$220	114
$240	130
$260	146
$280	160
$300	168

Determine the efficiency wage.

Answers to Problems

2 Table 27.5 shows the productivity-wage ratio. The efficiency wage is $1,300 per month, as shown in the diagram.

Table 27.5

Wage	Productivity	Productivity/wage
$ 900	800	0.89
$1,000	1,000	1.00
$1,000	1,320	1.20
$1,200	1,680	1.40
$1,300	1,950	1.50
$1,400	1,960	1.40

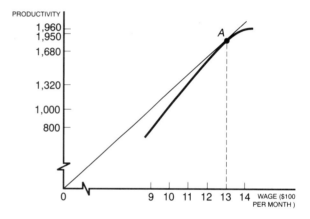

3 Table 27.6 shows the productivity-wage ratio.

Table 27.6

Wage	Productivity	Productivity/wage
$200	100	0.50
$220	114	0.52
$240	130	0.54
$260	146	0.56
$280	160	0.57
$300	168	0.56

The efficiency wage is $280 per week, as shown in the diagram.

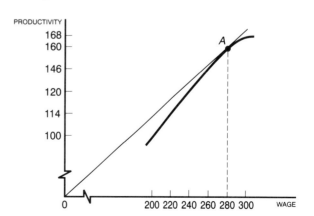

Chapter 28

AGGREGATE DEMAND

Chapter Review

Chapters 28 to 32 shift the emphasis from demand and supply in the aggregate labour market to the aggregate demand and supply of products, which determine the economy's output, or gross domestic product (GDP). Chapter 26 showed that product markets are governed by the interplay of aggregate supply and aggregate demand. In many cases, particularly in the short run, it is possible to be more specific: product markets are governed by aggregate demand. This chapter looks behind the aggregate demand curve and explains what it is composed of and how it is determined. The chapter develops income-expenditure analysis and uses it to show how the economy reaches an equilibrium on the demand side and why the equilibrium changes. The multiplier process, by which changes in spending ripple through the economy, is explained. The next two chapters continue the development of income-expenditure analysis with a detailed look at each component of expenditure. The full aggregate demand and supply model returns in Chapter 31.

ESSENTIAL CONCEPTS

1   **Income-expenditure analysis** starts with the assumption that the price level is fixed. Aggregate ex-

penditures then depend upon national income, and the **aggregate expenditures schedule,** drawn in Figure 28.1, shows how aggregate expenditures increase as national income increases. Because national income equals national output (GDP), the horizontal axis also measures output. Aggregate expenditures equal output where the aggregate expenditures schedule crosses the 45-degree line. This is the equilibrium, and at this point all the economy's output is purchased.

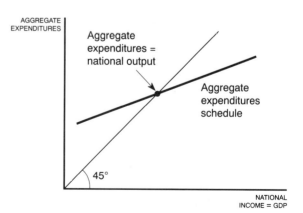

Figure 28.1

2 Aggregate expenditures are the sum of consumption, investment, government purchases, and net exports, as shown by the equation

$$AE = C + I + G + E.$$

Changes in any of the components of expenditure shift the aggregate expenditures schedule up or down and cause equilibrium output to change. In Figure 28.2 AE shifts up and output increases.

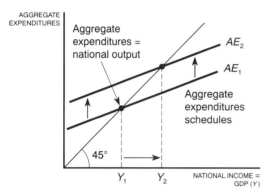

Figure 28.2

3 The **consumption function** describes the relationship between income and consumption. The additional consumption resulting from a one-dollar increase in income is the **marginal propensity to consume** (MPC), which is the slope of the consumption function. The **marginal propensity to save** (MPS) is the additional amount saved out of a one-dollar increase in income.

4 The **multiplier process** shows that when aggregate expenditures shift, the change in output is greater than the change in spending. It works as follows. Suppose investment increases. This investment causes incomes to rise and, through the marginal propensity to consume, causes a second round of extra consumption spending. This extra round of consumption further increases incomes and generates a third round of spending. The process continues, and the ultimate increase in output equals the multiplier times the initial change in spending. The formula for the multiplier is $1/(1 - \text{MPC})$.

5 Income taxation makes the consumption function flatter because some of the extra income is taken in taxes, rather than spent. Similarly, in an open economy, some spending leaves the economy for imported goods; this further flattens the aggregate expenditures schedule. Both taxes and imports cause the multiplier to be smaller.

BEHIND THE ESSENTIAL CONCEPTS

1 This chapter introduces a very important concept. Income-expenditure analysis is one of the central models in macroeconomics. It has three components.

a First, aggregate expenditures (what households and firms want to spend) are related to income. The relationship is summarized by the aggregate expenditures schedule. This is a behavioural relationship.

b Second, national income equals national output. This identity means that the horizontal axis also measures output.

c Third, when spending equals output, all the economy's goods and services are sold, and the economy is in equilibrium. This occurs at the intersection of the AE schedule and the 45-degree line.

2 You might wonder what role prices play in income-expenditure analysis. Prices are determined by supply and demand, but here we are concerned only with the demand side. At this level of analysis, prices are fixed; one way of thinking about this is that the economy is operating on the flat portion of the aggregate supply curve.

3 How does the economy reach equilibrium without price adjustment? **Inventories** play the key role.

a If GDP is below equilibrium, then households and firms want to buy more than the economy produces. Firms notice this when they sell the goods they have on inventory. Firms produce more to restore inventories, and GDP increases.

b If GDP is above equilibrium, the story is reversed. Households and firms buy less than the economy produces, inventories of unsold goods accumulate, and firms cut back on production. GDP falls.

4 A helpful way to understand the multiplier process and why the multiplier is smaller when there are taxes and trade is to think in terms of injections and leakages. Suppose that the economy gets an injection of new spending, say an increase in exports. Some people will receive this money, and they will save some and spend some. We say that the money that is saved "leaks" out of the system. The money that is spent becomes other people's income; they in turn save some and spend some, and the process continues. The total amount of spending generated is a multiple of the initial injection. But any leakage reduces the total amount of spending. Clearly, taxes go to the government. That is a leakage. Money spent on imports goes abroad—another leakage. More leakages means less spending and a smaller multiplier.

SELF-TEST

True or False

1 Aggregate expenditures include what households, firms, and government spend on goods and services produced in Canada.

2 As income increases by one dollar, aggregate expenditures increase by less than one dollar.

F 3 The statement that national income equals national output is an example of an equilibrium relationship.

T 4 The statement that aggregate expenditures equal national output is an example of an equilibrium relationship. AE = Y

T 5 Unplanned inventories equal zero in equilibrium. (p. 763-4)

F 6 The aggregate expenditures schedule gives total desired spending at each price level. (not)

T 7 Aggregate expenditures equal consumption plus investment plus government purchases plus net exports.

F 8 Net exports equal imports minus exports. X-M = E

T 9 The relationship between a household's income and its consumption is called its consumption function.

F 10 Disposable income equals national income plus taxes. minus

F 11 The marginal propensity to consume equals the marginal propensity to save. MPC = ? - 1

F 12 The multiplier equals 1 divided by the marginal propensity to consume. $\frac{1}{1-MPC}$

T 13 An increase in investment causes equilibrium output to increase by more than the change in investment. ↑I (multiplier)

F 14 A higher tax rate on income means that the multiplier is larger. smaller

T 15 Imports increase as income increases. ↑M

Multiple Choice

 AS / AD

1 This chapter focuses on aggregate demand and its intersection with

   a the entire aggregate supply curve.
   b the upward-sloping portion of the aggregate supply curve.
   c the horizontal portion of the aggregate supply curve.
   d the vertical portion of the aggregate supply curve.
   e none of the above.

2 The aggregate expendures schedule traces the relationship between the economy's total expenditures and national income. AE

   a keeping output fixed.
   b at a given price level.
   c as price changes to clear the product market.
   d holding consumption fixed.
   e holding net exports fixed.

3 As income increases, aggregate expenditures income↑ AE

   a increase.
   b decrease.
   c remain the same.
   d increase or decrease depending on how product prices change.
   e increase or decrease depending on events in the capital market.

4 The marginal propensity to consume gives MPC (wordy)

   a the fraction of extra income that will be consumed.
   b the ratio of consumption to income.
   c the fraction of extra consumption that comes from wage income.
   d the fraction of extra consumption that comes from interest and dividends.
   e the ratio of consumption out of wage income to consumption out of interest and dividend income.

5 The aggregate expenditures schedule AE

   a is horizontal.
   b is horizontal for low levels of output, upward sloping for intermediate levels of output, and steep at high levels of output.
   c is upward sloping.
   d is downward sloping.
   e is a 45-degree line.

6 If national income were zero, consumption would

   a be zero.
   b be positive because people would borrow or consume out of savings.
   c be less than autonomous consumption.
   d exceed autonomous consumption.
   e none of the above.

7 The statement that national income is equal to national output is an example of

   a an equilibrium relationship.
   b an identity.
   c a behavioural relationship.
   d a hypothesis.
   e an assumption.

8 The statement that aggregate expenditures equal aggregate output is an example of

   a an equilibrium relationship.
   b an identity.
   c a behavioural relationship.
   d a hypothesis.
   e an assumption.

9 Which of the following is not true? In equilibrium

   a the output of the economy must be purchased.
   b aggregate expenditures equal national output.
   c aggregate expenditures equal what households, firms, and government want to spend at the equilibrium level of national income.
   d unplanned inventories equal zero.
   e autonomous consumption equals zero. consumption depend on level of income. doesn't depend of income

10 An upward shift in the aggregate expenditures schedule occurs when

   a households, firms, and government spend more at each level of income.
   b households, firms, and government spend less at each level of income.

c households, firms and government spend less at each price level.

d households, firms and government spend more at each price level.

e the economy is in recession.

11 Which of the following is not a component of aggregate expenditures?

AE=C+I+G+E

a consumption
b investment
c government purchases
d net exports
e taxes

12 The household's consumption function traces the relationship between its consumption and its

a investment.
b income.
c taxes.
d inflation rate.
e total expenditure.

13 The slope of the aggregate expenditures schedule equals

AE slope = MPC

a zero.
b the average propensity to save.
c the marginal propensity to save.
d the average propensity to consume.
e the marginal propensity to consume.

14 The marginal propensity to save equals *MPS = 1 - MPC*

a the marginal propensity to consume.
b 1 plus the marginal propensity to consume.
c 1 minus the marginal propensity to consume.
d the reciprocal of the marginal propensity to consume.
e none of the above.

15 Autonomous consumption is

a the extra consumption out of an additional dollar of income.
b the ratio of consumption to disposable income.
c that part of consumption that does not depend on disposable income.
d the extra savings out of an additional dollar of income.
e the level of consumption when desired inventories equal zero.

16 When investment increases, equilibrium output

a increases by more than the change in investment.
b increases by less than the change in investment.
c increases by the same amount as the change in investment.
d decreases by less than the change in investment.
e decreases by more than the change in investment.

17 In the simple model without taxes, the multiplier equals

a 1 divided by the marginal propensity to consume.
b the marginal propensity to save.
c the marginal propensity to consume.
d 1 divided by the marginal propensity to save. *1/MPS*
e zero.

18 Which of the following is not true? Adding taxes to the income-expenditure model causes

a disposable income to be less than national income.
b the aggregate expenditures schedule to be flatter.
c the multiplier to be smaller.
d the aggregate consumption function to be flatter.
e a fall in autonomous consumption.

19 The amount of each extra dollar of disposable income spent on imports is the

a marginal propensity to import.
b marginal propensity to consume.
c marginal propensity to save.
d marginal propensity to export.
e marginal propensity to invest.

20 Adding international trade to the income-expenditure model causes

a the multiplier to be larger.
b the aggregate expenditures schedule to be flatter.
c the aggregate expenditures schedule to be steeper.
d the equilibrium level of output to be lower.
e none of the above.

Completion

1 The relationship between the economy's total expenditures and national income is summarized by the *AE = Y*.

2 The *consumption function* traces the relationship between consumption and disposable income.

3 The portion of consumption that does not depend upon income is called *autonomous consumption*.

4 The fraction of additional income that is consumed is called the *MPC*.

5 National output increases by more than the amount of a given increase in investment by a factor called the *multiplier*.

6 When firms cannot sell all that they produce, they experience an increase in *unplanned inventories*.

7 The relationship between national income and imports is summarized by the *import function*.

8 The proportion of a one-dollar increase in income spent on imports is called the *marginal propensity to import*.

9 An economy actively engaged in international trade and investment is called an *open econ*.

10 The difference between imports and exports equals a *trade deficit* *X-M*

Answers to Self-Test

True or False

1	t	6	f	11	f
2	t	7	t	12	f
3	f	8	f	13	t
4	t	9	t	14	f
5	t	10	f	15	t

Multiple Choice

1	c	6	b	11	e	16	a
2	b	7	b	12	b	17	d
3	a	8	a	13	e	18	e
4	a	9	e	14	c	19	a
5	c	10	a	15	c	20	b

Completion

1 aggregate expenditures schedule
2 consumption function
3 autonomous consumption
4 marginal propensity to consume
5 multiplier
6 unplanned inventories
7 import function
8 marginal propensity to import
9 open economy
10 trade deficit

Doing Economics: Tools and Practice Problems

The topic of this section is income-expenditure analysis. We begin with an explanation of the tools needed and follow with problems involving economies with no taxes or imports. For each, we find the consumption function, calculate the aggregate expenditures schedule, and solve for the economy's equilibrium output. We then study the multiplier process, which shows how a change in spending brings about a larger change in equilibrium output. Finally, we consider increasingly complicated problems with income taxes and imports, where the net export function must be calculated. An important lesson of these latter problems concerns how taxes and imports affect the multiplier and the stability of the economy.

Tool Kit 28.1: Finding the Aggregate Consumption Function

Aggregate expenditures equal the sum of consumption, investment, government spending, and net exports. The first step is to find the aggregate consumption function, which shows the level of consumption that corresponds to each level of national income.

Step one: Identify the marginal propensity to consume (MPC), autonomous consumption, and the income tax rate.

Step two: Calculate the aggregate consumption function by substituting various values of national income into the following formula:

Aggregate consumption = autonomous consumption + [national income (1 − tax rate)] × MPC.

(Note that the term in brackets is disposable income, which equals national income when the tax rate is zero.)

Tool Kit 28.2: Finding the Net Export Function

In an open economy, net exports must be included in aggregate expenditures. The **net export function** shows the level of net exports that corresponds to each level of national income.

Step one: Identify the marginal propensity to import (MPI), the tax rate, and the level of exports.

Step two: Calculate the import function by substituting various levels of national income into the following formula:

imports = [national income (1 − tax rate)] × MPI.

Step three: Find the net export function by subtracting imports from exports for every level of national income:

net exports = exports − imports.

Tool Kit 28.3: Finding the Aggregate Expenditures Schedule

With the aggregate consumption and net export functions in place, the aggregate expenditures schedule can be calculated. The aggregate expenditures schedule shows the level of aggregate spending corresponding to each level of national income.

Step one: Identify the aggregate consumption function, the level of investment spending, the level of government spending, and the net export function.

Step two: Calculate the aggregate expenditures schedule by summing consumption, investment, government spending, and net exports for each level of national income:

$$AE = C + I + G + E.$$

Tool Kit 28.4: Using Income-Expenditure Analysis to Determine the Equilibrium

We find the equilibrium level of output and national income (which are always equal), where the aggregate expenditures schedule crosses the 45-degree line. At this point, consumers, firms, government, and foreigners spend just enough to purchase the economy's output.

Step one: Identify the aggregate expenditures schedule.

Step two: Choose a level of national income, and find the corresponding level of aggregate expenditures. If they are equal, stop. This is the equilibrium level of output.

Step three: If aggregate expenditures exceed national income, then inventories will fall, firms will increase production, and output will expand. Choose a greater level of national income, and repeat step one. If aggregate expenditures are less than national income, then inventories will rise, firms will cut back production, and output will decrease. Choose a lower level of national income, and repeat step one.

Step four: Continue until the equilibrium is found.

Tool Kit 28.5: Using Multiplier Analysis to Find the Ultimate Change in Output Caused by an Initial Change in Spending

The great lesson of income-expenditure analysis is that an initial change in spending ripples through the economy and ultimately results in a larger change in output. The process by which this happens is the multiplier process, and the multiplier itself shows how much larger than the initial change in spending is the ultimate change in output.

Step one: Identify the marginal propensity to consume, the tax rate, the marginal propensity to import, and the initial change in spending.

Step two: Calculate the multiplier. Use the appropriate formula:

no taxes or imports: $1/(1 - MPC)$
income taxes: $1/[1 - MPC (1 - tax rate)]$
open economy
(no taxes): $1/[1 - (MPC + MPI)]$
open economy $1/[1 - (MPC - MPI)$
with taxes: $(1 - tax rate)]$.

Step three: Calculate the ultimate change in output by multiplying the initial change in spending by the multiplier:

change in output = (change in spending) × multiplier.

Step four: Verify the result in step three by adding the change in spending to the original aggregate expenditures schedule and solving for the new equilibrium level of output.

---

1 (Worked problem: income-expenditure analysis) For years, Costa Guano has remained closed to foreign trade and investment. The government of the isolated nation spends no money and collects none in taxes. Autonomous consumption is 300 million guanos (the currency of Costa Guano), and the marginal propensity to consume equals 0.8. Finally, domestic private investment equals 100 million guanos.

a Find the aggregate consumption function.
b Find the aggregate expenditures schedule.
c Calculate equilibrium output and national income.
d Brimming with confidence, Costa Guano's firms increase their investment spending by 100 million (for a total of 200 million). Calculate the multiplier and the ultimate change in output brought about by this increase in investment. The (mythical) unit of currency is the guano. See Table 28.1.

Step-by-step solution

Step one (a): Find the aggregate consumption function. Identify the MPC, autonomous consumption, and the tax rate. The MPC is 0.8, autonomous consumption is 300 million, but the tax rate is zero.

Step two (a): Calculate the aggregate consumption function. When national income equals zero, aggregate consumption equals autonomous consumption (300 million). At 500 million in national income, consumption equals 300 + .8 (500) = 700 million. Continuing, we derive Table 28.1.

Table 28.1

National income (millions of guanos)	Aggregate consumption (millions of guanos)
0	300
500	700
1,000	1,100
1,500	1,500
2,000	1,900
2,500	2,300
3,000	2,700

Step one (b): Find the aggregate expenditures schedule. Identify the aggregate consumption function, investment, government spending, and the net export function. The aggregate consumption function is given in Table 28.1, and investment equals 100 million. Government spending and net exports equal zero.

Step two (b): Calculate the aggregate expenditures schedule by adding consumption and investment, as shown in Table 28.2.

Table 28.2

National income	Aggregate consumption	Investment	Aggregate expenditures
0	300	100	400
500	700	100	800
1,000	1,100	100	1,200
1,500	1,500	100	1,600
2,000	1,900	100	2,000
2,500	2,300	100	2,400
3,000	2,700	100	2,800

Step one (c): Calculate equilibrium output and national income. Identify the aggregate expenditures schedule. It appears in Table 28.2.

Step two (c): Choose a level of national income. When national income is 2,000 million, aggregate expenditures equal 2,000 million. Consumers and firms exactly purchase the economy's output of 2,000 million.

Step one (d): Calculate the multiplier and the ultimate change in output brought about by this increase in investment of 100 million (from 100 to 200). Identify the marginal propensity to consume, the tax rate, the marginal propensity to import, and the initial change in spending. The MPC is 0.8, the initial change in spending is 100 million. There are no taxes or imports.

Step two (d): Calculate the multiplier. Because there are no taxes or imports, the multiplier equals

$$1/(1 - \text{MPC}) = 1/(1 - 0.8) = 1/0.2 = 5.$$

Step three (d): Calculate the ultimate change in output:

$$\text{change in output} = 100 \times 5 = 500 \text{ million.}$$

Step four (d): Verify the result in step three by adding the change in spending to the original aggregate expenditures schedule and solving for the new equilibrium level of output. The new aggregate expenditures schedule is given in Table 28.3.

Table 28.3

National income	Aggregate consumption	Investment	Aggregate expenditures
0	300	200	500
500	700	200	900
1,000	1,100	200	1,300
1,500	1,500	200	1,700
2,000	1,900	200	2,100
2,500	2,300	200	2,500
3,000	2,700	200	2,900

The new equilibrium level of output is 2,500 million, which is 500 million more than originally. It checks!

2 (Practice problem: income-expenditure analysis) El Dorado, an insular economy closed to foreign trade and investment, has no income-based taxes, and its government spends nothing. The marginal propensity to consume is 0.9, autonomous consumption is 5 billion dorals (the currency of El Dorado), and private investment totals 1 billion. (Hint: Choose national income in intervals of 10 billion; that is, 0, 10, 20, etc.)

  a Find the aggregate consumption function.
  b Find the aggregate expenditures schedule.
  c Calculate equilibrium output and national income.
  d After a period of stability, investment in El Dorado jumps to 2 billion dorals. Calculate the multiplier and the ultimate change in output brought about by this increase in investment.

3 (Practice problem: income-expenditure analysis) In Erehwemos, there is no taxation and also no government spending. The economy is closed to the outside world. All investment is undertaken by private domes-

tic firms, and the total is 2 billion wemos (the Erehwemosian currency). The marginal propensity to consume is 0.75, and the autonomous consumption is 2 billion. (Hint: Choose national income levels in intervals of 4 billion; that is, 0, 4, 8, 12, etc.)

  a Find the aggregate consumption function.
  b Find the aggregate expenditures schedule.
  c Calculate equilibrium output and national income.
  d Investment climbs to 4 billion. Calculate the multiplier and the ultimate change in output brought about by this increase in investment.

4 (Worked problem: income-expenditure analysis) This problem builds on problem 1. Recognizing the need for infrastructure investment, the government of Costa Guano institutes an income tax with a flat rate of 25 percent and spends 300 million. Private investment continues at 200 million, the marginal propensity to consume is 0.8, and autonomous consumption equals 300 million. The economy remains closed to foreign trade.

  a Find the consumption function.
  b Find the aggregate expenditures schedule.
  c Find the equilibrium level of output.
  d Suppose that the government raises its spending by 200 million (for a total of 500 million). Calculate the multiplier, and solve for the ultimate change in output brought about by the increase in government spending.

Step-by-step solution

Step one (a): Identify the marginal propensity to consume, autonomous consumption, and the income tax rate. The MPC is 0.8, autonomous consumption equals 300 million, and the income tax rate is 25 percent.

Step two (a): Calculate the aggregate consumption function. When national income equals zero, aggregate consumption equals autonomous consumption (300 million). At 500 million in national income, aggregate consumption = 300 + {[500 (1 − 0.25)] × 0.8} = 600. Continuing, we derive Table 28.4.

Table 28.4

National income (millions of guanos)	Aggregate consumption (millions of guanos)
0	300
500	600
1,000	900
1,500	1,200
2,000	1,500
2,500	1,800
3,000	2,100

Step one (b): Identify the aggregate consumption function, investment, government spending, and the net export function. The aggregate consumption function is given in Table 28.4, investment equals 200 million, and government spending equals 300 million. Net exports remain zero.

Step two (b): Calculate the aggregate expenditures schedule by adding consumption, investment, and government spending, as shown in Table 28.5.

Table 28.5

National income	Aggregate consumption	Investment	Government spending	Aggregate expenditures
0	300	200	300	800
500	600	200	300	1,100
1,000	900	200	300	1,400
1,500	1,200	200	300	1,700
2,000	1,500	200	300	2,000
2,500	1,800	200	300	2,300
3,000	2,100	200	300	2,600

Step one (c): Identify the aggregate expenditures schedule. It appears in Table 28.5.

Step two (c): Choose a level of national income. When national income is 2,000 million, aggregate expenditures equal 2,000 million. Consumers and firms exactly purchase the economy's output of 2,000 million.

Step one (d): Identify the marginal propensity to consume, the tax rate, the marginal propensity to import, and the initial change in spending. The MPC is 0.8, and the initial change in spending is 200 million. The tax rate is 25 percent, but there are no imports.

Step two (d): Calculate the multiplier. Because there is an income tax but no imports, the multiplier equals

$$1/[1 - \text{MPC} (1 - \text{tax rate})] = 1/[1 - 0.8 (1 - 0.25)]$$
$$= 1/(1 - 0.6) = 1/0.4 = 2.5.$$

(In problem 1, there was no income tax and the multiplier equalled 5. Here, the income tax reduces the multiplier to 2.5.)

Step three (d): Calculate the ultimate change in output:

change in output = 200 × 2.5 = 500 million.

Step four (d): Verify the result in step three by adding the change in spending to the original aggregate expenditures schedule and solving for the new equilibrium level of output. The new aggregate expenditures schedule is given in Table 28.6.

Table 28.6

National income	Aggregate consumption	Investment	Government spending	Aggregate expenditures
0	300	200	500	1,000
500	600	200	500	1,300
1,000	900	200	500	1,600
1,500	1,200	200	500	1,900
2,000	1,500	200	500	2,200
2,500	1,800	200	500	2,500
3,000	2,100	200	500	2,800

The new equilibrium level of output is 2,500 million, which is 500 million more than originally. It checks. The economy is more stable with the income tax, for it took a 200-million change in spending to change output by 500 million in problem 1, where there was no tax.

5 (Practice problem: income-expenditure analysis) This problem builds on problem 2. An income tax system is passed by El Dorado's Council of Ministers. The flat tax rate is 1/9 on all income, and the government plans to spend 3 billion. The marginal propensity to consume remains at 0.9, autonomous consumption is 5 billion, and private investment continues at 2 billion.

 a Find the consumption function.
 b Find the aggregate expenditures schedule.
 c Find the equilibrium level of output.
 d Suppose that the government raises its spending by 4 billion (for a total of 7 billion). Calculate the multiplier, and solve for the ultimate change in output brought about by the increase in government spending.

6 (Practice problem: income-expenditure analysis) This problem builds on problem 3. Erehwemos institutes an income tax with a flat rate of 1/3. The government spends 2 billion wemos. The marginal propensity to consume remains at 0.75, autonomous consumption equals 2 billion, and private investment equals 4 billion.

 a Find the aggregate consumption function.
 b Find the aggregate expenditures schedule.
 c Calculate equilibrium output and national income.
 d Responding to the war threat from neighbouring Erehwon, the government doubles spending. The increase in government spending is 2 billion (for a total of 4 billion). Calculate the multiplier and the ultimate change in output brought about by this increase in government spending.

7 (Worked problem: income-expenditure analysis) This problem builds on problems 1 and 4. Costa Guano has opened its economy to foreign trade. It exports 500 million in world markets. Its citizens have developed tastes for foreign goods, however, and their marginal propensity to import is 1/3. Autonomous consumption remains at 300 million, investment equals 200 million, government spending has returned to 300 million, the marginal propensity to consume is 0.8, and the tax rate is 25 percent.

 a Find the aggregate consumption function.
 b Find the net export function.
 c Find the aggregate expenditures schedule.
 d Find the equilibrium level of output.
 e Suppose that exports increase by 325 million (for a total of 825 million). Calculate the multiplier, and solve for the ultimate change in output brought about by the increase in exports.

Step-by-step solution

Step one (a and b): The aggregate consumption function is the same as in problem 4 and is given in Table 28.4. Identify the marginal propensity to import, the tax rate, and the level of exports. The MPI equals 1/3, the tax rate is 25 percent, and the level of exports equals 500 million guanos.

Step two (a and b): Calculate the import function. When national income is zero, so are imports. When national income is 500 million, imports = $[500 \times (1 - 0.25)] \times 1/3 = 125$ million. Continuing, we derive the import function in Table 28.7.

Table 28.7

National income (millions of guanos)	Imports (millions of guanos)
0	0
500	125
1,000	250
1,500	375
2,000	500
2,500	625
3,000	750

Step three (a and b): Find the net export function. When national income is zero, net exports are 500 – 0 = 500 million. When national income is 500, net exports are 500 – 125 – 375. Continuing, we derive the net export function in Table 28.8.

Table 28.8

National income	Exports	Imports	Net exports
0	500	0	500
500	500	125	375
1,000	500	250	250
1,500	500	375	125
2,000	500	500	0
2,500	500	625	–125
3,000	500	750	–250

Step one (c): Identify the aggregate consumption function, investment, government spending, and the net export function. The aggregate consumption function is given in Table 28.4, investment equals 200 million, government spending is 300 million, and the net export function appears in Table 28.8.

Step two (c): Calculate the aggregate expenditures schedule by adding consumption, investment, government spending, and net exports. Table 28.9 gives the results.

Table 28.9

National income	Aggregate consumption	Investment	Government spending	Net exports	Aggregate expenditures
0	300	200	300	500	1,300
500	600	200	300	375	1,475
1,000	900	200	300	250	1,650
1,500	1,200	200	300	125	1,825
2,000	1,500	200	300	0	2,000
2,500	1,800	200	300	–125	2,175
3,000	2,100	200	300	–250	2,350

Step one (d): Identify the aggregate expenditures schedule. It is given in Table 28.9.

Step two (d): Choose a level of national income. When national income equals 2,000 million, aggregate expenditures equal 2,000 million, and this is the equilibrium level of output.

Step one (e): Identify the marginal propensity to consume, the tax rate, the marginal propensity to import, and the initial change in spending. The MPC is 0.8, the tax rate is 25 percent, the MPI equals 1/3, and exports increase by 325 million.

Step two (e): Calculate the multiplier. The multiplier

= 1/[1 – (MPC – MPI)(1 – tax rate)]

= 1/[1 – (0.8 – 1/3)(1 – 0.25)] = 20/13 = 1.54.

Note that in the open economy, the multiplier is smaller than in the closed economy of problem 4.

Step three (e): Calculate the ultimate change in output:

change in output = 325 × 20/13 = 500.

Step four (e): Verify the result in step three by adding the change in exports to the original aggregate expenditures schedule (Table 28.9) and solving for the new equilibrium level of output. The new aggregate expenditures schedule is given in Table 28.10. (Note that the increase in exports increases net exports by 325 million.)

Table 28.10

National income	Aggregate consumption	Investment	Government spending	Net exports	Aggregate expenditures
0	300	200	300	825	1,625
500	600	200	300	700	1,800
1,000	900	200	300	575	1,975
1,500	1,200	200	300	450	2,150
2,000	1,500	200	300	325	2,325
2,500	1,800	200	300	200	2,500
3,000	2,100	200	300	75	2,675

The new equilibrium level of output is 2,500 million, which is 500 million more than originally. It checks. The open economy is yet more stable because it took a 325 million change in spending to change output by 500 million.

8 (Practice problem: income-expenditure analysis) This problem builds on problems 2 and 5. The new economics minister wins the day with a brilliant argument against protectionism, and El Dorado opens its economy. Its exports surge to 14 billion. The marginal propensity to import is 9/40, the marginal propensity to consume remains at 0.9, autonomous consumption is 5 billion, private investment is 2 billion, and the government spends 3 billion.

a Find the consumption function.
b Find the net export function.

c Find the aggregate expenditures schedule.

d Find the equilibrium level of output.

e Suppose that exports increase by 4 billion (for a total of 18 billion). Calculate the multiplier, and solve for the ultimate change in output brought about by the increase in exports.

9 (Practice problem: income-expenditure analysis) This problem builds on problems 3 and 6. With peace at hand, the Erehwemos economy is opened to foreign trade and investment. Exports equal 2⅔ billion, and the marginal propensity to import is 0.25. Government spending has returned to 2 billion, but private investment remains at 4 billion. Autonomous consumption is also 2 billion, and the marginal propensity to consume remains at 0.75. Finally, the tax rate is 1/3.

a Find the aggregate consumption function.

b Find the net export function.

c Find the aggregate expenditures schedule.

d Calculate the equilibrium output and national income.

e Exports increase to 5⅓ billion. Calculate the multiplier and the ultimate change in output brought about by this increase in exports.

Answers to Problems

2 Table 28.11 gives

a the aggregate consumption function and

b the aggregate expenditures schedule.

Table 28.11

National income (billions of dorals)	Aggregate consumption (billions of dorals)	Investment (billions of dorals)	Aggregate expenditures (billions of dorals)
0	5	1	6
10	14	1	15
20	23	1	24
30	32	1	33
40	41	1	42
50	50	1	51
60	59	1	60
70	68	1	69
80	77	1	78
90	86	1	87
100	95	1	96

c Equilibrium output is 60 billion.

d The multiplier is 1/(1 − 0.9) = 10. The change in output is 1 × 10 = 10. Table 28.12 shows that when investment increases to 2 billion, equilibrium output grows to 70 billion. It verifies that equilibrium output increases by 10 (from 60 to 70 billion), as indicated above.

Table 28.12

National income	Aggregate consumption	Investment	Aggregate expenditures
0	5	2	7
10	14	2	16
20	23	2	25
30	32	2	34
40	41	2	43
50	50	2	52
60	59	2	61
70	68	2	70
80	77	2	79
90	86	2	88
100	95	2	97

3 Table 28.13 gives

a the aggregate consumption function and

b the aggregate expenditures schedule.

Table 28.13

National income (billions of wemos)	Aggregate consumption (billions of wemos)	Investment (billions of wemos)	Aggregate expenditures (billions of wemos)
0	2	2	4
4	5	2	7
8	8	2	10
12	11	2	13
16	14	2	16
20	17	2	19
24	20	2	22
28	23	2	25

c Equilibrium output is 16 billion.

d The multiplier is 1/(1 − MPC) = 1/(1 − 0.75) = 4. The change in output is 2 × 4 = 8. This is verified by Table 28.14, which shows that the new equilibrium output is 24 billion.

Table 28.14

National income	Aggregate consumption	Investment	Aggregate expenditures
0	2	4	6
4	5	4	9
8	8	4	12
12	11	4	15
16	14	4	18
20	17	4	21
24	20	4	24
28	23	4	27

5 Table 28.15 shows

a the aggregate consumption function and

b the aggregate expenditures schedule.

Table 28.15

National income (billions of dorals)	Aggregate consumption (billions of dorals)	Investment (billions of dorals)	Government spending (billions of dorals)	Aggregate expenditures (billions of dorals)
0	5	2	3	10
10	13	2	3	18
20	21	2	3	26
30	29	2	3	34
40	37	2	3	42
50	45	2	3	50
60	53	2	3	58
70	61	2	3	66
80	69	2	3	74
90	77	2	3	82
100	85	2	3	90

c The equilibrium level of output is 50 billion.

d The multiplier is $1/[1 - \text{MPC} (1 - t)] = 1/[1 - 0.9(1 - 1/9)] = 5$. The change in output is $4 \times 5 = 20$ billion. Table 28.16 shows that when government spending is 7 billion, the new equilibrium output is 70 billion, which represents an increase of 20 billion.

Table 28.16

National income	Aggregate consumption	Investment	Government spending	Aggregate expenditures
0	5	2	7	14
10	13	2	7	22
20	21	2	7	30
30	29	2	7	38
40	37	2	7	46
50	45	2	7	54
60	53	2	7	62
70	61	2	7	70
80	69	2	7	78
90	77	2	7	86
100	85	2	7	94

6 Table 28.17 gives

a the aggregate consumption function and

b the aggregate expenditures schedule.

Table 28.17

National income (billions of wemos)	Aggregate consumption (billions of wemos)	Investment (billions of wemos)	Government spending (billions of wemos)	Aggregate expenditures (billions of wemos)
0	2	4	2	8
4	4	4	2	10
8	6	4	2	12
12	8	4	2	14
16	10	4	2	16
20	12	4	2	18
24	14	4	2	20
28	16	4	2	22

c Equilibrium output is 16 billion.

d The multiplier is $1/[1 - \text{MPC} (1 - t)] = 1/[1 - 0.75(1 - 1/3)] = 2$. The change in equilibrium output is $2 \times 2 = 4$ billion, as is verified by Table 28.18, which shows that the new equilibrium output is 20 billion.

Table 28.18

National income	Aggregate consumption	Investment	Government spending	Aggregate expenditures
0	2	4	4	10
4	4	4	4	12
8	6	4	4	14
12	8	4	4	16
16	10	4	4	18
20	12	4	4	20
24	14	4	4	22
28	16	4	4	24

8 Table 28.19 shows

a the aggregate consumption function,

b the net export function, and

c the aggregate expenditures schedule.

Table 28.19

National income (billions of dorals)	Aggregate consumption (billions of dorals)	Investment (billions of dorals)	Government spending (billions of dorals)	Net exports (billions of dorals)	Aggregate expenditures (billions of dorals)
0	5	2	3	14	24
10	13	2	3	12	30
20	21	2	3	10	36
30	29	2	3	8	42
40	37	2	3	6	48
50	45	2	3	4	54
60	53	2	3	2	60
70	61	2	3	0	66
80	69	2	3	−2	72
90	77	2	3	−4	78
100	85	2	3	−6	84

d Equilibrium output is 60 billion.

e The multiplier is $1/[1 - (\text{MPC} - \text{MPI})(1 - t)] = 1/[1 - (0.9 - 9/40)(1 - 1/9)] = 2.5$. The change in output is $4 \times 2.5 = 10$. Table 28.20 shows that the new equilibrium output is 70 billion, which indicates an increase of 10 billion.

Table 28.20

National income	*Aggregate consumption*	*Invest-ment*	*Govern-ment spending*	*Net exports*	*Aggregate expenditures*
0	5	2	3	18	28
10	13	2	3	16	34
20	21	2	3	14	40
30	29	2	3	12	46
40	37	2	3	10	52
50	45	2	3	8	58
60	53	2	3	6	64
70	61	2	3	4	70
80	69	2	3	2	76
90	77	2	3	0	82
100	85	2	3	−2	88

9 Table 28.21 shows

a the aggregate consumption function,
b the net export function, and
c the aggregate expenditures schedule.

Table 28.21

National income (millions of wemos)	*Aggregate consumption (millions of wemos)*	*Invest-ment (millions of wemos)*	*Govern-ment spending (millions of wemos)*	*Net exports (millions of wemos)*	*Aggregate expenditures (millions of wemos)*
0	2	4	2	2⅔	10⅔
4	4	4	2	2	12
8	6	4	2	1⅓	13⅓
12	8	4	2	⅔	14⅔
16	10	4	2	0	16
20	12	4	2	−⅔	17⅓
24	14	4	2	−1⅓	18⅔
28	16	4	2	−2	20

d Equilibrium output equals 16 billion.
e The multiplier is $1/[1 - (\text{MPC} - \text{MPI})(1 - t)] = 1/[1 - (0.75 - 0.25)(1 - 1/3)] = 1.5$. The change in output is $(8/3 \times 3/2) = 4$ billion. Table 28.22 shows that the new equilibrium output equals 20 billion, which is an increase of 4 billion.

Table 28.22

National income (millions of wemos)	*Aggregate consumption (millions of wemos)*	*Invest-ment (millions of wemos)*	*Govern-ment spending (millions of wemos)*	*Net exports (millions of wemos)*	*Aggregate expenditures (millions of wemos)*
0	2	4	2	5⅓	13⅓
4	4	4	2	4⅔	14⅔
8	6	4	2	4	16
12	8	4	2	3⅓	17⅓
16	10	4	2	2⅔	18⅔
20	12	4	2	2	20
24	14	4	2	1⅓	21⅓
28	16	4	2	⅔	22⅔

Chapter 29

CONSUMPTION AND INVESTMENT

Chapter Review

This chapter and the next move behind aggregate expenditures and give a deeper look at each of its components—consumption, investment, government expenditures, and net exports. Here the text focuses on consumption and investment. The important issues involve how consumption and investment are determined and the causes of shifts in the consumption and investment functions. Chapter 30 considers government and trade, before attention returns to the aggregate demand–aggregate supply model in Chapter 31.

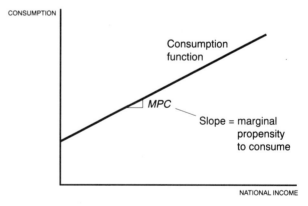

CONSUMPTION

Consumption function

MPC

Slope = marginal propensity to consume

NATIONAL INCOME

Figure 29.1

ESSENTIAL CONCEPTS

1   What determines **consumption** expenditures? The basic building block is the **Keynesian consumption function,** which gives the relationship between consumption and current income. Figure 29.1 shows that as current income increases by one dollar, consumption increases by the marginal propensity to consume. Other, more future-oriented theories of consumption are the **life-cycle hypothesis** and the **permanent income hypothesis.** These hypotheses shift the focus away

from current income to expected future income, interest rates, and prices.

2   The life-cycle hypothesis asserts that individuals plan their consumption over their entire lifetime. Thus, people save during their working years when income is high in order to provide for consumption during retirement. Because savings play such an important role, current and expected future interest rates as well as expected future income have significant effects on the

level of consumption. The life-cycle hypothesis is a future-oriented explanation. It implies that the relationship between consumption and current income would be quite flat, as shown in Figure 29.2.

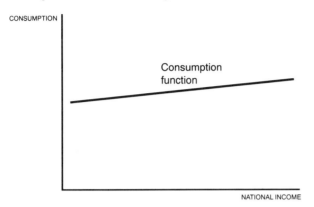

Figure 29.2

3   The permanent income hypothesis also argues that people rationally plan their present and future consumption; they save in good years to provide extra consumption in bad years. Again, the focus is on both current and future income, interest rates, and prices. The permanent income hypothesis reconciles the discrepancy between the aggregate and the individual: over time, aggregate consumption increases in the same proportion as income, while for individuals consumption increases by a smaller proportion than income.

4   In reality, the relationship between current income and consumption is not as flat as the future-oriented theories suggest. Two explanations of why consumption seems to be more dependent on current income involve **durable goods consumption** and **credit availability.** When incomes fall during recessions, individuals postpone purchases of durable goods. Because they are uncertain when and if good times will return, they take the safer alternative of making do with old durable goods. Further, when incomes fall, individuals find borrowing more difficult than the permanent income hypothesis asserts. Banks also are unsure of the future incomes of borrowers and are reluctant to lend money to the unemployed. It is safer for banks to lend money to those who do not need it!

5   **Investment** includes firms' purchases of new plant and equipment and inventories, and households' purchases of new houses, which are durable goods. Business investment in plant and equipment is based on the expectation that future profits from the investment will more than outweigh the current investment expenditure. Of course, the firm must discount future revenues and costs; therefore, the interest rate is important. The **investment function** gives the total value of investment at each rate of interest. Lower interest rates increase the present value of profits and lead to more investment. Nevertheless, most investment is financed out of retained earnings; thus, interest rates do not play as important a role in investment as the availability of funds. The reliance on available funds and expectations of future conditions and

risk make investment the most variable component of aggregate expenditures.

6   Firms hold inventories of inputs in order to **facilitate production;** a firm can be sure that the inputs will be there when needed. Firms may hold inventories of output in order to **smooth production;** that is, the firm can produce at a steady rate and always have enough to meet a highly variable consumer demand. Nonetheless, inventories are much more variable than output and contribute to the instability of the economy. During downturns, for example, it is less risky for firms to cut production and sell off inventories than to continue to produce in the hope that good times will return.

BEHIND THE ESSENTIAL CONCEPTS

1   The marginal propensity to consume out of current income is quite high, so that the consumption function slopes up rather steeply. Why, then, do we study the future-oriented theories of consumption, which stress the future and predict a flat consumption function? The answer is that the life-cycle and permanent income hypotheses provide a deeper understanding of consumption, especially of what factors might cause the Keynesian consumption function to shift and of the stability of the function. For example, in recessions, people become pessimistic about future incomes and postpone durable goods purchases; this shifts the consumption function and aggregate expenditures down. Remember that the central questions in macroeconomics involve the fluctuations in the economy; therefore, it is vital to understand the causes of the changes.

2   The life-cycle and permanent income hypotheses involve borrowing and savings; thus, they teach us the importance of capital markets. If you were always able to obtain credit, your consumption would not vary much. You could borrow in low-income years (such as when you were at university), live well, and repay during high-income years. But capital markets are not perfect; credit rationing suggests that banks are reluctant to make loans secured only against future earnings. When your income falls during recessions and you need money, the best available option is to postpone major purchases. Imperfect capital markets make consumption more variable, and thus they are at the centre of the discussion about economic ups and downs.

3   To see why business investment is volatile and why it fluctuates over the business cycle, put yourself in the shoes of a business owner. The economy is in recession, and customers are not buying your products. Profits are down, and you have few retained earnings to spend on investment. The bank will not lend to you because it perceives your precarious financial position. Even if you could obtain funds, a recession is not the time to take risks. During good times, a failed investment may only mean lower profits; during bad times, it may mean bankruptcy. The safest option is to postpone purchases of new plant and equipment, cut production, and sell off inventories.

4 While modern macroeconomists of every school think that a firm microeconomic foundation for their theories is essential, the differences between microeconomics and macroeconomics are interesting. Microeconomics focuses largely on prices. In the basic competitive model, prices always adjust and clear the market. Even when imperfect competition is the subject, economists focus on the failure of prices to capture all costs and benefits or to find the right level. In macroeconomics, especially the new Keynesian approach, prices do not do their job, and markets do not always clear. Consumption is driven by income, not so much by prices. There is still an equilibrium, but it is one in which income, not price, adjusts until desired aggregate spending equals output.

SELF-TEST

True or False

1 The Keynesian consumption function describes the relationship between consumption and permanent disposable income.

2 According to the life-cycle hypothesis, people save during working years to provide for consumption during retirement.

3 According to the permanent income hypothesis, people save during good years to offset low income during bad years.

4 The future-oriented theories of consumption imply that the consumption function is relatively flat.

5 The future-oriented theories of consumption imply that the multiplier is large.

6 Future-oriented consumption makes it more difficult for increases in government spending to stimulate national income.

7 Spending on durable goods is less variable than spending on nondurable goods.

8 A borrower who cannot afford the interest rate at which banks are willing to lend is credit rationed.

9 Consumption depends more on current disposable income than the future-oriented theories of consumption imply.

10 The investment spending relevant for aggregate expenditures includes purchases of capital equipment by firms and purchases of shares by individuals.

11 There has been considerable variation in real interest rates, and this explains the volatility of investment.

12 Firms finance most investment out of retained earnings.

13 Firms usually perceive that investment is riskier during recessions.

14 In the Canadian economy, inventories fluctuate less than output because firms try to smooth production and produce at a steady rate.

15 Government may increase business confidence by demonstrating a commitment to maintaining high employment and output.

Multiple Choice

1 The view that current disposable income determines current consumption is consistent with

a only the Keynesian consumption function.
b only the life-cycle hypothesis.
c only the permanent income hypothesis.
d the Keynesian consumption function and the life-cycle hypothesis.
e the life-cycle hypothesis and the permanent income hypothesis.

2 The idea that individuals save during working years in order to provide for consumption during retirement is incorporated in

a only the Keynesian consumption function.
b only the life-cycle hypothesis.
c only the permanent income hypothesis.
d the Keynesian consumption function and the life-cycle hypothesis.
e the life-cycle hypothesis and the permanent income hypothesis.

3 The idea that people save in good years to provide for extra consumption in bad years is incorporated in

a only the Keynesian consumption function.
b only the life-cycle hypothesis.
c only the permanent income hypothesis.
d the Keynesian consumption function and the life-cycle hypothesis.
e the life-cycle hypothesis and the permanent income hypothesis.

4 The idea that expected future income affects current consumption is emphasized in

a only the Keynesian consumption function.
b only the life-cycle hypothesis.
c only the permanent income hypothesis.
d the Keynesian consumption function and the life-cycle hypothesis.
e the life-cycle hypothesis and the permanent income hypothesis.

5 The idea that a temporary tax cut will significantly increase current consumption is implied by

a only the Keynesian consumption function.
b only the life-cycle hypothesis.
c only the permanent income hypothesis.
d the Keynesian consumption function and the life-cycle hypothesis.
e the life-cycle hypothesis and the permanent income hypothesis.

6 According to the future-oriented consumption theories, the multiplier is

a quite small.
b zero.
c large.

d small in recessions but large in booms.
e large in recessions but small in booms.

7 If there is a rise in the price of an asset that an individual owns, then that individual is said to receive

a human capital.
b capital gains.
c retained earnings.
d temporary income.
e disposable income.

8 If consumption is future-oriented, the aggregate expenditures schedule

a is flatter than if consumption depends only on current disposable income.
b is steeper than if consumption depends only on current disposable income.
c is horizontal.
d coincides with the 45-degree line.
e is vertical.

9 Which of the following is a reason why consumption depends more on current income than the future-oriented theories might suggest?

a Individuals can postpone purchases of durable goods when current income falls.
b Banks are reluctant to lend money to people who do not have a pressing need for a loan.
c Individuals can see through the corporate veil and reduce their consumption when profits fall.
d Government tax and spending policies do not affect individual consumption.
e None of the above.

10 An individual is credit rationed if

a the individual cannot afford the interest charged on a loan.
b banks charge a higher rate of interest to reflect their perception of the risk that the individual will not repay on schedule.
c the individual is unable to borrow even though willing to pay the interest, and the interest rate reflects the risk of lending to the individual.
d the individual has no savings.
e the individual has no current income.

11 The component of aggregate expenditures that is most variable is probably

a investment.
b consumption.
c government expenditures.
d net exports.
e savings.

12 For aggregate expenditure calculation, which of the following is not included in investment spending?

a purchases of new capital goods
b inventories accumulated in anticipation of sales
c purchases of used capital goods
d purchases of new homes
e none of the above

13 Before investing, which of the following would businesses not have to do?

a predict future revenues
b predict future costs
c adjust future revenues and costs for inflation
d compute the present value of profits using the real interest rate
e none of the above

14 The investment function describes the total value of investment at each

a price level.
b level of disposable income.
c level of national income.
d rate of interest.
e level of GDP.

15 Real interest rates

a are quite volatile; this reflects instability in the capital market.
b vary enough to provide a good explanation of short-term variations in investment.
c vary little.
d are irrelevant to the investment decision.
e change very little but lead to large changes in the level of investment because investment demand is quite elastic.

16 Tobin's *q* is

a the extra investment that a firm undertakes out of the next dollar of profits.
b the ratio of profits to investment expenditures.
c the ratio of the price of shares in the stock market to the underlying value of the firm's assets.
d the ratio of the real to the nominal interest rate.
e the elasticity of the investment function.

17 Most investment is financed

a out of retained earnings.
b by borrowing at the real interest rate.
c by issuing new shares.
d by selling bonds.
e by raising product prices.

18 Which of the following is not a reason why firms invest less during recessions?

a Retained earnings fall as revenues decline faster than expenses.
b As individual firms cut back on investment and inventories, national output falls owing to the multiplier effect; this further reduces the profitability of investment.
c Banks are less willing to lend because they foresee a greater risk that the loans will not be repaid.
d Firms' forecasts of the profitability of investment become more pessimistic.
e None of the above.

19 The theory that investment is more volatile than output because firms try to keep a constant ratio of their capital stock to output is called

a the investment accelerator.
b Tobin's *q*.
c the investment multiplier.
d the production-facilitating theory.
e the production-smoothing theory.

20 Which of the following is not true of the Canadian investment tax credit?

    a It effectively reduces the price of capital goods eligible for the credit, and thereby stimulates investment.

    b Before 1988, it applied to all forms of investments.

    c Since 1988, it applies only to certain forms of investments.

    d It allows firms to deduce from their tax bills a certain proportion of any eligible investment they have made.

    e None of the above.

Completion

1 The savings decision is a decision about _____ to consume.

2 The present discounted value of expected future wages is called _____ .

3 According to the _____ hypothesis, people save during their working years in order to increase consumption after retirement.

4 The _____ hypothesis argues that people save during good earning years to provide extra consumption during bad years.

5 The Keynesian consumption function stresses the relationship between consumption and _____ .

6 Future-oriented theories of consumption, such as the permanent income and life-cycle hypotheses, imply that the aggregate expenditures schedule is _____ .

7 The ability to postpone purchases of durable goods and the fact that it is difficult to borrow against future earnings make consumption _____ dependent on current income.

8 Changes in the level of _____ are the principal reason for the economy's instability.

9 Most firms finance most of their investment through _____ .

10 Since 1988, the _____ has been restricted to certain forms of investment, for example, investment in Atlantic Canada.

11 Inventories generally _____ during recessions.

Answers to Self-Test

True or False

1	f	6	t	11	f
2	t	7	f	12	t
3	t	8	f	13	t
4	t	9	t	14	f
5	f	10	f	15	t

Multiple Choice

1	a	6	a	11	a	16	c
2	b	7	b	12	c	17	a
3	c	8	a	13	e	18	e
4	e	9	e	14	d	19	a
5	a	10	c	15	c	20	e

Completion

1 when
2 human capital
3 life-cycle
4 permanent income
5 current income
6 relatively flat
7 more
8 investment
9 retained earnings
10 investment tax credit
11 increase

Doing Economics: Tools and Practice Problems

Using income-expenditure analysis is the first subject in this section. We see how factors that cause changes in consumption and investment bring about shifts in the aggregate expenditures schedule and new equilibrium levels of output. Next, we study how government fiscal policies might be offset by private savings and borrowing, without affecting consumption; this is sometimes referred to as Ricardian equivalence. In the real world, consumption is affected by government tax and spending policies. One important explanation involves the cost and availability of credit. Several problems show how imperfect capital markets lead to the failure of Ricardian equivalence.

Tool Kit 29.1: Using Income-Expenditure Analysis

Income-expenditure analysis can be used to answer such questions as "What is the effect on output of a change in interest rates?" In general, when some economic event causes a change in consumption or investment, the aggregate expenditures schedule will shift and bring about a change in the equilibrium level of output. Table 29.1 lists some important factors that change consumption and investment.

Table 29.1

Shifts in Aggregate Expenditures
  Changes in consumption, which are related to changes in wealth, real interest rates, credit availability, or estimates of future earnings.
  Changes in investment, which are related to changes in real interest rates, stock prices, credit availability, retained earnings, expectations of profitability, perceptions of risk, or willingness to bear risk.

Step one: Start with an equilibrium.

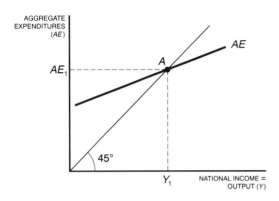

Step two: Identify a cause, and determine its effect on consumption, investment, or both.

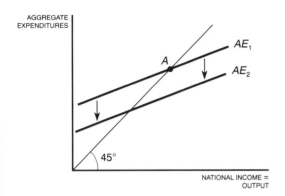

Step three: If consumption or investment increases, shift the aggregate expenditures schedule up; if either decreases, shift the schedule down.

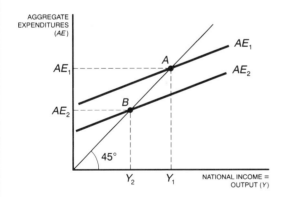

Step four: Find the new equilibrium level of output, and compare.

1 (Worked problem: income-expenditure analysis) Use income-expenditure analysis to explain the impact of a boom in the stock market.

Step-by-step solution

Step one: Start with an equilibrium.

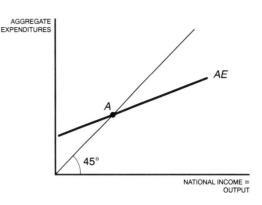

Step two: Identify a cause, and determine its effect on consumption, investment, or both. The increase in stock prices makes individuals wealthier, and so induces them to increase consumption. Firms can finance more investment by issuing new shares; thus, investment increases.

Step three: Shift the aggregate expenditures schedule. Because both consumption and investment increase, it shifts up.

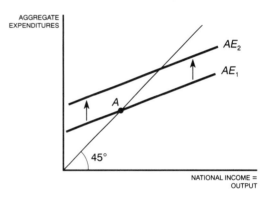

Step four: Find the new equilibrium, and compare. In the new equilibrium, output is greater. The increase in stock prices has brought about an increase in the economy's output.

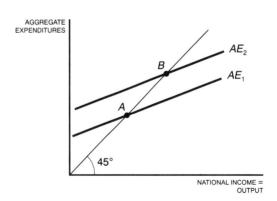

2 (Practice problem: income-expenditure analysis) Use income-expenditure analysis to determine the impact of an increase in real interest rates.

3 (Practice problem: income-expenditure analysis) Use income-expenditure analysis to determine the impact of each of the following.

a Firms anticipate an economic downturn accompanied by lower profits.

b The economy has fallen into recession, and because bankruptcies threaten, firms are less willing to bear risk.

c Believing that the defence budget will be cut, consumers fear layoffs.

d Retained earnings reach a four-year high.

e Tight monetary policy has limited the availability of credit for households and firms.

f Real interest rates fall by 2 percent.

g Uncertain about the consequences of NAFTA, firms perceive a risky future.

h Loose monetary policy increases the availability of credit.

Tool Kit 29.2: Exploring Ricardian Equivalence

When the government increases spending without a tax increase, it finances its deficit by selling bonds. Today's bonds must be repaid, however. This means that future taxpayers are liable for the debts incurred to finance current spending. The notion of Ricardian equivalence says that households will save now in order to be able to pay the future tax liability, and these savings will completely offset the effects of government deficit finance. In this section, we see how this might be true if capital markets were perfect, and several reasons why private savings do not offset government deficits in the real world: credit constraints and different interest rates for borrowing and lending. The lesson is that imperfect capital markets are an important reason why fiscal policy can be effective.

Step one: Draw the two-period budget constraint for the typical household. (Follow the procedure outlined in Chapter 9.)

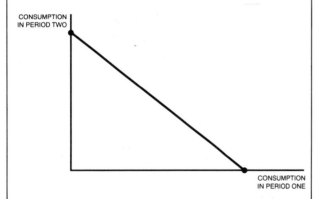

Step two: Choose a point that reflects the household's consumption and savings decisions. Label it *A*.

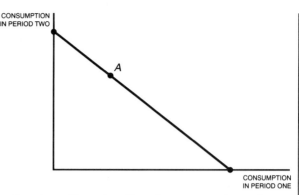

Step three: Show the effect of government borrowing by adding the extra spending to current consumption (the horizontal coordinate of *A*) and subtracting the future tax liability from future consumption (the vertical coordinate of *A*). Label the new point *B*.

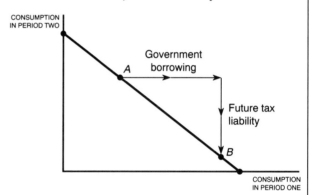

Step four: Determine if point *B* lies on or above the original budget constraint.

Step five: If *B* is on the original budget constraint, then Ricardian equivalence holds, and the household will save to return to point *A* because *A* indicates their preferred decision. If *B* is above the original budget constraint, Ricardian equivalence is not true, and the household may choose to consume more today.

---

4 (Worked problem: Ricardian equivalence) Doctor Campbell and her husband make $210,000 per year and expect that their real earnings will continue for at least 10 years. Although they expect a 50 percent real interest rate over the 10-year period, they neither borrow nor save. The government passes a subsidy program that will give the Campbells an extra $10,000 this year. It finances this program by issuing 10-year bonds that pay a 50 percent real rate of return over the period. The Campbells expect that they will pay their share of the tax liability when the bonds come due in 10 years. Analyze how the program will affect the Campbells' savings decision and whether Ricardian equivalence would hold.

Step-by-step solution

Step one: Draw the two-period budget constraint. The present discounted value of their income equals $210,000 +

[$210,000 × (1/1 + .50)] = $350,000, which is the horizontal intercept. The future equivalent is [$210,000 × (1 + .50)] + $210,000 = $525,000, which is the vertical intercept. The slope is 525,000/350,000 = 1.50, which is 1 plus the interest rate.

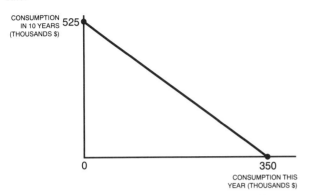

Step two: Choose a point that reflects the household's consumption and savings decisions. The Campbells neither save nor borrow, so they choose to consume $210,000 in each year.

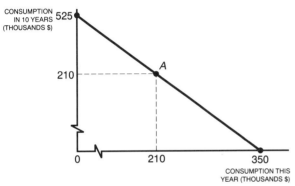

Step three: Show the effect of the program. It gives the Campbells $10,000 now, but it takes away $10,000 × (1 + .50) = $15,000 in 10 years. This moves their chosen point from A to B.

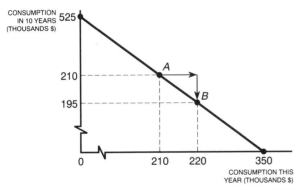

Step four: Determine if point *B* lies on or above the original budget constraint. Clearly, *B* is on the same budget constraint.

Step five: If *B* is on the original budget constraint, then Ricardian equivalence holds, and the household will save to return to point *A* because *A* indicates their preferred decision. The Campbells merely increase their savings to $10,000. The

principal and interest will be just enough to pay the tax increase that they expect in 10 years. The government borrowing is exactly offset by private savings.

5 (Practice problem: Ricardian equivalence) The typical person in Ricadonia earns 20,000 ricks (the local currency) annually. The real interest rate is 5 percent per year, and the typical person borrows 2,000 ricks. The government decides to stimulate the economy by giving each person 5,000 ricks. To finance this grant, the government sells one-year bonds that also pay 5 percent. Taxes will be increased next year to pay off the bonds. Analyze how the grant will affect the typical person's borrowing and savings decisions and also whether Ricardian equivalence would hold in Ricadonia.

6 (Worked problem: Ricardian equivalence) Return to the Campbells of problem 4. All information is the same except the real interest rate for borrowing, which is now 100 percent over the 10-year period. Analyze how the program will affect the Campbells' savings decision and whether Ricardian equivalence would hold.

Step-by-step solution

Step one: Draw the two-period budget constraint. The vertical intercept remains as in problem 4, but the horizontal intercept now equals the present value of income discounted at 100 percent = $210,000 + [$210,000 × 1/(1 + 1.00)] = $315,000.

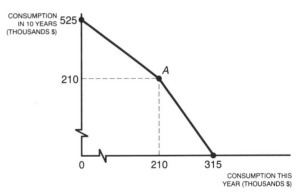

Step two: Choose a point that reflects the household's consumption and savings decisions. The Campbells continue to choose to consume $210,000 in each period.

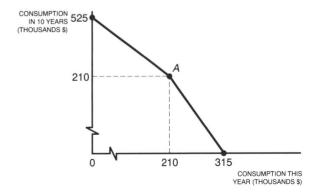

Step three: Show the effect of the government program. As in problem 4, it increases current consumption by $10,000 and reduces future consumption by $15,000, as shown by point *B*.

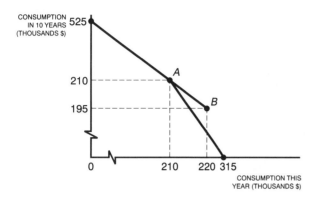

Step four: Determine if point *B* lies on or above the original budget constraint. It is now above.

Step five: If *B* is above the original constraint, Ricardian equivalence is not true, and the household may choose to consume more today. The deficit finance allows the Campbells to consume more today than it would if they had to borrow the money from a bank. They may choose any point on the line segment between *B* and *A,* and their choice will indicate more consumption. In this case, the government deficit increases consumption.

7 (Practice problem: Ricardian equivalence) Return to problem 5, and suppose that all information is the same except that the borrowing interest rate is 20 percent. Analyze how the grant will affect the typical person's borrowing and savings decisions and also whether Ricardian equivalence would hold in Ricadonia.

8 (Practice problem: Ricardian equivalence) Although the Johnsons earn $50,000 per year after taxes and expect to continue to earn the same in real terms for the next 5 years, they have a bad credit history and cannot borrow. They could earn 25 percent on their savings, but they do not have any. Analyze the effect on the Johnsons' budget constraint of a current tax cut of $10,000 financed by a five-year bond paying 25 percent over the period. The bond will be repaid with tax increases, and the Johnsons expect that their share of the tax increase will pay off the bonds issued to finance their share of the current tax cut.

Answers to Problems

2 The increase in real interest rates reduces consumption (durable goods purchases fall) and investment, shifts aggregate expenditures down, and reduces output.

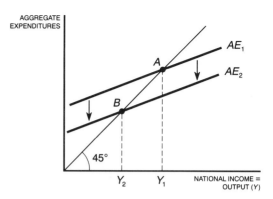

3 *a* Investment falls; this shifts aggregate expenditures down and reduces output.

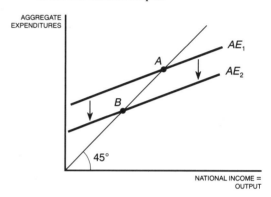

 b Investment falls, this shifts aggregate expenditures down and reduces output.

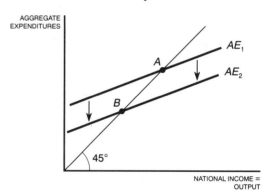

 c Consumption falls, this shifts aggregate expenditures down and reduces output.

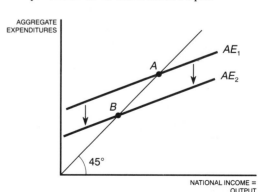

d Investment increases; this shifts aggregate expenditures up and increases output.

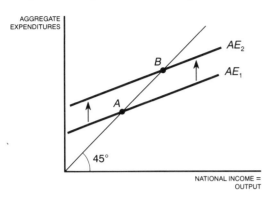

e Investment and purchases of durable goods fall; this shifts aggregate expenditures down and reduces output.

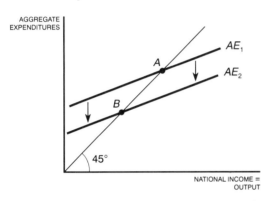

f Investment and purchases of durable goods rise; this shifts aggregate expenditures up and increases output.

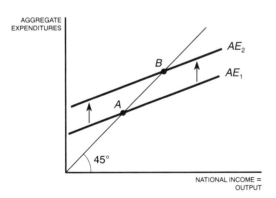

g Investment falls; this shifts aggregate expenditures down and reduces output.

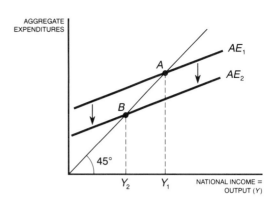

h Investment increases; this shifts aggregate expenditures up and increases output.

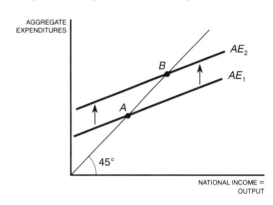

5

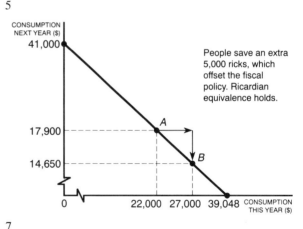

People save an extra 5,000 ricks, which offset the fiscal policy. Ricardian equivalence holds.

7

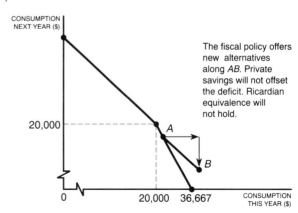

The fiscal policy offers new alternatives along *AB*. Private savings will not offset the deficit. Ricardian equivalence will not hold.

8

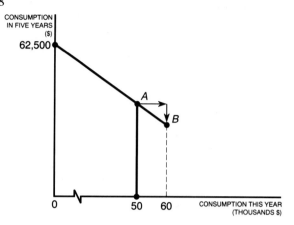

Chapter 30

GOVERNMENT EXPENDITURES AND TRADE

Chapter Review

Like Chapter 29, this chapter takes a deeper look at two of the four components of aggregate expenditures. Here the focus is on government expenditures and net exports. The goal is to understand how these two elements of the aggregate expenditures schedule work. The next chapter returns to the aggregate demand and supply model and shows more clearly how income-expenditure analysis and aggregate demand are related.

ESSENTIAL CONCEPTS

1   **Government expenditures** are one of the four components of aggregate expenditures. It follows that changes in government spending shift aggregate expenditures and cause changes in the economy's output. Government may help stabilize the economy during recessions by increasing spending when other forms of private spending are low.

2   Advocates of **balanced budgets** want the government to spend no more than it collects in taxes. Even while keeping the budget balanced, government can stimulate aggregate expenditures, although not as much as it can

with deficit spending. A simultaneous increase in government spending and taxes causes aggregate expenditures to rise by just the amount of the increase. The multiplier equals 1 in this case.

3   Keynes advocated using deficit spending, that is, running deficits in times of high unemployment, to stabilize the economy. Economists measure fiscal responsibility with the **full-employment deficit,** which is the deficit that would have occurred if the economy were at full employment. During recessions, the actual budget will be in deficit even though the full-employment budget is balanced.

4   Government deficits will not be effective in stimulating the economy if government borrowing **crowds out** private investment. Crowding out is unlikely to occur when there is excess capacity in the economy or if the borrowing is financed with foreign capital. An influx of foreign capital will reduce net exports, however.

5   Certain government programs, such as unemployment insurance and income taxes, act as **automatic stabilizers**; cause greater spending and reduced taxes during recessions, while creating less spending and more taxes during economic booms. Automatic stabilizers reduce the multiplier and smooth fluctuations in the economy.

Provincial governments, however, do not see stabilization of the economy and the maintenance of full employment as their responsibility. Indeed, fluctuations in their expenditures have probably exacerbated, rather than reduced, instability.

6 Since the 1980s, a sizeable trade surplus has disappeared and been replaced by a growing trade deficit. Canada has always used trade protection as a policy device, but calls for trade barriers have increased with the size of the trade deficit. Such barriers reduce imports, but they also raise prices and invite foreign retaliation. Additionally, protectionism may lead to changes in the exchange rate, which in turn could offset the creation of jobs in the domestic economy that the protectionism was supposed to foster.

7 The **net export function** shows how net exports (exports minus imports) change as income changes. Net exports can increase or decrease as tastes change. Relative incomes can also affect net exports. The marginal propensity to import is the amount spent on imports out of an extra dollar of income, and if Canadian incomes rise relative to foreign incomes, net exports will decrease. Finally, changes in relative prices are important, especially the exchange rate, which is the price of one currency in terms of other currencies. If the Canadian dollar becomes more expensive, so do our exports, and the net export function shifts down.

BEHIND THE ESSENTIAL CONCEPTS

1 The concepts of stocks and flows can help you distinguish between the deficit and the debt. The federal budget deficit is the difference between federal government taxes and its expenditures:

budget deficit = taxes − expenditures.

The budget deficit is a flow; you can think of it as a flow of red ink. After many years of budget deficits, the federal government has built up a rather large debt. The debt is the sum of the accumulated deficits, and it is a stock.

2 The net export function gives the relationship between national income and the level of net exports. It is downward sloping because as income increases, Canadians buy more imports. Any change in income brings about a movement along the net export function. As always, you must be clear about the difference between moving along a curve and shifting it. Other relevant changes, such as changes in tastes, changes in foreign income, or changes in the exchange rate, shift the net export function.

3 Government can smooth the economy in two ways. First, it can stimulate the economy during recessions. Here government takes an active role and makes up for the shortfall in private spending. Another approach works automatically. Taxes such as personal or corporate income taxes, which increase as income increases, and programs such as welfare and unemploy-

ment insurance act as automatic stabilizers. These programs provide additional spending during downturns and reduce spending in booms; they reduce the size of the multiplier and smooth the ups and downs of the private economy.

SELF-TEST

True or False

F 1 If government spending and taxes increase by the same amount, then the aggregate expenditures schedule will not change.

F 2 The real budget deficit equals what the deficit would be if the economy were operating at full employment.

T 3 The budget deficit is a flow, and the accumulated government debt is the corresponding stock.

T 4 Government borrowing to finance deficits may crowd out private investment.

T 5 Unemployment insurance helps to stabilize the economy by increasing government expenditures during recessions.

F 6 According to the political business cycle theory, government stabilizes the economy in order to win re-election.

F 7 The balanced budget requirements in some U.S. state constitutions help to stabilize the economy.

T 8 The expenditure cuts of the early 1990s shifted the aggregate expenditures schedule down, and so contributed to the recession.

T 9 A closed economy neither imports nor exports.

F 10 Protectionists advocate policies to promote imports.

T 11 An increase in national income will increase the trade deficit. ?

F 12 If the dollar appreciates, Canadian exports will increase. decrease

F 13 The real exchange rate is the exchange rate adjusted for changes in price levels in each country.

T 14 In an open economy, changes in the exchange rate can augment or offset the effectiveness of government attempts to stimulate the economy.

F 15 Downward shifts in the net export function stimulate the economy. ↓ exports

Multiple Choice

1 An increase in government spending, holding the level of taxes constant, will

a shift the aggregate expenditures schedule up.
b leave the aggregate expenditures schedule unchanged.
c shift the aggregate expenditures schedule down.
d rotate the aggregate expenditures schedule to the left.

e rotate the aggregate expenditures schedule to the right.

2 An increase in taxes, holding the level of government spending constant, will

    a shift the aggregate expenditures schedule up.
    b leave the aggregate expenditures schedule unchanged.
    c shift the aggregate expenditures schedule down.
    d rotate the aggregate expenditures schedule to the left.
    e rotate the aggregate expenditures schedule to the right.

3 An increase in both government spending and taxes, keeping the overall budget balanced, will

    a shift the aggregate expenditures schedule up.
    b leave the aggregate expenditures schedule unchanged.
    c shift the aggregate expenditures schedule down.
    d rotate the aggregate expenditures schedule to the left.
    e rotate the aggregate expenditures schedule to the right.

4 Deficit spending is financed by

    a taxes.
    b spending cuts.
    c government borrowing.
    d printing money.
    e the multiplier.

5 The deficit that would occur if the economy were at full employment under current spending and tax policies is called the

    a balanced budget multiplier.
    b full-employment deficit.
    c trade deficit.
    d total accumulated government debt.
    e real budget deficit.

6 The change in the inflation-adjusted level of accumulated government debt from year to year is the

    a balanced budget multiplier.
    b full-employment deficit.
    c trade deficit.
    d real budget deficit.
    e nominal budget deficit.

7 Crowding out refers to

    a the possibility that taxes reduce private investment.
    b the effect of inflation on the real value of the accumulated government debt.
    c the possibility that government borrowing may reduce private investment.
    d the effect of protectionism on the trade balance.
    e the effect of imports on the market share of domestic firms.

8 Mechanisms that increase the government deficit during recessions and decrease it during economic booms are called

    a balanced budget multipliers.
    b full-employment deficits.
    c automatic stabilizers.
    d political business cycles.
    e none of the above.

9 Which of the following is not an automatic stabilizer?

    a income taxes.
    b unemployment insurance.
    c defence spending.
    d Old Age Security benefits.
    e none of the above.

10 Provincial government spending tends to

    a increase in booms and decrease in recessions, and thus reduce the volatility of the economy.
    b increase in booms and decrease in recessions, and thus increase the volatility of the economy.
    c decrease in booms and increase in recessions, and thus reduce the volatility of the economy.
    d decrease in booms and increase in recessions, and thus increase the volatility of the economy.
    e be stable over the business cycle and neither increase nor reduce the volatility of the economy.

11 A closed economy

    a does not trade with the rest of the world.
    b exports but does not import.
    c imports but does not export.
    d exports and imports, but does not run a trade deficit.
    e none of the above.

12 Protectionists favour policies that

    a insulate domestic producers from foreign competition.
    b bring about an open economy.
    c lower taxes to protect business from insolvency.
    d regulate businesses to protect the safety of consumers and workers.
    e guarantee a balanced budget.

13 Which of the following can <u>increase</u> the trade deficit?

    a a downward shift in the import function.
    b an upward shift in the import function.
    c a decrease in foreign income.
    d an increase in foreign income.
    e none of the above.

14 The net export function gives the level of net exports corresponding to each level of

    a imports.
    b exports.
    c the exchange rate.
    d national income.
    e protectionism.

15 The marginal propensity to import is

    a the ratio of imports to exports.
    b the ratio of net exports to national income.
    c the ratio of imports to national income.
    d the proportion of an additional dollar of national income spent on imports.

e the extra imports that result from a 1 percent fall in the exchange rate.

16 An increase in Canadian income, together with unchanged income abroad, will

a increase the trade deficit. ↑M
b decrease the trade deficit.
c increase both exports and imports, and so leave the trade deficit constant.
d decrease both exports and imports, and so leave the trade deficit constant.
e have no effect on exports or imports.

17 The exchange rate is the

a price of domestic goods in terms of foreign goods.
b ratio of the domestic interest rate to the world interest rate.
c extra imports out of an additional one dollar of national income.
d cost of one currency in terms of another.
e ratio of taxes to government spending.

18 If the exchange rate changes from 200 yen per dollar to 250 yen per dollar, then

a the dollar appreciates and Canadian goods become cheaper to the Japanese.
b the dollar appreciates and Canadian goods become more expensive to the Japanese.
c the dollar depreciates and Canadian goods become cheaper to the Japanese.
d the dollar depreciates and Canadian goods become more expensive to the Japanese.
e none of the above.

19 Which of the following does not affect the prices of Canadian goods relative to those produced abroad?

a the exchange rate.
b the dollar prices of Canadian goods.
c the rate of inflation in Canada.
d the prices of foreign goods (measured in foreign currency).
e none of the above.

20 If increased government expenditures lead to an appreciation of the dollar, the

a net export function will shift up. ↑M
b net export function will shift down. ↑income
c net export function will rotate to the right.
d net export function will rotate to the left.
e dollar will depreciate.

Completion

1 If the government spends more than it raises in taxes, the deficit is financed by ___borrowing___ .

2 The ___full employment deficit___ equals the deficit that would have occurred if government revenues and spending were at their full-employment levels.

3 The ___real budget deficit___ is the yearly change in the real level of total accumulated government debt.

4 ___Crowding out___ refers to the possibility that government borrowing may reduce private investment.

5 Mechanisms that reduce government spending or raise taxes in recessions are called ___automatic stabilizers___

6 When the economy runs a trade deficit, ___exports___ are less than ___imports___ .

7 The view that trade policies should give advantages to domestic producers and inhibit foreign producers is called ___protectionism___

8 The ___net export function___ gives the level of net exports corresponding to each level of national income.

9 The ___marginal propensity to import___ is the proportion of a one-dollar increase in national income spent on imports.

10 The cost of one currency in terms of another is called the ___exchange rate___

Answers to Self-Test

True or False

1	f	6	f	11	t
2	f	7	f	12	f
3	t	8	t	13	t
4	t	9	t	14	t
5	t	10	f	15	f

Multiple Choice

1	a	6	d	11	a	16	a
2	c	7	c	12	a	17	d
3	a	8	c	13	b	18	b
4	c	9	c	14	d	19	e
5	b	10	b	15	d	20	b

Completion

1 borrowing
2 full-employment deficit
3 real budget deficit
4 Crowding out
5 automatic stabilizers
6 exports, imports
7 protectionism
8 net export function
9 marginal propensity to import
10 exchange rate

Doing Economics: Tools and Practice Problems

As in Chapter 29, this section uses income-expenditure analysis to understand fluctuations in the economy's level of output. The focus of this chapter is on government fiscal policies and international trade.

Tool Kit 30.1: Using Income-Expenditure Analysis

We use income-expenditure analysis to understand how changes in taxes, government spending, imports, and exports affect the output in the economy. When taxes, government spending, or foreign trade change, the aggregate expenditures schedule shifts and creates a change in the equilibrium level of output. Table 30.1

lists some important factors that shift aggregate expenditures.

Table 30.1
Shifts in Aggregate Expenditures

Changes in government spending.

Changes in taxes that affect consumption, such as changes in income tax rates, and those that affect investment, such as changes in the capital gains tax or the investment tax credit.

Changes in net exports that arise from changing tastes (of Canadian households) for imports, tastes (of foreign households) for Canadian exports, foreign incomes, or relative prices of Canadian and foreign goods. Relative prices may change as a result of inflation in Canada, inflation abroad, or changes in exchange rates.

Step one: Start with an equilibrium.

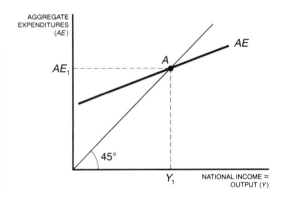

Step two: Identify a cause, and determine its effect on consumption, investment, government spending, or net exports.

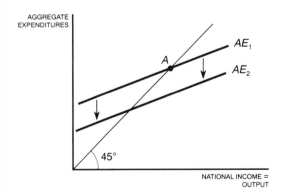

Step three: If any component of aggregate expenditures increases, shift the aggregate expenditures schedule up; if any decreases, shift the schedule down.

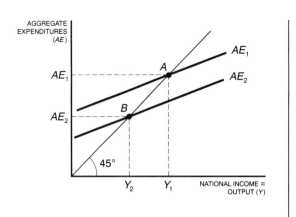

Step four: Find the new equilibrium level of output and compare.

1 (Worked problem: income-expenditure analysis) Use income-expenditure analysis to explain the impact of an increase in capital gains taxes.

Step-by-step solution

Step one: Start with an equilibrium.

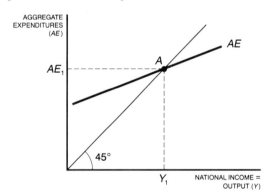

Step two: Identify a cause, and determine its effect on consumption, investment, government spending, or net exports. The increase in capital gains taxes reduces private investment.

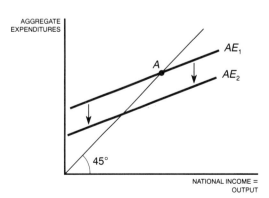

Step three: Shift the aggregate expenditures schedule. Because investment decreases, it shifts down.

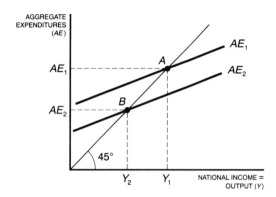

Step four: In the new equilibrium, output is less. The capital gains tax increase reduces the economy's output.

2   (Practice problem: income-expenditure analysis) Use income-expenditure analysis to determine the impact of an increase in Canadian exports.

3   (Practice problem: income-expenditure analysis) Use income-expenditure analysis to determine the impact of each of the following.

   a   A deep recession in Europe reduces foreign incomes.
   b   To reduce the budget deficit, the Canadian government increases income tax rates.
   c   Canadian exports fall dramatically.
   d   An investment tax credit is introduced that allows firms to deduct 10 percent of investment expenses from their tax bill.
   e   A "Buy Canadian" campaign motivates households to reduce their purchases of imported goods.
   f   The Canadian dollar appreciates in foreign currency markets.
   g   Serious inflation returns in Canada as prices rise at the rate of 10 percent per year.
   h   The Canadian dollar depreciates in foreign currency markets.
   i   After a change of government in Ottawa, defence spending falls when an order for 50 helicopters is cancelled.

Answers to Problems

2   Net exports increase, aggregate expenditures shift up, and output increases.

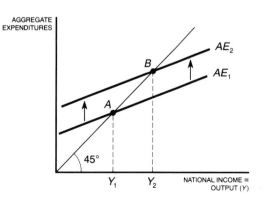

3   *a*   Exports fall, net exports fall, aggregate expenditures shift down, and output decreases.

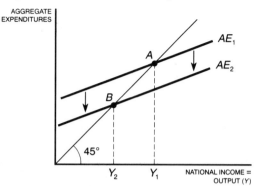

   b   Aggregate expenditures shift down, and so decrease output.

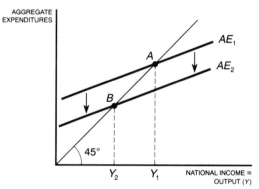

   c   Exports fall, net exports fall, aggregate expenditures shift down, and output decreases.

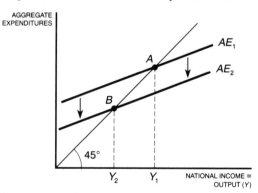

   d   Investment increases, aggregate expenditures shift up, and output increases.

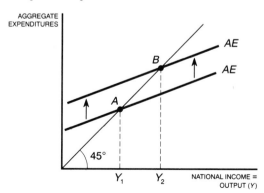

e Imports fall, consumption increases, aggregate expenditures shift up, and output increases.

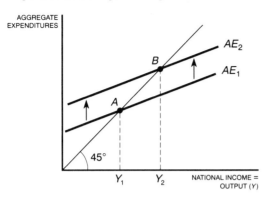

f Net exports fall, aggregate expenditures shift down, and output decreases.

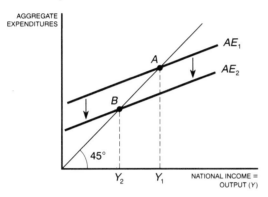

g Net exports fall, aggregate expenditures shift down, and output decreases.

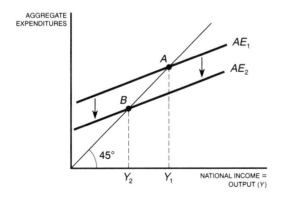

h Net exports increase, aggregate expenditures shift up, and output increases.

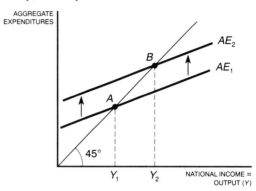

i Government spending falls, aggregate expenditures shift down, and output decreases.

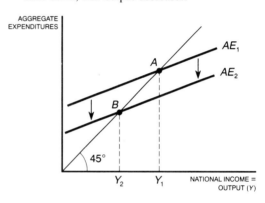

(handwritten notes at top of page:)
22.96
24.86
47.82

I = purchase of an asset that will provide a return over a long period of time

Firms put money elsewhere b/c it pays more than to ↓r→↑I. put it in the bank where the interest rate is low

Chapter 31

AGGREGATE DEMAND AND SUPPLY

Chapter Review

This chapter of the text uses the income-expenditure analysis developed in Chapters 28 to 30 to construct the aggregate demand curve. Together with the aggregate supply curve, the aggregate demand curve determines the economy's equilibrium level of output and its price level. Fluctuations in output and price levels are explained by shifts in the two curves. The final section of the chapter explores the interaction between the labour and product markets, focusing especially on the role of expectations. This chapter assumes that prices adjust to clear the product market. Chapter 32, the final chapter in this part of the text, turns to the possibilities and consequences of price rigidities.

ESSENTIAL CONCEPTS

1 The **aggregate demand curve** shows the level of aggregate demand at each price level. Income-expenditure analysis can be used to show that as the price level falls, aggregate demand increases. The intersection of aggregate demand with aggregate supply determines the economy's output and price level.

2 When prices fall, each component of aggregate demand changes for various reasons. Overall, aggregate demand increases by a small amount, and the aggregate demand curve is quite inelastic.

a The **real balance effect** denotes the rise in consumption that occurs when prices fall. As prices decrease, the *real* value of people's money holdings and any other dollar-denominated assets increases. Consumption increases, but only slightly.

b Falling prices affect investment in three ways. First, the **interest rate effect** shows that as the interest rate falls, firms are induced to increase investment. Second, as firms earn lower profits, and because profits are an important source of funds, investment falls as a result of the **credit constraint effect**. Finally, as firms' financial positions grow precarious, the **firm wealth effect** makes them less willing to bear the risk of investment.

c Net exports increase when prices fall because Canadian goods are relatively less costly.

3 The **aggregate supply curve** shows the output that all firms in the economy are willing to produce at each price level. It is derived by adding all the supply curves of all the firms. It is flat at low levels of output,

then upward sloping, and nearly vertical as the economy approaches its capacity.

4   The aggregate demand curve shifts because of changes in consumer purchases of durable goods, changes in investment demand, changes in net exports, and changes in government spending. The aggregate supply curve shifts because of natural and manmade disasters, changes in technology, changes in the prices of imported goods, changes in the perception of and willingness to bear risk, and changes in wage rates. Shifts in aggregate demand and aggregate supply explain the fluctuations in output and prices that occur in the economy.

5   If the economy is in deep recession, reductions in wage rates are unlikely to increase output enough to restore full employment. Firms are willing to produce more when the wage falls, and aggregate supply shifts to the right, as shown in Figure 31.1. But as wages fall, workers have less to spend, and aggregate demand shifts to the left. The price level falls, but there is little change in output.

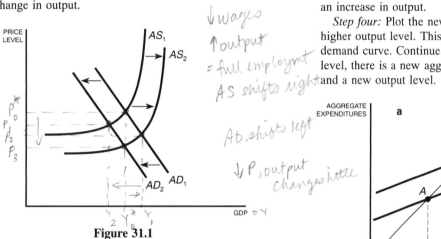

Figure 31.1

6   If current prices, current wages, and expectations of future prices and wages all change proportionately to one another, then output will remain constant. The new classical economists argue that while an unanticipated increase in prices may lead to more output in the short run, as workers learn of the price increase and demand higher wages, output will return to its original, market-clearing level. They argue that expectations are formed rationally and that the adjustment takes place relatively quickly. An extreme implication of this position is the **policy ineffectiveness proposition,** which says that in manipulating aggregate demand, government can only change the price level.

7   New Keynesian economists see the long run as too distant to be relevant and argue that for extended periods of time, the economy settles at low levels of output accompanied by high unemployment. According to the new Keynesian view, expectations adjust slowly in response to demand shocks, and in the short run, it is better to assume that they are either static or slow to adapt. For the new Keynesians, market clearing is more the exception than the rule.

BEHIND THE ESSENTIAL CONCEPTS

1   It is important to understand the relationship between the income-expenditure analysis developed in Chapters 28 to 30 and the aggregate demand curve. Income-expenditure analysis shows what the equilibrium level of output would be if prices were fixed. For every price level, there is a new *AE* curve and a corresponding equilibrium level of output. We derive the aggregate demand curve from the income-expenditure analysis in the following way.

Step one: Start with an equilibrium in the income-expenditure diagram, as shown by point *A* in Figure 31.2ᴀ. Remember that a price level corresponds to this equilibrium.

Step two: Plot the price level and output level, as shown in panel ʙ. This is point *A* on the aggregate demand curve.

Step three: Reduce the price level. This shifts the aggregate expenditures schedule up and brings about an increase in output.

Step four: Plot the new, lower price level and the higher output level. This is point *B* on the aggregate demand curve. Continue the process. For each price level, there is a new aggregate expenditures schedule and a new output level.

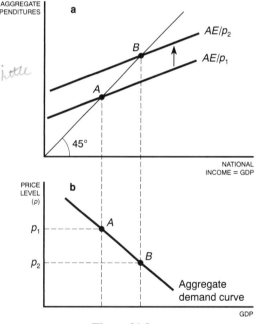

Figure 31.2

2   Anything that causes the aggregate expenditures schedule to shift up will increase aggregate demand. If the price level falls, then we move along the aggregate demand curve. If any other factor, such as investment or government spending, changes, then the aggregate demand curve itself shifts.

3   If you think that today's prices and wages will not change, then your **expectations** are **static.** If you think that today's prices and wages will continue to change at the same rate that they have changed in the recent

past, then your expectations are **adaptive.** But if you use all available information to form your expectations, then they are **rational.** The real question for macroeconomics, however, is how well do households and firms understand what is going on, how rapidly do they learn of new circumstances, and how quickly do they make the correct decisions?

4 Although there are important sources of disagreement among economists, most would accept this chapter's basic explanations of how the macroeconomy works. These include the relationship between income-expenditure analysis and the aggregate demand curve, the basic shapes of the aggregate demand and supply curves, the reasons for shifts in aggregate demand and supply, and the fact that these shifts explain the economy's ups and downs. The areas of disagreement involve the speed of adjustment and market clearing. Economists who lean towards the new Keynesian position believe that the economy may amplify disturbances, may cause them to persist, and will adjust slowly. As a consequence, the economy spends quite a bit of time away from full employment. The new classical position says that because of rational expectations, adjustments to shocks are quick, and the economy spends most of its time near full employment. One way to sum up the situation is to say that all agree where to look, but they do not agree exactly on what they see.

SELF-TEST

True or False

1 The aggregate demand curve is derived on the assumption that wages are fixed.

2 The aggregate supply curve is derived on the assumption that wages are fixed.

3 The real balance effect shows that as prices fall, the real values of individuals' money holdings increase, and they consume more.

4 Firms may reduce their investments when prices fall because as their revenues fall, there is less money available for investments.

5 As product prices fall, net exports decrease and the trade deficit widens.

6 The aggregate demand curve is relatively elastic.

7 An increase in purchases of durable goods will shift the aggregate demand curve to the right.

8 If the Canadian dollar appreciates, net exports will increase and shift the aggregate demand curve to the right.

9 A major improvement in technology will shift the aggregate supply curve to the left.

10 A change in wages shifts both the aggregate demand and supply curves.

11 Rational expectations are formed using all available information.

12 Historically, nominal prices and wages have moved in the same direction, and limited the changes in real wages.

13 New Keynesian economists emphasize that adjustment to full employment may be slow and uncertain.

14 The policy ineffectiveness proposition states that changes in government tax and spending policies can only affect the price level.

15 New classical economists believe that the economy operates at full employment almost all of the time.

Multiple Choice

1 Which of the following is not true? The aggregate supply curve

a is relatively flat at low levels of output.
b is upward sloping at intermediate levels of output.
c is vertical at the highest level of output.
d gives the output level that firms choose to supply at each price level.
e is upward sloping at all levels of output.

2 In deriving the aggregate demand curve, which of the following is not assumed?

a Expectations of future prices are fixed.
b Wages are fixed.
c The current price level is fixed.
d Interest rates are fixed.
e The exchange rate is fixed.

3 As the price level decreases,

a the aggregate expenditures schedule shifts up and the level of aggregate demand increases.
b the aggregate expenditures schedule shifts down and the level of aggregate demand increases.
c the aggregate expenditures schedule shifts up and the level of aggregate demand decreases.
d the aggregate expenditures schedule shifts down and the level of aggregate demand decreases.
e aggregate expenditures are unaffected.

4 According to the real balance effect, as prices fall,

a the real values of individuals' money holdings increase, and they consume some of this additional wealth.
b lower prices lead to lower interest rates and more business investment.
c firms' revenues and thus the money available for investment fall.
d firms become less willing to undertake the risks associated with investment.
e net exports increase.

5 According to the interest rate effect, as prices fall,

a the real values of individuals' money holdings increase, and they consume some of this additional wealth.
b lower prices lead to lower interest rates and more business investment.
c firms' revenues and thus the money available for investment fall.

d firms become less willing to undertake the risks associated with investment.

e net exports increase.

6 The firm wealth effect indicates that as prices fall,

  a the real values of individuals' money holdings increase, and they consume some of this additional wealth.

  b lower prices lead to lower interest rates and more business investment.

  c firms' revenues and thus the money available for investment fall.

  d firms become less willing to undertake the risks associated with investment.

  e net exports increase.

7 As prices fall, the credit constraint effect implies that

  a the real values of individuals' money holdings increase, and they consume some of this additional wealth.

  b lower prices lead to lower interest rates and more business investment.

  c firms' revenues and thus the money available for investment fall.

  d firms become less willing to undertake the risks associated with investment.

  e net exports increase.

8 The aggregate demand curve is

  a perfectly inelastic.

  b relatively inelastic.

  c perfectly elastic.

  d relatively elastic.

  e upward sloping.

9 An upward shift in the aggregate expenditures schedule leads to

  a a rightward shift in aggregate demand.

  b a leftward shift in aggregate demand.

  c a rightward shift in aggregate supply.

  d a leftward shift in aggregate supply.

  e a rightward shift in both aggregate demand and supply.

10 An increase in investment spending causes

  a a rightward shift in aggregate demand.

  b a leftward shift in aggregate demand.

  c a rightward shift in aggregate supply.

  d a leftward shift in aggregate supply.

  e a rightward shift in both aggregate demand and supply.

11 A decrease in government spending causes

  a a rightward shift in aggregate demand.

  b a leftward shift in aggregate demand.

  c a rightward shift in aggregate supply.

  d a leftward shift in aggregate supply.

  e a rightward shift in both aggregate demand and supply.

12 An earthquake, flood, or other serious natural disaster causes

  a a rightward shift in aggregate demand.

  b a leftward shift in aggregate demand.

  c a rightward shift in aggregate supply.

  d a leftward shift in aggregate supply.

  e a rightward shift in both aggregate demand and supply.

13 An increase in the price of an important imported good, such as oil, causes

  a a rightward shift in aggregate demand.

  b a leftward shift in aggregate demand.

  c a rightward shift in aggregate supply.

  d a leftward shift in aggregate supply.

  e a rightward shift in both aggregate demand and supply.

14 Which of the following is not true? In recessions, firms

  a grow less willing to bear risks.

  b postpone investment.

  c reduce inventories.

  d cut back on production.

  e none of the above.

15 When nominal wages fall,

  a aggregate supply shifts to the right, aggregate demand shifts to the left, and the price level falls.

  b aggregate supply shifts to the right, aggregate demand shifts to the left, and the price level rises.

  c aggregate supply shifts to the left, aggregate demand shifts to the right, and the price level falls.

  d aggregate supply shifts to the left, aggregate demand shifts to the right, and the price level rises.

  e none of the above.

16 Individuals who always expect today's prices to continue have

  a static expectations.

  b adaptive expectations.

  c rational expectations.

  d great expectations.

  e none of the above.

17 Individuals who always expect current trends in prices to continue have

  a static expectations.

  b adaptive expectations.

  c rational expectations.

  d great expectations.

  e none of the above.

18 Individuals who use all available information to make forecasts of future prices have

  a static expectations.

  b adaptive expectations.

  c rational expectations.

  d great expectations.

  e none of the above.

19 Classical economists do not believe that

  a individuals have rational expectations.

  b shifts in the aggregate demand curve only affect the price level.

    c wages adjust quickly to clear the labour market.

    d the economy almost always operates at or near full capacity.

    e none of the above.

20 Which of the following is not a tenet of the new Keynesian economists?

    a People take a significant amount of time to adjust expectations to changes in the economy.

    b Aggregate demand can have significant effects on output.

    c Wages may fail to adjust to clear the labour market.

    d Unemployment may persist.

    e Shifts in aggregate demand affect only the price level.

Completion

1 One reason for the downward slope of the aggregate demand curve is the _____, which says that people feel wealthier when prices fall and consume more.

2 Lower prices may reduce investment spending by reducing retained earnings, according to the _____ effect.

3 Lower domestic prices cause net exports to _____.

4 Increases in the prices of imported goods shift the _____ curve to the left.

5 If people use all available information to predict future prices, then their expectations are said to be _____.

6 If people expect current trends to continue, then their expectations are said to be _____.

7 If people expect that the future will look like the present, then their expectations are said to be _____.

8 The view that changes in aggregate demand change only the price level is called the _____.

9 _____ economists believe that expectations are revised quickly and that markets adjust quickly.

10 _____ economists believe that for extended periods of time, wages may fail to adjust to clear the labour market.

Answers to Self-Test

True or False

1	t	6	f	11	t
2	t	7	t	12	t
3	t	8	f	13	t
4	t	9	f	14	t
5	f	10	t	15	t

Multiple Choice

1	e	6	d	11	b	16	a
2	c	7	c	12	d	17	b
3	a	8	b	13	d	18	c
4	a	9	a	14	e	19	e
5	b	10	a	15	a	20	e

Completion

1	real balance effect
2	credit constraint
3	increase
4	aggregate supply
5	rational
6	adaptive
7	static
8	policy ineffectiveness proposition
9	New classical
10	New Keynesian

Doing Economics: Tools and Practice Problems

Having gained a deeper understanding of aggregate demand through the study of income-expenditure analysis, we return to the aggregate demand and supply model. In this problem set, we study how shifts in aggregate demand and aggregate supply lead to changes in output and in the price level. Changes in wages, perceptions of risk, and willingness to bear risk shift both the aggregate demand and aggregate supply curves. An increase in wages shifts aggregate demand to the right because wage earners typically consume more of their income than capital owners do, but it shifts aggregate supply to the left because it increases production costs. If firms perceive more risk ahead or become less willing to bear risk, they reduce investment; this shifts aggregate demand to the left. They also reduce production; this shifts aggregate supply to the left.

Tool Kit 31.1: Using Aggregate Demand and Supply

    Shifts in aggregate demand and aggregate supply explain the fluctuations in the economy's output and price level, but the impact of any given shift depends upon whether the initial equilibrium is on the flat, upward-sloping, or vertical segment of the aggregate supply curve. Table 31.1 summarizes the factors that shift the aggregate demand and supply curves.

Table 31.1

Shifts in aggregate demand arise from:

    changes in consumption, which in turn arise from changes in wealth, real interest rates, credit availability, uncertainty about future earnings, taxes (especially income tax rates), or wages.

    changes in investment, which in turn arise from changes in real interest rates, stock prices, credit availability, retained earnings, expectations of profitability, perceptions of risk, willingness to bear risk, or taxes (especially capital gains and the investment tax credit).

    changes in government spending.

changes in net exports, which in turn arise from changes in tastes (of Canadian households) for imports, tastes (of foreign households) for Canadian exports, foreign incomes, or relative prices of Canadian and foreign goods. (Relative prices change because of inflation in Canada, inflation abroad, or changes in exchange rates.)

Shifts in aggregate supply arise from:

changes in the economy's production capacity, natural or manmade disasters, changes in technology, changes in perceptions of risk, changes in willingness to bear risk, or wages.

Step one: Start with an equilibrium. This will be on the flat, upward-sloping, or vertical portion of the aggregate supply curve.

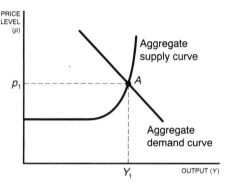

Step two: Identify a cause, and determine which curve or curves shift and in what direction.

Step three: Shift the curve or curves.

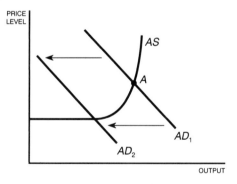

Step four: Find the new equilibrium, and compare the output and price level with those for the old equilibrium.

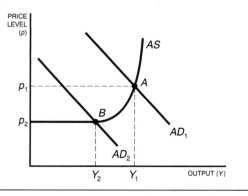

1 (Worked problem: aggregate demand and supply) Suppose the economy is in deep recession along the flat portion of the aggregate supply curve, and wages fall. Use aggregate demand and supply to show the effects on the output and price level.

Step-by-step solution

Step one: Start with an equilibrium.

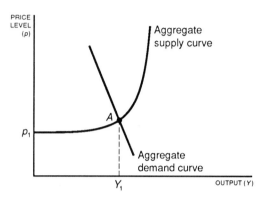

Step two: Identify a cause, and determine which curve shifts and in what direction. The fall in wages shifts aggregate supply down and aggregate demand to the left.

Step three: Shift the curves.

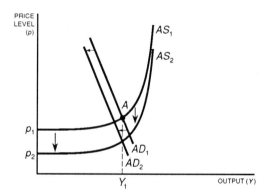

Step four: Find the new equilibrium, and compare the output and price level with those for the old equilibrium. The price level is now lower than before, but there is little, if any, effect on output.

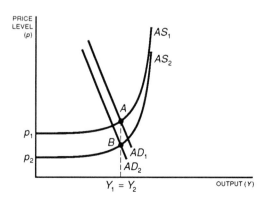

2 (Practice problem: aggregate demand and supply) Suppose the economy is operating at full capacity along the vertical portion of the aggregate supply curve. The government attempts to stimulate private investment with an investment tax credit. Use aggregate demand and supply to show the effects on the output and price level.

3 (Practice problem: aggregate demand and supply) Suppose the economy is operating at full capacity along the vertical portion of the aggregate supply curve. Use aggregate demand and supply to show the effects on the output and price level in each of the following situations.

   a Government spending increases.
   b Mortgage rates rise.
   c The Canadian dollar appreciates relative to foreign currencies.
   d Foreign demand for Canadian exports increases because of a change in tastes.

4 (Practice problem: aggregate demand and supply) Suppose the economy is in deep recession along the flat portion of the aggregate supply curve. Use aggregate demand and supply to show the effects on output and the price level in each of the following situations.

   a The Canadian dollar depreciates relative to foreign currencies.
   b Real interest rates fall.
   c The federal government significantly cuts income taxes.
   d Loose monetary policies increase the availability of credit.

5 (Practice problem: aggregate demand and supply) Suppose the economy is in equilibrium along the upward-sloping portion of the aggregate supply curve. Use aggregate demand and supply to show the effects on output and the price level in each of the following situations.

   a Individuals grow nervous about possible future plant closings and layoffs.
   b Foreign incomes fall as Europe and Japan slip into recession.
   c A boom on Bay Street increases stock prices.
   d Instability around the world leads firms to perceive greater risk ahead.

Answers to Problems

2 Aggregate demand shifts up, and so increases the price level but leaves output unchanged.

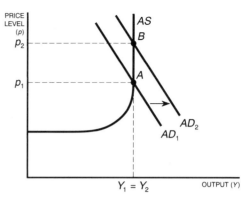

3 *a* Aggregate demand shifts up, and so increases the price level but leaves output unchanged.

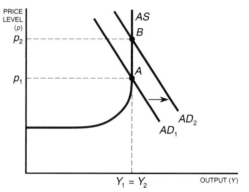

   b Investment and purchases of durable goods decrease, and so shift aggregate demand down and reduce the price level, but leave output unchanged.

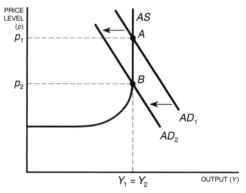

   c Net exports decrease, the price level falls, but output remains unchanged.

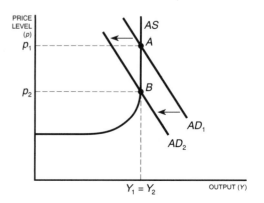

d Net exports increase, the price level rises, but output remains unchanged.

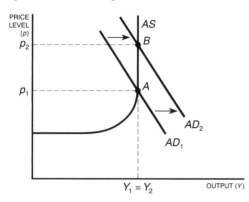

4 *a* Net exports increase, aggregate demand shifts up, the price level remains constant, and output increases.

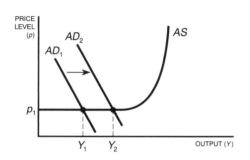

b Investment and purchases of durable goods increase, and so shift aggregate demand up and increase output but leave the price level unchanged.

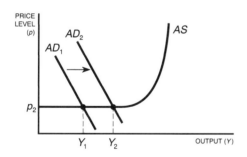

c Aggregate demand shifts up, and so increases output but leaves the price level unchanged.

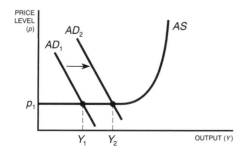

d Investment increases, and so shifts aggregate demand up and increases output but leaves the price level unchanged.

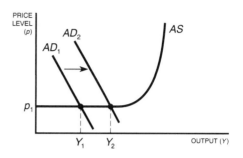

5 *a* Consumption falls and aggregate demand shifts to the left; this reduces output and the price level.

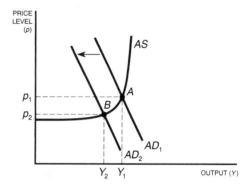

b Net exports fall and aggregate demand shifts to the left; this reduces output and the price level.

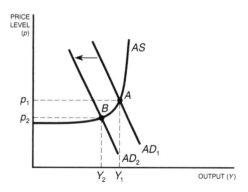

c Investment increases and aggregate demand shifts to the right; this increases output and the price level.

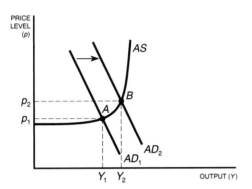

d Investment falls and aggregate demand shifts to the left. Also, firms supply less output and aggregate supply shifts to the left. Output decreases with little change in the price level.

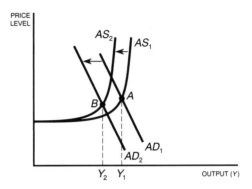

Chapter 32

STICKY PRICES

Chapter Review

Chapters 28 to 31 presented the model of the product market where output is determined by the intersection of the aggregate demand and aggregate supply curves. There are reasons, however, to think that prices may not adjust to this level, but rather remain stuck above or below the intersection. In this chapter, the text examines the reasons for sticky (as opposed to flexible) prices and the consequences for the economy and for macroeconomic policy. The detailed study of the product market, begun in Chapter 28, is completed here. The next part of the text considers the capital market and the role of money.

ESSENTIAL CONCEPTS

1 If the price level is stuck *above* where aggregate demand and aggregate supply intersect, then output equals aggregate demand, and output is below the level it would be at full employment. The resulting unemployment is called **Keynesian unemployment.** If the price level increases further, the economy moves along the aggregate demand curve, and output is re-

duced. An increase in wages shifts aggregate demand to the left, and also reduces output. Shifts in aggregate demand alter output, but unless prices change, aggregate supply shifts do not affect output.

2 If the price level is stuck *below* where aggregate demand and aggregate supply intersect, then output equals aggregate supply, but output is still below the level at which it would be at full employment. This type of unemployment is called **classical unemployment.** If the price level increases, the economy moves along the aggregate supply curve, and output increases. An increase in wages shifts aggregate supply to the left, and reduces output. Shifts in aggregate supply alter output, but unless prices change, aggregate demand shifts have no effects.

3 New classical economists believe that prices and wages adjust rapidly to clear the product and labour markets and that because of rational expectations, the economy usually operates near its vertical long-run aggregate supply curve. New Keynesian economists, on the other hand, believe that sticky prices are yet another reason why the economy may remain below full employment for a considerable period of time. Prices may eventually adjust, but the government may be

able to act more quickly and shift aggregate demand to restore full employment.

4 Firms may be reluctant to change prices for three reasons. First, changing prices is expensive. Economists refer to this reason as **menu costs,** analogous to the expense restaurants incur when printing new menus. Second, the uncertainties associated with changing prices may be greater than those associated with changing output. Customers may revise their expectations about prices and postpone purchases if they see prices falling. Finally, in oligopolies, firms may face **kinked demand curves.** Firms can facilitate cooperation by offering to match price cuts. This strategy puts a kink in each firm's demand curve at the current price. Cutting prices gains few extra customers, and firms may prefer to postpone price decreases.

BEHIND THE ESSENTIAL CONCEPTS

1 When the price is stuck at somewhere other than its market-clearing level, the quantity of output is determined by the short side of the market. If the price is too high to clear the market, then demand is the short side. Although suppliers would like to produce more, there is not enough demand, and thus the output equals the quantity demanded. On the other hand, when the price is too low to clear the market, supply is the short side. Demanders would like to purchase more goods, but only what suppliers can profitably produce is made available. In this case, the output equals the quantity supplied.

2 For the most part, both aggregate demand and aggregate supply affect the output of the economy. There are cases, however, when one or the other is irrelevant.

   a Demand determines the economy's output in two cases: when the price level is too high (the focus in this chapter) and when aggregate demand intersects aggregate supply along the flat portion of aggregate supply (covered in Chapters 28 to 30).

   b Supply also determines the economy's output in two cases: when the price level is too low (discussed in this chapter) and when aggregate demand intersects aggregate supply along the vertical portion of aggregate supply (covered in Chapters 28 to 30).

3 The main disagreement that economists have about the nature of the macroeconomy involves how much time the economy spends away from full employment. In Chapter 31, you learned that the two major schools (new classical and new Keynesian) differ on the shape of the aggregate supply curve. New classical economists believe in a world of rational expectations and vertical aggregate supply (at least in the long run, which occurs relatively quickly). New Keynesians see a flatter aggregate supply curve. In this chapter, another aspect of the dispute emerges: new Keynesian economists also doubt that prices adjust rapidly to the

intersection of aggregate demand and supply. They do not agree with the new classical view that the long run occurs relatively quickly, quoting Keynes himself who claimed that "in the long run we are all dead!"

SELF-TEST

True or False

1 When the price is stuck above the level at which aggregate demand and aggregate supply intersect, output equals aggregate supply.

2 When the price is stuck below the level at which aggregate demand and aggregate supply intersect, output equals aggregate supply.

3 In a demand-constrained equilibrium, the price level is below the level at which aggregate demand and aggregate supply intersect.

4 In a demand-constrained equilibrium, there is too much employment.

5 Keynesian unemployment occurs in a supply-constrained equilibrium.

6 Classical unemployment occurs when the price level is stuck above the level at which aggregate demand and aggregate supply intersect.

7 In a demand-constrained equilibrium, an increase in wages increases unemployment.

8 In a supply-constrained equilibrium, a decrease in wages increases unemployment.

9 Aggregate demand shifts have no effect on Keynesian unemployment.

10 Aggregate supply shifts have no effect on classical unemployment.

11 New classical economists, quite naturally, think that classical unemployment is important.

12 New Keynesian economists believe in the importance of rational expectations and therefore think that prices adjust quickly.

13 Menu costs refer to the expense of changing prices.

14 Firms perceive greater risk during economic downturns and may choose the safer path of reducing output rather than reducing price.

15 Firms facing a kinked demand curve are unlikely to change price when their costs decrease.

Multiple Choice

1 If the price level is stuck above the level at which aggregate demand and aggregate supply intersect, then

   a output is less than firms are willing to supply.
   b output is more than firms are willing to supply.
   c output is less than consumers are willing to purchase.

d output is more than consumers are willing to purchase.

e none of the above.

2 If the price level is stuck below the level at which aggregate demand and aggregate supply intersect, then

a output is less than firms are willing to supply.

b output is more than firms are willing to supply.

c output is less than consumers are willing to purchase.

d output is more than consumers are willing to purchase.

e none of the above.

3 In a demand-constrained equilibrium,

a output equals the level at which aggregate demand and aggregate supply intersect.

b the price level is stuck below the level at which aggregate demand and aggregate supply intersect.

c the price level is stuck above the level at which aggregate demand and aggregate supply intersect.

d output is greater than it is at the intersection of aggregate demand and aggregate supply.

e none of the above.

4 In a supply-constrained equilibrium,

a output equals the level at which aggregate demand and aggregate supply intersect.

b the price level is stuck below the level at which aggregate demand and aggregate supply intersect.

c the price level is stuck above the level at which aggregate demand and aggregate supply intersect.

d output is greater than it is at the intersection of aggregate demand and aggregate supply.

e none of the above.

5 In a demand-constrained equilibrium, there is

a Keynesian unemployment.

b classical unemployment.

c Keynesian overemployment.

d classical overemployment.

e no unemployment.

6 In a supply-constrained equilibrium, there is

a Keynesian unemployment.

b classical unemployment.

c Keynesian overemployment.

d classical overemployment.

e no unemployment.

7 Which of the following would not be observed in a constrained equilibrium?

a The price level is stuck at somewhere other than the intersection of aggregate supply and demand.

b There is unemployment.

c Shifts in either aggregate demand or aggregate supply have no effect.

d The level of output is either less than that which firms are willing to supply or less than that which households are willing to purchase.

e None of the above.

8 Which of the following would not be observed in a demand-constrained equilibrium?

a The price level is stuck above the intersection of aggregate supply and demand.

b There is classical unemployment.

c Shifts in aggregate demand have no effect.

d The level of output is less than that which firms are willing to supply.

e None of the above.

9 Which of the following would not be observed in a supply-constrained equilibrium?

a The price level is stuck below the intersection of aggregate supply and demand.

b There is Keynesian unemployment.

c Shifts in aggregate demand have no effect.

d The level of output is less than that which firms are willing to supply.

e None of the above.

10 In a demand-constrained equilibrium, when prices rise,

a output and real wages fall.

b output rises and real wages fall.

c output falls and real wages rise.

d output and real wages rise.

e none of the above.

11 In a supply-constrained equilibrium, when prices rise,

a output and real wages fall.

b output rises and real wages fall.

c output falls and real wages rise.

d output and real wages rise.

e none of the above.

12 In a demand-constrained equilibrium, a cut in wages

a might lower output as aggregate demand shifts left.

b shifts aggregate supply to the right, and increases output.

c shifts aggregate supply to the left, and decreases output.

d increases employment.

e none of the above.

13 In a supply-constrained equilibrium, a cut in wages

a might lower output as aggregate demand shifts to the left.

b shifts aggregate supply to the right, and increases output.

c shifts aggregate supply to the left, and decreases output.

d increases unemployment.

e none of the above.

14 Government tax and spending policies can effectively increase output

a if the economy is in a demand-constrained equilibrium, but not if it is in a supply-constrained equilibrium or unconstrained equilibrium.

b if the economy is in a supply-constrained equilibrium, but not if it is in a demand-constrained equilibrium or unconstrained equilibrium.

c   if the economy is in a demand-constrained equilibrium or an unconstrained equilibrium, but not if
it is in a supply-constrained equilibrium.

d   if the economy is in a supply-constrained equilibrium or an unconstrained equilibrium, but not if it
is in a demand-constrained equilibrium.

e   if the economy is in any equilibrium, constrained
or unconstrained.

15   Which of the following is true of new Keynesian
economists?

a   They believe that prices adjust rapidly.
b   They believe that wages adjust rapidly.
c   They believe that supply-constrained equilibria are
more likely than demand-constrained equilibria.
d   They believe that neither prices nor wages adjust
rapidly.
e   They believe that the economy is almost always
producing near the full-employment level.

16   The costs of changing prices are called

a   variable costs.
b   sunk costs.
c   fixed costs.
d   pricing costs.
e   menu costs.

17   During recessions, firms perceive that

a   cutting prices is riskier than cutting production.
b   increasing prices is riskier than increasing production.
c   cutting production is riskier than cutting prices.
d   increasing prices is riskier than increasing production.
e   none of the above.

18   Which of the following is not true of the beliefs of
firms facing a kinked demand curve?

a   Their customers will quickly learn of price increases, and they will lose business.
b   Other firms' customers will be slow to learn of
any price cuts, and so the firm will gain little new
business.
c   Rivals may match price cuts.
d   Rivals will not match price increases.
e   None of the above.

19   If marginal cost increases slightly for a firm that
faces a kinked demand curve, the firm will

a   increase the price of its product.
b   leave the price of its product unchanged.
c   reduce the price of its product.
d   increase its output.
e   reduce its output.

20   Which of the following is not a belief of new Keynesian economists?

a   Much of the economy is characterized by imperfect competition.
b   Prices are often inflexible.
c   Wages often fail to adjust to clear the market.

d   The economy is very well described by the perfectly competitive model.
e   The economy is sometimes demand constrained.

Completion

1   When the price level is stuck below the intersection
of aggregate supply and demand, the economy is said
to be in _____ equilibrium.

2   When the price level is stuck above the intersection
of aggregate supply and demand, the economy is said
to be in _____ equilibrium.

3   In a demand-constrained equilibrium, output is below
the full-employment level; this results in _____
unemployment.

4   In a supply-constrained equilibrium, output is below
the full-employment level; this results in _____
unemployment.

5   As the price level rises, the real wage _____.

6   _____ economists believe that product prices
adjust rapidly to clear product markets.

7   If the economy is in a demand-constrained equilibrium,
shifts in the _____ curve will have no effect.

8   If the economy is in a supply-constrained equilibrium,
shifts in the _____ curve will have no effect.

9   The costs of changing prices are called _____.

10   Firms that believe that rivals will match price cuts
but not price increases face a _____ demand
curve.

Answers to Self-Test

True or False

1	f	6	f	11	f
2	t	7	t	12	f
3	f	8	t	13	t
4	f	9	f	14	t
5	f	10	f	15	t

Multiple Choice

1	a	6	b	11	b	16	e
2	c	7	e	12	a	17	a
3	c	8	c	13	b	18	e
4	b	9	d	14	c	19	b
5	a	10	a	15	d	20	d

Completion

1   supply-constrained
2   demand-constrained
3   Keynesian
4   classical
5   falls
6   New classical
7   aggregate supply
8   aggregate demand
9   menu costs
10   kinked

Doing Economics: Tools and Practice Problems

In this section, we study when and how shifts in aggregate demand and supply affect the economy when the price level is stuck and does not clear the product market. If the price level is too high, equilibrium is demand constrained, and unemployment is called Keynesian unemployment. If the price level is too low, equilibrium is supply constrained, and we have classical unemployment.

Tool Kit 32.1: Using Aggregate Demand and Supply with Sticky Prices

When the price level is stuck away from the intersection of aggregate demand and aggregate supply, the economy's output will be determined by the short side of the product market. A shift in aggregate demand, for example, affects output only if at the given price level, aggregate demand is less than aggregate supply. This occurs if the price level is stuck above the market-clearing level. Similarly, shifts in aggregate supply have an impact only when the price level is below market clearing.

Step one: Start with an equilibrium. The price level will be stuck either above or below market clearing.

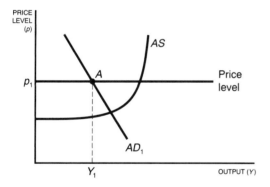

Step two: Identify a cause, and determine which curve or curves shift.

Step three: Shift the curve or curves, but keep the price level constant.

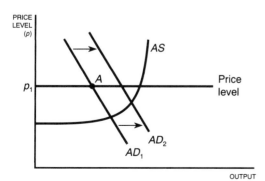

Step four: Find the new equilibrium, and compare output levels.

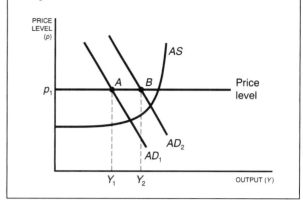

1 (Worked problem: sticky prices) Suppose the economy is in a supply-constrained equilibrium, and the price level is stuck. Wages fall. Show the effect on output.

Step-by-step solution

Step one: Start with an equilibrium. In a supply-constrained equilibrium, the price level is stuck at point *A*, below market clearing.

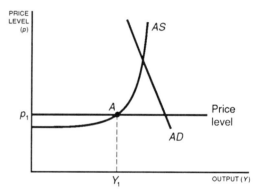

Step two: Identify a cause, and determine which curve or curves shift. A decrease in wages shifts aggregate demand to the left and aggregate supply to the right.

Step three: Shift the curve or curves, but keep the price level constant.

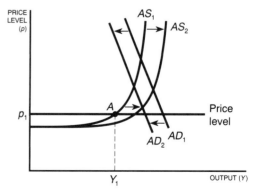

Step four: Find the new equilibrium, point *B*, and compare output levels. The new equilibrium entails greater output.

Although the fall in wages shifts aggregate demand to the left, the economy is ruled by supply. Aggregate supply shifts right because the fall in wages reduces costs for firms and increases the amount of output they are willing to sell at current prices. This shift in aggregate supply increases output.

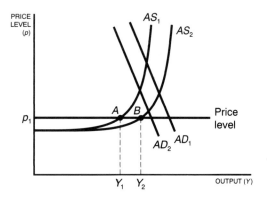

2 (Practice problem: sticky prices) Suppose the economy is in a demand-constrained equilibrium, and the price level is stuck. Wages fall. Show the effect on output.

3 (Practice problem: sticky prices) Suppose the economy is in a supply-constrained equilibrium, and the price level is stuck. Show the effect of each of the following on output.

a Real interest rates rise.
b The Canadian dollar appreciates against foreign currencies.
c Government spending increases.
d Firms become more willing to take risks.

4 (Practice problem: sticky prices) Suppose the economy is in a demand-constrained equilibrium, and the price level is stuck. Show the effect of each of the following on output.

a Households grow anxious about impending plant closings and layoffs.
b Share prices rise.
c Foreign purchases of Canadian exports increase.
d A series of natural disasters strikes the economy.

Answers to Problems

2 Aggregate demand shifts to the left, aggregate supply shifts to the right, output falls, and the price level remains stuck.

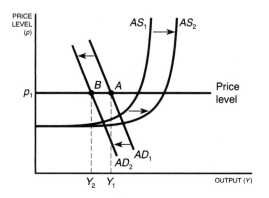

3 a Aggregate demand shifts to the left with no change in output or the price level.

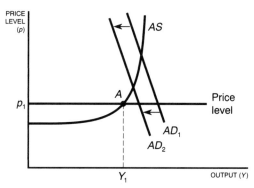

b Aggregate demand shifts to the left with no change in output or the price level.

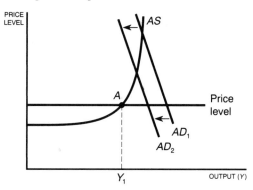

c Aggregate demand shifts to the right with no change in output or the price level.

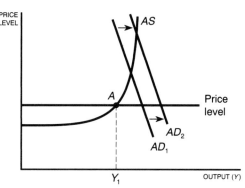

d Both aggregate demand and supply shift to the right, the price level remains stuck, and output increases.

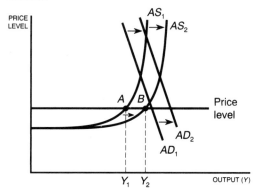

4   *a*   Aggregate demand shifts to the left, output falls, and the price level remains stuck.

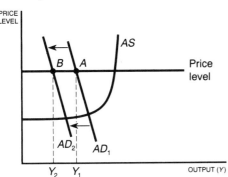

b   Aggregate demand shifts to the right, output rises, and the price level remains stuck.

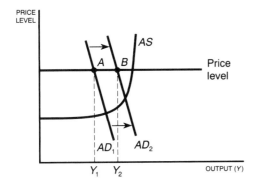

c   Aggregate demand shifts to the right, output rises, and the price level remains stuck.

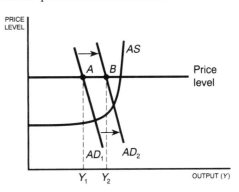

d   Aggregate supply shifts to the left with no change in output or the price level.

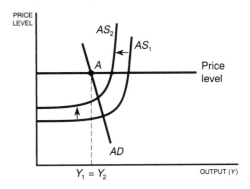

Money's Role

Chapter 33

MONEY, BANKING, AND CREDIT

Chapter Review

This chapter begins Part Five of the text, in which attention shifts to money and its influence on the third major market, the capital market. What money is and the purposes it serves in the economy are the first two topics. The chapter then introduces the concept of the money supply and explains how the banking system creates money. The chapter also discusses the Bank of Canada, the institution of government responsible for regulating the money supply and ensuring the availability of credit. Chapters 34 to 36, the remainder of Part Five, extend the insights of this chapter to consider monetary policy and its effects on unemployment, output, inflation, and the international economy.

ESSENTIAL CONCEPTS

1   Economists define **money** by what it does. Money serves three functions. It is a **medium of exchange,** which facilitates trades between firms and households. It is a **store of value,** which permits individuals to buy and sell at different times. Finally, it is a **unit of account,** which helps people measure the relative value of different goods.

2   Since there are many financial assets that perform money's three functions to some degree, the **money supply** is measured in several ways. The most important measure is **M1,** which includes currency outside the banks, and demand deposits (chequing accounts). Other measures, such as **M2** and **M3,** include progressively less liquid assets. The liquidity of an asset refers to how easy it is to convert to M1. The now rather common practice of buying on credit using credit cards or home equity loans makes specifying the size of the money supply more difficult.

3   The **financial system** includes all the institutions that help savers and borrowers transact. **Financial intermediaries** are the firms that stand between savers and borrowers. Traditionally, the financial system was synonymous with the **chartered banks,** but the so-called **near banks,** such as trust and mortgage loan companies, credit unions, and caisses populaires, have become an increasingly important part of the financial system and have assumed many of the functions previously only carried out by the chartered banks. The **Bank of Canada** is the central bank of Canada. It controls the money supply and availability of credit to promote and stabilize overall economic activity.

4   Though the Bank of Canada controls the money supply,

money itself is created by the banking system. Banks operate on the **fractional reserve system;** this means that they keep only a fraction of deposits on hand as reserves. (Until recently, the fraction was stipulated by the Bank Act. Now only the banks' prudence determines the reserves they hold.) Because only a fraction of any deposit is retained in the form of reserves, a new deposit allows a bank to make additional loans, which ultimately return to the banking system as more deposits. The process of deposit expansion continues until total deposits have grown by a multiple of the initial deposit. The **money multiplier** is the relationship between the initial deposit and the ultimate change in total deposits.

5   The Bank of Canada has two primary instruments for controlling the money supply. Most important, it buys and sells government bonds. This activity is called **open market operations.** The Bank also manipulates the **bank rate,** which is the interest rate charged to banks when borrowing from the Bank of Canada. The bank rate is set 25 basis points above the average yield of a three-month Treasury bill at the weekly auction. This yield is influenced by the Bank's open market operations; it rises if the Bank sells bonds and falls if it buys them.

BEHIND THE ESSENTIAL CONCEPTS

1   How do the Bank's instruments affect the money supply? Each works by increasing or decreasing banks' reserves, affecting the money available for loans.

   a   When the Bank engages in open market operations, it buys and sells bonds. If it buys a bond, for example, the money that it pays is deposited in a bank. The bank's reserves increase, and it in turn can grant new loans.

   b   When the Bank increases the discount rate, banks know that borrowing from the Bank will be more expensive. They guard against having to borrow by keeping more reserves and making fewer loans.

2   Figure 33.1 will help you keep straight how open market operations affect the money supply. On the left is the Bank's vault, where it keeps stacks of bonds and currency. The currency in the vault is not money, because it is not in the economy. On the right is the economy. If the Bank buys bonds, currency flows from the vault into the economy and increases the money supply. If the Bank sells bonds, the money it receives leaves the economy and goes into the vault, where it is no longer money.

3   Both the Bank of Canada and the government sell government bonds. You can keep the two straight if you remember why the bonds are sold. The government sells bonds to borrow money to finance government spending. When this happens, the money is spent, and it stays in the economy. The Bank sells bonds to reduce the money supply. When the Bank sells bonds, the money it receives goes into the Bank's vault and leaves the economy.

4   You should not confuse the money multiplier in this chapter with the fiscal multiplier introduced in Chapter 28. They are two different concepts. The fiscal multiplier shows that an increase in aggregate expenditures—for example, in investment—brings about a larger increase in output. The money multiplier shows that an increase in reserves leads to a larger increase in total deposits.

5   The *workings* of the fiscal and money multipliers, however, are similar. With the fiscal multiplier, an initial increase in spending creates additional income, which leads to a second round of spending in which some of the income is consumed. The sequence is spending—income—additional spending, etc. Each successful round of spending is smaller, and the process ultimately settles down.

   With the money multiplier, an initial increase in deposits leads to new loans, which ultimately are deposited back in the banking system. The sequence here is deposits—loans—additional deposits—additional loans, etc. Each successive round of deposits is smaller, and again the process ultimately settles down.

6   The formulas for the multipliers are also similar. The fiscal multiplier equals 1 divided by the marginal propensity to save. You can think of savings as a leakage, which makes the next round of spending smaller than the last one. The formula for the money multiplier is 1 divided by the reserve ratio. Again, in that they are not loaned out, reserves are like a leakage, and make the next round of deposits smaller than the previous round.

7   One of the fundamental trade-offs in economic life is risks and incentives. We have seen this notion many times, and it appears again in this chapter in the context of deposit insurance. The Canadian Deposit Insurance Corp (CDIC) protects your money against loss in case of bank failure. Because you know that your money is safe, you seek the highest rate of interest and have little incentive to worry about the financial health of the bank. Banks know how you think and are motivated to grant risky loans, because they seek high average returns so that they can afford to pay high rates of interest. Thus, deposit insurance reduces the risk for depositors, but it creates incentives that can lead to reckless lending.

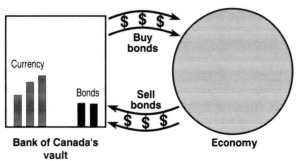

Figure 33.1

SELF-TEST

True or False

F 1   The term "money" refers only to currency and coins in circulation.

F 2   The store of value function of money refers to its use as a measure of the relative value of goods.

F 3   The money supply is an example of a flow variable.

T 4   M1 includes currency outside the banks and demand deposits.

T 5   An asset is liquid if it is easily converted into money (M1).

T 6   Financial intermediaries are firms that provide a link between savers and borrowers.

T 7   The Bank of Canada is the central bank of Canada.

T 8   The Bank of Canada has a large degree of independence from the federal government in setting monetary policy.

F 9   A bank's net worth equals its liabilities minus its assets.

T 10   Banks operate on the fractional reserve system; this means that they hold only a fraction of the amount of deposits in reserve.

T 11   The money multiplier implies that total deposits increase by a multiple of an initial deposit.

F 12   The Bank of Canada controls the money supply by mandating maximum interest rates that banks can charge their best customers.

T 13   The bank rate is the interest rate that the Bank of Canada charges on loans to banks.

T 14   Open market operations refer to the buying and selling of government bonds by the Bank of Canada.

T 15   Deposit insurance lessens the risk faced by depositors but also reduces their incentives to monitor the performance of banks.

Multiple Choice

1   Trade without the use of money is called

   a   double coincidence of wants.
   b   medium of exchange.
   c   barter.
   d   unit of account.
   e   multiple deposit.

2   Double-coincidence of wants refers to

   a   the fact that in order for two individuals to barter, each must have what the other wants and want what the other has.
   b   the fact that money must be both a store of value and a medium of exchange.
   c   the unlikely possibility that two individuals will have exactly the same tastes.

   d   the fact that dividends are taxed twice.
   e   the fact that the Bank of Canada engages in open market operations and sets the bank rate.

3   The use of money to facilitate exchange is its

   a   medium-of-exchange function.
   b   store-of-value function.
   c   unit-of-account function.
   d   double-coincidence-of-wants function.
   e   fractional reserve function.

4   The use of money to measure the relative value of goods and services is its

   a   medium-of-exchange function.
   b   store-of-value function.
   c   unit-of-account function.
   d   double-coincidence-of-wants function.
   e   fractional reserve function.

5   The use of money as a means of preserving purchasing power for a time period is its

   a   medium-of-exchange function.
   b   store-of-value function.
   c   unit-of-account function.
   d   double-coincidence-of-wants function.
   e   fractional reserve function.

6   The economic definition of money is

   a   currency and demand deposits.
   b   M1.
   c   anything that acts as a medium of exchange, store of value, and unit of account.
   d   anything that avoids the double-coincidence-of-wants problem.
   e   none of the above.

7   Which of the following is not included in M1?

   a   notes in circulation
   b   personal savings deposits
   c   coin in circulation
   d   demand deposits (chequing accounts)
   e   none of the above

8   Which of the following is not included in M2?

   a   M1
   b   nonpersonal notice deposits
   c   foreign currency deposits
   d   personal savings deposits
   e   none of the above

9   Which of the following is not included in M3?

   a   M1
   b   M2
   c   nonpersonal fixed-term deposits
   d   deposits in near banks
   e   none of the above

10   An agreement by a bank to lend up to some specified amount is a

   a   chequing account
   b   daily interest account

c line of credit
d savings account
e none of the above

11 Which of the following are not financial intermediaries?

a banks
b savings and loans
c mutual funds
d life insurance companies
e none of the above

12 The objectives of government involvement in the financial system include

a funding government spending.
b stabilizing the level of economic activity.
c protecting banks from unfair competition.
d creating jobs in the financial sector.
e none of the above.

13 The central bank of Canada is

a the Bank of Canada.
b the National Bank of Canada.
c the Canadian Imperial Bank of Commerce.
d the Royal Canadian Mint.
e none of the above.

14 The Bank of Canada is

a an agency funded and overseen by the chartered banks.
b an agency funded and overseen by the major players on Bay Street.
c a nationalized bank.
d a government ministry.
e an agent of regional policy.

15 The fractional reserve system in banking means that banks

a lend a fraction of their money to consumers and a fraction to businesses.
b hold a fraction of the amount on deposit in reserves.
c hold a fraction of the amount on loan in reserves.
d lend a fraction of their money to foreign businesses and a fraction to domestic businesses.
e none of the above.

16 The bank rate is

a the interest rate charged by the Bank of Canada on loans to banks.
b the interest rate paid by the Bank of Canada on deposits.
c the difference between the interest rate charged by the Bank of Canada and that charged in the market.
d the maximum allowable difference between interest charged on loans to consumers and loans to banks.
e the interest rate ceiling on credit card balances.

17 Which of the following is not a way in which the Bank of Canada can increase the money supply?

a Lower the bank rate.
b Reduce the reserve requirement.
c Buy Treasury bills.
d Transfer federal funds from the central bank to accounts in the chartered banks.
e None of the above.

18 The money multiplier shows that

a the rich get richer.
b an increase in aggregate expenditures brings about a larger increase in national income.
c an increase in reserves leads to a larger increase in total deposits.
d a multiple of deposits must be held as reserves.
e deregulation leads to instability in the banking system.

19 Open market operations, the most important means by which the Bank of Canada controls the money supply, involve

a changing the bank rate.
b setting interest rates.
c changing the reserve requirement.
d buying and selling government bonds.
e placing varying restrictions on foreign borrowing and lending.

20 The Canadian Deposit Insurance Corporation

a acts as the central bank of Canada.
b ensures that banks will not fail.
c insures deposits (of up to $60,000) in case of bank collapse.
d protects banks against unfair foreign competition.
e sets the reserve requirement for bank deposits.

Completion

1 For a trade to take place in a barter economy, each individual must have what the other wants and want what the other has; that is, there must be a _____.

2 Money facilitates exchange; it is performing its _____ function.

3 Money holds on to its purchasing power; it is performing its _____ function.

4 People use money as a measuring rod, taking advantage of the _____ function of money.

5 Currency and demand deposits are included in the _____ measure of money.

6 Firms that act as go-betweens for savers and borrowers are called _____.

7 The central bank in Canada is called the _____.

8 When the Bank of Canada buys and sells bonds, it is engaging in _____.

9 The minimum level of reserves that banks must keep on hand is _____.

10 The interest rate charged to banks by the Bank of Canada is called the _____.

Answers to Self-Test

True or False

1	f	6	t	11	t
2	f	7	t	12	f
3	f	8	t	13	t
4	t	9	f	14	t
5	t	10	t	15	t

Multiple Choice

1	c	6	c	11	e	16	a
2	a	7	b	12	b	17	b
3	a	8	c	13	a	18	c
4	c	9	d	14	c	19	d
5	b	10	c	15	b	20	c

Completion

1 double-coincidence of wants
2 medium-of-exchange
3 store-of-value
4 unit-of-account
5 M1
6 financial intermediaries
7 Bank of Canada
8 open market operations
9 zero
10 bank rate

Doing Economics: Tools and Practice Problems

In this section, we learn about the balance sheet of a bank, where assets, liabilities, and net worth are recorded, and use this tool to see how open market operations lead to changes in deposits, to trace through the deposit expansion process, and to compute the money multiplier.

1 (Worked problem: balance sheet) President's Choice Bank has $18 million in outstanding loans, $3 million in government bonds, reserves of $4 million, and deposits equal to $20 million. Compute its net worth, and construct the balance sheet.

Step-by-step solution

Step one: Make a T-account.

President's Choice Bank's Balance Sheet

Assets	Liabilities and net worth

Step two: Enter each of the assets (outstanding loans, bond holdings, reserves) in the left column, and sum the assets.

Tool Kit 33.1: Constructing the Balance Sheet

The balance sheet is a T-account, with assets listed on the left and liabilities and net worth on the right. When anything changes, net worth must adjust to keep the right and left sides in balance. To create a balance sheet, follow this procedure.

Step one: Make a T-account. Label the left column "Assets" and the right column "Liabilities and net worth."

Assets	Liabilities and net worth

Step two: Enter each of the assets (outstanding loans, bond holdings, reserves) in the left column, and sum the assets.

Assets	Liabilities and net worth
Loans Bonds Deposits	
Total assets	

Step three: Enter each of the liabilities (deposits) in the right column, and sum the liabilities.

Assets	Liabilities and net worth
Loans Bonds Deposits	Deposits
Total assets	

Step four: Compute net worth by subtracting liabilities from assets:

net worth = assets − liabilities.

Enter net worth in the right column.

Assets	Liabilities and net worth
Loans Bonds Deposits	Deposits Net worth
Total assets	

Step five: Sum the right and left columns, and check that the balance sheet is in balance.

Assets	Liabilities and net worth
Loans Bonds Deposits	Deposits
Total assets = Total liabilities + net worth.	

President's Choice Bank's Balance Sheet

Assets	Liabilities and net worth
Loans outstanding = $18 million Government bonds = $3 million Reserves = $4 million Total assets = $25 million	

Step three: Enter each of the liabilities (deposits) in the right-hand column, and sum the liabilities.

President's Choice Bank's Balance Sheet

Assets	Liabilities and net worth
Loans outstanding = $18 million Government bonds = $3 million Reserves = $4 million Total assets = $25 million	Deposits = $20 million

Step four: Compute net worth:

net worth = 18 + 3 + 4 − 20 = $5 million.

Enter net worth in the right-hand column.

President's Choice Bank's Balance Sheet

Assets	Liabilities and net worth
Loans outstanding = $18 million Government bonds = $3 million Reserves = $4 million Total assets = $25 million	Deposits = $20 million Net worth = $5 million

Step five: Sum the right and left columns, and check that the balance sheet is in balance.

President's Choice Bank's Balance Sheet

Assets	Liabilities and net worth
Loans outstanding = $18 million Government bonds = $3 million Reserves = $4 million Total assets = $25 million	Deposits = $20 million Net worth = $5 million Total liabilities plus net worth = $25 million

2 (Practice problem: balance sheet) First Bank has $220 million in outstanding loans, $10 million in government bonds, $25 million in reserves, and $240 million in deposits. Compute its net worth, and construct its balance sheet.

3 (Practice problem: balance sheet) Second Bank has $400 million in outstanding loans, $25 million in government bonds, $50 million in reserves, and $450 million in deposits. Compute its net worth, and construct its balance sheet.

Tool Kit 33.2: Understanding Deposit Expansion and the Money Multiplier

Using the fractional reserve system, banks create money. When banks receive a new deposit, they keep only a fraction on hand in reserve and loan out the remainder. But the loans find their way back into the banking system, and so increase deposits further, and set off a new round of loans. When the process settles down, total deposits in the banking system have increased by a multiple of the initial deposit.

Step one: Construct a combined balance sheet for the banking system.

Step two: Identify the initial deposit, and add it to the banking system's deposits.

Step three: Identify the reserve ratio. Calculate the required increase in reserves made necessary by the initial deposit, and add it to the banking system's reserves:

new required reserves = reserve ratio × initial deposit.

Step four: Calculate the new loans that the deposit allows, and add the amount to the banking system's loans:

new loans = initial deposit − new required reserves.

This completes round one of the deposit expansion process. (Remember to recompute the total assets and liabilities and net worth.)

Step five: Trace through a few more rounds by repeating steps two through four. The initial deposit for round two is the amount of new loans from round one.

Step six: Compute the final expansion in deposits. This will be the increase in the money supply:

final deposit expansion = initial deposit/reserve ratio.

Because there are no other leakages in this example, the money multiplier equals 1/reserve ratio.

√4 (Worked problem: deposit expansion and money multiplier) The banking system in Costa Guano has $4 billion in outstanding loans, $1 billion in government bonds, $1 billion in reserves, and deposits of $5 billion. Its reserve ratio is 0.20. (Monetary magnitudes are converted to dollar equivalents.)

a Construct the combined balance sheet.
b A new deposit of $1 billion arrives from abroad. Trace through three rounds of the deposit expansion process, and compute the final deposit expansion.

Step-by-step solution

Step one: Construct a combined balance sheet for the banking system.

Costa Guano's Combined Balance Sheet

Assets	Liabilities and net worth
Loans outstanding = $4 billion Government bonds = $1 billion Reserves = $1 billion Total assets = $6 billion	Deposits = $5 billion Net worth = $1 billion Total liabilities plus net worth = $6 billion

Step two: Identify the initial deposit, and add it to the banking system's deposits. The deposit is $1 billion.

Step three: Identify the reserve ratio. Calculate the required increase in reserves made necessary by the initial deposit, and add it to the banking system's reserves:

new required reserves = 0.20 × 1 = $0.2 billion.

Step four: Calculate the new loans that the deposit allows, and add the amount to the banking system's loans:

new loans = 1 – 0.2 = $0.8 billion.

Costa Guano's Combined Balance Sheet (round one)

Assets	Liabilities and net worth
Loans outstanding = $4.8 billion Government bonds = $1 billion Reserves = $1.2 billion Total assets = $7 billion	Deposits = $6 billion Net worth = $1 billion Total liabilities plus net worth = $7 billion

This completes round one of the deposit expansion process. (Note the new totals.)

Step five: Trace through a few more rounds by repeating steps two through four. The initial deposit for round two is the amount of new loans from round one.

Costa Guano's Combined Balance Sheet (round two)

Assets	Liabilities and net worth
Loans outstanding = $5.44 billion Government bonds = $1 billion Reserves = $1.36 billion Total assets = $7.8 billion	Deposits = $6.8 billion Net worth = $1 billion Total liabilities plus net worth = $7.8 billion

Costa Guano's Combined Balance Sheet (round three)

Assets	Liabilities and net worth
Loans outstanding = $5.95 billion Government bonds = $1 billion Reserves = $1.49 billion Total assets = $8.44 billion	Deposits = $7.44 billion Net worth = $1 billion Total liabilities plus net worth = $8.44 billion

Step six: Compute the final expansion in deposits. This will be the increase in the money supply:

final deposit expansion = 1/(0.2) = $5 billion.

5 (Practice problem: deposit expansion and money multiplier) In El Dorado, the banking system has outstanding loans of $200 million, government bonds of $10 million, reserves of $30 million, and deposits of $210 million. Its reserve ratio is 1/7. (Monetary magnitudes are converted to dollar equivalents.)

a Construct the combined balance sheet.
b A new deposit of $49 million arrives from abroad. Trace through two rounds of the deposit expansion process, and compute the final deposit expansion.

6 (Practice problem: deposit expansion and money multiplier) The Erehwemos banking system has outstanding loans of $45 billion, government bonds of $2 billion, reserves of $5 billion, and deposits of $50 billion. Its reserve ratio is 0.10. (Monetary magnitudes are converted to dollar equivalents.)

a Construct the combined balance sheet.
b A new deposit of $5 billion arrives from abroad. Trace through three rounds of the deposit expansion process, and compute the final deposit expansion.

Answers to Problems

2

First Bank's Balance Sheet

Assets	Liabilities and net worth
Loans outstanding = $220 million Government bonds = $10 million Reserves = $25 million Total assets = $255 million	Deposits = $240 million Net worth = $15 million Total liabilities plus net worth = $255 million

3

Second Bank's Balance Sheet

Assets	Liabilities and net worth
Loans outstanding = $400 million Government bonds = $25 million Reserves = $50 million Total assets = $475 million	Deposits = $450 million Net worth = $25 million Total liabilities plus net worth = $475 million

5 a

El Dorado's Combined Balance Sheet

Assets	Liabilities and net worth
Loans outstanding = $200 million Government bonds = $10 million Reserves = $30 million Total assets = $240 million	Deposits = $210 million Net worth = $30 million Total liabilities plus net worth = $240 million

b

El Dorado's Combined Balance Sheet (round one)

Assets	Liabilities and net worth
Loans outstanding = $242 million Government bonds = $10 million Reserves = $37 million Total assets = $289 million	Deposits = $259 million Net worth = $30 million Total liabilities plus net worth = $289 million

El Dorado's Combined Balance Sheet (round two)

Assets	Liabilities and net worth
Loans outstanding = $278 million	Deposits = $301 million
Government bonds = $10 million	
Reserves = $43 million	Net worth = $30 million
Total assets = $331 million	Total liabilities plus net worth = $331 million

Final deposit expansion = 49 /(1/7) = $343 million.

6 *a*

Erehwemo's Combined Balance Sheet (round one)

Assets	Liabilities and net worth
Loans outstanding = $45 billion	Deposits = $50 billion
Government bonds = $2 billion	
Reserves = $5 billion	Net worth = $2 billion
Total assets = $52 billion	Total liabilities plus net worth = $52 billion

b

Erehwemo's Combined Balance Sheet (round two)

Assets	Liabilities and net worth
Loans outstanding = $49.5 billion	Deposits = $55 billion
Government bonds = $2 billion	
Reserves = $5.5 billion	Net worth = $2 billion
Total assets = $57 billion	Total liabilities plus net worth = $57 billion

Erehwemo's Combined Balance Sheet (round three)

Assets	Liabilities and net worth
Loans outstanding = $53.55 billion	Deposits = $59.5 billion
Government bonds = $2 billion	
Reserves = $5.95 billion	Net worth = $2 billion
Total assets = $61.5 billion	Total liabilities plus net worth = $61.5 billion

Final deposit expansion = 5 /(0.1) = $50 billion.

Chapter 34

MONETARY THEORY AND POLICY

Chapter Review

Chapter 33 showed how the Bank of Canada can use its instruments to bring about changes in the money supply and the availability of credit. This chapter discusses how these changes affect the economy. The most important issues involve changes in the money supply that affect output, prices, or both, and the channels through which these changes operate. There is some disagreement among economists concerning the latter issue, and the chapter outlines the sources of contention and the consequences for monetary policy. The discussion in this chapter assumes the economy is closed; Chapter 35 explains how monetary policy works in the international monetary system of the world's interdependent economies.

ESSENTIAL CONCEPTS

1 If the money supply is increased, people may either hold onto the money or spend it. If they hold it, aggregate demand will remain unchanged. If they spend it, aggregate demand will shift to the right, and output, prices, or both will increase. This can be seen from the definition of **velocity:**

$$V = pQ/M,$$

where p is a price index, Q is output, and M is the money supply. An increase in M must result in a decrease in V or an increase in p or Q. The big question in this chapter is how a change in M can affect aggregate demand.

2 **Keynesian monetary theory** starts with the demand for money to facilitate transactions. The opportunity cost of holding money is the **nominal interest rate,** which is determined by the intersection of supply and demand for money. An increase in the money supply lowers interest rates, stimulates investment, and shifts aggregate demand. The main problem with this theory is that the supply of money affects the nominal interest rate, while investment is determined by the real interest rate.

3 Another view, held by monetarists, rearranges the definition of velocity as $M = pQ/V$ and interprets this equation as the demand for money. It assumes that velocity is constant (or at least predictable); therefore, an increase in money supply must increase p or Q by shift-

ing aggregate demand to the right. The problem with this theory is the assumption that velocity is constant.

4   New Keynesians agree that interest rate effects may be important but add that money can affect investment and consumption through changes in stock or bond prices (**portfolio theories**). They focus especially on how money affects credit availability. New Keynesians acknowledge that an increase in the money supply increases bank reserves and makes it easier for banks to lend, but they emphasize the need to motivate banks to lend and businesses to invest. A stable, secure banking system is important, but in deep recessions when banks and firms are pessimistic, monetary policy is likely to be ineffective.

5   Regarding monetary policy, most economists agree that in the long run, money affects only the price level. The main areas of dispute are whether money can affect output in the short run and whether the government should use monetary policy to reduce economic fluctuations or let the money supply grow at the rate of growth of output.

BEHIND THE ESSENTIAL CONCEPTS

1   There are areas of disagreement about monetary theory and policy, but there is also a good deal of common ground. Concerning monetary theory, most economists recognize that the Bank of Canada controls the money supply through its use of open market operations and the bank rate. Most economists also agree that the demand for money depends upon income. In the area of monetary policy, economists believe that in deep recessions increases in the money supply will likely be ineffective, in mild recessions increases will shift aggregate demand and help the economy recover when the economy is operating at capacity, they will result only in higher prices. Severely restricting the money supply and credit availability, on the other hand, will cause a recession.

2   There is no consensus about how credit availability and the money supply work their way through the economy, but there are four possibilities.

   a   A larger money supply lowers interest rates and increases investment.
   b   A larger money supply directly shifts aggregate demand because velocity is constant.
   c   A larger money supply brings about higher stock and bond prices, which lead to more consumption and investment.
   d   Looser credit motivates more lending.

3   Similarly, there is disagreement concerning monetary policy. There are four schools of thought.

   a   Real business-cycle theorists see money policy as largely irrelevant because it can only affect the price level.
   b   Monetarists and new classical economists believe

money policy is effective (although they disagree why) in the short run but dangerous, because a policy of tight money can cause serious economic downturns.
   c   New Keynesians advocate the use of monetary policy to smooth the economy, but doubt its effectiveness during deep recessions.

4   The logic of credit rationing resembles the logic in the efficiency wage theory of unemployment. Banks ration credit because they fear that raising the interest rate would attract low-quality (risky) borrowers, many of whom would default. Because the interest rate remains below market clearing, there is an excess demand for loans.

   As you will remember, in the labour market firms are reluctant to reduce wages because they anticipate that it would lead their best workers to quit. Because the wage rate remains above market clearing, there is an excess supply of workers (unemployment).

SELF-TEST

True or False

F 1   The velocity of money is the ratio of nominal GDP to the price level. *money*

F 2   The demand for money arising from its use as a unit of account is called the transactions demand for money.

T 3   The transactions demand for money increases as nominal income increases.

T 4   The opportunity cost of holding money is the nominal interest rate.

T 5   According to Keynesian monetary theory, the nominal interest rate is determined by the intersection of the supply and demand for money.

T 6   According to Keynesian monetary theory, an increase in the money supply will lower interest rates and increase investment except during deep recessions.

T 7   One problem with Keynesian monetary theory is that the money supply may affect the nominal interest rate, but it is the real interest rate that affects business investment.

T 8   The theory that the velocity is constant and thus that increases in the money supply bring about equal proportional increases in income is called the quantity theory of money.

F 9   Monetarists believe that money is important and that the government should use active monetary policy to influence the fluctuations in the economy.

T 10 Until recently, the velocity of money has increased steadily, although the upward trend slowed during recessions.

T 11 Bank of Canada policies may affect the ability of banks to make loans, but they cannot force banks to lend.

12 Because of credit rationing, interest rates may not rise even though there is an excess demand for money.

13 If the interest rate falls and banks are willing to lend, investment will increase unless firms have an elastic demand for loans.

14 Real business-cycle theories predict that output will usually increase if the money supply increases.

15 New Keynesian economists agree with Keynes that monetary policy can stimulate the economy, but they emphasize credit availability rather than interest rates as the important mechanism.

Multiple Choice

1 When the Bank of Canada increases the supply of money,

a individuals may hold the additional money, and so increases velocity, or spend it, which will result in lower prices and more output.
b individuals may hold the additional money, and so increase velocity, or spend it, which will result in higher prices and more output.
c individuals may hold the additional money, and so decrease velocity, or spend it, which will result in lower prices and more output.
d individuals may hold the additional money, and so decrease velocity, or spend it, which will result in higher prices and more output.
e none of the above.

2 Along the horizontal range of the aggregate supply curve, an increase in the supply of money will

a increase output.
b increase the price level.
c decrease output.
d decrease the price level.
e none of the above.

3 Which definition of money is used in this chapter?

a M1
b M2
c M3
d M2+
e none of the above

4 Velocity is defined as the ratio of

a GDP to the price level.
b the price level to GDP.
c GDP to the money supply.
d the money supply to GDP.
e M2 to M1.

5 According to Keynesian monetary theory, changes in the money supply affect the economy through

a the interest rates.
b the velocity.
c the foreign exchange market.
d the quantity theory of money.
e the credit availability.

6 The transactions demand for money refers to money held

a as a medium of exchange.
b as a store of value.
c as a unit of account.
d as a precaution against unexpected need such as illness or job loss.
e as a hedge against deflation.

7 Which of the following will cause an increase in the demand for money?

a an increase in real income
b an increase in nominal income
c an increase in velocity
d an increase in the nominal interest rate
e an increase in the real interest rate

8 The opportunity cost of holding money is

a the exchange rate.
b the velocity.
c the real interest rate.
d the nominal interest rate.
e none of the above.

9 Which of the following is not a principle of Keynesian monetary theory?

a The nominal interest rate is the opportunity cost of holding money.
b The demand for money decreases as the interest rate rises.
c The interest rate is determined by the intersection of money demand and money supply.
d The velocity of money is stable.
e None of the above.

10 Which of the following is a tenet of the Keynesian theory of monetary policy?

a Monetary policy is ineffective because it cannot affect the interest rate.
b Monetary policy is especially effective in deep recessions when money is scarce.
c Monetary policy is ineffective in deep recessions.
d Monetary policy is ineffective because investment is not affected by changes in interest rates.
e Monetary policy is effective but is too dangerous to use.

11 Portfolio theories of how monetary policy affects the economy focus on the role of money

a as a medium of exchange.
b as a store of value.
c as a unit of account.
d as a precaution against unexpected need such as illness or job loss.
e as a hedge against deflation.

12 Which of the following is not true? According to portfolio theories, the Bank of Canada can increase the money supply, lower interest rates, and shift aggregate demand because

a when interest rates fall, stock prices rise and firms invest more when stock prices are high.

b when interest rates fall, stock prices rise and people increase consumption because they are wealthier.

c open market operations increase banks' reserves, and their responses lead to higher stock prices.

d even in recession, monetary policy can be effective.

e none of the above.

13 Monetarists believe that

a the velocity of money is stable over time.

b the velocity of money is unpredictable.

c the quantity theory of money is no longer a sensible way to look at the economy.

d money serves no function as a store of value.

e the velocity of money increases as the money supply grows.

14 Which of the following is not a belief held by monetarists?

a The velocity of money is stable over time.

b The Bank of Canada should let the money supply grow at the rate of growth in full-employment output.

c Contractions of the money supply are largely responsible for many of the major economic downturns.

d The velocity of money increases as the money supply grows.

e Increases in the money supply increase output, the price level, or both.

15 When the money supply is increased, ↑M

a bank reserves and bank loans are increased and bank purchases of Treasury bills are decreased.

b bank reserves and bank loans are decreased and bank purchases of Treasury bills are increased.

c bank reserves and bank purchases of Treasury bills are increased and bank loans are decreased.

d bank reserves and bank purchases of Treasury bills are decreased and bank loans are increased.

e none of the above.

16 According to credit availability theories, an increase in the money supply will stimulate the economy when

a interest rates fall.

b stock prices rise.

c bond prices rise.

d interest rates rise.

e banks make more loans on easier terms.

17 According to credit availability theories, Bank of Canada policies

a affect the ability of banks to lend, but cannot force them to lend.

b affect the willingness of banks to lend, but cannot affect the ability of banks to lend.

c affect the ability and willingness of banks to lend by lowering interest rates.

d may not stimulate the economy if banks buy fewer Treasury bills.

e none of the above.

18 Which of the following is not true of the credit availability theories of why monetary policy may be ineffective in severe recessions?

a Banks may prefer holding Treasury bills to making loans if default rates are high.

b Banks may prefer holding Treasury bills to making loans if their net worth is low.

c Banks may prefer holding Treasury bills to making loans if other banks have gone bankrupt.

d Banks may prefer varying the terms of credit to changing interest rates to attract more borrowers.

e None of the above.

19 Even though there is an excess demand for credit, banks may not increase the interest rate if

a Treasury bill interest rates are high.

b increased interest rates have an adverse selection effect by attracting riskier borrowers.

c Treasury bill interest rates are low.

d credit rationing is illegal.

e borrowers cannot afford higher interest rates.

20 According to real business-cycle theorists, money

a affects only the price level in the long run but can have real effects on output in the short run.

b affects the economy by changing interest rates and investment.

c has no effect on either prices or output.

d affects only the price level in both the short and long runs.

e affects output but has no impact on the price level.

Completion

1 Gross domestic product divided by the money supply equals the _____.

2 Money held for use as a medium of exchange forms the _____.

3 The opportunity cost of holding money is the _____.

4 The view that money affects the economy through changes in interest rates and investment is the _____ monetary theory.

5 According to _____, velocity is constant and increases in the money supply bring about proportionate increases in national income.

6 _____ believe that there is a stable and predictable relationship between the money supply and national income.

7 _____ occurs when there is an excess demand for credit but banks do not raise interest rates for fear of attracting less credit-worthy borrowers.

8 According to _____ theories, changes in the money supply may lead to different levels of investment without changing interest rates.

9 New classical economists emphasize that individuals and firms have _____ and can understand government monetary policy, at least in the long run.

10 _____ economists see monetary policy as largely irrelevant, because it affects only the price level.

Answers to Self-Test

True or False

1	f	6	t	11	t
2	f	7	t	12	t
3	t	8	t	13	f
4	t	9	f	14	f
5	t	10	t	15	t

Multiple Choice

1	d	6	a	11	b	16	e
2	a	7	b	12	d	17	a
3	a	8	d	13	a	18	e
4	c	9	d	14	d	19	b
5	a	10	c	15	a	20	d

Completion

1 velocity
2 money supply
3 nominal interest rate
4 Keynesian
5 monetarism
6 Monetarists
7 Credit rationing
8 portfolio
9 rational expectations
10 Real business-cycle

Doing Economics: Tools and Practice Problems

The traditional theory of how changes in the money supply affect the economy is Keynesian monetary theory. Although there are problems associated with this theory, it represents the best starting point for the study of monetary policy. In this section, the problems trace the channels through which money moves to shift aggregate demand and alter the equilibrium output of the economy.

Tool Kit 34.1: Using Keynesian Monetary Theory

According to this view of money and the economy, the nominal interest rate, which is the opportunity cost of holding money, is determined by the intersection of the supply and demand curves for money. An increase in the supply of money shifts the supply curve to the right and lowers the interest rate. Finally, lower interest rates induce more investment and shift aggregate demand to the right.

Step one: Identify the demand curve for money, the supply curve for money, and the investment function.

Step two: Start with an equilibrium in which the supply and demand curves for money intersect at the nominal interest rate. The level of investment is read off the investment function at this interest rate.

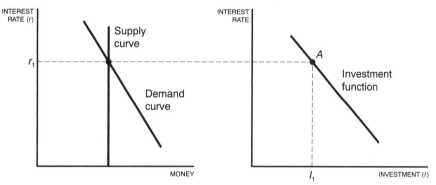

Step three: Shift the money supply curve to reflect the change in the money supply.

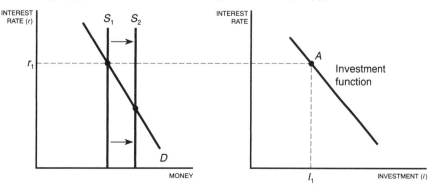

Step four: Find the new equilibrium interest rate.

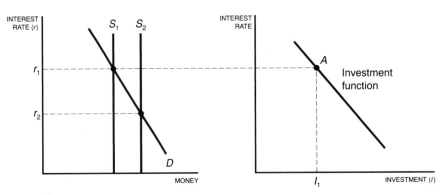

Step five: Determine the change in investment by reading the new level of investment off the investment function.

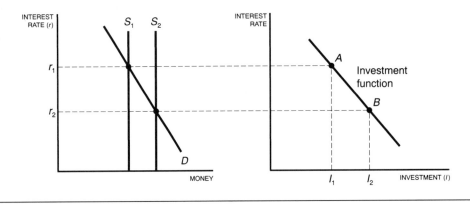

1   (Worked problem: Keynesian monetary theory) The money demand and investment function are given in Table 34.1. The initial money supply is $1.8 billion.

Table 34.1

Money demand		Investment function	
Nominal interest rate	Money demand (billions)	Real interest rate	Investment (100 millions)
10%	$1.0	10%	$2
9%	$1.2	9%	$3
8%	$1.4	8%	$4
7%	$1.6	7%	$5
6%	$1.8	6%	$6
5%	$2.0	5%	$7
4%	$2.2	4%	$8

a   Find the equilibrium interest rate and level of investment.
b   Suppose the Bank of Canada lowers required reserves, and the money supply increases to $2 billion. Determine the new interest rate and level of investment.
c   How does aggregate demand shift?

Step-by-step solution

Step one (a): Identify the demand curve for money, the money supply, and the investment function. See Table 34.1 for the money demand and the investment function. The money supply is $1.8 billion.

Step two: Start with an equilibrium in which the supply and demand curves for money intersect at the nominal interest rate. The level of investment is read off the investment function at this interest rate. The initial equilibrium interest rate is 6 percent, which induces firms to invest $600 million.

Step three (b): Shift the money supply curve to reflect the change in the money supply.

Step four: Find the new equilibrium interest rate. It is 5 percent.

§*Step five:* Determine the change in investment by reading the new level of investment off the investment function. Firms increase their investment levels to $700 million, which represents an increase of $100 million.

Step six (c): Aggregate demand shifts to the right.

2   (Practice problem: Keynesian monetary theory) The money demand and investment function are given in Table 34.2. The initial money supply is $4.2 billion.

Table 34.2

Money demand		Investment function	
Nominal interest rate	Money demand (billions)	Real interest rate	Investment (100 millions)
10%	$2.5	10%	$2.0
9%	$3.0	9%	$4.0
8%	$3.3	8%	$5.0
7%	$3.6	7%	$6.0
6%	$3.9	6%	$7.0
5%	$4.2	5%	$7.5
4%	$4.5	4%	$8.0

a Find the equilibrium interest rate and level of investment.

b Suppose the Bank of Canada sells bonds, and so causes the money supply to decrease to $3.6 billion. Determine the new interest rate and level of investment.

c How does aggregate demand shift?

3 (Practice problem: Keynesian monetary theory) The money demand and investment function are given in Table 34.3. The initial money supply is $5.5 billion.

Table 34.3

Money demand		Investment function	
Nominal interest rate	Money demand (billions)	Real interest rate	Investment (100 millions)
10%	$4.5	10%	$12.0
9%	$5.0	9%	$14.0
8%	$5.5	8%	$15.0
7%	$6.0	7%	$16.0
6%	$6.5	6%	$17.0
5%	$7.0	5%	$17.5
4%	$7.5	4%	$18.0

a Find the equilibrium interest rate and level of investment.

b Suppose the Bank of Canada buys bonds, and so cause the money supply to increase to $7 billion. Determine the new interest rate and level of investment.

c How does aggregate demand shift?

Answers to Problems

2 *a* Interest rate = 5 percent; investment = $750 million.

b Interest rate = 7 percent; investment = $600 million.

c Aggregate demand shifts to the left.

3 *a* Interest rate = 8 percent; investment = $1,500 million.

b Interest rate = 5 percent; investment = $1,750 million.

c Aggregate demand shifts to the right.

Chapter 35

MONETARY POLICY: THE INTERNATIONAL SIDE

Chapter Review

In this chapter, the discussion of monetary policy moves from the domestic arena to the international. Changes in the money supply, explored in the last two chapters, also affect the exchange rate, which is the price (or rate) at which a currency trades for other currencies. Important topics in this chapter include how the exchange rate is determined and how the effectiveness of monetary policy depends on foreign exchange markets. The chapter closes with an examination of attempts by governments to manage exchange rates. While this and the previous chapter focus on the effect of monetary policy on output, Chapter 36 turns to the questions of price stability and inflation.

ESSENTIAL CONCEPTS

1   International trade and investment require the exchange of currencies. One country's currency can be traded for another's on the **foreign exchange market.** Under the current **flexible exchange rate system,** the prices of currencies (**exchange rates**) are determined by supply and demand. Foreign households and firms demand

Canadian dollars in order to purchase Canadian exports, to invest in Canadian assets, and to speculate. Canadian households and firms supply dollars in order to import foreign goods, to invest in foreign assets, and also to speculate. Equilibrium in the foreign exchange market is shown in Figure 35.1.

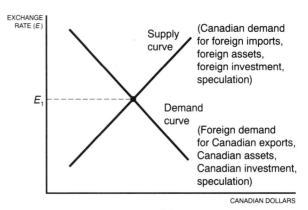

Figure 35.1

2   If there were no international borrowing or lending, then the demand for Canadian dollars would equal the

value of Canadian exports, and the supply of dollars would equal the value of Canadian imports. When the foreign exchange market reached equilibrium, trade would be in balance. But because international capital is mobile (although not perfectly), trade deficits and surpluses are possible. A country can import more than it exports (run a trade deficit) and make up the difference by borrowing from abroad.

3   The supply of and demand for a country's currency will shift when there are changes in the world demand for its exports, its citizens' demand for imported goods, the attractiveness of investing in its assets relative to foreign investments, or the expectations about changes in the exchange rate. Shifts in supply or demand will cause changes in the equilibrium exchange rate.

4   International borrowing and lending, as they work through international currency markets, can limit the effectiveness of domestic monetary policy. For example, if the Bank of Canada raises Canadian interest rates, firms may simply borrow overseas. Foreign capital, attracted by the higher Canadian interest rates, may bid up the price of the dollar and cause net exports to fall. Finally, current monetary policy affects expectations of future inflation and interest rates, and so leads to further changes in exchange rates. These changes may reinforce or work against the intended direction of monetary policy.

5   When the Canadian dollar appreciates, Canadian exports become more expensive to foreigners, while imported goods grow cheaper in Canada. Trade thus depends upon exchange rates. The volatility of exchange rates adds to the risks of importing and exporting, and also international borrowing and lending.

6   The **fixed exchange rate system,** under which governments pegged exchange rates at particular levels, has been abandoned. Still, governments try to influence and stabilize the level of exchange rates. Stabilizing exchange rates is difficult for two reasons: no one can be sure of the equilibrium exchange rate, and international cooperation in this area is problematic.

BEHIND THE ESSENTIAL CONCEPTS

1   International currency markets closely resemble other markets governed by supply and demand, but they use a lingo all their own. The price of one currency in terms of another is not called the price, it's called the "exchange rate." When this price rises, it "**appreciates.**" When it falls, it "**depreciates.**" A currency priced above equilibrium is "**overvalued.**" Under the abandoned fixed exchange rate system, when the government reduced the fixed price, it "**devalued**" its currency.

2   Do not confuse the supply of Canadian dollars in the international currency market with the supply of money you learned about in Chapters 33 and 34. The supply of *dollars* in currency markets shows for every exchange rate how much Canadian households and firms desire to spend in order to buy imported goods or invest abroad. The supply of *money,* on the other hand, is determined by the Bank of Canada. Although changes in the supply of money may bring about changes in the economy that affect the supply of dollars in international currency markets, the two supply curves are different animals. It's important to keep them straight.

3   The effects of changes in the demand for imports and exports in international currency markets are straightforward. If foreign nationals want to purchase more Canadian export goods, then they need Canadian dollars, and the demand for dollars shifts to the right. If Canadian citizens desire more imported goods, dollars must be traded for foreign currencies, and the supply of dollars shifts to the right. Notice that in each case, only one curve shifts.

4   When you analyze changes that affect international borrowing and lending, both curves will shift. The reason is that the capital flows towards the country that offers the higher *relative* return. If Canadian interest rates increase, for example, foreign investors will want to buy Canadian assets (lend in Canada) and will therefore demand more dollars. At the same time, Canadian investors will keep their dollars at home to take advantage of the high interest rates. They will supply fewer dollars. Thus, the demand shifts to the right, and the supply shifts to the left. Later in the chapter, you will get lots of practice working with demand and supply in international currency markets.

5   Why are exchange rates so volatile? Exchange rates go up and down because borrowing and lending involve expectations about the future, and our expectations change as we get new information. To see this, imagine that you are a Japanese investor thinking about buying a Canadian bond. You will earn the Canadian rate of interest, but to determine the rate of return in terms of your own currency, you must anticipate how the exchange rate will change. The following formula summarizes the issue:

rate of return in foreign currency = dollar interest rate − rate of change in exchange rate.

Thus, the rate of return and therefore your demand for dollars depend upon the future happenings in the currency market. Whenever expectations are involved, things are volatile. (Note that the exchange rate is measured in units of foreign currency per dollar.)

SELF-TEST

True or False

F   1   If the Canadian dollar depreciates relative to the French franc, then a dollar will buy more francs.
_{less}

2   If the Canadian dollar appreciates relative to the Japanese yen, then the yen must depreciate relative to the Canadian dollar.
T

3 An appreciation of the Canadian dollar makes Canadian exports more expensive for foreign households to purchase.

4 If there were no international borrowing or lending, then the money value of exports would equal the money value of imports.

5 If the exchange rate is below the intersection of supply and demand for Canadian dollars, then there is an excess supply of dollars.

6 International capital markets are highly but not perfectly mobile.

7 An increase in European interest rates makes investing in Europe more attractive, and shifts the supply of dollars to the right.

8 The supply of dollars in world currency markets is determined by the Bank of Canada.

9 The real exchange rate is the exchange rate adjusted for inflation.

10 The rate of return that a Brazilian investor earns on a Canadian Treasury bill is the dollar interest rate minus the rate of change in the exchange rate.

11 Apart from changes in expectations, the mobility of capital tends to make monetary policy less effective.

12 Under the fixed exchange rate system, speculation always destabilized currency markets.

13 If investors have rational expectations, then exchange rates will move like a random walk.

14 Firms that export or import can reduce but not eliminate risks by buying and selling currencies on futures markets.

15 Stabilizing the exchange rate is difficult because it is hard to know what the equilibrium exchange rate is.

Multiple Choice

1 If the Canadian dollar becomes more valuable relative to the Italian lira, then

  a the dollar appreciates and the lira depreciates.
  b the dollar depreciates and the lira appreciates.
  c the dollar and the lira appreciate.
  d the dollar and the lira depreciate.
  e the dollar is devalued.

2 The price of one currency in terms of another is called

  a the discount rate.
  b the inflation rate.
  c the exchange rate.
  d purchasing power parity.
  e the required reserve ratio.

3 Which of the following is not true? Foreigners demand Canadian dollars so that they can

  a buy Canadian goods.
  b invest in Canadian assets.
  c speculate, hoping that the dollar will appreciate.

  d convert them to their own currency.
  e none of the above.

4 If the Canadian dollar appreciates, Canadian goods become

  a more expensive in foreign currency.
  b less expensive in foreign currency.
  c more expensive in Canadian dollars.
  d less expensive in Canadian dollars.
  e none of the above.

5 If there is no foreign borrowing or lending, then a surplus of Canadian dollars means

  a Canadian imports exceed Canadian exports.
  b Canadian exports exceed Canadian imports.
  c the Canadian trade account is in balance.
  d the Canadian dollar will appreciate.
  e foreign firms are competing unfairly in Canadian markets.

6 If Canadian consumers increase their demand for foreign goods, then

  a the Canadian dollar will appreciate and foreign currencies will depreciate.
  b the Canadian dollar will depreciate and foreign currencies will appreciate.
  c the Canadian dollar and foreign currencies will appreciate.
  d the Canadian dollar and foreign currencies will depreciate.
  e none of the above.

7 An increase in foreign investment in Canada will

  a shift the demand for dollars to the left.
  b shift the supply of dollars to the left.
  c shift the demand for dollars to the right.
  d shift the supply of dollars to the right.
  e none of the above.

8 A German investor holding Canadian dollars for speculative purposes hopes that

  a the German mark appreciates.
  b the Canadian dollar appreciates.
  c the Canadian dollar depreciates.
  d the Canadian trade account is in balance.
  e purchasing power parity is restored.

9 An Italian investor who is holding a Canadian corporate bond earns in Italian lira

  a the rate of interest on the corporate bond.
  b the rate of interest on an equivalent Italian corporate bond.
  c the rate of change in the exchange rate.
  d the rate of interest on the corporate bond plus the rate of change in the exchange rate.
  e the rate of interest on the corporate bond minus the rate of change in the exchange rate.

10 If capital is perfectly mobile between Germany and Canada and if the inflation rate is 10 percent in Canada and 5 percent in Germany, the nominal interest rate in Germany

a will equal the interest rate in Canada.

b will exceed the interest rate in Canada by 5 percent.

c will be less than the interest rate in Canada by 5 percent.

d will equal 15 percent.

e will be twice as high as the interest rate in Canada.

11 If the Canadian interest rate increases, then

a foreign capital will flow into Canada.

b Canadian capital will flow abroad.

c the demand for Canadian dollars will decrease.

d the Canadian dollar will depreciate.

e the supply of dollars will shift to the right.

12 The world's capital markets, which make international capital more mobile,

a have little impact on the effectiveness of monetary policy.

b strengthen the effectiveness of monetary policy.

c weaken the effectiveness of monetary policy.

d are exactly like national capital markets.

e use only the U.S. dollar, which is the internationally recognized currency for capital markets.

13 Higher U.S. interest rates

a cause the Canadian dollar to appreciate.

b discourage Canadian exports through the change in the exchange rate.

c encourage Canadian imports through the change in the exchange rate.

d reduce Canadian investment.

e none of the above.

14 If speculators expect that the Canadian dollar will depreciate 5 percent over the next year, then

a they will want to buy dollars now to realize a capital gain.

b they will want to sell dollars now.

c the dollar will be devalued now.

d the dollar will first appreciate and ultimately depreciate after the speculators have sold their dollars.

e none of the above.

15 The system in which governments intervene in order to reduce the day-to-day variability of exchange rates is called the

a flexible exchange rate system.

b fixed exchange rate system.

c gold standard.

d dirty float system.

e purchasing power parity system.

16 Under the fixed exchange rate system, the equilibrium exchange rate (that is, the rate we would observe in a flexible exchange rate system) is

a irrelevant.

b always lower than the fixed exchange rate.

c always higher than the fixed exchange rate.

d always equal to the fixed exchange rate.

e none of the above.

17 The movement of exchange rates, like a random walk, is consistent with

a static expectations.

b adaptive expectations.

c rational expectations.

d great expectations.

e random expectations.

18 Volatile exchange rates make international trade

a more profitable.

b riskier.

c safer than domestic trade.

d impossible.

e none of the above.

19 The International Monetary Fund is

a a bank specializing in international investment.

b a mutual fund holding shares in all the world's major stock markets.

c an organization set up by the United Nations to promote the adoption of a single world currency.

d an international bank set up to lend to central banks of countries.

e an agency set up to finance development projects in the Third World.

20 The purchasing power parity theory says that

a exchange rates move as a random walk.

b exchange rates should adjust so that a certain sum of money could buy the same goods in any country.

c exchange rates should adjust to keep each country's balance of trade equal to zero.

d the rate of return equals the rate of interest minus the expected change in the exchange rate.

e if international trade is fair, then no country would have a trade deficit.

Completion

1 If the Canadian dollar becomes less valuable relative to the German mark, then we say that the dollar has _____ and the mark has _____.

2 The _____ allows exchange rates to be determined by the law of supply and demand.

3 If foreigners increase their demand for Canadian goods, the demand for dollars will shift to the _____.

4 Holding currency in anticipation of capital gains when it appreciates is called _____.

5 The rate of return that a French investor earns on a Canadian bond is the bond's interest rate minus the _____.

6 High inflation in Canada causes the dollar to _____.

7 The system under which exchange rates are pegged to particular levels is called the _____.

8 If governments take actions that cause the exchange rate to be higher than it would be in a free market, the currency is _____.

9 The international institution set up to provide loans to the central banks of member nations is the

_____.

10 The theory that the long-run equilibrium exchange rate should result in the same money buying equivalent bundles of goods in each country is called

_____.

Answers to Self-Test

True or False

1	f	6	t	11	t
2	t	7	t	12	f
3	t	8	f	13	t
4	t	9	t	14	t
5	f	10	f	15	t

Multiple Choice

1	a	6	b	11	a	16	e
2	c	7	c	12	c	17	c
3	d	8	b	13	e	18	b
4	a	9	e	14	b	19	d
5	a	10	c	15	d	20	b

Completion

1 depreciated, appreciated
2 flexible exchange rate system
3 right
4 speculating
5 change in the exchange rate
6 depreciate
7 fixed exchange rate system
8 overvalued
9 International Monetary Fund
10 purchasing power parity

Doing Economics: Tools and Practice Problems

Supply and demand in international currency markets is the topic of this section. This is an application of basic supply and demand, so we follow the usual four-step procedure. All the applications in this section deal with the market for Canadian dollars and the determination of the dollar exchange rate.

We will study three reasons for shifts in the supply and demand curves for foreign currencies. First, the demand for traded goods may change, and shift either the demand or supply curve for dollars. Second, interest rates may change, and because investors seek the highest relative return, both the supply and demand curves may shift. Finally, when

inflation changes, investors expect that the exchange rate will change to offset the inflation, and again both curves will shift. One thing to keep in mind when both curves shift is that the shifts reinforce each other. In other words, if the shift in the demand curve causes the dollar to depreciate, then the supply curve will shift to cause further depreciation. Table 35.1 summarizes the possible causes of shifts.

Table 35.1

Shifts in demand and supply curves for foreign currencies.

1 Traded goods and services: When the foreign demand for Canadian exports increases, demand for Canadian dollars shifts to the right; when it decreases, demand for Canadian dollars shifts to the left. When Canadian demand for imported goods increases, supply of Canadian dollars shifts to the right; when it decreases, supply of Canadian dollars shifts to the left.

2 Borrowing and lending: When Canadian interest rates increase, demand for Canadian dollars shifts to the right and supply shifts to the left. When they decrease, demand for Canadian dollars shifts to the left and supply shifts to the right. When foreign interest rates increase, demand for Canadian dollars shifts to the left and supply shifts to the right. When they decrease, demand for Canadian dollars shifts to the right and supply shifts to the left.

3 Expected change in exchange rates: When the Canadian inflation rate increases, demand for Canadian dollars shifts to the left and supply shifts to the right. When it decreases, demand for Canadian dollars shifts to the right and supply shifts to the left. When the foreign inflation rate increases, demand for Canadian dollars shifts to the right and supply shifts to the left. When it decreases, demand for Canadian dollars shifts to the left and supply shifts to the right.

Tool Kit 35.1: Supply and Demand for Currencies

Step one: Start with an equilibrium.

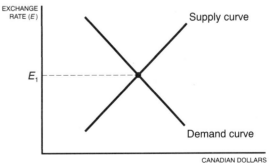

Step two: Observe the exogenous change, and determine which curve or curves shift.

Step three: Shift the supply curve, demand, curve, or both.

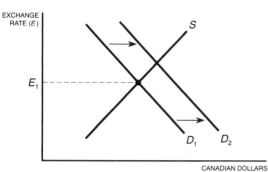

Step four: Find the new equilibrium exchange rate, and compare it with the original one.

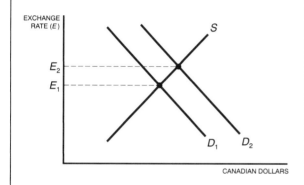

1 (Worked problem: supply and demand for currencies) What is the effect of an increase in German interest rates on the Canadian dollar exchange rate?

Step-by-step solution

Step one: Start with an equilibrium.

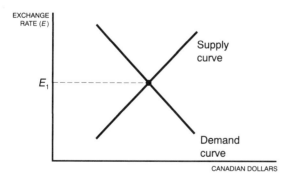

Step two: Observe the exogenous change, and determine which curve shifts. The increase in German interest rates shifts the demand for dollars to the left (because German investors keep their marks in Germany to earn high German interest rates), and the supply of dollars shifts to the right (because Canadian investors seek to trade dollars for marks and invest in Germany).

Step three: Shift the curves.

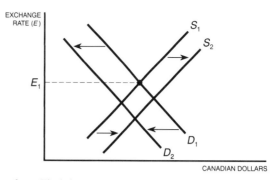

Step four: Find the new equilibrium, and compare. The Canadian dollar depreciates.

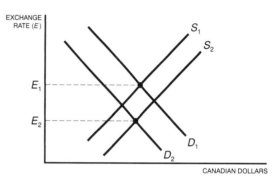

2 (Practice problem: supply and demand for currencies) Canadian energy conservation reduces the demand for imported oil. How does the exchange rate change?

3 (Practice problem: supply and demand for currencies) For each of the following, use supply and demand analysis to show the effect on the exchange rate for Canadian dollars.

a Foreign demand for Canadian movies skyrockets.
b Canadian demand for African music takes off.
c Japanese interest rates rise.
d European interest rates fall.
e Canadian interest rates increase.
f Canadian interest rates decrease.
g Inflation takes off in East Asia.
h South American inflation rates fall.
i Canadian inflation increases.
j Canadian inflation decreases.

Answers to Problems

2 The supply curve of dollars shifts to the left, and the Canadian dollar appreciates.

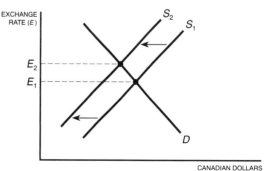

3 *a* The demand curve for dollars shifts to the right, and the Canadian dollar appreciates.

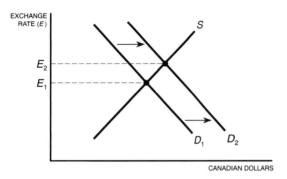

b The supply curve of dollars shifts to the right, and the Canadian dollar depreciates.

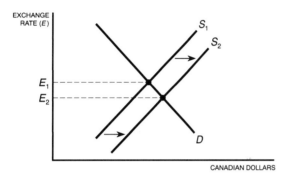

c The demand curve shifts to the right, the supply curve shifts to the right, and the dollar depreciates.

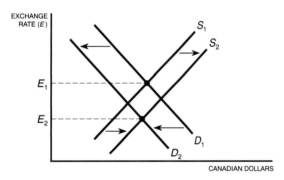

d The demand curve shifts to the right, the supply curve shifts to the left, and the dollar appreciates.

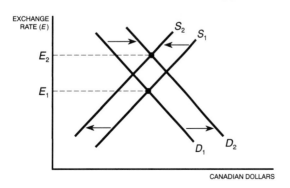

e The demand curve shifts to the right, the supply curve shifts to the left, and the dollar appreciates.

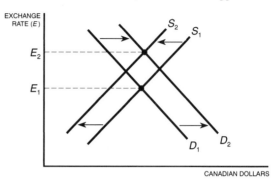

f The demand curve shifts to the left, the supply curve shifts to the right, and the dollar depreciates.

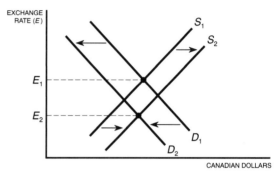

g The demand curve shifts to the right, the supply curve shifts to the left, and the dollar appreciates.

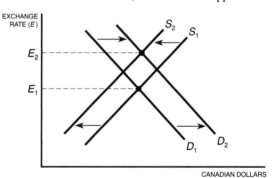

h The demand curve shifts to the left, the supply curve shifts to the right, and the dollar depreciates.

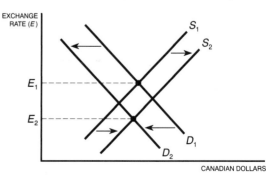

i The demand curve shifts to the left, the supply
curve shifts to the right, and the dollar depreciates.

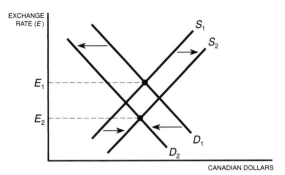

j The demand curve shifts to the right, the supply
curve shifts to the left, and the dollar appreciates.

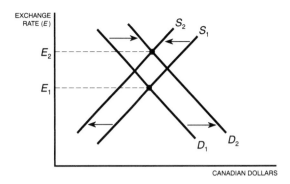

Chapter 36

PRICE STABILITY

Chapter Review

Inflation is frequently misunderstood, and is consequently much maligned. This chapter explains the costs of inflation and how inflationary episodes start and persist. Fighting inflation involves restricting aggregate demand, and thus there is a trade-off between inflation and unemployment, at least in the short run. The chapter discusses this trade-off and its implications for macroeconomic policy and price stability. Part Five and the detailed study of money and capital markets conclude with this chapter. In Part Six, all the parts of the macroeconomic model—the labour market, the product market, and the capital market—are assembled as we study several major issues: growth, budget, and trade deficits, stabilization policy, economic development, and alternative economic systems.

ESSENTIAL CONCEPTS

1 **Inflation** is a general rise in the price level over time and is costly in many ways. Inflation hurts lenders because they are repaid with cheaper dollars. It hurts investors because they are taxed on returns from their in-

vestments that barely compensate for the higher price level. It hurts individuals holding money in savings accounts, as it erodes the purchasing power of this money. Inflation causes further trouble because it distorts relative prices and, when variable, contributes to the riskiness of borrowing and lending. The costs of inflation can be softened somewhat by **indexing,** which means linking future payments to some measure of inflation.

2 Inflation can begin with a monetary or other **demand shock,** which shifts aggregate demand up and increases the price level. It can also begin with a **supply shock,** such as an increase in the price of imported oil, which shifts aggregate supply up, and thereby increases the price level. If expectations of inflation are built into an economy's institutions, the economy can move into an **inflationary spiral.** Continuing inflation can be of the **demand-pull** or **cost-push** variety, but monetary policy plays a key role. The Bank of Canada can either **accommodate inflation** by increasing the money supply and the availability of credit or choke it off by tightening money and credit, which shifts aggregate demand to the left.

3 The **Phillips curve,** shown in Figure 36.1, points out the costs of fighting inflation by showing the trade-off

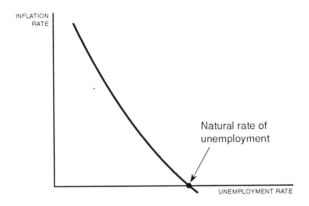

INFLATION
RATE

Natural rate of
unemployment

UNEMPLOYMENT RATE

Figure 36.1

between unemployment and inflation. Decreases in inflation increase unemployment (at least in the short run) until unemployment reaches its so-called **natural rate,** when the price level is constant.

4   The Phillips curve can shift because of real factors, as was the case in the 1970s when large numbers of baby boomers and women entered the labour force. Other reasons for a shift include unemployment insurance or laws restricting layoffs, both of which increase the natural rate of unemployment. Expectations can also shift the curve as workers adjust to inflation and insist on higher wages. The **natural-rate proposition** argues that this adjustment takes place relatively quickly, and thus any attempt to reduce unemployment only results in higher inflation.

5   Monetarists emphasize the costs of inflation, believe that the Phillips curve is close to vertical, and advocate abandoning discretionary monetary policy, simply letting the money supply grow at the rate of output growth. Keynesians, on the other hand, point out the costs of reducing inflation and advocate a more active policy to reduce unemployment. Few economists favour wage and price controls, however.

BEHIND THE ESSENTIAL CONCEPTS

1   When inflation is anticipated, its effects are limited. To understand this better, imagine that you are borrowing $2,500 from your uncle for this year's tuition. To compensate him for living without his money for a year, he wants a 3 percent real rate of return. If there is no inflation, you simply agree to pay him 3 percent interest. If inflation is expected to be 7 percent, you pay him 10 percent interest, which gives him 7 percent to make up for the increase in prices and leaves a 3 percent real return. All contracts can be indexed in this way: therefore a mild, steady rate of inflation does not impose serious costs on the economy.

2   An unpredictable rate of inflation is very costly. Suppose that inflation is uncertain, that it might be 14 percent or 0 percent with equal probability. The average

inflation rate is still 7 percent, but now when you borrow from your uncle, there is risk. If you pay the same 10 percent and inflation is zero, your uncle earns a 10 percent real return—a bonanza! On the other hand, if inflation turns out to be 14 percent, he nets negative 4 percent, and receives back less in real terms than he lent. You can see how a variable and unpredictable rate of inflation imposes risks on capital markets.

3   Another of the important costs of inflation involves the tax system. Most economists favour indexing. The tax structure is indexed to some extent; for example, income tax brackets are adjusted each year for inflation. Investment earnings, however, are not indexed. If you start a business for $100,000 and sell it for $150,000 in 5 years and if the inflation rate is 50 percent over those years, then your real return is zero. Nevertheless, you would be liable for taxes on your nominal gains of $50,000. A sensible reform would exempt nominal gains from taxes.

4   The natural-rate proposition is quite similar to the policy ineffectiveness idea introduced in Chapter 31. The former states that if government tries to reduce unemployment below the natural rate, it will get inflation. With no change in unemployment, there will be no change in output, which is exactly what the policy ineffectiveness proposition says: government policy at most brings about changes in prices.

inflation = 0, unemployment > 0

SELF-TEST

True or False

1   The Canadian tax system is <u>fully</u> indexed for inflation.

F

2   Inflation makes it expensive to hold money, because as the price level rises, money becomes less available.

T

3   Inflation persists because of demand and supply shocks.

F

4   The Bank of Canada accommodates inflation by letting the money supply grow at the rate of growth in output.

F

5   The natural rate of unemployment is the rate that would occur if inflation were zero.

T

6   If workers expect increased inflation, they will insist on higher wages, and shift the Phillips curve up and to the right.

T

7   The natural-rate proposition states that if government attempts to lower unemployment below the natural rate, it will only bring about inflation.

T

8   Keynesians advocate letting the money supply grow at the rate of growth in output.

F

9   Changes in the generosity of the unemployment insurance scheme have the potential to shift the Phillips curve.

T

F 10 Price controls effectively eliminate excess demands for goods.

T 11 Moral suasion refers to attempts by the government to convince firms to limit price increases voluntarily.

T 12 With rapidly adjusting expectations, the Phillips curve is likely to be nearly vertical.

T 13 Supply-side economists advocate fighting inflation by reducing marginal tax rates and thereby shifting the aggregate supply curve to the right.

F 14 A loss of confidence in a country's currency causes a fall in the inflation rate.

T 15 The openness of the economy reinforces the effectiveness of monetary policy in fighting inflation.

Multiple Choice

1 Periods of very rapid increase in the price level, such as occurred in Germany after World War I, are referred to as

a demand-pull inflation.
b cost-push inflation.
c hyperinflation.
d natural rate inflation.
e monetary inflation.

2 Cost-of-living adjustments, or COLAs, are a type of

a wage and price control.
b indexation.
c monetary target.
d discretionary monetary policy.
e inflation tax.

3 If not anticipated, an increase in inflation will

a hurt both borrowers and lenders.
b help both borrowers and lenders.
c hurt borrowers but help lenders.
d hurt lenders but help borrowers.
e have no effect on either borrowers or lenders.

4 Inflation

a does not affect taxpayers, because the tax system is fully indexed.
b does not affect taxpayers, because only real income is taxed.
c does not affect taxpayers, because only nominal income is taxed.
d frequently injures investors, who are taxed on high nominal incomes, even though inflation makes their real income small or even negative.
e hurts wage earners but not investors.

5 The inflation tax refers to

a the fact that inflation makes it expensive to hold money.
b the fact that the earnings of investors are not adjusted for inflation.
c the fact that wages are not adjusted for inflation.
d the injury suffered by borrowers in inflationary times.

e the injury suffered by lenders in inflationary times.

6 Inflation often distorts

a nominal prices.
b relative prices.
c absolute prices.
d average prices.
e none of the above.

7 Inflation can begin as a consequence of

a only demand shocks.
b only supply shocks.
c only monetary shocks.
d wage and price controls.
e demand shocks, supply shocks, or monetary shocks.

8 The economy is in an inflationary spiral if

a the inflation began with a demand shock.
b the inflation began with a supply shock.
c the inflation began with a monetary shock.
d people's expectations of inflation are built into institutional practices, such as COLAs.
e there are wage and price controls.

9 Inflation carried along by increased government spending is referred to as

a demand pull.
b cost push.
c monetary push.
d indexed.
e hyperinflation.

10 The Bank of Canada can accommodate inflation by

a initiating a monetary shock.
b increasing real interest rates.
c allowing credit to become tight.
d allowing the money supply to increase with the price level.
e increasing the money supply at the same rate as the increase in output.

11 Which of the following perpetuates inflation?

a accommodating monetary policy by the Bank of Canada
b an increase in prices of imports
c a monetary shock
d a demand shock
e none of the above

12 The trade-off between inflation and unemployment is illustrated by the

a aggregate demand curve.
b aggregate supply curve.
c Phillips curve.
d aggregate expenditures schedule.
e money demand curve.

13 The natural rate of unemployment is the rate that prevails

a when there is no inflation.
b during hyperinflation.

c when inflation equals its natural rate.

d when there are no wage and price controls.

e in inflationary spirals.

14 Stagflation refers to

a a period when the inflation rate does not change.

b a period of high inflation and high unemployment.

c a period when there are no monetary shocks.

d a period when the government institutes wage and price controls.

e a period when the Bank of Canada accommodates inflation.

15 The increase in the number of new entrants as baby boomers reached working age

a shifted the Phillips curve to the right.

b shifted the Phillips curve to the left.

c did not shift the Phillips curve.

d rotated the Phillips curve, and made it vertical.

e rotated the Phillips curve, and made it horizontal.

16 Along the short-run Phillips curve, expectations are

a indexed.

b fixed.

c rational.

d adaptive.

e volatile.

17 The natural-rate proposition argues that

a the Bank of Canada should always accommodate inflation.

b the Bank of Canada should never accommodate inflation.

c if the government attempts to reduce unemployment below the natural rate, it only causes inflation.

d if the government attempts to reduce inflation below the natural rate, it only causes unemployment.

e the long-run Phillips curve is horizontal.

18 If people expect inflation to be higher, then the Phillips curve

a is vertical in the short run.

b shifts to the right.

c shifts to the left.

d does not shift, because it assumes that expectations are always rational.

e is horizontal in the long run.

19 Monetarists argue that the Bank of Canada should

a increase the money supply at a rate equal to the rate of increase in output.

b accommodate inflation by letting the money supply increase at the rate of increase in the price level.

c use monetary policy to keep interest rates constant.

d use discretionary monetary policy to promote full employment.

e move the economy up and to the left along the Phillips curve.

20 If expectations adjust rapidly, then the Phillips curve will be

a flat.

b close to flat.

c close to vertical.

d upward sloping.

e none of the above.

Completion

1 Extremely high rates of increase in the price level are called *hyperinflation* .

2 Formally linking any payment, such as wages or taxes, to inflation is called *indexing* .

3 Inflation perpetuated by increases in government or investment spending is *demand-pull* inflation.

4 Inflation perpetuated by wage increases is an example of *cost-push* inflation.

5 The trade-off between unemployment and inflation is represented by the *Phillips curve*

6 The rate of unemployment that would result if there were no inflation is the *natural-rate*

7 The *natural-rate proposition* argues that if the government attempts to reduce unemployment below the natural rate, it simply brings about an increase in inflation.

8 Monetarists argue that the Bank of Canada should increase the money supply at the same rate as the increase in real output and abandon *discretionary* monetary policy.

9 If the government tries to persuade firms to limit price increases, then it is using *moral suasion*

10 *Supply-side* economists argued that the best way to fight inflation was to shift the aggregate supply curve by cutting taxes.

Answers to Self-Test

True or False

1	f	6	t	11	t
2	t	7	t	12	t
3	f	8	f	13	t
4	f	9	t	14	f
5	t	10	f	15	t

Multiple Choice

1	c	6	b	11	a	16	b
2	b	7	e	12	c	17	c
3	d	8	d	13	a	18	b
4	d	9	a	14	b	19	a
5	a	10	d	15	a	20	c

Completion

1 hyperinflation

2 indexing

3 demand-pull

4 cost-push

5   Phillips curve
6   natural rate
7   natural-rate proposition
8   discretionary
9   moral suasion
10 Supply-side

Doing Economics: Tools and Practice Problems

In Chapter 25, we learned how to measure inflation and construct the price index. In this chapter, we use those tools to study cost-of-living provisions in contracts and to make comparisons between prices at different times. The goals are to understand how the economy deals with steady and predictable inflation and to develop a feel for the difference between real and nominal values.

Tool Kit 36.1: Using Cost-of-Living Provisions to Adjust Wages and Prices

Wage agreements between employer and employees, contracts between firms and their suppliers, government entitlement programs, and even the income tax system are indexed for inflation with cost-of-living provisions. These provisions specify that wages, prices, or other important economic variables must be adjusted to reflect inflation. The problems in this section show how to do this using the consumer price index. Table 36.1 gives the consumer price index for every year since 1950. (You will find these data, and many other series, in the *Stiglitz Tutor*, a computerized self-test and Canadian data bank.)

Step one: Identify the dollar amount to be adjusted, that year's price index, and the current price index.

Step two: Convert the amount to current dollars:

current dollar equivalent = amount
    × (current price index/past price index).

---

1   (Worked problem: cost-of-living provisions) Dan's Steel Company offered a wage of $15 per hour in 1980. A cost-of-living provision in the contrast guaranteed that the nominal wage would be increased to compensate for inflation. Use the consumer price index given in Table 36.1 to calculate the wage in each year since 1980.

Step-by-step solution

Step one: The wage in 1980 was $15. To find the inflation-adjusted wage in 1981, we need the consumer price index in 1980, which is 67.2, and in 1981, which is 75.5.

Step two: Convert the wage to 1981 dollars:

wage in 1981 = $15 × (75.5/67.2) = $16.85.

Table 36.1
Annual Averages of the All-Items Consumer Price Index (1986=100)

Year	CPI	Year	CPI	Year	CPI
1914	9.2	1941	12.9	1968	28.7
1915	9.4	1942	13.5	1969	30.0
1916	10.2	1943	13.7	1970	31.0
1917	12.0	1944	13.8	1971	31.9
1918	13.6	1945	13.9	1972	33.4
1919	14.9	1946	14.3	1973	36.0
1920	17.3	1947	15.7	1974	39.9
1921	15.2	1948	17.9	1975	44.2
1922	14.0	1949	18.5	1976	47.5
1923	14.0	1950	19.0	1977	51.3
1924	13.7	1951	21.1	1978	55.9
1925	13.9	1952	21.6	1979	61.0
1926	14.0	1953	21.4	1980	67.2
1927	13.8	1954	21.5	1981	75.5
1928	13.8	1955	21.5	1982	83.7
1929	14.0	1956	21.8	1983	88.5
1930	13.9	1957	22.5	1984	92.4
1931	12.6	1958	23.1	1985	96.0
1932	11.4	1959	23.4	1986	100.0
1933	10.9	1960	23.7	1987	104.4
1934	11.0	1961	23.9	1988	108.6
1935	11.1	1962	24.2	1989	114.0
1936	11.3	1963	24.6	1990	119.5
1937	11.7	1964	25.1	1991	126.2
1938	11.8	1965	25.7	1992	128.1
1939	11.7	1966	26.6		
1940	12.2	1967	27.6		

Source: Statistics Canada CANSIM Database, Series P490000.

The wage in 1982 is $15 × (83.7/67.2) = $18.68, which we can also obtain by applying the ratio of the 1982 and 1981 price levels to the expression we used to calculate the 1981 wage: $15 × (75.5/67.2) × (83.7/75.5) = $18.68. Proceeding similarly, we derive the information in Table 36.2.

Table 36.2

Year	Wage
1980	$15.00
1981	$16.85
1982	$18.68
1983	$19.75
1984	$20.62
1985	$21.43
1986	$22.32
1987	$23.30
1988	$24.24
1989	$25.45
1990	$26.67
1991	$28.17
1992	$28.59

2 (Practice problem: cost-of-living provisions) The Canada Pension Plan (CPP) is financed, in part, by employee contributions of 2.5 percent of what is called "pensionable earnings." At the time the CPP came into effect (January 1, 1966), pensionable earnings were defined as earnings between $600 and $5,000 per year. The maximum has been increased over time, and the maximum monthly retirement pension has also been frequently adjusted. The levels for both, for various years from 1970 to 1993, are given in Table 36.3.

Table 36.3
Maximum Pensionable Earnings and Maximum Monthly Retirement Pension

Year	Maximum pensionable earnings	Maximum monthly retirement pension
1970	$ 5,300	$ 43.33
1975	$ 7,400	$122.50
1980	$13,100	$244.44
1985	$23,400	$435.42
1988	$26,500	$543.06
1989	$27,700	$556.25
1990	$28,900	$577.08
1991	$30,500	$604.86
1992	$33,400	$636.11

Source: *The National Finances, 1993*, Canadian Tax Foundation.

Adjust these numbers for inflation, taking 1970 as the base year; that is, express all figures in terms of 1970 dollars. Are maximum pensionable earnings keeping pace with the maximum pension? Is either keeping pace with inflation?

3 (Practice problem: cost-of-living provisions) The federal income tax brackets are adjusted in some, though not all, years. For 1991, the lowest rate of tax, 17 per-cent, was applied on taxable incomes up to $28,784; the next rate, 26 percent, was applied on taxable incomes beyond this point and up to $57,567; and beyond this point the third rate of 29 percent was applied. For 1992, the break points were raised to $29,950 and $59,180. Were these increases in line with inflation? It should be noted that the break points are set in the year preceding that to which they apply. If the 1991 figures are treated as 1990 figures, therefore, and the 1992 figures are treated as 1991 figures, does this change your answer?

Answers to Problems

2 The adjusted maximum pensionable earnings for 1975, in 1970 dollars, are $7,400 × (31.0/44.2) = $5,190.05; the adjusted maximum monthly pension for 1975 is $122.50 × (31.0/44.2) = $85.92. Between 1970 and 1975, therefore, the maximum pensionable earnings fell in real terms though the maximum pension rose. The adjusted maximum pensionable earnings for 1992 are $33,400 × (31.0/128.1) = $8,082.75. The adjusted maximum monthly pension for 1992 is $636.11 × (31.0/128.1) = $153.94. Between 1970 and 1992, therefore, both the maximum pensionable earnings and the maximum pension rose in real terms. The former has risen less dramatically than the latter, however. The calculations for other intervening years follow the same pattern and are left to the reader as an exercise.

3 To adjust for inflation, multiply the 1992 break points by (126.2/128.1) = 0.985. This yields figures in 1991 dollars of $29,500 and $58,292. These are higher than the 1991 figures. If the 1991 figures are treated as 1990 figures, and the 1992 figures are treated as 1991 figures, the adjustment for inflation is to multiply by (119.5/126.2) = 0.947. Now the later figures become $28,363 and $56,043, so in this case the break points are not keeping pace with inflation.

Part Six

Policies for Growth and Stability

Chapter 37

GROWTH AND PRODUCTIVITY

↑K ↑I ↑quality labour
↑efficiency resource allocation
↑ technology

Chapter Review

This chapter of the text begins Part Six, which builds on the lessons of the previous five parts and takes a detailed look at some major macroeconomic problems. The chapter focuses on the causes of growth and the potential for continued expansion. The key concept is productivity, defined as output per worker. The next two chapters turn to problems in recent Canadian macroeconomic policy and consider suggestions for improvement.

ESSENTIAL CONCEPTS

1   Although the Canadian economy has grown enormously in this century, the rate of growth in **productivity** (output per hour worked) has slowed in the last two decades. This slowdown mirrors what has happened in the U.S. economy, where the slowdown has led to a loss of confidence in U.S. technological leadership. In Canada, the slowdown has resulted in zero growth in real wages (though not family incomes); in the United States, real wages have declined. Additionally, in both countries, the growth slowdown has exacerbated inequality in living standards.

2   The four causes of growth in productivity are an increase in the accumulation of capital goods (investment), an improvement in the quality of the labour force, an increase in the efficiency of resource allocation, and improvements in technology, usually referred to as technological change. Concerns about productivity slowdown have led economists to propose policies designed to restore rapid growth.

3   Figure 37.1 represents the **production function,** which shows the relationship between inputs and outputs. It illustrates that the accumulation of capital goods per worker brings about an increase in output per worker; however, the increase is subject to the **law of diminishing returns.**

4   Although today's world capital market allows international borrowing, **capital accumulation** clearly requires more domestic savings and investment. Canadian savings rates have fallen because more generous public pension rights have reduced incentives to save for retirement, while improved capital markets have made borrowing easier. In addition, savings rates have suffered because the fraction of the population in the prime savings years (45 to 65) has declined. Canadian investment has fallen because of high real interest

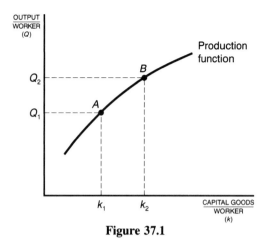

Figure 37.1

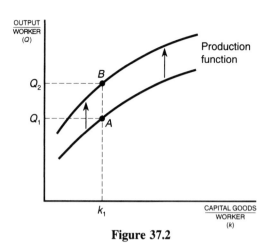

Figure 37.2

rates, an uncertain investment climate, and some increased government regulations.

5   Investment in skills and education improves the quality of the labour force. Economists call this **human capital.** Although the Canadian educational system has considerable strengths, especially in higher education, there is concern about whether it remains capable, among other things, of providing the most able students with the skills required to help Canada sustain technological excellence.

6   The economy expanded during this century as resources moved from traditional agriculture to higher productivity employment in manufacturing. Presently, the movement is towards the service sector, where some economists think the potential for productivity gains is more limited.

7   **Technological change** shifts the production function up and can outstrip diminishing returns. Although not everyone benefits from every innovation, technological change increases productivity, employment, and living standards overall. **Learning by doing** and **research and development** are important sources of technological progress. Sound macroeconomic policies that encourage full employment, R & D funding and tax subsidies, more science and technology education, and better government regulation all promote technological advance.

BEHIND THE ESSENTIAL CONCEPTS

1   You should be clear about the distinction between factors that lead to movements along the production function and those that cause shifts. Capital accumulation moves the economy along its production function, as shown in Figure 37.1. An improvement in technology, on the other hand, shifts the production function. In Figure 37.2, the technological advance increases output without increasing the capital stock.

2   Productivity equals output per worker. As population grows, capital goods must be accumulated for the new

workers to use. Because output per worker depends on how much capital each has to work with, this extra capital only keeps productivity constant. Additional capital goods must be accumulated to increase the amount of capital per worker, so that productivity can grow.

3   Some have argued that the available natural resources set up limits to growth. Certain natural resources, such as petroleum and agricultural land, are privately owned and traded in well-organized markets. These markets provide good incentives for conservation and preservation. If oil becomes scarce, for example, its price will rise, and world oil stocks will be conserved. This type of natural resource will probably not limit the world's growth. The ozone, oceans, and the genetic diversity in threatened natural habitats, on the other hand, are natural resources that are commonly owned and not traded in markets. The world's economy provides no incentive to conserve or preserve these resources. Their destruction is an external cost, not captured by prices. These global environmental problems may pose threats to increased living standards. Their solution requires cooperation among the world's governments.

SELF-TEST

True or False

F   1   Productivity means output per unit of capital goods. *worker*

F   2   Canadian productivity growth plummeted in the early 1980s.

T   3   Family incomes increased between 1973 and 1988. *women workers?*

F   4   The law of diminishing returns says that technological advance must bring about slower growth in the future.

F   5   Human capital refers to the plant and equipment that workers use on the job.

F   6   Because world capital is mobile, there is no relationship between domestic savings and investment.

7 The Canadian savings rate during the 1980s rose to offset government budget deficits. *F*

8 One reason for low Canadian savings rates during the 1980s is that the fraction of the population in the prime savings years declined. *T*

9 A country's infrastructure includes its roads, bridges, sewer systems, and airports. *T*

10 Investment in infrastructure has increased substantially during recent years. *F*

11 Looser monetary policies can lower interest rates and encourage investment. *T*

12 A great strength of the Canadian educational system is its commitment to egalitarianism. *T*

13 Unemployment affects the quality of the labour force in the long run as unemployed workers fail to acquire experience and lose human capital. *T*

14 Everyone benefits from each technological advance through higher productivity and growth. *F*

15 Market incentives ensure that such natural resources as rain forests and the global environment will be preserved. *F*

Multiple Choice

1 Productivity is

   a output per hour worked.
   b hours worked divided by output.
   c the extra output from the marginal worker.
   d the number of workers required to produce the next unit of output.
   e output divided by the total number of inputs.

2 The Canadian rate of growth in productivity

   a sped up in the late 1960s and 1970s.
   b has been nearly constant throughout the twentieth century.
   c slowed significantly in the late 1960s and 1970s.
   d increased steadily through the twentieth century.
   e fell dramatically in the 1980s.

3 Since the early 1980s, real wages have

   a fallen.
   b remained virtually constant.
   c risen for unskilled workers but fallen for the upper 40 percent in the income distribution.
   d fallen for both ends of the income distribution.
   e continued to grow at rates close to the previous period.

4 Since the early 1980s, household incomes in Canada have

   a fallen along with real wages.
   b fallen even though real wages rose.
   c risen chiefly because more women entered the labour force.
   d grown at the rate of growth of real wages.
   e grown at a slower rate of growth than that of real wages.

5 The causes of growth do not include

   a the accumulation of capital goods.
   b improvement in the quality of the labour force.
   c more efficient allocation of resources.
   d technological advance.
   e none of the above.

6 The production function shows the relationship between

   a the levels of inputs and the level of output.
   b technology and growth.
   c productivity and real wages.
   d learning and experience.
   e productivity and output.

7 According to the law of diminishing returns, as the economy accumulates more capital, output increases

   a at the same rate as capital grows.
   b at a slower rate than capital grows.
   c at a faster rate than capital grows.
   d only if new workers enter the labour force.
   e only if the new capital equipment takes advantage of new and better technologies.

8 Human capital refers to

   a the capital goods that individuals own.
   b education and skills that increase the productivity of individuals.
   c fertility.
   d output per hour worked.
   e the capital goods that workers use on the job.

9 Technological change

   a shifts the production function so that the same number of inputs produce more output.
   b shifts the production function so that more output is produced but only if additional capital goods are used.
   c shifts the production function so that more output is produced but only if additional workers are hired.
   d increases productivity for capital but not for workers.
   e increases productivity but does not shift the production function.

10 Which of the following is not a benefit of investment?

   a New entrants into the labour force are provided with capital goods.
   b Existing workers are provided with additional capital goods.
   c The new equipment takes advantage of new and better technologies.
   d Diminishing returns are postponed.
   e None of the above.

11 The law of diminishing returns implies that

   a investment cannot sustain higher rates of growth indefinitely.
   b technological advance cannot sustain higher rates of growth indefinitely.
   c investment does not cause growth.

d human capital is more important than physical capital.

e real wages cannot grow as fast as productivity.

12 According to the life-cycle theory, savings in Canada were low in the 1980s because

   a the fraction of the population that is retired decreased.

   b the fraction of the population in the prime savings years (45 to 65) increased.

   c the fraction of the population in the prime savings years (45 to 65) decreased.

   d the population as a whole increased.

   e the fraction of the population in the prime savings years (21 to 44) decreased.

13 During the 1980s, tax changes

   a encouraged savings by increasing the real after-tax rate of return to savings.

   b encouraged savings by decreasing the real after-tax rate of return to savings.

   c discouraged savings by increasing the real after-tax rate of return to savings.

   d discouraged savings by decreasing the real after-tax rate of return to savings.

   e had no impact on savings.

14 Which of the following did not contribute to the low level of investment in the 1980s?

   a favourable tax treatment for commercial real estate

   b frequent changes in tax laws

   c volatile exchange rates

   d high and variable real interest rates

   e none of the above

15 Which of the following contributed to the misallocation of investment in the 1980s?

   a favourable tax treatment for commercial real estate

   b frequent changes in tax laws

   c volatile exchange rates

   d high and variable real interest rates

   e none of the above

16 During the 1980s, investment in infrastructure

   a was adequate, but the level of business investment was low.

   b was inadequate but was offset by a high level of business investment.

   c was inadequate and exacerbated the effects of the low level of business investment.

   d was low because tax changes made it more expensive.

   e was adequate, as was the level of business investment.

17 Which of the following characteristics of the Canadian educational system is viewed as a major weakness?

   a the absence of early tracking of students in lower grades

   b the relative accessibility of higher education

   c the discoveries and innovations that flow from university research laboratories

   d the low percentage of students choosing majors in science and technology

   e none of the above

18 The notion that in the process of production firms gain experience and produce more efficiently is called

   a the law of diminishing returns.

   b learning by doing.

   c the productivity slowdown.

   d research and development.

   e eminent domain.

19 The obligation of producers to compensate victims of defective products is called

   a learning by doing.

   b eminent domain.

   c product liability.

   d precautionary savings.

   e diminishing returns.

20 Which of the following is true of the years following 1970?

   a The rate of growth in productivity decreased, while inequality increased.

   b The rate of growth in productivity increased, as did inequality.

   c Both the rate of growth in productivity and inequality decreased.

   d The rate of growth in productivity increased, but inequality decreased.

   e The rate of growth in productivity slowed down, with no appreciable change in inequality.

Completion

1 _____ is defined as output per hour worked.

2 The _____ relates the levels of inputs to the level of output.

3 A country's roads, airports, bridges, sewer lines, and railroads make up its _____.

4 Economists refer to education and skills as _____.

5 Discovering better ways of producing goods through experience is called _____.

6 The obligation of producers to compensate victims of a defective product is called _____.

7 The _____ of nineteenth-century England destroyed labour-saving machinery, hoping to protect their jobs.

8 According to the _____, successive increments in capital lead to smaller increases in output per worker.

9 The savings that a household sets aside in case of emergency or illness are called _____.

10 The _____ shows how production costs fall as a firm gathers more experience.

Answers to Self-Test

True or False

1	f	6	f	11	t
2	f	7	f	12	t
3	t	8	t	13	t
4	f	9	t	14	f
5	f	10	f	15	f

Multiple Choice

1	a	6	a	11	a	16	c
2	c	7	b	12	c	17	d
3	b	8	b	13	a	18	b
4	c	9	a	14	a	19	c
5	e	10	e	15	a	20	a

Completion

1 Productivity
2 production function
3 infrastructure
4 human capital
5 learning by doing
6 product liability
7 Luddites
8 law of diminishing returns
9 precautionary savings
10 learning curve

Doing Economics: Tools and Practice Problems

Two important factors in the Canadian productivity slowdown are low savings and misallocated investment. In this section, we study some reasons for low savings rates: demographic changes, improved opportunities for consumer borrowing, and more generous public pensions. Also, we see how favourable tax treatment of certain types of projects misallocates investment.

REASONS FOR LOW SAVINGS RATES: DEMOGRAPHIC CHANGES

One important fact about the current population of Canada is that generations, or cohorts, are of different sizes. The so-called baby boom generation, now around 35 or 45, is significantly larger than its parents' generation and also its children's generation. This fact has important implications for national savings because, as the life-cycle model predicts, individuals save at different rates during their lifetimes. Generally, people will save little in their early years, a great deal in middle age, and less when retired. When generations are of different sizes, then the national savings rate will fluctuate as the relatively large generation moves through the high-savings years.

1 (Worked problem: low savings rates) There was zero population growth in the state of Steady for centuries until now. People in Steady behave exactly as the life-cycle model predicts; they save at different rates dur-

ing the successive periods of their lives. The savings supply curves for three age classes of equal size are given in Table 37.1.

Table 37.1

	Savings		
Interest rate	Young	Middle	Old
4%	$1,000	$20,000	$5,000
6%	$1,100	$25,000	$5,000
8%	$1,200	$30,000	$5,000
10%	$1,200	$35,000	$5,000

a Suppose the generation that is now young is twice as large as the other generations, which are of equal size. Calculate the supply of savings for the economy.

b Twenty years from now, the large generation will be middle-aged. The currently old will die and be replaced by the cohort that is now middle-aged. Calculate the supply of savings for the economy in 20 years.

c Forty years from now, the large population will be old. The young and middle generations will be half the size of the large generation. Calculate the supply of savings in 40 years.

d Plot the three savings supplies, and notice the fluctuations in savings supply caused by the demographic transition.

Step-by-step solution

Step one (a): We find the market supply of savings by summing the total amount of savings at each interest rate. If the interest rate is 4 percent, then total savings will be

(2 × $1,000) + (1 × $20,000) + (1 × $5,000) = $27,000.

We multiply the $1,000, which is the savings of the young, by 2 because there are twice as many young people.

Step two: At a 6 percent interest rate, the supply of savings is

(2 × $1,100) + $25,000 + $5,000 = $32,200.

Continuing the process derives the entire supply of savings, which is as follows.

Interest rate	Savings
4%	$27,000
6%	$32,200
8%	$37,400
10%	$42,400

Step three (b): To find the total supply of savings 20 years from now when the large generation will be middle-aged, multiply the supply of savings in the middle-aged generation by 2 and add it to the others. For example, at a 4 percent interest rate, total savings are

$1,000 + (2 × $20,000) + $5,000 = $46,000.

Continuing gives the supply of savings in 20 years.

Interest rate	Savings
4%	$46,000
6%	$56,100
8%	$66,200
10%	$76,200

Step four (c): Total savings 40 years from now are found by multiplying the savings of the old by 2 and adding them to the savings of the others. The supply curve is

Interest rate	Savings
4%	$31,000
6%	$36,100
8%	$41,200
10%	$46,200

Step five (d): Plot the curves. Clearly, supply shifts to the right as the large generation moves into the high-savings years and shifts to the left when they retire.

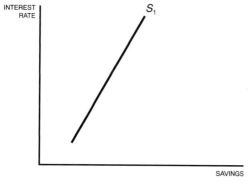

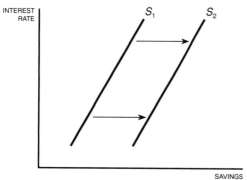

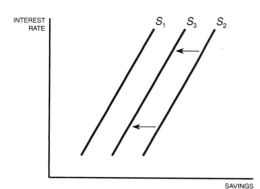

2 (Practice problem: low savings rates) Using the same data as in problem 1, suppose that a baby boomlet generation follows 40 years behind the large genera-

tion. In other words, every other generation will be twice as large as the generations were in Steady for centuries. Derive the supply of savings for the economy for 20-year intervals. Begin with a small young generation.

REASONS FOR LOW SAVINGS RATES: LOWER INTEREST RATES FOR BORROWING

One of the great strengths of the Canadian economy is its efficient capital market. Recently a combination of factors, for example credit cards, home equity loans, and bank deregulation, have increased access for borrowers. Lower interest rates for borrowers rotate part of the budget constraint out, and give the household more opportunities to consume more today. This is an application of the opportunity set with multiple constraints introduced in Chapter 2.

3 (Worked problem: low savings rates) Harold and Myla take home $60,000 each year. They can earn 4 percent on any savings, but they must borrow at 14 percent.

a Plot their two-period budget constraint.
b A preapproved application for a new credit card arrives. The interest rate on the unpaid balance will be 8 percent. Plot their new two-period budget constraint, and compare it with the answer to part a.

Step-by-step solution

Step one (a): Plot the budget constraint with the 4 percent interest rate. The slope is 1.04, and it passes through the point $60,000 now and $60,000 next year.

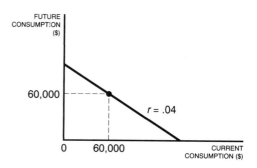

Step two: Plot the budget constraint with the 14 percent interest rate. The slope is 1.14, and it passes through the point $60,000 now and $60,000 next year.

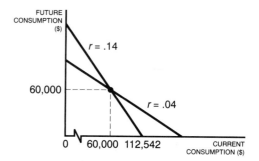

Step three: Darken the portion of each budget constraint that lies under the other constraint. This is the answer to part a.

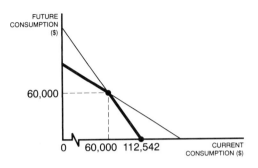

Step four (b): Again, plot the budget constraint with the 4 percent interest rate as in step one.

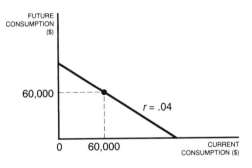

Step five: Plot the budget constraint with the 8 percent interest rate. The slope is 1.08, and it passes through the point $60,000 now and $60,000 next year.

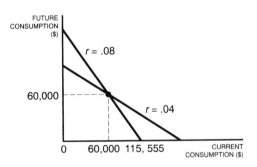

Step six: Darken the portion of each budget constraint that lies under the other constraint. This is the answer to part b.

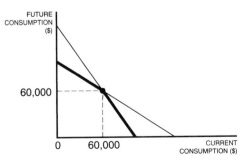

Step seven: Compare the two budget constraints. The lower interest rate gives Harold and Myla more opportunities, but the extra opportunities all involve borrowing.

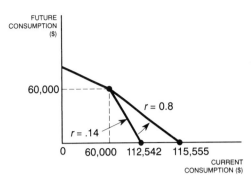

4   (Practice problem: low savings rates) Bill takes home $10,000 this year, but he anticipates taking home $30,000 next year. He can earn 8 percent on savings, but he has a poor credit rating and must pay 19 percent to borrow.

   a   Plot his two-period budget constraint.
   b   Through his credit union at his new job, Bill can obtain loans for 10 percent. Plot his new two-period budget constraint, and compare.

REASONS FOR LOW SAVINGS RATES: INCREASED PUBLIC PENSION RIGHTS

Public pensions certainly reduce people's incentives to save for retirement, and because they are financed on a pay-as-you-go basis, they reduce national savings. Improvements to public pensions during the 1970s further reduced savings incentives. The next two problems use the two-period budget constraint to illustrate this idea.

5   (Worked problem: low savings rates) Juwan has 10 years until retirement. He earns $40,000 after taxes and expects to receive $20,000 in public pension rights when he retires. He expects that over the 10-year interval until retirement he can earn a 100 percent rate of return, and he currently saves $5,000 per year.

   a   Calculate the present discounted value of his pension rights.
   b   Draw his two-period budget constraint, and plot his chosen point.
   c   Suppose that his pension rights are increased to $30,000. His taxes are also increased by $5,000; this reduces his current net income to $35,000. Draw his two-period budget constraint.
   d   How much does Juwan now save?

Step-by-step solution

Step one (a): The present discounted value of his benefit payment is $20,000/(1 + r) = $20,000/(1 + 1) = $10,000.

Step two (b): Draw his two-period budget constraint. Label the axes "Current consumption" and "Retirement consumption." The slope is 1 + r, and the interest rate for the 10-year period is 100 percent. The horizontal intercept is the present discounted value of all income, which is $40,000 + $10,000 = $50,000.

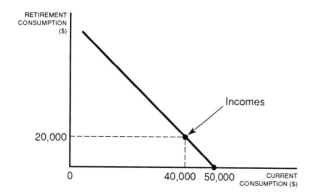

Step three: Plot his chosen point. Juwan chooses to save $5,000; thus, he consumes $40,000 – $5,000 = $35,000 now. The $5,000 grows to $10,000 in 10 years, which enables consumption of $20,000 + $10,000 = $30,000.

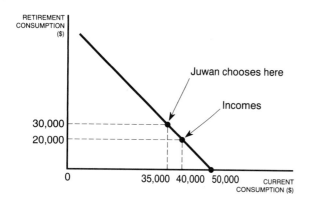

Step four (c): Plot his new budget constraint. The present discounted value of his benefits is now $30,000/2 = $15,000. The horizontal intercept is $15,000 + $35,000 = $50,000, which is unchanged. Because neither the present discounted value of his two-period income nor the interest rate changes, the budget constraint remains the same.

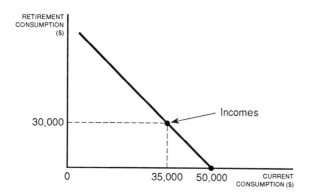

Step five (d): Because he has the same budget constraint, he chooses the same point. But he achieves this combination of current and retirement consumption by reducing his savings to zero. The increase in pension rights has reduced Juwan's savings by exactly $5,000.

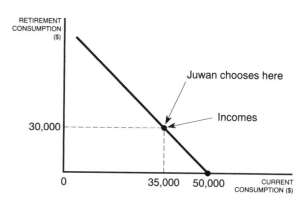

6 (Practice problem: low savings rates) Mai Lin is only 10 years from retirement. She can expect to receive $2 in interest for every $1 saved for retirement. She takes home $60,000 annually, saves $10,000 each year, and expects pension rights of $30,000 when she retires.

a Plot her two-period budget constraint.

b Suppose Parliament passes a 50 percent increase in benefits. Taxes also rise so that the budget constraint does not change. How will Mai Lin's consumption now and during retirement change? How will her savings change?

Tool Kit 37.1: Showing How Subsidies Can Misallocate Investment

Preferential tax treatment of certain types of investment can misallocate an economy's capital stock. A subsidy to a particular type of investment will raise its return, and since investors always seek the highest rate of return, they will reallocate their portfolio to take advantage of the subsidy.

Step one: Add up the demands of each sector for capital.

Step two: Find the market-clearing rate of interest.

Step three: Substitute the market-clearing rate of interest into each demand to determine the allocation of investment that occurs without subsidy.

Step four: Add the subsidy to the demand for capital in the subsidized sector.

Step five: Repeat steps one through three.

Step six: Compare the allocation found in step five with that found in step three.

---

7 (Worked problem: allocation of investment) The 1988 tax reform eliminated certain provisions that gave preferential tax treatment to real estate. To see the effect that these tax subsidies have, consider Table 37.2, which gives hypothetical demands for capital by the real estate and manufacturing sectors in billions of dollars. The supply of financial capital for the two sectors is $3,900 billion.

Table 37.2

Interest rate	Demand in the real estate sector (billions)	Demand in the manufacturing sector (billions)
10%	$1,000	$2,000
9%	$1,100	$2,200
8%	$1,200	$2,400
7%	$1,300	$2,600
6%	$1,400	$2,800
5%	$1,500	$3,000
4%	$1,600	$3,200

a Find the market allocation.
b Suppose the tax subsidy amounts to an extra 3 percent annual earnings for a real estate investment. Find the allocation.
c How does the tax subsidy alter the equilibrium allocation of capital?

Step one (a): Add the demands of each sector for capital. We choose an interest rate, and sum the quantity demanded in each sector. When the interest rate is 10 percent, the total quantity demanded is $1,000 + $2,000 = $3,000 billion. Continuing, we derive Table 37.3.

Table 37.3

Interest rate	Real estate (billions)	Manufacturing (billions)	Total
10%	$1,000	$2,000	$3,000
9%	$1,100	$2,200	$3,300
8%	$1,200	$2,400	$3,600
7%	$1,300	$2,600	$3,900
6%	$1,400	$2,800	$4,200
5%	$1,500	$3,000	$4,500
4%	$1,600	$3,200	$4,800

Step two: Find the market-clearing rate of interest. Quantity supplied, which is $3,900 billion, equals quantity demanded when the interest rate is 7 percent.

Step three: Substitute the market-clearing rate of interest into each demand to determine the allocation of investment. The 6 percent rate of interest brings about an allocation of $1,300 billion in real estate and $2,600 billion in manufacturing.

Step four (b): Add the subsidy to the demand for capital in the subsidized sector. Simply add 3 percent to the interest rate column for the real estate sector. Table 37.4 gives the result.

Table 37.4

Interest rate	Real estate (billions)
13%	$1,000
12%	$1,100
11%	$1,200
10%	$1,300
9%	$1,400
8%	$1,500
7%	$1,600

Step five: Repeat steps one through three. Table 37.5 gives the new total demand.

Table 37.5

Interest rate	Real estate (billions)	Manufacturing (billions)	Total (billions)
13%	$1,000	$2,000	$3,000
12%	$1,100	$2,000	$3,100
11%	$1,200	$2,000	$3,200
10%	$1,300	$2,000	$3,300
9%	$1,400	$2,200	$3,600
8%	$1,500	$2,400	$3,900
7%	$1,600	$2,600	$4,200
6%	$1,600	$2,800	$4,400
5%	$1,700	$3,000	$4,700
4%	$1,800	$3,200	$5,000

The market clears at an 8 percent interest rate with an allocation of $1,500 billion to real estate and $2,400 billion to manufacturing.

Step six (c): Compare the allocation found in step five with that found in step three. The tax subsidy increases the real estate sector's allocation from $1,300 billion to $1,500 billion, and reduces the manufacturing sector's allocation from $2,600 billion to $2,400 billion. In effect, $200 billion is reallocated from manufacturing to real estate.

8 (Practice problem: allocation of investment) Table 37.6 gives the demands for financial capital in the sector that produces goods for export and the sector that produces goods that compete with imports. The available supply of capital is $200 billion.

Table 37.6

Interest rate	Demand in the import-competing sector (billions)	Demand in the export sector (billions)
12%	$ 30	$ 40
11%	$ 50	$ 50
10%	$ 60	$ 60
9%	$ 70	$ 80
8%	$ 80	$ 90
7%	$100	$100
6%	$120	$110
5%	$140	$120

a Find the market allocation.
b Worried about lost market share to imports, a protectionist Parliament passes a series of tax subsidies and trade barriers. Suppose that the tax subsidies and import controls amount to an extra 5 percent annual earnings for import-competing investment. Find the new allocation.
c How does the tax policy alter the equilibrium allocation of capital?

9 (Practice problem: allocation of investment) Preferential tax treatment can reallocate investment capital across regions. The enterprise zone idea offers tax

breaks to firms that locate in specified areas such as impoverished inner cities. To see how this policy might work, consider Table 37.7, which gives demands for capital in enterprise zones and elsewhere. Assume that the tax breaks are worth 6 percent and the total quantity supplied equals $10 billion.

Table 37.7

Interest rate	Demand in the enterprise zones (billions)	Demand elsewhere (billions)
9%	$0.6	$ 8.2
8%	$0.8	$ 8.6
7%	$1.0	$ 9.0
6%	$1.2	$ 9.8
5%	$1.4	$10.8
4%	$1.6	$12.0
3%	$1.8	$15.0
2%	$2.0	$20.0

a   Find the market allocation without the tax breaks and the corresponding interest rate.
b   Find the demand curves with the tax breaks.
c   Find the new allocation brought about by the tax breaks. How does the tax policy alter the equilibrium allocation of capital?

Answers to Problems

2   With a small young cohort, a large middle-aged cohort, and a small old cohort, the supply of savings is as follows.

Interest rate	Savings
4%	$46,000
6%	$56,100
8%	$66,200
10%	$76,200

When the young cohort is large, the middle-aged cohort small, and the old cohort large, the supply of savings is as follows.

Interest rate	Savings
4%	$46,000
6%	$56,100
8%	$66,200
10%	$76,200

4   a
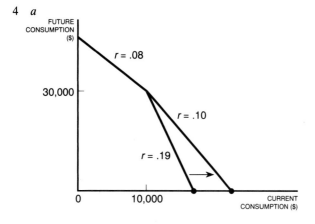

b   With the lower interest rate for borrowing, Bill's budget constraint rotates out, and gives him new opportunities, all of which involve borrowing more.

6   a
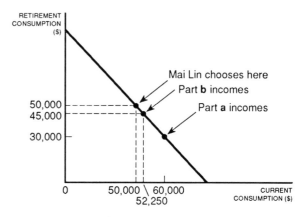

b   The budget constraint does not change, so neither do her current and retirement consumptions. The increase in pension rights reduces her savings by $7,500.

8   a   The equilibrium interest rate is 7 percent, and the allocation is $100 billion to each sector.
b   Table 37.8 gives the demands with the tax subsidy and trade protection policies.

Table 37.8

Interest rate	Imports (billions)	Exports (billions)	Total (billions)
17%	$ 30	$40	$ 70
16%	$ 50	$40	$ 90
15%	$ 60	$40	$100
14%	$ 70	$40	$110
13%	$ 80	$40	$120
12%	$100	$40	$140
11%	$120	$50	$170
10%	$140	$60	$200
9%	$140	$80	$220
8%	$140	$90	$230

c   The market clears at an interest rate of 10 percent with an allocation of $140 billion to the import-competing sector and $60 billion to the export sector. The policies shift $40 billion from the export to the import-competing sector.

9   a   The market allocation without the enterprise zone tax breaks is $1 billion in the zones and $9 billion elsewhere and the interest rate is 7 percent.
b   Table 37.9 gives the demands with the tax breaks.

Table 37.9

Interest rate	Demand in the enterprise zones (billions)	Demand elsewhere (billions)	Total (billions)
15%	$0.6	$ 8.2	$ 8.8
14%	$0.8	$ 8.2	$ 9.0
13%	$1.0	$ 8.2	$ 9.2
12%	$1.2	$ 8.2	$ 9.4
11%	$1.4	$ 8.2	$ 9.6
10%	$1.6	$ 8.2	$ 9.8
9%	$1.8	$ 8.2	$10.0
8%	$2.0	$ 8.6	$10.6
7%	$2.0	$ 9.0	$11.0
6%	$2.0	$ 9.8	$11.8
5%	$2.0	$10.8	$12.8

c The new equilibrium allocation is $1.8 billion to the enterprise zones and $8.2 billion elsewhere at an equilibrium interest rate of 9 percent. The tax breaks shift $0.8 billion to the zones from elsewhere in the economy.

Chapter 38

THE PROBLEM OF THE TWIN DEFICITS

Chapter Review

The Canadian budget and current-account deficits exploded during the 1980s. The insights of Parts Four and Five are used in this chapter to expose the connection between the two deficits and evaluate policies designed to correct them. Two key identities—the basic balance-of-payments identity and the savings-investment identity for an open economy—are introduced to organize the issues. This look at two specific problems sets the stage for a more general discussion of macroeconomic policy in Chapter 39.

ESSENTIAL CONCEPTS

1   Federal government spending rose in the 1980s, and taxes, already insufficient to cover spending levels at the beginning of the period, rose by less than spending. This led to huge **federal budget deficits,** financed by government borrowing. Each deficit increased the government's total **debt** burden (that is, the amount of borrowing outstanding), and interest on this debt itself contributed to further deficits. At the same time, the Canadian balance of payments began to slip from a surplus in 1984 to a **current-account deficit;** this

deficit reached $11 billion in 1986, and then almost tripled by 1991. This can be linked to a major outflow of net investment income, which rose from $13 billion in 1984 to $24 billion in 1990.

2   Government borrowing can affect future generations in three ways. First, the burden can be shifted directly to the future generation by increasing taxes after the current generation has retired. Second, borrowing drives up interest rates and crowds out private investment. Finally, since much of the borrowing comes from abroad and foreign investors are attracted by higher Canadian interest, current borrowing increases foreign indebtedness. Repayment of foreign debt then requires reduced future living standards.

3   The federal budget deficit contributed to the current-account deficit because government borrowing to finance the former drove up interest rates. This attracted foreign investment, which raised the value of the dollar, and made imports less expensive and exports more expensive than they would otherwise have been. In short, there was a shift in the demand for Canadian dollars, as a result of increased demand for funds to invest in Canada. This resulted in a current-account deficit; indeed, an investment inflow and a current-account deficit are just two sides of the same

coin. The overall balance of payments must, by definition, balance. So the only way that Canadian consumers and businesses can import more from abroad than they export abroad is if foreigners are willing to make up the difference by lending to, or investing in, Canada.

4 The connection between budget and current-account deficits can be seen by examining two identities: the **basic balance-of-payments identity** and the **savings-investment identity** for an open economy.

   a The basic balance-of-payments identity is

$$\text{current-account deficit} = \text{imports} - \text{exports}$$
$$= \text{capital-account surplus},$$

where the surplus on the capital account will be in the form of positive net capital inflows. This means that if foreign capital flows into Canada (in greater amounts than Canadian capital flows abroad), then Canada must run a current-account deficit.

   b The savings-investment identity for an open economy is

$$\text{private savings} + \text{net capital inflows}$$
$$= \text{investment} + \text{federal budget deficit}.$$

This identity says that unless investment falls and savings rise by enough to finance the budget deficit, the deficit results in positive net capital inflows, which the basic balance-of-payments identity says must equal the current-account deficit.

5 Trade restrictions are an ineffective and undesirable approach to the current-account deficit. They are ineffective because they set off changes in exchange rates that partially offset the restrictions, and they may lead to foreign retaliation. They are undesirable because they shield domestic firms from healthy competition and prevent Canada from taking advantage of specialization and the gains from comparative advantage. Most economists favour attacking the current-account deficit by reducing the federal budget deficit.

BEHIND THE ESSENTIAL CONCEPTS

1 The basic balance-of-payments identity is not an equilibrium relationship. An identity always holds; it is true by definition. An equilibrium relationship only holds in equilibrium. To see the difference, consider Figure 38.1. Suppose that the exchange rate is e_1, which is below the equilibrium. The price of the dollar is too low. Foreign households and firms would like to buy more dollars, so that they can buy more Canadian exports or invest in the Canadian economy. Although the currency market is not in equilibrium, the balance-of-payments identity is still true. Imports minus exports exactly equal foreign inflows of capital. The foreigners who would like to buy more Canadian goods, or invest more in the Canadian economy cannot obtain the necessary dollars that would enable them to do so. The quantity of dollars that foreigners actually buy is

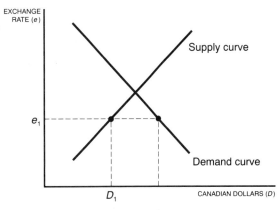

Figure 38.1

D_1, which is limited by the quantity that Canadian firms and households sell.

2 If you are the age of the typical university student, say 19 or 20, you will pay for some of the current federal budget deficit. Government borrowing is sopping up private savings and crowding out private investment. Currently capital goods are not purchased, research and development is not undertaken, and businesses are not started. Furthermore, the current-account deficit caused by the budget deficits is financed by selling off Canadian assets. Reduced investment and the sale of assets will result in lower living standards in the future.

3 The distinction between stocks and flows is important in this chapter. The annual federal budget deficit is a flow, and the corresponding stock is the federal debt, which is the sum of past accumulated deficits. The current-account deficit is also a flow variable. It is the difference between what Canadian households and firms import and export. The basic balance-of-payments identity makes it clear that the current-account deficit is financed by capital flows. Now capital flows into Canada when foreign nationals buy Canadian assets and when Canadian firms borrow from abroad. Both of these activities affect the credit position of Canada. The relationship between these current-account deficits and Canadian status as a debtor nation is that the accumulated current-account deficits have led to a stock of foreign indebtedness.

SELF-TEST

True or False

1 The Canadian budget deficit is high, but there have been other episodes of equally high peacetime deficits.

2 A budget deficit does not matter because we owe the money to ourselves.

3 Total federal government debt, expressed as a proportion of GDP, more than tripled between the mid-1970s and the early 1990s.

4 A major problem with reducing the debt is that so much of total government expenditure is nondiscretionary.

5 Government borrowing drives up the interest rate and crowds out private investment.

6 The current-account deficit always equals inflows of capital from abroad.

7 If a country runs a current-account surplus, then it must invest more abroad than it receives in foreign investment.

8 Investment can be financed by private savings, government savings, or capital flows from abroad.

9 Canada has always had a current-account deficit, though it is much larger now than it used to be.

10 Trade restrictions are a way to reduce imports without affecting the exchange rate.

11 The Canadian current-account deficit with Japan must be balanced by inflows of capital from Japan.

12 Most economists agree that the best way to reduce the current-account deficit is to reduce the budget deficit.

13 Most economists agree that the best way to reduce the budget deficit is to reduce the current-account deficit.

14 Most economists agree that the best way to reduce the current-account deficit is to reduce the budget deficit.

15 The largest single component of government spending is transfers to the provinces.

Multiple Choice

1 During much of the 1980s, Canada ran

 a federal budget deficits and current-account surpluses.
 b federal budget surpluses and current-account deficits.
 c federal budget and current-account surpluses.
 d federal budget and current-account deficits.
 e balanced federal budgets and current accounts.

2 The large federal budget deficits of the 1980s were a consequence of

 a increases in spending together with increases in taxation of a lesser magnitude.
 b increases in spending and decreases in taxation.
 c decreases in spending and decreases in taxation of a greater magnitude.
 d increases in spending without any changes in taxation.
 e decreases in taxation without any changes in spending.

3 The increase in the current-account deficit during the second half of the 1980s arose as a consequence of

 a decreases in the surplus on the merchandise trade account and increases in the deficit on the services trade account, but no change in the deficit on the investment-income account.
 b increases in the deficit on the merchandise trade account, decreases in the surplus on the services trade account, but no change in the deficit on the investment-income account.
 c decreases in the surplus on the merchandise trade account, increases in the deficit on the services trade account, and increases in the deficit on the investment-income account.
 d increases in the deficit on the merchandising trade account, decreases in the surplus on the services trade account, and increases in the deficit on the investment-income account.
 e none of the above.

4 Federal budget deficits

 a increase private investment by reducing the interest rate.
 b crowd out private investment by increasing the interest rate.
 c reduce future output if the borrowing finances government investments such as roads or research and development.
 d always reduce future consumption because future generations must pay taxes to repay the debt.
 e none of the above.

5 Government borrowing to finance the deficit

 a crowds out both foreign and Canadian private investment.
 b crowds out Canadian private investment by raising the interest rate but causes increased foreign investment.
 c crowds out foreign investment by increasing the exchange rate but has no effect on Canadian private investment.
 d attracts foreign investment, and the extra competition leads to increased Canadian private investment.
 e causes the exchange rate to depreciate.

6 Which of the following is not true?

 a The burden of current government deficits necessarily falls on the current generation.
 b The burden of current government deficits may be shifted to future generations if taxes are increased after the current generation retires.
 c The burden of current government deficits may be shifted to future generations if current borrowing replaces private investment.
 d The burden of current government deficits may be shifted to future generations if current borrowing increases foreign indebtedness.
 e None of the above.

7 The basic balance-of-payments identity says that

 a imports must equal exports.
 b imports must equal capital flows from abroad.
 c exports must equal capital flows from abroad.

d the current-account deficit must equal capital flows from abroad.

e capital flows from abroad must equal capital flows to overseas economies.

8 If a country invests more overseas than foreign countries invest in it, then

a its current account must be in balance.

b it must run a current-account surplus.

c it must run a current-account deficit.

d it must balance its government budget.

e its government deficit must equal the net flow of capital to other countries.

9 In an open economy, the savings-investment identity says that

a private savings must equal private investment.

b private savings plus capital flows from abroad must equal investment.

c private savings plus capital flows from abroad must equal investment plus the government deficit.

d private savings plus capital flows from abroad must equal the government deficits plus the current-account deficit.

e private savings plus capital flows from abroad must equal the government deficit plus the current-account deficit plus investment.

10 According to the savings-investment identity for an open economy, investment may not be financed from

a private savings.

b government savings.

c capital flows from abroad.

d government budget deficit.

e none of the above.

11 Typically, developing economies

a borrow less than mature economies.

b borrow while mature economies lend.

c lend while mature economies borrow.

d neither borrow nor lend.

e borrow or lend at the same rates as mature economies.

12 In the mid-1980s, Canada

a changed status from a creditor to a debtor nation.

b changed status from a debtor to a creditor nation.

c remained a creditor nation, while running current-account deficits.

d remained a debtor nation, and increased foreign indebtedness.

e saw no change in its foreign indebtedness.

13 Subsidizing exports will lead to

a an increase in the exchange rate.

b a decrease in the exchange rate.

c no change in the exchange rate.

d either an increase or a decrease in the exchange rate, depending on the size of the government budget deficit.

e an increase in the current-account deficit.

14 Which of the following is not true?

a Trade restrictions lead to an increase in the exchange rate, and so make imports cheaper.

b Trade restrictions reduce the gains from international trade.

c Trade restrictions may lead to foreign retaliation.

d Trade restrictions insulate domestic producers from foreign competition.

e None of the above.

15 Most economists agree that the appropriate way to reduce the current-account deficit is to

a reduce investment.

b reduce the federal budget deficit.

c increase household savings.

d increase business savings.

e impose trade restrictions.

16 The most likely attack on the budget deficit will come from

a increases in taxes alone.

b reductions in transfer payments alone.

c increases in taxes and reductions in transfer payments.

d the abolition of the GST.

e none of the above.

17 Of those listed, which represents the smallest component of federal government spending?

a payments to the elderly

b transfers to the provinces

c interest on the public debt

d unemployment insurance

e defence

18 Of those listed, which represents the largest component of federal government spending?

a payments to the elderly

b transfers to the provinces

c interest on the public debt

d unemployment insurance

e defence

19 Economists generally advocate

a free trade.

b running a current-account deficit to increase current consumption.

c running a current-account surplus to decrease current consumption.

d not trading with foreign nations.

e borrowing from abroad to finance the budget deficit.

20 Dumping refers to

a selling government bonds in foreign markets.

b eliminating public pensions.

c abandoning strategic trade policy.

d selling goods abroad at lower prices than at home.

e running a current-account surplus to accumulate wealth in the form of gold and silver.

Completion

1 The difference between government expenditures and revenues is the _____.

2 The total accumulated sum of past budget deficits is the _____.

3 The basic balance-of-payments identity says that the current-account deficit must equal _____.

4 In an open economy, private savings plus capital flows from abroad must equal investment plus the _____.

5 _____ are agreements by foreign countries to reduce the sales of their goods in the domestic country.

6 Economists generally agree that the best way to attack the _____ deficit is to reduce the _____ deficit.

7 Interest on the _____ absorbs more than 25 percent of federal government expenditures.

8 Government debt is a _____ and the government's budget deficit is a _____.

9 Selling goods abroad for lower prices than at home is called _____.

10 Subsidizing exports will ultimately result in an _____ of the exchange rate.

Answers to Self-Test

True or False

1	f	6	t	11	f
2	f	7	t	12	t
3	t	8	t	13	f
4	t	9	f	14	t
5	t	10	f	15	f

Multiple Choice

1	d	6	a	11	b	16	c
2	a	7	d	12	a	17	e
3	c	8	b	13	a	18	c
4	b	9	c	14	e	19	a
5	b	10	d	15	b	20	d

Completion

1 budget deficit
2 government debt
3 capital flows from abroad
4 budget deficit
5 Voluntary export restraints
6 current-account, budget
7 public debt
8 stock, flow
9 dumping
10 appreciation

Doing Economics: Tools and Practice Problems

The identities introduced in this chapter are among the most important ideas in macroeconomics. The basic balance-of-payments identity says that the current-account deficit must be balanced by capital inflows from abroad:

current-account deficit = imports − exports = capital inflows.

The savings-investment identify for an open economy requires that the capital flows from abroad combined with private savings equal private investment plus the federal budget deficit:

private savings + capital inflows =
       private investment + federal budget deficit.

Tool Kit 38.1: Understanding the Relationship between Budget and Trade Deficits

Step one: Start with an equilibrium in the product and foreign exchange markets.

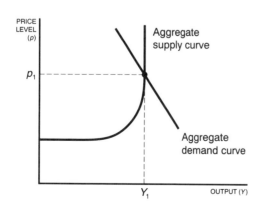

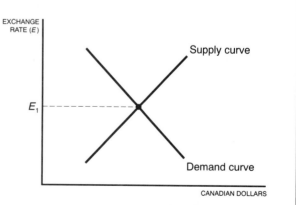

Step two: Identify a change, and determine which curves shift. Because of the identities, curves will shift in both markets.

Step three: Shift the curves.

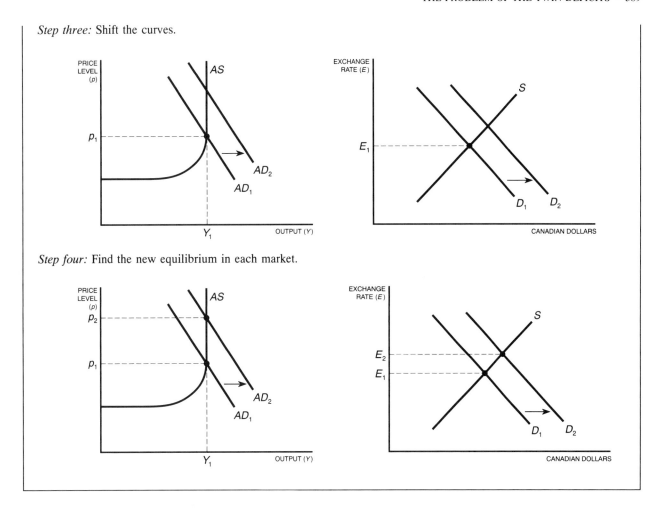

Step four: Find the new equilibrium in each market.

Together they establish that the current-account deficit and the federal budget deficit are inextricable.

Any change in the federal budget deficit not only shifts aggregate demand in the product market, but also affects the market for foreign exchange. Similarly, to understand how changes in imports or exports affect the economy, we must look at both the product and foreign exchange markets. For example, an increase in exports reduces the current-account deficit. This must also reduce capital inflows (by the basic balance-of-payments identity) and private investment (by the saving-investment identity). In this section, we explore this relationship.

1 (Worked problem: budget and current-account deficits) Suppose that, as a consequence of the cancellation of an order for new helicopters, the government sharply reduces defence spending with no change in tax rates. Show how the reduced federal budget deficit affects the product and foreign exchange markets.

Step-by-step solution

Step one: Start with an equilibrium in the product and foreign exchange markets.

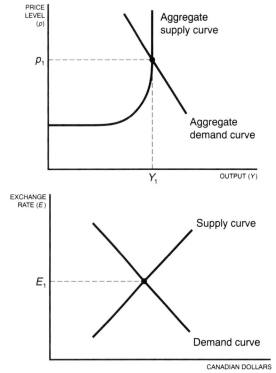

Step two: Identify a change, and determine which curves shift. The decreased budget shifts aggregate demand to the left in the product market. The savings-investment identity for an open economy says that there is less need for capital inflows from abroad, and the demand for dollars will fall.

Step three: Shift the curves.

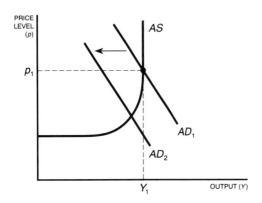

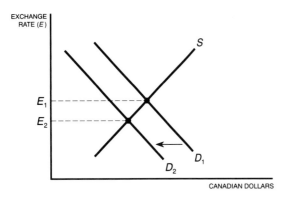

Step four: Find the new equilibrium in each market. The decline in aggregate demand brings about a fall in output, while in the foreign exchange market the Canadian dollar depreciates.

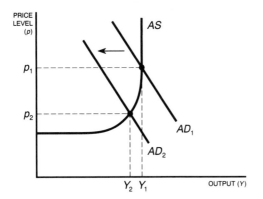

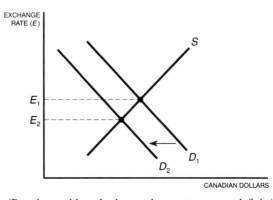

2   (Practice problem: budget and current-account deficits) Suppose lack of confidence in the new government causes private investment to fall. Show how this change affects the product and foreign exchange markets.

3   (Practice problem: budget and current-account deficits) Show how each of the following changes affects the product and foreign exchange markets.

   a   The demand for Canadian exports increases.
   b   Purchases of foreign goods by Canadian house-holds increase.
   c   Private savings increase.
   d   To reduce the federal budget deficit, the govern-ment passes a major tax increase.
   e   Instability abroad causes foreign capital to flow into Canada.

Answers to Problems

2   Aggregate demand shifts to the left, and reduces out-put and the price level; in the foreign exchange mar-ket, the demand for dollars decreases and the exchange rate depreciates.

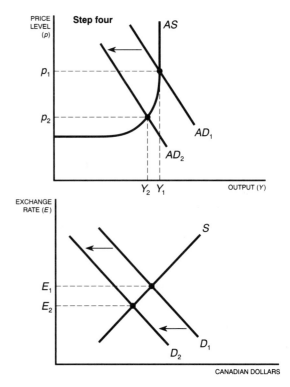

3 *a* Aggregate demand shifts to the right, and increases the price level; in the foreign exchange market, the demand for dollars increases and the exchange rate appreciates.

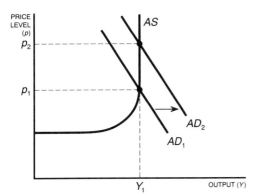

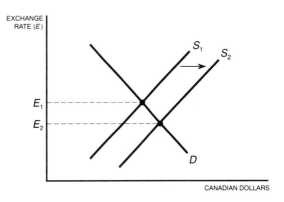

c As savings increase and consumption falls, aggregate demand shifts to the left, and reduces output and the price level; in the foreign exchange market, the demand for dollars decreases (increased savings replace foreign capital) and the exchange rate depreciates.

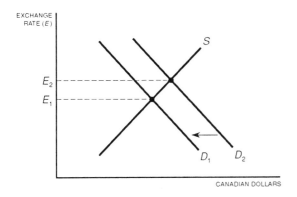

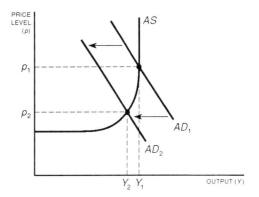

b Aggregate demand shifts to the left, and reduces output and the price level; in the foreign exchange market, the supply of dollars increases and the exchange rate depreciates.

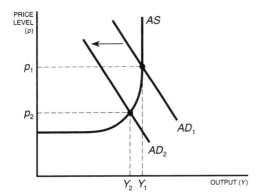

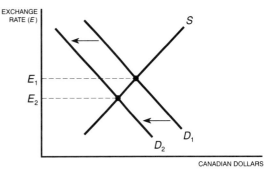

d Aggregate demand shifts to the left, and reduces output and the price level; in the foreign exchange market, the demand for dollars decreases and the exchange rate depreciates.

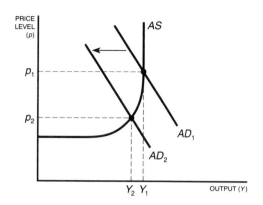

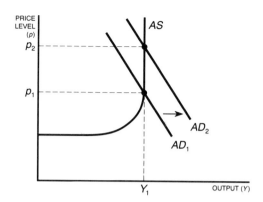

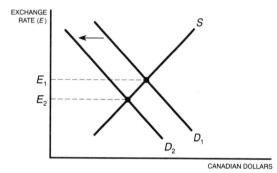

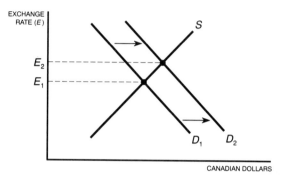

e The demand for dollars increases, and causes the dollar to appreciate. The savings-investment identity for an open economy says that either savings decrease or investment increases, either of which shifts aggregate demand up.

Chapter 39

DIFFERING APPROACHES TO MACROECONOMIC POLICY

Chapter Review

This chapter brings together the material studied in Chapters 25 to 38 to round out the discussion of the major issues of macroeconomics: the nature and causes of economic fluctuations and the role of economic policy. The key issue in economic policy is whether and to what extent the government should intervene to stabilize the economy's fluctuations. The chapter examines how differing views concerning the nature of the business cycle lead to disagreements about policy. The next two chapters consider the application of economics to alternative economic systems, notably socialism and communism, and to the situation of less-developed countries, which are home to three-quarters of the world's population.

ESSENTIAL CONCEPTS

1   Although the economy grows over time, it *fluctuates* around its long-term trend; sometimes it grows faster, other times more slowly, and, occasionally it even contracts. The most important theories of why the economy behaves the way it does are the traditional busi-ness-cycle, the real business-cycle, the monetarist/new classical, and the new Keynesian views.

2   According to **traditional business-cycle theory,** the economy is inherently unstable. The reasons for the instability are endogenous; that is, they lie within the economy itself. This view asserts that firms try to maintain a constant inventory-to-sales ratio (called the **accelerator**). The accelerator in turn causes output to fluctuate much more than sales. These variations are further amplified by the multiplier process discussed in Chapter 28. The economy expands rapidly until it bumps against capacity constraints at full employment, and then it slumps into recessions.

3   **Real business-cycle theory** attributes variations in economic activity to random, unpredictable shocks originating outside the economy (exogenous). This view stresses the importance of **supply-side shocks,** such as innovations and natural disasters, but insists that markets clear throughout the ups and downs. The economy thus responds rapidly to these exogenous shocks, and economic fluctuations are not an important matter for government policy.

4   **Monetarists** and **new classical economists** blame the government, especially its misguided monetary policy,

for economic fluctuations. Unanticipated **monetary shocks** confuse firms into thinking that changes in demand represent changes in consumer tastes. Thus, in the short run, firms respond incorrectly by changing output. Because their expectations are formed rationally, firms soon learn of the monetary supply change and adjust prices, and so restore the economy to its full-employment level.

5 Finally, the **new Keynesian view** says that a variety of exogenous shocks, from both the supply side and the demand side, may move the economy from its long-term trend, but various mechanisms in the economic system *amplify* these shocks and cause the variations in output to *persist*. Government can play an important role in offsetting these ups and downs. Recessions can endure for considerable periods of time with long-lasting consequences as investments are not made and unemployed workers lose their skills through inactivity.

6 The key question for economic *policy* is whether the government should intervene to smooth economic fluctuations. Several views of government intervention are described below.

   a First among the **noninterventionist** views is real business theory, which sees no role for government in stabilizing what is an already efficient economy. Monetarists and new classical economists side with them in recommending against government intervention. Although the economists believe that eventually private actions will offset the effects of government fiscal and monetary policies (the policy ineffectiveness proposition), they especially fear the detrimental, shorter-run effects of monetary policy and the long-run damage caused by inflation. They advocate **fixed policy rules,** such as balanced budgets and constant money-supply growth rates.

   b **Interventionists,** who include traditional business-cycle and new Keynesian economists, support the use of **discretionary fiscal and monetary policy.** In recessions, government should increase the budget deficit to stimulate the economy. These economists also advocate the use of monetary policy to counteract economic variations but doubt its effectiveness during recessions. In addition to the judicious use of discretionary policies, these views support the design and institution of **automatic stabilizers,** such as unemployment insurance and income taxes.

7 The instruments of government policy include fiscal policy measures such as tax rates and levels of expenditures, and monetary instruments such as open market operations and moral suasion. In different circumstances, some form of each policy may be appropriate. Policy instruments should be evaluated on the basis of their effectiveness; the induced change in the mix of output; the breadth of impact, flexibility, and speed of implementation; the certainty of consequences; and the potential side effects. For example,

monetary policy is flexible and can be swiftly implemented, but its effects are concentrated on certain narrow sectors of the economy. Income tax cuts may increase consumption, but the side effects of the resulting deficit crowd out private investment and reduce future growth.

BEHIND THE ESSENTIAL CONCEPTS

1 This is one of the text's most important chapters. To avoid getting bogged down in the four different views of the nature of economic fluctuations, the two camps with opposing policy prescriptions, and all the arguments and evidence, keep in mind the central questions presented in the chapter. Here are the important ones.

   a Are variations in the level of economic activity caused by exogenous shocks, or are they an inevitable result of endogenous mechanisms within the economic system?
   b If shocks are important, is their origin on the supply side, on the demand side, or with government policy?
   c Do people's rational expectations cause the economy to adjust quickly, or are there forces that amplify the disturbances and lead to persistence in economic fluctuations?
   d Is government policy quickly understood and offset by private actions, or is it effective in counteracting the economy's ups and downs?
   e Should the government use its instruments with discretion to smooth the economy, or should it bind itself with fixed policy rules?

2 As you read through the arguments and evidence, try to relate them to the appropriate questions. Also, find arguments and evidence to relate to each question listed above. Here are some examples of how to do this.

   a The view that exogenous shocks cause variations in the level of economic activity is bolstered by the fact that economists are reasonably sure about the causes of some recessions. For example, the 1973 oil price shock is a prime candidate for the cause of the slowdown that followed it.
   b Shocks to the economy seem to come from both sides of the economy and from government. Recessions have often followed reductions in military spending after wars, a fiscal shock. Tight monetary policy certainly played an important role in triggering the recession that began in 1981.
   c Not every shock to the economy causes a recession. For example, the stock market crash of 1987 had little impact on the level of real economic activity. While this fact supports the argument for quick adjustment, the Great Depression and Europe's recent experience with persistently high unemployment indicate that economic downturns can last for considerable time periods.

d The policy ineffectiveness proposition implies that private savings should have increased during the 1980s to offset the unprecedented large peacetime budget deficits. The fact that savings fell undermines the view that policy is offset by private actions.

e Advocates of fixed policy rules must believe that the government can deliver the promised policy. The **dynamic consistency problem** teaches that government may find that it is not in its own interest to follow its announced rules.

SELF-TEST

True or False

1 The traditional view of business cycles is that their causes are exogenous shocks.

2 According to real business-cycle theory, monetary policy is effective but dangerous; therefore, its adherents advocate fixed rules.

3 New Keynesian economists point out that the economy may amplify shocks and cause their effects to persist.

4 New Keynesian economists are optimistic about the possibility that governments will improve their ability to implement discretionary fiscal and monetary policies.

5 The failure of savings rates to increase as federal budget deficits increased during the 1980s is not consistent with real business-cycle theory.

6 The policy ineffectiveness proposition states that governments will have difficulty carrying out their promises.

7 Real business-cycle theory argues that politicians cause economic fluctuations in order to manipulate voters.

8 Monetary policy can have real effects if producers confuse an increase in the money supply with a change in consumer tastes.

9 An example of the type of policy rule advocated by noninterventionists is that government should cut taxes during recessions and increase taxes during economic booms.

10 Unemployment insurance is an automatic stabilizer.

11 An increase in the money supply may not stimulate the economy if producers simply raise prices.

12 Fiscal policy is inherently more flexible than monetary policy.

13 Increased government expenditures crowd out private investment regardless of the actions of the Bank of Canada.

14 Fiscal instruments like tax reductions have broader impact than monetary policies.

15 The recession of the early 1980s was probably due to tight monetary policy.

Multiple Choice

1 The traditional business-cycle view holds that economic fluctuations are

a due to endogenous forces and are predictable.
b due to random, exogenous shocks and are unpredictable.
c chiefly due to misguided monetary and fiscal policy.
d due to exogenous shocks but are amplified and made persistent by the economic system.
e none of the above.

2 The real business-cycle theory holds that economic fluctuations are

a due to endogenous forces and are predictable.
b due to random, exogenous shocks and are unpredictable.
c chiefly due to misguided monetary and fiscal policy.
d due to exogenous shocks but are amplified and made persistent by the economic system.
e none of the above.

3 Monetarists and new classical economists believe that economic fluctuations are

a due to endogenous forces and are predictable.
b due to random, exogenous shocks and are unpredictable.
c chiefly due to misguided monetary and fiscal policy.
d due to exogenous shocks but are amplified and made persistent by the economic system.
e none of the above.

4 The new Keynesian view is that economic fluctuations are

a due to endogenous forces and are predictable.
b due to random, exogenous shocks and are unpredictable.
c chiefly due to misguided monetary and fiscal policy.
d due to exogenous shocks but are amplified and made persistent by the economic system.
e none of the above.

5 The accelerator model of the economy assumes that firms want to keep the

a ratio of output to labour constant.
b ratio of investment to sales constant.
c level of unemployment constant.
d rate of growth in the money supply constant.
e level of full-employment GDP constant.

6 Which of the following would new Keynesians not regard as a cost of an economic downturn?

a the lost output from idle resources.

b the experience and skills lost by unemployed workers.

c innovations and inventions not discovered because firms cut research and development during recessions.

d the lost output from capital equipment not purchased during recessions.

e none of the above.

7 Noninterventionist economists view government as a source of instability and advocate

a binding fiscal and monetary policies with fixed policy rules.

b using fiscal and monetary policies with discretion.

c returning control of the money supply to the private sector.

d dynamic inconsistency.

e repealing the accelerator.

8 According to the policy ineffectiveness proposition, government monetary policy

a is the source of most economic slowdowns.

b should be used with discretion to counteract economic ups and downs.

c is offset by private actions.

d is effective in slowing the economy but ineffective in stimulating the economy.

e is driven by political motives.

9 Monetary policy can have real effects if

a producers are unable to distinguish between an increase in demand due to monetary growth and one due to changes in consumer tastes.

b it changes the price level but not output.

c the accelerator is greater than 1.

d markets anticipate it and change price appropriately.

e it follows policy rules rather than exercising discretion.

10 Which of the following is not an example of a policy rule advocated by noninterventionists?

a The money supply should increase at a fixed rate each year.

b The money supply should be adjusted to stimulate aggregate demand in recessions and constrain aggregate demand in inflationary times.

c The budget deficit should be zero.

d Government expenditures should be a fixed percentage of GDP.

e The money supply should increase with the rate of output.

11 Which of the following is not consistent with political business-cycle theory?

a People vote against incumbents during recessions.

b Politicians plan economic policies to ensure that the economy is booming at election time.

c Voters focus only on economic conditions during the election year.

d Economic policy causes business cycles.

e Economic fluctuations are caused by exogenous, mostly supply-side, shocks.

12 The policy ineffectiveness proposition would imply that

a monetary policy caused the 1981 recession.

b savings rates would have increased to offset federal budget deficits during the 1980s.

c the Great Depression was caused by a large contraction in the money supply.

d tax cuts stimulate the economy.

e none of the above.

13 The 1973 slowdown was probably caused by

a tax increases.

b bank failures.

c restrictive monetary policy.

d oil price shocks.

e tax cuts.

14 Dynamic consistency refers to

a the fact that most business cycles follow the same pattern.

b The recommendation that government policy follow certain fixed rules.

c the issue of whether the government will carry out its promises.

d the political business-cycle explanation for economic fluctuations.

e the need to harmonize fiscal and monetary policy.

15 Automatic stabilizers are

a programs, such as unemployment insurance or progressive taxation, that increase spending during recessions and reduce it during economic booms.

b policy rules that restrain the use of discretionary fiscal and monetary policy.

c the adjustments that individuals with rational expectations make to offset fiscal and monetary policies.

d market responses, such as increased interest rates, that limit the ability of government to stimulate the economy.

e none of the above.

16 The revisions of deficit targets that take place are examples of the problem of

a policy ineffectiveness.

b discretionary fiscal policy.

c dynamic consistency.

d the multiplier-accelerator process.

e the political business cycle.

17 Which of the following illustrates problems with the effectiveness of a policy instrument?

a Even though the Bank of Canada undertakes policies that increase bank reserves, it may not be able to motivate banks to make new loans.

b Looser monetary policy, even though it was designed to increase investment, might instead cause the dollar to depreciate and increase net exports.

c Monetary policy often concentrates its effects on particular sectors, such as export-competing industries or consumer durables.

d There are lags in the government's ability to recognize and implement fiscal programs.

e Individuals may treat tax cuts as temporary and increase consumption.

18 Which of the following illustrates a concern with the effect of a policy instrument on the composition of output?

a Even though the Bank of Canada undertakes policies that increase bank reserves, it may not be able to motivate banks to make new loans.

b Looser monetary policy, even though it was designed to increase investment, might instead cause the dollar to depreciate and increase net exports.

c Monetary policy often concentrates its effects on particular sectors, such as export-competing industries or consumer durables.

d There are lags in the government's ability to recognize and implement fiscal programs.

e Individuals may treat tax cuts as temporary and increase consumption.

19 Which of the following relates to the issue of the flexibility of a policy instrument?

a Even though the Bank of Canada undertakes policies that increase bank reserves, it may not be able to motivate banks to make new loans.

b Looser monetary policy, even though it was designed to increase investment, might instead cause the dollar to depreciate and increase net exports.

c Monetary policy often concentrates its effects on particular sectors, such as export-competing industries or consumer durables.

d There are lags in the government's ability to recognize and implement fiscal programs.

e Individuals may treat tax cuts as temporary and increase consumption.

20 Which of the following shows the importance of concern for the breadth of impact of a policy instrument?

a Even though the Bank of Canada undertakes policies that increase bank reserves, it may not be able to motivate banks to make new loans.

b Looser monetary policy, even though it was designed to increase investment, might instead cause the dollar to depreciate and increase net exports.

c Monetary policy often concentrates its effects on particular sectors, such as export-competing industries or consumer durables.

d There are lags in the government's ability to recognize and implement fiscal programs.

e Individuals may treat tax cuts as temporary and increase consumption.

Completion

1 According to the traditional business-cycle view, fluctuations in the economy are _____.

2 The _____ view of the economy places the blame for economic fluctuations on supply shocks, but believes that the economy adjusts quickly and efficiently.

3 New Keynesians stress that although externally generated shocks may hit the economy, the system can _____ them and cause the effects to _____.

4 New classical economists and monetarists see _____ as an important reason for economic instability.

5 New classical economists and monetarists also argue that government fiscal and monetary policies should follow _____.

6 Economic policies are said to be _____ if they change with economic circumstances.

7 The issue of whether government will actually carry out its promised economic policy is called _____.

8 _____ include tax and expenditure programs that work to smooth economic fluctuations.

9 One of the major advantages of monetary policy as opposed to fiscal policy is its _____.

10 Concerning the issue of using discretionary monetary and fiscal policies to smooth recessions, economists divide into _____ and _____.

Answers to Self-Test

True or False

1	f	6	f	11	t
2	f	7	f	12	f
3	t	8	t	13	f
4	t	9	f	14	t
5	t	10	t	15	t

Multiple Choice

1	a	6	e	11	e	16	c
2	b	7	a	12	b	17	a
3	c	8	c	13	d	18	b
4	d	9	a	14	c	19	d
5	b	10	b	15	a	20	c

Completion

1 endogenous
2 real business-cycle
3 amplify, persist
4 monetary shocks
5 fixed policy rules
6 discretionary
7 dynamic consistency
8 Automatic stabilizers
9 flexibility
10 interventionists, noninterventionists

Doing Economics: Tools and Practice Problems

Most economists share the common framework developed throughout this book. Nevertheless, there are differences, the most important of which concern how quickly (if at all) the economy returns from recessions and what the role of government is in restoring full employment. In this section, we study three approaches: the real business cycle, new classical, and new Keynesian. (In this area, monetarists would subscribe to the analysis of new classical economists.) Several exercises explore these economists' views on how the economy is affected by four likely causes of recession: tight monetary policy, a decline in government spending, an increase in import prices, and a fall in private investment spending following a stock market crash.

Tool Kit 39.1: Analyzing the Real Business Cycle

Step one: Start with an equilibrium in the product market. Note the vertical aggregate supply curve.

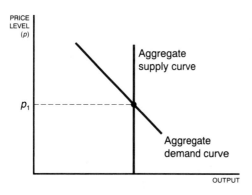

Step two: Identify a shock, and determine which curve shifts. (Note that while supply shocks always shift the aggregate supply curve, demand shocks may be offset by private savings and borrowings, and leave the aggregate demand curve unchanged.)

Step three: Shift the appropriate curve.

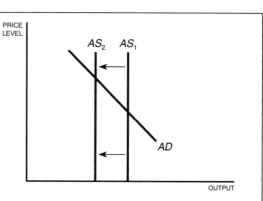

Step four: Find the new equilibrium. The quick adjustment of prices will ensure that full employment is restored, with no role for government intervention.

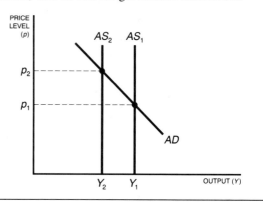

Tool Kit 39.2: Analyzing the New Classical Business Cycle

Step one: Start with an equilibrium in the product market. Note that the short-run aggregate supply curve is drawn, and the equilibrium is at the full-employment level of output.

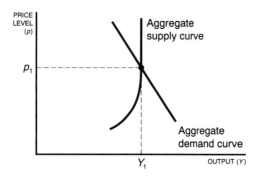

Step two: Identify a shock, and determine which curve shifts. Anticipated demand shocks may be offset by private savings and borrowing. Unanticipated demand shocks shift aggregate demand.

Step three: Shift the appropriate curve.

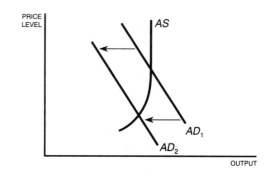

Step four: Find the new short-run equilibrium.

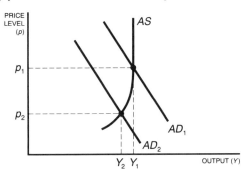

Step five: Shift the short-run aggregate supply curve until it intersects aggregate demand at the full-employment level of output. This shift, which occurrs rela-

tively quickly, reflects the rational expectations adjustment to the new economic conditions and makes any government intervention unnecessary.

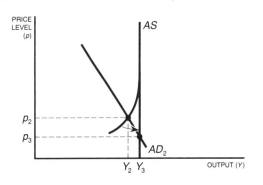

Tool Kit 39.3: Analyzing the New Keynesian Business Cycle

Step one: Start with an equilibrium in the product market.

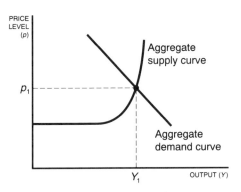

Step two: Identify a shock, and determine which curve shifts.

Step three: Shift the appropriate curve. Economic forces may amplify the impact of any shift in aggregate demand or supply.

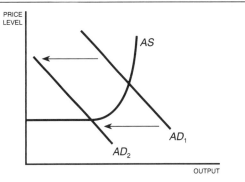

Step four: Find the new equilibrium. The effects are persistent, and the economy may settle at an under-employment equilibrium for a substantial length of time. Government fiscal or monetary policy intervention is recommended to restore full employment.

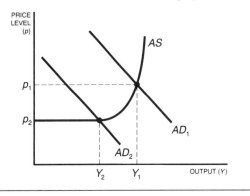

1 (Worked problem: comparing perspectives) Suppose that the Bank of Canada institutes a new tight-money regime.

 a   Analyze the impact on the economy from the real business-cycle perspective.
 b   Analyze the impact on the economy from the new classical perspective.
 c   Analyze the impact on the economy from the new Keynesian perspective.

Step-by-step solution

Step one (a): Start with an equilibrium in the product market.

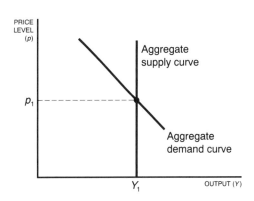

Step two: Identify a shock, and determine which curve shifts. The tight-money policy raises interest rates, reduces credit availability, and shifts aggregate demand to the left.

Step three: Shift the appropriate curve.

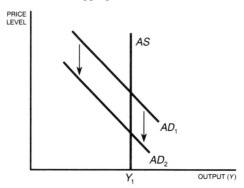

Step four: Find the new equilibrium. Full employment is maintained at a lower price level. There is no recession.

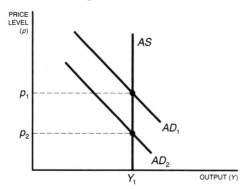

Step one (b): Start with an equilibrium in the product market.

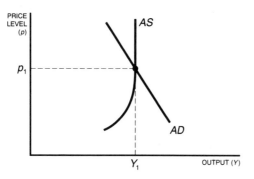

Step two: Identify a shock, and determine which curve shifts. The tight-money policy raises interest rates, reduces credit availability, and shifts aggregate demand to the left.

Step three: Shift the appropriate curve.

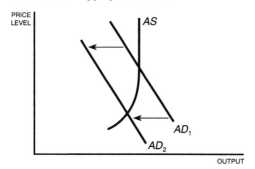

Step four: Find the new short-run equilibrium. The unanticipated monetary shock initiates a recession.

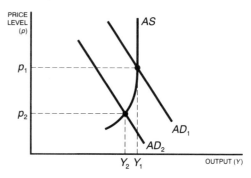

Step five: Shift the short-run aggregate supply curve until it intersects aggregate demand at the full-employment level of output. Full employment is restored relatively quickly at a lower price level.

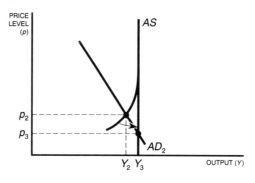

Step one (a): Start with an equilibrium in the product market.

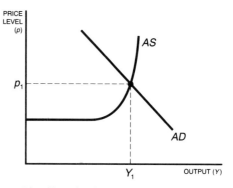

Step two: Identify a shock, and determine which curve shifts. The tight-money policy raises interest rates, reduces credit availability, and shifts aggregate demand to the left.

Step three: Shift the appropriate curve.

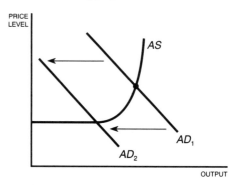

Step four: Find the new equilibrium. The economy settles in recession, and some fiscal or monetary stimulus is recommended to restore full employment.

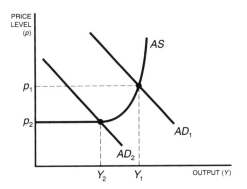

2   (Practice problem: comparing perspectives) Government spending is being curtailed sharply. Assume no change in tax rates.

   a Analyze the impact on the economy from the real business-cycle perspective.
   b Analyze the impact on the economy from the new classical perspective.
   c Analyze the impact on the economy from the new Keynesian perspective.

3   (Practice problem: comparing perspectives) Suppose that import prices of raw materials increase dramatically.

   a Analyze the impact on the economy from the real business-cycle perspective.
   b Analyze the impact on the economy from the new classical perspective.
   c Analyze the impact on the economy from the new Keynesian perspective.

4   (Practice problem: comparing perspectives) Suppose that following a stock market crash, business confidence plummets and investment spending decreases substantially.

   a Analyze the impact on the economy from the real business-cycle perspective.
   b Analyze the impact on the economy from the new classical perspective.
   c Analyze the impact on the economy from the new Keynesian perspective.

Answers to Problems

2 *a*   If the decline in government spending was unanticipated, aggregate demand shifts to the left, and the price level falls to clear the goods market. An anticipated fall in spending would be offset by increased consumption, and so leave aggregate demand unchanged.

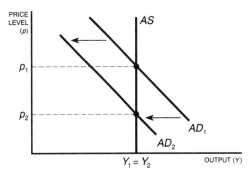

   b Aggregate demand shifts to the left, and the economy enters a recession until individuals and firms adjust. The price level falls, and full employment returns relatively soon.

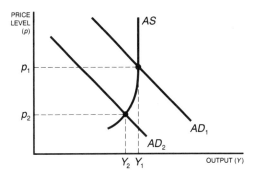

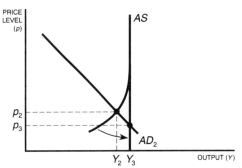

   c Aggregate demand shifts to the left, and the economy enters a recession. There is no natural mechanism to restore full employment in the near term. A fiscal or monetary stimulus is recommended to shift aggregate demand and achieve full employment.

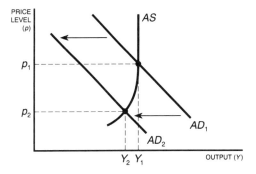

3   *a*   Aggregate supply shifts to the left, the price level increases, and the goods market clears at a lower level of output. The economy is still at full employment, but the full-employment level of output is now lower.

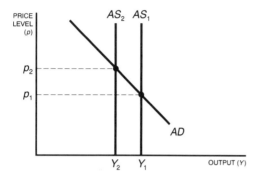

b   Aggregate supply shifts to the left, and initiates a recession. Soon individuals and firms adjust, and aggregate supply shifts to the right to restore full employment.

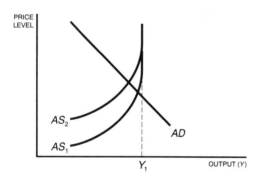

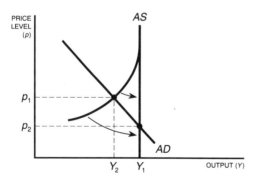

c   Aggregate supply shifts to the left, and the economy enters a recession. The economy will remain in recession for a considerable time. A fiscal or monetary stimulus is recommended to shift aggregate demand and achieve full employment.

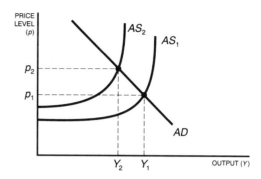

4   *a*   Aggregate demand shifts to the left, but prices adjust quickly to maintain full employment.

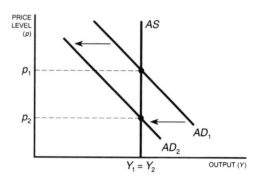

b   Aggregate demand shifts to the left, and initiates a recession. Aggregate supply soon shifts to the right as individuals and firms adjust their expectations to the new economic conditions.

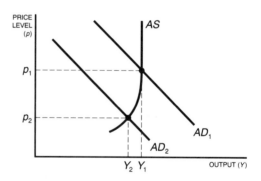

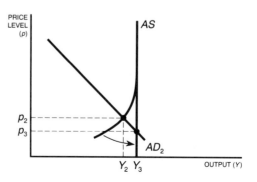

c Aggregate demand shifts to the left, and the economy enters a recession. A fiscal or monetary stimulus is recommended to shift aggregate demand and achieve full employment.

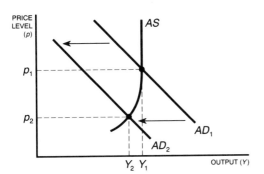

Chapter 40

ALTERNATIVE ECONOMIC SYSTEMS

Chapter Review

This chapter compares the nature and performance of the system we have studied throughout this book, the mixed economy, with some alternatives, namely the economic systems that evolved in the former Soviet Union and Eastern Europe in this century. The chapter includes some discussion of the worker-managed firms found in what used to be Yugoslavia as well as the incorporation of markets into the socialist economies of Hungary and communist China. The next, and final, chapter deals with the topic of developing economies.

ESSENTIAL CONCEPTS

1 In **socialist** economies, the government owns the means of production; in **communist** countries, it owns all property. Both systems have a high degree of government control of economic decisions, or **central planning,** which stands in contrast to the market system in **market economies** (also called capitalist because of the prominent role played by private capital). The economies of Western Europe, Japan, the United States, and Canada rely on private property and markets for most economic decisions.

2 Appalled by the extreme economic inequality that accompanied the industrial revolution, Karl Marx predicted the downfall of capitalism and its replacement by a communist state. The 1917 revolution in Russia that toppled the Czar (who was subsequently executed) and eventually brought the Bolsheviks to power under Vladimir Lenin used Marx's writings as its justification, and the country was until recently governed under a socialist system that some, at least, would term Marxist (or more commonly Marxist-Leninist, because of the influence of Lenin).

3 **Soviet-style socialism** coordinated economic activity through a series of centrally administered plans that answered the basic economic questions of what is to be produced, how it is to be produced, and for whom. A system of political controls and rewards backed up by force replaced market incentives. In the labour market, this system assigned workers to jobs and limited labour mobility. The capital market was replaced by central directions that pursued a low-consumption, high-investment strategy emphasizing heavy industry. Goods were produced according to the plan and sold at prices controlled below market-clearing levels; this led to shortages and long lines at stores. Despite the ideology of "to each according to his needs," much inequality remained.

4 Soviet-style socialism failed for at least two reasons. It provided no *incentives* to managers; they could not keep any profits, nor were they responsible for losses. Furthermore, the planning mechanism was unable to gather the needed *information* to allocate resources efficiently or to monitor workers and firms in order to ensure that the plan was carried through effectively. Prices, which were set arbitrarily, did not convey information about relative scarcity and value, as do market prices.

5 Under **market socialism** as in Hungary, the central planners set prices and ordered managers to maximize profits. This revision of the system performed only a little better than Soviet-style socialism; prices were set without good information, and managers, still without property rights, had no incentives to pursue profits. Some success was achieved with the "responsibility system" in China, where farmers were allowed to sell their produce and keep some of the proceeds. Yugoslavia instituted worker-managed firms as a partial step towards markets.

6 The transition from Soviet-style socialism to market economies is difficult and fraught with problems. The transition begins with a period of disruption and falling living standards as old, inefficient factories are closed and resources are reallocated. Unemployment and inflation rise as price controls are relaxed and the effects of **monetary overhang**, previously accumulated large holdings of money, are felt. Limiting budget deficits, controlling credit, and privatization of government-owned assets, including land, are difficult in countries making the transition. Finally, it takes a long time for all the various institutions that support market economies to evolve.

BEHIND THE ESSENTIAL CONCEPTS

1 The main disadvantages of central government control are gathering the information needed to determine the optimal decisions and giving incentives to managers and workers. Every organization, whether it operates within a market or a socialist economy, faces these problems. The difficulty with the socialist system is that the economy is simply too large an organization to control from the centre.

2 The experiment with worker-managed firms in Yugoslavia showed interesting results. Since workers shared the profits, their goal was not to maximize total profits but rather to maximize profits per worker. This reduced the incentive to hire additional workers, because any new worker would cause the profit pie to be sliced more thinly. Further, the incentives to invest and increase the value of the enterprise were limited because it could not be sold.

3 The Soviet-style socialist economies bottled up inflation by controlling prices below the market-clearing levels and by providing fewer goods than people wanted to buy. Because there were so few goods to spend money on, savings rates were especially high—a phenomenon known as monetary overhang. As prices are freed from government control, they rise to market-clearing levels, but inflation grows even more as people spend their monetary overhang.

4 Despite claims of eliminating unemployment, the Soviet-style socialist economies did have disguised unemployment. Workers were assigned to firms, and layoffs were banned. Plants with excess workers simply kept them on the payroll. Because they were subject to the **soft budget constraint,** any losses resulting from the excess payroll were covered by the central government.

SELF-TEST

True or False

1 Under socialism, the state owns the means of production.

2 In mixed economies, there is a reliance on markets for most decisions, but government also plays a substantial role.

3 Karl Marx led the Russian revolution of 1917, and established a Marxist state.

4 Under central planning, important decisions are made at the plant level.

5 In Soviet-style economies, incentives were provided by force.

6 In Soviet-style economies, there was little job mobility but some disguised unemployment.

7 The Soviet Union pursued a high-investment, low-consumption economic plan.

8 Soviet-style socialist economies nearly eliminated economic inequality.

9 Although socialist economies lost the competition for efficient production, they were able to protect their environment.

10 Most economists believe that the experiment in Soviet-style socialism was a failure.

11 Bureaucrats lacked the information to make efficient decisions under Soviet-style socialism.

12 Under market socialism, prices replace planning in determining investment decisions.

13 Worker-managed firms have little incentive to hire more workers.

14 The movement from socialism to a more market-oriented economy will cause prices to increase.

15 Privatization refers to the process of eliminating price controls and returning the function of setting prices to private firms.

Multiple Choice

1 Socialism is the system under which

   a the state owns all property, including the means of production and land.
   b the state owns the means of production.
   c there is a heavy reliance on firms and households interacting in markets.
   d there is a heavy reliance on markets and a considerable role for government.
   e workers own and manage the firms.

2 Under communism,

   a the state owns all property, including the means of production and land.
   b the state owns the means of production.
   c there is a heavy reliance on firms and households interacting in markets.
   d there is a heavy reliance on markets and a considerable role for government.
   e workers own and manage the firms.

3 In a mixed economy,

   a the state owns all property, including the means of production and land.
   b the state owns the means of production.
   c there is a heavy reliance on firms and households interacting in markets.
   d there is a heavy reliance on markets and a considerable role for government.
   e workers own and manage the firms.

4 The Russian revolution of 1917, which installed communism, was led by

   a Karl Marx.
   b Mikhail Gorbachev.
   c Vladimir Lenin.
   d Josef Stalin.
   e Boris Yeltsin.

5 The forced collectivization of agriculture was ordered by

   a Karl Marx.
   b Mikhail Gorbachev.
   c Vladimir Lenin.
   d Josef Stalin.
   e Boris Yeltsin.

6 Which of the following is not true? Marx believed

   a in the labour theory of value.
   b that human preferences and behaviour are largely determined by the economic system.
   c that economic factors govern the entire structure of society.
   d that capitalism would eventually collapse.
   e none of the above.

7 Under central planning,

   a the government makes all significant economic decisions.
   b government-owned property is sold or given to individuals.
   c workers own and manage their firms.
   d prices are set by the interplay of supply and demand.
   e land is redistributed to those who have worked it.

8 Under socialism, in the labour market,

   a wages adjust to clear the market.
   b firms pay efficiency wages to keep and motivate their best workers.
   c workers are assigned jobs, and there is very little labour mobility.
   d unions set wages through collective bargaining.
   e workers own and manage their own firms.

9 In Soviet-style socialist economies, the allocation of investment capital is determined by

   a workers who own and manage their own firms.
   b the capital market.
   c the government.
   d majority vote.
   e none of the above.

10 In Soviet-style socialist economies, prices

   a were outlawed.
   b were set equal to market-clearing levels.
   c were set above market-clearing levels.
   d were set below market-clearing levels.
   e were determined by the forces of supply and demand.

11 The Soviet Union pursued a policy of

   a high investment and low consumption.
   b high consumption and low investment.
   c high investment and high consumption.
   d low investment and low consumption.
   e none of the above.

12 Socialist enterprises often face soft budget constraints, which means that

   a workers share the profits equally.
   b firms that continue to make losses are absorbed by larger firms.
   c the government makes up any losses.
   d workers do not have to work unless the firm makes a profit.
   e workers are assigned jobs and thus are never unemployed.

13 Which of the following is not true? A problem with central planning is

   a the lack of incentives to encourage managers to operate firms efficiently.
   b the lack of information needed to make efficient decisions.
   c the fact that prices, not determined by markets, cannot provide informative signals.
   d the difficulty in monitoring the performance of managers and workers.
   e none of the above.

14 Under market socialism,

 a government makes the investment decisions.
 b firms do not maximize profits.
 c workers own and manage their own firms.
 d there are no profits.
 e none of the above.

15 In China, farmers were allowed to sell most of what they produced and keep the profits under

 a collectivized agriculture.
 b farmer cooperatives.
 c the responsibility system.
 d land reform.
 e privatization.

16 Worker-managed farms were instituted in

 a China.
 b the Soviet Union.
 c Poland.
 d Hungary.
 e Yugoslavia.

17 Which of the following was not a problem with worker-owned cooperatives?

 a Workers had little incentive to undertake investments that paid off after they left the firm.
 b Keeping a share of the profits motivated workers to work hard in smaller firms.
 c Cooperatives had little incentive to hire new workers.
 d The aging work force diminished investment incentives.
 e The reluctance to hire workers contributed to the unemployment problem.

18 The large holdings of money kept because there was little to buy were called

 a monetary overhang.
 b convertible currency.
 c the responsibility system.
 d the liquidity trap.
 e the inflationary spiral.

19 Privatization refers to

 a the transfer to individuals of property formerly owned by the state.
 b the fact that managers under Soviet-style socialism kept information private.
 c the consolidation of agriculture into large firms.
 d the policy that allowed private farmers in China to sell much of what they produced.
 e the attempt to combine the best features of socialism and private enterprise.

20 Which of the following is not a problem involved in the transition from socialism to market economies?

 a inflation.
 b unemployment.
 c the lack of a safety net.
 d falling living standards.
 e none of the above.

Completion

1 The government owns and operates the means of production under _____.

2 Under _____, the government owns all property.

3 The system of _____ gives the government and its ministries control over economic decisions.

4 Economies with a heavy reliance on markets but also a considerable role for government are referred to as _____.

5 _____ believed that wages would never rise above subsistence, that capitalists would exhaust investment opportunities, and that the capitalist system would eventually collapse.

6 _____ forced the collectivization of farms, and caused a famine in which millions died.

7 According to _____, economies can combine the advantages of market mechanisms with public ownership of the means of production.

8 Worker-owned _____, in which workers hired managers and received the profits, were encouraged in the former Yugoslavia.

9 Transferring businesses and property from public ownership to individuals is called _____.

10 In socialist countries, savings that are due to the lack of goods to buy and not to the desire to save are called _____.

Answers to Self-Test

True or False

1	t	6	t	11	t
2	t	7	t	12	f
3	f	8	f	13	t
4	f	9	f	14	t
5	t	10	t	15	f

Multiple Choice

1	b	6	e	11	a	16	e
2	a	7	a	12	c	17	b
3	d	8	c	13	e	18	a
4	c	9	c	14	a	19	a
5	d	10	d	15	c	20	e

Completion

1 socialism
2 communism
3 central planning
4 mixed economies
5 Marx
6 Stalin
7 market socialism
8 cooperatives
9 privatization
10 monetary overhang

Doing Economics: Tools and Practice Problems

In a planned economy, such as Soviet-style socialism, the state owns and must allocate the means of production. To gain some understanding of the allocation problem the state must solve, we first look at some relatively simple problems involving how to allocate a resource between different plants or regions that produce the same good. The next topic involves a Yugoslavian experiment with firms owned and managed by the workers. We explore the problem of how many workers to hire.

Tool Kit 40.1: Finding the Efficient Allocation of a Resource

When new productive resources become available, state bureaucrats must decide how to use them. The solution to this problem requires massive amounts of information, as the planner must know the production functions for each plant or region. As you have learned, markets can solve this problem with a minimum of information requirements.

Step one: Identify the production functions for each possible use.

Step two: Compute the marginal product for each quantity of the resource:

marginal product = change in output/change in input.

Step three: Allocate the first unit of the resource to the activity with the highest marginal product.

Step four: Allocate the second unit of the resource to the activity with the next highest marginal product.

Step five: Continue until the available supply of the resource is exhausted.

---

1 (Worked problem: planning and efficient allocation) The Commissar of Fishing has received eight new trawlers for cod. The commissar must decide how to allocate the new vessels between the Black Sea and Caspian Sea fleets. The production functions for each fleet are given in Table 40.1.

Table 40.1

Number of trawlers	Harvest of Black Sea cod (tonnes per week)	Harvest of Caspian Sea cod (tonnes per week)
1	9	20
2	17	36
3	24	50
4	30	62
5	35	72
6	39	80
7	42	86
8	44	90

a Find the efficient allocation of trawlers.

b Suppose the commissar simply allocates the trawlers equally between the fleets. How many fewer tonnes of cod will be harvested?

Step-by-step solution

Step one: Identify the production functions for each possible use. They are given in Table 40.1.

Step two: Compute the marginal product for each quantity of the resource. The first trawler in the Black Sea harvests 10 tonnes. The second one increases the harvest to 19, which is a marginal product of 19 − 10 = 9. Continuing, we derive Table 40.2.

Table 40.2

Number of trawlers	Harvest of Black Sea cod	Marginal product	Harvest of Caspian Sea cod	Marginal product
1	9	9	20	20
2	17	8	36	16
3	24	7	50	14
4	30	6	62	12
5	35	5	72	10
6	39	4	80	8
7	42	3	86	6
8	44	2	90	4

Step three: Allocate the first unit of the resource to the activity with the highest marginal product. The highest marginal product is 20 in the Caspian Sea.

Step four: Allocate the second unit of the resource to the activity with the next highest marginal product. The next highest marginal product is 16, again in the Caspian Sea.

Step five: Continue until the available supply of the resource is exhausted. If 6 trawlers are allocated to the Caspian, where the output is 80, and 2 to the Black Sea, where the output is 17, there the output of cod is 97. The allocation is efficient, and this is the answer to part a.

Step six: If 4 trawlers are sent to each region, total output is 30 + 62 = 92, which is 7 less than if the allocation were efficient.

2 (Practice problem: planning and efficient allocation) Nine new tractors roll off the assembly line at the huge state-owned tractor works in Braslov. Many cooperative farms have requested new tractors, and the minister in charge must allocate them. The production functions for three farms are given in Table 40.3. Output is measured as thousands of bushels of wheat.

a Find the efficient allocation of tractors.

b Compute the waste if the tractors are divided equally among the three farms.

Table 40.3

Tractors	Output at farm #1	Output at farm #2	Output at farm #3
0	30	100	50
1	40	150	90
2	49	180	120
3	57	200	140
4	64	210	150
5	70	215	155
6	75	218	160
7	79	220	164
8	82	220	166
9	82	220	167

3 (Practice problem: planning and efficient allocation) Six new locomotives are made available for either the north-south route or the east-west route. The production functions for each route are given in Table 40.4. Output is measured as numbers of standard containers per week.

Table 40.4

Locomotives	East-west route output	North-south route output
1	1,000	1,000
2	1,800	1,600
3	2,500	2,000
4	3,000	2,200
5	3,300	2,300
6	3,500	2,400

a Find the efficient allocation of locomotives.
b How much output is wasted if all are allocated to the east-west route?

Tool Kit 40.2: Finding the Level of Employment in a Worker-Managed Firm

One experiment in market socialism occurred in the former Yugoslavia when the government sanctioned the creation of firms owned and managed by workers. The profits from each firm were shared equally among the workers. Worker-managed firms do seek profits, but they do not maximize total profits; rather, their goal is to make profits per worker as large as possible. Generally, this practice results in fewer workers hired than under a full-fledged market system.

Step one: Identify the production function and the product price.

Step two: Compute the total revenue at each level of employment by multiplying the output by the product price:

revenues = output × product price.

Step three: Compute profits by subtracting costs from revenue:

profits = revenues − costs.

Step four: Compute profits per worker by dividing profits by the corresponding number of workers. This is the share of profits going to each worker.

profits per worker = profits/number of workers.

Step five: Find the level of employment for which profits per worker is highest. This is the equilibrium level of employment in the worker-managed firm.

---

4 (Worked problem: worker-managed firms) The new branch of the Hair Cuttery is ready to open. It will be owned and managed by the stylists. The price of haircuts is $10, and the production function is given in Table 40.5. Fixed costs equal $50 per day. Find the equilibrium number of stylists.

Table 40.5

Stylists	Haircuts per day
1	6
2	16
3	30
4	42
5	50
6	56
7	60

Step-by-step solution

Step one: Identify the production function and the product price. The production function is given in Table 40.4, and the price is $10.

Step two: Compute the total revenue at each level of employment by multiplying the output by the product price. When the number of stylists is 1, output is 6 and revenues equal 6 × $10 = $60. Continuing, we complete the column as shown in Table 40.6.

Step three: Compute profits by subtracting costs from revenue. We subtract $50 from the revenue column. The completed information is given in Table 40.6.

Table 40.6

Stylists	Haircuts per day	Revenues	Profits
1	6	$ 60	$ 10
2	16	$160	$110
3	30	$300	$250
4	42	$420	$370
5	50	$500	$450
6	56	$560	$510
7	60	$600	$550

Step four: Compute profits per worker by dividing profits by the corresponding number of workers. This is the share of profits going to each worker. For example, profits per worker when there is one stylist equal $10/1 = $10. Continuing, we derive Table 40.7.

Table 40.7

Stylists	Haircuts per day	Revenues	Profits	Profits per stylist
1	6	$ 60	$ 10	$10.00
2	16	$160	$110	$55.00
3	30	$300	$250	$83.33
4	42	$420	$370	$92.50
5	50	$500	$450	$90.00
6	56	$560	$510	$85.00
7	60	$600	$550	$76.57

Step five: Find the level of employment for which profits per worker is highest. The equilibrium level of employment is 4, where profits per worker equal $92.50.

5 (Practice problem: worker-managed firms) Moe's Lite-Brite Charcoal Company soaks charcoal in lighter fluid for $1 per bag. Its production function is given in Table 40.8. The business and all its equipment is being sold to the employees. Their fixed cost including the payment on the loan to finance the sale will be $500 per day. Find the equilibrium level of employment when Moe's becomes worker managed.

Table 40.8

Workers	Output per day
1	100
2	500
3	1,500
4	2,500
5	2,900
6	3,300

6 (Practice problem: worker-managed firms) The Thelonius Thimble Company is to become worker owned and managed next month when the likable Thelonius retires. The business is being given to the workers, and they will have no fixed cost. Thimbles sell for $0.10 each. The production function is given in Table 40.9. Find the equilibrium number of employees of the worker-managed thimble company.

Table 40.9

Workers	Thimbles
1	2,000
2	5,000
3	10,000
4	13,000
5	15,000
6	17,000

Answers to Problems

2 Table 40.10 gives the marginal product of tractors at each of the farms.

Table 40.10

	Farm #1		Farm #2		Farm #3	
Tractors	Output	Marginal product	Output	Marginal product	Output	Marginal product
0	30	30	100	100	50	50
1	40	10	150	50	90	40
2	49	9	180	30	120	30
3	57	8	200	20	140	20
4	64	7	210	10	150	10
5	70	6	215	5	155	5
6	75	5	218	3	160	5
7	79	4	220	2	164	4
8	82	3	220	0	166	2
9	82	0	220	0	167	1

a The efficient allocation is 1 tractor to farm #1, 4 tractors to farm #2, and 4 tractors to farm #3.
b The output if the tractors are divided equally is 57 + 200 + 140 = 397. The output at the efficient allocation is 40 + 210 + 150 = 400. The waste is 400 − 397 = 3, and since output is measured in thousands of bushels, this represents 3,000 bushels.

3 Table 40.11 gives the marginal product along each route.

Table 40.11

	East-west route		North-south route	
Locomotives	Output	Marginal product	Output	Marginal product
1	1,000	1,000	1,000	1,000
2	1,800	800	1,600	600
3	2,500	700	2,000	400
4	3,000	500	2,200	200
5	3,300	300	2,300	100
6	3,500	200	2,400	100

a The efficient allocation is 4 to the east-west route and 2 to the north-south route.
b Output is 3,500 if all are allocated to the east-west route. Output is 3,000 + 1,600 = 4,600 at the efficient allocation. The waste is 4,600 − 3,500 = 1,100.

5 Table 40.12 gives profits per worker, which are maximized when the firm includes 4 workers.

Table 40.12

Workers	Output per day	Revenues	Profits	Profits per worker
1	100	$ 100	-$ 400	-$400
2	500	$ 500	$ 0	$ 0
3	1,500	$1,500	$1,000	$333
4	2,500	$2,500	$2,000	$500
5	2,900	$2,900	$2,400	$480
6	3,300	$3,300	$2,800	$466

Table 40.13

Workers	Output per day	Revenues	Profits	Profits per worker
1	2,000	$ 200	$ 200	$200
2	5,000	$ 500	$ 500	$250
3	10,000	$1,000	$1,000	$333
4	13,000	$1,300	$1,300	$325
5	15,000	$1,500	$1,500	$300
6	17,000	$1,700	$1,700	$283

6　Table 40.13 gives profits per worker, which are maximized when the number of workers is 3.

Chapter 41

DEVELOPMENT

Chapter Review

This chapter looks at how economics is applied to the analysis of less-developed countries. It examines living standards in these countries as well as the causes of underdevelopment and the prospects for bringing the living standards up to those of the developed countries. The chapter closes with a look at the policies some countries have pursued, namely the relative advantages of the export-led and import-competing strategies.

ESSENTIAL CONCEPTS

1 In **less-developed countries (LDCs)** GDP per capita was less than U.S. $580 in 1989. The per capita income gap among developed countries has narrowed over the past century, but it has widened between the developed and less-developed world. Although a few countries have successfully raised their living standards, most of the LDCs remain in grinding poverty. Agricultural gains from the **green revolution,** improvements in health and life expectancy, and the emergence of the **newly industrialized countries** of East Asia are some examples of successful economic development. They are, unfortunately, the exceptions.

2 Although there is considerable variation among LDCs, agriculture dominates the economy in most. In the rural sector, farming takes place on small, labour-intensive farms with poorer techniques and less fertilizer than in the developed world. **Sharecropping** remains a widespread arrangement. Redistribution of land ownership through **land reform** has at times been successful, but dramatic inequality remains. In the urban sector, wages are far higher, and as a result many individuals have migrated to the cities. Such migration has caused massive unemployment and squalor. The term **dual economy** describes the vast difference between the rural and urban sectors.

3 The institutions and structures of economies in LDCs do not facilitate growth. Although savings rates are high, there is a shortage of capital. The absence of efficient capital markets keeps the limited capital from its most productive use. An inadequate supply of skilled workers accompanies burgeoning population growth, which reduces the ratio of capital to workers and lowers productivity. Also, ethnic divisions and language barriers work against the mobility of labour. Fi-

nally, many LDCs lack natural resources and modern technology.

4 Market failures also undermine the prospects for development. In addition to the imperfect labour and capital markets, there is widespread unemployment and a lack of entrepreneurs. Externalities prevent worker training. Finally, severe economic inequality has led to business practices that undermine incentives (such as share-cropping), much political instability, and an un-favourable climate for foreign investment.

5 The failure of markets has led many LDCs to adopt central planning. Because planners do not have sufficient information to make correct decisions, central planning has not, however, been successful. An overreliance on heavy industry, corruption, and widespread interference in trade and foreign exchange are common problems of LDC development efforts. The pervasive role of government also motivates wasteful rent seeking. Another clear failure has been in providing needed **infrastructure,** especially a sound legal system.

6 Two approaches designed to influence the direction of economic development are **export-led growth** and **import substitution.** The export-led strategy protects and encourages certain industries judged to be potentially successful against world competition. Import substitution emphasizes the development of domestic markets by substituting domestic production for imports. In addition, economists disagree about whether LDCs should focus on agriculture, where the current comparative advantage surely lies, or industry.

BEHIND THE ESSENTIAL CONCEPTS

1 The case for central planning in LDCs has always rested on pervasive market failures. Clearly, markets do a poor job allocating resources in these countries. Yet the failure of planning provides a salient example of government failure. Although the potential for beneficial government intervention exists, governments have made matters worse.

2 Real world markets are complicated, and the institutions that help them work have taken time to evolve. Reputations, repeated business arrangements, implicit contracts, and other institutions help ease the information problems that trouble imperfectly competitive markets. In the LDCs, these institutions are not present, and in their absence, resource allocation is worse.

SELF-TEST

True or False

1 Over the last century, the income gap between the industrialized and less-developed economies has narrowed.

2 One success story in the less-developed world has been the emergence of the newly industrialized countries, such as Singapore and Taiwan.

3 Increases in life expectancy and improvements in infant mortality have allowed rapid population growth in many LDCs.

4 In poor countries, agriculture plays a more prominent role, often accounting for 80 percent of GDP.

5 The LDCs have much less capital per person than Canada because their savings rates are very low.

6 The absence of capital markets in LDCs prevents the limited supply of capital from finding its most efficient use.

7 Land reform transfers agricultural land to those who work it.

8 Inequality can inhibit development by leading to political instability and a poor climate for foreign investment.

9 Sharecropping provides incentives for the tenant farmer to work hard and maintain the productivity of the land.

10 Central planning enables developing countries to coordinate all the related activities in a single coherent development strategy.

11 An important element of a country's infrastructure is its legal system.

12 A difficulty with the export-led strategy is that it protects inefficient domestic producers from the competition of foreign firms.

13 One problem with import substitution is that it is difficult to remove trade barriers once they are imposed.

14 The infant industry argument advocates protecting firms from competition until, through learning by doing, they become effective competitors in the world economy.

15 The comparative advantage of many LDCs lies in agriculture.

Multiple Choice

1 What fraction of the world's population lives in LDCs?

  a one-fourth
  b one-half
  c three-fourths
  d one-third
  e one-sixth

2 Over the past century, the income gap

  a has narrowed between countries with high incomes, but has widened between high- and low income countries.
  b has widened between countries with high incomes, but has narrowed between high- and low-income countries.

c has widened between countries with high income and between high- and low-income countries.

d has narrowed between countries with high income and between high- and low-income countries.

e has not changed between countries with high incomes or between high- and low-income countries.

3 The green revolution refers to

a the spread of concern for the environment in the LDCs.

b the World Bank's largely successful efforts to aid development by lending money for infrastructure investment.

c the development and spread to LDCs of new agricultural technologies, which brought about huge increases in output.

d improvements in life expectancy and infant mortality statistics in the LDCs.

e none of the above.

4 Agriculture in the developed countries

a uses smaller farms than in the LDCs.

b uses more workers per hectare than in LDCs.

c uses less fertilizer per hectare than in LDCs.

d is more mechanized than in LDCs.

e none of the above.

5 Sharecropping refers to

a the fact that much of the agricultural output in the LDCs is taken in taxes.

b the World Bank's policy of matching agricultural gains in LDCs with food shipments.

c the sharing of technological know-how between agricultural research centres in the developed world and the LDCs.

d the system in which the landlord takes a share of the output of a farm.

e the system in which farmers set aside a fraction of their output to support religious institutions.

6 Which of the following is not a disadvantage of sharecropping?

a Sharecropping reduces incentives to work hard, because the farmer does not receive the entire output.

b Tenants who do not own the land have less incentive to maintain its quality.

c Although tenant farmers must share the output with the landlord, they bear all the risk.

d Absentee landlords cannot monitor and reward the efforts of tenant farmers towards maintaining and improving the land.

e Landlords and tenant farmers share the risk of poor crops and low prices.

7 In LDCs, it is generally true that

a savings rates are low.

b because it is in short supply, capital is used very intensively.

c because the capital stock is so low, the marginal return to capital is much higher than in developed countries.

d the lack of effective capital markets keeps capital from its most productive uses.

e the stable political environments attract foreign investment.

8 Which of the following is not part of the explanation for the debt crises experienced by several LDCs in the 1980s?

a high interest rates

b the world recession in the early 1980s

c lack of prudence in lending by banks

d deposit insurance

e none of the above

9 In LDCs, the population

a is large and well educated.

b is falling because of the poor medical care and meagre diets.

c is growing too rapidly, and causing an excess supply of trained workers.

d is growing too rapidly, but includes too few vocationally trained, skilled workers.

e none of the above.

10 Natural resources are

a necessary but not sufficient for development.

b both necessary and sufficient for development.

c neither necessary nor sufficient for development.

d not necessary but sufficient for development.

e irrelevant to development.

11 In LDCs,

a both labour and capital markets work well.

b while labour markets work well, capital markets fail to allocate the scarce capital efficiently.

c while capital markets work well, ethnic divisions and language barriers hinder the labour market.

d neither capital nor labour markets work efficiently.

e there are no labour or capital markets.

12 The true social value of a resource is called its

a market price.

b shadow price.

c efficiency price.

d marginal price.

e average price.

13 Because of the massive unemployment and underemployment in LDCs, the shadow wage

a is less than the market wage.

b is equal to the market wage.

c is greater than the market wage.

d is less than the market wage in urban areas but greater in rural areas.

e is less than the market wage in rural areas but greater in urban areas.

14 The fact that once trained, a worker may move to another company implies that training workers is an example of a

a positive externality.

b negative externality.
c public good.
d shadow price.
e shortage.

15 Which of the following is not true? Inequality may inhibit development by

a leading to political instability and a poor investment climate.
b fostering the development of sharecropping.
c leading governments to impose high tax rates.
d forcing governments to spend money on food subsidies rather than investment.
e none of the above.

16 Most economists

a favour central planning by LDCs because planners can better coordinate all the aspects of major projects.
b favour central planning by LDCs because planners have better information about whether projects will be successful.
c are skeptical about central planning because planners lack the needed information.
d see no need for planning of any kind.
e view planning as neither beneficial nor harmful because of the policy ineffectiveness proposition.

17 Rent seeking refers to

a the payments made by sharecroppers.
b activities by individuals to get special benefits from governments.
c campaigns to attract foreign investment.
d the failure of sharecroppers to maintain the land.
e none of the above.

18 Which of the following is not part of a country's infrastructure?

a roads
b bridges
c ports
d legal system
e none of the above

19 Encouraging the production and export of goods in which the country has a comparative advantage is the strategy called

a export-led growth.
b central planning.
c dynamic comparative advantage.
d import substitution.
e *laissez-faire.*

20 Encouraging the development of a domestic market by substituting domestically produced goods for imports is called

a export-led growth.
b central planning.
c dynamic comparative advantage.
d import substitution.
e *laissez-faire.*

Completion

1 Economists refer to the poorest nations of the world as _____.

2 Nations that have recently moved from being quite poor to being middle-income countries, including South Korea and Hong Kong, are called _____.

3 The development of new seeds, fertilizers, and agricultural practices that brought about increases in agricultural output in the LDCs during the 1960s and 1970s was called the _____.

4 In many LDCs, there is a _____, which includes a poor rural sector alongside a relatively more advanced urban sector.

5 A country's roads, ports, bridges, and legal system are examples of its _____.

6 _____ is a strategy according to which governments encourage exports to stimulate growth.

7 _____ is a strategy whereby the focus is on substituting domestic goods for imports to develop self-sufficiency.

8 Countries that have large numbers of unemployed or underemployed workers are said to have _____.

9 The true social value of a resource is its _____.

10 The _____ is the most important of the international agencies that lend funds to LDCs to aid in development.

Answers to Self-Test

True or False

1	f	6	t	11	t
2	t	7	t	12	f
3	t	8	t	13	t
4	t	9	f	14	t
5	f	10	f	15	t

Multiple Choice

1	c	6	c	11	d	16	c
2	a	7	d	12	b	17	b
3	c	8	e	13	a	18	e
4	d	9	d	14	a	19	a
5	d	10	c	15	e	20	d

Completion

1 less-developed countries
2 newly industrialized countries
3 green revolution
4 dual economy
5 infrastructure
6 Export-led growth
7 Import substitution
8 labour surplus
9 shadow price
10 World Bank

Doing Economics: Tools and Practice Problems

Two important problems that impede growth in less-developed countries are the absence of markets to allocate resources efficiently, and the prevalence of institutions, such as sharecropping, that provide weak incentives. We study both of these problems in this section.

1 (Worked problem: absence of markets) Less-developed economies not only have limited supplies of capital and skilled labour, they also lack good markets to allocate what supplies they have. In this section, we consider the efficient allocation of resources, how markets achieve this allocation, and the losses that result from misallocation. The World Bank has made $10 million available for development projects in Costa Guano. Two possible uses for the money are building roads and building irrigation systems. The present discounted value of investments in each sector is given in Table 41.1. (Monetary magnitudes are converted to dollar equivalents.)

Table 41.1

Investment (millions)	Irrigation projects (millions)	Roads (millions)
$ 1	$10	$ 25
$ 2	$18	$ 45
$ 3	$25	$ 60
$ 4	$31	$ 72
$ 5	$36	$ 83
$ 6	$40	$ 93
$ 7	$43	$102
$ 8	$45	$110
$ 9	$46	$116
$10	$46	$120

a Find the efficient allocation of the $10 million.
b How would competitive markets allocate the money.
c The party in power in Costa Guano draws much of its support from agriculture. If it used the money for irrigation, how much less would the benefits be?

Step-by-step solution

Step one (a): To find the efficient allocation, we adapt the procedure outlined in Tool Kit 40.1. Identify the production functions for each possible use. Here we are given the relationship between investment and the benefits of investment in Table 41.1.

Step two (a): Compute the marginal benefit for each quantity of the resource. We compute marginal benefit in the usual way. For example, the marginal benefit of the first $1 million in investment in irrigation is $10 million. Continuing, we derive Table 41.2.

Table 41.2

Investment (millions)	Irrigation projects (millions)	Marginal benefit (millions)	Roads (millions)	Marginal benefit (millions)
$ 1	$10	$10	$ 25	$25
$ 2	$18	$ 8	$ 45	$20
$ 3	$25	$ 7	$ 60	$15
$ 4	$31	$ 6	$ 72	$12
$ 5	$36	$ 5	$ 83	$11
$ 6	$40	$ 4	$ 93	$10
$ 7	$43	$ 3	$102	$ 9
$ 8	$45	$ 2	$110	$ 8
$ 9	$46	$ 1	$116	$ 6
$10	$46	$ 0	$120	$ 4

Step three (a): Allocate the first unit of the resource to the activity with the highest marginal benefit. The first $1 million is allocated to road building, where it has a marginal benefit of $25 million.

Step four (a): Allocate the second unit of the resource to the activity with the next highest marginal benefit. The second $1 million is allocated to road building, where it has a marginal benefit of $20 million.

Step five (a): Continue until the available supply of the resource is exhausted. We allocate $8 million to roads and $2 million to irrigation.

Step one (b): To find the competitive market allocation, simply interpret the marginal benefits as the demand for the investment money, and follow the procedure in the first three steps of Tool Kit 37.1. Add each sector's demand for capital. When the price is $25 million, the total quantity demanded is $1 million by the road-building industry. When the price falls to $20 million, the quantity demanded is $2 million. Continuing, we derive the demand in Table 41.3.

Table 41.3

Price (millions/million)	Quantity (millions of investment)
$25	$ 1
$20	$ 2
$15	$ 3
$12	$ 4
$11	$ 5
$10	$ 7 ($1 each for roads and irrigation)
$ 9	$ 8
$ 8	$10
$ 7	$11 etc.

Step two (a): Find the market-clearing price. The market clears at a price of $8 million.

Step three (a): Substitute the market-clearing price into each demand to determine the allocation of investment. At a price of $8 million, road builders will purchase $8 million, and irrigation firms will purchase $2 million. This is exactly the efficient allocation.

Step one (c): If all the investment money is used in irrigation projects, then the total benefit will be $46 million. The efficient allocation gives benefits equal to $18 million (irrigation) + $110 million (roads) = $128 million. Thus the waste that is due to misallocation is $118 − $46 = $72 million.

2 (Practice problem: absence of markets) Eight engineers return to Zaire with their diplomas from McMaster University (the MIT of the North). They can work for the government building bridges or in the mining sector. The (Canadian dollar equivalent) value of output produced in each sector is given in Table 41.4.

Table 41.4

Engineers	Roads	Mining
1	$200,000	$100,000
2	$280,000	$190,000
3	$350,000	$270,000
4	$410,000	$330,000
5	$450,000	$360,000
6	$480,000	$380,000
7	$500,000	$400,000
8	$500,000	$400,000

a Find the efficient allocation of the 8 engineers.
b How would competitive markets allocate the engineers?
c The president for life likes roads. How much is wasted if all 8 engineers are sent to build roads?

3 (Practice problem: absence of markets) The Zambesi River can provide up to 100 million litres annually for irrigation. Both the cotton and the millet crops would benefit from irrigation, and the benefits are given in Table 41.5.

Table 41.5

Water (millions of litres)	Cotton (millions)	Millet (millions)
1	$ 50	$ 25
2	$ 95	$ 50
3	$135	$ 75
4	$170	$100
5	$200	$125
6	$225	$150
7	$245	$175
8	$260	$190
9	$270	$200
10	$275	$200

a Find the efficient allocation of the water.
b How would competitive markets allocate the water?
c The president for life allocates 80 million to millet and the rest to cotton. How much value is wasted?

Tool Kit 41.1: Analyzing Sharecropping

In less-developed economies, much farming takes place under conditions of sharecropping, where the landlord receives a fixed percentage of the output of the farm. The landlord's share of output is an externality from the point of view of the tenant, and as in all similar situations, there are incentive problems.

Step one: Find the full marginal benefits and costs of the tenant's effort.

Step two: Find the efficient level of effort, which is the level at which marginal benefits equal marginal cost.

Step three: Calculate the tenant's marginal private benefits multiplying the full marginal benefits by the tenant's share.

Step four: Find the equilibrium level of effort, which is the level at which marginal private benefits equal marginal cost.

Step five: Compare the equilibrium and efficient levels of the activity.

4 (Worked problem: analyzing sharecropping) Mahragh grows sorghum on 20 hectares in Chad. He gives one-half of his output in rent to the landlord. The current price is $1 per bushel, and Table 41.6 gives the production function. Finally, Mahragh could devote time each day to his wife's bicycle manufacture business, where he could earn $30 for each daily hour.

Table 41.6

Effort (hours per day)	Sorghum (bushels)
1	120
2	210
3	270
4	300
5	315
6	321
7	324

a Find the efficient level of effort.
b Find the equilibrium level of effort.

Step-by-step solution

Step one: Find the full marginal benefits and costs of the tenant's effort. We first compute the marginal product in bushels of sorghum and then multiply by the price of sorghum to find the dollar value. The first 2 hours of daily effort increase output to 120 bushels, which sell for $120. Continuing, we derive Table 41.7.

Table 41.7

Effort (hours per day)	Sorghum (bushels)	Marginal product (bushels per daily hour)	Marginal benefits (per daily hour)
1	120	120	$120
2	210	90	$ 90
3	270	60	$ 60
4	300	30	$ 30
5	315	15	$ 15
6	321	6	$ 6
7	324	3	$ 3

Step two: Find the efficient level of effort, which is the level at which marginal benefits equal marginal cost. The marginal cost, which is $30, equals marginal benefits at 4 hours per day.

Step three: Calculate the marginal private benefits by multiplying the full marginal benefits by the tenant's share. Mahragh's share is one-half; so if he works 1 hour each day, his marginal private benefits equal $120 × 1/2 = $60. Continuing, we derive Table 41.8.

Table 41.8

Effort	Marginal private benefits (per daily hour)
1	$60.00
2	$45.00
3	$30.00
4	$15.00
5	$ 7.50
6	$ 3.00
7	$ 1.50

Step four: Find the equilibrium level of effort, which is the level at which marginal private benefits equal marginal cost. The marginal private benefits equal marginal cost at 3 hours per day.

Step five: Compare the equilibrium and efficient levels of the activity. Mahragh works 3 hours each day, which is 1 less than the efficient number of hours.

5 (Practice problem: analyzing sharecropping) Mr. Droulig is a sharecropper on a farm owned by the bank. He pays one-third of his revenues from farming 20 hectares in rural Mali to the bank. Table 41.9 gives the relationship between his effort and the revenues from the farm.

Table 41.9

Time (hours)	Total revenues
1	$18
2	$33
3	$45
4	$54
5	$60
6	$63

Mr. Droulig, when not sharecropping, can work in town and make $6 per hour.

a If he owned the farm himself and did not share revenues with the bank, how much would he work on the farm?
b How much does Mr. Droulig choose to work on the farm?

6 (Practice problem: analyzing sharecropping) Protecting farms against soil erosion is vital in the Sahel region of sub-Saharan Africa. The benefits of effort (in dollars) for a typical farm are given in Table 41.10. Assume that the marginal cost of effort is $100 and that sharecroppers pay one-half their yield in rent.

a Find the level of effort for owners.
b Find the level of effort for sharecroppers.

Table 41.10

Effort (days)	Benefits
1	$ 500
2	$ 900
3	$1,200
4	$1,400
5	$1,500
6	$1,500

Answers to Problems

2 The marginal benefits of the engineers in each sector are given in Table 41.11.

Table 41.11

Engineers	Roads	Marginal benefits	Mining	Marginal benefits
1	$200,000	$200,000	$100,000	$100,000
2	$280,000	$ 80,000	$190,000	$ 90,000
3	$350,000	$ 70,000	$270,000	$ 80,000
4	$410,000	$ 60,000	$330,000	$ 60,000
5	$450,000	$ 40,000	$360,000	$ 30,000
6	$480,000	$ 30,000	$380,000	$ 20,000
7	$500,000	$ 20,000	$400,000	$ 20,000
8	$500,000	$ 0	$400,000	$ 0

a The efficient allocation is 4 engineers to each sector.
b The market would allocate 4 to each sector with a wage of $60,000.
c The total benefits if all the engineers are sent to build roads equal $500,000. At the efficient allocation, the total benefits equal $410,000 + $330,000 = $740,000. The waste is $740,000 − $500,000 = $240,000.

3 Table 41.12 gives the marginal benefits of irrigation water for each crop.

Table 41.12

Water (millions of litres)	Cotton (millions)	Marginal benefit (millions)	Millet (millions)	Marginal benefit (millions)
1	$ 50	$50	$ 25	$25
2	$ 95	$45	$ 50	$25
3	$135	$40	$ 75	$25
4	$170	$35	$100	$25
5	$200	$30	$125	$25
6	$225	$25	$150	$25
7	$245	$20	$175	$25
8	$260	$15	$190	$15
9	$270	$10	$200	$10
10	$275	$ 5	$200	$ 0

a The efficient allocation is 6 million litres to cotton and 4 million to millet.

b The market would allocate 6 million to cotton and 4 million to millet with a price equal to $25.

c Using 8 million for cotton and 2 million for millet gives benefits equal to $260 + $50 = $310. Since benefits are being represented in millions of dollars, this represents $310 million. The efficient allocation gives benefits equal to $225 + $100 = $325 million. The waste is $325 − $310 = $15. Since benefits are being represented in millions of dollars, this represents $15 million of waste.

5 Table 41.13 gives the full marginal benefits and the private marginal benefits of time.

Table 41.13

Time	Total revenues	Full marginal benefits	Private marginal benefits
1	$18	$18	$12
2	$33	$15	$10
3	$45	$12	$ 8
4	$54	$ 9	$ 6
5	$60	$ 6	$ 4
6	$63	$ 3	$ 2

a The efficient amount of time is 5 hours.

b Mr. Droulig works 4 hours each day.

6 Table 41.14 gives the owner's and sharecropper's marginal benefits of efforts to reduce soil erosion.

Table 41.14

Effort	Benefits	Owner's marginal benefits	Sharecropper's marginal benefits
1	$ 500	$500	$250
2	$ 900	$400	$200
3	$1,200	$300	$150
4	$1,400	$200	$100
5	$1,500	$100	$ 50
6	$1,500	$ 0	$ 0

a The owner would devote 5 days.

b The sharecropper would devote 4 days.